THE ECONOMICS OF
NONPROFIT INSTITUTIONS

YALE STUDIES ON NONPROFIT ORGANIZATIONS

Program on Non-Profit Organizations
Institution for Social and Policy Studies
Yale University

JOHN G. SIMON, CHAIRMAN
PAUL DIMAGGIO, DIRECTOR

The Economics of Nonprofit Institutions

Studies in Structure and Policy

Edited by

SUSAN ROSE-ACKERMAN

Columbia University

New York · Oxford
OXFORD UNIVERSITY PRESS
1986

Oxford University Press

Oxford   New York   Toronto
Delhi   Bombay   Calcutta   Madras   Karachi
Petaling Jaya   Singapore   Hong Kong   Tokyo
Nairobi   Dar es Salaam   Cape Town
Melbourne   Auckland

and associated companies in
Beirut   Berlin   Ibadan   Nicosia

Published by Oxford University Press, Inc.,
200 Madison Avenue, New York, New York 10016

Oxford is a registered trademark of Oxford University Press

Library of Congress Cataloging-in-Publication Data
Main entry under title:
The Economics of nonprofit institutions.
   Includes index.
   1. Corporations, Nonprofit—United States—Addresses, essays, lectures.
2. Corporations, Nonprofit—Taxation—United States—Addresses, essays, lectures.
I. Rose-Ackerman, Susan.
HD2785.E28   1986   338.7'4   85-15342
ISBN 0-19-503709-X

Printing (last digit): 9 8 7 6 5 4 3 2

Printed in the United States of America
on acid-free paper

Series Foreword

This volume and its siblings, comprising the Yale Studies on Nonprofit Organizations, were produced by an interdisciplinary research enterprise, the Program on Non-Profit Organizations, located within Yale University's Institution for Social and Policy Studies.[1] The Program had its origins in a series of discussions initiated by the present author in the mid-1970s while serving as president of Yale. These discussions began with a number of Yale colleagues, especially Professor Charles E. Lindblom, Director of the Institution, and Professor John G. Simon of the Law School faculty. We later enlisted a number of other helpful counselors in and out of academic life.

These conversations reflected widespread agreement that there was a serious and somewhat surprising gap in American scholarship. The United States relies more heavily than any other country on the voluntary nonprofit sector to conduct the nation's social, cultural, and economic business—to bring us into the world, to educate and entertain us, even to bury us. Indeed, the United States can be distinguished from all other societies by virtue of the work load it assigns to its "third sector," as compared to business firms or government agencies. Yet this nonprofit universe had been the least well studied, the least well understood aspect of our national life. And the nonprofit institutions themselves were lacking any connective theory of their governance and function. As just one result, public and private bodies were forced to make policy and management decisions, large and small, affecting the nonprofit sector from a position of relative ignorance.

To redress this startling imbalance, and with the initial assistance of the late John D. Rockefeller III (soon joined by a few foundation donors), the Program on Non-Profit Organizations was launched in 1977. It seeks to achieve three principal goals:

1. to build a substantial body of information, analysis, and theory relating to nonprofit organizations;

[1] The sharp-eyed editors at Oxford University Press requested that we explain the presence of an intrusive hyphen in the word "Non-Profit" in the Program's title, and suggested that the explanation might be of interest to this volume's readers. The explanation is simple: At the Program's inception, it adopted the convention, in wider currency than it is today but even at that time incorrect, of hyphenating "non-profit." Since then the Program has mended its ways wherever the term "nonprofit" is not used as part of the Program's title. But in the Program's title, for reasons both sentimental and pragmatic, the hyphen remains, as a kind of trademark.

2. to enlist the energies and enthusiasms of the scholarly community in research and teaching related to the world of nonprofit organizations; and
3. to assist decision makers, in and out of the voluntary sector, to address major policy and management dilemmas confronting the sector.

Toward the first and second of these goals the Program has employed a range of strategies: research grants to senior and junior scholars at Yale and at forty-one other institutions; provision of space and amenities to visiting scholars pursuing their research in the Program's offices; supervision of graduate and professional students working on topics germane to the Program's mission; and a summer graduate fellowship program for students from universities around the country.

The Program's participants represent a wide spectrum of academic disciplines—the social sciences, the humanities, law, medicine, and management. Moreover, they have used a variety of research strategies, ranging from theoretical economic modeling to field studies in African villages. These efforts, supported by fifty foundation, corporate, government, and individual donors to the Program, have gradually generated a mountain of research on virtually every nonprofit species—for example, day-care centers and private foundations, symphony orchestras and wildlife advocacy groups—and on voluntary institutions in twenty other countries. At this writing the Program has published 100 working papers and has sponsored, in whole or in part, research resulting in no fewer than 175 journal articles and book chapters. Thirty-two books have been either published or accepted for publication. Moreover, as the work has progressed and as Program-affiliated scholars (of whom, by now, there have been approximately 150) establish links to one another and to students of the nonprofit sector not associated with the Program, previously isolated researchers are forging themselves into an impressive and lively international network.

The Program has approached the third goal, that of assisting those who confront policy and management dilemmas, in many ways. Researchers have tried to design their projects in a way that would bring these dilemmas to the fore. Program participants have met with literally hundreds of nonprofit organizations, either individually or at conferences, to present and discuss the implications of research being conducted by the Program. Data and analyses have been presented to federal, state, and local legislative and executive branch officials and to journalists from print and electronic media throughout the United States, to assist them in their efforts to learn more about the third sector and the problems it faces.

Crucial to the accomplishment of all three goals is the wide sharing of the Program's intellectual output not only with academicians but also with nonprofit practitioners and policy makers. This dissemination task has been an increasing preoccupation of the Program in recent years. More vigorous promotion of its working paper series, cooperation with a variety of non-academic organizations, the forthcoming publication of a handbook of research on nonprofit organizations, and the establishment of a newsletter (published with increasing regularity for a broad and predominantly non-academic list of subscribers) have all helped to disseminate the Program's research results.

These efforts, however, needed supplementation. Thus, the Program's working papers, although circulated relatively widely, have been for the most part drafts rather than finished papers, produced in a humble format that renders them unsuitable for the relative immortality of library shelves. Moreover, many of the publications resulting from the Program's work have never found their way into working paper form. Indeed, the multidisciplinary products of Program-sponsored research have displayed a disconcerting tendency upon publication to fly off to separate disciplinary corners of the scholarly globe, unlikely to be reassembled by any but the most dogged, diligent denizens of the most comprehensive of university libraries.

Sensitive to these problems, the Lilly Endowment made a generous grant to the Program to enable it to overcome this tendency toward centrifugality. The Yale Studies on Nonprofit Organizations represent a particularly important part of this endeavor. Each book features the work of scholars from several disciplines. Each contains a variety of papers, many unpublished, others available only in small-circulation specialized periodicals, on a theme of general interest to readers in many regions of the nonprofit universe. Most of these papers are products of Program-sponsored research, although each volume contains a few other contributions selected in the interest of thematic consistency and breadth.

The present volume, edited by Susan Rose-Ackerman, Professor of Law and Political Economy at Columbia University and a long-time participant in the work of the Program on Non-Profit Organizations, deals with economic theory and policy—the exploration of various economic rationales for the role of voluntary organizations in America and abroad and the examination of subsidy and regulatory policies (through the tax system and otherwise) that affect the size, shape, and behavior of the nonprofit sector.

As the reader will already have observed, I do not write this foreword as a stranger. I am very much a member of the family, someone who was present at the creation of the Program of Non-Profit Organizations and continues to chair its Advisory Committee, and who also serves Oxford as Master of University College. What this extended family is doing to advance knowledge about the third sector is a source of considerable satisfaction. From its birth at a luncheon chat more than a decade ago, the Program on Non-Profit Organizations has occupied an increasingly important role as the leading academic center for research on voluntary institutions both in America and abroad. And now the publication by Oxford University Press of this volume and the other Yale Studies on Nonprofit Organizations enlarges the reach of the Yale Program by making its research more widely available within the scholarly community and to the larger world beyond.

London   Kingman Brewster
October 1985

Preface

Social science research on the nonprofit sector has multiplied in recent years. Even economists, used to concentrating on the private for-profit sector, are beginning to recognize the importance of studying organizational alternatives to conventional business firms. Yet, while a scholarly literature is rapidly developing, it is not easily accessible either to faculty members seeking to assemble course materials and to introduce themselves to a new field for original research or to thoughtful nonprofit managers and sponsors wishing to reflect on the strengths and weaknesses of the sector.

In this volume I attempt to respond to some of these needs by assembling a series of economically oriented articles that cover a range of theoretical and policy-oriented topics. The articles vary in technical and economic sophistication from quite theoretical pieces using the mathematical apparatus of modern economics to entirely verbal presentations written by economists for an audience of lawyers, nonprofit managers, and policy analysts. Thus, technically trained economists can see how their tools are being used to analyze nonprofit organizations while noneconomists can gain an appreciation of the way economic arguments can contribute to our understanding of the sector.

The book is organized into two parts. The first half outlines several different economic rationales for the existence of nonprofits: nonprofits may provide supplemental public services, they may be established as a response to information imperfections when trust and altruistic motives are important, or they may be vehicles for a diverse set of entrepreneurial objectives other than profit maximization. The second half concentrates on a series of policy issues: the tax deductibility of contributions, the link between government grants and private donations, the regulation of fundraising, and the exemption of nonprofits from the corporate income tax.

This volume is one of a series of edited books containing recent scholarship on the private nonprofit sector and includes a number of papers originally supported by Yale University's Program on Non-profit Organizations (PONPO). The series, which is under the general sponsorship of PONPO, has been made possible through a generous grant from the Lilly

Endowment Incorporated. The authors of papers included in this volume also benefited from a workshop based on the book manuscript and held in May 1984 at Columbia University. The workshop was sponsored jointly by PONPO and Columbia's Center for Law and Economic Studies.

I wish to thank several people for their help in the preparation of this volume. Fall Fergueson put the manuscript in the form required by Oxford. Yvonne Tenney, my assistant, read the galleys and Kuen Lee, a graduate student in the Columbia Economics Department, prepared the index. Finally, I am very grateful to John Simon and Paul DiMaggio of PONPO for asking me to prepare a volume in the PONPO series and to PONPO itself for supporting my own research on charities over the past several years.

Contents

VII. Corporate Tax Benefits

Contributors

Burton A. Abrams is Professor of Economics at the University of Delaware. His research interests are in the areas of public choice and public finance.

Avner Ben-Ner is Lecturer in Economics at the University of Haifa, Visiting Assistant Professor of Economics at the University of California at Davis, and a former research assistant of the Program on Non-Profit Organizations and lecturer in economics at Yale University. His work focuses on theoretical and empirical aspects of organizational life cycles (especially cooperatives, communes, and nonprofit organizations) as well as on the economics of trade unions and comparative economics systems.

Charles T. Clotfelter is Professor of Public Policy Studies and Economics at Duke University. His research interests include public finance and tax policy. He has recently completed *Federal Tax Policy and Charitable Giving*, a National Bureau of Economics Research Monograph.

David Easley is Associate Professor of Economics at Cornell University. His research and teaching interests are in microeconomic theory, particularly the effect of differential information on markets.

Henry B. Hansmann is Professor of Law and Economics at Yale Law School. His research interests are focused on the law and economics of alternative organizational forms, especially nonprofit and cooperative organizations.

Harold M. Hochman is Professor of Economics and Public Administration and Director of the Center for the Study of Business and Government at Bernard Baruch College of the City University of New York. His current research interests include regulatory policy and methods of private and public choice.

Estelle James is Professor of Economics and Chair of the Economics Department at the State University of New York, Stony Brook. She is the author of numerous articles on nonprofit organizations, the economics of education, and applied welfare economics. She is currently studying the public/private division of responsibility for education in a variety of modern industrial and developing societies.

Michael Krashinsky is Associate Professor of Economics and has been Associate Dean at the Scarborough Campus of the University of Toronto. He has written books on day care and on user charges in the social services. His current research interests include optimal taxation, education, electoral incumbency, and the nonprofit sector in Canada.

Judith Manfiedo Legoretta is a graduate of the W. Averell Harriman College for Policy Analysis and Public Management. The paper included is this volume reflects the field work she carried out in fulfillment of her internship requirements for the M.S. degree, which she received in 1981.

Maureen O'Hara is Associate Professor of Finance at the Johnson Graduate School of Management, Cornell University. Her research focuses on financial intermediation and the effect of regulation on the behavior of financial institutions.

Sharon Oster is a professor at the School of Organization and Management, Yale University. Her research is in the fields of industrial organization and management.

James D. Rodgers is Professor of Economics and Chairman of the Department of Economics at the Pennsylvania State University. His research is in the areas of welfare economics and public finance.

Susan Rose-Ackerman is Professor of Law and Political Economy at Columbia University and Director of Columbia Law School's Center for Law and Economic Studies. She is the coauthor of *The Uncertain Search for Environmental Policy* (1974), the author of *Corruption: A Study in Political Economy* (1978), and a writer of numerous articles in professional journals. Her current work involves the relationship between administrative law and social science.

Lester M. Salamon is Director of the Center for Governance and Management Research at the Urban Institute in Washington, D.C. Prior to joining the Institute, he was Deputy Associate Director of the U.S. Office of Management and the Budget and Associate Professor of Policy Science at Duke University. His most recent publications include *The Federal Budget and the Nonprofit Sector* (1982), *The Illusion of Presidential Government* (1981), and articles in the *National Tax Journal, World Politics,* the *American Political Science Review, Public Policy,* and other journals.

Mark Schlesinger is a Macy Fellow at the Center for Health Policy and Management, J. F. Kennedy School of Government, Harvard University.

Mark Schmitz is a private consultant in Seattle, Washington. He was previously on the economics faculties of Washington State University and the University of Delaware.

John G. Simon is Augustus Lines Professor of Law at Yale Law School, and Chairman of the Program on Non-Profit Organizations at Yale University.

Richard Steinberg is Assistant Professor of Economics at Virginia Polytechnic Institute and State University. He has written a number of papers on the role and functioning of nonprofit organizations and is engaged in continuing research on these topics.

Jeff Strnad is Associate Professor of Law at the University of Southern California and Assistant Professor of Law and Economics at the California Institute of Technology. His research is in the areas of public finance and social choice theory with special emphasis on tax policy.

Burton A. Weisbrod is Professor of Economics and Director of the Center for Health Economics and Law at the University of Wisconsin–Madison. A former senior staff member of the President's Council of Economic Advisers, Weisbrod is currently undertaking research in two principal areas: health economics and comparative behavior of for-profit and nonprofit institutions. He is the author or coauthor of twelve books and over one hundred articles on a variety of public sector economic problems.

Jeffrey H. Weiss is an assistant professor of economics and finance at Baruch College, City University of New York. He has also been associated with Baruch's Center for the Study of Business and Government. Weiss has published numerous articles in the field of cooperative game theory.

Dennis R. Young is a professor at the W. Averell Harriman College for Policy Analysis and Public Management of the State University of New York at Stony Brook. He is also a visiting faculty member of the Institution for Social and Policy Studies, Program on Non-Profit Organizations, at Yale University. His principal research interests are the economic organization of public services and the theory and management of nonprofit organizations. His books include *How Shall We Collect the Garbage?; Foster Care and Nonprofit Agencies* (coauthored with Stephen Finch) and *If Not for Profit, For What?*

THE ECONOMICS OF
NONPROFIT INSTITUTIONS

Introduction

SUSAN ROSE-ACKERMAN

Economic analyses of private, nonprofit firms can enrich and complement the new scholarship in industrial organization and political economy. This work, which promises to change the way economists think about both markets and government, concentrates on a fuller consideration of alternative institutional forms and types of markets. Thus, the private nonprofit firm can be seen as an important organizational option different from both for-profit firms and public agencies. Three themes are important. First, work on nonprofits is closely linked to the work of both the new institutional economists and those who study the relationship between the forms of public organizations and their behavior. The former study for-profits; the latter, public bureaucracies and legislatures, but their basic modeling strategies are similar.[1] Second, another line of research analyzes the selection mechanisms which sort people across institutions. Entrepreneurs who are especially interested in high levels of personal income will gravitate to jobs in the for-profit sector while ideologists and altruists will choose nonprofits.[2] Third, the study of markets where nonprofit firms are active is analogous to analyses of monopolistically competitive markets with imperfect information.[3]

Economic analyses of nonprofit firms generate insights both for those whose primary interest is the voluntary nonprofit sector and for economists whose main concern is the private market economy. Thus, a sensitivity to the opportunities for private gain even within nominally charitable organizations leads to a focus on the structure of nonprofit firms and on the incentives faced by those who work for them. Conversely, an understanding of the independent rule of trust, loyalty, and altruism can inform our understanding of organizations ostensibly concerned only with profit maximization.[4]

In the past several years a group of economists, many of them supported by Yale University's Program on NonProfit Organizations, has pursued these themes in a series of independent, but interrelated, studies. Their work emphasizes the relationship between organizational form, market structure,

and firm behavior but is also sensitive to the complex motivations of donors, customers, and managers. This book collects several of these studies,
currently available in widely dispersed journals or unpublished working
papers. Many of the papers in the book were discussed during a one-day
conference, organized by Columbia University's Center for Law and Economic Studies. A few of the discussants prepared formal remarks, and these
are also included in this volume.

By presenting a variety of theoretical approaches in one place, the first
half of the book attempts to show the reader the range of modeling possibilities currently being pursued. The second half suggests the way economic analysis enlightens a series of policy issues: the charitable deduction, government grants to nonprofits, the regulation of fundraising, and
nonprofit exemption from the corporate income tax.

THEORY

I distinguish between four types of models: (1) models which are relatively
institution free and concentrate on voluntary provision as a response to
government failure; (2) models which see nonprofits as a response to information asymmetries and transaction costs in the private for-profit marketplace; (3) models of entrepreneurs and managers who view the nonprofit firm as a way to further their own goals; and (4) models which
emphasize the competitive interactions between nonprofit firms producing
close substitutes.

Nonprofits as a Response to Government Failure

The papers by Burton Weisbrod, Jeffrey Weiss, and work on the charitable
deduction all concentrate on nonprofits which provide collective goods and
are financed by voluntary donations from people dissatisfied with low levels of government activity. In the papers by Weisbrod and Weiss nonprofit
organizations are not modeled explicitly; they are merely conduits which
efficiently convert gifts into services demanded by donors. Donors obtain
exactly the type of services they most prefer, given their willingness to pay.
Since students of the charitable deduction are mainly interested in the deduction's effect on the price of charitable giving, they also assume away
other influences on giving such as the range and quality of charitable outputs. In these models donors can observe the quality and quantity of output, and their charitable giving is a response to government's political
choices.

Despite its lack of institutional detail and its unconcern with product
differentiation in the nonprofit sector, Weisbrod's model is a seminal contribution. He points out that even in a very simple direct democracy, which
makes choices by voting and levies taxes which do not reflect marginal
benefits, a significant proportion of the population could believe that the

level of public services is too low. This is especially likely if demands are very heterogeneous at the given set of tax prices. As a consequence, some of the dissatisfied people might make charitable contributions to private organizations willing to produce incremental units of the service. Of course, it is not enough to point out that some people are undersupplied with public goods; one must also explain why donations are made. Here narrow economic reasoning is inadequate because of free-rider problems. While Weisbrod does not entirely resolve this issue, he does point to social pressure, tied private benefits, and the possibility of voluntary redistributions which benefit both donor and recipient. On the basis of his modeling efforts, he argues for the public subsidy of gifts to organizations which produce collective benefits.

Weisbrod's theory seems to imply that a world with both a government and a voluntary sector will have higher levels of public services than one with only a government and will produce Pareto Superior outcomes where everyone is at least as well off as in a world with no voluntary sector.[5] Jeffrey Weiss, however, demonstrates that this is not necessarily true. If both charities and the government provide the same type of "public" service, then gifts to charity reduce people's demands for government-provided goods and may lead to an overall reduction in public services. Those with high demands for public services who contribute to charity could end up worse off when voluntary organizations exist. In the case that Weiss develops, donations are individually rational for these people, but all high demanders could be made better off if charitable gifts were made illegal.

Jeffrey Strnad's article on the charitable deduction is discussed below in the policy section, but its theoretical perspective is similar to Weiss's work in its concentration on the political bargains which may be struck between high and low demanders. In both models low demanders may ultimately be made better off from the presence of a charitable deduction. In Weiss's model this result occurs because high demanders finance activities which directly benefit everyone. In Strnad's work the benefit comes from the higher marginal tax rate that wealthy, high demanders accept along with the deduction.

Contract Failure and Information Asymmetries

The second and largest body of theory emphasizes the tasks which nonprofit organizations can perform better than for-profit firms. If the quality of output is difficult to measure, and if contracts for future delivery are difficult to enforce, the nonprofit form may act as a signal assuring people that quality will not be sacrificed for private monetary gain. Thus, Henry Hansmann argues that this signal is believable because of the nondistribution constraint that prevents private individuals from claiming a share of the firm's profits. Nonprofits arise because of the failure of contractual arrangements in the for-profit sector. In developing this argument Hansmann presents a fourfold categorization of nonprofits that will help organize my discussion of the other papers in this section. Firms are labeled "donative" or "commercial" depending upon whether funds come mostly from donations (e.g., charities which aid the poor) or mostly from the sale of services (e.g., hospitals). Nonprofits are "mutual organizations" in Hansmann's terminology if they are controlled by their patrons, be they donors or paying customers. In contrast, "entrepreneurial firms" are controlled by people without a financial stake in the enterprise.

Donative nonprofits arise in response to contract failure because donors have great difficulty monitoring the quality and quantity of services provided by charities which aid the needy. Similarly, following Weisbrod's argument, nonprofits have a comparative advantage over for-profits in the production of collective goods. Such firms will generally be donative nonprofits (to use Hansmann's terminology) because donors also consume the collective good. Hansmann then goes on to discuss the advantages of commercial nonprofits in providing difficult to evaluate personal services such as health care or education. Here, however, competition with for-profit firms is common and both types coexist in a number of industries (see Table 1). Coexistence is possible because of product differentiation. For example, nonprofits may specialize in expensive, high-quality services while for-profits provide lower-quality, less expensive outputs.

Hansmann's functional argument hinges on the effectiveness of the non-distribution constraint and on the difficulty of evading its strictures. While Hansmann recognizes that the nondistribution constraint can sometimes be evaded and is not well enforced, he argues that, on balance, it operates to produce a sector that consumers believe to be more trustworthy than the for-profit alternative.

David Easley and Maureen O'Hara also base their analysis on contract failure, but their emphasis is different from Hansmann's. For them, a nonprofit firm is defined as one in which the manager receives a fixed reward. They assume that, given this definition, nonprofits have no incentive to distort information. The authors, therefore, postulate that since managers are indifferent between lying and telling the truth, they will always tell the truth. Thus, in markets with asymmetric information, customers believe that the information nonprofit firms provide is more credible than that provided by for-profit competitors.

Easley and O'Hara justify the resulting distribution of nonprofits across industries by showing that nonprofits are the preferred form in some industries. They then argue that if "society" negotiated with managers over the form of their reward, the optimal structure would result. This argument, however, to the extent that it attempts to rationalize the facts, fails to explain how "society," a rather amorphous and poorly managed entity, is able to negotiate with firm managers. The modeling exercise, while interesting, is an "as if" exercise (i.e., the existing pattern of organizational forms can be understood *as if* it resulted from such a negotiation).

By focusing entirely on "mutual" nonprofits, Avner Ben-Ner attempts to remedy this modeling deficiency by analyzing firms in which customers (or donors) control managers directly instead of through arms-length contracts. They may, in fact, even become the managers themselves. Ben-Ner is also concerned with quality control and contract failure, but he puts relatively little emphasis on the nondistribution constraint itself. Customer control is paramount. Such control may be expensive, however, since buyers must spend time monitoring managers. Thus, mutual nonprofits will only be established where quality control problems are severe.

Ben-Ner also demonstrates that the problem with for-profit provision is not limited to managers' incentives to misrepresent quality. First, since quality is a public good, profit-seeking firms may produce too little of it, and production under the control of consumers may be superior. Second, for-profit sellers may be unable to estimate individual demands for quality well enough to price discriminate. If so, a monopolist may ration high-demand consumers by quantity rather than price. Consumer control could remedy this inadequacy; however, if only one type of consumer (say high demanders) manage to dominate the mutual nonprofits, other consumers could lose. Ben-Ner's analysis is full of insights, but it is largely based on a monopolized market structure with no competition. He has not fully resolved the question of whether his arguments for consumer control in the presence of asymmetric information would carry over to a more competitive structure where for-profits and "mutual" nonprofits compete.

Michael Krashinsky attempts a broad overview and critique of the entire line of work reported here. He is basically supportive of the authors' emphasis on transaction costs and information asymmetries, but he points to some limitations of these theories. His major problem is their failure to distinguish sharply between problems which lead to the formation of nonprofits and those which lead to other adaptations such as detailed contracts, professionalism, government regulation, or public production. Krashinsky then goes on to sketch some of the factors which favor the nonprofit form over the alternatives of private for-profit or public production. The private, for-profit firm is, he points out, a response to the transaction costs of organizing all production through contracts between producers. Nonprofits, in contrast, become important in situations where transaction costs and information asymmetries exist between producers and consumers and among consumers. Nonprofits do not, however, arise in all such cases. Instead, Krashinsky argues that the nonprofit form tends to dominate other responses to high transaction costs when there is a separation between the purchaser and the direct beneficiary.[6] This form is especially likely to dominate when one's initial purchase decision is not easy to change. Consumers become essentially "locked in" to particular suppliers because of the cost of investigating and moving to another producer. In addition, nonprofits tend to arise as a way to overcome free-rider problems among consumers. Krashinshy does not, however, believe that Avner Ben-Ner's characterization of nonprofits as consumer-controlled organizations has widespread validity. Instead, he pictures consumers as having a more limited role in influencing these organizations.

Table 1. Service Industries Where Taxable and Tax-Exempt Firms Coexist (U.S. Totals: Establishments with Payroll, 1977)[a]

SIC Codes	Industry	Taxable		Tax-Exempt[b]		Tax-Exempt Share of Total	
		Number	Receipts[c] $1000	Number	Expenses[d] $1000	Number	Revenues[e]
7032	Sporting and recreational camps	2249	230,273	826	82,661	26.9	26.4
702, 704	Rooming houses and other lodging places[f]	3116	234,411	3096	219,861	49.8	48.4
7391	Commercial R&D laboratories	1784	2,025,573	268	1,148,222	13.1	36.2
7397	Commercial testing laboratories	1924	686,010	178	66,171	8.5	8.8
Health:							
8051	Skilled nursing care facilities	5733	5,190,993	1258	1,615,259	18.0	23.7
8059	Nursing and personal care facilities	5046	2,003,888	1073	600,607	17.5	23.1
8062	General medical and surgical hospitals	779	4,281,837	3296	37,186,364	80.9	89.7
8063	Psychiatric hospitals	128	300,899	86	328,330	40.2	52.2
8069	Other specialty hospitals	79	161,153	242	1,681,961	75.4	91.3
808	Outpatient care facilities	3239	997,356	4178	1,805,082	56.3	64.4
Education:							
821	Elementary and secondary schools[g]	2237	273,109	3297	1,296,078	59.6	82.6
8221	Colleges, universities, professional schools and junior colleges	40	57,593	1537	11,730,047	97.5	99.5
8222	Junior colleges and technical inst.	101	93,040	218	297,581	68.3	76.2
823	Libraries and information centers	183	9,887	1386	178,358	88.3	94.7
824	Correspondence and vocational schools	2571	841,028	790	160,362	23.5	16.0

Social services:						
832	Individual and family social services	1986	201,524	12,440	2,236,902	86.2	91.7
833	Job training and vocational rehab. serv.	736	187,081	3396	1,048,367	82.2	84.9
835	Child day-care services	14,172	759,554	10,641	829,218	42.9	52.2
836	Residential care	4600	666,042	5603	1,857,437	54.9	73.6
839	Social services	1610	224,267	8903	2,322,984	84.7	91.2
Culture, amusements, and recreation:						
7922	Theatrical producers and misc. services	2713	917,366	651	206,312	19.4	18.4
929	Bands, orchestras, dance groups, actors, and other entertainers and groups	4008	850,838	577	317,824	12.6	27.2

Sources: Table 1, Summary Statistics for the United States: 1977, pp. 53-1-2, 53-1-3, in U.S. Department of Commerce, Bureau of the Census, *1977 Census of Service Industries: Other Service Industries,* SC77-A-53, and *United States Report (Selected Service Industries)* SC77-A-52.

[a] For detailed definitions of terms, see the sources cited above.

[b] Excludes governmental organizations but includes (a) establishments owned by a government but operated by a private organization or (b) funded by government but operated independently (p. A-2)

[c] Receipts (Basic dollar volume measure for taxable establishments) include receipts from customers or clients for services rendered and merchandise sold during 1977 whether or not payment was received in 1977, except for health practitioners, who reported on a cash basis (payments received regardless of when services were rendered), and educational institutions, which were instructed to report for the fiscal year ending in 1977. Total receipts do not include local and state sales taxes or federal excise taxes collected by the establishment directly from customers and paid directly by the establishment to a local, state, or federal tax agency; nor do they include nonoperating income from such sources as investments, rental of real estate, etc. Receipts in this report do not include service receipts of manufacturers, wholesalers, retail establishments, or other businesses whose primary activity is other than service. However, they do include receipts other than from services rendered (e.g., sales of merchandise to individuals or other businesses) by establishments primarily engaged in performing services covered in this segment of the census. Rents and receipts of separately operated departments, concessions, etc. (e.g., a hospital gift shop or a commercially operated university dormitory), are excluded. These operations would be classified according to their major activity and separately tabulated. Although the count of establishments in this report represents the number in business at the end of the year, the receipts figures include receipts of all establishments in business at any time during the year.

[d] Expenses (Basic dollar volume measure for tax-exempt organizations). Expenses include payroll, employee benefits, interest and rent, taxes, cost of supplies used for operation, depreciation expense, fees paid for fundraising, and other expenses allocated to operations during 1977. (Educational institutions were instructed to report for the fiscal year ending in 1977.) Expenses in this report exclude outlays for purchases of real estate, construction and all other capital improvements, funds invested, assessments or dues paid to the parent or other chapters of the same organization, and funds transferred by fundraising organizations to charities and other organizations.

[e] Tax-exempt establishments' expenses divided by sum of receipts of taxable establishments and expenses of tax-exempt firms.

[f] Taxable firms include 702 (rooming and boarding houses) and 704 (organization hotels and lodging houses operated by membership organizations for the benefit of their constituents and not open to the general public). Nonprofits are active only in sector 704 but may compete with organizations in 702. Sector 704 includes fraternity and sorority houses and the residence houses and hotels of other organizations. The data in the table overstate the importance of tax-exempt firms since they may actually compete with portions of the for-profit rental housing market and with for-profit hotels and motels.

[g] Excludes schools operated by religious organizations.

The one empirical piece in the section, by Weisbrod and Schlesinger, directly addresses the question of whether for-profit firms are more likely than nonprofit firms to take advantage of the poor information of consumers. Using the nursing-home industry in Wisconsin as an example, they find that for-profits seem to perform more poorly when quality is difficult for outsiders to observe but are equivalent to nonprofits along other dimensions. The authors' empirical tests were complicated by the inevitable difficulty of measuring intangible aspects of quality, but the paper does provide a suggestive first step.

Of course, as most of these authors recognize, the nonprofit corporate form has problems which counteract some of its advantages even in markets with imperfect and asymmetric information. First, because profit sharing is illegal, managers may not pursue efficiency as actively as their for-profit counterparts and, in fact, people who prefer a quiet, pleasant life or else have particular ideological axes to grind may self-select into the nonprofit sector (cf. Dennis Young's piece in this volume). Second, capital may be difficult to raise because nonprofits do not have access to equity capital. Nonprofit and for-profit firms may be quite similar in form and behavior when scale economies are unimportant. The need for capital, however, may lead to a distinction between those firms which can raise money from profit-oriented investors and those which can generate voluntary donations.[7] Third, because service quality is frequently unobservable, the trustworthy reputation of nonprofit providers may be undermined by people who use nonprofits as shells for private gain. Direct donor or customer control can minimize this possibility, but that solution is also costly in both time and money.

The possibility of coopting nonprofit firms for private gain suggests a reason for avoiding policies which outlaw for-profit firms in particular industries or otherwise favor nonprofits with government grants and regulatory laxity. Such special treatment may simply encourage profit-oriented entrepreneurs to hide their goals behind the smokescreen of the nonprofit form. Therefore, in each market where nonprofits compete with for-profits (e.g., day care, general hospitals, summer camps, private psychiatric hospitals; see Table 1) it is necessary to demonstrate anew that the nonprofit form is genuinely associated with reliability and high quality. The nondistribution condition, taken alone, does not assure that a firm can be trusted.

Nonprofit Entrepreneurs and Managers

The models based on government failure and contract failure are essentially demand-side models which emphasize the reasons why individuals may prefer to deal with nonprofit organizations. The supply side has been less well examined. We need a more well-developed theory of nonprofit entrepreneurship. Given the lack of high monetary gains, what motivates people to become nonprofit entrepreneurs? Do these entrepreneurs, as theory suggests, behave differently from those in the for-profit sector? How do individuals who control nonprofit organizations act to further their own ends?[8] Why do some organizations change form, e.g., from for-profit firms or from government entities to nonprofit corporations? Research here is at an early stage, but both Dennis Young and Estelle James have produced worthwhile analyses. Young has carried out a series of detailed case studies of nonprofit entrepreneurs which show the wide range of their motivations and backgrounds. Some are committed ideologists, others seem to be budget maximizers.[9] Recent work by Estelle James, summarized in her comments on the preceding section, emphasizes the importance of religious faith as a primary motivating ideology. Especially outside the United States, religious groups provide a major source of entrepreneurial energy as they seek to make converts and maintain adherents through establishing schools and health-care facilities.

Young's article in this volume draws on his extensive case study experience in the social science area. He characterizes entrepreneurs as artists, professionals, believers, searchers, independents, conservers, power seekers, controllers, players, and income seekers. He then argues that people with different entrepreneurial traits will be attracted to different types of firms or industries. The motivation of a firm's entrepreneur obviously has a great deal to do with whether the firm can, in fact, be "trusted" in Hansmann's sense. Young's ideas carry over to his joint paper with Judith Legoretta which presents several examples of public and for-profit organizations which became nonprofits. In those examples the main motivation was an enterpreneur's attempt to maintain control of an organization even as he or she gave up direct day-to-day oversight.

Estelle James' paper is concerned not with entrepreneurs who found institutions but with individuals in powerful positions *within* nonprofit organizations. While Young's theory is linked to his case studies of private social-service agencies which are often small, highly personalized organizations, James' model is the large, decentralized university. She is interested in the common and important phenomenon of cross-subsidization. Those who control the organization (tenured professors) hire temporary workers (untenured faculty) to engage in revenue producing activity (teaching the basics to large classes of undergraduates). The revenue generated from this activity (tuition payments) is used to subsidize the professional activities of the controllers (research and graduate education). Such cross-subsidization is not always possible, however, because the temporary workers may be able to form their own institutions and keep the surplus. Nevertheless, in the current university setting James' model is plausible because of the prestige which junior faculty obtain from being part of an institution with a distinguished senior faculty.

Market Models

The papers in the theoretical section of the book, while economic in approach, do not analyze the interaction of nonprofit firms in a market. The research explains how nonprofits can arise in response to market failures or government failures, and it analyzes the motivations of entrepreneurs and managers, but it ignores competition. A market perspective is, however, central to my own papers which are included in the public policy section. In my models nonprofits are a diverse group of firms producing similar outputs on the basis of different ideological principles. Ideological product differentiation is central. The firms may seem to be producing close substitutes (day care, education, health services, counseling, etc.), but because of differences in philosophy, particular donors and consumers will be enthusiastic about one provider and wish to drive another out of business. A conservative Christian who believes in "creationism" may eagerly support private schools which refuse to teach evolution and hope to close down schools run by the Ethical Culture Society. Those who control these charitable organizations are modeled as pragmatic ideologists with an interest in the survival of their firms. They have a most preferred philosophical position, but they may shift the organization's ideological perspective if this is required in order to obtain funds. Therefore, if there are fixed costs to setting up an organization, then not all donors and customers will be able to find exactly the mixture of service type and ideology they most want. People willing to sacrifice personal financial rewards in order to be nonprofit entrepreneurs have some freedom to fulfill their own ideological preferences.

In my paper on government grants and philanthropy, however, I show how competition for scarce donations, government grants, and customers constrains the choices of entrepreneurs. Similarly, the presence of for-profit competitors can modify the behavior of nonprofit firms. In industries such as day care where both types of firms coexist, nonprofits may specialize in one type of service (e.g., services for subsidized children and wealthy, paying customers), while for-profits concentrate on another (e.g., low-cost services for the middle-class children of working parents).[10]

Suppose, in contrast, that no entry barriers exist. There are no fixed costs in setting up an organization and no shortage of nonprofit entrepreneurs. In my paper on fundraising I show that these conditions, thought to be desirable in an ordinary market, can destroy the viability of the charitable sector. Firms compete for charitable donations by spending money on advertising brochures and new entrants compete away any surplus available for providing services to the needy. Competition is genuinely "destructive" under these conditions.

POLICY

Governments affect the behavior and growth of nonprofit firms in three ways: (1) through the tax system, (2) through direct spending programs, and (3) through regulations. While economists and tax analysts have studied the charitable deduction, economists have focused little scholarly attention on the other, equally important, policy issues. In the past, discussions of federal spending and regulatory policy have either ignored nonprofits or lumped them in with other types of providers. While this treatment may sometimes be justified, the papers included here take some first steps toward disentangling the distinctive features of government–nonprofit relations.

The Charitable Deduction

We begin, however, with a familiar topic: the charitable deduction. Clotfelter and Salamon's paper predicts the effects of the 1981 tax act on charitable contributions by individuals.[11] Gifts will increase but at a slower rate than with no change in the law, and the balance will shift toward lower income taxpayers. This implies an increase in gifts to religious groups and a likely fall in gifts to health and education. Besides the presentation of empirical results the paper has the further advantage of summarizing and referencing past work on the price and income elasticity of giving.

Hochman and Rodgers argue that a tax credit is superior to a deduction because it may well approximate the efficient solution in which marginal payments for collective goods (both taxes and gifts) reflect marginal benefits. John Simon, in a longer piece excerpted here, focuses more on distributive equity than on allocative efficiency. He worries about the elitism involved in encouraging voluntary donations through charitable deductions, although he ultimately concludes that it is not the proper focus of attention for those concerned either with correcting income inequalities or with assuring legislative equity and fairness.

These papers provide a background for Jeffrey Strnad's attempt to rationalize the existing tax law in public choice terms. He argues that the deduction may be part of a broad political bargain between the rich and the poor. If so, the poor must believe that they gain on balance from the continuation of the present law. He goes on to show that, in contrast to Hochman and Rodgers' result, a tax credit does not necessarily represent a Pareto Superior result under which everyone gains.

When Strnad turns to a positive analysis of the political system, however, he is unable to conclude that the charitable contribution deduction is necessarily Pareto Superior to a world with no deduction. Nevertheless, he defends the deduction by focusing on the political compromise of which it is a part. Thus, Strnad would hesitate to overturn the deduction because this act could upset other parts of the existing political bargain.

Government Spending

Especially in the social welfare field, government transfer programs substitute for private charity. Recently, however, some of this public spending, particularly for social services, has been channeled through nonprofit organizations. Some scholars have been interested in the impact of this spending on private giving.

The work of Abrams and Schmitz emphasizes the level of public spending and does not deal explicitly with the fact that some government money is being spent by nonprofit organizations. Recognizing that both income and substitution effects will reduce spending, they find that a one percent increase in government transfers (per person) leads to about a 0.2 percent reduction in an individual's private charitable giving.

My own theoretical effort moves beyond this highly aggregated effort to consider government grants made directly to nonprofit organizations. Here the effects on charitable giving are more complex and may be positive. Obviously, if the funds are provided in the form of matching grants, they reduce the price of giving to that charity below the "tax-price" and may well stimulate giving. (Gifts to other organizations not eligible for grants might, of course, fall.) However, this is not the only situation in which gifts may increase. Thus, lump sum grants may be given with strings attached. These conditions may lead the charity to engage in better record keeping and reporting or to produce services favored by existing small donors who lack the government's leverage. A large public grant may also permit the nonprofit to realize scale economies or to select clients more carefully. In all of these circumstances public grants might stimulate private giving as donors benefit from the conditions attached to the public monies. Of course, the reverse result is possible too: an agency may have to choose between accepting public support or retaining its private donors. For example, as a condition of support, the government may require the agency to undertake certain programs or adopt broad-based eligibility criteria which conflict with donors' wishes.

Regulation of Fundraising

Several state governments regulate charities' solicitation practices and fundraising percentages. My paper in this section shows that these laws may be counterproductive. Without controls on entry, charities cannot directly determine the share of resources spent on fundraising. In one section of the paper I assume that donors use the average fundraising share to estimate the marginal share. While it is a mistake for donors to do this, their behavior is based on the fact that the average share is generally the only information available.[12] Even when donors react to high shares by reducing their donations, however, the fundraising share will remain at high levels as new charities enter. Thus, if the entry of new charities is easy, a law establishing a fundraising percentage may be unenforceable. There is an inevitable tension between, on the one hand, encouraging diversity and fostering the growth of new charities and, on the other, establishing a voluntary system that can provide high levels of services.

Richard Steinberg criticizes my contention that donors confuse average and marginal fundraising shares. He demonstrates that, in general, the average share is a poor proxy for the marginal share. Charities with high average shares may spend marginal dollars almost entirely on services. Thus, information on a charity's fundraising share is unlikely to prove useful to rational donors. Steinberg's preliminary empirical work, in support of his theoretical efforts, shows that charitable giving appears to be sensitive to marginal dollars spent on fundraising but not to the average share. He does not, however, have any independent information on whether donors actually are aware of any of this information.

Corporate Taxation

Nonprofit organizations are exempt from the corporate profits tax unless they engage in "unrelated" business activities. Hansmann seeks a rationale for this basic exemption. My paper concentrates on the unrelated business income tax and claims of "unfair" competition made by firms which compete with nonprofits.

Hansmann rationalizes the exemption as a partial compensation for nonprofits' difficulties in obtaining access to the capital markets. Therefore, these firms are more dependent on internally generated capital, and exemption from tax assures them of a larger supply of capital.

My article discusses the issue of "unfair" competition between nonprofit and for-profit firms. I isolate situations in which it is plausible to contend that such competition occurs and then go on to argue that the tax on unrelated business income is misguided. It is likely to induce nonprofit organizations to concentrate their moneymaking activities in "related" areas (e.g., gift shops, travel tours, restaurants) so that they have a relatively large impact on businesses in a relatively few areas. Repeal of the tax could spread nonprofits' revenue-raising activities more broadly and prevent them from having a large impact on any one industry. One would then only need to be sure that nonprofit subsidiaries were not being used by profit-seeking individuals to circumvent the tax laws.

CONCLUSIONS

This volume presents a new field of study for economists and demonstrates the fruitful multiplicity of approaches that exists.[13] The work parallels and intersects with much recent work in industrial organization, price theory, and public finance. It is my hope that the papers included here will be useful both to those with a substantive interest in the nonprofit sector and to economists working in other fields who may discover a new subject for analysis. The papers do not represent a finished and unified body of work. Instead, each one, in the process of developing its own arguments, raises and leaves unanswered other important questions. We are at the beginning of an ongoing research endeavor.

NOTES

1. The former include, for example, Richard R. Nelson and Sidney G. Winter, *An Evolutionary Theory of Economic Change*, Cambridge: Harvard University Press, 1982; and Oliver Williamson, *Markets and Hierarchies*, New York: Free Press, 1975. For examples of the latter see Richard Barke and William Riker, A political theory of regulation with some observations on railway abandonments, *Public Choice* 39:33–66 (1982); William Niskanen, *Bureaucracy and Representative Government*, Chicago: Aldine-Atherton, 1971; Susan Rose-Ackerman, *Corruption: A Study in Political Economy*, New York: Academic Press, 1978. Closely related to this work is research that emphasizes the importance of property rights in determining behavior. See, for example, Armen Alchian and Harold Demsetz, Production, information costs and economic organization, *American Economic Review* 62:777–795 (December 1972); Eugene Fama and Michael Jensen, Separation of ownership and control, *J. of Law and Economics* 26:301–325 (June 1983). A previous compilation of articles reflects this research perspective: Kenneth Clarkson and Donald Martin, eds., *The Economics of Nonproprietary Organizations*, Greenwich, Connecticut: JAI Press, 1980.

2. See Burton A. Weisbrod with Joel F. Handler and Neil Komesar, *Public Interest Law: An Economic and Institutional Analysis*, Berkeley: University of California Press, 1978.

3. A monopolistically competitive market consists of a large number of firms, each producing a slightly different product. The goods are close, but not perfect, substitutes. See B. Curtis Eaton and Richard Lipsey, The principle of minimum differentiation reconsidered, *Review of Economic Studies* 42:27–49 (January 1975); Kelvin Lancaster, *Variety, Equity and Efficiency*, Cambridge: Cambridge University Press, 1979; and Steven Salop and Joseph Stiglitz, Bargains and ripoffs: A model of monopolistically competitive price dispersion, *Review of Economic Studies* 44:493–510 (October 1977).

4. See Kenneth Arrow, *The Limits of Organizations*, New York: Norton, 1974.

5. Situation A is Pareto superior to another situation, B, if everyone is at least as well off at A as at B and if at least one person is better off. Situation A can then be described as more efficient than Situation B.

6. For a related view see Eugene Fama and Michael Jensen, Agency problems and residual claims, *J. of Law and Economics* 26:341–345 (June 1983).

7. Professor Kelvin Lancaster of Columbia University made this point in his remarks at the May conference. See, also, Henry Hansmann's piece in this volume on nonprofit's exemption from the corporate income tax.

8. The use of boards of directors as a way to control managers is an important issue not discussed by the authors included in this volume. For a preliminary attempt, however, see Fama and Jensen supra note 1 at 318–321 and Oliver Williamson's critique of their analysis in Organizational form, residual claimants, and corporate control, *J. of Law and Economics* 26:358–360 (June 1983).

9. Dennis Young, *Casebook of Management for Non-Profit Organization: Entrepreneurship and Organizational Change in the Human Services*, New York: Haworth Press, 1984. Also, Dennis Young, *If Not For Profit, For What?* Lexington: Lexington Books, D. C. Heath Co., 1983.

10. For a fuller discussion of day care see Susan Rose-Ackerman, Unintended consequences: Regulating the quality of subsidized day care, *Journal of Policy Analysis and Management* 3:14–30 (Fall 1983).

11. An expanded treatment of the effects of tax changes on giving appears in Charles Clotfelter, *Federal Tax Policy and Charitable Giving*, Chicago: University of Chicago Press, forthcoming 1985.

12. It is possible, however, that donors care directly about total spending on fundraising. This could occur if donors believe that their gifts permit them to "buy-in" to the charity, i.e., a gift gives one the right to feel good about all the services provided by the charity. Then, if two charities have the same overall budget, donors will prefer the one with the lower fundraising share. In a comment at the May conference Michael Krashinsky made a complementary point. He suggested that low fundraising expenses are associated with the ability to use

volunteers to help raise money. Donors may believe that an organization which is able to attract such volunteers is of higher quality than one which must depend on paid fundraisers.

13. For literature reviews which complement the collection presented here see Henry Hansmann, Economic theories of nonprofit organization, in W. Powell, ed., *Handbook of Nonprofit Organizations,* New Haven: Yale University Press, 1986; Estelle James and Susan Rose-Ackerman, The private nonprofit firm, in M. Montias and J. Kornai, eds., *Economic Systems,* a volume in J. Lesourne and H. Sonnenshein, eds., *Fundamentals of Pure and Applied Economics* and *Encyclopedia of Economics,* Harwood Academic Publishers, forthcoming, and Richard Steinberg, Nonprofit organizations and the market, in Powell, ed.

Models of Nonprofit Firms

I

GOVERNMENT FAILURE

1

Toward a Theory
of the Voluntary Nonprofit Sector
in a Three-Sector Economy

BURTON A. WEISBROD

This chapter is an exploratory effort to examine the role of a voluntary, "nonprofit" sector in an economy with public and private (for-profit) sectors and with collective-consumption and private-consumption goods. More generally, we seek to discover those factors that determine which goods will be provided governmentally, which privately in for-profit markets, and which in voluntary markets. The approach is primarily positive, attempting particularly to predict the circumstances under which the voluntary sector will develop, grow, and decline. A model will be fashioned in which certain behavioral and organizational constraints limit public-sector and for-profit sector activities and stimulate the voluntary sector; and in which the demand for collective-consumption goods is not sufficient to ensure governmental production or provision. The existence of voluntary organizations will thus be explained with a minimum of institutional assumptions. In effect, we set forth the logic behind a hypothesis that there are nongovernmental, voluntary organizations providing collective goods—goods that enter, positively, the utility functions of more than one person simultane-

From *The Voluntary Nonprofit Sector,* ed. by Burton A. Weisbrod, D. C. Heath, Lexington, Mass., pp. 51–76. Revision of paper presented at the Conference on Altrusim and Economic Theory, Russell Sage Foundation, New York, March 3–4, 1972, and published in *Altruism, Morality and Economic Theory,* ed. by Edmund S. Phelps, Russell Sage Foundation, N.Y., 1975, pp. 171–95. © 1975 Russell Sage Foundation. This research received a variety of support: from funds granted to the Institute for Research on Poverty by the Office of Economic Opportunity pursuant to the provisions of the Economic Opportunity Act of 1964; from the University of Wisconsin Graduate School; and from Guggenheim Foundation and Ford Foundation fellowships. In connection with various parts of the research the author has been very fortunate to be assisted by Jennifer Gerner, A. James Lee, Marc Bendick, Jr., and Donna Beutel. Eugene Smolensky, Mark Menchik, and Donald Nichols provided helpful comments on an earlier draft. The conclusions contained herein are the author's sole responsibility.
  Reprinted by permission of the author.

ously. Some normative judgments will be reached regarding efficient public policy toward certain types of voluntary organizations.

The analysis presented here is essentially static. There is some consideration, however, of the effects on the distribution of economic activity among the three sectors—government, for-profit, and voluntary—that result from changes in population characteristics and in the level and inequality of income.

The interest that is now developing in organizations variously referred to as voluntary, nonprofit, collective, charitable, nonmarket or philanthropic is overdue, for there is no doubt that a wide array of economic activity is undertaken outside the private profit-seeking sector and outside the public sector. Contemporary economics includes a long-established theory of the private (profit) sector, the rationale for its existence, and the mode of its equilibrium behavior; more recently a theory of the public (government) sector has evolved, emphasizing the existence of "public," "collective-consumption" goods for which the private sector is an unsatisfactory production vehicle that is likely to produce suboptimal quantities.[1] Yet the reality of goods and services that are provided neither governmentally, in the sense of being financed through taxation, nor privately, in the sense of being financed through user charges and operated for "profit," confronts us with a gap in our theories.

But the goal here is less ambitious than to explain the existence, let alone the behavior, of *all* of the many kinds of organizations that are found outside the private for-profit and the public sectors. Rather, it is to identify one class of such activities—the provision (financing) of public-type, collective-consumption goods by nongovernmental enterprises. Thus, this chapter examines some interrelations between the public sector, the private sector, and the voluntary sector, focusing on the provision of collective-consumption goods outside the government.

We begin with an analysis of governmental behavior. The existence of certain constraints on governments will be seen to result in what might be termed government market failure, analogous to the conditions causing private market failures. Development of a voluntary sector will be posited as an adjustment to the restricted capabilities of the other two sectors.

THE ELEMENTS OF A SIMPLE MODEL OF OUTPUT DETERMINATION IN THE GOVERNMENT SECTOR

Assume a society exists in which: people behave rationally in pursuit of their individual objectives of utility maximization; a given state of technology and set of production possibilities exist, and these permit production of some collective-consumption and some private-consumption goods; each person's utility is a function of both his private goods and the collective-consumption goods that are available to him; utility functions are not the same for all people.

One question with which we want a behavioral model to deal is: How much of the demand for collective-consumption goods will be satisfied by government? "Satisfied" by a government is defined as financed by a government, no distinction being made between government production (ownership) of some good and provision via purchase or contracting-out—that is, paying a private producer to supply it.[2] Henceforth, the term *government provision* will be used to describe both types of arrangements.

A rule or behavioral assumption is needed for determining how government will finance any given level of output for a specified good, and a rule is also required for specifying how voter demands will influence the level of government provision. Both of these are important and, given the present state of economic understanding, controversial issues. While particular assumptions will be stated shortly, it is desirable to relax the assumptions in order to determine the sensitivity of our results to the particular assumptions. Regarding the finance mechanism we postulate:

Any tax (and perhaps user-charge) system may be used by government to finance a particular expenditure program, subject to the constraint that the system does not permit every, or nearly every, consumer to equate the tax he pays with the marginal benefit of the good to him. Such a relatively weak assumption will not permit strong statements about government output levels, and more attention should be given to the implications of more specific requirements, but some interesting conclusions can nonetheless be reached. It should be noted, however, that the assumption is less innocuous than it might appear. It rules out vote trading, selling, or logrolling *if* the effect would be to leave each person with a *net* tax price—net of "bribe"—that is equal to his valuation of marginal output. While such trading activities do occur to some extent and they do tend to reduce divergencies between marginal benefit and marginal price among consumers, the combination of information costs, strategic behavior (transaction costs) and, in most instances, legal prohibition (against "selling" votes) sustain significant divergencies.

We turn now to the need for a rule regarding how consumer-voter demands influence decisions by government to supply a good. This has received growing attention in recent years but consensus has not yet been reached.[3] In this chapter, however, we begin with the following assumption.

Government will supply a quantity and quality of any commodity that is determined by a political voting process. One such process would involve majority vote, according to which the demands of the median voter would determine the outcome.[4] An alternative would be a *weighted*-majority decision rule in which the weight attached to each person's "vote" is some function of the "loudness" of his "squawk" (intensity of dissatisfaction with a given tax-and-provision decision).[5] The latter model might predict that mean, rather than median, demand determines levels of government provision, and that the dispersion to the right and to the left of the mean might have asymmetrical effects. But these are little more than plausible speculations concerning political processes. For our present purpose we require only that the political process leaves significant numbers of voters dissatisfied with government output and taxation levels.

Summing up: if consumer-voters know the rule by which government will allocate costs among them, their utility functions will generate a set of demand functions for governmentally provided goods which, with the government-supply decision-rule, will determine a level of government provision.

While each of our assumptions may reasonably be questioned as to its realism, there is particular reason to question whether consumer-voters know how the cost of any increased government output provision will be distributed among taxpayers.[6] Nevertheless, it is perhaps reasonable to believe that whatever cost-distribution rule taxpayers expect to be used, few persons expect a rule that (even roughly) equates tax liability with the value of benefits from a marginal unit of the good. This is especially true for the host of governmentally provided goods for which there are no user charges.

The assumption of *non*benefit-principle tax-pricing is critical to the argument that follows. The reason is that a tax-pricing system that does not equate, for each voter, his marginal tax with the marginal benefit he receives from each collective-consumption good, will produce in general a level of government provision that exceeds what some voters demand and that falls short of what others demand. Not only is such a result nonoptimal, as is well known,[7] but as we shall see its occurrence can be expected to set in motion forces that will influence the aggregate allocation of resources among the three economic sectors. The assumption of nonbenefit tax-pricing is quite general, permitting a wide range of tax systems. It rules out only a system in reality is not available anyway, given that little is known about individuals' marginal valuation of particular public goods, and given that the free-rider problem leads people to hide their true valuations, even if they know them, when a benefit-based tax system is known to be used for financing a collective-consumption good.

Figure 1–1 illustrates a situation in which: (a) voter demands for public provision of a specific good vary among the seven persons portrayed; and in which (b) the tax-finance price rule specifies that costs are borne equally by all,[8] with each taxpayer paying P per unit of output provided by the government. This simple, but realistic tax rule is used for its simplicity only; it is not implied by our assumptions. The good may be thought of as a collective-consumption good, although it need not be. Later, we will consider briefly the demand for governmental provision of noncollective-consumption goods.

It is apparent from the diagram that, with each consumer-taxpayer paying the same tax, P, per unit of output, a majority of consumers (persons 4–7) would prefer the output to be at least at the level Q_1. At that level, consumers 1, 2, and 3 prefer to reduce the total tax and the quantity of output, while consumers 5, 6, and 7 prefer to increase both the total tax and the quantity supplied, but they are in the minority. Assuming a majority-

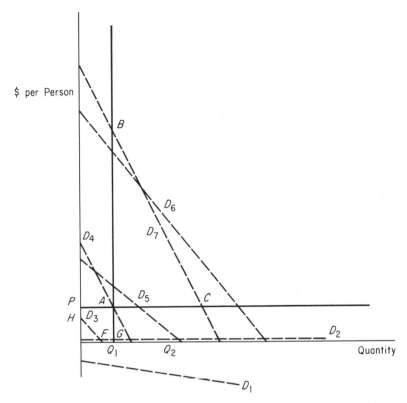

Figure 1-1 Hypothetical individual demand curves for a collective good.

vote rule, person 4, the median voter, has his way. In general, however, whether a majority vote or some other rule is operative, in the absence of marginal-benefit taxation the political process of determining an output level is likely to leave some consumers dissatisfied because they are receiving and paying for too much of the good, while others are dissatisfied because they are receiving too little—that is, they would prefer to have the total tax payment and output level increased.[9] The relative numbers of the two dissatisfied groups depend, of course, on the particular tax-pricing system and the political decision process. The simple majority-vote rule, for example, would satisfy only the median consumer, and so the population would be split evenly between those who demand more and those who demand less at the prevailing marginal tax-prices.

The *intensities* of individuals' dissatisfactions will also generally vary; for a person who demands *more* than the quantity supplied, the intensity can be measured by the area under his demand curve, above the tax-price curve, and to the right of the quantity supplied. For person 7 in Figure 1-1, this is the area *ABC*. For a person who demands *less* than the quantity supplied, the intensity of dissatisfaction may be measured, in corresponding fashion, by the area above the demand curve, below the tax-price curve, and to the left of the quantity supplied (*PAGFH* in Figure 1–1, for person 3).

REACTIONS OF DISSATISFIED CONSUMERS

With many consumers being either undersatisfied or oversatisfied, adjustments can be expected to occur.[10] Before turning to the nature of the adjustment possibilities, note that the relative numbers of persons who desire any adjustment, and the degree of adjustment desired, depend on the variation in demands of the tax price(s) that each consumer assumes he confronts. Thus, of major importance, in addition to the tax system, is the degree of demand homogeneity of the population. The greater the homogeneity within a political unit—that is, the greater the similarity in income, wealth, religion, ethnic background, education level, and other characteristics influencing demand for any collective-consumption good—the smaller the expected variation in individual demands and hence, the smaller the likely degree of dissatisfaction with the politically determined level and quality of output.

If (1) tax prices varied systematically with such population characteristics, and if (2) demand were a function of those same characteristics, then population heterogeneity in such a characteristic would not necessarily imply heterogeneity in quantities demanded. Heterogeneity of quantities demanded at the same tax price could be offset by corresponding, offsetting heterogeneity of tax prices. Thus, it might be argued that heterogeneity of income or wealth, for example, would be an unsatisfactory proxy for heterogeneity of quantities of collective goods demanded because tax prices are typically a function of income and wealth. But unless demands for a particular collective good vary with income or wealth in approximately the same way as tax prices vary with income and wealth, it remains true that heterogeneity of income or wealth proxy heterogeneity of quantities demanded and, in turn, proxy the extent of dissatisfied demand. However, other population characteristics—those that are highly correlated with demand for public goods but are not highly correlated with tax prices (religion, for example)—are still better proxies for diversity of quantities demanded and, hence, of oversatisfied and undersatisfied demand. The point is that diversity of population characteristics is not, ipso facto, equivalent to heterogeneity of quantities demanded. As a first approximation, though, it seems reasonable to assume that differences across political units in the degree of population heterogeneity are useful proxies for differences in the degree of undersatisfied demand.

There are several adjustment possibilities available to the dissatisfied consumers, including migration, formation of lower-level governments, resort to private market alternatives, and resort to voluntary organizations. Each will be discussed in turn, but the attempt is to describe not a sequential process but rather a general equilibrium adjustment process in which all of these organizational forms for satisfying consumer demands are simultaneously operative.[11]

One option for the dissatisfied consumer is *migration* to another governmental unit in which output and tax-pricing systems lead to an improvement in his economic welfare. The viability of this adjustment option is, of course, considerably greater if local governmental units are being considered than it is if higher-level governments are the focus.[12] In any case, since moving is not costless and since locational decisions reflect many considerations other than governmental outputs and taxes, we can think of Figure 1–1 as portraying the likely type of situation even after migration adjustments—a situation of diverse demands, some "oversatisfied" consumers, and some "undersatisfied" consumers.

Beyond migration, the undersatisfied and the oversatisfied consumers do confront somewhat different options. The oversatisfied consumers (persons 1–3 in Figure 1–1), if they do not move out, will have few options other than to bear the burden or to exert political pressure to alter either the tax-price system or the output-determination system. The undersatisfied consumers, however, have other alternatives, and this chapter focuses on them.

A second adjustment outlet, open to all those who want and are willing to pay for added output, is *to form lower-level governments*. Thus persons 5, 6, and 7, in Figure 1–1 might organize an additional government unit including only themselves, to provide additional units of the commodity in question. They could not entirely avoid the free-rider problem, of course— other persons would use some of the lower-level government's output if they could do so without paying (or by paying less than P). Neither could the undersatisfied demanders avoid the cost of organizing the new governmental unit. We can expect, therefore, that while (1) some lower-level government supplementation of output will take place—and this can be illustrated by parks and libraries, which are provided by federal, state, county, and local governments—at the same time, (2) some undersatisfied demand will remain.

As we consider adjustments in the several economic sectors, it should be noted that because we are considering collective goods, which benefit more than one person simultaneously, the provision of such goods in one sector may well reduce the demands for it in the other sectors. If the good were a pure collective good—involving no congestion whatsoever—then an increment of output of the good in one sector would presumably bring about an *equal* decrement in another sector, at least in equilibrium. When the collective good is anything short of pure, however, the provision of an additional unit of output in one sector will not lead to an equal decrease in the level of output provided in another sector.

In addition to migration and formation of lower-level government units, the third and fourth adjustment outlets for the undersatisfied demanders, the two on which this chapter focuses, are the *private* (for-profit) market and the *voluntary* (nonprofit) markets.

Consider, first, the private market. The currently prevailing view among economists regarding the role of private markets in the provision of public, collective-consumption goods is simply that those markets will produce suboptimal quantities of such goods, and that, therefore, governments may be, and from an allocative-efficiency standpoint should be, called upon to take steps to see that the output level is increased. Implicit in this view is an assumption that the private and the public markets are alternate organizational mechanisms for providing the *same* good.

PUBLIC- AND PRIVATE-GOOD SUBSTITUTES

We find that to be an invalid assumption. As an alternative we can think of the production-possibility set at a given point in time as including collective-consumption goods and private-good *substitutes* for them, as well as "ordinary" private goods, Thus, for example, the collective good, lighthouse, has a private-good substitute, shipboard radar; the collective good, provision of clean air, has private good substitutes in air filters and purifiers for home, automobile, and place of work; the collective good, standby fire department, has a private good substitute, sprinkler systems; the collective good, generic information (on drugs for example), has the private-good substitute, brand-name advertising; and the collective good, police department, has private good substitutes that include alarms, locks, guards, and dogs.[13]

To observe that there are often private-good substitutes for collective goods by no means says, however, that they are perfect substitutes. In fact, as the examples just given suggest, these substitutes are generally different in a particular and important way, which will be discussed shortly, and this difference has a notable implication for any attempt to understand and predict the degree of public sector involvement in the provision of a good.[14]

Observing that there are private-good substitutes for collective goods suggests that it would be useful to study the "industry" comprising: (1) each good or service provided by the public sector; plus (2) the substitutes provided by the private sector; plus—for the reason explored in the discussion that follows—(3) the substitutes provided by the voluntary sector.

It is presumably true that there is no technological constraint that prevents the private sector from producing collective goods. If that is so, then any observed difference in the "type" of goods provided by the private and the government sectors of an industry are likely to reflect consumers' preferences and/or relative prices. From the consumer-preference viewpoint, a collective-consumption good is likely to have one important disadvantage compared with a private-good substitute. The disadvantage of the collective good—whether it is governmentally or privately operated—is the lesser degree of individual control that each consumer can exercise over its form, quality, and utilization or deployment. Even the classical lighthouse and national defense activities must take particular forms, must be located in particular places, and must be activated and deactivated at particular times and under particular circumstances.

Rarely, if ever, will all consumers agree about how any of these decisions should be made, and yet, by the very nature of collective goods, the decisions, once made, affect all persons. A given lighthouse cannot be located differently for different users, nor can it be turned on and off at different times to satisfy conflicting preferences. (This is to observe once again the heterogeneity portrayed in Figure 1–1.)

Why, in the face of this disadvantage, inherent in sharing, should a good be demanded of government when a private-good substitute exists? One answer is that the private-good substitute may be a very poor substitute—as is the case with national defense, where hand guns (private goods) are poor substitutes for such collective good as hydrogen bombs, and where a social judgment has apparently been made that devastating weapons should not be purchasable by private consumers at any price. In many and perhaps most other cases, however, where private goods are available that can achieve virtually the same objective as the public-good version, the only significant advantage of the public good would seem to be its relative price. That is, some people may prefer to pay for a marginal unit of the public-good version at its associated tax price rather than a unit of the private good version at its market price. (The particular tax-price system that is used will, thus, affect the number of persons who opt for the public good or the private good substitute.)

We can now return to analysis of the choices open to consumers whose demands for any collective good are undersatisfied through government markets. The consumer who turns to the private-market option is, in effect, choosing an option that often involves a different form of the good in question. He may be expected to select a form which, while providing its owner with greater individual control, does so by providing smaller external benefits to other consumers. After all, if a consumer must bear the total cost rather than share the cost with others, then he will presumably tend to choose a form of the good that maximizes internal benefits, including his individual control, paying little attention to the external benefits that might be provided in greater measure by some other, collective-consumption form of the good.

The point to emphasize is that such a choice may be socially nonoptimal, albeit privately optimal in an economy with only two sectors—private and public—and with output in the public sector being constrained. Purchases of private-good substitutes may not reflect simply the interaction of preferences and production costs; rather they can reflect, and, in the situation depicted in Figure 1–1 actually do reflect, an adjustment to the nonoptimal level of provision of the collective good by government.[15] The analysis suggests, at this point, that consumers are likely to be left in nonoptimal positions in both private and government markets, being over or undersatisfied in government markets and making socially inefficient choices in private markets.

THE VOLUNTARY SECTOR

This brings us to a potential rationale for the development of other organizational mechanisms, including voluntary nonprofit organizations.[16] The reasoning above suggests the hypothesis that a class of voluntary organizations will come into existence as *extragovernmental providers of collective-consumption goods*.[17] These organizations will "supplement" the *public* provision (which can be zero) and provide an alternative to the *private*-sector provision of the private-good substitutes for collective goods.[18] The proposition that there exists a voluntary sector that specializes in the provision of collective-type goods may be termed our "output hypothesis."

   If voluntary organizations do in fact provide collective goods, they may be expected to confront financial problems, given free-rider behavior. However, since all the alternatives available to undersatisfied demanders also involve inefficiencies, it could be worthwhile (that is, efficient) to form and maintain voluntary organizations as a "second best" solution.[19]

   This exposition has seemingly implied that the initial response to demands for collective consumption goods is sought in the public sector, with subsequent adjustments reflecting dissatisfaction with that response. Such a sequence may or may not be accurate as a description of real-world behavior—although a little evidence on this will be cited later—but in any case the sequencing is only an expositional convenience. Although the public sector has some clear advantage in the provision of collective goods, it may also have a disadvantage in the form of organizational costs.[20] When the differential costs of organizing economic activity in the various sectors (and at various governmental levels) is considered—a factual matter about which little is known—it is no longer apparent in which sector the initial response to collective-good demand will occur. It is likely, however, that the government sector will *not* be the first to respond to consumer demands for collective goods. The reason is that demands by all consumers do not generally develop simultaneously, and so the political decision rule will at first determine a zero level of government provision, leading the undersatisfied demanders to nongovernmental markets.

   Not all governmentally provided goods and services have a significant collective-consumption component. Publicly provided employment services and library provision of current best-seller novels (but not research materials), for example, are not easily explainable as responses to this source of market failure.[21]

   Why governments provide noncollective goods is a matter deserving further scrutiny, and we will only touch on the question here. One potential justification for public provision of a private-consumption good is the saving in private-market transaction costs (or enforcement costs) in cases where there is widespread agreement regarding the quantity of an individual-consumption good that each consumer wishes to consume. As long as tax bills are being paid to finance government provision of collective goods, there may be advantages to adding to the bill a sum to finance the "minimum" level of a private good that the political majority prefers.

While more study is needed of the rationale for government provision of goods having little or no collective character, it is important to note that governments do provide them. For if this is the case, then the voluntary sector, if it is indeed providing collective-consumption goods, as the output hypothesis states, will be found to be more prominent in supplementing those government activities having the "largest" collective-consumption component. By contrast, we may expect that the *private*-good activities of government will be supplemented to a relatively greater extent in the private for-profit sector.

Since the undersatisfied demanders have been portrayed as the group that gives rise to the voluntary sector, it follows that the relative size of the voluntary sector in an industry can be expected to be a function of the heterogeneity of population demands. That is, the amount of collective good provision by the voluntary sector as compared with the public sector depends on the degree to which the public sector is able to satisfy the diverse demands of its constituents. The larger the quantity of collective good demand that is undersatisfied at the tax price scheme used by government, the larger the expected size of the voluntary sector, ceteris paribus. Thus, for any given level of governmentally provided output, the larger the variance of demand, the greater the amount of voluntary-sector output that can be expected. Similarly, the more homogeneous are consumers' demands—the more alike are quantities demanded at the governmentally prescribed tax prices—and the closer the tax system is to approximating marginal benefit pricing, the less will be the undersatisfied demand and the smaller will be the size of the voluntary sector relative to the government sector, again ceteris paribus. If, as we believe, taxes are rarely equated with marginal benefits, the market share of the voluntary sector in the provision of collective goods will vary directly with the heterogeneity among individual demand schedules for these goods.[22]

Note that it is not heterogeneity of consumers that counts, nor even heterogeneity of consumer demand functions (somehow measured), but heterogeneity of quantities demanded for the given set of tax prices. A population could be very heterogeneous with respect to some demand parameter (for example, income) and yet demand identical quantities of a particular collective good at the respective tax prices. Conversely, a population could be quite homogeneous in its demand functions and yet demand varied quantities if tax prices varied among persons. Only if tax prices were all Lindahl-equilibrium prices—equating for each consumer the marginal tax price with his marginal valuation of output—would consumers all demand the same quantity of the collective good.

With a collective-consumption good and substitutes for it being provided in two or even three economic sectors, there is no easy answer to the normative question of whether such a good is likely to be provided in optimal, suboptimal, or superoptimal total quantities. What is needed is a more general theory that goes beyond the *private* market's tendency to under-provide collective-consumption goods, and explains the public and voluntary markets' supplemental activities.

PRIVATE- AND PUBLIC-GOOD SUBSTITUTES, SOME DYNAMICS

Up to this point we have assumed that the set of collective-consumption and individual-consumption goods from which consumers could choose was given exogenously. Now we will drop the static assumption of a predetermined set of goods, instead examining some determinants of what is included in the set. Specifically, is there a basis for predicting that in the course of time the menu of collective-consumption goods will expand more, or less, rapidly than the menu of private goods? What determines such changes?

It was stated above that a major distinction between public goods and their private good substitutes is the greater individual control offered by the latter and preferred by consumers generally. Granted such a difference, it would seem likely that if consumers at a given level of income are found to be purchasing a particular ratio of a public good to its private-good substitute, then at sufficiently higher income levels that ratio is likely to fall, as demand shifts in favor of the private goods. This is not to say the the income elasticity of demand for any collective good is necessarily negative at some income levels.

The income hypothesis, then, is: at very low income levels the income elasticity of demand for a given collective good is positive and large; as income increases people shift expenditures from a pattern in which neither a collective good nor a private-good substitute is purchased, to a pattern that includes some collective goods. And as incomes rise further, the demand for collective goods rises, but at some point the private-good substitutes will come to be bought instead of the collective good. (This point may differ, of course, for different goods.) That is, the income elasticity of demand for collective goods may be positive but lower than that for private-good substitutes at sufficiently high levels of income. Thus, the relationship between the level of per capita income and the relative size of the government sector is likely to be that of an inverted U.[23]

SOME BITS OF EVIDENCE

This brief section provides a number of scraps of "evidence" on the notions presented earlier. None of the evidence, individually or in total, is offered as "proof" of the propositions we have discussed. Rather, they are intended to be suggestive of the types of research that would be useful to better understand the role of voluntary organizations in a three-sector economy that also includes government and private for-profit sectors.[24]

Private-Good Substitutes for Collective Goods

We now consider the effects of relaxing the initial assumption of an exogenously determined set of collective and private goods. If the hypothesis is correct that beyond some level of income for any given person, private goods are demanded in preference to collective goods, then as such an income level is approached by increasing numbers of persons, we should expect an increase in the amount of private-market resources devoted to research and development of private-good substitutes. Thus, the set of private, individual-consumption goods that are available would expand in response to increased incomes. This may be one of the factors explaining: (a) the growing number of inventions to provide home and business security—in addition to the expanded governmental provision of the traditional collective good, police protection; (b) the development of home garbage disposers, incinerators, and, now, trash compactors as substitutes for the more-collective good, trash collection; and (c) the development of electronic air filters as substitutes for cleaner air in the environment.

In more general terms, there are many examples of how increased incomes are reducing consumers' relative demands for "shared" goods, which they can utilize only under particular conditions and at particular times—urban mass transit and public libraries, for example—and are increasing demands for nonshared goods that are fully under the individual's control—for example, private autos and paperback books. We do not suggest that the distinction between shared and nonshared goods is synonymous with the distinction between collective-consumption and individual-consumption goods. Nevertheless, there is a relationship: collective-consumption goods, except for the pure case, do require sharing.

**A Fragment of Historical Evidence on Voluntary Provision
of Public Goods**

Our analysis concerning undersatisfied demanders of collective goods and their relationship to voluntary organizations portrays the latter as nongovernmental providers of collective goods that are normally identified with governments. Historical events provide one test of our view, which implies that before a political majority comes to demand governmental provision, the minority that demands governmental provision of a good will be undersatisfied and will turn to voluntary organizations. Thus, *provision by voluntary (nonprofit) organizations is hypothesized to precede governmental provision historically.* It is noteworthy, therefore, that in sixteenth-century England, where governmental provision of any civilian goods or services was very modest, private "philanthropies" (voluntary organizations) were providing funds for such wide-ranging collective activities as schools, hospitals, nontoll roads, fire-fighting apparatus, public parks, bridges, dikes and causeways, digging of drainage canals, waterworks, wharves and docks, harbor cleaning, libraries, care of prisoners in jails, and charity to the poor[25]—in short, for the gamut of nonmilitary goods that we identify to-day as governmental responsibilities. Such voluntary-sector giving even included support for such charitable causes as "houses for young women convinced of their folly."[26] At the same time we are told that private interests "sought to prod the central government to carry forward needed projects . . ."[27]—behavior that we would anticipate since collective-type goods were involved and those persons having the greatest demands would be expected to wish to share the cost burdens broadly.

The relationship between governmental and voluntary provision of goods has also been noted by historians of Elizabethan England. According to one author, "The various philanthropic activities, which we have been reviewing [including highways, police, charity, hospitals and schools] were supplemented in some important respects by the corporate action of the towns."[28] Whether the public sectors "supplemented" the voluntary, or vice versa, is an insignificant distinction.

Note that it is quite consistent with our theoretical model that the level of politically determined governmental provision of a collective good can be zero, even though a large minority (or even a majority, if a political decision rule other than majority vote is used) has positive demands. If the undersatisfied demanders turn to the voluntary sector, as is likely, then this sector will develop first. Later, perhaps in response to economic development, the number of positive demanders might increase and so the government sector would become a provider of the good involved. Thus, in general, we might expect the voluntary sector to precede the government sector in the provision of collective goods.

An historical perspective on public-sector activities raises the question of to what extent any observed changes in the relative size or scope of government are the results of changes in the magnitudes of variables—for example, incomes—or changes in the magnitudes of parameters—such as those mirroring attitudes toward the "appropriate" role of government. Both, of course, may be important. The view (hypothesis) being set forth here, however, is that the varying roles of government over time, as well as across countries, are not a consequence of exogenously determined "attitudes" toward government; rather that such attitudes are themselves endogenously determined by changes in incomes, in other demand variables, and in the state of technology and factor prices. Depending on stages of development and on population demand characteristics, different roles for government can be expected.

Financing Voluntary Provision of Collective Goods

If our identification of voluntary organizations with the provision of public, collective goods is valid, we should expect these organizations to confront financing problems. Indeed, because these organizations share with private-sector firms ". . . the absence of the coercive and compulsive powers of government," Buchanan and Tullock have grouped those two types of organizations terming them "voluntary groups," and distinguishing them from governments.[29]

It is important, however, to distinguish between any differences among organizations in the types of their *outputs,* and differences in the methods of their *finance,* although the two are not entirely independent. Our emphasis here is on the nature of outputs, and on this basis the similarity of government and voluntary organizations is significant, as is the difference between both of these and the private for-profit organizations. The free-rider problem associated with collective goods does lead us to expect that nongovernmental providers of such goods face a financial obstacle.

Upon further study, however, it turns out that voluntary organizations do employ "coercive and compulsive powers," just as do governments, although the penalties are social rather than governmentally sanctioned fines or imprisonment. While pressures to "donate" to the United Fund, Red Cross, Cancer Society, or private colleges, are (sometimes) somewhat more subtle than the pressure to pay ones's taxes, the difference is one of degree, not of kind.[30]

There are several plausible reasons why people may give to a voluntary organization when there is neither compulsion of law nor any apparent quid pro quo. One is the social pressure just noted.[31] A second reason, very closely related to the first, is captured by the recent conception of Pareto-optimal redistribution—individuals' utility functions may be such that they derive benefit from either the act of giving or from seeing someone else benefited.[32] That is, the *apparent* lack of a quid pro quo may be misleading. A donor to a voluntary organization may derive satisfaction from the act of giving to a worthy cause. Also, he may benefit from the gratitude, esteem, and plaudits of his neighbors and fellow citizens—rewards which to some extent even show up as financial returns and act to internalize what would otherwise be external benefits to the donor.

Sometimes the benefit from giving is quite direct and in a private-good form; thus, a giver may receive a tangible gift in return for his donation. One organization offers a "free" road atlas for a $3 donation; in other cases the donor may have his name inscribed on a plaque or even on a college library or hospital wing.[33]

The question *why* people like such social-reinforcement rewards and, hence, are willing to pay for them, is an important matter of utility-function determination that economists have avoided too long. Utility functions are not determined entirely by forces exogenous to the economic system, and —even if they were—economic analysis could still contribute to understanding the process of their formation. In any case, there can be no doubt that there are very many transactions in the economy that involve no binding quid pro quo—there are many things that people do which, like supporting voluntary organizations, bring little or no clear and certain reward. One example is truly voluntary giving to charity or to a blood bank.[34] Another is the support by young people for old-age pensions through the social security system, support which appears to hinge on the hope and faith that future generations of young people will be willing to finance the retirement of the aged just as the current generation of young people is doing. It is by no means obvious why young people have such faith, but apparently it is a real force influencing actions. It seems to apply not only to retirement pensions, but also to the support for public education. There appears to be a "social compact" such that each generation of adults agrees to support the education of the younger generation.

This analysis suggests that there is an efficiency basis for some public subsidization for voluntary giving, even when there is no basis for complete government financing. We have seen in Figure 1–1 that of the seven (groups of) people portrayed, only three demand more than Q_1 level of provision at the price P. A fourth, however, consisting of people such as person 4, would derive *some* positive benefit from additional output. It might be expected, therefore, that a majority of voters would favor a government program that financed, in addition to Q_1, a *part* of the cost of output in excess of that quantity. Given consumer awareness of the free-rider problem and its likely resolution in the diversion of nongovernment resources from collective goods to private-good substitutes, a political majority of voters would be rational to agree not only to *full governmental* financing of some output but also to *partial* government subsidy for some additional *nongovernmental* provision of collective goods.

Such a subsidy could take various forms, being an explicit grant or a tax subsidy. Both, in fact, are employed. The voluntary hospital industry in the United States, for example, has received *partial* government support through outright cash grants from the federal government for construction, through the Hill-Burton Act, and also has benefited from the income tax deductibility of private contributions to voluntary nonprofit hospitals. By contrast, the public hospitals are financed *fully* by government.

It is noteworthy that such governmental subsidies, and in particular the income-tax deductibility subsidies, are extended only to some of the nongovernmental organizations providing goods that are also provided governmentally. In general, only organizations in the health, education, charity, and religious areas can qualify for such government subsidies—not, by contrast, the nongovernmental organizations that either do, or might, provide trash collection, roads, fire or security services, or other services that have counterparts in the public sector. It would seem that the magnitude of the subsidy ought to depend (from the standpoint of allocative efficiency) on the severity of the free-rider problem—that is, on the quantity of external benefits that would be generated by individuals' private decisions to purchase (or supply) the good. We argued earlier that governments provide some noncollective-consumption goods, but subsidies would be widely supported (and would be efficient) only for the nongovernmental providers of *collective* goods, and not for the nongovernmental providers of private goods that substitute for collective goods.

Under current federal income-tax law, there are only two "levels" of such subsidization through the deductibility route: either zero, with gifts and grants to the organization not qualifying for tax deductibility, or full deductibility. (Of course, the importance of the latter from the *giver's* viewpoint depends on his marginal tax rate and whether he itemizes his deductions.) While a binary subsidy schedule would surely not be economically efficient under conditions of perfect information, it *could* be a reasonably good rule-of-thumb basis for setting subsidies to stimulate nongovernmental provision of public goods.

How efficient is the present subsidy mechanism? How effective is it? We make no attempt here to answer these questions carefully. While further study is needed, it seems that the kinds of activities for which private giving does qualify for tax deductibility do have a larger collective-good component than is the case for other activities—that is, they enter the utility functions of more persons and enter more "importantly." If this is so, then there is at least some efficiency basis for the voluntary-donations deductibility feature of our tax system.

Heterogeneity of Demand

Just as the model sketched earlier in this chapter predicts that there will often be private-market or voluntary-market supplementation of governmental provision of goods, so it also predicts that there will be little or no undersatisfied demand—and, hence, little or no extragovernmental provision—if all consumers demand essentially the same quantity of a given collective good at the particular tax price that each consumer confronts (that is, if tax prices are Lindahl prices). It is difficult to measure the actual extent of heterogeneity in quantities demanded. But the following simplifying assumptions permit a test of the hypothesis that the extent of extra governmental provision of collective goods depends on the degree of that heterogeneity in quantities demanded at the tax prices faced by taxpayers: assume (1) tax prices either are the same for all persons, or they are unequal but not in such a way as to be Lindahl prices, at which all taxpayers have the same marginal valuations of output; (2) the degree of heterogeneity in quantities demanded is positively correlated with the degree of heterogeneity in preferences, and this, in turn, may be proxied by the degree of heterogeneity of the population in the given governmental unit—for example, by the degree of diversity of religious preferences, urban-rural location preferences, cultural heritages, and other demand-determining variables that are not so highly correlated with tax prices as to violate assumption (1). Granted these assumptions, we predict that if two political units (such as countries) differ in the degree of heterogeneity of their populations, the more homogeneous unit will, ceteris paribus, have a lower level of voluntary-sector provision of collective-type goods or their private-good substitutes.[35] In short, that country will tend to have relatively smaller voluntary and private sectors, and a relatively larger public sector. Conversely, in a country or smaller political unit, with greater inequality in individuals' demands for collective goods, the level of private and voluntary sector supplementation of public-sector provision will be larger and the public sector will be relatively smaller.[36]

The governmental "provision" (that is, support) of, say, church activities—which have a significant public-good component for persons of that faith but not for others—is apparently great in countries where virtually the entire population shares one religion (for example, Spain and Ireland). Similarly, the public provision (financing) is far lower in a country such as the United States, where religious preferences (including atheism) are more diverse; it seems likely that no religion in the United States could win the support of a majority of voters to the cause of substantial public financing of its activities.

If our hypothesis is correct and the heterogeneity of quantities demanded of collective goods influences the degree of supplementation in private and voluntary markets, then the relative size of the government sector would be expected to be a function of that heterogeneity. One test of this hypothesis is an exploratory analysis of determinants of the changing relative size of the total nondefense government sector (federal, state, and local) in the United States for various years over the time period 1929–1969. Explanatory variables in the model include, as proxies for heterogeneity of demand, the variances in income, age, and education, and measures of diversity of religion, race, and urbanness; *mean* or other average values (for example, percent of population that is urban) for these six variables were also included. Of particular interest are the variance measures, for our model suggests negative signs for them. That is, it predicts that government (nondefense) expenditures as a percentage of total GNP will be a negative function of the variation in demand for collective-consumption goods, and we are taking heterogeneity of population characteristics to reflect such variation.

The regression model we used is handicapped by having only 10 degrees of freedom (twenty-four observations and thirteen independent variables); nonetheless, our findings, while not overwhelming, are encouraging. First, inclusion of the heterogeneity measures actually increases the significance levels of the variables reflecting mean values. Second, the F ratio is extremely significant (0.0000 level). Third, of the six heterogeneity variables, five were negative, as hypothesized. Only two of the five—religion and race— were significant, however, a result that may reflect the multicollinearity and the relatively small number of degrees of freedom. Variance in income, for example, had the anticipated negative relationship with the relative size of the government sector, but the coefficient was significant at only the 0.33 level.

Further analysis of time series data would be useful in order to test for the impact of population heterogeneity. Similarly, cross-country comparisons of the size of the government sector would be useful. Lack of data on dispersions of demand variables, however, is an obstacle to such studies.

Industry Analyses—The Market Niches of the Public, Private, and Voluntary Sectors

The emphasis on the respective roles of the private and voluntary sectors vis-à-vis the public sector has led me to a new type of "industry study." Each service provided by governments (at this stage no distinctions between *levels* of government are being made) can be usefully thought of as a portion of an industry that also may include a voluntary and a private for-profit sector.

One principal hypothesis is that in such industries in which the government is providing essentially a *private* good, the undersatisfied demand will be manifest principally in the private for-profit sector, and the voluntary sector will be comparatively small. Similarly, if the government services are substantially *collective*, then supplementation will tend to be in the voluntary sector, with the private for-profit sector component being relatively small.

Several such three-sector industry studies for the United States have been undertaken to shed light on this hypothesis—including the hospital industry, the education industry, and, more superficially, the library and employment-service industries.[37]

CONCLUSION

To summarize: first, the expectation is that supplementation of public-sector provision (that is, financing) of any good, will either be overwhelmingly in the voluntary sector or overwhelmingly in the private, for-profit sector, depending on whether the publicly provided good is primarily a collective or an individual-type good. In addition to the extent of "collectiveness" of the governmentally financed good, the relative size of the voluntary and private sectors in any industry will depend on the state of technology—specifically on the degree of similarity between collective goods and their private-good substitutes, and on the relative production costs.

Second, in a model attempting to explain the relative size of the government sector in some industry (or for some country), a significant variable is likely to be the heterogeneity of quantities demanded—the smaller the heterogeneity, the smaller the nongovernmental sector. In a simple majority-vote model without vote trading, the level of governmental provision is a function of the median demand; thus, the greater the undersatisfied demand—that is, the demand in excess of the median—the larger will be the combined private and voluntary-sector outputs, and, hence, the smaller will be the proportion of output that is governmentally provided. In another model that, for example, weighted voters by intensity of preference, the resulting predictions would differ quantitatively; yet we would still expect that greater variance in consumers' demands would lead to relatively greater extragovernmental provision and a relatively smaller role for the public sector.

Third, consumer preference for private goods does not imply that consumers will always buy private-good substitutes and never purchase collective goods. At relatively low levels of income, consumers may purchase neither collective goods nor their private-good substitutes. At higher levels of income, consumers may purchase the "inferior" collective goods because the advantages of private-good substitutes are outweighed by their higher unit cost per consumer. With a sufficiently high level of income, however, we expect cost considerations to be swamped by the positive income effect so that purchases of the preferred private-good substitutes will grow relative to the purchases of collective goods. Thus, the demand for collective goods is hypothesized to be a nonlinear, peaked function of income, increasing through part of the income range but decreasing, at least relatively, at upper income levels.

Our focus on the role of the voluntary sector and on the substitutability of private and collective-type goods seems to suggest that a new type of industry study is warranted. Such studies would be concerned with the relative sizes and market niches of each of the three sectors—public, private, and voluntary. In general, the industries that have been conventionally studied—for example, steel, cement, beer—exist only in the private for-profit sector in the United States. But there are many other "industries" including hospitals, colleges, libraries, employment agencies, research, fire protection, and security, that comprise organizations in at least two, and sometimes three sectors of the economy. If our model of the undersatisfied demanders has merit, each industry in which public provision occurs is likely also to have a counterpart in the voluntary sector.

The analytic approach suggested here points to a number of testable propositions, involving historical, international, and three-sector industry studies (governmental, for-profit, and voluntary). Much more research is needed, however, both positive and normative, on the interrelated roles of the governmental, private, and voluntary sectors of the economy.

NOTES

1. For a useful survey of the varied conceptions of "public" goods, see Steiner (1969).

2. This is not to suggest that the distinction is an insignificant one, but it is not examined in this paper. Indeed, there does not appear to be an accepted theory of the choice between government production and purchase.

3. See Downs (1957); Black (1958); Buchanan and Tullock (1962); Jerome Rothenberg, A model of economic and political decision-making, in Margolis (1965); McKean (1968), especially Chapter nine; and Kasper (1971).

4. The majority rule approach may produce intransitive orderings. Moreover, since specific issues are generally decided by political representatives, not by voters—at least not *directly* by voters, ". . . the link between individual utility functions and social actions is tenuous, though by no means completely absent." [Kenneth Arrow, The organization of economic ac-

tivity: Issues pertinent to the choice of market versus non-market allocation, in Haveman and Margolis (1971), p. 70].

5. Albert Breton (1966) posits that individuals are more likely to engage in political activity the greater the difference between their actual and their desired position.

6. For a recent discussion of the issue see Hansen and Weisbrod (1971).

7. See Samuelson (1954).

8. The horizontal price function assumes implicitly that the cost of supplying marginal quantities of the good (national defense, a park, or anything else) is constant, but this is simply for convenience of exposition and is in no way required.

9. In this model each consumer is seen essentially as a price taker and quantity adjuster; the tax-price rule, although a variable, is constrained. For a related discussion see Johansen (1963).

10. The emphasis in the public goods literature has been on the quantity of the good *supplied* being equal for all consumers [Samuelson (1954); Buchanan (1970), esp. p. 30]. The comparative lack of attention to inequality in *demands* (as portrayed in Figure 1.1) is, in my view, unfortunate. If some particular national defense expenditure, or some lighthouse—to use two favorite examples of public goods—were demanded by only one person while all other persons were indifferent to them, these goods would presumably be provided in optimal quantities in the private sector. The point is not that such examples are realistic, but only that insofar as the key concern of analysts is the efficiency of private markets—the market-failure issue—the crucial characteristic of a "public" (collective-consumption) good is *not* its technical *availability* to many persons simultaneously, but the number of simultaneous *beneficiaries*—persons into whose utility functions it actually enters.

In Figure 1.1 for example, the good is, we suggest, *not* a "public good" for person 2, and is not a public good for person 3 in quantities greater than Q_1. Rather than regard a particular good as simply a public good, it is useful to think of women's public goods, water-sports enthusiasts' public goods, Catholic public goods, "hawks" and "doves" public goods, etc. [See Albert Breton (1965) who refers to local, metropolitan, state, national, and world goods, but not to the aggregations of consumers (beneficiaries) discussed here.] The figure also illustrates that a commodity can be a public good for some persons—entering all of their utility functions simultaneously—and also a public "bad" for others, such as person 1, entering negatively into their utility functions.

Samuelson has also come to the conclusion that a public good is most usefully defined in utility terms, not in terms of "technological" characteristics of a good. See his Pure theory of public expenditure and taxation, in Margolis and Guitton (1969).

The *extent* of benefits to each consumer is a second determinant of the degree of private-market failure. If, for example, a lighthouse entered positively into the utility functions of a number of consumers, but was of trivial value to most, the "few" large demanders might well reach a bargain that led to essentially an optimal level of provision.

11. This paper does not explore the possible game-theoretic aspects of decision-making in the three sectors when collective-consumption goods are involved.

12. This was discussed at the theoretic level by Tiebout (1956). See Oates (1969) for an empirical examination of the Tiebout model of choice among local governmental units. Jerome Stein (1971), in an analysis of optimal policy toward environmental pollution, has assumed away the issue of heterogeneous demands among consumers by assuming that ". . . each locality is composed of identical households. . . ." (p. 534).

13. Discussing the exclusion principle with regard to collective goods, Kenneth Arrow illustrates the problem with the example of pollution: ". . . it would have to be possible in principle to supply [clean air or water] to one [person] and not the other . . . But this is technically impossible." (In Haveman and Margolis, 1971, p. 65.)

But it is *not* impossible. Air and water filters, air conditioning, and bottled water perform precisely this exclusionary function, as do vacations to places "where the sky is not cloudy (or smoggy) all day."

14. A striking illustration of the difference between a public-good solution to a problem

and a private-good solution is the adjustment to environmental hazards in less-developed areas. Where malaria-carrying mosquitos breed, the public goods, area-wide DDT spraying and swamp drainage, might be used; and among the private-good substitutes are mosquito nets and migration away from the area.

An incisive analysis of the difference between public sector and private sector rationing policies, involving money prices, and waiting-time prices is in Nichols, Smolensky, and Tideman (1971).

15. A vertical summation of the seven demand curves in the diagram would intersect with the commodity cost curve, $7P$, at quantity Q_2, the output level that would be Pareto optimal if tax prices were set equal to marginal valuations of each consumer. While the optimal output exceeds the "actual" in this illustration, this would not be the case under some other political-decision rule.

16. For a useful introduction to some issues in this area, see Vickrey (1962).

17. Eli Ginzberg et al. (1965) discuss a wide range of "nonprofit" organizations. The authors observe that "Many non-profit organizations perform functions that are identical or closely allied to those performed by government. In fact, many governments weigh carefully whether to establish or expand certain activities under their own aegis; whether to seek to accomplish their goals by relying on non-profit organizations; or whether, as frequently happens, to do part of the work themselves and to look to non-profit organizations to do the rest" (p. 23).

On the relationship between the activities of nonprofit and private for-profit organizations, however, Ginzberg et al. are not in agreement with the analysis in this paper. They state: "The key difference between the private sector and the not-for-profit sector is not in the economic activities which they undertake, but in whether they are organized in order to seek a profit from their efforts" (p. 30). These authors make no distinction between collective-consumption goods and their private-good substitutes.

18. If it is true that there exists a nonpublic voluntary sector that provides collective-consumption goods, as do governments, then it really is ". . . a shame that public goods are called 'public'." (Davis and Winston, 1967, p. 372.)

19. Our emphasis on the similarity of outputs of the government and voluntary sectors, and on the similarity of outputs of the private-sector substitutes, may be contrasted with the dichotomization presented by James Buchanan and Gordon Tullock (1962). They emphasize the distinction between *government* provision and "private," where the latter includes both for-profit and "voluntary, but cooperative" organizations. (Buchanan and Tullock, 1962, p. 50.) The similarity of voluntary, "philanthropic" activities and the activities of the "free market" is also expressed by Robert A. Schwartz (1970) who states that individual philanthropic efforts "supplement the functioning of the free-market system. . . . ," rather than supplementing the outputs of public markets, the emphasis suggested in the present paper (p. 1291).

20. For a theoretical analysis of organizational costs, related to both population heterogeneity and the nature of political decision rules, see Buchanan and Tullock, 1970, especially p. 115.

21. James M. Buchanan (1970) focused attention on "the effects generated by governmental organization of the supply of goods and services that are largely, if not wholly, 'private,' that is, fully divisible into separate and distinguishable units of consumption," (p. 29).

22. The notion of heterogeneity of demand *schedules* is ambiguous and requires more study. It involves, however, the existence of unequal quantities demanded by consumers facing the governmentally determined tax prices. The "ambiguity" results from the likelihood that the variance of quantities demanded by various consumers will, in general, not be the same at all prices.

23. Compare "Wagner's Law" which, though variously interpreted, predicts that the public sector will grow with per capita income. For the original exposition see Wagner (1890); for discussions in English see Bird (1971) and Herber (1971), pp. 371–381.

24. See also Benedick (1977) and Lee and Weisbrod (1977).

25. See Jordan (1959).

26. Robert Nelson, An address to persons of quality and estate, ways and methods of doing good, published in 1715, cited by Gray (1905), p. 95.

27. See Jordan (1959).

28. See Gray (1905), p. 25.

29. Buchanan and Tullock (1962), p. 49.

30. At the theoretical level this similarity has been discussed by Ireland and Johnson (1970).

31. John Stuart Mill (1965) recognized that societal reinforcement could serve as a possible inducement to people to incur costs for which there was otherwise little or no private benefit. Although arguing that ". . . it is a proper office of government to built and maintain lighthouses . . . [since] no one would build lighthouses from motives of personal interest . . .", and that few people would undertake scientific research without government support, he also mentioned the possibility that "great public spirit" might motivate some persons to undertake activities that are "of great value to the nation" (p. 968).

32. See Hochman and Rodgers (1969); Schwartz (1970); and Ireland and Johnson (1970).

33. Note that income tax deductibility of such "donations" would never be a sufficient inducement for giving, as long as marginal tax rates confronting an individual were less than 100 percent.

34. The market for human blood is discussed in the most thought-provoking book by Titmus (1971).

35. The influence of "subcultures," defined by homogeneity of ethnicity and income, on voting behavior is examined in Wilson and Banfield (1964).

36. The relationship between population heterogeneity and degree of public-sector activity has also been considered in terms of the costs of organization; the greater the heterogeneity, the larger the prospective costs of organizing through political markets relative to the costs of organizing private firms. (See Buchanan and Tullock, 1962, especially Chapter 8.)

For an interesting paper describing the variation in size of public sectors among a number of countries, and attempting to explain it by "ideological differences," see King (1971).

37. See the studies by Lee and Weisbrod (1977), Benedick (1977), and Weisbrod and Long (1977), respectively.

REFERENCES

Benedick, Jr., Marc. 1977. Education as a three-sector industry, In *The Voluntary Nonprofit Sector,* ed. B.A. Weisbrod. Lexington, Massachusetts: D.C. Heath, pp. 101–42.

Bird, Richard M. 1971. Wagner's law of expanding state activity. *Public Finance,* 26 (1).

Black, Duncan. 1958. *The Theory of Committees and Elections.* Cambridge, England: Cambridge University Press.

Breton, Albert. 1966. A theory of the demand for public goods. *Canadian Journal of Economics and Political Science* (November): pp. 455–67.

Breton, Albert. 1965. Theory of government grants. *Canadian Journal of Economics and Political Science* (May): pp. 175–87.

Buchanan, James. 1970. Notes for a theory of socialism. *Public Choice* (Spring): pp. 29–43.

Buchanan, James, and Gordon Tullock. 1962. *The Calculus of Consent.* Ann Arbor: University of Michigan Press.

Davis, Otto A., and Andrew B. Whinston. 1967. On the Distinction Between Public and Private Goods. *American Economic Review* (May): pp. 360–73.

Downs, Anthony. 1957. *An Economic Theory of Democracy.* New York: Harper and Row.

Ginzberg, Eli, Dale L. Hiestand, and Beatrice J. Reubens. 1965. *The Pluralistic Economy.* New York: McGraw-Hill Book Co.

Gray, B. Kirkman. 1905. *A History of English Philanthrophy.* London: Frank Cass and Company Limited.

Hansen, W. Lee, and Burton A. Weisbrod. 1971. Who pays for a public expenditure program? *National Tax Journal* (December): pp. 515–17.

Haveman, Robert, and Julius Margolis, eds. 1971. *Public Expenditures and Policy Analysis.* Chicago: Markham Publishing Company.

Herber, Bernard P. 1971. *Modern Public Finance: The Study of Public Sector Economics.* Homewood, Illinois: Richard D. Irwin, Inc.

Hochman, Harold, and James Rodgers. 1969. Pareto optimal redistribution. *American Economic Review* (September): pp. 542–557.

Ireland, Thomas R., and David B. Johnson. 1970. *The Economics of Charity.* Blacksburg, Virginia: Center for the Study of Public Choice.

Johansen, Leif. 1963. Some notes on the Lindahl theory of determination of public expenditures. *International Economic Review* (September): pp. 346–58.

Jordan, W.K. *Philanthropy in England, 1480–1660.* London: George Allen and Unwin, Ltd.

Kaspar, Hirschel. 1971. On political competition, economic policy, and income maintenance. *Public Choice* (Spring): pp. 1–19.

King, Anthony. 1971. Ideologies as predictors of public policy patterns: A comparative analysis. Paper presented at Meetings of American Political Science Association, Chicago, September.

Lee, A. James, and Burton A. Weisbrod. 1977. Collective goods and the voluntary sector: The case of the hospital industry, In *The Voluntary Nonprofit Sector,* ed. B.A. Weisbrod. Lexington, Massachusetts: D.C. Heath, pp. 77–100.

Margolis, Julius, ed. 1965. *The Public Economy of Urban Communities.* Washington, D.C.: Resources for the Future, Inc.

Margolis, Julius, and H. Guitton, eds. 1969. *Public Economics.* Proceedings of a Conference held by the International Economic Association. New York: St. Martin's Press, pp. 98–123.

McKean, Roland N. 1968. *Public Spending.* New York: McGraw-Hill, Inc.

Mill, John Stuart. 1965. *Principles of Political Economy,* Vol. III. Toronto: University of Toronto Press.

Nichols, Donald, Eugene Smolensky, and Nicholas Tideman. 1971. Discrimination by waiting time in merit goods. *American Economic Review* (June): pp. 312–23.

Oates, Wallace. 1969. The effects of property taxes and local public spending on property values: An empirical study of tax capitalization and the Tiebout hypothesis. *Journal of Political Economy* (November–December): pp. 957–71.

Samuelson, Paul A. 1954. The pure theory of public expenditure. *Review of Economics and Statistics* (November): pp. 350–56.

Schwartz, Robert A. 1970. Personal philanthropic contributions. *Journal of Political Economy* (November–December): pp. 1264–91.

Stein, Jerome. 1971. Micro-economic aspects of public policy. *American Economic Review* (September): pp. 531–37.

Steiner, Peter O. 1969. *Public Expenditure Budgeting.* Washington, D.C.: The Brookings Institution.

Tiebout, Charles. 1956. A pure theory of local government expenditure. *Journal of Political Economy* (October): pp. 416–24.

Titmus, Richard. 1971. *The Gift Relationship.* London: George Allen and Unwin.

Vickrey, William. 1962. One economist's view of philanthropy. In *Philanthropy and Public Policy,* ed. Frank Dickinson. New York: National Bureau of Economic Research.

Wagner, Adolf, 1890. *Finanzwissenschaft,* 3rd ed. Liepzig: C.F. Winter.

Weisbrod, Burton A., ed. 1977. *The Voluntary Nonprofit Sector.* Lexington, Massachusetts: D.C. Heath.

Weisbrod, Burton A., and Stephen Long. 1977. Further explorations. In *The Voluntary Nonprofit Sector,* ed. B.A. Weisbrod. Lexington, Masschusetts: D.C. Heath, pp. 143–70.

Wilson, James Q., and Edward C. Banfield. 1964. Public-regardingness as a value premise in voting behavior. *American Political Science Review.* (December): pp. 876–87.

2

Donations: Can They Reduce a Donor's Welfare?

JEFFREY H. WEISS

Scholars commonly assume that voluntary contributions toward the provision of some public good increase the contributors' welfare. Weisbrod (1975) makes this assumption in explaining the effects of voluntary, not-for-profit organizations if both governmental and voluntary provision of public goods occurs.[1] He argues that, because of informational constraints and for other reasons, governments must adopt nonbenefit taxes for the financing of public goods. This adoption leads, in general, to a nonoptimal result, and in particular, to a situation in which certain "high" demanders of public goods are not fully satisfied with the low level of governmental provision. These persons then turn to voluntary provision to increase their utility. Implicit in Weisbrod's argument, however, is the additional assumption that the donors supplement a given level of governmental provision. This assumption may be appropriate under certain circumstances. Here, though, I show that if the levels of voluntary and governmental provision are determined simultaneously, then a high demander may be worse off with voluntary provision than without it.

To obtain this result I compare the outcomes of two related three-person games. Each player's utility depends on the level of his personal wealth and the level of public-good provision. The players' preferences differ in their evaluations of wealth relative to the public good: two of the players are "low" demanders of the public good, while the third is a "high" demander. We can think of each player as representing a relatively homogeneous group of people. For example, the high demanders might represent the New York City Upper-Eastside donors to the Metropolitan Museum of Art, while the low demanders might represent the rest of the city's citizens. How much

This chapter is a modified version of "Can Donations Reduce a Donor's Welfare?" which is forthcoming in *Public Choice*. The author gratefully acknowledges Susan Rose-Ackerman's insightful comments.

of the public good is provided depends, in part, on who is allowed to provide it. In Game A only governmental provision is permitted and its level is determined by majority rule. Minorities dissatisfied with the majority's decision must nevertheless accept it: voluntary provision, emigration, vote-selling, and the setting up of lower-level governmments for the purpose of supplementing the majority's choice are not permitted.[2] In Game B, voluntary provision is permitted and its level is determined simultaneously with the level of governmental provision. In this setting I show that, in at least one payoff vector in the core of Game B, the high demander achieves a level of utility lower than the level that he achieves in Game A.

We can analyze the interaction of voluntary provision and governmental provision in either a noncooperative or a cooperative setting.[3] I choose a cooperative setting because it seems more appropriate to the decision context under study. In a noncooperative setting players take others' donations and votes as given while making their choices. There is no communication among the players and, therefore, the players can make no threats and achieve no mutually beneficial compromises. But, because of the presence of Pareto "relevant" externalities, noncooperative decision-making would result in inefficient equilibria. If transaction costs are not prohibitive, then we should see a movement away from noncooperative decision-making to cooperative decision-making.[4] Here, the players communicate, they exchange threats and demands, and they achieve mutually agreeable compromises. While transaction costs could be prohibitive for individual voters, they would not necessarily be prohibitive for coalitions of voters, for their representatives, or, for that matter, for government agencies. The same could be true for donors: individual costs could be high, but if these were shared among the coalition's donors, then per capita costs could be relatively low. The donors could also have their agent, the voluntary organization, bargain for them. Therefore, we might observe government agencies bargaining with voluntary organizations, as well as, although perhaps less often, individual voter-donors bargaining directly with other voter-donors, and these voter-donors bargaining with their agents.

Finally, I abstract from principal-agent problems. Therefore, whenever I speak of the government raising taxes or voluntary organizations increasing their provision of the public good, for example, I mean nothing more than that a majority of persons has voted for an increase in taxes, and the total amount of voluntary provision by individual contributors has increased.

Essential preliminaries, as well as Game A, are presented in the next section. The section following analyzes the voluntary provision game and the last section briefly discusses the main result.

PRELIMINARIES AND GAME A

The grand coalition, N, is composed of two low demanders, players 1 and 2, and one high demander, player H. Players 1 and 2 each have the utility function $U^\ell(g,x)$, where g is a pure public good, and player i's wealth, x_i, is a pure private good. H's utility function, $U^H(g,x)$, is such that at any consumption bundle, (g,x), he would be willing to give up more x for an additional unit of the public good than would either players 1 or 2. That is, for any (g,x), $\text{MRS}^H > \text{MRS}^\ell$.[5]

In each game, each player has an endowment of m units of the private good. At the outset of either game, society's endowment of the public good is zero, but there exists a technology, characterized by a constant marginal rate of transformation of one, for transforming the private good into the public good.

In both games each player's wealth is taxed at the same proportional rate $t \in [0,1]$. Any majority may pick this rate. In the first game, players cannot provide g voluntarily, or emigrate, or sell their votes if they are dissatisfied with the level of provision that the majority chooses. The second game allows voluntary provision of g. Let $y_i \geq 0$ denote player i's donation of the private good for the voluntary provision of g. Let $(t,\bar{y}) = (t,y_1,y_2,y_H)$ denote a *strategy* for the grand coalition, N, and associate with it the *allocation* $(g,\bar{x}) = (g,x_1,x_2,x_H)$, such that

$$g = 3tm + \sum_{j\epsilon N} y_j \qquad (2\text{--}1)$$

and

$$x_i = (1-t)m - y_i, \ i \epsilon N \qquad (2\text{--}2)$$

Equation (2–1) makes use of the taxation and equal endowment assumptions, as well as the assumption that for every unit of the public good produced, one unit of the private good must be given up. Note that this last assumption implies that y_i can also be interpreted as the amount of g provided voluntarily by player i. Equation (2–2) is simply player i's after-tax and postdonation wealth.[6] From these equations, we can express each player's utility as a function of t and $\bar{y}$,

$$U^i(3tm + \sum_{j\epsilon N} y_j, \ (1-t)m - y_i), \ i \epsilon N \qquad (2\text{--}3)$$

In Game A voluntary provision of g is forbidden. Hence, the entire game is reduced to the choice of a tax rate t. Which t will be chosen can be easily determined by first noticing that, for $y_i = 0$, $i \epsilon N$, Equations (2–1) and (2–2) define (parametrically in t) identical "budget lines" for each of the players (labeled G in Figure 2–1). Any element of G, (g,x_i), is equal to $(3tm,(1-t)m)$. If, for example, $t=0$ were chosen, then the players would consume the bundle $(0,m)$. If $t=1$ were chosen, then each would consume $(3m,0)$. Clearly, intermediate values of t imply bundles between these two extremes. Note also that the slope of G is

$$\frac{dx_i/dt}{dg/dt} = \frac{dx_i}{dg} = -1/3$$

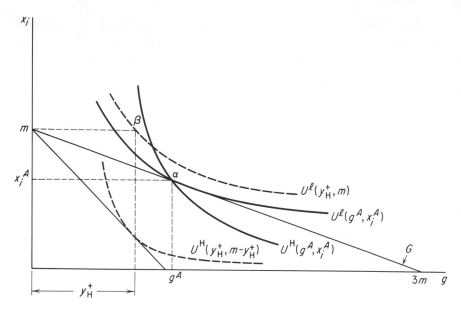

Figure 2–1

which is simply the per-person cost of an additional unit of governmentally provided g.

In this situation, players 1 and 2 maximize their utilities by voting for t^A, which gives each of them the bundle $(g^A, x_i^A) = (3t^A m, (1 - t^A)m)$, and the utility $U^\ell(g^A, x_i^A.)$.[7] In addition, $MRS^\ell(g^A, x_i^A) = 1/3$, since this is a maximizing choice for 1 and 2. At their choice, H achieves the utility $U^H(g^A, x_i^A)$, and since he is a "high demander", [that is, $MRS^H(g^A, x_i^A) > MRS^\ell(g^A, x_i^A)$], he would prefer a tax rate greater than t^A. But since he is the only person who would vote for such a change, and since t^A is unanimously preferred to lower tax rates, t^A is the majority-voting equilibrium of Game A.

This is exactly the situation as described by Weisbrod (1975): at the choice of the low demanders, H is "undersatisfied"; in addition, the equilibrium is inefficient because $MRS^1 + MRS^2 + MRS^H > MRT = 1$, since $MRS^H > MRS^1 = MRS^2 = 1/3$. That is, the players value, as a group, an additional unit of the public good more highly than they value the private good which would be given up to produce the public good.

GAME B

Game B permits voluntary provision. This complicates the game's structure because each player's utility is a function not only of what happens politically, but also of the total level of voluntary provision in society, as well as the level of his total contributions to voluntary organizations. Finding the entire core of Game B is equally complicated, and I do not present such an analysis here.[8] Instead, I show that under certain situations there can exist at least one payoff vector in the core of this game in which H receives less utility than the amount he achieves in Game A.

The key to understanding how this result could come about is recognizing that the utility levels achieved by the players in Game A would not necessarily be the status quo point from which they would bargain in Game B. What would be, or most likely be, cannot be determined a priori. However, a quite plausible candidate is contained in the following heuristic scenario.[9] Player H, being less than fully satisfied at (g^A, x_i^A), decides to provide y_H' *units of G* voluntarily. Players 1 and 2, taking y_H' as given, vote for less governmental provision. Player H then responds with a new level of voluntary provision, $y_H'' > y_H'$, which again results in a fall in the tax rate. This process continues until, perhaps, the situation depicted by the dashed indifference curves in Figure 2–1 obtains. In it, H, taking $t = 0$ as given, maximizes his utility by providing y_H^+ units of g voluntarily. This contribution gives him the utility $U^H(y_H^+, m - y_H^+) < U^H(g^A, x_i^A)$.[10] Players 1 and 2 have voted for no governmental provision, and each achieves the utility $U^\ell(y_H^+, m)$. Note that even with $t = 0$, they still consume the public good, because they free ride on H's voluntary provision.[11] But such behavior results in an inefficient allocation of resources, since g is a public good and since 1 and 2 place a positive value on additional units of g. Consequently, with nonprohibitive transactions costs, H and {1,2} begin bargaining over t and y_H. This results in a compromise choice of t and y_H, (which is not shown in Figure 2.1), and which gives 1 and 2 each a utility greater than $U^\ell(y_H^+, m)$, and H a utility greater than $U^H(y_H^+, m - y_H^+)$, but less than $U^H(g^A, x_i^A)$. Moreover, this payoff vector is a stable one for this society, that is, it cannot be improved upon by any coalition $S \subseteq N$.

Before proving that this payoff vector is in the core of Game B, I first prove that the noncooperative allocation $(y_H^+, m, m, m - y_H^+)$ cannot be a bargaining equilibrium, and then, I will illustrate the exact nature of the compromise choice worked out by H and {1,2}. First, consider Figure 2–2, where I again show the utility levels achieved by the players when 1 and 2 vote for $t = 0$ and H voluntarily provides y_H^+ units of g. Also shown is the graph of the function $T(g, h^+) = x_\ell$, [in the (g, x_ℓ) plane], that is a set of consumption possibilities for 1 and 2, each element of which arises, in general, from the following possible bargain with H: 1 and 2 provide nothing voluntarily, but they vote for a positive tax rate t; H, in turn, given this t, provides the largest amount of y_H consistent with his achieving the utility level $h^+ = U^H(y_H^+, m - y_H^+)$.[12] The one element of $T(g, h^+)$ that does not arise from this kind of bargain is the bundle (y_H^+, m), that comes about when $t = 0$ and $y_H = y_H^+$. For some $t^0 > 0$, $x_\ell = (1 - t^0)m$ and $g = 3t^0 m + y_H^0$, which is the point marked C. For still larger t's, 1 and 2 could consume the bundles D and E. Notice that in each of these bargains, since H only gets h^+ utility, the total "gains" from cooperation accrue to 1 and 2 and they are split evenly.

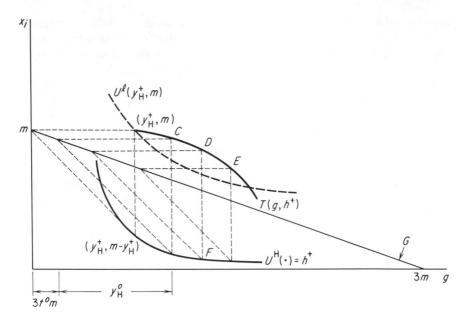

Figure 2–2

The slope of $T(g,h^+)$ can be shown to be

$$\frac{dx_\ell}{dg} = \frac{MRS^H - 1}{2} \qquad (2\text{-}4)$$

$MRS^H - 1$ is the difference between the most H would pay for an additional unit of g, thereby keeping him at the utility level h^+, and the cost of g. If an increase in g is desired and if H is to remain at this utility level, the difference must be "picked up" by players 1 and 2. Equation (2–4) then says that, under the terms of these bargains with H, this remaining cost is split evenly between these two players.

It is now clear that the noncooperative allocation, $(y_H^+,m,m,m-y_H^+)$, cannot be a bargaining equilibrium: the slope of $T(g,h^+)$ at $g=y_H^+$ is zero, but 1 and 2 would be willing to give up a positive amount of x_ℓ for an additional amount of g. Consequently, there exist allocations (such as D for 1 and 2, and F for H) where H gets the same utility as at $(y_H^+,m-y_H^+)$, but where 1 and 2 are better off than at (y_H^+,m).

I now illustrate the exact nature of the desired bargaining solution. Clearly, there must exist bargaining solutions in which some of the gains from cooperation accrue to H (that is, he does better than h^+). To find one such solution, pick h^B to be less than $U^H(g^A,x_i^A)$, and just "slightly" greater than h^+.[13] H's indifference curve corresponding to h^B, as well as $T(g,h^B)$, is shown in Figure 2–3. From the construction of $T(g,h)$, it is clear that $T(g,h^B)$ will be "below" $T(g,h^+)$, and the "closer" h^B is to h^+, the closer $T(g,h^B)$ will

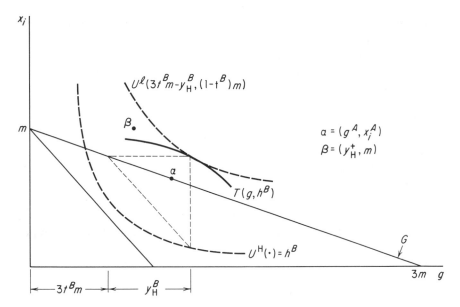

Figure 2–3

be to $T(g,h^+)$. Maximizing 1's utility over $T(g,h^B)$ gives him the utility $U^\ell(3t^Bm + y_H^B,(1-t^B)m)$ and H the utility $U^H(3t^Bm + y_H^B,(1-t^B)m - y_H^B) = h^B$. This level of utility for 1 is greater than $U^\ell(y_H^+,m)$, because h^B is just slightly greater than h^+. Since 1's maximizing choice is $(t^B,0,0,y_H^B)$, 2 achieves the same utility as does 1. I will prove below that this payoff vector is in the core of Game B.[14]

The most interesting feature of this bargaining solution, besides the fact that H achieves a lower level of utility than in Game A, is that he is not in a "price-taking" equilibrium with respect to his level of voluntary provision. That is, y_H^B does not maximize his utility, given t^B. But as we showed earlier, such a position for H, cannot be part of a bargaining solution for N.[15] More important, however, there is no reason why the players should be in such a configuration at a bargaining solution. In such a solution, H does not pick y_H^B taking t^B as given, nor does {1,2} pick t^B taking y_H^B as given. Rather, the players jointly choose t^B and y_H^B simultaneously.

To show that $(t^B,0,0,y_H^B)$ is a stable bargaining solution, it is necessary to prove that no coalition, S, will drop out of the bargain, because it believes it can do better for all its members by not cooperating with the rest of society. When a coalition chooses this option, it is still subject to the rules of the society. For example, if a minority coalition, S, drops out of the bargain, its endowment remains subject to taxation by the majority $(-S)$, and the majority is still constrained to spend these tax revenues on the provision of the collectively consumed public good. Note that by losing S's cooperation, $-S$ loses its input into S's voluntary provision decision, while

S loses its input into what tax rate will be chosen, as well as $-S$'s voluntary provision decisions.

I now prove that no coalition, S, $S \subseteq N$, will drop out of the bargain.

H: Since $\{1,2\}$ could pick the strategy $t = y_1 = y_2 = 0$, the best that H could achieve would be $U^H(y_H^+, m - y_H^+)$. Furthermore, there may exist other strategies for $\{1,2\}$ that would imply even lower levels of utility for H. Therefore, H will not block $(t^B, 0, 0, y_H^B)$.

$\{\ell\}$, $\ell = 1$ or 2: $\{j, H\}$, $j \neq \ell$, could pick the strategy $t = t^A$, $y_j = y_H = 0$. At the implied consumption bundle, $MRS^\ell = 1/3$, in which case ℓ would pick $y_\ell = 0$. This then gives him a utility of $U^\ell(g^A, x_\ell^A)$, which is less than he gets in the bargaining solution.

$\{1,2\}$: For both players to do better than $U^\ell(3t^B m + y_H^B, (1 - t^B)m)$, each must consume a bundle "above" G. Equations (2–1) and (2–2) imply that this result can occur only if $y_H > 0$. But, H could pick $y_H = 0$ for any choice by $\{1,2\}$.[16]

$\{\ell, H\}$, $\ell = 1$ or 2: Suppose $\{\ell, H\}$ could block $(t^B, 0, 0, y_H^B)$ with some other strategy (t, y_ℓ, y_H), such that $U^\ell(3tm + y_\ell + y_H, (1 - t)m - y_\ell) > U^\ell (3t^B m + y_H^B, (1 - t^B)m)$ and $U^H(3tm + y_\ell + y_H, (1 - t)m - y_H) > U^H(3t^B m + y_H^B, (1 - t^B)m - y_H^B)$. But $j \neq \ell$ could then pick $y_j = 0$, which would imply that $U^j(3tm + y_\ell + y_H, (1 - t)m) \geq U^\ell(3tm + y_H, (1 - t)m - y_\ell)$. These inequalities then imply that the payoff vector associated with $(t^B, 0, 0, y_H^B)$ is not Pareto optimal. But, as I prove in the related article in *Public Choice*, this solution's associated payoff vector is Pareto optimal. Therefore, there exists no such blocking strategy for $\{\ell, H\}$.

N: Since the solution is Pareto optimal, N does not block it.

DISCUSSION

What can be concluded about the effects of voluntary provision? Weisbrod (1975) has argued that voluntary provision allows for a greater revelation of consumers' preferences, with the resulting outcome Pareto superior to the outcome in which the government alone is proving the public good (that is, the outcome of Game A). I prove elsewhere (Weiss, 1981) that this is a possibility, by showing that the core of Game B always contains such payoff vectors.[17]

However, this conclusion is not valid in every situation since the players would not necessarily take the utility levels achieved in Game A as the status quo point from which they would bargain in Game B. Since a priori considerations do not determine this point, I presented the following plausible candidate. The low demanders vote for no governmental provision of the public good, and the high demanders, given this fact, voluntarily provide a utility maximizing amount of the collectively consumed public good. Here, the high demander achieves a level of utility less than what he achieves in Game A, and because of the public-good externality, the situation is inefficient. Since using the core (as the solution concept) implies that transactions costs are not prohibitive, the players would bargain to an efficient outcome. I then proved that at such an outcome it would be possible for everyone's welfare to be greater than at the status quo point, but the high demander's utility could still be less than the amount he achieved in Game A. Finally, I proved that such a bargaining solution is in the core of Game B.

NOTES

1. See Hansmann (1980) and Weisbrod (1979) for alternative, although not inconsistent, explanations of the effects of not-for-profit organizations.

2. See Weiss (1984) for an analysis of the impact of vote-selling on Game A.

3. For an analysis of this interaction in a noncooperative setting see YoungDay (1978) and Roberts (1984). The analysis of noncooperative voluntary provision alone has been done by Buchanan (1968), McGuire (1974), and Young (1982), among others.

4. This, of course, will more likely happen, the smaller the number of people involved. See Olson (1965).

5. Each player's utility function is twice-continuously differentiable, strictly quasiconcave, and strictly monotonic.

6. In this formulation contributions are not tax-deductible.

7. I assume here that $t^A \epsilon$ (0,1).

8. See Weiss (1981) for the complete analysis.

9. That is, this scenario provides us with an informal "dynamics" to what is, formally, simply a comparison of the payoff vector in the core of Game A with a payoff vector in the core of Game B.

10. It is assumed here that $U^H(y_H^+, m - y_H^+) < U^H(g^A, x_i^A)$ and $U^\ell(y_H^+, m) > U^\ell(g^A, x_i^A)$. As the reader can see, however, doing so involves nothing unusual about $U^\ell(\cdot)$ or $U^H(\cdot)$.

11. If $MRS^\ell(y_H^+, m) \leq 1/3$, then the situation depicted by the dashed indifference curves in Figure 2-1 is a (Nash) noncooperative equilibrium between H and (1,2), when the latter plays as a single player.

12. Formally, $T(g, h^+)$ is defined by the equations

$$x = (1-t)m$$
$$g = 3tm + f(t)$$

where $f(t) = y_H$ is defined implicitly by the relationship $U^H(3tm + y_H, (1-t)m - y_H) - h^+ = 0$. I assume that H's indifference curves never intersect the axes.

13. In the related article in *Public Choice*, I prove that such an h^B exists.

14. In Weiss (1981) I show that payoff vectors "near" this one, but where the low demanders get "marginally" unequal payoffs, are not in the core of Game B. Rather surprisingly, however, payoff vectors quite "distant" from this one, where the low demanders get extremely different payoffs, may be in the core of Game B.

15. Whether it could be under a different set of rules which allowed, for example, contributions to be tax-deductible, is clearly an interesting issue, but it is not considered here.

16. Whether such a threat by H is credible cannot be decided here, since there is no consensus in the literature as to what exactly is a credible threat. See Schelling (1960) for a discussion of this issue.

17. One such payoff vector can be found by constructing $T(g, A^+)$, where A^+ is a utility level just "slightly" greater than $U^H(g^A, x_i^A)$, and then proceeding as in the text.

REFERENCES

Buchanan, J. 1968. *The Demand and Supply of Public Goods*. Chicago: Rand McNally.

Hansmann, H. 1980. The role of the nonprofit enterprise. *Yale Law Journal* 89(5):835–901. Reprinted as Chapter 3 of this volume.

McGuire, M. 1974. Group size, Group homogeneity and the aggregate provision of a pure public good under Cournot behavior. *Public Choice* 18:107–26.

Olson, M. 1965. *The Logic of Collective Action*. Cambridge: Harvard University Press.

Roberts, R. 1984. A positive model of private charity and public transfers. *Journal of Political Economy* 92:136–48.

Schelling, T.C. 1960. *The Strategy of Conflict*. Cambridge: Harvard University Press.

Weisbrod, B. 1975. Towards a theory of the voluntary non-profit sector in a three sector economy. In *Altruism, Morality and Economic Theory*, ed. E. Phelps. New York: Russel Sage Foundation.

Weisbrod, B. 1979. *Economics of Institutional Choice*. Paper presented at the conference on Institutional Choice and the Private Non-Profit Sector. Madison, Wisconsin.

Weiss, J.H. 1981. The ambivalent value of voluntary provision of public goods in a political economy, unpublished Ph.D. dissertation, University of Wisconsin, Madison.

———. 1984. Is vote selling desirable? Baruch College, Department of Economics and Finance Working Paper.

Young, D. 1982. Voluntary purchase of public goods. *Public Choice*, 38:73–85.

YoungDay, D. 1978. *Voluntary Provision of Public Goods: A Theory of Donations*, unpublished Ph.D. dissertation, University of Wisconsin.

II

CONTRACT FAILURE
AND INFORMATION ASYMMETRY

3

The Role
of Nonprofit Enterprise

HENRY B. HANSMANN

Private nonprofit institutions account for a sizable and growing share of our nation's economic activity.[1] The sectors in which these institutions are most common—education, research, health care, the media, and the arts—are vital elements in the modern economy. Moreover, these are sectors that present particularly pressing and difficult problems of public policy. The existing literature in law and economics, however, has largely overlooked nonprofit institutions; while we are reasonably well supplied with positive and normative perspectives on both profit-seeking and governmental organizations, to date there has been extraordinarily little effort to understand the role of nonprofits.[2]

This lack of understanding is reflected in the substantial confusion that characterizes policymaking concerning nonprofits. Nonprofit corporation law is poorly developed and varies in significant respects from one state to the next. Even the Model Nonprofit Corporation Act exhibits uncertainty about such basic issues as the purposes for which nonprofit corporations may be formed. Large classes of nonprofits receive special treatment in almost all areas in which federal legislation impinges upon them significantly, including corporate income taxation, Social Security, unemployment insurance, the minimum wage, securities regulation, bankruptcy,

From *The Yale Law Journal* 89 (April 1980): 835–98. Preparation of the original article was supported in part by a grant from the Alfred P. Sloan Foundation to the Program on Nonprofit Organizations at the Institution for Social and Policy Studies, Yale University.

A number of people have offered useful comments on earlier drafts of this paper, both individually and as participants in workshops and seminars. I am particularly indebted, however, to Richard R. Nelson, who first aroused my interest in nonprofits and whose ideas have provided the starting point for much of my own thinking in this area, and to John G. Simon, who has been an important source of intellectual, moral, and material support throughout the course of this research.

Reprinted by permission of the author, the Yale Law Journal Company, and Fred D. Rotham and Company. Portions of text and footnotes omitted. Remaining footnotes have been re numbered.

antitrust, unfair competition, copyright, and postal rates. Yet the principles on which such special treatment is based are nowhere clearly formulated. Similarly, there continues to be debate concerning the action of the National Labor Relations Board in shifting radically, over the past decade, from a policy of excluding nonprofits entirely from coverage under federal labor law to a policy of including them under the law on the same terms as profit-seeking enterprise.

In this chapter, I seek to develop a broad perspective on the economic role that nonprofit organizations perform. My purpose is both to fill some of the gaps in our positive theories of institutions and to provide a basis for informed policymaking. This chapter discusses the entire spectrum of nonprofit organizations, though it focuses primarily upon nonprofit corporations that produce goods and services. This class of institutions, sometimes referred to as "operating" nonprofits, includes, for example, colleges, hospitals, day-care centers, nursing homes, research institutes, publications, symphony orchestras, social clubs, trade associations, labor unions, churches, and organizations for the relief of the needy and distressed. I shall devote correspondingly little attention to foundations, which for the most part are simply philanthropic intermediaries that produce no goods and services of their own. My concern is, moreover, with private nonprofit organizations, not with governmental enterprise.

THE ESSENTIAL CHARACTERISTICS OF NONPROFIT ENTERPRISE

Before examining the purposes served by nonprofit organizations, it is necessary to have a clear image of their essential structural features.

What Makes an Organization Nonprofit?

A nonprofit organization is, in essence, an organization that is barred from distributing its net earnings, if any, to individuals who exercise control over it, such as members, officers, directors, or trustees. By "net earnings" I mean here pure profits—that is, earnings in excess of the amount needed to pay for services rendered to the organization; in general, a nonprofit is free to pay reasonable compensation to any person for labor or capital that he provides, whether or not that person exercises some control over the organization. It should be noted that a nonprofit organization is not barred from earning a profit. Many nonprofits in fact consistently show an annual accounting surplus. It is only the distribution of the profits that is prohibited. Net earnings, if any, must be retained and devoted in their entirety to financing further production of the services that the organization was formed to provide. Since a good deal of the discussion that follows will focus upon this prohibition on the distribution of profits, it will be helpful to have a term for it; I shall call it the "nondistribution constraint."

Most nonprofits of any significance are incorporated. For these organizations, the nondistribution constraint is imposed, either explicitly or implicitly, as a condition under which the organization receives its corporate charter. Thus a nonprofit corporation is distinguished from a for-profit (or "business") corporation primarily by the absence of stock or other indicia of ownership that give their owners a simultaneous share in both profits and control.

In most other respects, the nonprofit corporation statutes closely parallel the statutes that provide for business corporations. In fact, they are, if anything, even more permissive. Thus a nonprofit corporation may have a membership that, like the shareholders in a business corporation, is entitled to select the board of directors through elections held at regular intervals. But the statutes typically do not make this a requirement, so that the board of directors may, alternatively, simply be made an autonomous, self-perpetuating body.

Sometimes nonprofit organizations are formed as charitable trusts without being incorporated, although for operating nonprofits this approach is uncommon in the United States. In such cases, control over the organization lies with the trustees, and the nondistribution constraint is imposed by the law of trusts, which prohibits trustees from taking from the trust anything beyond reasonable compensation for services rendered.

Unincorporated associations can sometimes also be appropriately labeled "nonprofit." Their status is problematic, however, for there is no well-developed body of statutory or case law dealing with them, and in particular, no simple mechanism whereby the nondistribution constraint can be imposed and enforced. Because of this, and because incorporation is relatively simple, it is uncommon to encounter substantial organizations that are operated as unincorporated nonprofit associations.

A Categorization of Nonprofit Organizations

The flexibility of the corporation statutes permits nonprofit organizations to assume a wide variety of forms. Consequently, for the sake of simplifying exposition and analysis, it will help us to develop a basic subcategorization of nonprofits according to the manner in which they are financed and controlled.

Financing: donative versus commercial nonprofits
Nonprofits that receive most or all of their income in the form of grants or donations I shall call "donative" nonprofits. Organizations for the relief of the needy, such as the Salvation Army, the American Red Cross, and CARE, are perhaps the most obvious examples. Those nonprofits that, on the other hand, receive the bulk of their income from prices charged for their services I shall call "commercial" nonprofits. Many nursing homes, most hospitals, and the American Automobile Association would clearly fall within this latter category.

Of course, not all nonprofits fit neatly into one or the other of these two categories. For example, most universities rely heavily upon donations as well as upon income from the sale of services—that is, tuition—and, thus, lie somewhere between the two. Consequently, donative and commercial nonprofits should be considered polar or ideal types rather than mutually exclusive and exhaustive categories.

In this chapter I shall use the word "patrons" to refer to those persons who constitute the ultimate source of a nonprofit's income. Thus, in the case of a donative nonprofit, by "patrons" I mean the organization's donors, while in the case of commercial nonprofits I use the term to refer to the organization's customers; when the organization receives income from both customers and donors, the term comprises both.

Control: mutual versus entrepreneurial nonprofits
Nonprofits that are controlled by their patrons I shall call "mutual" nonprofits. Country clubs provide an example: generally their directors are elected by the membership, which comprises the organization's customers. Common Cause, the citizens' lobby, presents another example: the board of directors of that organization ultimately is selected by the membership, which consists of all individuals who donate at least fifteen dollars annually to the organization. On the other hand, nonprofits that are largely free from the exercise of formal control by their patrons I shall term "entrepreneurial" nonprofits. Such organizations are usually controlled by a self-perpetuating board of directors. Most hospitals and nursing homes, for example, belong within this latter category. Again, the two categories are really the ends of a continuum. For example, the board of trustees of some universities is structured so that roughly half is elected by the alumni—which constitutes the bulk of past customers and present donors—while the other half is self-perpetuating.

It is important to recognize that, while the organizations that I have termed "mutual" nonprofits may bear some resemblance to cooperatives, they are by no means the same thing. Cooperatives are generally formed under state cooperative corporation statutes that are quite distinct from both the nonprofit corporation statutes and the business corporation statutes. Cooperative corporation statutes typically permit a cooperative's net earnings to be distributed to its patrons or investors, who may in turn exercise control over the organization. Thus, cooperatives are not subject to the nondistribution constraint that is the defining characteristic of nonprofit organizations. Mutual nonprofits should also be distinguished from entities such as mutual insurance companies and mutual savings and loan associations, which generally are structured essentially as cooperatives.

The Four Resulting Categories
The intersection of the preceding divisions in terms of finance and control produces four categories of nonprofits: (1) donative mutual; (2) donative entrepreneurial; (3) commercial mutual; and (4) commercial entrepreneurial. The following diagram displays some typical examples of these four types of organization.

	mutual	entrepreneurial
donative	Common Cause National Audubon Society political clubs	CARE March of Dimes art museums
commercial	American Automobile Association Consumers Union* country clubs	National Geographic Society** Educational Testing Service community hospitals nursing homes

* Publisher of *Consumer Reports*
** Publisher of *National Geographic*

With these bits of nomenclature at our service, we can now turn to more substantive matters.

TOWARD A GENERAL THEORY OF THE ROLE OF NONPROFIT ENTERPRISE

Undoubtedly many factors help explain why nonprofit institutions have proliferated in some areas of activity and not in others. Some of these factors are peculiar to particular types of nonprofits and will be considered below when we focus on individual sectors. There is, however, a rather general answer to the question, what makes a given activity more suitable to nonprofit than to for-profit organization?[3]

Economic theory tells us that, when certain conditions are satisfied, profit-seeking firms will supply goods and services at the quantity and price that represent maximum social efficiency. Among the most important of these conditions[4] is that consumers can, without undue cost or effort, (a) make a reasonably accurate comparison of the products and prices of different firms before any purchase is made, (b) reach a clear agreement with the chosen firm concerning the goods or services that the firm is to provide and the price to be paid, and (c) determine subsequently whether the firm complied with the resulting agreement and obtain redress if it did not.

In many cases—most notably with standardized industrial goods and farm produce—these requirements are reasonably well satisfied. Yet occasionally, due either to the circumstances under which the product is purchased and consumed or to the nature of the product itself, consumers may be incapable of accurately evaluating the goods promised or delivered. As a consequence, they will find it difficult to locate the best bargain in the first place or to enforce their bargain once made. In such circumstances, market competition may well provide insufficient discipline for a profit-seeking producer; the producer will have the capacity to charge excessive prices for inferior goods. As a consequence, consumer welfare may suffer considerably.

In situations of this type, consumers might be considerably better off if they deal with nonprofit producers rather than with for-profit producers. The nonprofit producer, like its for-profit counterpart, has the capacity to raise prices and cut quality in such cases without much fear of customer reprisal; however, it lacks the incentive to do so because those in charge are barred from taking home any resulting profits. In other words, the advantage of a nonprofit producer is that the discipline of the market is supplemented by the additional protection given the consumer by another, broader "contract," the organization's legal commitment to devote its entire earnings to the production of services. As a result of this institutional constraint, it is less imperative for the consumer either to shop around first or to enforce rigorously the contract he makes.[5]

Of course, one would expect that when the profit motive is eliminated a price is paid in terms of incentives. For example, nonprofit firms might be expected to be slower in meeting increased demand and to be less efficient in their use of inputs than for-profit firms. In addition, in spite of the limitations imposed upon them, nonprofits may succeed in distributing some of their net earnings through inflated salaries, various perquisites granted to employees, and other forms of excess payments. However, in situations in which the consumer is in a poor position to judge the services he is receiving, any approach to organizing production is likely to be a question of "second best." Moreover, it is plausible that the discipline of the market is in many cases sufficiently weak so that the efficiency losses to be expected from an industry of for-profit producers are considerably greater than those to be expected from nonprofit producers. In sum, I am suggesting that nonprofit enterprise is a reasonable response to a particular kind of "market failure," specifically the inability to police producers by ordinary contractual devices, which I shall call "contract failure."

It follows from these basic notions that the corporate charter serves a rather different function in nonprofit organizations than it does in for-profit organizations. In the case of the business corporation, the charter, and the case law that has grown up around it, protect the interests of the corporation's shareholders from interference by those parties—generally corporate management and other shareholders—who exercise direct control over the organization. In the case of the nonprofit corporation, on the other hand, the purpose of the charter is primarily to protect the interests of the organization's *patrons* from those who control the corporation. For this fundamental reason, the corporate law that has been developed for business corporations, and particularly that which concerns the fiduciary obligations of corporate management, often provides a poor model for nonprofit corporation law. Unfortunately, this fact has not always been appreciated.

APPLICATIONS OF THE THEORY

Contact failure occurs in a number of different forms and contexts. Some of the most common and most interesting of these contexts will be discussed here, in order to clarify the notion of contract failure and to shed some light on the economic problems peculiar to some important industries in which nonprofits play a significant role.

In some instances, the circumstances that give rise to contract failure are simple and reasonably obvious. This is the case, for example, with institutions such as redistributive philanthropies and with institutions that provide complex personal services. In other instances, the problems of contract failure that give rise to nonprofits are embedded in, or are the product of, various peculiar market conditions. This is the case with institutions in which contract failure is bound up with problems of public goods, price discrimination, and imperfect loan markets. In considering these latter institutions, it will be necessary to examine in some detail the full complex of factors that give rise to the need for nonprofit organizations.

Separation Between the Purchaser and the Recipient of the Service

Donative nonprofits provide the simplest and clearest applications of the contract-failure theory outlined in the preceding section. Of the various types of donative nonprofits, it is the most traditional of charities—namely those organizations that provide relief for the needy—that appear to be the easiest to understand.

Consider, for example, CARE, which obtains much of its funding from personal contributions. These contributions finance a relatively simple service, namely shipping and distributing foodstuffs and other supplies to needy individuals overseas. Why is this service provided by a nonprofit organization rather than a for-profit one? That is, why do we not have profit-seeking firms that make essentially the same kind of offer that CARE does— that in return for payment to them of ten dollars, say, they will ship and distribute a given quantity of fortified milk to hungry children in India?[6] Shipment and distribution of food, after all, is an activity commonly performed by for-profit firms. If you rely on a for-profit food distributor to provide the food you feed to your own children, why should you not also turn to a for-profit firm to provide the food you purchase for children overseas?

The answer, it appears, derives in large part from the fact that the individuals who receive the supplies distributed by CARE have no connection with the individuals who pay for them. Because of this separation between the purchasers and the recipients of the service, the purchasers are in a poor position to determine whether the service they paid for was in fact ever performed, much less performed adequately. If CARE were organized for profit, it would have a strong incentive to skimp on the services it promises, or even to neglect to perform them entirely, and, instead, to divert most or all of its revenues directly to its owners. After all, few of its customers could ever be expected to travel to India or Africa to see if the food they paid for was in fact ever delivered, much less delivered as, when, and where specified. The situation is quite different, of course, when an individual buys food for his own children. In that case, it is perfectly easy for him to rely on a for-profit grocer; he can check for himself whether he is getting his money's worth.

Thus, for a service of the type that CARE provides, it stands to reason that an individual would prefer to deal with a nonprofit firm, because in that case he has the additional protection provided by the nondistribution constraint: he needs an organization that he can trust, and the nonprofit, because of the legal constraints under which it must operate, is likely to serve that function better than its for-profit counterpart.

This does not mean, of course, that a nonprofit supplier is necessary or even appropriate in all situations in which one person subsidizes another's consumption. Indeed, such subsidies are often thoroughly compatible with for-profit enterprise. Thus, if goods rather than services are involved, the donor often has the option of simply taking delivery of the goods himself, thus ensuring that the producer has performed adequately, and then sending them personally to the donee—the procedure followed with most ordinary personal gifts. Further, in some cases, there are few problems with having a for-profit producer make delivery directly to the donee. For example, profit-seeking florist shops commonly arrange to have flower arrangements delivered all over the country as gifts. Because the arrangements involved are standardized and can be selected by picture, and because the donor is likely to hear from the recipient whether, and how well, the service was performed, there is only limited opportunity for abuse on the part of the florists.

Still another common approach to charity that utilizes for-profit producers involves subsidizing demand—that is, consumers—rather than supply. Redeemable coupons, such as food stamps or housing vouchers, are examples of a subsidy on the demand side. Gift certificates are a private counterpart to these government subsidy schemes. In situations in which demand-side subsidies are employed, the vigilance necessary to discipline for-profit producers comes from the donee rather than from the donor. It is only when the donor cannot contact the intended beneficiary of his gift directly, but instead must rely upon the producer of the subsidized service to act as the sole intermediary, that contract failure becomes a serious problem and a nonprofit producer seems necessary.

Public Goods

The concept of contract failure also helps to explain the prevalence of nonprofits as private-market producers of what economists term "public goods." Public goods, in the language of economics, are goods or services that exhibit two particular attributes: first, it costs no more to provide the good to many persons than it does to provide it to one person, because one person's enjoyment of the good does not interfere with the ability of others to enjoy it at the same time: and second, once the good has been provided to one person there is no way to prevent others from consuming it as well. Hamburgers are clearly "private goods," since they satisfy neither criterion: if I eat a hamburger you cannot eat it too—that is, hamburgers for two cost twice as much as hamburgers for one—and it is relatively easy for me to keep you from eating my hamburger. Air pollution control is commonly cited as an example of a public good; it costs as much to clean up the air for one citizen of Los Angeles as it does to clean it up for the whole city, and once the air has been cleaned up it is hard to prevent any individual from enjoying it.

If a public good is to be provided at the optimal level, and in the most efficient fashion, each individual should contribute toward its production a sum equal to the marginal value he places upon it. However, individuals have an incentive to contribute little or nothing toward the cost of producing such a good for two reasons: first, the individual's contribution is likely to be so small in proportion to the total that it will not appreciably affect the amount of the good that is provided, and second, the individual will in any case be able to enjoy the amounts of the good that are financed by the contributions of others. Thus, there is little relationship between the size of an individual's contribution and the amount of the good that he enjoys. Assuming all individuals follow this logic and become "free riders," then little or none of the good will be supplied, even though collective demand for the good is in fact quite high. Thus, economists generally have concluded that the private market is an inefficient means of providing public goods, and have looked to alternatives such as public financing as a better approach.

In fact, however, the free-rider psychology is far from universal; in many situations people *are* willing to contribute toward the production of public goods. And what is important for our purposes—though it has generally been overlooked in the existing literature on public goods—is that even in these cases profit-seeking firms probably will constitute an unworkable means of providing public goods. Contract failure is likely to be a problem if consumers seek to purchase public goods from profit-seeking producers, and hence nonprofits are likely to be more suitable suppliers.[7]

Contract failure in a public-goods context

Consider, for example, a listener-supported radio station of the type that now exists in many of the nation's larger cities. These stations carry no advertising, so that they may provide programming both uninterrupted by commercials and free of pressure from sponsors. They rely for most of their income upon direct contributions solicited from their listeners by over-the-air appeals.

Such stations are providing the listening audience a public good. It is no more costly to make the radio signal available to all individuals living within a given radius of the broadcasting station than it is to provide the signal to one individual within that radius. Furthermore, with present technology, it is infeasible to bar an individual within the broadcast area from tuning in and listening until he makes a payment to the radio station. It is, in fact, precisely these characteristics of the service that have led commercial radio stations to foresake any effort to collect payment for their programming from listeners; instead, they have adopted the technique of selling their audience to advertisers. However, this expedient changes the nature of the service and the incentives of the broadcaster in a way that many listeners find unpleasant. The listener-sponsored radio stations, in order to avoid such a result, carry no advertising and seek to "sell" their programs directly to the listeners by soliciting voluntary payments from them. Interestingly, in many large cities such stations have succeeded, by exhorting their listeners a bit, in overcoming the free-rider problem sufficiently to keep in business.

This is, then, a situation in which enough people are willing to contribute voluntarily so that provision of a public good is economically viable on a nongovernmental basis.[8] But the private organizations that provide this public good are all nonprofit. Why are there not some listener-supported for-profit radio stations as well? Silly as the question may seem, it is instructive to be precise about the answer.

Imagine that such a for-profit station were to be formed, and that it sought voluntary contributions from its listeners to cover its costs—including a reasonable return on the owners' investment. Could it count on as high a level of voluntary payments as its nonprofit counterpart would receive? Undoubtedly it could not. The reason is simply that contributors would have little or no assurance that their payments to a for-profit station were actually needed to pay for the service they received. A for-profit station would have every incentive to solicit payments far in excess of the total needed to pay for its broadcasts, and simply to distribute the difference to the owners as profits. With a nonprofit station, on the other hand, the listener has some assurance that all of his payment will in fact be used to pay for the broadcasts.

The difference between the radio station and the CARE example discussed above is that with the former the contributor is also the ultimate recipient of the organization's services. Thus, the problem with a for-profit radio station, unlike overseas charity, does not stem from the fact that the contributor cannot determine whether the services promised are in fact being provided. Rather, the problem here is related to the indivisible nature of the service involved, which is what makes it a public good. The listener knows what quality of broadcast is being provided, but he does not know whether his contribution is being used to pay for it. There is no observable connection between the amount of the individual's contribution and the quality of the broadcast.[9] The virtue of the nonprofit form of organization is that it can provide some assurance that in fact such a connection exists.

It should be clear by now in what way the contract failure problem that we are focusing on here is distinct from the standard public goods market failure—the freerider problem. The latter is concerned with the lack of incentive to contribute to the cost of a public good, while the former is concerned with the inability to control the use to which a contribution is put once it is made.

Contractual alternatives

The nature of the contract-failure problem, and the way in which non-profits provide a response to that problem, may become clearer if we focus more closely upon the contractual difficulties involved in the example just developed. In particular, let us consider whether it might not be possible for the owners of a commercial-free broadcasting station to devise a contract for services that would give the consumer as much security as does the nonprofit form.

Obviously a contractual promise by the owners simply to spend all or most of individual patron's payment upon production of broadcast services will be meaningless in itself. Because the services financed with the payment from the patron in question are undifferentiated from the services financed by other income, such a promise can have significance only if it is accompanied by an understanding that the compensation taken by the owners from other income will not be increased upon receipt of the patron's payment. It appears, then, that any contractual promise made by the owners to a given patron must make reference to the uses they will make of all of the organization's income, from whatever source it may derive. Such a promise might, for example, take one of the following forms:

1. The owners could promise that no more than, for example, five percent of the income they receive from all sources will be distributed to the owners as compensation and profits.
2. The owners could promise that the total amounts distributed to themselves as compensation and profits will not exceed a given dollar limit.
3. The owners could promise that the amounts distributed to themselves will not exceed "reasonable" compensation for the services and capital they contribute to the organization.

In each case it would need to be promised further that all amounts not distributed to the owners would be devoted to other expenses necessary for the production of broadcasts of the highest quality that those amounts permit.

It is immediately apparent that all three of these approaches convert the nominally profit-seeking firm producing the broadcasts into what is essentially a nonprofit organization. That is, all three devices effectively limit the amount of the organization's income that can be appropriated by the owners. The third approach, limiting compensation to amounts that are "reasonable" for the services rendered, is in fact roughly the interpretation given to the nondistribution constraint by the law. Approaches (1) and (2), so long as they are consistent with (3), can be seen simply as more specific versions of the latter standard and, therefore, are also just private-contract versions of the nondistribution constraint.

The difference between the contractual devices just mentioned and a formal nonprofit lies, then, not in the nature of the limitations imposed upon the managers but rather in the means by which they are established and enforced. Under the contractual approach, the patrons would need to insist upon receiving regular, audited financial statements from the firm containing sufficient detail to permit the patrons to determine whether the owners are adhering to the contractual constraints. Should it appear to a given patron at any point that the owners are not keeping their promises, then the patron would need to bring suit to enforce the contract. In contrast, under the nonprofit form, the state is empowered to bring suit if the organization's management compensates itself too generously.

The advantage of the nonprofit form, then, is that it economizes on contracting and enforcement. Under the private contractual approach each individual patron not only must understand and agree to a complex contract but also must police the organization's finances as a whole—or rely upon other patrons to do so. Moreover, to the extent that patrons do engage in such policing, they may be duplicating each other's actions, since the activity that constitutes breach of the contract is presumably the same for all. Consequently, considerable economies can be realized by placing all such transactions under one collective contract between the organization and its patrons: the contract determined by the state's nonprofit corporation law and policed by the state.

If "pay radio" were to become commercially feasible—that is, if there were some inexpensive means of making receipt of a radio station's broadcasts conditional upon payment of a periodic charge—then profitseeking firms also would be able to engage in commercial-free broadcasting simply by charging their listeners directly, as is already happening in the television industry via cable TV. The result presumably would be a reduction in the willingness of listeners to make voluntary contributions to nonprofit stations, since such stations would no longer be as necessary to fill the need for commercial-free programming. Thus pay radio might be expected to supplant nonprofit listener-supported stations. Such a result would be more efficient, in fact, since the free-rider problem would be eliminated. In this case, therefore, it seems that nonprofit enterprise is simply a response to technical problems in pricing services.

Other types of public goods

Many other public goods also are supplied by nonprofits. A familiar example is basic scientific and medical research, which, to the extent that it is performed by nongovernmental organizations, is conducted in large part by nonprofits, such as universities and independent research laboratories. In addition, there are a number of nonprofit organizations, such as the March of Dimes and the American Heart Association, that collect funds for such research and distribute them to the research institutions. Organizations that seek to influence the political process, such as Common Cause, the Sierra Club, and the Republican Party, also provide a public good to those individuals who share the organization's views. Similarly, organizations that lobby for particular sectors of industry, such as the American Petroleum Institute and the Motor Vehicle Manufacturers Association, provide public goods to the firms that are in the particular industry involved. These organizations are all nonprofit, rather than for-profit, for the same reason as in the case of the listener-supported radio stations discussed above.

Price Discrimination

There are further situations in which, as with public goods, the contract failure that ultimately gives rise to nonprofit producers grows out of other kinds of market failure. One of the more interesting of these, related to the public goods case just discussed, involves nonprofit organizations in the performing arts.

As it is, the high-culture, live performing arts—including symphonic music, ballet, and opera—are provided almost exclusively by nonprofit institutions, while in other areas of the performing arts, such as Broadway theater and movies, proprietary firms are the norm. This pattern can be explained superficially by the observation that firms in the high-culture performing arts depend upon donations for a substantial fraction of their income, and, for the reasons of contract failure discussed above, donors are likely to be willing to give to a firm only if it is nonprofit. What is more difficult to understand is why these particular forms of entertainment ever came to depend upon donative financing. The answer appears to be that, in this industry, donations serve as a means of implementing a form of voluntary price discrimination, and that such price discrimination is essential for survival in an industry, such as this, in which demand is heterogenous and limited, and in which fixed costs are high relative to variable costs.

Museums and libraries provide other examples of industries in which nonprofits have risen in part, it appears, because of the need for voluntary price discrimination.

Implicit Loans

Nonprofit organizations arise in certain situations as a response to legal and practical imperfections in loan markets. Private education provides an example. Institutions of higher education commonly depend heavily on voluntary private contributions to cover their expenses. Why are these contributions necessary, and why do people make them? In part, such contributions undoubtedly reflect motivations similar to those we have already surveyed. Certainly some gifts are intended to help cover costs for students who come from families that would not otherwise be able to afford such schooling. To this extent, colleges play a role as philanthropic intermediaries in somewhat the same way that CARE does. To some extent, too,

donations to colleges and universities are intended to help support the provision of public goods such as scientific research.[10] Yet these factors do not
seem to account for the bulk of donations to institutions of higher education.

In essence, the donations received by private colleges and universities are
in large part simply a response to a real failing in our market mechanisms—namely, the lack of an adequate system of educational loans. For
most people it would be worthwhile to borrow against their future earnings in order to pay the cost of higher education. Yet private lending institutions generally have not been willing to make such loans, due to problems in arranging for adequate security where the assets that the borrower
is acquiring with the loan involve human rather than physical capital.

The resulting unavailability of private loans means that, if private colleges and universities were to charge through tuition the full cost of the
education they offer, they would be able to educate only the children of
unusually prosperous families. Instead, the private schools have in effect
adopted a loan program with voluntary payback. Schools charge their students through tuition payments less than the full cost of education, but then
impress upon their graduates their moral obligation to repay the loan that
they have in effect received. Or, put differently, alumni contributions can
be seen as essentially a means by which college students pay for their college educations on a voluntary installment plan. Of course, there is no legally enforceable obligation to pay anything to the school once an individual has graduated, and many alumni give nothing. But the schools constantly
remind alumni of their moral obligation, and many alumni do give.[11] The
nonprofit form is undoubtedly important in encouraging alumni to make
the contributions on which the system depends, for reasons similar to those
for listener-supported radio stations. An individual will be more willing to
give money to a school if he knows that it will be devoted to providing
education. Yet the contributor cannot tell whether his donation was used
to further the educational goals of the institution, or whether, conversely,
it simply went into someone's pocket. The nonprofit form provides some
assurance to the donor in this regard.

I do not mean to suggest that if the imperfections in the market for educational loans could be eliminated—as, for example, through an expanded system of federal loan guarantees—then we could expect for-profit
colleges and universities to begin to proliferate. There are undoubtedly other
reasons, unconnected with alumni donations, why higher education is typically nonprofit. Some of these reasons are explored below.

Complex Personal Services

The preceding examples have all involved nonprofits that would be classified as donative under the categorization offered above.

At first glance, commercial nonprofits raise different issues. By definition, the patron of a commercial nonprofit is engaged in a straightforward

commercial transaction, purchasing a good or service provided exclusively to him for his personal consumption. Nevertheless, commercial nonprofits seem to respond to contract-failure problems similar to those found in the case of donative nonprofits. Commercial nonprofits typically arise in industries that provide complex personal services, as opposed to standardized industrial or agricultural goods. Often the complexity of these services, their nonstandardized character, and the circumstances under which they are provided make it difficult for the consumer to determine whether the services are performed adequately. Thus, the patron has an incentive to seek some constraints on the organization's behavior beyond those that he is able to impose by direct, private contract. Put differently, the services provided by commercial nonprofits commonly require that the consumer entrust to the producer a great deal of discretion that the consumer is in a poor position to police. The nondistribution constraint limits the opportunity for the managers of the organization to abuse this discretion and consequently offers the consumer additional protection.

It is true, however, that when an individual is purchasing for his own personal consumption, as is generally the case with the services provided by commercial nonprofits, he is necessarily in a better position to police the transaction than when, as is commonly the case with donative nonprofits, he is purchasing public goods or services that are to be delivered to others. Consequently, while the problems of market failure that give rise to commercial nonprofits can be serious, they are, in contrast to the problems that give rise to donative nonprofits, rarely of such magnitude as to prevent patrons from ever turning to a profit-seeking provider. Thus, we find that commercial nonprofits almost always operate in competition with proprietary firms that provide similar services, suggesting that the competing advantages and disadvantages of the two types of firms are closely balanced. In fact, profit-seeking firms have a significant, and frequently a dominant, share of the market in all of the important industries in which commercial nonprofits are to be found. Donative nonprofits, on the other hand, rarely have proprietary counterparts.

Some examples
The following examples of industries composed at least in part of commercial nonprofit institutions may help to illustrate these points.

Nursing care   Many of the nation's privately operated nursing homes for the elderly are nonprofit, though the majority are still proprietary. Nonprofit nursing homes commonly receive little or no income from donations and thus fall in the category of commercial nonprofits.

Nursing home patients who receive the services often are too enfeebled to be able to judge effectively the quality of care they receive, or to press complaints against managers or to seek out an alternative institution. Furthermore, payment for the services often comes not from the patient himself, but instead, as in the CARE example, from a third party such as a

medical insurance plan. In such cases only the third-party billpayer may
have the leverage to insist upon adequate performance. Yet such a third
party commonly has a much less direct stake in the quality of care provided than does the patient and may make little effort to inspect the home
firsthand or even to communicate with patients competent to offer a useful
critique. Moreover, even if the paying party is a relative of the patient and
does seek to ensure that performance is adequate, contract failure may result. The patient may not be a useful source of information and it may be
impossible to obtain an accurate idea of the quality of care through occasional visits. Because the quality of the nursing services and medication
provided by a nursing home might be difficult to judge, a proprietary nursing home operator can often get away with providing low-quality services
while charging exorbitant prices, or providing unneeded services and bill-
ing the patient for the cost. Worse, an unscrupulous operator may even use
medications to sedate complaining patients. For all of these reasons an individual might reasonably prefer to entrust his care and health, or those of
a relative, to a nonprofit nursing home, whose managers are prohibited from
appropriating earnings derived from deficient service.

Unfortunately, in the nursing home business many operators have found
it relatively easy to circumvent, via various forms of self-dealing, the nondistribution constraint that is supposed to characterize nonprofit enterprise. The rationale for nonprofit enterprise suggested here does not lose
its force, however, simply because the nonprofit form has at times been
abused. People undoubtedly patronize nonprofit nursing homes in the expectation that such institutions will be less likely than proprietary institutions to take advantage of the discretion that must necessarily be granted
to them. The fact that such expectations are sometimes ill-founded does
not belie the argument that they are a major source of the demand for the
services of nonprofit institutions. In any case, nursing homes seem to be a
deviant example in this regard. In no other important sector do nonprofit
institutions appear to be so frequently just a cover for proprietary activity.

Day care Day care for young children, like nursing care for the elderly,
is often provided by nonprofit institutions, though again proprietary organizations account for more than half of the existing facilities. The factors responsible for the substantial proportion of day-care centers that are
nonprofit seem similar to those just considered in the case of nursing homes.
While it is the parent who pays for the services rendered by a day care
center, it is the child to whom these services are immediately rendered.
Children typically are not very discriminating consumers, nor even, in many
cases, good sources of information about the nature of the services they
receive. In such circumstances it is natural for a parent to turn to a nonprofit provider on the assumption that such an institution will be less likely
to abuse the trust that must necessarily be placed in it.[12]

Education It has been noted above that it is often advantageous for educational institutions to be nonprofit so that they can have access to do-

native financing. Yet there are reasons even for schools that are commercial, receiving most or all of their income from tuition payments, to be nonprofit. For private primary and secondary schools, considerations similar to those just suggested for day care centers apply: the parents are paying while the child is the direct recipient of the services, and the parents may not want to rely exclusively on the child for an evaluation of the quality of education provided. Moreover, education at all levels is a complex and subtle service, and in many cases a parent or a student may not feel competent to make adequate judgments about the quality of the teaching and facilities that an institution offers.

Hospital care   Hospitals are perhaps the most common example of commercial nonprofits. Roughly ninety percent of all nongovernmental general hospitals are nonprofit. Although a few hospitals, particularly the large teaching hospitals, might be classified as donative, the vast majority of nonprofit hospitals receive virtually all of their income from payments made by patients—either directly or through insurance plans—for services rendered.

It can be argued that hospitals are commonly nonprofit for reasons similar to those just advanced to explain the presence of commercial nonprofits in other fields. The patient is commonly in a poor position to judge the quality of care he receives. The treatment administered is technical, and the patient is often not in any position to make consumer decisions. Consumers of hospital services might therefore appear to have a strong incentive to seek a supplier with a minimal incentive to take advantage of them. Yet here this line of reasoning is not entirely convincing. When a patient enters a hospital, he generally continues to be cared for by a private physician who is not an employee of the hospital, but rather bills the patient separately for his services. Moreover, it is the physician, not the hospital, who administers or is responsible for most of the crucial services received by the patient. The hospital, for the most part, provides relatively routine services, such as room and board, laboratory tests, and nursing care. Furthermore, it is the physician rather than the patient who generally orders particular hospital services, and who acts on behalf of the patient to make sure that the services are performed properly. That is to say, the physician acts essentially as a very sophisticated purchasing agent for the patient in the latter's dealings with the hospital. Thus the consumer appears to be no more at the mercy of a for-profit hospital than he is at the mercy of a for-profit manufacturer of prescription drugs.

Instead, historical factors probably play a large role in explaining why hospitals are typically nonprofit. In the nineteenth century, hospitals were almost exclusively charitable institutions serving as sickhouses for the poor and, thus, were donative institutions. In the twentieth century, however, changes in medical science and in the availability of insurance plans took hospitals almost entirely out of the business of charity and put them on a paying basis. Yet, while private hospitals seldom take charity cases any more, so far they have remained largely nonprofit. This is probably not simply a matter of inertia and tradition. Doctors undoubtedly find this state of affairs profitable and, thus, have a strong interest in seeing it continued. So long as hospitals bill patients at no more than cost for their services, doctors have a bit more freedom to raise their own fees. It is rather as if a foundation, tax-exempt and supported in part by public contributions, were to build office space and then lease it at cost, or less, to Wall Street law firms. One would not expect to see the lawyers in a hurry to have the foundation converted into an ordinary profit-making landlord.

In any event, a shift in the organization of the hospital sector is taking place. In the past, proprietary hospitals were typically small institutions, serving only the patients of the handful of doctors who owned them. As such hospitals grew, they were commonly converted into nonprofits.[13] Since 1967, however, publicly traded for-profit corporations have begun entering the hospital industry, acquiring ownership of large chains of hospitals, many of them formerly nonprofit. If the trend continues, the hospital industry may someday cease to be dominated by nonprofits—though other factors, such as national health insurance, may also have a strong influence on the future organization of hospitals.[14]

Comparison with services provided for profit

There are, of course, many goods and services that are not easily evaluated by consumers, yet are commonly provided by for-profit firms. Medicinal drugs, and the services of doctors, lawyers, automobile repairmen, and television repairmen provide examples. What distinguishes these services from those provided by nonprofits, and by commercial nonprofits in particular?

To begin with, while the consumer may be more or less at the mercy of the supplier in any given transaction involving drugs or the services of professionals and repairmen, such transactions are generally small and discrete and the costs of switching to another supplier are typically limited. As a consequence, the potential hazards involved in any given transaction are often relatively small. Further, in such circumstances the consumer has, as a means of disciplining the supplier in addition to enforcement of the original contract for services, the threat of taking his future business elsewhere if he should have reason to doubt the quality of performance. And finally, by switching suppliers from time to time the consumer may be able to educate himself somewhat about their services.

Further, in many cases, special institutions other than those with nonprofit status have arisen to provide consumers additional protection. Doctors and lawyers, for example, must be licensed and are subject to some degree of supervision and discipline from their respective professional associations. Ethical drugs are subject to federal regulation for quality and efficacy, and are available to the consumer only with a doctor's prescription.

In other industries, consumers seem to be at the mercy of for-profit providers, yet protective institutions have not developed to any significant degree. Among the services mentioned above, automobile and television repair fall into this category. In cases such as these, however, the mere possibility of developing special policing mechanisms may help to explain the relative absence of nonprofits. Thus, in the case of automobile and television repair—as opposed to the complex human services commonly provided by commercial nonprofits—it appears that a simple inspection and certification scheme probably would be sufficient to eliminate most of the problems that consumers face. The apparent lack of demand for such inspection schemes suggests that, for good reasons or bad, consumers are not overly concerned about their ability to judge the cost and quality of service that they receive from automobile and television repairmen.

The nature of the risks confronting the consumer also may be important in distinguishing those cases in which consumers turn to nonprofit producers. Where the services provided by for-profit producers are concerned, it appears that the major risk facing the consumer is generally that the producer will charge for work that was unnecessary and perhaps that was not done, rather than that the basic problem that caused the consumer to seek the service will not be solved—at least eventually. Thus, the customer's television probably will come back from the shop in decent working order, a result that he is easily able to check. The risk he runs is that he will be charged $100 for a $5 adjustment. When we look at the types of services provided by the major categories of commercial nonprofits, on the other hand, it seems that the producer is often in a position to get away with providing less than the minimal service the consumer requires. A day care center may be able to provide less nutrition, education, recreation, affection, or discipline for the children in its care than the parents would willingly tolerate, yet run only a minimal chance that many of the parents will become aware of it.[15] Since the value of such services to the consumer often is far in excess of their cost of production, to be deprived of the service itself can be far more damaging than simply to be overcharged for it.[16]

The prevailing size of the organizations in an industry seems to be another significant factor. The distinction between the for-profit and nonprofit forms becomes blurred when the organizations in question are small in scale, and thus the nonprofit form tends to lose its distinctive advantage in such cases. Consider, for example, a lawyer in solo practice who bills his clients by the hour. Since he only gets paid at what is presumably the going rate for his labor services, his law office is, in a sense, conducted on a nonprofit basis. Thus his business might not operate much differently if he were to establish it formally as a nonprofit rather than as a sole proprietorship. Similarly, if a person operates a small day care center out of his own home, employing few or no persons other than himself, the flow of funds and even the bookkeeping might look much the same whether the organization is formally created as a nonprofit or a for-profit entity. The nondistribution constraint that characterizes the nonprofit form has real meaning only when an enterprise is of sufficient scale to develop large earnings that cannot easily and plausibly be paid out simply as reasonable salaries to the individuals in control of the enterprise. This may be an important reason why the service industries that are dominated by nonprofits, such as education and hospital care, are those that exhibit substantial economies of scale, while the service industries in which nonprofits are significantly outnumbered by proprietary firms, such as day care and nursing care, are those in which the efficient scale of enterprise is rather small.

Finally, two other considerations may play a role here: first, it may be that, for reasons rooted in cultural norms or individual preferences, the constraints of the nonprofit form operate more effectively for some types of services than for others; and second, the liabilities that accompany the nonprofit form may vary from one industry to another.

We should not, in any case, be surprised that there are service industries in which there is evidently some degree of contract failure, but in which nonprofit firms have not come to play a significant role. As I have already noted, when an individual is purchasing private goods for his personal consumption, contract failure is unlikely to achieve such proportions as to make for-profit producers completely unworkable. In such circumstances, the extra degree of protection afforded by the nonprofit form is at best marginal. This is particularly evident when we consider that the nondistribution constraint is a rather crude consumer protection device; it may be an appropriate counter to the gross forms of contract failure that characterize the situations in which donative nonprofits are found, but it is a blunt instrument with which to attack the more limited forms of contract failure involved in the private provision of personal services. We have seen that there is no important service industry in which commercial nonprofits have entirely supplanted proprietary firms, and that in a number of industries in which commercial nonprofits are found, such as day care and nursing care, the nonprofit firms are substantially outnumbered by their for-profit competitors. It is therefore understandable that, when the complex of factors that determine the degree of contract failure in a given industry and govern the effectiveness of the nonprofit form in that industry assume a slightly different configuration, nonprofit firms are found to occupy no significant niche at all.

A CLOSER LOOK AT THE NONDISTRIBUTION CONSTRAINT

In the preceding discussion I have stressed the nondistribution constraint as the essential characteristic that permits nonprofit organizations to serve effectively as a response to contract failure. The extent to which the managers of nonprofits actually adhere to this constraint is therefore an issue of some importance.

The Effectiveness of Legal Sanctions for Distributing Profits

Although the prohibition on distribution of profits is more or less clearly embodied in the nonprofit corporation law of nearly all the states, most states in fact make little or no effort to enforce this prohibition. As a rule, its enforcement is placed exclusively in the hands of the state's attorney general; private parties, such as donors and consumers, generally lack standing to bring suit against the organization or its officers on this issue.[17] Yet in most states neither the office of the attorney general nor any other office of the state government devotes any appreciable amount of resources to the oversight of nonprofit firms.[18]

If, however, the organization is exempt from the federal corporate income tax, as most nonprofit enterprise is, then the Internal Revenue Service may well take an interest in whether there is any distribution of profits. Any organization that violates the nondistribution constraint imposed by its corporate charter is also likely to run afoul of the parallel provision in the tax law, and thereby run the risk of losing its exemption. Yet even the IRS has not been particularly zealous in this area[19]—perhaps because its primary sanction, denial of exemption, seems too drastic a response to a bit of self-dealing on the part of an institution's managers, particularly when it may well be the patrons of the institution who will suffer the most from the IRS's action.[20]

With such limited policing, it is not surprising that the managers of many nonprofit organizations succeed, to a greater or lesser extent, in evading the nondistribution constraint and in enriching themselves at the expense of the organizations and their patrons. The means used may be excessive salaries, low-interest loans from the organization, personal services and amenities paid for out of the organization's funds, excessively generous contracts for services provided to the organization by businesses owned by the managers, or the purchase or lease of real estate by the organization from its managers at inflated prices, mortgage interest, or rents.

It has already been noted that such devices seem to be disturbingly common in the nursing home industry. In addition, allegations of profiteering have been leveled at a variety of other types of nonprofits, including hospitals,[21] private schools,[22] and workshops for the blind.[23] Obviously such abuses, or even the potential for them, weaken the nonprofit form by undermining its effectiveness as a response to contract failure.

Normative Constraints on Profiteering

Nevertheless, these abuses appear to be the exception rather than the rule; in spite of minimal policing of the nondistribution constraint, nonprofit institutions in most industries evidently are operated on a fairly circumspect basis. Such broad compliance with a poorly policed constraint is presumably due to adherence to social norms that reinforce the legal restraints on profiteering by conditioning individual behavior even when the legal constraints are unlikely to be enforced. Indeed, such ethical constraints may be far more important than legal sanctions in causing the managers of nonprofits to adhere to their fiduciary responsibilities.

Of course, such normatively conditioned behavior is important in all areas of economic life.[24] The successful operation of any economy requires a general willingness to play by the rules of the game even when the umpire is not watching.[25] What is of particular interest here is that, where non-profits are concerned, such norms may have achieved more substantial development in some industries than in others. For example, in such areas as hospital care and higher education, which have been predominantly non-profit for centuries in Anglo-American society, it appears that norms prohibiting profiteering have taken deep root. Yet in more recently developed, and therefore less tradition-bound, sectors, such norms may be weaker. Perhaps this explains in part the difficulties in the nursing home sector, which has grown from almost nothing into a large industry in the past forty years.[26] Also, in industries such as nursing homes, the presence of a substantial number of for-profit competitors may weaken normative restraints; the standards of service and conduct set by the proprietary firms eventually may be taken as an acceptable minimum even among the nonprofits. The importance of such ethical constraints may also explain why so many non-profit institutions—including, for example, schools, hospitals, nursing homes, foster homes, and even housing project sponsors—are affiliated with religious groups. For such an association may help to keep the norms intact and at the same time assure potential patrons that in fact they *are* intact.[27]

Further, it seems likely that normative constraints operate more effectively in large organizations than they do in small ones, since in large organizations the activities of managers are exposed to the scrutiny of a larger number of other employees, and are also subject to the limitations imposed by bureaucratization. Thus, this is another reason why the typical size of organizations in a given sector, which is determined in large part by economies of scale, seems positively correlated with the extent to which nonprofits are established in the sector.

Screening Phenomena

Finally, the nondistribution constraint may gain added strength by screening selectively for a class of entrepreneurs, managers, and employees who are more interested in providing high-quality service and less interested in financial rewards than are most individuals. That is, the nonprofit form both may restrain the managers of the organization, whatever their personal desires, from profiteering at the expense of the organization's patrons and may select as managers precisely that class of individuals whose preferences are most in consonance with the fiduciary role that the organization is designed to serve. Such screening might also have consequences for the competition that takes place between nonprofit and for-profit firms within a given sector.

SOME PROBLEMS WITH THE NONPROFIT FORM

As suggested in the second section, there are liabilities as well as benefits to the nonprofit form of organization.

Limitations on Raising Capital

Because nonprofits are unable to sell equity shares, they must rely largely upon donations, retained earnings, and debt for capital financing. The funds available from these sources may, however, be poorly matched to the capital needs of the organization. Donations may reflect merely the whims of contributors. Sufficient retained earnings to finance major capital expansion may take too long to accumulate and of course are not available at all to a newly founded organization. Debt financing, which generally is available for only a fraction of the investments made by for-profit firms, is even more limited for nonprofits because of the poor fungibility of the organization's assets and the negative effect on the creditor's public relations in case of foreclosure. Thus, while some institutions have accumulated endowments in excess of their needs, many others are sorely strapped for the capital funds necessary to meet the burgeoning demand for their services.

Cross-Subsidization

The nondistribution constraint provides the consumer with some assurance that the sums he pays to a commercial nonprofit will go in their entirety to the production of services. It offers no assurance, however, that the services he pays for will be provided to *him*. In general, a nonprofit remains relatively free to use the sums paid by one consumer to subsidize another, especially if, as is often the case, the consumer is in a poor position to determine whether he is getting exactly what he paid for. As one example, it appears that nonprofit hospitals commonly use profits derived from some of their routine services to finance other services, such as open-heart surgery units, that are characterized by such high costs and low demand that they cannot pay for themselves. Similarly, some nonprofit hospitals use profits from services provided to paying patients to cover the cost of serving indigent patients. Whether such cross-subsidization is undesirable as a matter of policy depends upon the degree to which it fosters the provision of services whose costs exceed their benefits and the nature of the interpersonal redistribution to which it gives rise.

Incentives for Managerial Efficiency

The profit motive encourages efficient production. A profit-seeking entrepreneur has an incentive to choose the least costly means of producing a given service. Nonprofits might therefore be expected to be less vigilant in eliminating unnecessary expense than are their for-profit counterparts. Whether this is so depends upon the factors that actually motivate the managers of for-profit and nonprofit firms. Thus, the familiar separation of ownership and control in large publicly held corporations may sometimes leave the management of such firms as free as the management of a nonprofit to select the goals to be served by the firm and to decide how efficiently it will be run. Some data suggest that, in the hospital industry at least, nonprofits are in fact managed somewhat less efficiently than their for-profit counterparts.[28]

Incentives for Entry and Growth

The profit motive also provides a mechanism for ensuring that firms enter an industry and expand when demand for that industry's products or services increases. Nonprofits may, therefore, be less responsive to changes in demand, even when the availability of capital is not a constraint.

Implications for the General Theory

If there were no special disadvantages to the nonprofit form of organization, one would expect nonprofit firms to displace profit-seeking firms in all industries. That is, if the only thing distinguishing nonprofit firms from for-profit firms was the fact that, by virtue of the nondistribution constraint, in the nonprofit firm price never exceeds cost, then there would be no situation in which a for-profit firm would have a competitive advantage over a nonprofit firm.

As the preceding discussion suggests, however, nonprofit firms are at a disadvantage relative to for-profit firms in various respects, including access to capital, efficiency of operation, and speed of entry and growth in expanding markets. Consequently, whether nonprofit firms are more suitable than for-profit firms in any given industry depends upon the balance of competing factors. Only if, in any given case, the protection afforded patrons by the nondistribution constraint is so valuable as to outweigh the disadvantages just mentioned will nonprofit firms have a competitive edge. Conversely, where, as in the case of most industrial goods, contract failure is not much of a problem, and hence the nondistribution constraint gives the consumer little added protection, the balance clearly tips in favor of proprietary firms.

LAW, ECONOMICS, AND INDIVIDUAL BEHAVIOR

In this chapter I have offered, in essence, a positive theory of consumer demand. That is, I have argued that nonprofits tend to produce particular services, those characterized by "contract failure," because consumers prefer to deal with nonprofits in purchasing those services. This preference, I have suggested, is based upon a feeling that nonprofits can be trusted not to exploit the advantage over the consumer resulting from contract failure. This trust derives its rational basis from the nondistribution constraint that characterizes the nonprofit form.

One might object that consumers do not, in fact, think this way. Surely the average consumer, if asked why he deals with a nonprofit rather than a for-profit firm in a given situation, would be unlikely to elaborate the theory of contract failure offered above. Indeed, one suspects that most people are vague about precisely what it is, from a legal point of view, that makes an organization nonprofit.

The theory outlined in this chapter, however, does not require that every consumer, in choosing whether to deal with a nonprofit organization, perform an elaborate cost-benefit analysis concerning the type and degree of market failure involved, the effectiveness of the nondistribution constraint, possible offsetting inefficiencies of the nonprofit form, and so forth. Rather, it is sufficient that experience in the long run leads consumers as an overall group to develop a sense that in certain circumstances it is most appropriate to deal with nonprofits. Undoubtedly for most consumers such attitudes are learned from others rather than based upon conscious reflection. I am suggesting only that for those consumers who do exercise judgment, the decision to patronize a nonprofit versus a for-profit firm is based either upon some previous experience with both nonprofit and for-profit firms in various circumstances, or upon a more or less conscious realization that in purchasing the service one is to some degree at the mercy of the producer, and that therefore one may be better served by a firm in which the profit motive has been curtailed. Similarly, the arguments advanced in the preceding sections do not lose force merely because many individuals who patronize nonprofits have at best only a vague understanding of the nondistribution constraint. It suffices that some subset of patrons has a general notion that when an organization is nonprofit it is somehow committed to operating for some purpose other than profit maximization. In general, social institutions and patterns of behavior may represent a reasonable degree of economic rationality even when most of the individuals involved are not self-consciously engaged in intricate processes of economically rational thought.

I do not, of course, pretend to have explained here everything important that there is to know about the nonprofit sector. For one thing, it takes supply as well as demand to make a market; to understand the nonprofit sector in full, one must know not only the circumstances under which patrons will seek the services of nonprofits, but also the factors that determine whether and how nonprofit organizations will develop to meet that demand. In this chapter I have focused heavily on the demand side, primarily because this seems the best way to illuminate the general role served by the nonprofit form. Questions of supply response have been touched upon only briefly, and much remains to be said.

Moreover, I have by no means given a complete picture even of the demand side. In particular, I have made little effort here to explore the sources of donative behavior—those factors, for example, that lead an individual to contribute voluntarily toward the financing of a public good, or to repay voluntarily the implicit loan he received from his undergraduate college.[29] Rather, I have taken such behavior for granted and have simply asked: given that people are prepared to donate in such circumstances, what is the structure of the organizations to or through which they will choose to direct their contributions?

CONCLUSION

There is a tendency to view nonprofit organizations as institutions that defy systematic, and particularly economic, analysis—because either, on the one hand, they are thought to be the product of arbitrary historical processes, or, on the other hand, they are thought to be invested with an ethical quality that places them beyond mere utilitarian concerns. I have suggested here, instead, that we should view the nonprofit organization as a reasonable response to a relatively well-defined set of social needs that can be described in economic terms. It follows that it is the responsibility of lawmakers to review and reform the hodge-podge of organizational and regulatory law that applies to nonprofits to ensure that it is well-designed to assist nonprofits in serving those needs. The ideas advanced here will, I hope, serve as a useful guide in that process.

NOTES

1. At present there are no accurate and comprehensive published data on the size and growth of the nonprofit sector. Some estimate, however, can be made from the National Income Accounts. See U.S. Dep't of Commerce, Bureau of Economic Analysis, The National Income and Product Accounts of the United States, 1929–74, at 16–19, 88–89, 326, 336 (1977). These accounts include income derived from nonprofit institutions within the total for a category denominated "households and institutions," which also contains such household-generated income as compensation of domestic servants. The portion of this total that is attributable to nonprofit institutions can be estimated by subtracting from it the figure reported in the accounts for compensation paid by private households. Since the figure for households and institutions itself is derived as a residual—that is, is not built up separately from primary data— the accuracy of the resulting estimate is difficult to judge; nevertheless, it appears to be the best estimate obtainable.

The data suggest that the nonprofit sector accounted for roughly 2.8 percent of national income in 1974. More dramatic than the absolute size of the sector has been its growth. It has more than doubled as a percentage of national income since 1929, when the figure was 1.2 percent. Furthermore, the growth of the sector has been particularly rapid in recent years: the share of national income it represents increased by roughly 33 percent in the period 1960– 1974. The growth of the sector in absolute terms, of course, has been even more dramatic.

Because nonprofits are concentrated in the labor-intensive service industries, the share of total direct employment accounted for by nonprofits is even larger than its contribution to GNP, amounting to 5.9 percent in 1973. See Ginzberg, The pluralistic economy of the U.S., Scientific American, Dec. 1976, at 25, 26.

A considerable fraction of the current size and recent growth of the nonprofit sector derives from the preponderance of nonprofit institutions in two important areas, hospital care and private education, particularly postsecondary education. See (1964) and (1973) National Center for Education Statistics, Projections of Education Statistics; Cooper, Worthington, & Piro, National health expenditures, 1929–1973, 37 Soc. Security Bull. 3, 3–19 (February 1974).

2. Two notable exceptions are B. Weisbrod, The Voluntary, Nonprofit Sector (1977); Nelson & Krashinsky, Two major issues of Public policy: Public subsidy and organization of supply, in Public Policy for Day Care of Young Children 47 (R. Nelson & D. Young eds. 1973), discussed in notes 5 and 7 infra.

3. The way I am approaching this question may appear a bit backward from a historical perspective. At least where corporations are concerned, nonprofits long antedate their for-profit counterparts, which are in fact relative latecomers on the organizational scene. Thus, while the modern American university can trace its ancestry directly to the chartering of the University of Oxford in the twelfth century, and ecclesiastical corporations such as monasteries go back even further, the first charters for profit-seeking corporations were not issued until nearly half a millennium later. Viewed historically, then, we might well be tempted to ask why it was that large profit-seeking organizations arose. Yet today we are confronted with a well-articulated rationale for organizing economic activity along profit-seeking lines, and it is the nonprofits that seem to call for explanation. That explanation, I believe, can in large part be discovered by considering some of the limitations of the for-profit form.

4. Other, more familiar conditions are, for example, the absence of monopoly or collusive behavior among producers or purchasers.

5. Similar arguments have been advanced before with respect to particular services. For example, several authors have argued that, because hospital services are beyond the capacity of individual patients to judge effectively, nonprofit hospitals are preferable to profit-seeking hospitals, which might exploit the patient's ignorance and helplessness. See A. Somers, *Hospital Regulation: The Dilemma of Public Policy* 200–01 (1969); Arrow, Uncertainty and the welfare economics of medical care, 53 *Am. Econ. Rev.* 941 (1963); Titmuss, Ethics and economics of medical care, in R. Titmuss, *Commitment to Welfare* 247, 254–55 (1968); Note, The role of prepaid group practice in relieving the medical care crisis. 84 *Harv. L., Rev.* 887, 981 n.179, 995 (1971). Interestingly, hospital care is one of the areas of nonprofit activity in which this theory appears weakest. Such a theory also has been offered for children's day care. *See* Nelson & Krashinsky, *supra* note 2.

None of these discussions explains, however, why nonprofit institutions provide the consumer with greater protection. Nor do they explore the connection between the role of non-profits in such areas as hospital care and child care and the role they play in other areas such as the performing arts and relief of the poor.

6. In its solicitations, CARE has always been quite explicit about just what a contribution "buys"; a recent appeal states, "$5 serves 100 children a daily bowl of nourishing porridge for a week. $10 gives 2,000 children each a glass of fortified milk. $25 provides wheat flour for 3,000 nutritious biscuits in a school feeding program." CARE, Promotional Brochure (on file with *Yale Law Journal*).

7. One economist has argued that nonprofit firms arise generally as private-market providers of public goods. *See* B. Weisbrod, *supra* note 2. Weisbrod does not, however, explain why the nonprofit form is more suitable in this area than the for-profit form. Moreover, although I agree that the provision of public goods is a significant role for nonprofits, I do not feel that it has the overall importance that Weisbrod assigns to it; rather, I see public goods simply as a special case of the more general contract failure theory.

8. Many nonprofit radio stations now receive some financial support from the federal government through the Corporation for Public Broadcasting. However, a number of stations, such as those in the Pacifica group, arose long before any governmental support was available. Even today, public subsidies are only a small portion of the income of many listener-supported radio and television stations.

9. When an individual can determine the incremental amount of the public good that he has purchased, there is no reason to prefer a nonprofit supplier to a for-profit supplier. For example, for-profit providers are common where the purchaser takes delivery of the incremental amount of the public good himself before contributing it to the public stock—as when someone buys confetti that he then throws out the window on a parade, where it merges with the confetti thrown by thousands of others for a grand overall effect.

10. In general, education itself is not a public good, although there may be some public benefits associated with it.

11. Undoubtedly other factors are also important. For example, an individual will to some extent be labeled throughout life as a graduate of the particular school he attended, and therefore has an incentive to see to it, through contributions, that the school remains as prestigious as possible. Since the school's prestige is a public good for its graduates, the analysis above, *see*

pp. 64–67 *supra,* applies to contributions made for this purpose. Alumni contributions also serve as a form of voluntary price discrimination, much as in the case of the performing arts.

12. *See* Nelson & Krashinsky, The demand and supply of extra-family day care, in *Public Policy for Day Care of Young Children* 9, 18 (R. Nelson and D. Young eds. 1973).

13. *See* Steinwald and Neuhauser, The role of the proprietary hospital, 35 *Law & Contemp. Prob.* 817, 820 (1970).

14. The widespread use of third-party payment systems for hospital expenses may be eroding further any differences between the quality and cost of services provided by non-profit and for-profit hospitals. The incentives for a hospital's management created by the third-party payment schemes may dominate any differences in incentives that derive from the form of incorporation.

15. The relative magnitude of the risks involved may be another important factor. A person may be more willing to take chances on the quality of care given to his ailing television or to his automobile than to his ailing heart or to his only child.

16. Furthermore, when an individual is simply overcharged for a service, then, particularly if the price has been agreed to in advance, the price is still generally less than the value to the individual of having the service performed, and therefore he still derives a net benefit from the transaction. To put the point in technical terms, the individual has simply been deprived of some of his potential consumer surplus. When, on the other hand, an individual pays for a service that in fact is not performed, or at least not performed adequately, the transaction can be a net loss for him, depriving him not only of all of his potential consumer surplus but of some or all of the value of the purchase price as well.

17. *See* Karst, The efficiency of the charitable dollar: an unfulfilled state responsibility, 73 *Harv. L. Rev.* 433, 445–49.

18. *See* Karst, *supra* note 17, at 449–60; Office of the Ohio Attorney General, The status of state regulation of charitable trusts, foundations, and solicitations, in *V Comm'n on Private Philanthropy and Public Needs, Research Papers* 2705, 2710–25 (1977).

19. The state tax authorities concerned with administering the exemption of nonprofits from state property, sales, and income taxes generally become concerned in a particular case, it appears, only after the Internal Revenue Service has acted, and therefore do not constitute a substantial independent means of enforcement. *See* Karst, *supra* note 17, 442–43.

20. *See The role of private foundations in today's society: Hearings before the Subcomm. on Foundations of the Senate Comm. on Finance,* 93d Cong., 1st Sess. 271–74 (1974) (statement of Sheldon Cohen).

21. *See* Kenner v. Commissioner, 318 F.2d 632 (7th Cir. 1963).

22. *See* N.Y. *Post,* Oct. 27, 1977, 1, col. 6.

23. *See Wall St. J.,* Jan. 24, 1979, 1, col. 1.

24. *See* K. Arrow, *The Limits of Organization* 23–29 (1974).

25. *See* McKean, Economics of trust, altruism, and corporate responsibility, in *Altruism, Morality, and Economic Theory* 29 (E. Phelps ed. 1975).

26. Dept of Health, Education, and Welfare, Public Health Service, Pub. No. 616, *The Nation's Health Facilities, Ten Years of the Hill-Burton Hospital and Medical Facilities Program,* 1946–56, 83–86 (1958).

27. I am indebted to Robert C. Clark for this point.

28. *See* Clarkson, Some implications of property rights in hospital management, 15 *J. Law & Econ.* 363 (1972).

29. Economic models commonly assume that individuals act in an "economically rational" manner in that they choose to engage only in those activities that promise to yield benefits to the individual that exceed their costs. Such an assumption, simplistically applied, might lead one to conclude that individuals will seldom undertake activities, such as voluntary support for public goods, for which the costs far exceed the direct material benefits to the individual, and to label such behavior as "economically irrational" when it is observed. Yet in fact, such altruistic or socially cooperative behavior is extremely common, and, once we change our unit of analysis from the individual to the society as a whole, it typically represents a very high level of economic rationality.

4

Optimal Nonprofit Firms

DAVID EASLEY and MAUREEN O'HARA

The theory of the firm is one of the central paradigms of economic theory. By analyzing the microeconomic foundations of decision-making, economists have provided major insights into the operation and behavior of profit-seeking firms. The operation and behavior of nonprofit firms, however, have received little attention, despite the fact that nonprofits produce a wide variety of goods and services in the economy. Indeed, economists usually view nonprofits as economic anomolies, organizations outside of the "real" economic system.

Recently, this view of nonprofits has been challenged in the works of Weisbrod (1979), Hansmann (1980), and Easley and O'Hara (1983a; 1983b). These authors argue that nonprofits exist not only because of altruistic or historical reasons but also because the nonprofit represents the optimal institution for providing particular goods and services. Because nonprofits operate under different constraints than do for-profit firms, the nonprofit can be thought of as representing a different "contract" from that characterizing the for-profit firm's operations. In this paper, we demonstrate how contract theory can be applied to determine the conditions under which the nonprofit contract dominates the for-profit contract.

The contractual approach to economic institutions provides not only a cogent rationale for the existence of nonprofit firms, but also allows insights into their operating behavior. Perhaps more importantly, this approach demonstrates that nonprofits are not merely alternative economic institutions but can, in some circumstances, be the *optimal* method of organizing production.

A CONTRACTUAL APPROACH TO ECONOMIC INSTITUTIONS

For-profit and nonprofit firms have many common characteristics. Both organizations use inputs (labor, capital, etc.) to produce outputs (goods and services). Both organizations produce a wide variety of such goods and services. Both organizations are also typically operated by managers who make the firm's operating decisions subject to the constraints imposed upon them.[1]

The operative constraints, however, differentiate for-profit from non-profit firms. In the for-profit firm the manager (or owner) is free to operate the firm subject only to market forces. This is not true for the nonprofit firm. Generally, society, acting through state-imposed nonprofit regulations, attempts to control the firm by specifying fixed returns to its operators. Typically, a nonprofit is barred from distributing any "profits" to its operators, and, to make this "nondistribution" constraint effective, a further constraint is imposed on management salaries and expenses (the "reasonable compensation" constraint).

These added constraints on the nonprofit led Hansmann (1980) to hypothesize that nonprofits arose in response to "contract failure." That is, the added control in the nonprofit firm was necessary because it was not possible to obtain the desired goods and services using the standard profit contract. Since the nonprofit contract imposes different limitations on the manager, under some circumstances this alternative contract could become valuable.

In our earlier papers (1983a; 1983b) we applied mechanism, or contract, theory to determine the socially optimal mechanisms for the production of various goods. The optimal contract can then be interpreted as a type (profit, nonprofit, etc.) of firm. The intuition behind contract theory is that all optimal contracts between society and the manager of a firm possess certain properties. Since market conditions may differ, the type of contract that will possess these properties may also differ. Given these market conditions and optimal contract properties, we can solve for the implied contract structure.

Before specifying these properties and conditions in more detail, let us first consider what is meant by a contract. We view society and the manager of a firm as playing a noncooperative game. The manager wants to maximize his own welfare or utility; society wants to maximize collective welfare or utility.[2] A mechanism specifies the rules of this game between society and the manager and the allocations to each player given their respective moves. The outcome of a mechanism is a contract. For example, a contract could specify the return a manager may have if he produces a particular amount of goods in a certain state of the world.

As noted previously, all contracts (no matter how they arise) must possess certain properties.[3] These properties can be divided into those necessary for feasibility and those necessary for optimality. Feasibility requires that two conditions hold. First, any contract must provide the manager with a return at least equal to his reservation level. If the manager is "underpaid" relative to his other alternatives, he will quit and no production will take place. This return to the manager may include factors other than money. If the manager's utility is a function of both his income and his work effort, then his required return must also incorporate these two factors.

A second feasibility requirement is known as the incentive compatibility constraint. If the production process involves a variable whose true value is known to the manager but not to society, then any feasible contract must make it in the manager's best interest to reveal this information.[4] For example, suppose that the output of a firm depends both on the manager's effort and on a variable such as average input cost that varies with the state of nature. If society desires different allocations to the manager depending on the state, then a feasible contract must induce the manager to tell the truth about the state. If a proposed contract does not satisfy this incentive compatibility requirement, then in some states of the world the manager will lie and the proposed state-contingent contract then cannot be implemented.

These feasibility conditions determine which contracts are technologically possible. However, we are also interested in which contract results in the "best" outcome. We say that a contract is "best" or *Pareto optimal* if there exists no other contract that can make society better off without making the manager worse off.

While any optimal contract must possess these feasibility and optimality properties, there could exist hundreds or even thousands of different mechanisms, and thus contracts, to consider. Fortunately, we need not consider all such possibilities. Instead, we can utilize the "revelation principle" to restrict our attention to a much smaller set of contracts.[5] The revelation principle states that the equilibrium resulting from any contract satisfying the minimum utility and incentive compatibility constraints is equivalent to the equilibrium resulting from a very simple mechanism. This simple mechanism has the following form: the manager reports a value for the state of nature and, given his report, a prespecified allocation to the manager and society is then selected.

By examining this much simpler contractual structure we can determine the optimal contract given any set of market conditions. For example, if the optimal contract allows the manager to take any salary or reward consistent with a specific output or benefit level to society, then we say that a for-profit contract is selected. Alternatively, if the optimal contract specifies the manager's reward, then a nonprofit contract is selected. This specification of the manager's reward corresponds to the "nondistribution" and "reasonable compensation" constraints that legally define the nonprofit firm.

OPTIMAL PROFIT AND NONPROFIT FIRMS

In the previous section, we outlined a methodology for determining when a nonprofit firm is the preferred economic institution. In this section, we apply this methodology to determine the actual conditions under which nonprofits prevail.

Perhaps the simplest starting point for such an analysis is a market in which every participant has full information on all aspects of production. If there is no asymmetry in information about the production process, then the incentive compatibility constraints need not be considered because there is nothing for the manager to report. As a result, the only feasibility constraint is the minimum utility constraint for the manager. Optimality is then determined by analyzing the resulting allocations to the manager and society from various contract structures.

It is easy to demonstrate that with no information problems the profit firm is always Pareto-optimal. This results because with full information society can always specify its required benefit level such that the manager receives only his reservation utility level. With the manager receiving the smallest amount possible, there can exist no other contract that makes society any better off.

In fact, any time the incentive compatibility constraints need not be considered, it can be demonstrated that the profit contract is Pareto-optimal. While this occurs with full information, it also results if the value of the underlying information is known to more than one manager. In this case, a contract can be structured so that competition between the managers will reveal the underlying information. Once this occurs, we are back to a full-information world in which for-profit firms are Pareto-optimal.

Although in these cases no other contract can improve upon the for-profit firm outcome, it may be possible to replicate these allocations with an alternative contractual structure. Specifically, the alternative contract fixes the manager's return at his minimum utility level in every state of the world. Since the manager's utility is a function of both money and work effort, if his effort depends on the state of the world so, too, must his monetary return. This suggests that while contracts specifying a fixed return across states would not be optimal, contracts with state-varying returns could be. In an earlier paper we defined such contracts as "variable return nonprofit" contracts and demonstrated that such contracts are never dominated by profit contracts.

The preceding discussion suggests that if there is symmetric information (either because of no private information or because competition reveals such information) then either for-profit firms or variable return nonprofit firms are optimal. In the variable return nonprofit contract, however, the manager's return must be prespecified for every possible state of the world. If the contracting costs of writing such a contract are considered, then the choice of the optimal organizational structure is clear: the for-profit firm dominates all other options.

If we are to establish a role for nonprofit firms, therefore, we must look to markets characterized by asymmetric information. If the production process involves factors whose value is known by the manager but not by society (i.e., the manager has private information) then the added control of the nonprofit contract may become valuable.

In a world of asymmetric information, the crucial questions become: (1) who knows what and (2) when do they know it. Suppose that the production process depends on the manager's work effort and some input variable (e.g., productivity) whose value differs across states of the world. The manager knows which value prevails but society does not. In states where productivity is high the manager can work less than in states where productivity is low to produce the same output. Therefore, society may want allocations to differ across the various states. In order to do so society must select a contract that satisfies the incentive compatibility constraint. This constraint requires the manager's payoffs to be structured so that his utility is highest if he tells the truth about the state.

In addition, the contract selected by society must satisfy the manager's minimum utility constraint. The form of this constraint depends on when the manager learns the true value of the input variable. We focus on the case where the manager learns the true value only after entering the contract. In this case the minimum utility constraint need only guarantee the manager that his expected utility be greater than or equal to his reservation utility level. As the manager's utility may be low in some states, the manager faces the risk that such an adverse state will occur. Thus the optimal contract will involve both incentive and risk-sharing considerations.[6]

If the manager is risk-neutral, then a for-profit contract specifying a fixed output for the firm and requiring the manager to take all of the variance through his reward and effort is optimal. In fact, this type of contract yields a first best result (i.e., the same outcome as is possible without asymmetric information) and so it clearly cannot be dominated by any alternative form of contract. The for-profit contract could be duplicated by a variable return nonprofit contract, but such a contract would be costly to write and enforce.

If the manager is risk averse, however, nonprofit contracts are likely to be strictly preferred to for-profit contracts. This happens because the additional control over the manager's reward in a nonprofit contract makes it possible to provide the manager some insurance against adverse states and still satisfy the incentive compatability constraints. As a result, the nonprofit contract may provide more total output across states than does a for-profit contract. This variable return nonprofit contract may be expensive to write and enforce, but even a constant return nonprofit contract may dominate a for-profit contract if the potential gains are large enough.

While this insurance role for nonprofit firms is theoretically valid, a cursory examination of actual nonprofit operations suggests that this is not their definitive role. It is not obvious to us that nonprofits operate in areas that are unusually risky. To establish the optimality of nonprofit firms, we must consider other sources of asymmetric information.

One such source may be the observability of a firm's output. If important characteristics of a firm's output are unobservable or observable only with great cost, then the contracting problem between society and the manager becomes much more complex. This unobservability problem could arise, for example, if donors to charity are unable to observe the charity's actual recipients. This same problem also arises, however, if important product characteristics such as quality are difficult to observe or measure.

If a firm's output cannot be observed, then the optimal contract between society and the manager is a nonprofit contract.[7] This results because only a contract specifying a constant return across states can satisfy the incentive compatibility constraints. Any contract that specified different returns would provide an incentive to the manager to always lie about the state. When output was observable, an optimally structured contract would reveal the lie because the actual output would be inconsistent with the reported state. If output is unobservable, this inconsistency cannot be detected, and the manager will always report the state most favorable to his interests.

The nonprofit contract removes this incentive to lie by making the manager indifferent to which state occurs. Since his monetary return in each state is the same and output is unobservable, the manager will maximize his utility by working as little as possible.[8] With some production technologies, this will result in positive output. For example, if total output is an additive function of manager effort and the input value that prevails in each state, then even with minimum effort some output will be produced. This contrasts with the outcome from a for-profit contract which never results in positive output for society. Since the for-profit manager's return is unconstrained, the manager simply takes all of the output of the firm for himself. This difficulty with the for-profit contact was the basis for Hansmann's theory of "contract failure."

However, while a nonprofit contract may result in positive output, this is not guaranteed. If the production process is a multiplicative function of effort and inputs, then applying zero effort will result in zero output for society. Since this is the same outcome as occurs with the for-profit contract, there may be no gain at all to employing a nonprofit firm. Only if positive output results from minimum effort can the nonprofit firm outperform the for-profit firm.

THE OPTIMALITY OF NONPROFIT FIRMS

The preceding section outlined the conditions under which nonprofit firms are optimal. The analysis suggests that nonprofits can only be optimal if there is asymmetric information in the production process. If information is asymmetric, then nonprofits may be preferred if managers are risk averse or if the output of a firm is difficult or costly to observe.

One aspect of this analysis that seems important to us is that nonprofits appear not as alternatives to for-profit firms, but rather as the *optimal* structure for production. This distinction is important because it implies that nonprofits are necessary for the efficient operation of the economic system. This optimality of the nonprofit structure appears in stark contrast to the standard view of nonprofits found in the economics literature. In that literature, the nonprofit firm is rarely even mentioned, let alone modeled and explained. Our analysis suggests one reason for this failing. If firms are analyzed only under conditions of symmetric information then, indeed, nonprofit firms will be economic anomolies. If, however, a more realistic view permitting asymmetric information is allowed, then nonprofits appear to be not only viable but, in fact, optimal economic organizations.

The following examples illustrate this finding by considering the method of providing goods and services in several industries.

Blood Banks

If the output of a firm is unobservable, or observable only at great cost, then the optimal contract may be that of a nonprofit organization. One example of such a contract is the operation of blood banks. Until the early 1970s, a substantial amount of blood was provided by for-profit firms. Such firms provided blood by paying donors and then reselling the blood to hospitals. Although the output quantity (the blood) was clearly observable to buyers (the hospitals), its quality was not easily determined. Because of adverse selection problems, the blood produced by for-profit firms tended to possess undesirable properties such as hepatitis. In the absence of costless procedures to verify the blood's quality, many states enacted legislation effectively precluding for-profit firms from the blood bank industry.[9]

The nonprofit contract may have improved social welfare for two reasons. First, with firms unable to profit from transacting in blood, the incentive to collect "bad" blood and sell it as good was diminished. Second, owners of "good" blood might prefer to donate to nonprofit firms rather than to profit-seeking enterprises. If blood banks were operated for profit, in some states of the world they may obtain large returns. If motivations to donate were humanitarian, individuals would prefer to give to blood banks that were prohibited from such bloodthirsty behavior. The nonprofit contract, therefore, alleviates both the incentive to "cheat" on the output and the adverse selection problem.

Nursing Homes

Nursing homes provide another example of firms producing an output which is not easily observed. In many cases, the purchaser of the firm's services is not the recipient; a nursing home may be paid by a relative or financial guardian to provide services to an elderly patient. If the patient is unable to report on the services rendered (because of senility, etc.) then the nursing home may have an incentive to provide minimal benefits. In such a situation, the nondistribution constraint in the nonprofit contract may provide some protection.[10] However, a constant return nonprofit contract may result in a loss of productive efficiency. If monitoring is not too costly (i.e., the relative can visit and observe the output), then the greater efficiency of the for-profit institution may be preferred to the performance of the nonprofit firm and, therefore, for-profit firms may be preferred. At present, both for-profit and nonprofit nursing homes exist, suggesting that the monitoring costs may be low for some individuals.

Medicare Payments

The quality of medical care is often difficult to determine. If quality is unobservable then a fixed fee or nonprofit contract is the optimal payment structure. Medicare payments are an example of this type of payment. Starting in September 1983, the Medicare system began phasing in a new system of compensation for medical care providers.[11] This new system involves the use of Diagnosis Related Groups or DRGs. Under this system, a patient is classified into a DRG and, based on this diagnosis, the hospital is then paid a fixed fee for treating the patient. The fee is independent of both the length of time the patient stays in the hospital and the quantity of services the patient actually receives. This payment is also independent of whether the services were provided by a for-profit or a nonprofit hospital. Notice that this effectively turns the contract for providing Medicare services by proprietory hospitals into a nonprofit contract. Although *legally* a firm may be a proprietory enterprise, accepting a Medicare patient results in its receiving only the same reasonable return that the nonprofit receives. Such fixed fee or constant return contracts characterize the provision of many products where output quality is hard to measure.

Religion

Religious organizations are all established as nonprofit institutions. Although tax-exemption is often cited as the reason for such organizational structure, another explanation may be the unobservability of the output. Presumably some contributions finance "salvation" related activities; by definition, individuals who contribute are unable to judge accurately the efficiency or even the delivery of such output. An important consideration is that when the service can be observed (e.g., a marriage), an explicit payment to the religious organization is often expected. Again, as noted in this chapter, the nondistribution constraint merely guarantees that contributions are not usurped for the management's profit; it does not guarantee the efficiency of the church's operations.

NOTES

1. We assume that owners run for-profit firms and we make no distinction between owners and managers. In effect we apply the analysis normally used to study the interactions between managers and owners to study the interactions between owner-managers and society. Alternatively, our focus on for-profit firm managers can be interpreted as assuming that the agency problem between owners and managers has been solved with a contract requiring a fixed return on capital to the owners. We also implicitly assume, counterfactually, that for-profits and nonprofits face the same input costs and, thus, can, raise capital (through debt) at the same cost.

2. If nonprofit managers are not as "greedy" as for-profit managers (i.e., do not have the same utility over effort and personal income) then society would prefer nonprofit managers as they need not be paid as much. However, this argument yields no insight into which sec-

tors will have nonprofits. Our analysis shows not only that nonprofits will exist with "greedy" managers, but it also suggests in which sectors of the economy we would expect to find nonprofits.

3. This discussion is based on Harris and Townsend's (1981) analysis of resource allocation under asymmetric information.

4. The reason to have a random variable in the technology is that otherwise observations of output and the manager's reward would reveal the manager's effort to society. If effort is observable to society, then society can always obtain a first-best solution [see Shavell (1979) or Holmström (1979)].

5. See Myerson (1979) or Harris and Townsend (1981).

6. If the manager learns the true state before entering the contract there are no risk sharing considerations. However, the incentive problems may still result in the optimality of nonprofit contracts. See Easley and O'Hara (1983b) for further analysis.

7. This does not necessarily imply that a legally-structured nonprofit firm is necessary. Our argument is that any firm accepting such a contract is, by our economic definition, a nonprofit firm. For example, consider sponsored research projects. Cornell University (a nonprofit) and Mathematica Policy Research (a for-profit) could well bid on the same government research project. The return to the researcher will not be state-contingent and such contracts are equivalent to constant return nonprofit contracts. In this case, there is little economic difference between the two organizations, but there is a large legal difference.

8. This does not mean that the manager is idle. Effort is measured as an amount above the minimum level necessary to be a manager (for example, effort may represent quality or intensity of work during the manager's necessary eight-hour day).

9. For a discussion of the blood bank problem see Hough (1978).

10. Hansmann (1980) provides a similar explanation for the existence of nonprofit nursing homes. Weisbrod and Schlesinger (1986) consider the effectiveness of nonprofit nursing homes and provide a description of the industry.

11. This new system was mandated by Congress in March 1983 as part of the Social Security Amendments of 1983.

REFERENCES

Easley, D., and M. O'Hara. 1983a. The economic role of nonprofit firms. *Bell Journal of Economics* 14(Autumn): 531–38.

———. 1983b. Profit, nonprofit, and constrained-profit firms: A new look at firm structure. (August).

Hansmann, H.B. 1980. The role of nonprofit enterprise. *Yale Law Journal* 89(April): 835–98. Reprinted as chapter 3 of this volume.

Harris, M., and R. Townsend. 1981. Resource allocation under asymmetric information. *Econometrica* 49: 33–64.

Holmström, B. 1979. Moral hazard and observability. *Bell Journal of Economics* 10(Spring): 74–91.

Hough, D.E. 1978. *The Market for Human Blood*. Lexington, Massachusetts: D.C. Heath.

Myerson, R.B. 1979. Incentive Compatibility and the bargaining problem. *Econometrica* 47: 61–73.

Shavell, S. 1979. Risk sharing and incentives in the principal and agent relationship. *Bell Journal of Economics* 10(Spring): 55–73.

Weisbrod, B.A. 1979. Economics of Institutional Choice. Working Paper, University of Wisconsin.

Weisbrod, B.A., and M. Schlesinger. 1986. Public, private, nonprofit ownership and the response to asymmetric information: the case of nursing homes, chapter 7 in this volume.

5

Nonprofit Organizations: Why Do They Exist in Market Economies?

AVNER BEN-NER

Nonprofit organizations are firms which do not seek to generate monetary profits for distribution to their owners or officers. This chapter proposes an explanation for the formation of nonprofit organizations in market economies, where the prevalent form of organization is the profit-seeking and profit-distributing capitalist firm.

The explanation focuses on the relations between consumers and the firms from which they purchase. Because consumers and firms pursue different objectives, a potential conflict of interest exists between them. When certain circumstances prevail this conflict induces firms and consumers to exploit special advantages or information they hold in order to enhance their welfare (profits or consumer surplus, respectively) at the expense of the other party. If the two parties are integrated so that one party dictates the other party's objectives and controls the integrated organization, the antagonistic relations between them will be eliminated, all gains are internalized, and the incentives to withhold information and exploit special advantages disappear. The integrating party obtains information that cannot be transmitted on the anonymous market and requires the organization to maximize joint surplus (profits plus consumer surplus). The increase in joint surplus due to the integration is appropriated by the integrating party.

Since firms cannot take the initiative and integrate consumers, integration can be achieved only by consumers. The integrated organization may

Helpful comments on previous versions were made by J. Foreman-Peck, H. Hansmann, E. James, E. Neuberger, J. Roemer, J.G. Simon, T. Van Hoomissen, anonymous referees, and participants at workshops at the University of Pennsylvania, Yale University, Technion, Tel-Aviv University, Ben-Gurion University, and the University of Haifa. The incisive comments of S. Rose-Ackerman have been particularly helpful. Support from the Program on NonProfit Organizations at Yale University and use of research facilities at the University of California, Davis, are gratefully acknowledged. Errors are my responsibility.

be called a consumer cooperative by analogy with producer cooperatives controlled by their workers. This chapter focuses on nonprofit organizations in which consumer surplus maximization subject to a zero-profit constraint is preferred to joint surplus maximization.

Thus, the central argument of this chapter is that nonprofit organizations may be established when direct consumer control of firms enhances consumers' welfare relative to control through the market. Three general types of circumstances are studied: when capitalist firms have better information than consumers concerning product characteristics; when capitalist firms incorrectly supply quality and other product characteristics; and when capitalist firms ration high-demand consumers of excludable public goods by quantity rather than by price. Potential benefits from the operation of nonprofit organizations are not distributed evenly across all consumers. Therefore, I also discuss the issue of who is most likely to form and control a nonprofit organization.

A nonprofit organization is formed when consumers' net gain from being its customers exceeds the benefit of purchasing from a capitalist organization. I show, in the final section of the chapter, that the costs of formation and operation are generally higher for nonprofit organizations than for capitalist firms. This disadvantage prevents their establishment in all cases when incentives for integration by consumers exist.

THE CHOICE BETWEEN NONPROFIT ORGANIZATION AND CONSUMER COOPERATIVE

A consumer-controlled organization distributes among its consumers the joint surplus of the organization (i.e., the consumer surplus and the profits generated by the organization). Therefore, it is in the consumers' best interest for the organization to maximize the joint surplus. This section focuses on general cases in which the objective of joint surplus maximization either coincides or is replaced with the objective of consumer surplus maximization subject to a zero-profit constraint. For purposes of definition, I will call a consumer-controlled organization that pursues the first objective a consumer cooperative, and that which pursues the second objective a nonprofit organization.

Members of a consumer cooperative purchase goods and share in the profit or losses of the organization by receiving dividends or paying fees. A nonprofit organization sets prices so that it makes no profits or losses.[1] The two solutions are identical if the maximization of joint surplus yields zero profit—a condition that occurs if the organization is established at "optimum scale" (the scale at which the aggregate demand curve intersects the average cost curve at its minimum) or if the marginal cost of production is constant.

Frequently, the distribution of dividends is undesirable in consumer-controlled organizations because it requires the existence of memberships and ownership shares which, through trade, may eventually be concentrated in a few hands. These few shareholders may then maximize their personal welfare by maximizing profit at the expense of consumers as a group. If the concentration of shares can be restricted, dividends can be distributed, and consumers prefer a consumer cooperative over a nonprofit organization.

The rest of this chapter focuses explicitly on nonprofit organizations. However, most of the analysis applies with minor modifications to consumer cooperatives as well.[2]

INFORMATIONAL ASYMMETRY WITH RESPECT TO PRODUCTS

The Capitalist Firm

An informational asymmetry before purchase is said to exist when individual sellers know the characteristics, say quality, of their own output, while buyers know only the average quality of that product offered on the market. If there are numerous sellers, each has an incentive to sell low-quality products, since the return to high quality cannot be captured by an individual high-quality seller but is shared by all firms through its impact on average quality. The overall size of such markets may shrink as bad products drive out good ones, and markets for certain products may not exist at all. George Akerlof, who originally analyzed this case, summarized his findings as follows:

> There may be potential buyers of good quality products and there may be potential sellers of such products in the appropriate price range; however, the presence of people who wish to pawn bad wares as good wares tends to drive out legitimate business. The cost of dishonesty, therefore, lies not only in the amount by which the purchaser is cheated; the cost also must include the loss incurred from driving legitimate business out of business (Akerlof, 1970, p. 459).

The problems created by the combination of profit-seeking coupled with dishonesty, quality variation, and informationally weak consumers can be ameliorated if certain conditions are met or institutional arrangements are provided. These include costless access by consumers to prepurchase information, restriction of competition (such that the few sellers' decisions on quality appreciably affect the average quality of the product on the market), licensing, mandatory disclosure of information by sellers, direct regulation of product quality, industry self-regulation, quality guarantees, and brand-names (Akerlof, 1970; Leland, 1979; and Stuart, 1981).

Nevertheless, these solutions cannot be used in all situations where profit-maximizing dishonesty may occur. In particular, the state will rarely use its resources to resolve quality problems when the number of affected consumers is small or when the costs of monitoring and enforcing quality standards or disclosing information about quality are very high. This will be particularly true of products sold in local markets (such as local public goods) and of products whose quality is difficult to assess. When the state does undertake quality-assurance activities it may, because of limited information or because of its need to respond to the average consumer, impose standards that do not reflect closely the demand in affected markets. Similarly, industry self-regulation will not eliminate the suboptimality caused by asymmetric information (Leland, 1979).

A more complicated situation exists if some asymmetry in information persists after the purchase has been made. This may happen, for example, if the direct consumer (a recipient of aid) is not able to communicate to the purchaser (a charitable donor) all the pertinent information regarding the product. Informational asymmetry will also persist if some desirable or undesirable aspects of the product cannot be fully evaluated by the consumer, or when a long time passes before these aspects are revealed. The problems generated by postpurchase asymmetry in information coupled with individual profit-seeking are similar to those created by prepurchase asymmetry, but the solutions are fewer and more costly.

The Nonprofit Organization

When the solutions proposed by Akerlof and others are infeasible or significantly suboptimal, it may still be possible for consumers to form a nonprofit organization and gain access to the information they lack, thereby eliminating both pre- and postpurchase asymmetry in information and the incentives to create or use such asymmetry.

To maximize consumer surplus subject to a nonprofit constraint, prices are set in a way which emulates the market mechanism. The nonprofit organization cannot use prevailing market prices which reflect the asymmetric information between capitalist firms and consumers. It must obtain information from its consumers about their demands and establish the price such that supply equals demand.[3] Hence, a nonprofit organization formed in response to asymmetric information cannot operate as a perfectly competitive firm; this organization must be related to its consumers in a non-market fashion in order to obtain information about their demands.

Private goods will generally provide the least focus for consumer interest and organization. Consider, for example, a market for leather shoes where consumers have less information than sellers. Suppose that only leather-like shoes are sold on the market in spite of the fact that the existing demand for real-leather shoes could be satisfied in the absence of dishonesty of profit-seeking sellers. Consumer control of a shoe store which sells real-leather shoes may solve the problem. However, these consumers will soon discover the benefits of portraying leather-like shoes as real-leather shoes and selling them to other consumers for profit, and will transform the store into a capitalist firm. The quick demise of the nonprofit organization comes about because of the possibility of selling different shoes to different consumers—the privateness of shoes. This scenario would fail if all consumers had to use the same shoes, that is, if shoes were a public, joint consumption good.[4]

In contrast, consider mixed goods—those that have both private and public aspects, such as the services of day-care centers, nursing homes, and psychiatric hospitals. Many aspects of the "treatment" provided in these organizations are necessarily identical in quality and quantity for all consumers by the nature of the production technology, giving it a public aspect. In general, such services are particularly vulnerable to market informational asymmetry because those who pay for the service are not the same as those who consume it. If purchasers form a nonprofit organization, they cannot take advantage of the informational asymmetry they enjoy since this would require subjecting all consumers, including those they care about, to suboptimal treatment.

VARIATION IN QUANTITY, QUALITY, AND OTHER PRODUCT CHARACTERISTICS

The Capitalist Firm

This section focuses on products that possess multiple characteristics and are produced under conditions of symmetric information. If a whole gamut of products bearing different combinations of all characteristics can be provided on competitive markets,[5] consumer welfare cannot be increased by circumvention of the market through vertical integration. The discussion below concentrates on situations in which this is not the case. I explicitly analyze the monoplistic case, but similar results can be reached under the assumption of competition.[6] While the analysis deals explicitly with private goods, it can be easily shown that it applies to excludable local public goods (of the kind analyzed in the succeeding section) as well.

Consider a good with just two characteristics, quantity and quality. Buyers' may consume different quantity levels, but quality is identical for all units of consumption. Quantity is a private good—each consumer may purchase the quantity he or she demands at the quoted price—but quality, which is identical for all consumers and all units of consumption, resembles a public good.

A profit-maximizing monopolist, facing the entire market demand function for a product, considers the influence of both quantity and quality on profit. The profit-maximization problem of the monopolist can be written as follows: maximize $P(x,q)x - C(x,q)$, where $P(x,q)$ is the inverse market demand function for quality (q) and quantity (x), and $C(x,q)$ is the monopolist's cost function. Using subscripts to denote partial derivatives, the monopolist's rules for provision of quality and quantity are summarized by the following expressions:

$$P(x,q) + x\, P_x(x,q) = C_x(x,q) \text{ and } P_q(x,q)x = C_q(x,q)$$

This solution does not maximize the joint surplus: the firm undersupplies quantity by exploiting its power over price and incorrectly supplies quality. If social welfare were maximized, quantity would be set such that $P_x(x,q) = C_x(x,q)$. For quality, profit maximization introduces an additional "failure": the marginal cost of quality is set equal to marginal revenue (the market valuation of quality times the quantity sold). Joint surplus maximization calls for equating the marginal cost of quality with the total of the marginal valuation of all the units sold, that is, $\int_0^x P_q(x,q)\mathrm{d}v$. Unless $P_q(x,q)$ does not depend on q, the profit-maximizing provision of quality and quantity are not those which maximize joint surplus.

Spence (1975), Sheshinski (1976), and others have shown that price, quantity, quality, and rate-of-profit regulation may improve the profit-maximization solution, but will constitute only second-best solutions. Joint surplus maximization necessitates perfect price discrimination which cannot be attained with ordinary market information and market tools.

Social welfare could be increased if consumers "submitted" their demand functions to the capitalist firm that would set a separate price for each unit sold—thus, extracting the entire consumer surplus. Although this amounts to total surplus maximization, most consumers have nothing to gain from revelation of their demands and, in fact, are better off when charged a single price by an ordinary firm.[7] If consumers could bargain with the firm, they could trade the revelation of their preferences for some of their consumer surplus. However, individual bargaining requires that each consumer bargain directly with the firm, and is therefore likely to result in very little, if any, surplus remaining with the consumers. Alternatively, consumers could organize to bargain collectively (resembling a bilateral monopoly) and retain some of their surplus.[8] However, bargaining between the firm and consumers cannot assure the latter the entire joint surplus, and even their bargained-for share is not guaranteed because the firm may renege on its agreement and use the information it has obtained from consumers for price discrimination without surplus sharing.

The Nonprofit Organization

If consumers can organize, they may attain a better solution than through bargaining: formation of a nonprofit organization which is then operated to maximize consumer surplus subject to the zero-profit constraint. To achieve that result, consumers have to reveal their demands in order to permit price discrimination implemented through personalized prices.

To illustrate the case analyzed in this section, consider a day-care center that maximizes profits by providing certain characteristics (teacher-student ratio, kind and amount of toys, educational philosophy, etc.). Suppose that some parents are discontent with the level of characteristics and are able to form a nonprofit day-care center and reveal their demands to its appointed management. In such a case they may attain different and better levels of provision of the various characteristics, supported by a discriminatory price schedule which, as an approximation, may be linked to parents' incomes rather than their actual demands.

PROVISION OF EXCLUDABLE LOCAL PUBLIC GOODS UNDER CONDITIONS OF HETEROGENEOUS DEMAND

Price discrimination never benefits all consumers of *pure* private goods. In particular, high-demand consumers will never voluntarily subject themselves to such discrimination. In the previous section it was shown that when goods bear both private (quantity of a good) and public (quality of a good) goods' characteristics all consumers may benefit from demand revelation and price discrimination. The present section focuses more explicitly on the provision of goods that have strong public goods' characteristics: excludable local public or joint consumption goods such as performing arts and parks (a detailed example appears at the end of this section). The very same units of such goods may be provided to more than one consumer, although in addition to costs of production there may be costs of provision (associated with making the good available to different consumers) and costs of exclusion (associated with charging consumers relative to their consumption). This section analyzes provision by a monopolist who cannot price-discriminate, and by a nonprofit organization that can discriminate between its consumers because it is controlled by them. A more detailed treatment can be found in Ben-Ner (1985).

The Model of the Profit-Maximizing Monopolist[9]

Consider a monopolist that produces an excludable public good and that has constant marginal costs of production as well as of provision and exclusion. There are only two classes of consumers, each with a fixed number of identical consumers, N_1 and N_2, respectively. Consumers have linear demand functions originating from the same point on the price axis but the demand curves of Class 2 ("high demand") consumers lie above the demand curves of Class 1 ("low demand") consumers. These assumptions permit convenient mathematical and diagramatic exposition without significant loss of generality.

$$\Pi = P(N_1 L_1 + N_2 L_2) - c\bar{L} - b(N_1 L_1 + N_2 L_2) \qquad (5\text{--}1)$$

$$D_1 - L_1 \geq 0 \qquad (5\text{--}2)$$

$$D_2 - L_2 \geq 0 \qquad (5\text{--}3)$$

$$\bar{L} - L_1 \geq 0 \qquad (5\text{--}4)$$

$$\bar{L} - L_2 \geq 0 \qquad (5\text{--}5)$$

$$D_i, P \geq 0 \qquad (5\text{--}6)$$

The firm maximizes profits (Π), defined in expression (5–1) as sales to consumers (L_1 to each class i consumer) at the uniform price P minus costs of production of total output (c is the constant marginal cost of production and $\bar{L}$ is total output where $\bar{L} = \max[L_1, L_2]$) and minus costs of exclusion and provision of the output (b for each consumer). The firm will not provide a consumer with more output (L_i) than he or she demands (D_i) at the profit-maximizing price. This reflects the excludability of the good and is represented by expressions (5–2) and (5–3) above. The publicness of the good is represented by expressions (5–4) and (5–5), which indicate that consumption by each individual must be no more than the total amount produced, and by the production cost function, $c\bar{L}$. A consumer of class i $(i=1,2)$ has a demand function $D_i=a_i-f_iP$ $(a_i,f_i>0)$, such that $a_1/f_1=a_2/f_2=d$ (a constant) to reflect the assumption that demand curves originate from the same point on the price axis. The assumption that Class 2 consumers are the high-demand class implies that $D_2>D_1$ for all $P<d$.

By maximizing profits, subject to constraints (5–2) to (5–6), the firm derives the optimal uniform price P and output level $\bar{L}$. Regarding the constraints (5–2) to (5–5), two different cases may arise:

Case I:	Case II:
$D_1-L_1=0$	$D_1-L_1=0$
$D_2-L_2=0$	$D_2-L_2>0$
$\bar{L}-L_1>0$	$\bar{L}-L_1=0$
$\bar{L}-L_2=0$	$\bar{L}-L_2=0$

In the first case both classes consume the quantity they desire at the given price. Total output is set according to the demand of Class 2 consumers who consume more than Class 1 consumers. In Case II all consumers are treated as if they were of Class 1; the consumption of both classes is equal. Class 2 consumers find that the quantity offered on the market falls short of the quantity they demand at the price established by the firm; that is, they are rationed by quantity.[10]

Case II is unique to public goods as it is never profitable to ration consumers of pure private goods by quantity but only by price. The intuition behind the rationing outcome can be illustrated with a simple example. Suppose that there are numerous Class 1 consumers and only one Class 2 (high-demand) consumer who has excess demand at the profit-maximizing price and quantity. Thus the total marginal willingness to pay of all consumers exceeds marginal cost, but each individual person's marginal willingness to pay is below marginal cost. Raising the price to absorb the excess demand will depress Class 1 consumers' demand and reduce revenue by more than the increase caused by the higher revenue derived from the Class 2 consumer. Increasing production to satisfy the excess demand at the given price will also yield a marginal loss because the single high-demand consumer's willingness to pay is, by hypothesis, below the additional cost of this production.

Whether or not the rationing outcome will be chosen—and the extent of rationing itself—depends on cost and demand conditions (represented by the parameters c, b, N_1, N_2, a_1, a_2, f_1, and f_2). This dependence is summarized briefly below (a detailed analysis is presented in Ben-Ner, 1985).

The likelihood that high-demand consumers will be quantity-rationed increases with the marginal cost of production, c. The intuition for this result is that the higher the marginal cost the higher the price required to cover the provision of additional units of the output to high-demand consumers and the greater the revenue loss from low demand consumers caused by such a price increase. The privateness of the good, represented by the marginal cost of provision and exclusion b, is inversely related to the rationing outcome. That is, if c is zero while b is positive, the good in question is purely private and, therefore, quantity-rationing will not occur. The relative sizes of consumer classes affect the likelihood of rationing in opposite ways. The fewer there are Class 2 consumers relative to Class 1 consumers, the less likely it is the firm will find it profitable to satisfy their higher demand (the intuition can be derived from the example above). If the demand of both classes increases (i.e., if the demand curves shift to the right), the likelihood of quantity rationing will diminish. The intuition is that this is equivalent to a reduction in the marginal cost of production. However, if the difference in the demand patterns of the two classes increases (i.e., if the difference in the slopes of the demand curves increases), the likelihood of rationing Class 2 consumers increases. The intuition can be seen with an extreme example: if the two classes were identical, no rationing would occur.

When high-demand consumers are rationed by quantity, they are willing to pay the firm to produce more. However, the firm cannot take advantage of that willingness because it cannot distinguish between Class 1 and Class 2 consumers, and market channels will typically carry information only about aggregate demand. Moreover, as noted earlier, voluntary demand revelation by consumers to capitalist firms will be frequently undesirable to consumers. In consequence, high-demand consumers have incentives to establish a firm to which they can reveal their demands without fear. Demand revelation will permit price discrimination among consumers and allow high-demand consumers to pay higher prices and consume the larger quantities they desire.

The Nonprofit Organization

This subsection analyzes the working of a nonprofit organization to which both classes of consumers reveal their preferences so that price discrimination is possible.[11] Denoting by P_i the class-specific price and recalling that $D_2 > D_1$, the zero-profit constraint is:

$$P_1 N_1 D_1 + P_2 N_2 D_2 - c D_2 - b(N_1 D_1 + N_2 D_2) = 0$$

The addition of this constraint implies a nonunique solution to the problem and determines a range of feasible price-quantity pairs for each class.[12] The price paid by class i can range between some $P_i(\min)$ and $P_i(\max)$, where the minimum price paid by one class corresponds to the maximum price paid by the other class. A similar situation exists with respect to quantities. Moreover, it is easy to see that for class i $P_i(\min)$ implies its maximum consumption and maximum consumer surplus, which correspond to the other class' maximum price, minimum consumption, and minimum consumer surplus. Consumer surplus and consumption are a monotonically decreasing function of the price the consumer pays.

Different types of nonprofit organizations can now be defined relative to their goals. An organization that maximizes the consumer surplus (or, identically, the consumption) of class i will be termed a "class i dominated nonprofit organization." An organization that aims at maximizing a function of the consumption of both classes will be called a "jointly dominated nonprofit organization."

The theoretical discussion can be illustrated with an example drawn from the performing arts. Performance halls are used frequently as an example of an excludable public good. However, the performing arts themselves produce an even more important public good: the productions they mount. The number of different productions mounted during a given period of time is represented by $\bar{L}$. The marginal cost of mounting a production (rehearsals, costumes, scenery, copyrights, etc.) is represented by c. The production is akin to a mold which is not consumed directly; consumers consume *performances* of a given production, not the production itself. Presentation of performances also requires resources: use of a theater hall, wages of actors and stage hands, and costs of exclusion such as wages of ticket sellers and ushers. The cost of presenting a performance per consumer—member of the audience—is b. Consumers pay P for attending a performance (they attend only one performance of a given production). Not all consumers will attend all productions mounted by the organization: $\bar{L} \geq L_i$. It is possible that some classes of consumers will have excess demand at the uniform price charged by a capitalist firm: $D_i > L_i$. This will occur when the marginal cost of production is "high," when the number of high-demand consumers is low relative to other consumers, and when other circumstances described earlier in this section prevail. These circumstances motivate consumers to form and control nonprofit performing-arts organizations. The next section analyzes which consumers have incentives to form nonprofit organizations, who will control these organizations, and who will gain from their operation.

INCENTIVES FOR ESTABLISHING AND CONTROLLING NONPROFIT ORGANZATIONS

There are two sources of possible benefits for consumers controlling nonprofit organizations. First, a nonprofit organization distributes among consumers what would otherwise be the profits of a monopolistic capitalist firm. Second, the internalization of conflicts increases the joint surplus by inducing consumer demand revelation and by eliminating the incentive to cheat consumers. The present section analyzes the incentives that different classes of consumers may have for forming nonprofit organizations, and

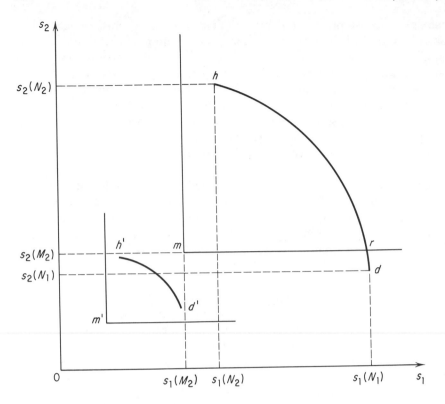

Figure 5–1

their relative powers of controlling these organizations and appropriating the gains from operating them. The discussion focuses explicitly on the model of the previous section although its conclusions can be adapted to other circumstances as well.

The conditions under which consumers have an incentive to be customers of a nonprofit organization dominated by Class 1, Class 2, or a jointly dominated nonprofit organization, or of a capitalist firm, can be introduced with the aid of Figure 5–1. The axes record the consumer surplus of a Class 1 consumer (s_1) and of a Class 2 consumer (s_2). Point m represents the surplus of each type of consumer as a customer of a quantity-rationing, capitalist monopolist. If, given the same cost and demand parameters, these consumers were customers of a Class 1 dominated nonprofit organization, their respective consumer surplus would be $s_1(N_1)$ and $s_2(N_2)$, as reflected by point d. If they were customers of a Class 2 dominated nonprofit organization, their respective consumer surplus would be represented by point h. Points that lie on the boundary hrd represent solutions of jointly dominated nonprofit organizations biased to various degrees in favor of one class or the other. The origin 0 represents the case when cost and demand conditions are such that there can be no provision by any type of organization, or when only a nonprofit organization is feasible but one class attempts to exclude the other class. If conditions would lead a capitalist firm to ration Class 2 consumers "stringently," point m' would obtain and the segment $h'd'$ would represent the nonprofit's possibilities.

If cost and demand conditions do not induce quantity-rationing of Class 2 consumers, the point m and the boundary hrd would shift upward and to the right while maintaining their relative positions.

The diagrammatic exposition can be generalized by stating the following results (proved in Ben-Ner, 1985):

1. Class 1 (low demand) consumers prefer a nonprofit organization dominated by themselves to one dominated by Class 2, and any nonprofit organization to a capitalist firm.

2. (a) Class 2 (high demand) consumers prefer a nonprofit organization dominated by themselves to any other type of organization. This class's interest in a Class 1 dominated nonprofit organization is contingent upon conditions detailed below.

(b) If conditions lead a capitalist firm to behave so that no quantity-rationing occurs, Class 2 consumers would prefer such a firm to a Class 1 dominated nonprofit organization.

(c) At relatively low marginal costs of production, Class 2 consumers gain more surplus by being customers of a for-profit quantity-rationing firm rather than of a price-discriminating nonrationing Class 1 dominated nonprofit organization. When the marginal cost of production exceeds a certain level, and as the publicness aspect of the product increases, Class 2 consumers prefer to be discriminated against by a Class 1 dominated nonprofit organization rather than losing more consumer surplus by being treated like Class 1 consumers by a quantity-rationing capitalist firm. Class 2 consumers are more likely to prefer a Class 1 dominated nonprofit organization to a quantity-rationing capitalist firm the lower the marginal cost of provision and exclusion, the smaller the number of Class 2 consumers relative to Class 1 consumers, the smaller (more to the left) the demand of both classes, and the larger the difference in the demands (the slopes of the demand curves of the two classes).

(d) From the above discussion it follows that there exist jointly dominated nonprofit organizations preferred by Class 2 to a capitalist firm.

Suppose now that cost and demand conditions are such that a capitalist firm would have generated a solution at point m in the diagram. What type of nonprofit organization is likely to emerge? Consider first the possibility that Class 2 consumers get together to form a nonprofit organization dominated by themselves. They know their own demand, and they can act jointly as a monopolist with respect to the rest of the market which consists of Class 1 consumers. If consumers of different classes cannot be distinguished at the point of distribution (where the product is purchased), price discrimination can be effectuated only if class 2 consumers voluntarily disclose their identity; then a uniform price will be charged while Class 2 consumers make an additional direct payment to the organization, perhaps in form of donations (see Hansmann, 1981).[13] If price discrimination is possible at the point of distribution, different prices will be charged there. Thus, if Class 2 consumers form a nonprofit organization, the solution will be at point h in Figure 5–1; this solution will benefit both classes relative to the capitalist firm solution, and will be stable.

Consider next the possibility that Class 1 consumers wish to establish a nonprofit organization dominated by themselves. They too know their own demand and could act jointly as a monopolist with respect to the rest of the market, now consisting of Class 2 consumers. If identification of consumers and price discrimination at the point of distribution is possible, different prices will be charged by the two classes. Class 1 consumers will gain relatively to the capitalist firm solution, but Class 2 consumers will lose (point d in Figure 5–1). Hence, the latter will not patronize the Class 1 dominated nonprofit organization and will force it out of business, leaving room for a capitalist firm with solution at m. Similarly, Class 2 consumers will block any solution of jointly dominated nonprofit organizations that lie on rd. Class 1 consumers will opt for a feasible jointly dominated organization that is biased as much as possible in their own favor (i.e. an organization represented by point r). This organization will be stable.

If discrimination is not feasible at the point of distribution, Class 2 consumers must pay the uniform price and make an additional direct payment to the organization. Since this payment is voluntary and its magnitude must be negotiated between Class 1 founding consumers and Class 2 customers, it is unlikely that r will be a stable solution as it was earlier. Rather, the solution will lie somewhere on hr.

When cost and demand conditions are such that the relevant points are m', h', and d' in the diagram, any nonprofit organization is preferred over a capitalist firm by both classes. The previous discussion pertains, mutatis mutandis, to this case as well.

Focusing on three parameters of main interest—the marginal cost of production, c, the relative size of classes of consumers, N_2/N_1, and the relative strength of their demand, f_2/f_1 $(= a_2/a_1)$—the following conclusions can now be suggested: the higher c, the lower N_2/N_1, and the higher f_2/f_1, the more interest Class 2 consumers have in forming a nonprofit organization of any type. Since a Class 2 dominated nonprofit organization cannot be challenged by Class 1 consumers, and because of the higher likelihood that, with small N_2, Class 2 consumers find it easier to organize (see next section), the expectation is that under such conditions a Class 2 dominated organization will emerge. A Class 1 dominated organization may be formed on rare occassions only (when conditions are such that points m', h', and d' are relevant). In general, if a nonprofit organization is not dominated by Class 2 consumers, it will be dominated by them jointly with Class 1, with a greater weight to the former.

The discussion of different types of nonprofit organizations, the incentives different classes of consumers may have for vertical integration, and the relative bargaining powers they may possess was directly based on the analysis of excludable local public goods. However, since the central features that generated the results above were demand revelation and price discrimination, these results pertain also to the case discussed earlier, where individual (or group) demand revelation and price discrimination are at the core of the nonprofit organization.[14]

THE NONPROFIT ORGANIZATION CALCULUS

Consumers will participate in the formation of a nonprofit organization if they expect to obtain a net gain from being its customers over purchasing from a capitalist firm. A net gain is achieved if the consumer surplus—derived from the operation of a nonprofit organization less the costs of its formation and operation—is greater than the net benefits from purchasing from a capitalist firm. In the previous sections I identified circumstances when nonprofit organizations are more beneficial than capitalist firms and investigated the distribution of the benefits across consumers. In the present section I analyze the special costs of forming and operating nonprofit organizations and the distribution of these costs across consumers.

Formation and Operation of Nonprofits

The formation and operation of a nonprofit organization rests on the successful completion of three main steps: (1) the identification of consumers with an interest in such an organization: (2) the creation of a coalition of consumers for the purposes of demand revelation and control of the organization; and (3) the assemblage of inputs needed for production. A capitalist firm is likely to have a cost advantage at each of these steps.

First, while a capitalist firm needs to identify a demand for its intended product, it does not have to identify consumers individually in order to learn about their demands. Although it could benefit from such information, the existence of a capitalist firm, unlike that of a nonprofit organization, is not predicated upon individual identification.

Second, a capitalist firm does not have to enforce demand revelation and execution of direct payments, while this possibly costly activity is the rationale for the existence of the nonprofit organization. (Of course, the flip side of this issue is that the nonprofit organization generates more benefits the more it succeeds in preventing free-ridership.) Furthermore, officers of a nonprofit organization are likely to have more opportunity than officers of a capitalist firm to pursue their personal objectives at the expense of the organization. Officers of a capitalist firm may be subject to the control of a few owners or to the "discipline" of the market for stocks. In contrast, the main control over the activities of a nonprofit organization's officers rests with consumers who, in general, have limited incentive to exercise control (Fama and Jensen 1983).

Third, certain inputs may be more expensive for a nonprofit organization than for a capitalist firm. Because of the relative scarcity of the nonprofit form of organization, skills required for its formation and operation may be scarce and command special returns. In addition, capitalist entrepreneurs may have better access to capital than nonprofit organizers. Counteracting these difficulties, however, a nonprofit organization may be able to obtain volunteer labor from its consumers which is cheaper than the labor available to capitalist firms.

Costs and Benefits

In the previous sections I argued that under certain circumstances the benefits generated by nonprofit organizations exceed those of capitalist firms. However, as suggested above, the costs of formation and operation are likely to be higher for the former type of organization. The net benefits to consumers depend on the relative magnitudes of the benefits and costs involved in the two types of organization. In the present subsection I comment briefly upon the relationship between certain characteristics of consumers and of products, on the one hand, and the costs of formation and operation of nonprofit organizations, on the other hand.

Costs

A correlation between consumers' interest in a nonprofit organization and their social, economic, residential, cultural, ethnic, religious, or political background will reduce the costs of formation and operation of nonprofit organizations. Such correlation facilitates consumers' identification and the communication among them, especially if consumers are already affiliated with an existing organization.[15] Also, a common background—and an affinity among consumers—helps to create the social cohesion that enhances the enforcement of demand revelation and the execution of direct payments when these are needed.[16]

Better-educated and wealthier consumers are more likely to possess organizational skills and other human capital that enable them to form consumer coalitions and maintain them more easily than other consumers. These consumers are also less restricted geographically in their efforts to form coalitions because they participate more often in organizations (e.g., social clubs or alumni associations) of wider geographical scope. Moreover, wealthier and better-educated consumers have better access to competent administrators and to capital markets. Consequently, other things being equal, the costs of formation and operation of nonprofit organizations are likely to be lower for these consumers.

Another important factor that contributes to the reduction of formation and operation costs is the small size of the demand class. The smaller the number of consumers the more likely it is that a feasible mechanism for truthful relevation of demands will be found and that voluntary payments will be effectuated (see, e.g., Groves and Ledyard, 1977, and Olson, 1971). Furthermore, the smaller the size of the high demand class the greater its benefits are from the formation of a nonprofit organization.

Consumers and Products

Nonprofit organizations are more likely to be formed in industries which have relatively strong local-public, rather then pure-private, good characteristics. As I indicated above, when informational asymmetry stimulates the formation of nonprofit organizations, these organizations can be formed and maintained only if they provide goods that are not pure-private, but mixed, goods. In earlier sections I have shown that goods with public characteristics provide incentives for consumers' vertical integration. In addition, such goods present more opportunity for the formation and maintenance of consumer coalitions and, therefore, it is more likely that a nonprofit organization specializing in their provision will form.

Local public goods are public goods produced for consumption by a locality or community.[17] Consumers of local-public goods are more likely to know each other than consumers of nonlocal-public or private goods.[18] This facilitates identification and communication and reduces the costs of coalition formation and maintenance (see Olson, 1971, p. 47, for a related analysis).[19]

The likelihood that the costs of formation and operation of nonprofit organizations will be low enough to permit the formation of such an organization increases with the social cohesion of consumers, and is higher the more local and public the good is. Since the benefits from nonprofit organizations are also larger for goods with public aspects, we may conclude (along with Weisbrod, 1975, although for different reasons) that local public goods are the best candidates for provision by nonprofit organizations.

CONCLUSIONS

When detailed information about consumer demand is unavailable or when capitalist firms have an incentive to cheat their consumers, the conflict of interest between consumers and capitalist firms who meet on the market can reduce both consumer welfare and profits below their potential levels. In the spirit of Williamson's (1975) analysis, I suggested that this conflict of interest and its consequences can be eliminated by consumers' backward vertical integration; that is, by consumer control of firms as nonprofit organizations. Consumer control guarantees that consumers will receive the nonprofit organization's surplus (distributed in form of lower prices, larger quantities, or higher qualities—rather than monetary dividends) and provides incentives for consumer demand revelation and honest treatment of consumers.

Control by consumers takes three forms: demand revelation, participation in the determination of the organization's goals, and monitoring of the organization's performance. Not all consumers actively participate in controlling a nonprofit organization. First, controlling consumers may exclude other consumers from control and treat them as would a capitalist firm.[20] Second, control may be delegated explicitly through elections, or through implicit consent to let more active consumers control the organization. In fact, the more public the product of the nonprofit organization the less necessary is the participation of consumers.[21] Third, some consumers may "free ride" on other consumers' control. Furthermore, technological, cost, and demand changes during the life cycle of a nonprofit organization may bring about a reduction in consumer interest and consumer control, a concomitant increase in control by the organization's officers, and, therefore, induce a change in the character of the organization (see Ben-Ner, 1984b).

This chapter concentrated on reasons for the formation of nonprofit organizations by studying a relatively limited range of possibilities from which, it is hoped, one can generalize to other cases.[22] Despite the different approach adopted in the present study, its findings strengthen and complement conclusions of other studies regarding the formation of nonprofit organizations in market economies. The conclusion reached here that nonprofit organizations will supply mostly local-public goods echoes Weisbrod's (1975) original conclusion that nonprofit organizations are established to supplement governmental provision of public goods.[23] Hansmann's (1980) and Nelson and Krashinsky's (1973) theory that when informational asymmetry exists, nonprofit organizations provide the trust consumers cannot find in capitalist firms receives strengthening in the present study. Easley and O'Hara's (1984) suggestion that nonprofit organizations can be viewed as being based on contracts between society and managers regarding the rate of return permitted to firms has its counterpart in the present chapter in the form of consumer control. The active role of consumers indicated by Badelt (1982) and Krashinsky (1986) was found here to be essential for the formation of nonprofit organizations.

The discussion in this chapter has been essentially theoretical; nevertheless, a series of empirical hypotheses can be generated from it. In a nutshell, these hypotheses concern (1) the characteristics of products provided by nonprofit organizations; (2) the identity of controlling consumers and the process of formation and governance of nonprofit organizations; (3) the characteristics of consumer coalitions that control these organizations; and (4) the relationship between technological and market developments, and the change in the locus of control over nonprofit organizations.

NOTES

1. The maximum joint surplus, regardless of whether consumers receive dividends or cover losses, is always at least as large as the maximum consumer surplus.

2. In several respects, including the possibility of trading in membership shares, consumer cooperatives resemble producer cooperatives. For an analysis of the formation of producer cooperatives see Ben-Ner (1986).

3. In the next section I suggest that information about individual demands and multiple prices will assure a better outcome for consumers.

4. This process of organizational transformation is similar to that described by Pauly (1970) and Ben-Ner (1984a) in contexts different from the present one.

5. Strictly speaking, the requirement regards all possible combinations of characteristics; if characteristics are continuous, this requirement cannot be met.

6. See Dreze and Hagen (1978).

7. Low-demand consumers would prefer an imperfect price-discrimination scheme even by a capitalist firm: one which differentiates them from higher-demand consumers but does not take away their entire consumer surplus by charging a different price for each unit of product. If these consumers reveal their demands they implicitly reveal the aggregate demand of the rest of the consumers. A later section, entitled "Incentives for Establishing and Controlling Nonprofit Organizations," discusses these issues in the context of excludable local public goods. Situations approximating this case arise when low-demand consumers, such as students and pensioners, can be identified.

8. Indeed, bargaining associations exist; for example, some purchases and sales executed by American farmers are carried out through such organizations; see Heflebower (1980).

9. The model builds on Brito and Oakland (1980), Brennan and Walsh (1981), and Burns and Walsh (1981). A similar formulation in a general equilibrium framework can be found in Dreze (1980).

10. A third, intermediate case may arise under rising marginal costs of production. The quantity supplied would then still fall short of that demanded by Class 2 consumers but would be larger than that demanded and consumed by Class 1 consumers.

11. In the next section it is shown that similar results can be reached with only some of the consumers revealing their demands.

12. The ranges can be represented by an ellipse. The efficient quantities' range is contained in the northeast segment of the ellipse and looks exactly like the segment hd in Figure 5–1 (the difference is that segment hd in the figure is in the pay-off space rather than the quantities space).

13. The possibility of free-ridership attempts by Class 2 is discussed later.

14. That case, which also involves the provision of goods characterized by some publicness aspects, can be represented diagramatically as the point m' and the segment $h'd'$ in Figure 5–1.

15. For example, parents of a certain religious denomination residing in the same neighborhood may know each other from church meetings and be interested in similar day-care center characteristics.

16. For example, wealthy opera-lovers may be socially and economically related to each other so that those who do not comply with acceptable norms of voluntary donations that reflect their wealth may be held in disrepute. This is probably the function of publicized donations.

17. The "community"—or what Ruys (1974) called the "consumption-collectivity"—might refer to those inhabitants of an urban area who have a demand for opera and who support the same opera house and company, or those within a neighborhood who demand day care and who are interested in the same day-care or community center. The boundaries of the community are determined, in part, by costs of transportation to alternative sources of supply and by the size of local demand and supply. These are the same factors that determine the market power of firms.

18. As an example, consider two cases, one with N_1 and N_2 reflecting relatively small numbers of local consumers of a public good and one with N_1 and N_2 reflecting the same or larger number of geographically dispersed consumers, such that the utility gains to consumers from the formation of a nonprofit organization are identical in both cases. Clearly, the costs of organization in the second case will be higher and consequently the capitalist firm may be preferred to the nonprofit organization.

19. Castells (1981) argues theoretically (in the "Afterward") and shows empirically (Ch. 14) that successful urban movements are organized around issues regarding collective consumption (roughly equivalent to local public goods) but not private consumption (private goods).

20. Controlling consumers, the members, appropriate most of the joint surplus of the organization, although often other consumers' welfare is also improved relative to the capitalist firm.

21. Outside the framework of nonprofit organizations, the opposite occurs: for public goods there is need for public participation, whereas for private goods none is necessary, because control is exercised through the market. "Full" control by all or very many people is not even remotely the case in democratic political systems, in corporations, producer cooperatives, or consumer cooperatives—all cases with formal and legal provision for broad participation. See Cole (1980) and Milofsky (1979) for studies of control in nonprofit organizations, and Ostergaard and Halse (1965) for a study of control in British consumer cooperatives.

22. For instance, only excludable public goods were mentioned in this essay, although a similar analysis could be applied to nonexcludable public goods such as broadcasting. The difference between the two types of public goods lies essentially in the greater problems of demand revelation and payment enforcement presented by nonexcludable goods. Similarly, the relationship between the state and nonprofit organizations has not been explored.

23. There is much empirical support for the hypothesis regarding public-goods supply by nonprofit orgnizations. For data on the industrial concentration of nonprofit organizations, see Rudney (1981) and Weisbrod (1980).

REFERENCES

Akerlof, George. 1970. "The market for "lemons": Quality uncertainty and the market mechanism." *Quarterly Journal of Economics* 84: pp. 487–500.

Badelt, Christoph. 1982. A public choice view of volunteer groups. Mimeo (April), University of Economics, Vienna.

Ben-Ner, Avner. 1984a. On the stability of the cooperative type of organization. *Journal of Comparative Economics* 8 (September): pp. 247–60.

Ben-Ner, Avner. 1984b. A model of nonprofit organizations' life cycle. Paper prepared for presentation at the American Economics Association Meetings, Dallas, December.

Ben-Ner, Avner. 1985. Public goods and the formation of nonprofit organizations. Mimeo.

Ben-Ner, Avner. Producer cooperatives: Why do they exist in capitalist economies? In *Between the Public and the Private: The Nonprofit Sector. Handbook of Nonprofit Organizations,* ed. Walter Powell. New Haven: Yale University Press, 1986.

Brennan, Geoffrey, and Cliff Walsh. 1981. A monopoly model of public goods provision: The uniform pricing case. *American Economic Review* 71 (March): pp. 196–206.

Brito, Dagobert, and William Oakland. 1980. On the monopolisitic provision of excludable public goods. *American Economic Review* 70 (September): pp. 691–704.

Burns, Michael, and Cliff Walsh. 1981. Market provision of price-excludable public goods: A general analysis. *Journal of Political Economy* 89 (February): pp. 166–191.

Castells, Manuel. 1979. *The Urban Question.* Cambridge, Mass: MIT Press.

Cole, Richard L. 1980. Constituent involvement in non-profit organizations, a study of twelve participation experiments. Working Paper-18, PONPO, Institution for Social and Policy Studies, Yale Univeristy.

Dreze, Jacques. 1980. Public goods with exclusion. *Journal of Public Economics* 13: pp. 5–24.

Dreze, Jacques, and K. Hagen. 1978. Choice of product quality: Equilibrium and efficiency. *Econometrica* 46 (May): pp. 493–513.

Easley, David, and Maureen O'Hara. 1984. The economic role of the nonprofit firm. *Bell Journal of Economics* 14 (Spring): pp. 531–38.

Fama, Eugene F., and Michael C. Jensen. 1983. Separation of ownership and control. *Journal of Law and Economics* 26: pp. 301–25.

Groves, T., and J. Ledyard. 1977. Optimal allocation of public goods: A solution to the "free rider" problem. *Econometrica* 45: pp. 783–809.

Hansmann, Henry. 1980. The role of nonprofit enterprise. *The Yale Law Journal* 89 (April): pp. 835–901. Reprinted as Chapter 3 of this volume.

Hansmann, Henry. 1981. Nonprofit enterprise in the performing arts. *Bell Journal of Economics* 12 (Autumn): pp. 341–61.

Heflebower, Richard B. 1980. *Cooperatives and Mutuals in the Market System.* Madison, Wisconsin: University of Wisconsin Press.

Krashinsky, Michael. 1986. Transactions costs and a theory of nonprofit organizations. Chapter 6 of this volume.

Leland, Hayne E. 1979. Quacks, lemons, and licensing: A theory of minimum quality standards. *Journal of Political Economy* 87: pp. 1328–46.

Milofsky, Carl. 1979. Not-for-profit organizations and community: A review of the socialogical literature. Working Paper 816, PONPO, Institution for Social and Policy studies, Yale University, February.

Nelson, Richard, and M. Krashinsky. 1973. Two major issues of public policy: Public subsidy and the organization of supply, In *Public Policy for Day Care of Young Children*, eds. Dennis Young and Richard Nelson. Lexington Massachusetts: D.C. Heath.

Olson, Mancur. 1971. *The Logic of Collective Action.* Cambridge Massachusetts: Harvard University Press.

Ostergaard, G.N., and A. Halsey. 1965. *Power in Cooperatives.* Oxford: Basil Blackwell.

Rudney, Gabriel. 1981. A quantitative profile of the nonprofit sector. Working Paper 40, PONPO, Institution for Social and Policy Studies, Yale University.

Ruys, P.H.M. 1974. *Public Goods and Decentralization.* Tilburg, The Netherlands: Tilburg University Press.

Sheshinski, Eytan. 1976. Price, quality and quantity regulation in monopoly situations. *Economica* 43: pp. 127–137.

Spence, Michael. 1975. Monopoly, quality, and regulation. *Bell Journal of Economics* 6: pp. 417–29.

Stuart, Charles. 1981. Consumer protection in markets with informationally weak buyers. *Bell Journal of Economics* 12 (Autumn): pp. 526–73.

Weisbrod, Burton. 1975. Toward a theory of the voluntary nonprofit sector in a three-sector economy. In *Altruism, Morality and Economic Theory*, ed. Edmund Phelps. New York: Russell Sage Foundation, pp. 171–95.

Weisbrod, Burton. 1980. Private goals, collective goals: The role of the nonprofit sector. In *The Economics of Non-Proprietary Organizations*, eds. K. W Clarkson andD. L. Martin. Greenwich, Connecticut: JAL Press.

Williamson, Oliver. 1975. *Markets and Hierarchies: Analysis and Antitrust Implications: A Study in the Economics of Internal Organization.* New York: Free Press.

6

Transaction Costs and a Theory
of the Nonprofit Organization

MICHAEL KRASHINSKY

While economists have long been interested in the way society organizes production, comprehensive analysis of one important option—the private nonprofit firm—has begun only recently. The analytical efforts generally have used the concept of market failure to explain why nonprofit rather than for-profit firms dominate certain parts of the economy (see Weisbrod, 1977; Hansmann, 1980, and Ellman, 1982 for variations on this approach[1]). Markets made up of for-profit firms are taken to represent the "normal" mode of production, but are subject to certain types of market failure. Nonprofit firms are a way to overcome this failure.

This approach is unsatisfying for three reasons. First, for-profit firms themselves exist and expand because of failures of contractual arrangements in the marketplace (see Williamson, 1975). In fact, as Arrow (1974, p. 33) has pointed out, all organizations exist because of failures of the price system to achieve necessary collective action—that is, because of "market failure." Thus the choice among various forms of organization (between for-profit and nonprofit firms, for example) depends upon the relative advantages of those organizations in overcoming the variety of factors, called "transaction costs," that make contractual arrangements among factors of production and consumers unwieldy. Thus explaining nonprofit firms in terms of the failure of for-profit firms is not wrong, but it does tend to obscure certain insights that can be obtained by addressing transaction costs more directly.

Second, production by for-profit firms is far from the norm historically. Cooperative production within tribes preceded for-profit firms, and only in the last few hundred years have large profit-making enterprises dominated

Work on this chapter was supported by the Program on Non-Profit Organizations at the Institution for Social and Policy Studies at Yale Univeristy. The author would like to thank Susan Rose-Ackerman, Paul DiMaggio, and Henry Hansmann for their detailed and helpful comments on an earlier draft of this chapter.

the market economy.[2] Thus, there are no strong historical reasons to begin with for-profit firms in building an explanation of the nonprofit sector.

Third, the notion of market failure can obscure the critical role of government in the development of the nonprofit sector. Nonprofit firms benefit from a variety of tax expenditures, including various tax exemptions and, in many cases, tax deductibility of contributions. Also, governments frequently give explicit preference to nonprofit firms when contracting for certain products. Thus two separate issues arise in discussing nonprofits: first, in the absence of subsidies, what forces lead nonprofit firms to emerge in certain sectors; second, what properties of nonprofit firms lead governments to subsidize them.

The next section of this chapter discusses the various transaction costs that give rise to nonprofit firms. The third section discusses some of the public policy issues that arise, and considers, in particular, when nonprofit firms might effectively supplement the activities of various public agencies. The final section discusses three specific sectors—education, the performing arts, and day care—in order to illustrate this paper's approach to nonprofit organizations.

TRANSACTION COSTS AND ORGANIZATIONAL FORM

In simple microeconomic theory, there are no transaction costs and, as a result, no need for any organizations.[3] When consumers desire particular commodities, they simply purchase the services of the factors necessary to produce those items. Alternatively, one productive factor may temporarily hire other factors, produce output, and then sell that output to consumers.

Of course, in an uncertain world, continual contracting and assembling of factors is expensive. Uncertainty makes contracts expensive by requiring provision for complex contingencies and by opening the way for opportunistic behavior when unanticipated contingencies occur. As Williamson (1975) points out, vertical integration may then become an attractive alternative. In other words, the transaction costs of producing output are significant and give rise to for-profit firms as a way to reduce those costs.

Transaction costs occur not only among the factors of production, but also between those factors and the consumers of final goods, and among consumers themselves. Since "production" and "consumption" are simply sequential acts in the process of transforming inputs into utility,[4] transaction costs should be similar whether they exist among producers, between producers and consumers, or among consumers. The peculiar assumption implicit in the conventional discussions of market failure is that these last two sets of transaction costs are unusual, while the first set (transaction costs among the factors of production) is not. Hence, for-profit firms which overcome transaction costs in production are normal, while nonprofit institutions which overcome the other kinds of tranaction costs are unusual and require "special" treatment. I do not find this approach useful, and the rest of this section will explore these other transaction costs as they relate to the nonprofit sector.

Transaction Costs Between Producers and Consumers

The most obvious transaction cost between producers and consumers is the cost of monitoring output. When this cost is significant, suppliers may try to fool consumers by reducing quality, thereby cutting costs and increasing profits. The predictable result is that market transactions become unattractive and either cease or involve significant losses for consumers.

One possible response to this problem is the nonprofit firm. Hansmann (1980), in one of the best "market failure" approaches to the nonprofit sector, argues that this difficulty in monitoring quality is at the root of the existence of the nonprofit sector. That of course is true, since these contracting problems explain the existence of all organizations. But one needs to ask why the nonprofit firm is a better solution to these problems than the wide variety of other institutions which exist to help consumers deal with uncertainty about quality, and what conditions make the nonprofit firm superior to these other institutions. An answer requires an understanding of the various gains and losses of using nonprofits as opposed to other institutions.

Let us begin by considering the nonprofit firm. Such a firm supposedly lacks the incentive to exploit the consumer's inability to judge quality.[5] Consumers might seek to constrain for-profit firms by writing contracts that restrict the profits that the firm can earn on particular transactions. But such contracts would be expensive to design and to enforce, since it would be difficult to prevent the use of "creative" accounting by the firm to divert profits to other transactions where such restrictions are not in force. In this sense, the law restricting the distribution of profits can be seen as a "standard contract" that firms can offer to consumers, one that commits the firm to zero—or at least undistributable—profits and guarantees that this commitment extends to all the firm's other contracts. Both this standard contract and the limited actions taken by governments to enforce it reduce transaction costs.[6]

Unfortunately, abandoning the profit motive is also costly. The same drive for profits that induces entrepreneurs to cut corners or quality also induces them to cut costs, adopt new technology, and respond rapidly to changes in demand. Of course, managers of nonprofit firms also have uses within their firms for any surplus they may earn, and they do seek to serve consumers. But these incentives may be less effective than the drive to earn "distributable" profits, and so the gains to consumers in the nonprofit firm may be outweighed by these losses. Furthermore, the absence of a profit potential may make it significantly harder for nonprofit firms to raise capital both initially and to finance any expansion. Given these problems, it is not surprising that a number of other "solutions" have arisen to the problem of quality uncertainty among consumers.

One solution is professionalism. In medicine, for example, the consumer has great difficulty in evaluating output. Doctors continue to operate as independent profit-making entrepreneurs, but band together into a profession which restricts entry and requires doctors to constrain themselves to act in the interests of patients. This constraint may not be particularly well monitored, but social pressures on doctors to act in a responsible manner are not ineffective, especially given the fact that entry restrictions also guarantee that scrupulous doctors can still earn significant economic rents.

Professionalism does not work perfectly, but it may be superior to other alternatives. For example, requiring doctors to act as nonprofit firms is hardly meaningful in an industry of small proprietorships or partnerships, since any "profits" could be appropriated as wages in ways that would be extremely difficult to control. The commitment to professionalism—to not exploiting consumers—enforced however imperfectly through a nonprofit medical association, is probably the best that can be done in the private sector. The same argument applies to a different degree to other professionals like lawyers, architects, or teachers.

Because information about quality has public good aspects, another solution is public regulation. Regulation is a more common solution to consumer concerns than the nonprofit firm, despite critics who suggest that such regulation serves producers more than consumers (see, for example, Friedman, 1962). The role of government is discussed more extensively in the third section.

The market itself also has developed a number of institutions specifically designed to deal with consumers' difficulty in monitoring quality. Warranties, liability laws, insurance against liability (with the accompanying role of insurance companies to minimize risk), reputation, franchising, department stores (which can serve as middlemen for consumers), and so on all deal with uncertainty in different ways.

In short, nonprofit firms are just one of a wide variety of institutions that have evolved to deal with high-transaction costs between producers and consumers. Consumer uncertainty about quality explains why these various institutions have developed—it remains to determine the particular aspects of that uncertainty that favor the emergence of nonprofit organizations.

I would argue that the critical aspect is a separation between the purchaser and the direct beneficiary of the output. When buyer and consumer are two different people, the market institutions that address quality uncertainty work far less effectively. Virtually, all Hansmann's (1980) examples of quality uncertainty feature this separation, and it is this separation rather than quality uncertainty per se, that makes the nonprofit firm attractive. The splitting of payer and user generally occurs in two ways. The first involves an externality, where the individual or group that enjoys the external benefit subsidizes the relevant commodity.[7] The second involves a purchase by a family where the ultimate consumer does not make the consumption decision.

Consider first externalities. A single individual immediately affected by an externality does not require a nonprofit firm since that individual can provide the subsidy directly to the recipient and monitor its use without an intermediary. For example, someone who derives pleasure when poor urban children have a place to swim can simply build a pool where those children live and open it to them, perhaps hiring a for-profit firm to maintain the facility.[8]

The situation differs when the subsidy must be provided over time, especially beyond the lifetime of the donor. Circumstances are likely to change dramatically and in unpredictable ways over the period of the subsidy. This would make it impractical to draw up a contract adequately covering all contingencies, and thus it may be impossible to avoid situations in which a for-profit entrepreneur could increase his profits by frustrating the intent of the donor. The nonprofit institution lacks this incentive and thus may be the most effective way for the donor to overcome these transaction costs and protect his long-run interests in a rapidly changing world.

In the more general case, the externality affects many individuals. For example, many donors may support the activities of recreation centers in poor areas. Hansmann (1980, pp. 843–48) emphasizes that here the principal problem lies in monitoring quality, since the individual has no easy way to ensure that his donation is actually used to increase quality. This analysis is correct but may be misleading, since it suggests that the problem lies between producers and consumers. In fact, consumers as a group have no difficulty in monitoring quality, but the information necessary to do that monitoring is a public good. Therefore it is inefficient for each consumer to do his own monitoring,[9] and the problem (addressed below) is one of transaction costs among consumers.

Now consider the second type of separation of consumer and payer—purchases within the family. Adults frequently pay for things consumed by their children or elderly parents. Where the product in question is difficult to evaluate even by an aware consumer, this separation of consumer and decision-maker will make any sort of evaluation that much more difficult.

These factors may explain the prevalence of nonprofit firms in day care, education, and nursing homes. In each case the commodity is purchased by one family member and used by another, and these goods can be most easily evaluated by experience (see Nelson, 1970). But the direct consumer may not be competent either to make decisions about quality or to communicate them to the decision-maker. Even without that separation, quality is difficult to measure, since the effects of bad day care or education may not become evident for years. And once bad quality is recognized, switching firms can be rather costly. Thus, in Hirschman's (1970) terms, there is a great advantage to using voice rather than exit.

In addition to the separation emphasized above, the output in these industries tends to be a service (rather than a good) produced in a very labor-intensive way. The process of production is hard to separate from the product itself.[10] Consumers concerned about quality will want a direct involvement with producers—that is, voice—a process that is encouraged by the nonprofit form in which consumers often have direct input into the management of the firm.

It is interesting that many of the nonprofits involved in these sectors have some religious affiliation (or began that way). The involvement of consumer and producer make these areas attractive to religious organizations seeking both to serve their communities and to attract new members. And consumers may naturally trust such organizations, especially if they already belong to that religion.

All these factors do not make nonprofit firms the only alternative. Day care, education, and nursing home care are also produced by public agencies and for-profit firms. The responsiveness and flexibility of for-profit institutions can overcome a significant number of disadvantages, and government agencies may be well equipped to monitor performance. Nonprofit institutions dominate only if they minimize the transaction costs we have been discussing.

Transaction Costs Among Consumers

The standard proofs of the efficiency of for-profit firms assume that goods are private so that one consumer's actions do not affect others. When this assumption is violated (when consumption externalities exist), markets may fail. The extreme case, public goods, is most relevant for nonprofits. Here, a particular group consumes a commodity in common, but members of the group have no incentive to help purchase the commodity because each individual benefits whether or not he pays. Economists call this the free-rider problem. The result is that too little of the commodity is purchased unless transaction costs among consumers are so low as to allow effective bargaining. This is unlikely in a large group because of the difficulty of simultaneously negotiating with each consumer what his contribution should be.

Buchanan (1965) argues that this problem can be overcome by forming clubs to collect dues and exclude nonmembers from the benefits of the public good. Such a club would be a nonprofit organization that would economize on transaction costs among consumers by centralizing negotiations. The possibility of exclusion makes negotiations much simpler by eliminating the free-rider problem. But Buchanan's model is not generally applicable to most sectors of the economy because of its strongly limiting assumptions.

First, Buchanan assumes that the cost of serving all additional consumers is relatively low. In other words, the average cost per consumer continues to fall until all consumers interested in the good have been satisfied, a feature that makes the industry a natural monopoly. Thus, a principal reason consumers prefer nonprofit to for-profit firms is that the former permits the consumers to retain the profits that a profit-seeking natural monopolist might otherwise extract.[11]

When no natural monopoly exists, the attractiveness of nonprofit clubs declines. For example, although health spas can, in the short run, service new members at low cost if the firm is below capacity, average costs in the long run level off at a size well below most local markets. Given the various problems involved in setting up and administering nonprofit clubs, consumers seem to prefer for-profit firms. Even when a natural monopoly exists, clubs can be too complex if the market is large and geographically diffuse, and capital constraints may not favor the nonprofit mode. This explains why the telephone company is not a nonprofit firm and why clubs usually produce output that is either limited geographically or of limited general interest.

Second, Buchanan's assumption that exclusion of nonmembers is practical holds only occasionally: public television cannot exclude viewers, although use of cable technology might make that possible in some areas; charities can hardly avoid helping people that non-contributors would like helped; advocacy groups cannot avoid representing the interests of non-contributors who share the goals of the organization. But without exclusion, the free rider problem reappears.

Fortunately, the inability to exclude can be partially overcome. Rose-Ackerman suggests that although potential donors benefit from an organization's activities whether or not they donate, the psychological benefits they obtain are higher if they have "bought in" by giving at least a certain amount (Rose-Ackerman, 1982, p. 195). Thus, by not donating, consumers exclude themselves from some of the benefits of the organization. Organizations will try to encourage this phenomenon by suggesting that donors are part of a community and by organizing appeals by neighbors and friends to reinforce that feeling. Individual consumers may also contribute towards public goods because they believe that it is fair to help pay when one receives benefits, despite what economic models predict. This weakness in the free-rider phenomenon is supported in some recent research.[12]

Finally, even where exclusion is technically possible, Buchanan's assumption that all consumers receive identical benefits from the public good is problematic. Consumers generally will assign very different money values to the public good both because of different tastes and because of different incomes. If the organization is constrained to collect the same dues from each member, it will be unlikely to produce the optimal level of output. Hansmann (1981, p. 343) even suggests that in some cases (the performing arts, for example) the inability to collect different amounts from consumers in some proportion to the value of the benefits received may result in a failure to cover costs and, hence, an inability to produce the public good in question. He then posits that contributions by those deriving higher benefits can be seen as voluntary price discrimination.

The problem of uniform fees is the same analytically as the inability to exclude. Although the organization can exclude those who do not pay the minimum dues, it cannot exclude those who receive higher benefits but decline to pay more. In some sense, the latter are partial free riders and organizations attempt to deal with them as discussed above. Donors are encouraged to believe that the psychic benefits of donation depend on giving in some proportion to the benefit received. Different types of memberships are produced, providing (in Rose-Ackerman's terms) different levels at which one may buy in. If the organization knows its members' unrevealed preferences and can put pressure on those members to increase their donations (with the implicit threat of partial exclusion for those who underdonate), more funds can be raised.

Hansmann (1980, p. 849–51) argues that private organizations which produce public goods are nonprofit because donors must believe that their contributions are going toward the cost of production rather than toward increased profits. This argument is correct. Where exclusion is possible, consumers prefer nonprofits in order to avoid exploitation by a natural monopolist. Where exclusion is not possible, consumers willingness to contribute depends on their sense of "buying in" (Rose-Ackerman's argument). Consumers prefer nonprofits because that is the only way to be sure that contributions advance the stated goals of the organization rather than just increasing the profits of entrepreneurs.

On Consumers and Donors

This chapter has emphasized the two different types of transaction costs that might favor nonprofit organizations. Since Hansmann tends to treat the two together as one theory of "contract failure," the question is whether the distinction is productive.

Ellman suggests that the duty owed to donors by a "donative" nonprofit is very different from that owed to customers by a "mutual benefit" nonprofit, and that Hansmann lumps customers and donors together in his theory because he does not understand the need for these two types of nonprofit corporations (Ellman, 1982, pp. 1023–31). There may well be a need for different legal structures,[13] but not because customers and donors are so different. As Hansmann points out, both are buying something from the organization—the customer buys a private consumption good while the donor buys a public good (even if it be only membership in some "community"). In arts organizations, where donors tend to be the most dedicated customers, even that distinction is hard to maintain.

The more useful distinction is between types of transaction costs. Transaction costs between consumers and producers arise because of uncertainties that make it impractical for consumers to monitor output. This applies whether the consumer is a conventional customer buying, for example, day care, or a donor buying, for example, a perpetual scholarship in his name. Transaction costs among consumers arise because of the free-rider problem in public goods. Again this applies whether the public good is consumed by those who pay for it or by other recipients.

Nonprofit firms economize on both types of transaction costs. Nonprofits address monitoring problems by reducing the return to producers who engage in opportunistic behavior. The government enforces the nondistribution constraint and restricts nonarm's-length transactions, and legal structures encourage both the direct involvement of consumers in the decision-making apparatus of the firm and the openness of the firm to consumer overview.[14] Nonprofits address free-rider problems by gathering consumers together into organizations that emphasize community and responsibility. The government again enforces the nondistribution constraint, and the legal structures emphasize the duty of producers to consumers, thereby economizing on the information that each consumer must accumulate on each organization.

Hansmann is correct that each case is similar because of the element of trust. What differs is the kind of transaction costs that limits the market's ability to produce trustworthy results. Understanding those transaction costs gives us more insight into the behavior of nonprofit organizations.

Consumers, Families, and Other Organizations

Producers vertically integrate to overcome transaction costs caused by uncertainty, a process extensively studied by Williamson (1975) and others. Consumers are similar to producers in that each produces output from inputs. Naturally, the same kinds of transaction costs arise between consumers and producers, and among consumers, as among producers. Yet the institutions designed to overcome these transaction costs are quite different, and, in particular, vertical integration involving consumers is far less common.

One reason is that consumers, viewed as organizations, are very small and unspecialized relative to firms. Integrating backward with producers is impractical because the producing unit small enough to integrate with a single consuming unit would be much too small to produce efficiently. And integration among consumers requires a communality of purpose not generally present. In theory, a large commune of consumers could integrate with efficient producing units (a doctor or an auto mechanic could be part of the commune), but the diverse goals of consumers and the unwillingness of individuals in Western society to surrender their autonomy make the decision-making structures of communes more costly in general than the transaction costs they seek to overcome.

One type of integration among consumers is the family. This small version of the commune avoids the enormously complex contracts that would be necessary if individuals attempted to negotiate long-term family activities (like child rearing) in the marketplace. The stresses in many families may provide some insight into why large communes have in general proven impractical.

The problem is that unlike most firms, consumers are unspecialized. The integration of firms provides benefits in most of the areas in which the firm operates. But communes provide benefits in the production of public goods that make up only a small part of the consumption bundles of most individuals. These benefits are small relative to the command and control problems that result.

When producers can derive benefits by acting together, but where the activities concerned are not a major part of the firms interests, firms also find that use of a nonprofit is more effective than full integration. For example, firms form nonprofit trade associations to lobby governments and perform other useful but nonessential services. There are free-rider problems that could be eliminated by integration, but the benefits would occur in a relatively small part of the firms' activities, while the command and control costs of integration would affect all the firms' activities.

Ben-Ner (1986, pp. 14–20) characterizes many nonprofit organizations as "backwards integration" by consumers. But while consumers are represented on the boards of directors of many nonprofit organizations, it is rare outside of small clubs to find a level of direct consumer control that is consistent with the usual definitions of backward integration. What nonprofit firms do is make voice easier by reducing the tensions between producer and consumer implicit in a market relationship.[15]

Voice is critical when consumers have a long-run interest in the output of a particular organization, a situation which arises when consumption takes place over time and exit is very costly. In Williamson's terms, this will produce market power that producers could exploit, and uncertainty and the cost of contracting may make it impossible for consumers to protect themselves in conventional markets. Examples include day care, religion, and the relationship between alumni and their university. In the latter two cases, the consumer forms a social relationship with the producer and wants to be assured either that major changes in the character of the output will not occur, or, if changing circumstances require such changes, that the consumer will be involved in the choices that must be made.

If General Motors decrees that its divisions specialize, a consumer with brand loyalty to a discontinued model may be disappointed, but he hardly suffers a major loss. Yet alumni of colleges that have gone coeducational or congregants of churches that have made major changes react in ways that suggest that real harm has occurred. No institution can insure against change, but nonprofit organizations offer at least the guarantee of consultation and involvement.

Polanyi (1944, pp. 68–76) suggests that the marketplace transforms into purely economic commodities things that have a critical social dimension and that society finds this transformation intolerable. He was referring to labor, land, and money, but the general point applies to social commodities like education, day care, and religion where the relationship between buyer and seller does not fit easily into a competitive market. An opportunistic attempt by a producer to lower quality and extract higher profits has very different implications for these social commodities than for normal consumer goods. Polanyi argues that market destroys community; in this context, the role of the nonprofit organization in protecting community becomes evident.

NONPROFITS AND THE PUBLIC ALTERNATIVE

The public sector addresses the same kinds of transaction costs that give rise to nonprofit organizations, and the public sector is much larger than the nonprofit sector. Regulation deals with transaction costs between producers and consumers, while government production of public goods overcomes transaction costs among consumers. Why then do nonprofits persist? The answer is that using the public sector itself involves transaction costs which may make nonprofit organizations a more efficient alternative.

Consider, first, transaction costs between producers and consumers, an especially important concern when it is very costly for consumers to monitor quality. Because information about quality is a public good that can be produced centrally, regulation can reduce transaction costs by centralizing monitoring and enforcement. But regulation itself involves transaction costs. First, producers attempt to capture regulatory bodies. Thus, consumers must expend real resources in the political arena to try to prevent this.[16]

Futhermore, while regulatory agencies do economize by centralizing the monitoring of quality, these public agencies must establish objective criteria for measuring quality.[17] When what is being produced is not physical output but rather a relationship between the consumer and the producer, such objective criteria will not be available. For example, a knowledgeable day-care inspector usually can tell quickly whether a center is providing quality care for children. But this judgment is based upon a sensitivity to the dynamics of the relationships between children and care-givers. Since these can hardly be specified in the regulations, the licensing requirements usually focus on physical aspects of the center itself (floor space, bathrooms, windows, etc.) and on the number and training of those providing the care. In areas like this, regulation will not be entirely satisfactory and nonprofit organizations, with all their inefficiencies, become a viable alternative.

Now consider transaction costs among consumers. These involve public goods, and public provision financed by taxes is an obvious solution to the free-rider problem. But mobilizing the public sector to produce the optimal amount and type of the public good itself involves political—that is, transaction—costs.

Weisbrod (1977) suggests a role for nonprofit firms by arguing that elected governments must respond to the tastes of the median voter. When a group of voters want a better quality product than is supplied by government, they band together in a nonprofit organization to obtain this product. Weisbrod is correct to argue that nonprofits serve the special needs of small groups, but this is not the result of government policy which serves only the median voter.[18] Governments provide all kinds of public goods that appeal primarily to relatively small groups of voters, including national parks, marinas, support for the arts, flood control, federally funded "local" projects, and other government actions catering to special interests. A rational government interested in reelection would not always respond to the median voter on each separate issue, but would try to build a winning coalition by taking into account the intensity of preferences of the various special interest groups.[19]

The logrolling described above involves significant transaction costs because each special interest group must form an effective lobby. Downs (1957, pp. 77–95) suggests that these lobbies are necessary to influence politicians because of uncertainty. Politicians are uncertain about the desires and intentions of voters and must be informed and convinced of the intensity of voter's preferences, while the voters themselves must be informed of how politicians have acted and what effect those actions have had. But lobbying is itself a public good and so involves significant transaction costs, including the usual free-rider problems within the interest group.[20] Moreover, lobbying involves ongoing negotiations with politicans and other lobbying groups and so can be costly. Becker (1983, p. 391) suggests that a change in behavior by any single pressure group—or, by inference, the emergence of a new pressure group—could result in an extensive general equilibrium change in the output of the political system. But such a change must involve significant negotiation costs.

In order to avoid the government, interest groups will sometimes form nonprofit organizations to provide the public good themselves, judging that the free-rider and other transaction costs of nonprofit firms are less than the cost of turning to the public sector. It is thus the cost of using the government and not the unwillingness of governments to serve "nonmedian" voters that leads to the establishment of nonprofits to provide public goods.

One way to use government, without the kind of logrolling suggested above, is for the group in question to agree to pay differentially higher taxes to cover the cost of the desired public good. For example, municipalities can provide to a local group of residents standard services (sidewalks, sewers, etc.) paid for by a special property tax in that area. Residents request these services by referendum or petition and the coercive nature of taxation eliminates the free-rider problem. Unfortunately, it is not as easy to identify the relevant group for more general public goods, such as ballet or university education or national parks.[21]

The high cost of using government is related to the overall size of the public sector: as government produces more public goods, coalition building becomes increasingly expensive. This is due in part to "bounded rationality"—the limited ability of those in government to process information effectively. This is an argument for the devolution of responsibility to lower levels of government as well as for production of public goods by other (that is, nonprofit) organizations. Thus, state and local governments may cater to geographic special interests (until in turn transaction costs rise for these governments too) while nonprofits may serve special interest groups that have no geographic component.

Transaction costs will tend to be larger if the public good involves moral values, because governments will be less certain about the impact of their actions on all groups in the country. For example, while a publicly funded marina will benefit only those who use it, an abortion clinic may influence the votes of many different interest groups. Given the risks, politicians will prefer to cede these areas to nonprofit firms.[22]

There may also be a sense in society that government involvement in certain moral areas may threaten freedom of expression. Thus, government may be specifically excluded from support for particular religions or advocacy groups[23] although general support to all such groups (operating as nonprofits) may be offered through the tax system.

Finally, some writers suggest that the size of government itself is an obstacle to freedom (see Friedman, 1962), so that any increase in the public sector itself involves a cost to society. If this view differs among countries, it may be an important explanation of the different relative roles of governments and nonprofits in different countries.

In summary, governments can overcome the free-rider problems that affect nonprofits, but only at the expense of a wide variety of transaction costs that occur when government is used. The extensive role of governments suggests that these costs are certainly not overwhelming, but there are a number of areas in which nonprofit organizations will have a comparative advantage over both the public sector and for-profit firms. To use the negative terms which I have tried to avoid, nonprofits are a reaction to both market failure *and* government failure.

This argument explains why the government offers tax relief to nonprofit organizations in a number of sectors. If the actions of a particular group in providing a public good for themselves also have spillover effects to the rest of society, but if transaction costs in the public sector restrict the use of governments, subsidies are efficient. In a sense, these subsidies avoid free-riding by individuals whose relatively minor interest in the good makes their participation in its voluntary financing unlikely. In addition, these general subsidies encourage a diversity of provision that is itself productive.[24]

CONCLUSION—THREE APPLICATIONS

I conclude by applying my arguments to three sectors in which nonprofit firms are important. In each case, the treatment is not meant to be exhaustive, but rather is used to illustrate the usefulness of the approach developed above.

Higher Education

Hansmann (1980, p. 861) suggests that universities are nonprofit because of the need to encourage donations. He goes on to argue that these donations are a way for alumni to pay for their college education on a voluntary installment plan, since tuition is below the average cost of education.

This situation arises because capital market imperfections make it impossible for students to borrow in order to pay the full cost of their educations.

Douglas (1980, p. 44) finds Hansmann at times overingenious, and I agree here. Loans by governments or by the universities themselves would overcome capital market imperfections, and in many cases the families whose children attend private universities are well able to finance (or at least guarantee) the loans necessary to cover full cost. While these approaches have transaction costs, they do not approach the free-rider costs implicit in a voluntary installment plan.

Donors often want to repay the university for what it has provided them, but fundraisers also try to tap the more general sense of community that exists between alumni and their schools. Donors remain part of a university community (as in the earlier discussion, the benefits are larger if one buys in by donating) whose continuity is maintained by the donations. Proof can be found on a number of fronts: large donors do far more than just pay their implicit loans; alumni take pride in the athletic and scientific accomplishments of their schools;[25] alumni send their children back to their old schools as a way of continuing an intimate involvement in that community; alumni return for reunions and join alumni clubs in other cities.

Once one accepts the more general explanations for donations, Hansmann's original argument for nonprofit firms applies. Such institutions are essential if donors are to be sure that their donations are not misused. Also, alumni want a say in how the university evolves in a changing world and the nonprofit organization is well suited to this type of voice.[26]

The government allows for tax deductibility of alumni donations because there exist externalities in education and research that extend beyond the alumni-university community (these externalities lead to the public financing of state universities). The subsidy of tax deductibility is available only to nonprofit educational institutions because the government must also be assured that its contributions do not inflate entrepreneurial profits.

The Performing Arts

The standard arguments for subsidies to the performing arts usually involve complex statements about externalities. These generally boil down to an assertion that culture is somehow in the public interest. Hansmann suggests another explanation for nonprofits, arguing that most of the performing arts have marginal costs well below average cost, and "that for most productions . . . the demand curve lies below the average cost curve at all points, so that there exists no ticket price at which total admission receipts will cover total costs" (Hansmann, 1981, p. 343). This, suggests Hansmann, leads nonprofit firms to promote voluntary price discrimination to capture enough consumer surplus to support production.[27] The argument for nonprofits is again that they are required because of the cost of monitoring a for-profit entrepreneur's use of donations.

Hansmann's argument is ingenious and correct, but it does not explain why the demand curve inevitably lies below the average cost curve. He argues that production costs have risen over time (Hansmann, 1981, p. 345), but since demand curves might be expected to vary by city size, one would expect to observe a need for voluntary price discrimination in certain cities but not in others. This is not the case. The explanation is that when demand lies above average cost, consumers prefer a nonprofit, since nonprofit firms will increase quality rather than increasing profits as in a natural monopoly situation (see the section titled "Transaction Costs and Organization Form"). In each city, these nonprofits raise quality and prices so long as demand continues to lie above average cost. But even when demand falls below average cost, it may be efficient to continue to raise quality if the value of that extra quality to the inframarginal consumer is high enough.[28] Thus, there are natural forces that may make it necessary to lose money and seek donations in cities of all sizes if efficiency is to be achieved. The nonprofit firm can collect donations from these inframarginal consumers to subsidize the increase in quality.

The critical assumption here is that high quality is worth far more to inframarginal (elite) consumers than to the general ticket buyer. This is the normal situation in the arts and the nonprofit firm provides a vehicle for those who love quality to subsidize its production. The phenomenon affects only public goods. For private goods, average cost curves tend to be flat, there are many producers, and each consumer buys the level of quality that he desires. In the performing arts, production is private rather than public (although governments provide subsidies because there do exist externalities) because the special-interest group of quality-lovers is dispersed and finds it cheaper to subsidize nonprofits directly than to lobby the government to finance greater quality.

Day Care for Young Children

In the day-care industry, nonprofit firms, for-profit firms, and government agencies coexist, so the advantages of the three modes can be compared (see Nelson and Krashinsky, 1974; and Krashinsky, 1977). For-profit firms have the advantage of responding quickly to the demands of parents (see Rose-Ackerman, 1983a) without the need for costly coordination by central agencies. But the danger is that entrepreneurs can lower quality because consumers find it difficult to monitor output. The buyer (the parent) is not the direct consumer and working parents have little spare time to shop around (in any case, exit is costly to children). The result is that profit-seeking centers tend to pay staff close to the minimum wage and tolerate rapid staff turnover. Although the center operators claim that experience is unimportant in day care, turnover in staff is itself unhealthy for young children. But low wages raise profits and parents have difficulty measuring the quality of day-care workers themselves (Krashinsky, 1977; see also Rose-

Ackerman, 1983b). These centers are regulated, but it is difficult to specify in regulations the factors that make for high-quality day care.

Public centers do pay high wages and provide quality care that can serve as an example to other centers. But public centers do not respond quickly to changes in consumer demand. Centers tend to be captured by professionals who demand subsidies and increases in quality beyond what parents are willing to pay for. Parents who want changes must work through the political system, a process which requires real resources of time and money.

All this is consistent with the discussion in earlier sections and seems to suggest nonprofit day care as the obvious alternative. Abandoning the profit motive reduces the incentive for opportunistic profit-seeking and provides for parental input into the running of the center. Dedicated day-care workers can interact with parents in a meaningful way and competition among centers will restrain prices and prevent capturing of the centers by professionals seeking to raise quality "too" high. Furthermore, those interested in the welfare of children will want to donate money to improve day care and will not do so to for-profit centers. Even governments turn to nonprofit centers with subsidies in order to escape the public responsibility and costs that come with public provision.

But nonprofit centers are not a panacea. They do not respond quickly to increases in demand and there is no mechanism for generating new day care in areas where it is required. It appears that the three sectors complement each other, with the strengths of one mode of provision compensating for the weaknesses of the others (see Nelson and Krashinsky, 1974).

Concluding Remarks

The essence of my argument is that nonprofit organizations overcome one set of transaction costs only to create another, as do all organizations. The relative sizes of those costs will depend on the details of each sector. Thus, the search for a single simple explanation of the nonprofit sector cannot be successful. What the transaction cost approach provides is not a unitary explanation but rather a framework in which to analyze the issues affecting any particular sector in the economy.

NOTES

1. Hansmann's concept of "contract failure" is closer to the argument in this paper and will be developed and critiqued more completely below.

2. Contemporary analysis also has largely neglected the production that takes place within families (that are not treated as nonprofit organizations) and that, if measured, would account for a significant fraction of GNP.

3. In perfect competition, the size of the firm is indeterminate, so that firms can be set up

instantly to produce any amount of output and then disassembled, while still being competitive in costs with larger and more permanent entities.

4. Cairncross (1958) suggests that producers and consumers are really similar units of administration, while Lancaster (1966) emphasizes the productive role of consumers in transforming purchased goods into the characteristics that they value.

5. Of course nonprofits can mask unscrupulous entrepreneurs, but the law against distributing profits and the monitoring of that law by the government makes those entrepreneurs more likely to seek enrichment elsewhere (of course such fraud may still occur).

6. The notion that standard contracts reduce transaction costs and that public enforcement of certain types of contracts also reduces transaction costs is a well-developed concept in law and economics—see for example, Posner (1977).

7. In the case of a negative externality, the individual or group might provide bribes to reduce production of the commodity.

8. Of course the donor may want to use a nonprofit organization in order to qualify for a tax deduction, but that is another issue entirely.

9. Information is what Baumol and Oates (1975, p. 19) would call an undepletable externality. Of course, donors might require from recipients a statement of all donations received. Each donor could then evaluate the impact of all donations on the quality of the output. For a small donor, such activity is costly relative to the donation, but the same is not true if all donors act together.

10. Baumol (1967) has suggested that these types of products are prevalent in the public sector. This may also be because of the importance of voice, although voice by individual consumers is not always easy in the public sector.

11. It should be noted that clubs often form for other reasons, for example, a desire by consumers for tight control of the firm when exit is costly.

12. Schneider and Pommerehne (1981) report on their own and other experiments that suggest that the free-rider problem cannot always be presumed to occur. Marwell and Ames (1981) also conducted experiments that suggest that while some free-riding will occur, it is not at the level predicted by economic theory. Put another way, their experiments are not consistent with the strong version of the free-rider hypothesis, which suggests that virtually no public goods will be provided voluntarily, although they may be consistent with a weaker version predicting simply that voluntary provision will be suboptimal. Interestingly, of all the student groups used in the experiments, economics graduate students were the most prone to free ride! (Marwell and Ames, 1981, p. 306–10).

13. For one thing, donative nonprofits give tax receipts and, thus, in effect spend government money.

14. Nelson and I have suggested that day-care firms, whether nonprofit or not, should be forced to operate in a completely open fashion (Nelson and Krashinsky, 1974).

15. The profit motive implies that producers will do whatever is required to increase profits, even if consumers are harmed. The only protection for consumers is producers' fears of being found out and suffering a loss of reputation and business.

16. Nonprofits themselves are of course also regulated to ensure that they do not serve as fronts for profit-making. But the agencies that do the monitoring are not industry-specific and thus may be less prone to capture by those being regulated.

17. Since the regulatory agency determines who can operate in a given industry, principles of natural justice must apply, and arbitrary decisions based upon the nonquantifiable impressions of knowledgeable agents are not acceptable.

18. Where there are many issues and preferences that are not single-peaked, it is impossible even to define the median voter.

19. The success of the gun lobby in opposing the gun-control legislation that is supported by a large majority of voters is an example of this phenomenon.

20. It is something of a paradox that in using the government to provide a public good the beneficiaries must form a nonprofit group to produce "lobbying" which is a public good.

21. Of course, interested parties can be identified when they use the commodity, but taxes

linked to use (user charges) will tend to discourage the consumption of the commodity by marginal users, an inefficient result for a public good.

22. If, overall, a good is beneficial for society but is strongly opposed on moral grounds by a small group, politicians know that they will lose that group's support by providing the public good, but may not be sure that the benefits will be sufficiently evident to everyone else to overcome this loss. For example, if medical research on animals has substantial benefits, the harm to antivivisectionists may be justified, but a politician may have reason to fear that he will win few votes by supporting such research. Alternatively, nonprofit organizations collecting funds for medical research need not have equivalent fears. And politicians may wish to fund such nonprofits in order to obtain the public good while distancing themselves politically from decisions on the use of animals.

23. However, government agencies may end up serving as advocacy groups in certain situations, and may even end up opposing each other.

24. See Simon (1978) on the value of this kind of diversity.

25. Donations rise after a successful football season, a phenomenon that is hardly consistent with repayment of implicit loans.

26. Alumni who opposed coeducation felt that it changed the institution in ways that reduced their sense of community (making the current school a very different place than when they had been there). Yet most alumni accepted the decision and continued to donate, in large part, because they were convinced that those running the university in a changing world had the best interests of the institution at heart. This trust would make a lot less sense if the university were run by entrepreneurs interested only in profits.

27. In the earlier discussion on clubs, the commodity would be a public good with the possibility of exclusion but with different levels of benefits among consumers.

28. Suppose that a town consists of 100 people all interested in a particular performance. When a production costs $2000, 80 residents are prepared to pay a maximum of $20 per ticket, while the remaining elite group of 20 is prepared to pay a maximum of $60 per ticket. Absent price discrimination, tickets sell for $20 and the performance breaks even. Now suppose that an increase in quality that raises the cost of production to $2100 increases the maximum that the 80 residents will pay to $20.99 and increases the maximum that elite group will pay to $65 (the elite love quality). Now no single price will support production, but the increase in quality is efficient because the $100 increase in costs generates $179.20 in increased consumer benefits. This increase in quality can be financed if tickets sell for $20.99 and each member of the elite chips in a donation of 5 cents. This leaves the marginal consumer no worse off (he still gains no consumer surplus), but raises the consumer surplus of each elite consumer.

REFERENCES

Arrow, K.J. 1974. *The Limits of Organization.* New York: W.W. Norton & Company, Inc.

Baumol, W.J. 1967. Macroeconomics of unbalanced growth: The anatomy of urban crisis. *American Economic Review* 57:415–26.

Baumol, W.J., and W.E. Oates. 1975. *The Theory of Environmental Policy.* Englewood Cliffs, New Jersey: Prentice-Hall, Inc.

Becker, G.S. 1983. A theory of competition among pressure groups for political influence. *Quarterly Journal of Economics* 98(3):371–400.

Ben-Ner, A. 1986. Nonprofit organizations. Why do they exist in market economies? Chapter 5 in this volume.

Buchanan, J.M. 1965. An economic theory of clubs. *Economica* 11:1–14.

Cairncross, A.K. 1958. Economic schizophrenia. *Scottish Journal of Political Economy* (February). 5:15–21.

Douglas, J. 1980. Towards a rationale for private non-profit organizations. Program on Nonprofit Organizations Working Paper No. 7, Institution for Social and Policy Studies. New Haven, Connecticut: Yale University.

Downs, A. 1957. *An Economic Theory of Democracy.* New York: Harper and Row.

Ellman, I.M. 1982. Another theory of nonprofit corporations. *Michigan Law Review* 80(5):999–1050.

Friedman, M. 1962. *Capitalism and Freedom.* Chicago: University of Chicago Press.

Hansmann, H.B. 1980. The role of non-profit enterprise. *Yale Law Journal* 89(5):635–901. Reprinted as Chapter 3 of this volume.

Hansmann, H.B. 1981. Nonprofit enterprise in the performing arts. *The Bell Journal of Economics* 12(2):341–61.

Hirschman, A.O. 1970. *Exit, Voice, and Loyalty.* Cambridge, Massachusetts: Harvard University Press.

Krashinsky, M. 1977. *Day Care and Public Policy in Ontario.* Ontario Economic Council Research Study No. 11. Toronto: University of Toronto Press.

Lancaster, K.J. 1966. A new approach to consumer theory. *Journal of Political Economy* 74:132–57.

Marwell, G., and R.E. Ames. 1981. Economists free ride, does anyone else? Experiments on the provision of public goods, IV. *Journal of Public Economics* 15(3):295–310.

Nelson, P. 1970. Information and consumer behavior. *Journal of Political Economy* 78(1):311–29.

Nelson, R.R., and M. Krashinsky. 1974. Public control and economic organization of day care for young children. *Public Policy* 22(1):53–75.

Polanyi, K. 1944. *The Great Transformation.* Boston: Beacon Press.

Posner, R.A. 1977. *Economic Analysis of Law.* 2nd ed. Boston: Little Brown and Company.

Rose-Ackerman, S. 1982. Charitable giving and 'excessive' fundraising. *Quarterly Journal of Economics* 97(2):193–212. Reprinted as Chapter 19 in this volume.

Rose-Ackerman, S. 1983a. The market for lovingkindness: Day care centers and the demand for child care. New Haven, Conn.: PONPO Working Paper.

Rose-Ackerman, S. 1983b. Unintended consequences: Regulating the quality of subsidized day care. *Journal of Policy Analysis and Management* 3:14–30.

Schneider, F., and W.W. Pommerehne. 1981. Free riding and collective action: An experiment in public microeconomics. *Quarterly Journal of Economics* 96(4):689–704.

Simon, J.G. 1978. Charity and dynasty under the federal tax system. *The Probate Lawyer* 5:1–92. Reprinted as Chapter 14 in this volume.

Weisbrod, B.A. 1977. *The Voluntary Non-Profit Sector.* Lexington, Massachusetts: D.C. Heath.

Williamson, O.E. 1975. *Markets and Hierarchies: Analysis and Antitrust Implications.* New York: The Free Press.

7

Public, Private, Nonprofit Ownership and the Response to Asymmetric Information: The Case of Nursing Homes

BURTON A. WEISBROD and MARK SCHLESINGER

INTRODUCTION

When private markets are inefficient, economists normally think about mechanisms that attack the problem directly—taxes, subsidies, or other regulations. If information is inadequate, subsidize its provision (or tax its nonprovision); if quality is "too low," regulate it; if working conditions are "unsatisfactory," regulate them. In a world of costless regulation such direct approaches are optimal. More generally, though, the cost of regulation is nontrivial, so that indirect mechanisms may be the most efficient policy response.

If regulation were costless, levels of profit or their distribution would never be regulated, since any allocative inefficiencies could be corrected by changing quantities or qualities of inputs or outputs, not profits per se. If, however, quantities or qualities of inputs or outputs were sufficiently costly to monitor and, hence, to regulate directly, then indirect regulation—perhaps of the uses to which profit might be put—could be efficient. Thus, nonprofit

Much of this work was completed while Weisbrod was Visiting Scholar at the Center for Health Policy and Management, J.F. Kennedy School of Government, Harvard University, and Ziskind Visiting Professor of Economics, Brandeis University. The authors thank Gary Chamberlain, John Goddeeris, Estelle James, Richard Nelson, Edgar Olsen, and Susan Rose-Ackerman for helpful comments, and James Alm, Stephen Bell, and Jerald Schiff for research assistance. Financial assistance was provided by the Foundations Fund for Research in Psychiatry, the Ford Foundation, the National Institute of Mental Health, the Graduate School of the University of Wisconsin-Madison, and the Division of Health Policy, Research and Education, Harvard University. The paper benefited from comments from seminar participants at Brandeis, Harvard, and Yale Universities.

forms of organization could be allocatively preferred to regulation of the private, for-profit market.

This chapter analyzes the comparative behavior of proprietary firms, government agencies, and private nonprofit organizations in markets with asymmetric information. When informational asymmetries exist, so too does the potential for "misrepresentation"—a promise to deliver one level of quality but actual delivery of a lower, less costly, level. If contingent contracts can be formulated and enforced, information asymmetries at time of purchase would not be of great concern. When such contracts cannot easily be drawn, misrepresentation may represent a problem for consumers who, as underinformed parties, can be expected to seek protective mechanisms. Government regulation may be sought; agents may be used to narrow the information gap; attempts may be made to limit entry into the industry to those providers whose behavior is believed to be incompatible with taking advantage of their informational superiority.

It has been argued that restricting the entry of proprietary enterprise serves the last purpose (Summary Report of New York State Moreland Act Commission on Nursing Homes and Residential Facilities, 1976). Underlying this claim is the notion that public and private nonprofit ownership provides incentives that limit the extent of misrepresentation or, as it is sometimes termed, "opportunistic behavior." In this chapter we evaluate this claim—generally, that institutional form matters, and more specifically, that proprietary firms are more likely to take advantage of an informational superiority. First, we consider the plausibility of the argument in theoretical terms. Second, we attempt to validate this claim empirically. While neither of these issues can be resolved conclusively by a single study, the answers developed here can improve our understanding of the influence of ownership form on organizational behavior.

THEORETICAL PERSPECTIVES

Previous theoretical and empirical work suggests that ownership form—and the associated reward structure—does influence organizational behavior. In nonproprietary organizations the absence of property rights in any organizational profit has been viewed as restricting productive efficiency of the firm (Frech and Ginsburg, 1981; DeAlessi, 1980; Bishop, 1980). This chapter extends previous analyses of ownership to the consequences of asymmetric information.

We utilize the following framework:

1. Every good, i, can be defined by attributes or dimensions, $j = 1 \ldots$, n. These vary in the cost, c, to buyers of measuring them, from zero to infinity—that is, $0 < c_{ij} < \infty$.

2. Sellers can measure all attributes at zero cost.

3. Buyers (assumed identical) place a value on full information about each attribute—$0 < v_{ij} < \infty$.

To simplify the analysis, we distinguish four classes of attributes: (I) "low" cost, "high" value attributes; (II) high cost, high value; (III) low cost, low value; and (IV) high cost, low value. Classes III and IV are uninteresting in the limit, since the value of information is low. Therefore, we focus on the first two classes of attributes, labeled hereafter Type I and Type II attributes or outputs.

4. Every good may be arrayed on a spectrum according to the ratio of its Type I (easy to monitor) to its Type II (hard to monitor) attributes. At one extreme, all characteristics of the good are readily monitored; this is the "textbook" case of full information or, more generally, symmetric information, buyers and sellers being equally informed. At the other extreme, all important characteristics are opaque to the consumer. This is perhaps illustrated by national defense—where the relevant good is not the military hardware or manpower, but "security"—or by certain complex, technology-intensive medical procedures.

Most goods fall somewhere between the two extremes. The used car, for example, has a number of easily monitored (Type I) attributes, including model, color, appearance, the presence of a manual transmission, and so forth. Other attributes are of the costly-to-monitor (Type II) sort. It is these that have given rise to the problem of buying a "lemon" and to jokes such as "Would you buy a used car from this person?"

The existence or nonexistence of informational asymmetries clearly hinges on the nature of the product and the market conditions under which it is exchanged. If buyers purchase the product frequently, if the cost of a mistaken purchase of the product is small relative to buyers' incomes, if buyers can eventually judge quality so that a contract could be written to specify contingent payments or penalties in the event of noncompliance, or if the cost of buyer mobility is low, so buyers can change suppliers easily, then no supplier—proprietary, governmental, or private nonprofit—will be able to be "untrustworthy," that is, to take advantage of a temporary informational advantage. Later we examine behavior in an industry, nursing homes, in which these conditions do not hold.

Although misrepresentation has been viewed as an important issue in "mixed" industries—in which private nonprofit, proprietary, and public enterprise coexist[1]—formal analyses of the impact of ownership form on organizational behavior have not considered the impact of information asymmetries. This literature, however, does serve as a useful point of departure for our attempt to understand the interplay of informational asymmetries and ownership form. We proceed now to examine certain dimensions of behavior in a mixed industry in which both Type I and Type II attributes are present, but where Type II attributes are especially important.

The study of ownership has been conducted largely within the "property rights" model. The focus of this model is on the incentives that particular types of ownership provide for managers and employees. Any arrangement other than proprietary ownership is characterized by a "nondistribution constraint"—the prohibition against distributing profits to those associated with the firm. This constraint, insofar as it is binding, is argued to have two effects. First, managerial efficiency suffers, since greater efficiency cannot be rewarded financially. Second, compensation shifts to inefficient forms, with a substitution of nonpecuniary for pecuniary benefits. Such nonpecuniary rewards—thought largely to be embodied in plush offices or ostentatious buildings—circumvent the letter of the law establishing the nondistribution constraint. According to the property rights model, inefficient nonproprietary organizations persist in the face of competition from more efficient proprietary providers only because they are protected by government subsidization. These subsidies offset the costs created by inefficient management, and make the output of nonprofit and public producers attractive to consumers (Nichols, 1972, p. 83; Frech and Ginsberg, 1981, p. 70).

The typical property rights model assumes that all producers have homogeneous preferences. If in fact preferences differ among individuals, ownership form could induce differences in organizational behavior in yet another way. Suppose that there are two types of potential managers—one characterized by a relatively strong preference for pecuniary rewards, the other by a relatively strong preference for nonpecuniary rewards. These nonpecuniary rewards may include a concern for "honesty," for the level of product quality, or for other factors that might preclude or mitigate the exploitation of an informational superiority.

Differences in managerial preferences are likely to interact with differences in institutional constraints. Individuals whose objectives are weighted heavily toward nonpecuniary benefits are more likely to choose nonprofit settings than are their fellows favoring monetary reward (Hansmann, 1980; Weisbrod, 1983).[2] The nondistribution constraint represents a greater relative loss of utility to the latter group. A self-selection process, therefore, can be expected to occur, the result being that nonproprietary organizations come to be managed by persons whose utility functions are most congruent with the constraints confronted by the organization. Under these conditions the nondistribution constraint may not be binding for those employed in nonproprietary settings. If this were the case, nonproprietary firms might be no less efficient socially than proprietary organizations, given managerial objectives.

A sorting model of this nature has implications for the connection between ownership and the propensity to misrepresent. Managers controlling an organization can be expected to misrepresent so long as this behavior is compatible with their objectives, taking into account the expected penalties if misrepresentation is discovered either by consumers or by regulators. Thus, nonproprietary organizations will be more likely or less likely to misrepresent than proprietary organizations, depending on whether misrepresentation is more or less consistent with nonpecuniary or pecuniary forms of rewards.

A review of the literature on industries that have substantial nonproprietary ownership suggests that opportunistic behavior has been perceived to be linked to monetary incentives.[3] In the nursing home industry, for instance:

> . . . for the proprietary nursing homes in particular, both opportunity and incentive exist to seek profits through reducing direct care costs (and hence reducing quantity and/or quality of services) for the in some degree captive population. Such reasoning has led to considerable concern about possible exploitation of frail and vulnerable patient populations by proprietary operations (Greene and Monahan, 1980, p. 7).

Thus there exist two models of the influence of ownership, one focusing on constraints, and the other on objective functions. These provide a basis for predicting—and testing—differences in behavior among ownership types in markets for goods that exhibit both Type I and Type II attributes.

Type I attributes are relatively easily monitored and enforceable in contracts. There are not, therefore, likely to be significant gains from deliberate deviations between delivered and promised levels of quality, regardless of ownership type. Not all deviations that occur, however, are deliberate. Organizations controlled by administrators who face inadequate incentives will be prone to such deviations. Clarkson has argued that this is exactly what one would expect to find in nonproprietary organizations. Unmotivated by a share of the profits, administrators in public and private nonprofit enterprises are predicted to be inefficient—avoiding working unpleasant shifts and less carefully monitoring the behavior of employees (Clarkson, 1972). To the extent that this property rights model accurately describes nonproprietary behavior, deviations between delivered and promised Type I attributes of quality should be smaller in proprietary than in nonproprietary settings.

By contrast with a model that focuses on the *constraints* limiting rewards, a model that focuses on the possible public interest *goals* of nonprofit organization administrators would predict that these administrators would work to minimize the deviation of actual from promised quality, simply because doing so entered positively into their utility functions. This model would predict no systematic difference between proprietary and nonprofit organizations in the closeness of actual to promised quality of Type I attributes; proprietary firms would provide the promised quality because they would be rewarded financially, while nonprofits would behave similarly because they would be rewarded in nonmonetary, utility terms.

To summarize, with respect to Type I attributes there are two competing hypotheses: (A) proprietary firms provide output that is closer to the quality "promised," and expected by consumers, than is the case for nonprofit, governmental, or private organizations, because the proprietaries are more efficient (the "property rights" model); and (B) there is no difference between actual and promised quality in the proprietary compared with the nonprofit sector because managers in each one face effective, although different, rewards (the "public interest" model). In distinguishing between these models, empirical findings can shed light on the relative importance of pecuniary incentives, which are constrained in the nonprofit sector but are unconstrained in the proprietary sector, and the public interest rewards, which are constrained in both sectors but, because of managerial sorting, may be more important in the nonprofit sectors.

With respect to Type II attributes, our hypothesis is more clearcut. These attributes, being by definition costly to monitor, present providers with opportunities to misrepresent quality; they can provide less than what was promised, and go undetected often enough to generate added profits. This potential exists for all providers, regardless of ownership.

Our maintained hypothesis, however, is that (C) the deviation of actual from promised quality in Type II dimensions is greater for proprietary firms. This would hold if either (1) the nondistributive constraint on profits is binding on the nonprofit organizations, so that their managers cannot benefit from reaping additional profits, and/or (2) the managers of nonprofits were more public spirited or honest. Note that if (1) holds, the managers of nonprofits would not be rewarded for cutting costs by delivering less than what was promised, and that their resulting failure to maximize profit could be socially efficient; the social inefficiency resulting from the profit distribution constraint on nonprofits could offset the inefficiency resulting from the proprietary firms' taking advantage of their informational superiority over their customers.

Thus, regarding Type II attributes, Hypothesis C would hold either if the *preferences* of managers of nonproprietary, as compared with proprietary organizations, were more inconsistent with "misrepresentation"—that is, with taking advantage of their informational superiority; or it would hold even if preferences were homogeneous among managers, if the nondistribution *constraint* on nonproprietary organizations was sufficiently enforced that it blunted incentives to utilize informational superiority. Thus, a finding that Hypothesis C holds cannot distinguish between these two models. Such a finding, however, would not be consistent with the view that legal constraints on nonprofit organizations are so poorly enforced or so easily circumvented as to be meaningless, and that institutional form is simply irrelevant as a predictor of behavior.

EMPIRICAL ANALYSIS

We test these hypotheses, using data from the nursing home industry in Wisconsin. The market for nursing home service is characterized by substantial information asymmetries. Consumers—patients, friends, and family members—are generally ill-informed about important dimensions of the commodity (Fraundorf, 1977). The commodity is purchased infrequently—once or twice during a typical person's lifetime—and each "purchase" (patient entry) has a large idiosyncratic component resulting from uncertainty regarding the probability distribution of an individual's service "needs" in the future. Particularly important is the high cost of patient mobility, resulting from the poor physical and mental health that characterizes most nursing home patients. Entry to a nursing home is thus tantamount to a lifetime contract.[4] If a buyer later discovers that an "error" was made at the time of purchase, the "exit" option is largely foreclosed. The option of "voice," or complaint (Hirschman, 1970), remains, however, and we use this as a source of information on perceived misrepresentation—which we identify with Type II attributes of nursing home services.

Not all nursing home services are equally associated with Type II attributes. Some aspects of life in a nursing home (for example, the age of the building and the beauty of the grounds) are readily assessed by potential residents at little or no cost. Some aspects, such as the availability of particular therapeutic services, may be enforceable through contingent contracts. Information about others may be learned from friends and relatives. Still other dimensions of "quality," however, are neither readily observed nor easily cast in contingent contracts. The quality of both medical care and of "tender loving care" fall into this category, Type II.

We use information collected by state regulators as measures of deviations of actual from anticipated Type I quality. That is, *regulatory violations* are taken as a measure of breaches of an implicit contract in Type I dimensions. Our reasoning is as follows. To be enforceable, formal regulations necessarily focus on the readily monitored aspects of nursing home quality (Vladeck, 1980, pp. 167–68; Ruchlin, 1979, p. 99). Although these are the characteristics of quality most readily observed by consumers, economies of scale in information-gathering may motivate "collective monitoring." (The question of whether such monitoring is most efficiently done by the proprietary sector or by some other type of institution is a related matter, but is beyond the scope of this chapter.) We postulate that regulations represent the minimum quality levels that would be sought by well-informed consumers. The total number of regulatory violations is our measure of the deviation of actual from anticipated quality in the more easily monitored, Type I, dimensions of output.

Aggregate violations are an imperfect measure of the true deviation between "promised" and "actual" quality in Type I dimensions. One reason is that not all violations have an equally large impact on resident welfare. Some regulations cover less important aspects of performance—that is, those having low value to consumers. Second, the number of violations tells us nothing about the magnitude of the deviations from standards. Finally, some nursing homes may, in the implicit contract, "promise" quality well above the minimum standards, while others claim simply to provide lower levels of care. Any given number of violations represents a larger deviation from promised quality by the first type of seller than by the second.

These imperfections in measurement are important in this context, however, only if they are systematically related to type of ownership. It is quite possible that homes with particular forms of ownership do promise, on average, higher-quality care—that is, occupy a higher-quality niche in the market—than do homes operating under other auspices. If, for example, managers of nonproprietary and proprietary organizations do have systematically different preferences, and if the former derive relatively more utility from, say, the prestige of associating with a "high quality" supplier, then this difference in goals would lead managers of nonprofit and public organizations to promise higher quality care. In our statistical work, below, we attempt to control for such a tendency for promised levels of attributes to vary systematically among institutional types.

We use the number of *complaints* lodged with state regulators as a measure of violations of Type II dimensions of quality. "Complaints"—by letter, telephone call or personal visit to a state agency, from patients, family members, or others—are postulated to occur when residents or their families perceive a breach of the implicit contract with the nursing home. Such "contracts," we assume, cover both Type I and Type II aspects of quality. We are principally concerned, however, with measuring the latter. Therefore, we analyze the relationship between complaints and form of ownership within a regression model which controls for those complaints that are found to be regulatory violations. Since regulations are oriented principally to Type I aspects of quality, this procedure allows our analysis of complaints to reflect the hard-to-measure quality characteristics, Type II.[5]

With such adjustments, the number of recorded complaints seems to be a useful proxy for Type II misrepresentations, but it is certainly imperfect. We have suggested that complaints result from breaches of Type II contractual terms, but it is arguable that such breaches are neither a necessary nor a sufficient condition for a complaint to be made. Residents may complain simply because they believe doing so will prompt some favorable response even if there were no deviation from promised quality care. Conversely, actual deviations may go unreported because residents fear retaliation by staff members or because they feel that complaints would not prompt useful action by state regulators. Again, for our purposes, it does not matter if such factors influence the complaint process—indeed, they surely do— as long as they do not exert a differential impact across ownership types.

It is difficult to know whether this assumption of a zero partial correlation between the propensity of a dissatisfied person to complain and organizational ownership type is valid. Evidence and theory are sketchy or nonexistent concerning the complaints-generation process.[6] Those knowledgeable about the nursing home industry in Wisconsin suggest, however, that our assumption about one part of the process is reasonable, that the response by state regulators or staff members to complaints does not vary with ownership (Zitske, 1979; McKenzie, 1979). Nor would one expect to find the use of complaints for strategic manipulation linked to the type of ownership of the home.[7]

In short, we model the process of misrepresentation and, hence, complaints, as follows: (1) A complaint occurs whenever there is a perceived breach of contract. (2) Breaches that are relatively easily monitored (Type I) are covered by government regulations, and when detected by regulatory agencies appear as regulatory "violations." (3) Breaches that are costlier to monitor—Type II (for example, tender loving care)—are not covered by regulations, and, when detected by patients, family members, and so forth, are reflected in "complaints."

We use this model to test the connection between ownership form and the performance of nursing homes: The deviation of actual from anticipated quality in Type I dimensions is proxied by regulatory violations; we use this measure to test Hypotheses A and B. The deviation of actual from promised or anticipated quality in Type II dimensions is proxied by consumer complaints; this is employed to test Hypothesis C. In each case, our methodology is to regress the dependent variables—violations or complaints—on dummy variables representing ownership form and on a set of additional variables to standardize for exogenous factors that may be correlated with both the dependent variable and with organizational ownership type.

REGRESSION SPECIFICATION

Violations Regression: Behavioral Variation with Respect to Type I Variables

As we noted above, to interpret regulatory violations as a measure of breaches of Type I contract variables, other factors must be controlled. These include both the promised level of quality and the stringency of regulatory codes. The former we proxy by the home's revenue per patient day, on the assumption that the higher this "price" the higher the implicitly promised level of services. Behavioral differences among suppliers due to differences in the source of funds are controlled by including variables measuring the proportion of a home's revenue that is derived from private payments and from Medicaid. Regulatory stringency is reflected by certification as either a "skilled nursing," "intermediate," "personal," or "residential" care facility, in decreasing order of standards (the latter two classes, having similar standards, have been grouped in our empirical work), and by whether it is certified to accept a large proportion of mentally retarded residents.

Other control variables are included to capture some of the complexities of markets for nursing home services. These include the extent of competition a particular home has, proxied by whether the home is in a community with a population over 10,000 (the largest class for which data were available); and by whether the home is affiliated with a hospital, in which case it has a somewhat captive population, but also has an incentive to behave in a manner satisfactory to the hospital.

Complaints Regression: Behavioral Differences with Respect to Type II Variables

The complaints regression contains many of the variables included in the violations regression. The interpretations, however, are somewhat different. Certification levels are included to capture, in part, residents' expectations of quality of the supplier's Type II output characteristics. Urban location and hospital affiliation are likely to reflect the close availability of facilities which might serve as standards of comparative information and, hence, would affect perceived violations of Type II outputs. Variables measuring the proportion of residents supported through Medicaid and private sources are included to capture the effect on residents' expectations—and, hence, on complaints—of who is paying for the care; services purchased by one's own resources, for example, might be scrutinized more closely and criticized more freely.[8] Finally, an independent variable is included measuring the percentage of complaints that were subsequently identified as regulatory violations. This controls—albeit imperfectly—for the mix of Type I and Type II breaches of contract that generated complaints.

Data

The data for nursing homes in Wisconsin in 1976 come from the State Division of Health, which regulates the industry. As of that year, there were 601 nursing homes in Wisconsin, with complete data available for 431. Regulatory "violations" were detected on the basis of an annual, announced inspection, with follow-up inspection if significant violations were detected. "Complaints" were reported by patients, family members, or other parties and could have been reported in written or oral form, in person or by telephone, by a named or anonymous person.

Some 7 percent of the homes had zero violations during the study year, and 60 percent had zero complaints. Because of the sizable number of such limit observations, we used the Tobit form for the regression, in order to avoid the bias that would result from using the OLS form.

EMPIRICAL RESULTS

Our findings are in Table 7–1, and mean values for the variables are in Table 7–2. The estimates of the violations regression suggest that, as predicted by the property rights model (Hypothesis A), some nonproprietary organizations (private, nonchurch-owned) have significantly more regulatory violations than do their for-profit counterparts. The Tobit estimates indicate that in terms of the underlying, latent model, a nonchurch-owned nonprofit home would be expected to have some 32 more regulatory violations per year than a proprietary home having similar size and other characteristics in Table 7–1; this is about 20 percent more than the simple mean numbers of violations shown in Table 7–2. These nonprofits appear, thus, to operate with greater "organizational slack" than do their for-profit counterparts, which permits greater unintended shortfalls of Type I aspects of quality.[9] Interestingly, this greater number of regulatory violations is not found for the church-owned nonprofits or for public nursing homes. This finding, predicted by Hypothesis B, suggests that religiously affiliated non-

Table 7–1. Tobit Coefficients and *t*-Statistics (in parentheses) from Violations Regression and Complaints Regression, Wisconsin Nursing Homes, 1976 *(Dependent Variable: Total Number of Violations or Complaints)*

	Tobit Estimates	
Independent Variables	Violations (1)	Complaints (2)
Constant	206.41[a]	−1.86
	(11.64)	(−1.51)
Ownership type (omitted category: "Proprietary")		
Governmental	15.96	−1.94[a]
	(0.95)	(−1.99)
Private nonprofit		
Church-owned	−0.47	−3.49[a]
	(−0.03)	(−2.45)
Nonchurch-owned	31.64[a]	−2.44[a]
	(2.14)	(−2.61)
Average revenue	−0.00	
	(−0.25)	
Certification level (omitted category: "Intermediate")		
Skilled	−58.95[a]	2.69[a]
	(−4.21)	(3.05)
Personal and residential	−228.64[a]	−7.02[a]
	(−10.43)	(−3.68)
Mental retardation certification	−77.74[a]	−1.26
	(−3.10)	(0.66)
Located in community with population over 10,000	25.42[a]	0.64
	(2.17)	(0.89)
Hospital-affiliated	−17.50	−3.85[a]
	(−0.95)	(−2.68)
Number of licensed beds	0.03	0.00
	(1.46)	(0.16)
Revenue source (omitted category: "Medicare")		
Proportion from private sources	7.14	
	(0.94)	
Proportion from medicaid	−5.65	
	(−0.71)	
Population mix (omitted category: "Medicare")		
Proportion of residents supported by Medicaid		0.09
		(0.78)
Proportion of residents supported by private funds		−0.15
		(1.29)
Proportion of complaints identified as regulatory violations		1.58[a]
		(5.14)

[a]Significant at .10 level or better.

profits and governmental organizations attract administrators who are relatively unaffected by the nondistribution constraint, perhaps because they are less motivated by financial incentives.

The estimates of the complaints equation (Table 7–1, col. 2) contrast

Table 7–2. Means of Variables

Variable	Nonprofit, Religious	Nonprofit, Nonreligious	Public	Proprietary
Percentage of total homes	8	25	15	51
Violations per home	144	163	161	170
Complaints per home	0.92	1.21	1.65	2.45
Percentage of complaints substantiated	0.59	0.42	0.46	0.46
Beds	52.3	73.3	156.7	88.3
Proportion of residents supported by private sources	0.45	0.51	0.46	0.52
Proportion of residents supported by Medicaid	0.46	0.41	0.49	0.41
Proportion of revenues from private sources	0.50	0.65	0.55	0.61
Proportion of revenues from Medicaid	0.41	0.27	0.34	0.32
Proportion of homes in urban settings	0.54	0.65	0.43	0.63
Proportion with hospital affiliation	0.07	0.26	0.07	0.00
Proportion with skilled nursing certification	0.66	0.65	0.82	0.63
Proportion with intermediate care certification	0.11	0.14	0.11	0.25
Proportion of homes certified for care of mentally retarded	0.37	0.42	1.00	0.74

with the violations regression. All three forms of nonproprietary organizations—public and both types of private nonprofit—had significantly fewer complaints, ceteris paribus, than did proprietary firms (as predicted by Hypothesis C). The significant negative coefficients on the "ownership type" variables in that regression are consistent with the interpretation that proprietary organizations do take more advantage than do other institutional forms of their informational superiority in Type II terms. The estimated coefficients are proportionately very large. Were it not for the observational problem that constrains the number of complaints to be nonnegative, the three types of nonprofits would be estimated to have 2–3 fewer complaints per home per year, numbers that exceed the actual sample means of 1–2 complaints shown in Table 7–2.

There are, of course, other interpretations of our findings. Similar regression coefficients would result if consumers believed systematically that their complaints would lead to a more satisfactory response from a proprietary firm. Such coefficients would also be found if residents expected less from nonproprietary administrators. Hence, there were fewer perceived breaches of contract for given actual behavior.

The complaints equation contains some other estimates, for certification level, which are consistent with the findings for ownership type. There are essentially three classes of nursing homes defined in terms of input of skills provided—"skilled" (the highest), "intermediate," and "personal and residential" (the lowest). (Mental retardation certification is defined along another dimension.) It seems likely that skilled homes would be expected to provide relatively more Type II attributes (for example, tender loving care) than would the personal and residential level homes. Thus, it is noteworthy that Table 7–1, column 2, shows that, ceteris paribus, skilled homes do have the most complaints, and personal and residential have the fewest.

The significant positive coefficient on the variable, "Proportion of Complaints Identified as Regulatory Violation," is also of interest. It suggests that if a Type I violation is believed by a patient, family member, or other person to have occurred, it is more likely to generate a formal complaint than is a perceived Type II violation. This would be expected insofar as discovery of a Type I violation is more likely to lead to corrective action.

No empirical study can hope to distinguish among alternative models that generate the same behavioral implications; neither can it disentangle true causality from correlations in the data. Nonetheless, our findings do suggest systematic patterns of behavior associated with the ownership form of an organization, at least in the nursing home industry.

LONG-RUN EQUILIBRIUM

If we are correct in believing that the differences between proprietary and nonproprietary organizations do become manifest when informational asymmetries—Type II outputs—are present, the question arises as to whether such differences in institutional behavior are consistent with long-run equilibrium in which the various forms of institutions coexist. It seems likely that the answer is no. Over time, consumers can be expected to learn about the signal value of institutional-ownership form with respect to Type II outputs, and as this occurs the less satisfactory institutional forms will tend to be driven from the market. But this, and the following remarks in this section, are speculative; the nature of the process of adjustment to long-run equilibrium in mixed industries should be the subject of further study.

As recognition of the signal value of institutional form grows, and organizations enter the industry with the "preferred" form, we can expect "debasement of the currency" of that form. Organizations will tend to "disguise" themselves, taking on the formal trappings of the preferred form while behaving differently. There are barriers to such misrepresented entry in the form of IRS regulation of private suppliers, and legislative oversight of public enterprise. Nonetheless, disguised entry of this sort is likely to narrow the differences in organizational behavior.

In markets where information flows slowly, the movement toward equilibrium may be greatly retarded. In the market for nursing home care, for example, the process of accretion of information by consumers is likely to be slow, indeed, for the reasons we gave earlier: infrequency of purchase, idiosyncratic demand, and consumer immobility. For other goods, with less severe informational problems for consumers, the speed of adjustment will be greater. Nonetheless, differences in the propensity to misrepresent are likely to remain important issues of public policy.

The question of when organizations with two or more forms of ownership are likely to coexist in a single industry is important. If one ownership form is preferred by consumers in the market for some particular good, why would other forms be present? An answer is suggested by the differences in organizational constraints. Consider the cases of hospitals or nursing homes and assume that, for reasons discussed above, consumers prefer the nonprofit organizations. Assume, further, that from an initial steady-state population, demand for health-care services begins to grow rapidly. It is likely, under these circumstances that entry to the industry will consist disproportionately of proprietary organizations rather than nonprofit; this is due to (1) the constraints on the nonprofits' access to the capital market—they cannot sell stock, nor borrow on the strength of their equity capital—and (2) the constraints on their decision-making procedures—they may be required to consult widely with their varied constituencies. Thus, proprietary firms, not being hobbled by such constraints, are, we conjecture, likely to respond more promptly to the increase in demand.

Given our assumption, however, that consumers prefer the nonprofit firms, we expect that such organizations will, despite responding more slowly, gradually enter the industry and will displace the proprietaries. In a steady-state equilibrium, only the preferred form of institution will remain (assuming equal costs), but as long as demand is growing, the greater adaptability of the proprietary form can lead to maintenance of a mixed industry, comprising both proprietary and nonprofit organizations. Superficial analysis of the geographic distribution of proprietary and private nonprofit organizations in the short-term hospital industry is consistent with such a model; the relative importance, in terms of number of beds, of proprietary hospitals is greatest in the rapidly growing states of the sunbelt.

Nonprofit and proprietaries will coexist in equilibrium despite consumer preferences for nonprofits, if the proprietaries have a cost and, hence, price advantage. If, for example, the freedom of proprietaries to reward managers who generate profit enhances their organizational efficiency—by contrast with governmental and private nonprofit organizations, which do not have such freedom—these organizations would be able to produce the services they do provide at lower cost.

Finally, coexistence of ownership-forms is possible even in long-run equilibrium insofar as consumer demands vary. In our model the nonprofits are most useful as mechanisms for providing information to consumers searching to avoid losses from informational handicaps. Better-informed consumers, thus, have less demand for utilizing the nonprofit form of provider, and so they may prefer to deal with proprietary sellers who would, in equilibrium, cater to this better-informed niche in the market. The industry would then consist of providers of two different quality levels—a proprietary sector specializing in Type I outputs and a nonprofit sector that is relied upon particularly for its Type II outputs.

CONCLUDING REMARKS: INFORMATIONAL ASYMMETRY, TRUST, AND THE DESIRABILITY OF REWARDING INCOMPLETELY MEASURED PERFORMANCE

It is commonplace in the workaday world to refer to one's "trust" in some individual or institution. The need for such trust—that is, for relying on some agent or mechanism for coping with informational asymmetry—exists only when one transactor cannot monitor the behavior of another at low cost. Like brand-name advertising, the type of institutional ownership may or may not signal relevant information.

Among the types of organizations examined—governmental, church-affiliated nonprofits, other nonprofits, and proprietary—we found that the proprietary type was clearly distinguishable from each of the other types when we considered the Type II dimensions of output. These findings are consistent with the view that under the conditions of substantial informational asymmetry, other forms of institutions are more "trustworthy" than is the proprietary form of institution in the sense that they are less likely to take advantage of their informational advantage to the detriment of their consumers.

The importance of this trust, or informational, phenomenon should not be underestimated. Where product quality is difficult to assess—including much of the health and education industries as well as the quality of corporate reports and information about environmental hazards—intervention through governmental regulation of product quality is often a costly exercise of questionable efficacy. An alternative in the form of designing institutions to reduce the cost of monitoring outputs could be an efficient means for reducing informational costs. It is noteworthy that public and nonprofit forms of enterprise are common in industries in which such services are produced (Table 7–3). As Heiner (1983) has recently suggested, such information-conserving institutions are likely to become more common as the perceived complexity of society increases.

It is interesting in this regard that the total number of nonprofit organizations has been growing rapidly. The number of tax returns filed by nonprofit organizations has increased from some 100,000 in the early 1950s to more than 300,000 twenty years later (Internal Revenue Service, various years). Moreover, the number of new applications for nonprofit, tax-exempt status, has increased from about 5000 per year in the late 1950s and the early 1960s to 15,000 in 1968 and to 35,000 in 1979.

On the other hand, trust can be misplaced. If consumers believe in some informational signal and conclude that additional monitoring is not needed,

Table 7–3. The Distribution of Ownership in Selected Mixed Industries in the 1970s

Industry	Percentage of Output Produced by Sector			Measure of Output
	Government	Proprietary	Nonprofit	
Nursing homes	11.2	68.8	20.0	Number of beds
Psychiatric hospitals, short-stay	59.8	23.8	16.3	Number of beds
Homes for mentally handicapped	16.1	46.2	37.7	Number of facilities
Day-care centers	8.8	50.7	40.5	Population served
Postsecondary education (including vocational)	46.9	33.5	19.6	Revenues
Research and development	16.1	67.6	16.4	Revenues

Sources: Nursing homes, psychiatric hospitals, and homes for mentally handicapped, U.S. Department of Health Education, and Welfare (1978); day-care centers, Keyserling (1972); postsecondary education, Bendick (1975); research and development, National Science Foundation (1972).

inefficiencies and inequities will result. Whether informational mechanisms that generate information and trust are best left to the private market is an important question that has been given little attention.

Our study also highlights the likelihood that organizations with different ownership forms may differ in some dimensions of performance but not in others. This holds important implications for the ways in which organizational performance is rewarded, and for the design of ownership and regulatory mechanisms. There is a growing empirical literature attempting to compare the efficiency of proprietary organizations with either public or private nonprofit institutions (Davies, 1971; Borcherding, Pommerehne, and Schneider, 1982). These studies recognized the possibility that outputs might not be identical across the sectors, and they made efforts to control for such differences. None of the studies, however, dealt with the possibility, suggested here, that there are systematic differences in the measurability of outputs across sectors, the proprietary sector being the institutional locus for provision of the more easily observed outputs.

Consider a variable, R_j, which is the ratio for any given good, j, of the "importance" to consumers of its Type I dimensions relative to the total importance of Type I and Type II dimensions of output. At one extreme would be a good for which there are no Type II dimensions ($R = 1$): all relevant aspects of such goods—for example, chocolate cookies—can be measured costlessly. At the other extreme would be a good for which there are no Type I outputs: all dimensions that enter consumers' utility functions are infinitely costly to monitor. A good approaching this polar case of maximum informational asymmetry, $R = 0$, would be national defense; the nursing home is a less extreme example.

The cost of monitoring outputs holds implications for the cost of rewarding "performance." Generally, Type I dimensions of performance can be rewarded easily, while Type II dimensions, being costly to monitor, are similarly costly to reward. Thus, rewarding "performance" has two countervailing effects: since only Type I dimensions of performance can be monitored and hence rewarded, a performance-reward system (1) encourages efficiency with respect to Type I dimensions, but (2) distorts the allocation of resources toward Type I outputs relative to what the allocation would be in a full-information world. Thus, as we "move" from cases of $R = 1$ (the full-information case) toward $R = 0$, we reach an optimum, R^*, at which the marginal efficiency-*inducing* effects of rewarding "performance" are equated with the marginal efficiency-*reducing* effects of allocational distortions. For goods with $R < R^*$, rewarding "performance"—as measured—is counterproductive, given that only some dimensions of total performance can be rewarded. For such goods, it is more efficient not to reward performance at all than to reward only the Type I dimensions.

This model can explain a number of seeming anomalies in various markets. (1) Civil service rules, frequently criticized on the grounds that they restrict the rewarding of performance, *may* reflect recognition of hard-to-monitor goals such as treating citizens "equitably" and "humanely." (2) Restrictions on political terms of office (for example, for the president of the United States) may reflect recognition of the dangers of rewarding elected officials with additional terms in office when some potential critical elements of their total performance—e.g., corruption—are costly to monitor. (3) Formal job tenure—whether for federal judges or academics—may reflect decisions to forego the opportunity to reward (or punish) measured performance, given the difficulty of measuring "wise" judicial decisions and violations of "academic freedom."

In all these cases, opportunities to reward performance are intentionally foregone. The seeming irrationality of divorcing rewards from performance is understandable, however, and indeed could be efficient insofar as Type II dimensions of performance are important but cannot be rewarded. Contemporary debate over the rewarding of "excellence" in public school teaching is yet another manifestation of the general problem of how to devise efficient reward structures in a world in which information about some relevant dimensions of performance is available at low cost while other information is available only at high cost, if at all.

NOTES

1. See Vladek (1980), pp. 174–91) and Nelson and Krashinsky (1973, p. 55).

2. Weisbrod (1983) presents a recent empirical analysis of such sorting, as illustrated by lawyers. For a more general discussion of this phenomenon, see Young (1983).

3. Misrepresentation can also be compatible, however, with nonmonetary objectives. For example, administrators of nonprofit teaching hospitals often indicate a need to charge patients at relatively high rates in order to subsidize teaching and research programs. Such subsidies tend not to be itemized on the patient's bill. Patients may well believe that they are simply paying for services rendered to them; whereas, in fact, misrepresentation may be occurring to further the nonpecuniary objectives of the administrator (Clark, 1980).

4. Less than 15 percent of nursing home discharges other than death involve transfers to other homes (Vladeck, 1980, p. 140). The majority of these transfers are not the result of choice by residents, but are transfers forced by their inability to pay for care. Those that do switch venues often suffer deleterious effects on health, a phenomenon which has come to be known as "transfer trauma" (Vladeck, 1980, pp. 140–41; Pegels, 1980, pp. 74–7).

5. If we are right in believing that nonprofit managers take less advantage of their informational advantages than do the proprietaries, and if complaints proxy such behavior, it is noteworthy that the differences in behavior among ownership forms should be largest for those elements of quality that are hardest to observe, even by patients or family members. Thus, observed differences in complaints will be biased downward relative to the true differences in interinstitution behavior when informational asymmetries are present; consequently, our findings, reported below, of significantly more complaints against proprietaries would be even stronger were it not for this expected reporting bias. (We owe this point to Susan Rose-Ackerman.)

6. More research is needed about this process in general. Complaint statistics were also gathered by the Civil Aeronautics Board about commercial airlines, and crime statistics are also essentially complaints. Little work has been done to model and estimate the systems that generate reported statistics.

7. It is possible that residents fail to complain due to fear of retaliation. Although this perceived threat could be linked to the type of ownership of the institution, there exists no evidence regarding such a connection.

8. The violations and complaints regressions use slightly different specifications for payor mix of residents. In the latter regression, we have used proportion of *residents* falling into each payor class, on the theory that the number of residents determines the probability that a complaint will be voiced. In the former regression, payor mix is proxied by proportion of *revenue*, on the theory that the incentives for administrators have been influenced by the dependency of their budgets on a particular source of payment.

9. This finding is in contrast to the simple means, in Table 7–2, which show proprietary homes to have the most violations per home. One important source of the change seems to be associated with the types of certification. Intermediate care facilities—the omitted class—are the recipients of the greatest number of violations, and these are predominantly proprietary. Why the proprietary homes are relatively concentrated in this class is another matter, possibly related, however, to the importance of Type II dimensions of outputs.

REFERENCES

Bendick, Marc. 1975. Essays on education as a three-sector industry. Ph.D. dissertation, University of Wisconsin, 1975. (A portion of this work appears in B. Weisbrod, *The Voluntary Nonprofit Sector,* Lexington, Massachusetts: Lexington Books, 1977.)

Bishop, C. 1980. Nursing home cost studies and reimbursement issues. *Health Care Financing Review* 1:47–64.

Borcherding, T., W. Pommerehne, and F. Schneider. 1982. Comparing the efficiency of private and public production: The evidence from five countries. *Zeitschrift fur Nationalokonomie* Supplement 2:127–56.

Clark, R. 1980. Does the nonprofit form fit the hospital industry? *Harvard Law Review* 93:1417–489.

Clarkson, K. 1982. Some implications of property rights in hospital management. *Journal of Law and Economics* 15:363–84.

Davies, D. 1971. The efficiency of public vs. private firms: The case of Australia's two airlines. *Journal of Law and Economics* 14:149–65.

De Alessi, L. 1980. The economics of property rights: A review of the evidence. *Research in Law and Economics* 2:1–47.

Fraundorf, Kenneth. 1977. Competition and public policy in the nursing home industry. *Journal of Economic Issues* 11:601–34.

Frech, H.E., and P.B. Ginsburg. 1981. The cost of nursing home care in the United States: Government financing, ownership, and efficiency. In *Health, Economics, and Health Economics*, eds., J. van der Gaag and M. Perlman. Amsterdam: North Holland.

Greene, Vernon, and Deborah Monahan. 1980. Predicting quality of care in skilled nursing home facilities: A multivariate analysis. Paper presented at the 33rd Annual Meeting of the Gerontological Society, San Diego, California, November 21–25.

Hansmann, Henry B. 1980. The role of nonprofit enterprise. *The Yale Law Journal* 89:835–901. Reprinted as Chapter 3 in this volume.

Heiner, R. 1983. The origin of predictable behavior. *American Economic Review* 73:560–95.

Hirschman, A. 1970. *Exit, Voice, and Loyalty.* Cambridge, Massachusetts: Harvard University Press.

Internal Revenue Service. *Tax Commissioner's Annual Report.* various years.

Keyserling, M. 1972. *Windows on Day Care.* New York: National Council of Jewish Women.

McKenzie, Greg. 1979. Executive director of the Wisconsin Association of Nursing Homes, personal interview (August 2).

National Science Foundation. 1972. *National Patterns of R&D Resources.* Washington, D.C., Report NSF70-46.

Nelson, Richard, and Michael Krashinsky. 1973. Two major issues of public policy: Public subsidy and the organization of supply. In *Public Policy for Day Care for Young Children*, eds., Dennis Young and Richard Nelson. Lexington, Massachusetts: Lexington Books.

Nichols, A. 1972. *Management and Control in the Mutual Savings and Loan Association.* Lexington, Massachusetts: Lexington Books.

Pegels, C. 1980. *Health Care and the Elderly.* Rockville, Maryland: Aspen Systems Corp.

Ruchlin, H. 1979. An analysis of regulatory issues and options in long-term care. In *Reform and Regulation in Long-Term Care*, eds. V. LaPorte and J. Rubin. New York: Praeger Publishers.

Savas, E. 1977. Policy analysis for local government: Public vs. private refuse collection. *Policy Analysis* 3:49–74.

Spence, Michael. 1974. *Market Signaling: Information Transfer in Hiring and Related Processes.* Cambridge, Massachusetts: Harvard University Press.

Summary Report of the New York State Moreland Act Commission on Nursing Homes and Residential Facilities. 1976. *Long Term Care Regulations: Past Lapses, Future Prospects,* New York: Albany.

U.S. Department of Health, Education, and Welfare. 1979. *Health, United States, 1978.* DHEW Publication No. (PHC) 78-1232, December.

Vladeck, B. 1980. *Unloving Care: The Nursing Home Tragedy.* New York: Basic Books.

Weisbrod, B. 1983. Nonprofit and proprietary sector behavior: Wage differentials among lawyers. *Journal of Labor Economics* 1:241–63.

Young, Dennis. 1983. *If Not for Profit, for What?* Lexington, Massachusetts: Lexington Books.

Zitske, Judith. 1979. Wisconsin State Nursing Home Ombudsman's Office, personal interview, March 8.

8

Comments

SHARON OSTER and ESTELLE JAMES

SHARON OSTER

My comments are addressed to the three theoretical chapters by Krashinsky, Ben-Ner, and Easley-O'Hara. All begin with the same familiar question: Why do we have nonprofit organizations? The approaches taken in response to this question, however, differ significantly, although all three lean heavily on asymmetric information arguments.

Krashinsky begins well with what I think is a central observation one needs to make in this literature: It is not enough to point to contract failure to explain the existence of nonprofits. We must present a convincing argument explaining why nonprofits are best able to master the failure. In particular, in the U.S. economy there is a rich array of organizational forms: public, private-regulated, private-owner controlled, nonprofit, and so on. Ideally, one would like a theory that begins to explain the mapping between organizational type and specific market failure.

While I think Krashinsky has done excellent service in pinpointing the right questions, I found his potpourri of answers less compelling. In large measure, Krashinsky's justification for the nonprofit form rests on the need for "trust" in particular transactions, especially transactions in which the buyer and user are separated. However, separation of user and buyer seems to me to be neither necessary *nor* sufficient to create strong trust needs. I buy mail-order presents for a distant niece through a conventional for-profit store. Similarly, it is surely not the fact that we buy day care for our children (that is, user/buyer separation) that creates a need for trust, but the vulnerability and innocence of the user. The elderly often buy their own nursing care, yet their vulnerability, too, is thought to create some additional need for trust. Moreover, even if trust *does* play an important role in some sectors of our economy, it is not at all obvious that the nonprofit is the only (or even the most) trustworthy organizational form. In many circumstances we have learned to "trust" the for-profit firm. When does this trust break down?

Day care is a common example in the nonprofit literature and appears again in both Krashinsky and Ben-Ner. I am struck in the day-care example by the survival of many different organizational types in this field: day-care providers include public agencies, nonprofits, for-profit small firms (that is, neighborhood care) and increasingly for-profit chains.[1] The coexistence of multiple forms is something neither Krashinsky nor Ben-Ner deal with in much detail. In Krashinsky's terms, we need to examine the way in which each of the day-care forms establishes "trust" for its buyers. I think an intriguing and useful empirical study could be done, for example, tracing the reliance of different organizational forms on tangibles versus intangibles as a way to develop trust and reputation.

In many ways, Easley-O'Hara have a more convincing answer to Krashinsky's very insightful question. In their interesting model, commodities are unobservable and this unobservability creates a dilemma for the consumer. In the for-profit firm, managers will work hard to produce output but appropriate all the benefits for themselves, since consumers have no way of measuring output. In the nonprofit organization this appropriation is not possible. Instead, managers will do little work, since again consumers have no easy way to measure output. In short, unobservability leads one to a choice of theft or sloth by the provider. The optimal organizational form (nonprofit or for-profit) then depends on the underlying production function. In particular, in a world in which output is produced with little effort, nonprofits may dominate since here the sloth of the manager has little consequence.

In the main I found the Easley-O'Hara model a quite useful one. I think, however, the model could have been pushed a lot further. For example, in some situations inputs may be observable even when output is not (that is, we can see work hours). In situations in which inputs are observable and a good indictor of output, trust may be less of an issue. Easley and O'Hara should move away from total reliance on production function structure and consider the ability of various monitoring techniques for ameliorating the theft versus sloth failures.

Ben-Ner, too, is searching for a rationale for the nonprofit, but I find his explanation in some ways the least satisfying. Ben-Ner argues that in some circumstances consumers seek control over their organizations and that nonprofits are a by-product of this search for control. The Ben-Ner thesis requires two steps. First, one needs to explain why consumers seek control (that is, what's the problem); and, second, an argument has to be made as to how consumer control solves the problem. In Ben-Ner's chapter, consumers seek control for one of three reasons: the need for trust, the desire of high demanders to supplement public goods, and an attempt to improve quality. All three are, to some extent, familiar problems.

How is it that consumer control solves any of those three problems? It is clear that backward integration—perfect consumer control—would indeed go some way toward solving the trust and quality problems in particular. For most nonprofits, however, users and providers are not completely overlapping groups. Ben-Ner argues that the few may be able to "represent" the many, but, as his own model of a world of differentiated tastes suggests, this will not always be true. We need to return to Krashinsky's question and ask whether a few consumers on a nonprofit board really overcome the kinds of market failure identified here.

I found all three papers quite interesting. Nevertheless, I think all three could use a good dose of attention to the institutions, the kind of empirical awareness found in the earlier Young-Nelson[2] book on day care.

NOTES

1. Susan Rose-Ackerman, 1983. Unintended consequences: Regulating the quality of subsidized day care. *J. Policy Anal. Management* 3:14–30.
2. Dennis Young and Richard Nelson, eds., 1973. *Public Policy for Day Care for Young Children*, Lexington, Mass.: Lexington Books.

ESTELLE JAMES

Although the variety of theoretical papers on the general topic of "why nonprofits exist" adopt somewhat different theoretical paradigms, they have certain common themes. First, most theories of nonprofits concentrate on the comparative advantage of nonprofit organizations (NPOs) versus profit-making organizations (PMOs), rather than nonprofits versus government. For reasons I shall discuss below, I believe this misses an important part of the picture. Second, most theories stress that NPOs arise in response to asymmetric information between producer and consumer, by removing the incentive that profit-maximizing managers have to downgrade quality. Nonprofits may be more trustworthy and the nonprofit contract more efficient, under these circumstances. Unfortunately, this hypothesis is nontestable because we have no independent, objective measure of informational asymmetries. Third, because of the nondistribution constraint, nonprofits are considered more likely to use donations for the intended purpose. Therefore, people are allegedly willing to make humanitarian donations through NPOs, and this is seen as another raison d'etre for their existence.

The points I have just listed are so commonly made, in these papers and elsewhere, that they may be considered part of the "conventional wisdom" about NPOs. In this comment I want to raise two sets of questions about them, one from a theoretical and one from an empirical point of view.

First, on theoretical grounds, I believe the trustworthiness of NPOs and their lack of incentive to downgrade quality or divert donations is overestimated. While NPO managers cannot distribute profits directly, they can do so indirectly in the form of high wages, expense accounts, and plush working conditions. It has been noted by several economists that we would expect more of this behavior from NPOs than from profit maximizers.

In addition, another phenomenon frequently observed in NPOs undercuts the "trustworthiness" argument—the practice of cross-subsidization. In a separate chapter in this volume[1] I have argued that we would expect multiproduct NPOs to engage in two sets of activities: one set on which they earn a profit and another set, yielding direct utility to them, on which they spend this profit. With respect to the first set NPOs have as much incentive as PMOs to downgrade quality and, therefore, they are neither more nor less optimal than PMOs for these goods. Similarly, they have as much incentive as PMOs to divert donations away from such goods and toward the other set of goods from which NPO managers derive utility. Once we accept the fact that NPOs will find it in their utility-maximizing interest to cross-subsidize, and will engage in some activities simply to earn a profit (but won't tell you ahead of time which these are), the alleged superiority of NPOs under asymmetric information disappears.

Cross-subsidization does, however, give us a different efficiency rationale for the existence of NPOs. Perhaps we find NPOs in areas where cross-subsidization is desired by society, as a means of funding the production of certain public goods which would otherwise require tax funding. As we know, tax financing also has a distortionary impact that, in some cases, may be worse than that of cross-subsidization—so we are in a second-best world where NPOs may have a comparative advantage.

The second general point I wish to make is empirical rather than theoretical, and stems from my study comparing the role of NPOs in a variety of industrialized and developing countries.[2] While there are important differences across countries, the universal elements are most striking. One common observation is that nonprofit schools, hospitals, and other social services are usually founded by organized religious groups, particularly proselytizing religions, and others as a defensive reaction. There are, of course, some secular founders, also, but these are most often found in areas of excess demand, where easy opportunities exist for disguised profit distribution. Overall, religious founders have played a major role throughout the world. We see this in the origin of many private nonprofit schools and hospitals in the U.S., church schools in Catholic countries, services provided by Hindu caste groups, Moslem foundations and waqfs, etc.

Why is this important for NPO theory? It explains why nonprofits are concentrated in areas such as education and health and it suggests a particular reason why the nonprofit form is chosen by the founders. On the first point, the object is not to maximize profits but to maximize religious faith or religious adherents, and schools are one of the most important institutions of taste formation or socialization. Similarly, hospitals are a service for which people will have an urgent need at times, and so constitute a good way for religious groups to gain entry. The nonprofit form is chosen because the main objective is often not compatible with profit-maximizing behavior. For example, religious schools, set up to keep their members within the fold, may have to charge a price below the profit-maximization level in order to entice the largest numbers to enroll.

Once these religious schools and hospitals are founded, why do people attend them rather than some public or secular profit-maximizing alternative? First, many religious groups in effect have a captive audience. Parents may prefer to send their children to a school with other children who have a similar religious orientation. This tendency may be reinforced by the suppliers of the service, the religious group itself. Second, some parents may "trust" such schools because they are run by religious groups, not because of their nonprofit legal status. Third, religious groups have had access in the past to low-cost volunteer labor (for example, priests and nuns) which allows them to undercut their secular rivals. Once a school or hospital is founded by a religious group, it develops a "reputation" that may enable it to continue attracting a clientele even if its cost advantage later disappears. For all these reasons nonprofit schools and hospitals may be preferred to for-profit organizations and may be able to coexist with cheap government alternatives.

The important point is that, without resort to abstract notions of asymmetric information and avoidance of quality deterioration, this simple empirical observation can explain why the nonprofit form was chosen by founders and was able to attract consumers and why it is concentrated in certain key human-services sectors. Consumer control, also, does not play an important role (as it does in Ben-Ner) although producer control does, based on the formation of coalitions of people with similar tastes.

Second in importance to religious groups as NPO founders are other "ideological" organizations—political groups, particularly in colonial countries such as pre-independence India and Kenya, or Socialist labor unions, as in Sweden today. In both cases the nonprofit form was used, and education was a logical focal point, since taste-formation and building group membership, not profit-maximizing, was the object.

Another common empirical observation emerging from my international study is that outside of the U.S. private donations are very small. Instead, many nonprofits rely on fee-financing; and, invariably, if the nonprofit sector is large, it receives substantial government subsidies, either directly through grants or (as in the U.S.) indirectly through tax privileges. This happens particularly often in the field of education, the most common service provided by nonprofits. Thus, the major donor whose attitude we must examine is the government. Specifically, since the government is financing, why does it choose to delegate production rather than producing itself, and why does it often delegate to nonprofit rather than for-profit organizations?

The point here is that nonprofit production in many cases should be seen as an alternative to public production rather than to production by for-profits. However, these nonprofits are not funded privately but are instead heavily dependent upon public financing. My own work suggests two important reasons why subsidized private production of education is sometimes chosen by the government over pure public production. First, the cost to the government is often less. Private schools and hospitals face less political pressure against imposing fees and are able to take advantage of volunteer labor, market imperfections, etc., that help keep costs down. Second, certain groups, often religious, want to control the schools and may engage in logrolling to get this control together with full or partial government subsidies. Both producer as well as consumer interests are involved in government subsidies and a coalition of these two often brings subsidies about.

When the government subsidizes services such as education or health care, it often requires that the private schools and hospitals be nonprofit. This suggests another reason for the choice of nonprofit status by founders: they are then eligible to receive government grants and tax privileges. Why does the government prefer to donate to nonprofits rather than to for-profits? I have two tentative explanations. First, if nonprofits were established first (e.g., by religious groups), they may pressure the government to impose the nonprofit constraint, to protect them from competition. Second, I would suggest that in concentrated industries (for example, defense, space) the government deals with profit-maximizing firms since it can indeed monitor and/or regulate a small number of large firms. However, in industries characterized by many small enterprises monitoring each one by the government would be very costly. Requiring nonprofit status is an easier alternative, affording some assurance that the subsidy will indeed be spent on the intended purpose. Thus, asymmetric information and transactions costs do enter after all, once we begin to analyze government behavior. The problem, however, is not one stemming from many small donors operating in a competitive market but, rather, from one large donor—the government—with the power to set certain basic contractual terms.

Of course, given the possibility of disguised profit distribution (e.g., via higher wages) in small enterprises and cross-subsidization in larger ones, government subsidies can be diverted from their original intent just as private donations can. Thus, requirements tying subsidies to NPO status may not always be well-founded.

In summary, I have argued that the prevalence of cross-subsidization means that NPOs are not more "trustworthy" than PMOs and that the predominance of religious founders explains the choice of nonprofit status and the sectoral distribution of NPOs without reference to problems of informational asymmetry. Informational asymmetry reappears however, when government subsidies are important and provides a reason why the public sector may require NPO status as a condition for receiving subsidies.

NOTES

1. James, E. 1983 How nonprofits grow: A model. *Journal of Policy Analysis and Management* 3:350–65. Reprinted as Chapter 10 of this volume.
2. See, for example, E. James and G. Benjamin, Pubic versus private education: The Japanese experiment, PONPO Working Paper No. 81, 1984; E. James, Benefits and costs of privatized services: Lessons from the Dutch educational system, *Comparative Education Re-*

view, Dec. 1984; The private provision of public services: A comparison of Sweden and Holland, PONPO Working Paper No. 60, 1982; The nonprofit sector in comparative perspective, in W. Powell, ed. *Between the Public and the Private: The Nonprofit Sector,* New Haven: Yale University Press, 1986.

III

ENTREPRENEURSHIP AND PROFESSIONAL CONTROL

9

Entrepreneurship and the Behavior of Nonprofit Organizations: Elements of a Theory

DENNIS R. YOUNG

A fascinating divergence exists in the economic literature on nonprofit organizations between those who attempt to explain the existence of the nonprofit sector and those who model the behavior of nonprofit organizations. In particular, the rationales for nonprofits offered by Weisbrod (1975), Hansmann (1980), Douglas (1983), and others have a selfless, public-spirited quality to them. Nonprofits are seen as providers of semipublic goods, or as agents of trust for consumers whose abilities to discern quality differences are impaired. Yet those who have developed explicit models of the behavior of nonprofit organizations set quite a different tone. Scholars such as James (1983), Pauly and Redisch (1973). Niskanen (1971), Feigenbaum (1979), Tullock (1966), and Rose-Ackerman (1980) basically have assumed revenue enhancing or other self-seeking objectives on the part of management of various types of nonprofit organizations—universities, hospitals, and charities among them.

The two schools of thought are not necessarily inconsistent. One can conceive that nonprofits are established in response to particular public needs—the provision of certain public goods or the delivery of certain services that require a fiduciary relationship with the consumer. In recognition of human frailities, tax advantages are granted and certain requirements—notably the nondistribution constraint—are imposed to ensure compliance with the intended purposes. Nonetheless, some nonprofit par-

From *Nonprofit Firms in a Three-Sector Economy*, ed. by M. White, Urban Institute, Washington, D.C., 1981, pp. 135–62. The author wishes to thank John G. Simon for his encouragement, and Richard R. Nelson and Michelle J. White for their helpful suggestions. Lois Pieretti is also thanked for typing several drafts. This chapter is based on work supported by the Program on Nonprofit Organizations, Institute for Social and Policy Studies. Yale University.
Reprinted by permission of the Urban Institute.

ticipants severely test the imposed constraints and manipulate them toward selfish ends. In doing so, they may be more successful in ensuring their survival than their more selfless colleagues.

Such a view gives rise to the homogeneous (selfish) behavior school of economic modeling, which has enjoyed success in application to the profit-making sector (that is, the assumption of profit-maximization) and some popularity in public sector applications (for example, budget-maximizing models). The aforementioned nonprofit modeling efforts also derive their lineage from this school. However, as we shall suggest, the nonprofit sector seems considerably more complex in its behavior patterns than single objective function models assume. Furthermore, the preceding rationalization notwithstanding, the "selfish" models do not ultimately appear to be fully consistent with the more benevolent theories of existence. (If selfish behavior is pervasive, why does the public benefit rationale persist?) As an alternative, we sketch the beginnings of a theory based on the screening of entrepreneurs with a variety of objectives, operating in an environment which allows considerable room for discretion and alternative pursuits.

ENTREPRENEURSHIP

Although there is some variety in the literature in interpreting the concept of entrepreneurship, we shall abide here by the widely accepted definition of Joseph Schumpeter (1949) that an entrepreneur is an individual who carries out "new combinations of means of production." As such, the entrepreneur is distinguished from the ordinary manager in the sense that the entrepreneur is engaged in breaking new ground in his administrative or organizing role rather than engaging simply in customary managerial practice or routine decision-making. Thus, it is entrepreneurs who found new organizations, develop and implement new programs and methods, organize and expand new services, and redirect the activities of faltering organizations. Entrepreneurs are just one group of organizational participants, and thus entrepreneurship is but one determinant of organizational behavior. Nonetheless, entrepreneurship is a particularly strategic focal point for attempting to characterize the more global and externally visible aspects of organizational performance that concern economists and policymakers— for example, the extent to which expansion, innovation, self-aggrandizing, quality emphasizing, cost inflating, or socially responsive organizational behavior is exhibited, or not exhibited. The reasons for this are twofold: First, entrepreneurs often play the role of "founding fathers" of their organizations and leaders in their respective industries. As such, their personal values and motivations can be transferred to, and shape in a significant way, the organizations they are instrumental in establishing, building, or altering. Second, enterprise itself is the very means through which the global objectives of organizations are displayed. If an organization is growth-oriented, it will grow through enterprise. If it is self-aggrandizing or aspires to market dominance, these goals will be sought through the implementation of new enterprise. And if such characteristics are lacking, there will be a dearth of entrepreneurial activity.

Focusing on entrepreneurship implies, almost by definition, a behavioral rather than maximizing theory of organizational behavior.[1] In particular, since a conventional maximizing theory focuses on what managers routinely do, on a day-to-day basis within accepted rules and technical constraints, such a theoretical framework cannot accommodate the entrepreneurial function which is specifically oriented to changes in the ends and means of production. (This is why the entrepreneurial function is essentially ignored in classical microtheory.) Thus, our end product in this present exercise must necessarily be a description of the dynamic (motivational) tendencies of (entrepreneur-driven) agencies, rather than an end-state characterization of static equilibrium. (Hence, in the final section of this chapter, we consider tendencies toward organizational "trustworthiness" and "responsiveness" rather than an assessment of global, static efficiency.)

A complete entrepreneur-based behavioral theory would have several parts. In particular, the role of entrepreneurs and the incidence of venture must be placed in perspective. Thus, one must discern where entrepreneurship is likely to occur, how entrepreneurs will vary from one context to another, and how ventures conceived by entrepreneurs will be shaped and modified by environmental circumstances. Thus, despite the likelihood of a presumed wide margin of entrepreneurial discretion, a theory of nonprofit behavior must still focus on how entrepreneurs interact with their environments, rather than naively assume that entrepreneurial motives are reflected in pure form by the organizations and sectors they lead.

STRATEGY OF THEORY CONSTRUCTION

Our theory construction requires several interlocking steps. First, we must discover what motivates entrepreneurs to do what they do. Here we must squarely face the questions of modeling strategy referred to above. We could select a single dominant entrepreneurial objective that we may believe characterizes all entrepreneurs (analogous to the income maximizing notion implicit in the microeconomic theory of the firm) or we can identify a variety of objectives (for example, income, power, status, etc.), any of which might describe the driving motives of a given entrepreneur. An intermediate approach would be to identify instrumental or proxy variables which capture various entrepreneurial goals in a single index. For example, Niskanen's (1971) notion of budget-maximizing is actually intended to represent a package of status, power, and income seeking by bureaucrats. Another example is found in the theory of managerial discretion by Williamson (1967), Migué and Bélanger (1974), and others. In this literature, the corporate manager is assumed to maximize his own utility. However, the arguments of the postulated utility function include a few key variables such as organizational staff and emoluments which are designed as stand-ins for the status, income, and power objectives of management.

For several reasons, the single objective and proxy index approaches are rejected here as strategies for characterizing the motivations of nonprofit entrepreneurs. In the first place, these frameworks are basically oriented to managers. Yet, field work investigations have indicated that entrepreneurs need not always become managers of their enterprises. Indeed, sometimes entrepreneurs develop their ventures with the specific intent of turning them over for others to administer, and these nonmanagerial entrepreneurs are likely to have different motives than managerial types. [See Young (1985) and Grennon and Barsky (1980)]. Secondly, field work also suggests that entrepreneurial motivations are quite varied and not easily captured by one or two proxy indexes such as staff, emoluments, or profits. As noted below, there appear to be strong elements of belief orientation and even self-lessness on the part of some important entrepreneurial characters.

Economists, of course, argue that in a competitive, profit-making sector, any variety of entrepreneurial or managerial motives is of little consequence since those who choose not to maximize profits will be driven out of business. (Note this idea is at odds with the reality of entrepreneurship which inherently involves search and experimentation as opposed to the possibility of operating on some mythical absolute norm of efficient production). This argument is hedged in a less than perfectly competitive profit sector by those of the managerial discretion school who argue that while profit-making is still of paramount importance, profit levels above some acceptable minimum may be exchanged for items of personal utility. This idea has even been extended to the public sector by Roger Parks and Elinor Ostrom (1980) who model the public sector officials as trading off a certain level of net public benefits (called a "benefits residuum") against personal utility, as proxied by staff levels.

In the nonprofit sector, there certainly seems to be a large margin of entrepreneurial "discretion." However, it is not clear that there is anything closely resembling a profit criterion or a benefits residuum to which entrepreneurs are held by market or political forces, nor is it clear that proxy indicators of personal utility (such as staff or emolument levels) can adequately capture or represent the motivations which, in general, drive entrepreneurial initiatives. (Furthermore, on a more general plane, any fixed notion of maximum or discretionary profits or benefits must be based on some precise criterion of "efficient production." As such, it is necessarily at odds with the phenomenon of entrepreneurship which itself represents the very process of defining the technological frontiers and institutional conditions upon which "efficient" operation is predicted.)

This is not to say that nonprofit entrepreneurs face no constraints or are completely unaccountable for their actions. Rather, we assert that the sources of accountability and constraints on ventures are sufficiently loose, diverse, and ill-defined, as to allow for a wide spectrum of motivations and resultant behaviors. For this reason we think it is sensible to follow a more general approach to modeling entrepreneurial motivations than a single objective or managerial discretion approach would allow. In particular, we propose to specify a set of entrepreneurial stereotypes each of which personifies an important entrepreneurial objective, such as the pursuit of income, power, autonomy, security, professional accomplishment, creative achievement, strong beliefs, or simply self-identity. With this as a basis, we hope ultimately to create a theoretical structure which will specify how entrepreneurs of different stripes become sorted into various sectors, what stimulates them to venture, what constraints inhibit their actions, and how significant a long-term imprint such enterprising leaves on their organizations and sectors.

The present chapter is limited to presentation of the first two parts of such a theory—the specification of entrepreneurial prototypes, and the nature of the selection process through which entrepreneurs are filtered into particular economic sectors. A sketch of these two elements is sufficient to provide some initial insights into the behavior of nonprofits and how that behavior may be affected by public policies that alter sectoral structure.

MODELS OF ENTREPRENEURS

Next, we postulate a set of stereotypical models that seem to capture the driving motivations and styles of entrepreneurs who conceivably may choose the nonprofit sector as their base of operations. For a fuller development of the ideas presented here see Young (1983). Young (1985) and Grennon and Barsky (1980) contain the case study materials alluded to in the discussion below.

It is important to emphasize that the following models are "pure types" in the sense that each stereotype personifies a particular variety of internal motives and drive. Naturally, most real people are more easily thought of in terms of some combination of the postulated models. The models themselves are simply analytical devices for helping to derive the behavioral implications for organizations and sectors. Thus, we will analyze the world as if it were populated with a distribution of the following characters.

The *artist* is an entrepreneur who derives satisfaction directly from the creative act, that is, his own (organizational and programmatic) constructs. There are basically two types of artist: the *architect* subtype is a builder, craftsman, or tinkerer who likes to "play" with organizational "blocks." He may view his organization as a workshop for building better structures, both physical and organizational. In one case study for example, the entrepreneur takes special pride in having nurtured a small, faltering agency into a multicampus organization featuring modern facilities, computerized record-keeping, and a unique umbrella-like organizational structure.

The *poetic* subtype is a less structured and less meticulous but more cerebral entrepreneur. He may view his agenda as a blank canvas to be filled with a painting of his own conception. In one case of a Catholic sister who established a child-care agency in the South Bronx, the venture is viewed as a personal expression of individual religious philosophy and social expression.

Both types of artist like to create, to nurture, and to see things grow. And both types seek artistic expression, need to be able to identify products (ventures) as their own work, and require the freedom to pursue their initiatives in relatively unharnessed settings without restrictive oversight.

The *professional* is highly attuned to the controversies and debates that characterize his intellectual discipline and derives his satisfaction from the pursuit and development of new ideas. He will pursue ventures at the leading edge of current professional thinking in his discipline and look to that discipline for reinforcement, recognition, and direction. In the case studies, for example, entrepreneurs of this type experiment in a careful, calculated manner with such leading edge concepts as outpatient clinical services for autistic children, and common shelter care for unmarried mothers and babies.

The *believer* is an entrepreneur who is unshakably devoted to a cause and formulates his ventures and focuses his energies primarily in pursuit of that cause. The cause may be defined (as in various case studies) as help for a particular (needy) constituency (e.g., members of an orthodox community), it may be a civil libertarian or social justice concept (e.g., fighting racial discrimination), a methodological panacea (e.g., interracial adoption), or a particular strategy of social reform (e.g., community control). Or the believer may simply have a religious resolve to be of service (as in the case of various church-based entrepreneurs and one deeply religious college professor).

The *searcher* is someone who is out to prove himself and to find his niche in the world. Often, the searcher is a young person, perhaps even moderately successful in what he is doing, but unhappy and critical in his present employment and anxious to resolve the tensions between his aspirations and uncertain self-confidence. Searchers will normally shun security to find opportunities where they can better satisfy their internal yearnings for recognition and identity. In some cases, however, the searcher may be trying to resolve a midlife crisis and attach to an institutional structure that provides a new source of direction. (In one case, a searcher-entrepreneur left his post in a university to help found a Youth Bureau. In another case, such an entrepreneur left his teaching post in a private school in New York and ultimately established a therapeutic camp in North Carolina.)

The *independent* is an entrepreneur who seeks autonomy and wants to avoid shared authority and decision-making. This may derive from strong-mindedness about how things should be done and/or frustration from working under the constraints of others. The independent basically seeks to set up an organization where he or she is his own boss, free of direct internal interference or overwhelming external constraints. (In one case, a headmaster of a private school left in conflict with his proprietor and went on to establish his own institution. In another case, the entrepreneur left his post in a state children's mental hospital to form his own child-care agency.)

The *conserver* is an organizational loyalist who carries out entrepreneurial activity (during the crisis period) in order to preserve the character and viability of his agency, with which he has long been affiliated. The loyalty of the conserver derives from some combination of personal economic interest and cherished ideas, both of which have, in his mind, become embodied in or associated with the organization itself. (In one case, a career employee who had risen through the ranks of a large child-care agency, helped initiate a new program on campus to help alleviate certain criticisms the agency was subjected to by its government funding source.)

The *power seeker* derives satisfaction from climbing to the top and gaining control over large organizations. There are essentially two kinds of power seekers:

Controllers who gain satisfaction directly from having authority over others, calling the shots, and having the security of knowing what is going on under them. Such power seekers (like the one who heads one of the largest adoption agencies in New York) prefer to run tightly, centrally controlled organizations and seek to expand those organizations only so long as they can maintain the feeling of control; and

Players who like the stage or platform their organization gives them to wield power, play high-stakes poker, and gain respect and acclaim within their organizations and in the world at large. Players are more willing to delegate authority than controllers and, hence, prefer larger and larger organizations. (In two cases, for example, entrepreneurs who have expanded two of the largest social agencies have used this base to become prominent personalities in New York public affairs.)

Income seekers are those entrepreneurs primarily driven by the motive of material reward, in the form of income, future capital gain, and perquisites of office that substitute for personal expenditure. In one nursing home case, for example, the entrepreneurs are not health or social work affiliated and view their venture basically as a business enterprise. In extreme (maximizing) form, such characters constitute the basic stereotype model implicit in the conventional theory of the firm of microeconomic theory.

Note that while the list of different entrepreneurial types is rather long, there is some overlapping and gradation of objectives from one type to another. For example, controllers may be thought of as some combination of players and independents. Furthermore, believers, poets, and professionals are similar to one another in their pursuit of concepts and ideas, albeit for different reasons and via different styles. Nonetheless, for purposes of analyzing screening decisions and behavioral implications, we find it useful to maintain the distinctions.

In order to distinguish among the qualities of entrepreneurship that we may expect to find in different parts of the economy, we postulate (in the manner of Weisbrod, 1979, and Hansmann, 1980) that a "screening process" takes place which filters the various entrepreneurial types into sectors of alternative structural characteristics. Potential entrepreneurs are presumed to make career choices early in their working lives, leading to employment in particular industries. Given this selection of industries, potential entrepreneurs are seen to further sort themselves by economic sector (profit, nonprofit, and public), by becoming employed in specific organizations.

The foregoing selection decisions are hypothesized to be based on a variety of structural characteristics of industries and sectors, as elaborated below. These characteristics may be viewed as decision variables upon which potential entrepreneurs choose careers and industries in which to work. We presume that within (wide) bounds of extant opportunity and personal talent, potential entrepreneurs select careers in industries (and sectors within industries) whose characteristics most closely accommodate their basic personality types as described above. In reality this is probably an oversimplification. That is, to some degree, personal motivations may be defined and developed within field and sector contexts rather than prior to selection (for example, one might act like a believer in one context, but an income seeker in another). However, for purposes of theory construction we assume here that the latter process is of secondary importance.

SCREENING BY FIELD OR INDUSTRY

Screening at the field or industry level can be seen to depend on four structural characteristics of industries: the intrinsic character of services produced; the degree of control by professions; the degree of economic concentration; and the social priority attached to the field.

Nature of the Service

Services can be characterized as having various degrees of social involvement, technical sophistication, and requirements for creative expression. These dimensions of service character can be seen to differentially appeal to the principal motivations represented by the postulated stereotype entrepreneurs. For example, believers will be drawn to fields like social service involving high levels of social involvement, where "causes" are clear and easy to articulate, and where "crusading" is an accepted form of behavior. Searchers might also find fields of social involvement conducive to helping them find a place for themselves, by identifying with positions on social issues or with organizations having a strongly defined social purpose. Conservers may also be disproportionately drawn to such fields because it is more likely that organizations with cherished traditions of service develop in such contexts. (The settlement house provides an example of this phenomenon.)

To the contrary, fields like medical care or research characterized by high levels of technical sophistication become the domain of the professional. Here, *believerism,* at least in blatant form, is discouraged in favor of rational discourse, methodological standards, and scientific patience and scrutiny. (Believers may operate in technical fields, espousing strongly held theories and methods, but they need to cloak these concepts in the form of rationally derived proposals.)

Technically sophisticated fields may also be attractive to artistic types of the architectural variety. Sophisticated technologies—in engineering, research, or the health fields, for example—appeal to architects and can provide them with the means to create new structures, products, and services. Thus, for example, new intensive-care or computer-research technologies become the basis for building up and reorganizing whole new organizational units.

Clearly, however, fields like the arts that emphasize creativity per se, are more likely to attract the artist entrepreneurial character, especially the poetic variety. Traditionally, for example, artistically trained personnel have been the primary management and entrepreneurial source for museums, theatre, and musical enterprise. The same creative, expressionistic urges that underlie performance in the artistic fields are likely to motivate and underwrite entrepreneurial enterprise via projects that strike out in new directions and bear messages of philosophic meaning or emotional content.

Professional Control

The degree to which organized professions control employment and maintain fundamental authority and power within a given field affects the pool of entrepreneurial talent available to that field in two ways. First, disciplinary control tends to institutionalize the nature of the service as described and protect it from degradation or corruption from extradisciplinary influences (for example, the influences of commercialism or the perspectives of other disciplines). Thus, the professions reemphasize the labeling of services as technical, helping, or creative undertakings. In part, therefore, social work is a helping profession, with its implications for self-sacrifice and public service, by self-definition of the profession itself as well as the inherent character of the work. Hence, those who would enter without this perspective are discouraged (by elders and peers) from doing so. Similarly, medicine or law are self-defined as technical professions, thereby limiting entry of those with other points of view. Finally, the arts require a creative, artistic viewpoint in a vein similar to those taken by helping and technical professions. The result is to channel, even more strongly than might otherwise be the case, believers and conservers into the helping fields, professionals into the technical fields, and artists into the creative fields.

A second important way in which professional control influences the formation of the entrepreneurial pool is through the imposition of ethical values. The altruism of the helping professions, the emphasis on intellectual honesty and technical competence of the technical professions, and the elevation of artistic expression by the creative professions, constitute only part of this ethical structure. Various professions also promulgate different values with respect to money-making and achievement of power. The helping professions by virtue of their self-sacrifice ethic will tend to deemphasize wealth and power accumulation, thus discouraging power and income seekers or moderating their desires in these dimensions. Technical professions will tend to promote income enhancement as a virtue, signifying societal recognition of their importance, competence, special skills, and investments in advanced training and education. The creative fields will be relatively neutral in these domains, neither recognizing money and power as symbols of status, nor disdaining them as sins. (The exception here is the discouragement of power seeking or income seeking undertaken at the sacrifice of originality or artistic freedom.)

In practice, of course, fields or industries are controlled by discipline-oriented professions in varying degrees. Professions do tend to seek exclusive control over particular fields or industries, but the degrees of dominance they achieve vary considerably from field to field.

INDUSTRY CONCENTRATION

Service industries in which nonprofits participate vary in the degree to which they are dominated by a few large organizations. Some fields such as day care or nursing home care are characterized by the presence of many, relatively small producing organizations, none of which represents a significant proportion of the total activity. In other fields (teaching hospitals or opera companies, for example), providers are relatively few, and activity is more concentrated in a small number of organizations (in a given locality).

Related to the question of concentration is the ease of entry into a given field for new agencies or organizations. If activity is concentrated in a few organizations, this condition may reflect relatively large capital requirements for operation which in itself represents a barrier to new entry. Or, economic concentration may reflect regulatory controls which attempt to ensure, in the absence of price competition, that facilities are efficiently utilized. Thus, government may restrict the entry of new hospitals, nursing homes, day-care centers, or foster-care agencies, to those which can demonstrate need and ensure that they will not simply dilute the occupancy of existing agencies. (The case studies in child welfare reveal numerous instances of entry impediments by city and state regulatory agencies in the form of administrative and financial requirements for incorporation and proof of need for proposed services.)

As a relevant aside, we may observe that there is a rough correlation between industry structure and the distribution of activity in a given field among profit-making, nonprofit, and public sectors. Within the service fields in which nonprofits tend to participate, there is a definite tendency for activity to become more concentrated within a few organizations as one moves from the profit-making, to nonprofit, to governmental form.[2] Government tends to locate most of the activity related to a particular function (for example, child welfare or health) within a single hierarchical structure, for example, a department of health. In contrast, the proprietary services are generally not the domain of the large corporation but rather that of the small independent operator—the doctor, the educator, or the consultant who is in business for himself or with a partner or small company. Nonprofits, partly because they are often required by government to meet various organizational standards of community involvement (e.g., advisory boards) and service regulation, tend to represent a middle ground—larger and more bureaucratic than proprietaries but smaller and more fragmented than governmental agencies. In addition, ease of entry will tend to increase as one moves from government, to nonprofit, to proprietary form, at least in terms of the governmental requirements that must be fulfilled.

The effect of industry concentration is simply to make particular fields more or less attractive to each of the entrepreneurial character types. If we assume that potential entrepreneurs have some appreciation of the current (and likely future) of the structure of the fields they select or reject, then several types of potential entrepreneurs may be screened on the dimensions of industry concentration and ease of entry.

- Independents will prefer fields which are relatively unconcentrated, where small organizations are common, and where new entry is relatively easy.
- Searchers may begin their careers in concentrated fields in which they become overwhelmed or frustrated by large organizations that impose fixed career ladders and authoritarian oversight. Ultimately, they may move to fields where new entry is possible or where many small agencies exist which may be explored for their career potential.
- Power seekers will prefer concentrated fields featuring large organizations, where opportunities abound for assuming more and more responsibility over larger and larger groups of people. Player-type power seekers will prefer more concentrated fields than controller-type power seekers, because the latter fears the feeling of losing tight control as organizations grow too large. Player types, in contrast, benefit from the larger and larger platforms (more and more notoriety) provided by bigger and bigger organizations.
- Conservers will prefer fields of modest concentration which feature organizations large, stable, and mature enough to have established traditions and provide a sense of economic security but which are not so large as to have become impersonal and institutional or mechanical in character.
- Professionals will tend to select fields which are moderately to highly

concentrated so as to provide adequate resource bases to pursue their endeavors. However, professionals may seek to avoid very highly concentrated fields if they perceive the large organizations within those fields to be inimical to the flexibility required for professional development. Professionals will also avoid fields which are so fragmented as to offer little promise of resource aggregation sufficient to support experimental activity.

• Artists will tend to select fields which exhibit a moderate to low concentration of activity. Like the professional, the artist will tend to seek sectors in which organizations have access to a resource base sufficient to support his penchant for building and program development, yet which are small enough so that new endeavors are both noticeable and identifiable as one's own product. The architect-type of artist prefers a sector that will utlimately support programs of significant size, while the poet normally prefers sectors with small agencies, preferring to be unencumbered by administrative responsibilities and constraints and free to explore a variety of ideas.

• The income seeker has no intrinsic preferences regarding the relative concentration of activity, size of organizations, or entry possibilities in a given field. Unconcentrated fields can present income opportunities through investment in the formation or building up of small enterprises, while concentrated fields may present opportunities for internal advancement in large agencies, matched by salary and benefit increases. Once having entered a weakly concentrated field, however, an income seeker may work toward its concentration, as a strategy of income maximization.

Social Priority

In terms of both the allocation of economic resources and the more elusive concept of prestige, society tends to attach greater importance and social status to some fields than others. For example, among fields in which nonprofits tend to participate, health and scientific research tend to be elevated (in the U.S. at least), while education and social service have had more precarious positions in the public's mind and in the economy. In any case, it is logical that the status of a given field will influence career choices and, hence, the types of entrepreneurs available to particular fields.

Differences in social priority among fields will have the strongest effects on two entrepreneurial types—income seekers and power seekers. Income seekers will look toward rich or expanding fields as presenting the greatest opportunities for material reward. Power seekers, especially those of the player variety, will see such fields as the locus of "where the action is." That is, they will seek the largest stage for achieving notoriety and influence over the largest and most important sets of people and resources.

Other entrepreneurial types may also be influenced in their career choice by the social status of alternative fields, but to a lesser extent than power or income seekers. Professionals and artists may see the more prestigious fields as providing stronger resource bases on which they can pursue intellectual or creative activity. Alternatively, searchers may see the higher status fields as larger vistas to explore in their efforts to find more satisfying careers.

The independent and believer types will be relatively indifferent to the social priority attached to alternative fields. The independent essentially seeks autonomy and may indeed tend to avoid fields that are in the spotlight, preferring more staid environments, although initially he may find the opportunity to establish himself in a high-status field where resources are available. The believer is even more predictable in this dimension. While fields of greater social priority may provide wider vistas for the taking up of social causes or the sponsorship of particular policies, the believer may just as well attach himself to fields he feels are underserved and require new attention by society.

SCREENING BY SECTOR

The foregoing field (industry) choice process, is one of two basic (intermingled) processes of selection through which the pool of entrepreneurial talent available for enterprise in a given sector is formed. The second process is employment choice in which individuals select organizational contexts in which to work and gain (preentrepreneurial) experience. This employment choice implies a decision on sector, that is, whether a given individual chooses to work in the commercial, nonprofit, or government sector, since any organization will necessarily fall into one of these categories. That is, once having selected a field, the potential entrepreneur will often have some choice of sector at the employment stage, since many fields are not totally dominated by a single sector. This seems especially true of fields in which nonprofits tend to participate.[3]

There is, however, a "chicken and egg" quality to the field and sector selection process. We observed earlier, for instance, how the selection by field may be strongly influenced by sectoral considerations. In particular, the predominance of a given sector in some field is likely to reflect itself in certain structural characteristics (for example, the concentration of economic activity, entry conditions, and size of organizations) upon which field selection may be based. In a similar manner, sector choice may depend on the opportunity structure of a field. That is, as a historical matter, within any given field, one sector may be larger and more vital than another, at a given point in time. The frequency of employment opportunities will vary accordingly. For example, until the mid-twentieth century when public universities began to develop, opportunities in higher education were concentrated very heavily in the nonprofit sector. In child care, a similar pattern holds, while for nursing homes, the proprietary sector developed much later than the nonprofit or public sectors.

Government funding or licensing policies often underlie these patterns. For example, some states (such as New York) refuse to certify proprietary foster care agencies. To the contrary, programs such as Medicaid have underwritten the growth of proprietary enterprise, while other legislation (for example, state higher education programs) has sponsored the development of public systems (universities).

While latent entrepreneurs of various types may have strong leanings by sector, they may have selected their fields for other reasons. If those fields are dominated by one sector or another, the potential entrepreneurs will be limited in their ability to exercise their sector preferences and will be forced to become employed in less preferred sectors. As we discuss later, the selected sector will then include motivational types that it would not otherwise attract. Given a more open opportunity structure, latent entrepreneurs would be sorted into more homogeneous motivational sets by sector.

Given some global distribution of opportunities, however, and assuming some choice of sector does obtain, there are various other factors that will tend to sort out entrepreneurial types. These factors—income potential, internal bureaucratic structure, and service ethic—tend to vary fairly systematically by sector across a wide range of fields.

Income Potential

The nonprofit sector is by definition restrainted by the so-called nondistribution constraint which formally precludes appropriation of differences between revenues and expenditures as "profits," by managers or trustees. As Hansmann and others have argued, the existence of this constraint discourages income enhancing in the nonprofit sector by providing a "signal" for expected (normative) behavior and the threat of legal penalties for blatant violation.

Thus, income potential is nominally more restricted and blunted in the nonprofit sector than it is in the profit sector. To the contrary, income maximizing behavior in the proprietary sector is the prescribed norm and may be (legally) implemented directly through profits, appreciation of capital (that is, capital gains), as well as through salary and perquisite enhancement and control over input factors. Of course, the relative potentials for income enhancement between the profit and nonprofit sectors will depend on market factors, including the marketability of services and the level of competition, as well as on tax and other revenue considerations. In some fields, nonprofits can conceivably combine tax concessions and access to philanthropy, to generate income potentials in excess of proprietary capabilities. However, the appropriation of surpluses as personal income will presumably be discouraged by legal restraints and accountability to the groups (government, donors, consumers) which implicitly enforce the conditions under which such special advantages are granted.

Income potentials and (normative) expectations in the public sector are the least systematic of the three sectors. Corruption and remuneration levels of public employees tend to vary considerably over time and place. Significantly, in some parts of the public sector (for example, within the federal government and some state and large local governments) civil service and political appointee pay scales may be sufficiently attractive to warrant the attention of those whose career objectives center heavily on income enhancement. Much depends on the particular political conditions associated with given parts of the public sector, including the wealth and level of demand for public goods by the relevant constituencies, the strength of public sector unions, and the tolerance levels for corruption.

Bureaucratic Structure

Within a given field, the profit-making, nonprofit, and public sectors tend to vary according to their dependence on hierarchy and political entanglement and, hence, the flexibility, independence, and authority levels which staff members and officials can maintain. Earlier, for example, we noted the tendency of economic activity in service fields to become more concentrated and, hence, more hierarchical, as one moved from the proprietary to nonprofit to government sector.

It is not simply the dependence on hierarchy, however, that differentiates the organizational (bureaucratic) structure of the three sectors. The degree of interaction and restraint from oversight bodies, and with the body politic at large, also varies fairly systematically by sector. Agencies in each sector are normally associated with a board or council of trustees in one form or another. In the public sector, a government bureau is accountable to a legislature, or subcommittee thereof. Nonprofit agencies are normally required to have boards of directors or trustees composed of responsible community members, in whom the ultimate well-being of the corporation is entrusted. In the proprietary sector, corporate responsibility resides in a board of directors composed of shareholders, usually including the executive director himself.

Within each sector, the authority asserted by these oversight bodies varies considerably, perhaps most widely in the nonprofit sector. Nonprofit agency boards of directors are known to range from those whose officers insist on major day-to-day influence on policymaking to those which are virtually rubber stamps for the executive director. Within the public and proprietary sectors there is less variance. Legislative committees tend to assert a reasonable level of interference, if not control, over an agency's budget, and executives are normally well advised to pay homage to their legislative benefactors. In the proprietary sector, the executive usually has very strong, often dictatorial control, commensurate with his financial interest and/or ability to keep the enterprise remunerative. Thus, in general it may be asserted that the requirement of executives to share authority and to be constrained by oversight bodies increases systematically from proprietary, to nonprofit, to public sectors.

A similar spectrum obtains with respect to entanglement of a more general political nature. The proprietary agency director must be careful to cultivate certain relationships in order to secure zoning, licensing, or other approvals that he may need for operation. He may have to be careful not to arouse community opposition to his operation if he is dealing with sensitive areas such as services to the retarded or delinquent. He may also be required to follow particular rules and reporting protocols if he decides to accept government funding. However, the proprietary director will be fundamentally less entangled and constrained by political considerations and government regulation than his nonprofit or public sector counterparts.

The nonprofit agency is based on the notion of a public purpose for some constituency whether it be a particular neighborhood, ethnic or religious group, or those interested or needing a particular type of service. As such, its board of directors, staff and volunteers are more likely to have roots in this constituency and to bring a strong element of political responsiveness and responsibility to the agency itself. Even those nonprofit agencies which might be incorporated without such grassroots support will normally be required by government to constitute a board of trustees representative of the public purpose for which nonprofit status is granted. As such there will at least be a nominal sensitivity to political pressures and community interests by the nonprofit. Furthermore, in the now common case where the nonprofit receives public funds and/or is chosen by government as a vehicle for public service delivery, the nonprofit will tend to become enmeshed in the broader spectrum of political interests and regulatory requirements of the granting government agency.

By far the most overwhelming set of political constraints is faced by decision-makers and program developers in public agencies whose actions must often reflect partisan, geographic, ethnic, and other political sensitivities. Thus, new policies or program initiatives must be checked or modified for their effects on multiple groups before action can be taken.

Overall, therefore, sectoral differences in organizational structure provide differential opportunities to those potential entrepreneurs whose ultimate motives concern power, autonomy, and flexibility. In general, the public sector is the most concentrated in terms of hierarchy and outside restraint on freedom of action. The proprietary sector tends to be least intense in these dimensions. The nonprofit sector constitutes a broad middle ground.

Service Ethic

Just as the different sectors vary in the norms which they promote (signal) with respect to money-making, they also vary in the ideals or service orientation they purport to stand for. While such normative codes may not in themselves be powerful influences on behavior, their importance as signaling devices for latent entrepreneurs at the stage of employment choice cannot be ignored.

Each sector has its lofty traditions and positive self-images. In government, it is the notion of public service—devotion to country and community through the competent provision of essential services. The concept of "public interest" nominally underlies the value system for government work.

Traditionally, the profit-making sector has been the domain of the rug-ged individualist, the self-made man who works hard for his living and makes it on his own. It is the domain of commerce, subject to the harsh discipline of the marketplace, where activity is frankly viewed as business and only secondarily as service. It is where the fortunes may be made, but where every cent must be earned; where free enterprise holds court and govern-ment is viewed as an intrusive and corrupting influence. In the modern era of large, multinational corporations and complex entanglements between government and private industry, this image has faded, but it still main-tains an essence of viability, especially in the arena of small business.

The nonprofit sector has its roots in voluntarism, charity, and commu-nity. It is a mode of organization based on the notion of voluntary mobi-lization of close-knit communities to assist those of its members in need or in trouble. Whether it be a social agency, hospital, or volunteer fire de-partment, the nonprofit agency is seen to be supported by contributions, manned by volunteers or those who would work for some sacrifice in pay, controlled by community elders, and administered by those whose interests are benevolent and specifically attuned to local needs. As with the folklore imagery of other sectors, the nonprofit's idealized image has also been tar-nished, as the application of this organizational device has been modified, extended, and intertwined with other sectors over time. Still, the imagery continues to bear some semblance of fact and, hence, to serve as a signal to community-minded, socially concerned idealists.

The relatively systematic differences in income potential, bureaucratic structure, and service ethic across sectors serve as screening factors at the employment stage for latent entrepreneurial types along the following ba-sic lines:

Income seekers will tend to be attracted to the proprietary sector where the avenues for money-making are more numerous and open and where profit-making per se is a socially approved (and legal) mode of behavior. This tendency will of course be modified to the degree that the market or regulatory environment restricts financial gain in the profit sector, and/or generous income streams and salary opportunities are channeled to the nonprofit or government sectors.

Independents will also tend to gravitate to the proprietary sector because of the less overbearing requirements in that sector for shared decision-making, and accountability to others, and because the lower concentration (less hierarchy, easier entry) of activity in that sector provides greater op-portunity for achieving positions of executive autonomy. This tendency will be modified to the extent that small nonprofits with rubber stamp boards in some areas are able to insulate themselves from outside pressures and, hence, attract independents. In few cases, however, will independents be attracted to government, where hierarchical and political accountability arrangements are omnipresent.

Power seekers will generally gravitate to the public sector for the same reasons that independents reject this alternative. Government exhibits ma-jor hierarchical structures and arenas of public visibility in which power seekers may climb to greater and greater heights of control and notoriety. This will be especially appealing to the player-type power seeker. The controller type of power seeker is more complex, however. While the opportunities for expanding control in the public sector appeal to him, at some level it becomes overwhelming. Major departments may be too large to control, and accountability relationships too complex to manage. The latent controller type, therefore, may decide that organizations in the nonprofit sector present more tenable alternatives.

The latent believer is an idealogue who is most likely to be attracted by the service ethic of the nonprofit or public sectors, but whose uncompromising social reform/social change attitudes are more likely to be accommodated by the less overbearing accountability structure of the nonprofit arena. Thus, the nonprofit sector is likely to employ more than its share of believers.

Conservers, too, are most likely to be employed in the nonprofit sector, for two reasons. First, conservers have a loyalty to organizations and traditions more consistent with the nonprofit and public sectors than the proprietary sector. (An exception here is the proprietary "family business" which may invoke conserver-type loyalties in the profit sector.) Second, conservers are more likely to be attracted by the smaller size and greater informality of organizations in the nonprofit sector, where traditions and personal relationships are more easily cultivated and maintained.

Like the power seekers, the two varieties of artist are also somewhat different in their likely employment preferences. Neither the poet nor architect is likely to be heavily attracted to the public sector since each desires to use activities as personal expressions of accomplishment. In the public sector, more hands are likely to stir the stew because of the greater hierarchy and complexity of accountability arrangements, with consequently less opportunity for personal identification with the product. Both artist types can be accommodated by the relatively less encumbered structure of the nonprofit sector, but the poetic type may be more confined to this sector than the architectural type. In particular, the architectural type is more concerned with the fact that he is building than what he is building. Hence, opportunities in the profit sector can be as appealing as those available in the nonprofit sector. For the poetic type, however, activity is more a matter of personal feeling and expression of values than pride of technique. The poetic type is more likely to feel inhibited by the rigor and restraint of the profit criteria than his architectural counterparts and more comfortable in the nonprofit sector where the diversity of support sources is more likely to yield organizations indulgent of diverse ideas, irrespective of direct market potential or political content.

Post-Employment-Choice Sector Mobility

By focusing on sector choice at the employment stage, we do not wish to imply that sector selection is necessarily made, once and for all, at an early stage of career development for latent entrepreneurs. Indeed for certain types, notably searchers, entrepreneurship occurs in the process of sorting out personal proclivities through employment change. Furthermore, for other entrepreneurial types, employment and sector change may represent a career pattern consistent with clear personal objectives. The most obvious example of this is the case of power seekers. The careers of power seekers are likely to exhibit a "climbing" pattern, with each successive job representing a step upward in terms of status, position, and authority over people and resources. This ladder may involve crossovers between sectors. For example, a power seeker may begin in a relatively small nonprofit agency, move to another more important one, and ultimately move into government at a high level. Or the pattern may crisscross sectoral borders several times, depending on the timing of opportunities. Because more open advancement opportunities may exist at the lower rungs of the nonprofit sector but more powerful positions at the top of the public sector, the careers of power seekers often do begin in the nonprofit sector but ultimately gravitate toward government. For reasons noted, this will tend to be more strongly the case for player than controller types.

A similar argument may be made for income seekers, with different directional patterns, however. This variety of entrepreneur may begin his career in a public agency, or perhaps nonprofit, where initial salaries may be better and where he can gain professional experience and "learn the ropes" of service provision. Later, having gained experience and perhaps accumulated some capital, he may decide to move his career into the proprietary domain. This is a common career pattern for physicians, psychologists, and academic consultants, for example. Overall, the mixed-career patterns of power seekers and income seekers complicate the basic sorting tendencies discussed earlier, by postponing and inhibiting them to a degree, rather than changing the basic directions.

Finally, it is worth reiterating certain points concerning the fineness with which potential entrepreneurs are able to match their preferences with the structural characteristics of different fields and sectors. Clearly, given the multiple dimensions on which screening decisions take place, and the relatively few distinct choices a given individual can make, the matches between entrepreneurial objectives and sectors will necessarily be imperfect. Furthermore, given the time span that may transpire between employment screening and enterprise, it is likely that some entrepreneurs will undergo changes in preferences as they become locked into particular sectors, resulting in additional matching imperfections.

IMPLICATIONS

There are several related inferences upon which we may speculate regarding the behavior of nonprofit organizations, given the nature of motivation and selection phenomena suggested in this chapter. In the most general terms, we can conclude that behavior of organizations in the nonprofit sector is not a fixed, immutable phenomenon; rather, it is a relative matter which depends substantially on both the nature of an industry and the parallel opportunities and characteristics of adjacent activity in the proprietary and public sectors as well. As such, we may surmise that public policies which affect the relative character of an industry and/or the relative opportunities among sectors, will change nonprofit behavior by altering the screening of different entrepreneurial types. Several such policies may be contemplated. For example, a policy which requires rigorous professional credentialing of managerial industry personnel may be expected to differentially screen out certain entrepreneurial types (e.g., searchers) and, hence, affect aggregate behavioral outcomes.

Of perhaps greater interest, some government policies are specifically directed toward the nonprofit sector. For example, government funding programs (such as arts funding by the National Endowment) may require nonprofit status as a condition of eligibility. Alternatively, government may simply require (as it does for child care in some states, and has been proposed for nursing homes) that all suppliers in a given industry be nonprofit. For purposes of illustrating how our theory potentially leads to empirically testable and socially relevant hypotheses, we shall briefly analyze implications of the latter policy.

Government policies which require that certain services be provided on a nonprofit basis and which proscribe the delivery of those services through other sectors, can be expected to have two possible (conflicting) effects:

1. Such policies may discourage certain entrepreneurial types from entering a given field or industry entirely; and
2. Such policies will result in a more heterogeneous entrepreneurial mix within the nonprofit sector.

Given that industry structure is only one of several important variables that we have hypothesized to screen entrepreneurial types in the choice of fields, it seems highly likely that the second of the above effects will dominate the first. Thus, for a given field, a nonprofit sector which operates in parallel with a profit-making and/or governmental sector will tend to be more homogeneous in its motivational tendencies than it would be if it monopolized the field. This could have several specific implications:

Income maximizing behavior can be expected to be more intense in nonprofit sectors which do not compete with a proprietary sector offering similar services. In such nonprofit sectors, the nondistribution constraint may be severely tested. Thus, as an empirically testable matter, we would expect that given a fixed level of policing and regulation of the nondistribution constraint, there would be a greater incidence of indirect profiteering and fraud in such nonprofit sectors. In particular, we may anticipate more indulgence in such practices as the inflation of managerial salaries and managerial self-dealing in the supply of inputs to nonprofits in this case, compared to the circumstances where the profit sector is available for parallel activity.

• Power-seeking (empire-building, expansive) behavior may be more intense in a nonprofit sector that does not compete with a public sector. Thus, as an empirical matter, we would expect to observe a growing concentration of activity in such a nonprofit sector, that is, an increasing in size and decreasing in the number of nonprofit organizations, relative to what would occur if there were a competing public sector.

• Autonomy-seeking (independent) behavior may be more intense in a nonprofit sector that does not compete with a proprietary sector. This may take the form of pressure to create new agencies within the nonprofit arena. Or, if new entry is discouraged by government controls or high cost, it may take the form of creating semiautonomous enclaves within larger, hierarchical nonprofit structures. Thus, as an empirically observable matter, we would expect to see decentralization and fragmentation of such a sector over time, manifested in terms of declining size, increasing number, and/or flattening of the hierarchical structure of member organizations, relative to what would occur if there were a competing proprietary sector.

For other types of entrepreneurial motivation, it is less clear whether confinement of industry activity to nonprofits would have a significant effect on the behavior of that sector. Artists, professionals, believers, searchers, and conservers, for example, seem likely to be fairly concentrated in the nonprofit arena, assuming available opportunities, no matter what other choices exist. Nonetheless, the sectorwide behavioral implications of these motivational types are also important. For example, in the event that the nonprofit accountability structure permits substantial internal entrepreneurial discretion, we may anticipate the following kinds of potentially worrisome patterns (in addition to those posed above for income and power seekers and independents):

• Artists of the architect variety may tend to build programs, facilities, and organizational structures beyond the requirements of client groups;

• Professionals may pursue esoteric programs of intellectual interest but marginal value to the constituent groups sponsoring the nonprofit organizations in which they operate;

• Believers and poets may lead organizations to overinvest in pet strategies, ideas, or causes, which from a more global point of view may be wasteful or misguided; and

• Conservers may delay hard decisions concerning the redirection of obsolescent policies or programs, by appealing to conservative constituent elements in their organizations and failing to provide an accurate picture of internal difficulties. Such potential behaviors raise the further policy question of how effectively the nonprofit accountability structure can control discretionary activity for those enterpreneurs screened into that sector. In particular we may inquire as to what effects particular policing initiatives—such as the strengthening of accountability relationships between executives and the boards of directors of nonprofit organizations, or the superimposition of community planning agencies (e.g., health and welfare councils) onto nonprofit sector decision-making regimes—may be expected to have in restraining the different varieties of potential entrepreneurial excess. Such an analysis is beyond the scope of the present paper and requires a detailed consideration of how each type of entrepreneur interacts with other constituents of the nonprofit organization. As presented above, our screening and motivation theory is essentially positive in thrust (that is, descriptive of the behavioral patterns likely to emerge under alternative policies and structural conditions). For policy purposes, however, a normative view would also be useful. In particular, we may ask if delivery of services via nonprofits produces outcomes which are in some sense more "socially desirable." This requires that we evaluate the various patterns of discretionary behavior that are predicted to take place under particular conditions of screening and policing of nonprofit constraints. Clearly, however, differentiating "unproductive" discretionary behavior from that which is nominally desirable is a very tenuous exercise. Not much can be said in the abstract, without reference to the constituent groups (clients, donors, trustees, funders) responsible for holding nonprofit organizations accountable or to some overriding social criteria. Nonetheless, the issue of potentially wayward discretionary behavior is a useful one to raise because it relates to two normative criteria of fundamental importance to researchers and policymakers concerned with the nonprofit sector. Specifically,

1. Under what circumstances can nonprofits be considered "trustworthy" in delivering services as promised and avoiding fraud and quality depreciation as strategies of self-aggrandizement?
2. Under what circumstances will nonprofits be "responsive" to demands for new, altered, or expanded services as expressed by market forces or governmental funding programs?

The motivation and screening of entrepreneurial activity is not a sufficient basis for providing a complete perspective on these questions. For example, it remains to be determined what specific conditions are responsible for igniting such initiative, what kinds of boundaries are set on enterprise by constituent and regulating groups, and how the initial intent of entrepreneurs becomes dispersed or diffused over time. But the screening and motivation processes described here may be a reasonable starting point. In particular, each variety of entrepreneur—potentially selected into or out of the nonprofit sector—has been seen to imply a particular behavior pattern (i.e., one that is more or less inspiring of trust and sensitive to current exigencies as expressed by economic demands.) Thus, policies which affect the alternative opportunities in industries and sectors may, conceivably at least, be adjusted or "tuned" to achieve some socially desired balance in these performance criteria for the nonprofit sectors or for industries as a whole.

NOTES

1. This point was suggested to me by Richard R. Nelson.
2. Evidence on this matter may be gathered from scattered and spotty sources. For hospitals in 1976, the *Statistical Abstract of the U.S.* (1978) indicates that for-profit institutions averaged 98.3 beds, compared to 195 for nonprofit, 119 for local government, and 611 for state government.

For nursing homes in 1973, Dunlop (1979) documents average sizes 69, 85, and 110 beds, for proprietary, nonprofit, and governmental, respectively.

In education in 1976, the *Statistical Abstract* (1978) indicates enrollments only for public vs. private (including nonprofit and proprietary) institutions. For elementary schools the figures are 422 public vs. 218 nonpublic; for secondary schools, 573 public vs. 324 nonpublic; for higher education, 6317 public vs. 1423 nonpublic.

For museums, size measurement is complicated by difficulties in reconciling estimates of full-time, part-time, and volunteer staff, and institutional definitions. In terms of operating budget for 1971–1972, *Museums USA* (1974) reports that private nonprofits slightly outnumber public museums in the category under $100,000, whereas the reverse holds for the $100,000–$250,000 category. Equal representation is found in the category over $250,000. In the special category of museums attached to educational institutions, a sharp differential exists between larger public and smaller private museums.

In general, better definitions are needed to effect realistic size comparisons of public, nonprofit, and proprietary activities. For example, in day care for young children, the postulated intersector size differentials would be clearer if public kindergartens were compared to nonprofit day-care centers and nursery schools, and to proprietary nursery schools and day-care homes. In museums, proprietary art galleries might be compared to nonprofit museums, to government departments responsible for public museums, and so on.

3. For example, according to the American Hospital Association (see Miller, 1980), general hospitals were distributed across sectors in 1976 as follows: 35 percent government, 52 percent nonprofit, 13 percent proprietary. For psychiatric hospitals, the figures are 59 percent, 17 percent, and 23 percent, respectively. For nursing homes the distribution is 8 percent, 19 percent, and 73 percent.

In education, according to U.S. HEW statistics in 1976 (see Miller, 1980), elementary schools split 82 percent/18 percent public vs. nonpublic, whereas secondary schools divided 87 percent/13 percent.

In higher education, according to Nielsen (1979), the division in enrollments between public and private, nonprofit institutions has gone from 50 percent/50 percent in 1950 to 78 percent/22 percent in favor of public institutions in 1977. For medical schools in 1977, the division was 57 percent/43 percent in favor of public institutions.

According to Netzer (1978), 85 percent of the arts sector (broadly defined) in terms of annual expenditure is commercial, as opposed to nonprofit or public. In museums, according to *Museums U.S.A.* (1974) for 1971–72, about 56 percent of museums were private nonprofit, compared to 34 percent government, and 5 percent attached to private educational institutions. (Proprietary galleries or exhibitions are excluded from the count.)

REFERENCES

Douglas, James. 1983. *Why Charity? The Case for a Third Sector,* Beverley Hills, Sage.
Dunlop, Burton. 1979. *The Growth of Nursing Home Care,* Lexington, Massachucetts: D.C. Heath and Company.
Feigenbaum, Susan. 1979. Some inter-industry relationships in the nonprofit sector: Theory and empirical testing. Department of Economics. Claremont Men's College.
Grennon, Jacqueline, and Robert Barsky. 1980. An exploration of entrepreneurship in the

field of nursing home care for the elderly. Institution for Social and Policy Studies. Yale University. Draft.

Hansmann, Henry. 1980. The role of non-profit enterprise. *Yale Law J.* 89:835–98. Reprinted as Chapter 3 of this volume.

James, Estelle. 1983. How nonprofits grow: A model, *J. of Policy Analysis and Management*, 3:350–63. Reprinted as Chapter 10 in this volume.

Migué, Jean-Lui, and Gerard Bélanger. 1974. Toward a general theory of managerial discretion. *Public Choice*, 17:27–47.

Miller, Lohr E. 1980. A quantitative guide to the non-profit sector of the U.S. economy. Institution for Social and Policy Studies. Program on Nonprofit Organizations. Yale University. Draft.

Museums U.S.A.: A Survey Report. 1974. National Research Center of the Arts for the National Endowment for the Arts.

Netzer, Dick. 1978. *The Subsidized Muse.* Cambridge: Cambridge University Press.

Nielsen, Waldemar A. 1979. *The Endangered Sector.* New York: Columbia University Press.

Niskanen, William. 1971. *Bureaucracy and Representative Government.* Aldine-Atherton.

Parks, Roger B. and Elinor Ostrom. March 1980. Towards a model of the effect of inter- and intraorganizational structure on public bureau service outputs. Workshop in Political Theory and Policy Analysis, Indiana University. Paper no. T-80.

Pauly, Mark and Michael Redisch. March 1973. The not-for-profit hospital as a physician's cooperative. *American Economic Review.* 63:87–99.

Rose-Ackerman, Susan. 1980. United Charities: an Economic Analysis. *Public Policy* 28:325–50.

Schumpeter, Joseph A. 1949. *The theory of economic development.* Cambridge: Harvard University Press.

Statistical Abstract of the United States. 1978. U.S. Department of Commerce. Bureau of the Census. Washington, D.C.

Tullock, Gordon. 1966. Information without profit. *Papers on Non-Market Decision Making*, Blacksburg, Va.: Center for the Study of Public Choice.

Weisbrod, Burton. Toward a theory of the voluntary nonprofit sector in a three-sector economy. In Edmund S. Phelps, ed. *Altruism, morality, and economic theory.* New York Russell Sage Foundation, 1975.

———. October 1979. Economics of institutional choice. Conference on Institutional Choice and the Private Nonprofit Sector, University of Wisconsin, Madison.

Williamson, Oliver. 1967. *The economics of discretionary behavior.* Markham.

Young, Dennis R. 1983. *If Not for Profit, for What?* Lexington, Mass.: D.C. Heath.

———. 1985. *Casebook of Management for Non-Profit Organizations: Entrepreneurship and Organizational Change in the Human Services,* New York: Haworth Press.

10
How Nonprofits Grow: A Model

ESTELLE JAMES

In recent months much attention has been focused on the possibility that nonprofit organizations might help to fill the void, as federal and state governments curtail some of their programs in education, housing, health services, support for the arts, and similar areas.

To evaluate the desirability of a public policy that shifts responsibility from government toward nonprofit organizations, one needs to understand how such organizations function. There have been numerous studies of how business organizations operate, presumably bent on producing the largest possible profit over the long run. And the number of studies of the operations of government agencies is rapidly growing. But only recently have economists paid much attention to the nonprofit sector.[1]

Nonprofit organizations are, in a sense, a hybrid of business enterprise and government, and different from both. Unlike the for-profit organizations (but like government), the nonprofit entity has no owners to whom it distributes its profits; instead, all of the organization's resources must be used internally. Unlike the government (but like for-profit organizations), nonprofit entities must raise their funds on a voluntary basis; they do not enjoy the powers of compulsory taxation. The net effect is to produce a pattern of behavior in the nonprofit organization that differs from the behavior of the other two.

The author gratefully acknowledges support received on this project from the Program on Non-Profit Organizations, Yale University. Suggestions for improving an earlier draft were received from a PONPO Workshop, a Wilson Center workshop, and from my colleague, Egon Neuberger.

Reprinted by permission of John Wiley & Sons. From *Journal of Policy Analysis and Management* 2 (1983):350–65. The Appendix, which appeared in the original article and which develops the proofs for some of the arguments made about cross-subsidization and NPO response to price changes, has been omitted from this volume.

CHOOSING ITS SERVICES

How It Chooses

What distinguishes the nonprofit organization most clearly from the other two organizational types are the factors it takes into account in deciding what services to produce and in what quantities. For example, a nonprofit organization may run a school of some stated capacity for handicapped children, and a convalescent home of some given capacity for the elderly; it may provide standard or deluxe service in either institution. These decisions may be made by a group of members, by a professional staff, or by a voluntary board of trustees. There may be struggles among them over the choice of services; but for present purposes, let us assume that eventually they speak with one voice, the voice of the manager. How is the manager likely to make these choices?

The manager has preferences regarding the services that the organization produces because he cares which activities he spends his time on, because certain products are considered more prestigious than others, or because he harbors a genuinely altruistic belief that these products are important to society. These preferences may be influenced by the background and training of the manager, by the internal structure of the organization, by the source of the volunteered time and money, or by other factors. The manager's job is to satisfy these preferences to the highest possible degree; in economic jargon, the manager wishes to maximize the utility function of the organization.

Assume that the nonprofit organization receives revenues that vary according to the level of services delivered, either because the organization charges a fee for such services or because it receives subsidies that are based on the level of services; private hospitals are a case in point. In addition, some of the organization's revenue may be fixed irrespective of the level of its services; this holds, for example, for well-endowed private universities and museums. The manager (our collective designation for the director, board members, and professional staff) has no way of altering the prices, subsidies, or costs associated with the services being delivered. Then the only way in which he can increase his benefits is by altering the mix of services to emphasize those that best reflect his preferences. This will lead him to produce more than a profit-making firm would of certain services, and less of others. (It follows that in situations where the profit-making firm produces the "right" amount of a service—that is, at the point where marginal social benefit equals marginal social cost—turning the output decision over to a nonprofit organization would probably produce a less desirable result.)

But there is a limit to which the manager can respond to his preferences—a limit imposed by the fact that the aggregate income of the organization, variable or fixed, must cover the aggregate variable and fixed costs of the organization. This brings us to one of the fundamental characteristics of nonprofit organizations. Because the manager has tastes, preferring to deliver one service rather than another, and because some of the preferred services may not cover their own costs, these organizations characteristically find themselves taking on profit-making activities that will cover the deficit incurred in other activities. This phenomenon, of course, represents the classic case of cross-subsidization; and it is a factor that must be given substantial weight in projecting how nonprofit organizations are likely to perform when providing public services.

Cross-Subsidization in Practice

The concept of cross-subsidization helps us understand certain well-known behavioral characteristics of nonprofit organizations in the fields of education, health, and the arts.

Consider the case of university education. Assume that undergraduate education, graduate training, and research can be viewed as separable activities. On this assumption, if one measures the resources (especially faculty time) devoted to each, it turns out that the average tuition paid by undergraduates exceeds the cost of their education, while the opposite is the case for graduate students. The undergraduate program employs large classes, and the graduate program small classes, while research is achieved mainly by diverting the faculty from teaching through a reduced teaching load. Teaching undergraduates, therefore, is often a profitable activity carried out in order to obtain the resources for the loss-making graduate and research programs.[2] Moreover, undergraduate class sizes are higher at universities than at colleges and have risen through time as graduate studies and research have grown. Finally, although nonprofit institutions can be found that specialize entirely in undergraduate education, very few can be found that specialize entirely in graduate education or basic research. All these observations are consistent with the notion that nonprofit organizations regularly engage in cross-subsidization, and the more they wish to carry out loss-making activities, the more they must seek out profitable activities to provide them with the necessary resources.

The coupling of profitable with unprofitable activities is observed not only in education but also in health. Nonprofit hospitals often couple loss-making activities that generate prestige with more routine profitable activities; for example, profits from appendectomies may be used to finance research and to maintain expensive underutilized facilities such as open heart surgery units.[3]

Similarly in the arts: in recent years, museums have heavily promoted gift shops and special exhibitions; these have been looked on as the financial salvation of these organizations, while being criticized for drawing attention from other pursuits on which curators place a higher artistic value. At a recent symposium attended by museum curators, the director of the Metropolitan Museum voiced his concern about the "exhibition fever that has gripped today's museum scene, often working to the detriment of the institution's own permanent collections." But, he added, "We would go bankrupt if we lost the exhibitions."[4]

The Metropolitan Opera sells tote bags, T-shirts, and posters in order to earn a profit that supports its main interest, the opera. Ballet programs held at the Met in 1978 yielded $1 million profit, which helped to cover its $11 million deficit from opera. The absolute rule of Anthony Bliss, director of the Met, was that opera could run a deficit but dance companies could not. "They must be run at least at a no-loss basis," he is quoted as saying, "because our primary responsibility is presenting opera."[5]

National Public Radio is planning to raise money for its radio productions through a variety of projects, including the sale of audio cassettes of NPR programs and the transmission of business information by satellite communication. "We're prepared to enter almost any profession except the oldest one," declared the president of NPR, as he announced his plans to rely on cross-subsidization increasingly in the years ahead.[6]

What do these examples, drawn from diverse fields, have in common? They all demonstrate that cross-subsidization in nonprofit organizations is not an accidental or short-run occurrence. Instead, it is part of a deliberate long-term strategy by management for financing the consumption of loss-making activities they care about most. This strategy is feasible where the organization provides services for whose costs individuals are willing to pay; that means, in turn, a service which individuals value and which they can be denied. Those criteria apply to an art exhibit, for instance, but not to the St. Patrick's Day parade. It means also that the manager must be in a position to transfer revenue between activities, whether from tickets of admission, subsidies, donations, or volunteered time.

Of course, the activities that the manager chooses in order to earn surplus revenues must be of a kind that is capable of generating a profit. This means as a rule that barriers to entry must exist: otherwise, profit-making firms would spring up, and eventually compete away the profits. Some of those barriers are "natural," visible in the unique reputation of the Met or the Smithsonian Institution. In other cases, the entry barriers stem from public decisions, such as legalizing bingo games in churches or granting accreditation certificates to schools.

Finally, this analysis helps explain another empirical observation—the chronic shortage of funds of nonprofit organizations. Managers of such organizations are chosen in part for their ability to provide services such as art exhibits or musical events or medical care, whose value will be judged by factors other than the willingness of the public to pay; they are chosen also for their ability to raise the money that will bridge the differences between income and cost; but they are not chosen for their ability to make a profit.[7] Given the relative value that their institutions place on the alternative activities and given the incentive system under which the managers work, we would hypothesize that most nonprofit organizations will face a perpetual shortage of funds, a hypothesis that seems supported by the facts.

The root of this situation is not, as has been suggested previously, that these are labor-intensive service industries with a chronic productivity lag.[8] More simply and fundamentally, nonprofit organizations should be regarded as consumption-oriented institutions; and consumers never have "enough" income. So long as the marginal utility of any good exceeds zero there is always a "need" for more, a pressure for the organization to expand some of its activities, and a consequent pressure to expand its resources to finance those desired activities.

PREDICTABILITY AND PLANNING

The same process that leads nonprofit organizations to subsidize one activity from the profits of another allows us to anticipate the responsiveness of such organizations to changes in economic circumstances.

To explore this issue, think of three different kinds of services. One kind yields profits to the organization, but is perceived as having no utility (for example, selling T-shirts to museum visitors); a second also yields a profit, but is thought of as having negative utility at the margin (for example, selling poorly made prints of famous paintings); and a third yields a loss to the institution but has positive utility (for example, providing free museum trips for disadvantaged children).

Picture a case in which the institution with services of all three types receives an unrestricted grant from a wealthy philanthropist who hopes to increase the services provided by the museum. The response of the museum, in view of the utility it assigns to each of its three programs, will be to increase the number of museum trips for disadvantaged children, to reduce the sale of poorly made prints, and to continue selling its T-shirts as it had in the past.

Now change the circumstances that the institution faces. Suppose that the institution's various selling prices all rise, increasing its profits in all the profit-making services and decreasing its losses on the others. Once again, it is likely to increase its program of trips for the disadvantaged, as long as such trips are seen as having positive utility. And it is likely to expand its sale of T-shirts to help pay for the trips. Whether the institution will increase or reduce its sale of poor prints is less clear. Athough the increased price of those prints will make them more profitable, thus providing more funds for the museum trips, the negative utility of that activity may mean that now the organization can afford to produce less of it despite the increase in price.

What if the price commanded by some of these activities changes differently from the others? Suppose, for instance, it becomes feasible to charge a small fee for the museum trips without reducing the demand for such trips. Then the museum will continue to sell its T-shirts, while reducing the sale of poor prints. On the other hand, if the price of T-shirts alone goes up, the trips will be increased and the print sales once again will be reduced. Finally, a rise in the price of poor prints will also increase the museum trip program while leaving T-shirt sales unchanged.

Responses such as these help to explain a number of widely observed reactions among nonprofit organizations. When the number of persons of college age increased in the 1950s, it was not at all clear that private institutions would want to expand rapidly enough to take on the increased demand. Instead, they may have preferred to become more selective and to raise their price of and profits from undergraduate education.[9] This is one possible reason why politicians felt the strong pressure to build new state universities to accommodate the "baby boom." At the same time, the higher profits from undergraduate education allowed an increase in the preferred activities of graduate training and research, in both absolute and relative terms. I would also predict that as universities grow less affluent in the 1980s than they were in the 1960s and early 1970s, they will seek to become more attractive to undergraduates, will place a greater weight on teaching, and will constrict their graduate programs. We already notice an increased emphasis on part-time adult education, a clear case of an activity that is taken on for its profit-making potential, rather than for the utility it provides to the faculty and school administrators.

The usefulness of looking at the behavior of nonprofit organizations in this way is highlighted by observing what it implies for various proposed policies in education, such as a voucher scheme in which nonprofit tuition-charging private schools are permitted to enroll. If such a scheme existed, it would give private schools a basis for increasing their tuition; and that in turn could lead such schools to reduce their enrollments by shutting out their least-desired students. This perverse supply response would leave many frustrated would-be customers with no place to go—less choice instead of more. Would new private schools then start up to accommodate this left-over demand? When the profit motive has been ruled out, it is difficult to predict the incentives for founding new enterprises. At best, any positive supply response coming from new schools would be slow and uncertain.

WHY PEOPLE DONATE

The foregoing analysis also helps to explain why people sometimes donate to nonprofit organizations, but rarely to profit-making organizations or government. When donors make gifts they are generally in a poor position to determine if the gift will be well used. If the donor cannot monitor the response, there is a risk that the gift will be absorbed into the organization without any change in its services; for-profit organizations will simply add to their profits, while governments will simply reduce their deficits. But nonprofit organizations derive utility from the delivery of services, not from the generation of profits or surpluses. Thus, donors who are not in a position to monitor the behavior of the recipient may feel safer contributing to the nonprofit entity. Some economists have pointed to increased "trust-worthiness" as a reason why people donate to nonprofit rather than to for-profit organizations. Trustworthiness, however, is an amorphous concept which is difficult to observe and measure; moreover, it is not immediately obvious that nonprofit organizations are more trustworthy than for-profit entities. It does, however, follow from the logic of the different constraints facing the two kinds of organizations that nonprofit organizations will increase their output in response to a donation while profit-making organizations will not. (This point is demonstrated more rigorously in the Appendix.)

Governments too are in a poor position to attract donations. If we think of government as a giant multipurpose nonprofit organization, the ability of potential donors to predict the use of their donations may be even smaller than in the case of for-profit organizations. Thus, even though individuals might see themselves deriving some utility from increasing some of government's activities, they are unlikely voluntarily to contribute money to government, aware that they cannot predict which activity will be increased.

Nonprofit organizations, therefore, can be expected to capture the lion's share of the donations of those who want to encourage the delivery of a certain group of services, especially if the donor is in no position to monitor the institution's response. By a Darwinian process, such organizations will dominate over profit-maximizing firms in these areas. The legal constraint on distributing profits serves the purpose of giving nonprofit organizations this comparative advantage in capturing donations and some organizations will voluntarily take on the constraint for that reason; the existence of potential donations can then be seen as a raison d'etre for the development of the nonprofit institutional form.

In the case of a nonprofit entity with several different service activities, however, the donor's trust may be partially misplaced. We have observed that larger donations will increase the output of the organization overall; but the activity that the donor had in mind may not be the one that is actually increased. If the donor hoped to finance more appendectomies, he might actually be helping to expand the open heart surgery unit. The resulting allocation effect, therefore, may be very different from the donor's intent.

DISTRIBUTION AND EQUITY

It is clear that the activities of nonprofit organizations involve a different distribution of decision-making power than do the analogous activities of for-profit organizations or government agencies. A shift from government agencies or for-profit organizations to nonprofit organizations reallocates some decision-making power from the political apparatus to donors, fee payers, and managers. Inasmuch as managers of nonprofit organizations are presumed to derive some of their returns from the job through their power to determine the mix of their services, the final mix will be affected by their preferences. The efforts of such managers to increase their level of satisfaction produce the phenomenon in which customers of one (profitable) activity subsidize customers of another (loss-making) service. Indeed, this method of financing activities in nonprofit organizations has recently been attacked on precisely these grounds; although the complaint was directed at nonprofit hospitals, it could as well have been applied to other organizations. According to the author,[10]

> . . . those who control the nonprofit hospital exploit the vulnerability of consumers as potential taxpayers. They charge for hospital services at rates that allow some funds to be directed toward research, teaching, favored patients, and favored departments of the hospital; they do not advertise or fully disclose this practice; and they do not give consumers any choice in the matter . . . The point is simply that the controlling group constitutes an undemocratic ruling class with respect to the hospital's minigovernmental functions . . . [And] in acting as minigovernments, they employ an unjust method of taxation . . . If it should happen that the latter (taxpayers) are taxed according to a plausible ideal of tax policy, the result would be fortuitous. It is far more likely that the non-profit's method of taxation will violate principles of horizontal and vertical equity.

Is it wrong for nonprofit organizations to make a profit in one service in order to subsidize another? Profits abound in our society among for-profit organizations, and these are rarely viewed as a form on unjust taxation. What, if anything, makes profits generated by a nonprofit organization different?

First, of course, is the fact that the organizations concerned hold themselves out as nonprofit; this representation may make those who provide donations or pay its fees more trusting in their approach. Second, the nonprofit status of the organizations affords them exemption from the income tax laws. Finally, in some instances such status also goes hand in hand with exclusive rights of various kinds, such as the right of accrediting boards to determine the status of college programs and the right of church groups to sponsor legal bingo games. All these factors help to differentiate profits in the nonprofit organization and provide a basis for raising questions about the practice of cross-subsidization.

Some observers have proposed that nonprofit organizations should be required to disclose that they were cross-subsidizing their services whereever that occurred, in order to control such practices. The difficulties in implementing such a policy, however, should not be minimized. Many products at a hospital or a university are jointly produced, so the calculation of their separate costs entails some unavoidably arbitrary allocations. At best, the process would be costly; at worst, meaningless to the average consumer and subject to extensive litigation.[11] The disclosure problem is compounded by the fact that the fields of health and education consist of many small units, each of which would have to go through an elaborate cost analysis; in this respect, they stand in contrast to public utilities, which are much more highly concentrated and can therefore analyze their financial performance without prohibitive expense. Besides, it is not at all clear that students would change colleges or patients hospitals, upon learning that the colleges or hospitals were earning a profit from the services they provided. In any event, the important point in the present context is the difference between nonprofit organizations on the one hand and government agencies or for-profit firms on the other, when making decisions on the mix of those services and the prices to be charged. In the case of the nonprofit organizations, the decisions are affected heavily by the preferences of the institutions that deliver the services, while the political process and the incentive of maximizing profits take lesser roles.

SOME CRITICAL IMPLICATIONS

What light does this analysis throw on the likely impact of reducing government subsidies and increasing the public's dependence on nonprofit organizations and voluntary contributions? In general, we have observed that the nonprofit organization chooses its mix of activities differently from a for-profit organization or a government agency. Variations among the organizations within the nonprofit sector make it difficult to anticipate their behavior. However, certain generalizations are possible.

The for-profit entity presumably seeks to maximize profit, while the government agency presumably responds in some degree to the mandates of its political masters. In this respect, the activities of both for-profit organizations and government agencies are governed to some extent by criteria that relate to social utility: the activities of the for-profit organization must survive the test of the marketplace, while those of the government agency must survive the scrutiny of the political structure. The activities of the nonprofit organization, however, are determined by criteria and processes that are more ambiguous in their results, and the social utility of the outcome depends upon the "validity" of their manager's preferences.

If government reduces the subsidies that it gives organizations which provide public services, such as education or health, some activities will decline but others will, for the same reason, expand. Those organizations that prospective donors prefer will have the better chance of surviving, although the favored organizations may sometimes choose to deliver services different from the donor's intent or expectation.

Perhaps as significantly, many organizations will seek out activities that are profitable in order to finance those that are not. The organizations that find such profitable activities will thrive and cross-subsidization will become even more important in the future than it has been in the past. The temptation and search for profitable activities has arisen in a particularly controversial way in the academic world, in connection with biomedical research. Attracted by the possiblity of large profits, Harvard University considered creating a genetics engineering company but ultimately abandoned the idea, fearing that the commercial motive would run counter to its traditional academic role; on the other hand, Massachusetts General Hospital, which is affiliated with the Harvard Medical School, accepted $50 million from a German chemical firm in return for priority access. While the president of Stanford University has expressed concern about potential conflicts of interest, Stanford recently entered into an agreement with several private firms to build a new biotechnical research center.[12]

An important limiting factor, from both the organization's and society's point of view, is the entrepreneurship and risk captial that new ventures require. When the supply of entrepreneurial resources is limited, the optimum allocation between profitable production and loss-making consumption activities becomes a crucial issue. If the organization does "too much" of the former, it has insufficient entrepreneurship left over for the latter; but if it does "too little" it cannot afford the latter at all. As nonprofit organizations face the task of delivering more services, some may find themselves devoting so much effort and energy to their profit-making activities as to alter their fundamental character. Paradoxically, they may operate more like profit-maximizing firms even as they are expected to take on more governmental functions.

NOTES

1. For studies that focus on particular organizations or industries see Baumol, W., and Bowen, W., *Performing Arts—The Economic Dilemma* (New York: Twentieth Century Fund, 1966); Hansmann, H., Non-profit enterprise in the performing arts, *Bell Journal of Economics* 12 (Autumn 1981):341–61; Newhouse, J.P., Toward a theory of nonprofit institutions: An economic model of a hospital, *American Economic Review* 60 (March 1970):64–75; Hall, T., and Lindsay, C., Medical schools: Producers of what? Sellers to whom?, *Journal of Law and Economics* 23 (April 1980): 55–81; James, E., and Neuberger, E., The University department as a non-profit labor cooperative, *Public Choice* 36 (1981):585–612; Pauly, M., and Redisch, M., The not-for-profit hospital as a physician's cooperative, *American Economic Review*, 63 (March 1973): 87–100; Rose-Ackerman, S., United charities: An economic analysis, *Public Policy* 28 (Summer 1980): 323–50. For important contributions using a more general approach see Clarkson, K., and Martin, D.L., eds., *The Economics of Nonproprietary Organizations* (Greenwich, CT: JAI Press, 1980); and Weisbrod, B., *The Voluntary Nonprofit Sector* (Lexington, Massachusetts: Heath, 1977).

2. James, E., Product mix and cost disaggregation: A reinterpretation of the economics of higher education, *Journal of Human Resources*, 13 (Spring 1978): 157–86; James, E., and Neuberger, E., The university department as a non-profit labor cooperative, *Public Choice*, 1981. In 1966–1967, undergraduate students in the lower division of private universities in the United States were more than paying their own way while upper-division students had just passed the break-even point; on the other hand, the cost for graduate students exceeded tuition by over $1500 per year. In the same period at public universities, undergraduate students were paying a much higher percentage of their real costs than were graduate students.

3. Hansmann, H., The role of nonprofit enterprise, *The Yale Law Review* 89 (April 1980): 835–99 (reprinted as Chapter 3 in this volume); Newhouse, Toward a theory of nonprofit institutions: An economic model of a hospital; and Clark, R.C., Does the nonprofit form fit the hospital industry?, *Harvard Law Review* 53 (7) (May 1980): 1416–89.

4. European museum aides told of Met's financial woes, *New York Times*, September 16,

1980, p. C8. His optimum solution: a $100 million endowment which would allow the museum to forego the exhibitions and return to its primary purpose of providing educational enlightment.

5. How ballet helps foot the bill for opera, *New York Times*, June 10, 1979, p. D1, 29. However, there are certain exceptions to this rule. "The exception is something that will make a strong artistic impact for the Met—there we'd be prepared to take a greater risk."

6. *Newsweek*, December 7, 1981, pp. 105–6.

7. As one case in point: *The Omaha Sun*, in 1972, ran a Pulitzer Prize-winning article on Boys Town, maintaining that it had raised "more money than it knows what to do with." Its annual income of $8 million from investments amply covered operating expenses, yet it continued to collect more than twice this amount from annual contributions. Shortly after this "unfavorable" publicity, a new director was appointed for Boys Town, and a large spending program began, including long-term donations to Catholic University and Stanford University, construction of a Center for the Study of Youth Development and an Institute for Learning Disorders in Children. By 1976, a million dollar deficit had been achieved by the highly regarded new manager. See *Newsweek*, October 25, 1976, p. 18.

8. For a discussion of the chronic impoverishment of nonprofit organizations in the performing arts, an impoverishment which they attribute to a productivity lag, see Baumol and Bowen, *Performing Arts*.

9. The prevalence of very inelastic and even backward-bending supply curves has also been noted with respect to certain hospital activities. See Pauly and Redisch, The not-for-profit hospital as a physician's cooperative.

10. Clark, Does the nonprofit form fit the hospital industry?, pp. 1439, 1468.

11. For a discussion of some of these problems with respect to calculations of educational costs, see James, Product mix and cost disaggregation.

12. For a discussion of these issues as they have arisen recently in the academic world, particularly in connection with biomedical research, see Tinkering with life, *Chronicle of Higher Education* 23 (December 9, 1981): 56; Donors and campuses, *New York Times*, October 9, 1981, p. A16; and Corporate links worry scholars, *New York Times* October 17, 1982, p. F4.

11

Why Organizations Turn Nonprofit: Lessons from Case Studies

JUDITH MANFREDO LEGORRETA
and DENNIS R. YOUNG

Over the last decade, social scientists have begun to address the question: Why do nonprofit organizations exist? Two principal answers are of central importance in this literature. The first is Weisbrod's (1975) hypothesis that nonprofit organizations are vehicles for voluntary provision of public goods that emerge in circumstances where government fails to satisfy the demands of certain subgroups in the community. The second is Hansmann's (1980) argument that nonprofit organizations are "trusted" institutions that are preferred as vehicles of service provision where consumers, for a variety of reasons, are not competent to judge the quality or effectiveness of services delivered.

These theories are both static and global; they offer seemingly universal explanations of the existence of all nonprofit organizations, for all time. More precisely, they assume that organizations exist in a steady-state equilibrium that logically reflects the reasons for which they were established. Existing theories also tend to be "demand-side oriented." That is, they are grounded in consumer preferences for public goods or for the trustworthy provision of services. However, the decision to form a nonprofit (or other type of) organization is made on the supply side by an entrepreneur and his or her associates who must evaluate a number of factors (personal preferences, barriers to entry, ease of operation, etc.) in addition to consumer preferences and other characteristics of demand (see Young, 1983).

Empirically, the current theories imply that one ought to be able to establish strong connections between the mission and services of an organization and the sector in which it is located. Weisbrod and others have had some success in making these connections. But the fact that many industries contain organizations belonging to two or three different sectors still presents a substantial puzzle. In particular, one must ask—why are there variations in sector status within a given industry? Are the variations in the character of services *within* an industry really large enough to account for the bulk of intra-industry sector differentiation? Perhaps there are dynamic or supply-side factors that help account for some of this variation.

All this is not to argue that the foregoing theories lack basic validity, only that there are many other factors underlying the observed distribution of organizations by sector. This situation makes it difficult to look to the "real world" for verification. Moreover, because the theories are static, they ignore the possibility that the rationale for establishing a nonprofit organization may be connected with the prior sectoral experience of the people and organizations involved. In particular, nonprofit organizations are sometimes formed not from scratch, in circumstances where the choice of sector may be an open question, but as a spin-off from, or conversion of, an existing organization. Thus, some organizations may be nonprofit simply because they are spun-off from other nonprofit organizations or formed by individuals experienced in the nonprofit world. Alternatively, a nonprofit organization may be formed by conversion of a unit of government or a firm in the commercial sector. In such cases, the choice of nonprofit status seems more likely to be viewed in terms of problems to be escaped in the incumbent sector, and to be influenced by supply-side as well as demand-side considerations. But where you stand depends on where you sit, that is, the explanation for nonprofit status may differ, depending on the previous history and circumstances of the particular organizational unit or its sponsors.

Thus, an alternative view of the world is possible, one that is useful for understanding why nonprofit organizations come into being. Specifically, there may be a myriad of idiosyncratic institutional and circumstantial reasons why organizations are formed in one sector or another. But organizations are dynamic and they exist in a changing economy that is not in equilibrium. There is no perfect mechanism for optimal placement of an organization into its "theoretically appropriate" sector, but there are incremental processes by which organizations select their initial sector status or change that status once in existence. We argue here that the latter phenomenon—conscious change of sector by an existing organization—may be a particularly fertile one to explore for understanding the rationales for nonprofit organization. Unlike organizations which may have been nonprofit for a long time, or even new organizations for which choice of sector status is just one of many factors that may have been deliberated at the time of establishment, cases of transition are explicitly focused on the question of sector. Such cases thus provide a direct line into the issue of nonprofit rationales, as well as an opportunity to determine whether governmental agencies which become nonprofit have different rationales from commercial firms which make the same shift.

This paper analyzes five case studies of organizations that switched to

private, nonprofit status: three of these organizations changed from proprietary form, and two changed from governmental status. These cases were
selected on the basis of accessibility to people and documentation after a
search identified nine such cases nationwide. The information for each case
study was obtained through personal interviews with executives and employees, and through documents provided by these individuals. (See Manfredo, 1980)

In the next section, each of the cases will be described, including a review of the reasons underlying the decisions to change sector. In the final
section of this chapter, we review the factors that induce government agencies on the one hand, and commercial firms on the other, to become private, nonprofit organizations.

CASE STUDIES

The three commercial to nonprofit sector cases are Gallery North, Hillcrest
Hospital, and Green Chimneys School. The two government to nonprofit
sector cases are the Urban Academy and the Chapter Ten mental health
agency.

Gallery North. Gallery North is an art gallery in East Setauket, Long
Island which serves as a resource center for the community. The gallery
provides slide registration and art purchasing consultation services, sponsors craft demonstrations and talks by artists, and is a vehicle through which
local artists can exhibit and sell their works. The gallery was originally established as a private, profit-making organization in 1965, but incorporated as a nonprofit organization in 1975.

The proprietor, a Mrs. Fuller, established the gallery because of her strong
personal interest in the arts, and her desire to bring "quality art" to her
community. She supplied the capital investment and was supported by the
volunteer labor of friends who shared her convictions. The gallery also derived support from revenues on sales by local artists, as well as gift shop
sales.

Over time it became more difficult for the proprietor to devote full time
to the gallery, and to finance operating deficits incurred periodically by the
organization. Yet she wanted to ensure that the gallery would continue to
operate as a service to the community. She preferred not to sell the gallery
for fear its philosophy would be altered. Nor did the volunteers who helped
with the gallery want to see it radically changed. Incorporation as a nonprofit provided the appropriate solution. In particular, this change allowed
the gallery to sustain itself through charitable contributions and eligibility
to receive governmental grants. It is interesting, however, that Gallery North
was not granted 501(c)3 status as a charitable organization by the IRS,
which considered the gallery to be a means of generating income for artists
who sold their works through the gallery. Still, the nonprofit status facili-

tated eligibility for some grants and it enabled the formation of a fund-raising arm, "Friends of Gallery North", to attract donations from members of the local community at large.

Moreover, the change to nonprofit status permitted the proprietor, and her volunteer friends, to retain a high degree of organizational control by becoming trustees of the organization, while at the same time it relieved them of personal financial responsibility.

In summary, it may be observed that although Gallery North was initially established as a for-profit organization, its basic philosophy has always been nonprofit in character. In particular, making money was never a strong motivation, and fostering the development of art in the community was always the underlying thrust. From the beginning, the gallery received community support through volunteers. But when the proprietor could no longer support the gallery herself, the nonprofit corporate form provided the means to do so without losing control of the organization or altering its basic operation.

Hillcrest Hospital. The 250-bed Hillcrest Hospital in Flushing, New York, was established in 1962 as a proprietary institution by a group of five physicians who owned the majority of shares. In 1974 it was sold to Group Health Incorporated (GHI), a large nonprofit health care organization. During the 1969 to 1974 period, the hospital experienced financial difficulties emanating from governmental regulations, particularly the wage and price controls of 1971 which allowed wage and supply costs to rise faster than hospital rates. Eventually these cost pressures lead to the decision to sell.

As part of the agreement with GHI, the original five proprietors retained majority control on the hospital's board of directors. This provision reflected these doctors' interests in guiding future policies of the hospital. Moreover, it relieved them of financial responsibility and pressures from other stockholders, while enhancing the chances of the hospital's survival. In particular, as part of a nonprofit organization, the hospital would have a better chance to affiliate with a medical school, and to utilize interns, which in turn could increase its rate of reimbursement.

Green Chimneys School. Green Chimneys is a child-care institution and elementary school located in Brewster, New York. It was established as a proprietary school in 1947, financed by tuition payments. In the early 1950s it converted to nonprofit status. The proprietor, Sam Ross, retained his position as headmaster after the transition and indeed into the 1970s, as the agency developed into a certified residential child-care agency serving the New York foster-care system.

Prior to the sector change, the school was financed by tuitions alone. Afterward, it was able to diversify its support to include foundation grants and private donor contributions. The proprietor identified the school's "public image" as an important motivation for the change, not only to attract philanthropic support but also to become more attractive to parents considering placement of their children at the school. In particular, Mr. Ross perceived parents as having suspicions about proprietary education; the nonprofit form, he felt, provided a higher degree of assurance.

Like the Gallery North and Hillcrest cases, the transition of Green Chimneys to nonprofit status allowed the proprietor to retain essential control of the organization. Although a more broadly based board of directors was required (indeed, as a proprietary agency the board consisted totally of family members) Ross maintained his role as chief executive and developed a good working relationship with a newly appointed board representative of the surrounding community. Since development of the school was his principal concern, and financial gain a secondary matter, the change to nonprofit status appears to have served Mr. Ross's purposes well.

The Urban Academy. The Urban Academy is a management training organization that provides technical assistance to government agencies. It was established in 1974 by New York City as a unit operated through the Research Foundation of the City University. In 1975–76, the Academy took on a major project involving the implementation of a new financial management system for New York City. This caused the Academy to expand rapidly. In 1977, the Academy left the university and incorporated as a nonprofit organization.

There were several reasons for this change. In order to accommodate the Academy's growth, additional personnel and other purchases were required. Recruitment, hiring, and purchasing proved to be highly cumbersome within the governmental system. Nonprofit status permitted the bypassing of this red tape.

Independent nonprofit status presented other advantages as well. It permitted the Academy to receive grants and donations from private foundations, and it allowed the Academy to diversify its clientele to jurisdictions and organizations outside New York City, thus providing a greater degree of stability.

In summary, the transition to independent nonprofit status permitted the Academy (under an entrepreneurial executive) to better control its own destiny by providing the autonomy to choose new projects and programs. Moreover, the move facilitated growth by relieving governmental purchasing and civil service constraints, and it provided greater financial security through diversification of clientele and sources of support. The basic mission to provide technical assistance and management training remained relatively unchanged.

Chapter Ten, Inc. The Fairfax-Falls Church Community Mental Health and Mental Retardation Services Board (hereafter referred to as the Services Board) is a local mental-health service board appointed by the supervisors of Fairfax County and the City Councils of Falls Church and Fairfax in Virginia. In 1979, the Board's Community Residence Program (CRP) was grouped with three other board programs and incorporated as an independent nonprofit organization called Chapter Ten, Inc. There were a number of important administrative reasons for the change.

The CRP was plagued with a cumbersome personnel system in the public sector. Nonadministrative (contracted, direct-care) employees were not considered County workers, hence, they received no County fringe benefits such as sick leave or medical insurance. Yet these employees were still subject to the financial restrictions of County policies such as constraints on use of performance-based compensation or bonuses. In addition, tenure was granted to CRP administrative staff, but not to direct-care workers. Thus, unproductive administrators had to be tolerated, while direct-care workers were demoralized by being subject to thirty days termination notice. Finally, the process for hiring an administrator was a time-consuming and inefficient one for CRP in the public sector.

Purchasing problems also hampered CRP's operation in the public sector. There was a long lag time in processing purchase orders, for example. This required that large sums of petty cash be kept on hand to compensate for the delays in reimbursement. The system for replacing capital equipment was also cumbersome, involving long review periods before approvals were granted.

Finally, financing and budgeting problems plagued CRP's operation in the public sector. For example, CRP was not eligible to receive philanthropic funds and, hence, was heavily dependent on federal, state, and local funding. Finally, the budgeting system was overbearing. Expenditure items of $1000 or more required prior approvals. And funds were sometimes spent hastily and ineffectively because budgets were required to "zero out" at the end of the fiscal year.

The purpose of changing the CRP to nonprofit status was to eliminate the administrative and financial difficulties experienced through the County system. In particular, the change allowed all CRP employees to receive fringe benefits. It allowed for autonomy in purchasing, enabling CRP to save money by buying items on sale and receiving them within a reasonable time frame. In general, the change provided for considerably more autonomy and flexibility in administration.

However, not all of the expected advantages of nonprofit status materialized. Outside funding was not attracted because Chapter Ten maintained a close affiliation with the Services Board and was perceived not to be independent of it.

Common Themes

There are several common themes linking the five cases of conversion to the nonprofit form. However, the commercial and governmental cases also differ substantially from each other.

In the commercial to nonprofit sector cases, there are several common factors. For example, in all three cases, the proprietors were interested in sustaining the purposes and operations of their organizations in a manner consistent with their personal preferences. The nonprofit form permitted them to relinquish ownership without relinquishing control, by becoming trustees or executive directors. Moreover, in all cases, the objectives of the proprietors seemed more closely tied to providing the service for which the organization was intended, than in making money. This explains why retaining control was so important. In most cases, the motivation for changing status was to relieve financial pressures; however, simply selling out would provide no assurance that the organization would continue to operate as intended or that the proprietor would retain a role in it.

In addition, the nonprofit form provided access to new sources of funds (grants and contributions) not available in proprietary form, funds that could sustain the organization more effectively. Relatedly, the nonprofit form appeared to enhance these organizations' public images, improving their marketability to potential customers by presenting a more trustworthy image as in the case of Green Chimneys, or a more prestigious one, for example, by improving chances for affiliation with a university, as in the case of Hillcrest.

In contrast, the public to nonprofit sector cases reflect different advantages of the nonprofit form. Becoming private, nonprofit firms provided these agencies and their executives with substantially more autonomy to develop and implement programs and considerably more flexibility, efficiency, and control in hiring, purchasing, financing, and budgeting. In these cases also, the change to nonprofit form was intended to increase the potential for diversifying sources of support and, hence, enhancing financial stability. However, this potential was realized in only a limited way. The Urban Academy was able to expand its clientele beyond New York City. But neither the Urban Academy or Chapter Ten succeeded in attracting significant levels of private grants or contributions. In the case of Chapter Ten this appeared to be related to the perception of potential contributors that the organization was still controlled by its sponsoring government agency.

The five case studies do provide support for explanations of nonprofit organizations found in current theory. Each of the organizations scrutinized here, for example, can be described as a vehicle for the voluntary provision of a public good or service. More precisely, the three cases originating in the commercial sector involve organizations whose proprietors were primarily dedicated to the service they were providing rather than simply viewing that service as instrumental to profit-making. Ultimately, this fact helped explain the transition to nonprofit status.

Clearly, the two cases emanating in the government sector are grounded in public service provision as well. In both these cases, the transition to nonprofit status did not lead to an abandonment of that mission but rather to a more efficient means of carrying it out. But as the classical theory of collective action would have it (Olson, 1965), public goods are not efficiently provided voluntarily because of free-rider problems. Hence, government provision is required for efficiency. The two public to nonprofit sector cases here seem to contradict this hypothesis. Actually, this is only partly so, as both the organizations studied provide services paid for by government. Still, the conversions to nonprofit form did reflect not only a desire for greater internal efficiency but also an attempt to obtain voluntary donations.

The cases also lend support to the trustworthiness theory. This is most directly seen in the Green Chimneys case where nonprofit status was viewed as a means of image-building to attract clientele. But this rationale is also reflected, though more weakly, in the other commercial sector-based cases. Hillcrest's proprietors thought nonprofit status would enhance chances of a teaching affiliation, again an exercise in image-building. Gallery North maintained a strong bond of trust between the proprietor and her close friends, even in proprietary form. However, nonprofit status enabled the organization to expand its aura of trust to the community at large, thus facilitating community-wide support.

However, as suggested in the introductory section, these demand-side elements of current theory do not fully capture or explain the use of the nonprofit form. The cases presented here exhibit even more cogent, pragmatic supply-side factors influencing choice of sector. For the proprietary-based cases, the nonprofit form allowed maintenance of control by the (former) proprietor, and, hence, the ability to keep the organization to a chosen course, while relieving the financial and administrative burdens of ownership. Similarly, the public sector-based cases provided the executive leaders with the autonomy and flexibility they wanted and needed to operate efficiently, while maintaining, even expanding upon, their public missions. In an important way, these supply-side factors reveal the essential inner drives motivating those who lead nonprofit organizations. The commercial to nonprofit cases demonstrate an underlying dedication to service provision per se, coupled with pragmatic risk aversion behavior, the change to nonprofit form involves the sacrifice of some autonomy and control in exchange for greater personal as well as organizational security. By contrast, the public to nonprofit sector cases reflect executives' desires for more risk and less security in exchange for greater flexibility and control. One's view does indeed depend on one's current position. Thus, all is relative, since the public and commercial organizations start at very different points on the risk/control/security/flexibility spectra. Perhaps the nonprofit form represents a "golden mean" for those with moderate preferences along these dimensions.

Finally, the five cases illustrate that the real world can be only imperfectly reflected in the theoretical explanations of nonprofit form. Organizations may be born into the "wrong" sector, and they may maintain such affiliations for long periods of time. Alternatively, organizations may be initially more appropriate for one sector, but as conditions change the sector location may fit less well. Yet, it takes time and effort for transitions to take place, and some appropriate transitions may never occur. The cases examined here include organizations that initially may have been misplaced outside the nonprofit sector. But the opposite phenomenon also occurs: organizations in the nonprofit sector that fit better, and may ultimately move to, another sector. Research groups in nonprofit universities may break away and become proprietary consulting firms, for example, and nonprofit social agencies may be taken over by government. Thus, examining a cross-section of organizations populating a given sector at any one time may not accurately reveal the set of rationales underlying sectoral affiliation. As indicated above, examining sector transitions provides another window, one that might be more fully exploited in future research that could focus not only on transitions *to* the nonprofit sector, but transitions *from* this sector as well.

REFERENCES

Douglas, James. 1983. *Why Charity?* Beverly Hills: Sage Publications.

Hansmann, Henry B. 1980. The role of non-profit enterprise. *Yale Law Journal* April. 89:835–98. Reprinted as Chapter 3 of this volume.

Manfredo, Judith K. 1980. Case studies of organizations which have undergone a sectoral change. Internship Report, W. Averell Harriman College, State University of New York at Stony Brook, December.

Olson, Mancur. 1965. *The Logic of Collective Action.* Cambridge: Harvard University Press.

Weisbrod, Burton A. 1977. *The Voluntary Non-Profit Sector.* Lexington, Massachusetts: D. C. Heath.

Young, Dennis R. 1983. *If Not For Profit, For What?* Lexington, Massachusetts: D. C. Heath.

PUBLIC POLICY TOWARD NONPROFITS

IV
THE CHARITABLE DEDUCTION

12

The Impact of the
1981 Tax Act on
Individual Charitable Giving

CHARLES T. CLOTFELTER and LESTER M. SALAMON

On August 13, 1981, President Reagan signed into law the Economic Recovery Tax Act of 1981, one of the central pillars of the economic program he had unveiled six months earlier. Among the provisions of this law were an across-the-board reduction of 25 percent in marginal tax rates for individuals over three years, a reduction in the maximum tax rate on individual income from 70 to 50 percent, liberalized depreciation allowances, and sizable reductions in estate taxes, an "above-the-line" charitable deduction for nonitemizers to be phased in over a period of years, and a provision to index tax rates beginning in 1985.

The purpose of this paper is to assess the probable impact of this new tax law on individual charitable giving over the next several years. This impact is worth exploring not simply because of the magnitude of the resources involved, but even more so because of the special role that charitable giving plays in the private, nonprofit sector of American life, and because of the special implications it consequently has for the Administration's overall economic strategy.

The nonprofit sector is a vast amalgam of organizations, ranging from

From National Tax Journal 35 (1982):171–87. Appendices omitted. Reprinted by permission of the NTA-TIA.

This chapter is a revised version of "The Federal Government and the Nonprofit Sector: The impact of the 1981 Tax Act on Individual Charitable Giving," an Urban Institute working paper, August 1981. In conducting this study, we benefited greatly from the programming assistance of Melodie Feather and Keith Fontenot, the helpful comments of Michael Moorman and Randall Weiss, and the production skills of Harriett Page, Janet Haynes, and Ellen McLamb. Research support was provided by Independent Sector and the Institute for Research in Social Science, University of North Carolina at Chapel Hill. The analysis and conclusions presented here are ours alone and do not necessarily represent the views of Independent Sector, The Urban Institute, or any other organization or individual.

museums, art societies, universities and civic clubs, to social welfare agencies, neighborhood organizations, public interest groups, and churches. Historically supported largely from private sources, these organizations have come to rely increasingly over recent years on government support and commercial revenues and fees. Of the $85.3 billion in expenditures that nonreligious nonprofit organizations reported in 1977, for example, only $19.1 billion, or 22 percent of the total, came from private giving.[1] Yet, it is still private contributions that give these organizations their distinctive character as independent, private institutions performing essentially public purposes. With private giving so small a share of nonprofit revenues, therefore, anything that threatens private giving threatens the very essence of the nonprofit sector.

The potential impact of the 1981 tax act on private giving takes on special meaning, however, in the context of the broader economic strategy being pursued by the Reagan Administration. One of the central tenets of this strategy, of which the tax act is a pivotal part, is that the role of government should be reduced and the private sector encouraged to fill whatever real gap in services occurs as a result. To the extent that the tax act turns out to discourage such private action by discouraging private giving, it would pose a significant challenge to this strategy and add further strain to nonprofit organizations already burdened by budget cutbacks. Under these circumstances, it becomes all the more urgent to assess what the impact of this act on charitable giving is likely to be.

This paper addresses the effect of the 1981 tax act on individual giving. We make no attempt to predict the effect of the law on contributions by corporations, estates, or foundations.[2] This approach is dictated by the limited economic analysis of the giving behavior of these other three sources and is justified by the fact that individual giving accounts for some 84 percent of total private giving. At the same time, however, this focus probably understates the potential negative impact of the 1981 tax law on charitable giving. This is so because the new tax law contains three features that are likely to discourage these other forms of giving. In the first place, bequest giving is likely to be adversely affected by the act's virtual elimination of taxation of estates, which will significantly reduce the tax incentives for charitable bequests. In the second place, corporate giving is likely to be adversely affected by the new law's massive reform of depreciation rules, which will reduce taxable corporate profits and lower corporate tax liabilities. Finally, giving by foundations is likely to be reduced because of the law's easing of the so-called payout requirement imposed on private foundations by the 1969 tax act.

The provisions of the act most likely to influence individual giving are the tax rate cuts, the new charitable deduction for nonitemizers,[3] and, beginning in 1985, the indexing of tax rates. The body of this chapter is organized into three major sections. The first section discusses the analytical problem in assessing the impact of taxes on individual giving. The second section describes the data and methodology used in the present study; and the third section presents the results of the simulation, focusing on the level and distribution of contributions resulting from the 1981 tax act and then examining separately the impact of the above-the-line charitable deduction. A brief concluding section summarizes the findings and their implications.

THE RELATIONSHIP BETWEEN TAXES AND GIVING

Any tax change such as the 1981 tax act has multiple effects on giving, some of which operate in opposite directions. For example, the taxable reductions that are a principal feature of the 1981 law will automatically increase after-tax income, which should encourage giving. However, lower tax rates also mean an increase in what economists term the "price of giving," the net, out-of-pocket cost of giving a dollar to charity. Because charitable contributions are deductible from income in computing tax obligations, it does not really cost those who itemize their deductions a full dollar to contribute a dollar to charity. In fact, the higher the tax bracket, the lower the real cost of giving. For a taxpayer in the 70 percent tax bracket, for example, the actual, out-of-pocket cost of giving a dollar to charity (the price of giving) is really 30 cents, since 70 cents would have gone to the federal government anyway. Reduce the tax rate to 50 percent, and the price of giving that same dollar to charity rises to 50 cents, an increase of 67 percent.

By reducing the maximum tax rate on unearned income from 70 percent to 50 percent, cutting marginal tax rates by 25 percent between 1981 and 1984, and indexing tax rates after 1985, the 1981 act promises to have effects of precisely this kind. At the same time, however, the act will permit those who do not use the standard deduction to claim deductions for their charitable contributions while still taking the standard deduction. This provision, which goes into effect in stages between 1982 and 1986, will lower the price of giving for these taxpayers, and thus encourage giving.

In addition to these tax-rate effects, charitable giving is also affected by inflation and economic growth, which increase before-tax income, shift some taxpayers into higher tax brackets and induce some taxpayers who now take the standard deduction to itemize their deductions instead, reducing their cost of giving and thus encouraging them to give more. These effects are particularly important in the case of the 1981 tax act because of the role this act is supposed to play in a broader economic strategy that its advocates claim will contribute significantly to overall economic growth.

Therefore, to capture the full effects of the 1981 tax act on charitable giving it is necessary to sort out and assess a wide assortment of relationships, and take account of the interactions among them. To do so, it is helpful to differentiate two broad kinds of effects that are at work. The first are price effects, which influence the cost of giving. Included here are changes in tax rates, as well as changes in income that move taxpayers into different tax brackets or affect their decisions on whether to itemize deductions. The second are income effects, or features that affect the income available for charitable giving. Included here are changes in general economic conditions that affect the level of before-tax income, and changes in tax rates that affect the level of after-tax income. A complete assessment of the impact of the 1981 law must take both of these kinds of effects into account.

To do this, a simulation model of charitable giving behavior by taxpayers was developed based on economic analysis of individual giving and using conventional simulation techniques. These techniques draw on econometric evidence from literature spanning more than a decade.[4] These studies have established the existence of strong, independent links between levels of giving, on the one hand, and changes in the tax-defined price of giving and income levels, on the other.

To say that giving levels are affected by income and the price of giving, of course, is not to say that no other factors are involved, or even that these two factors are the most important. Individuals give to charitable purposes for a variety of reasons. Since such contributions have a net cost even for taxpayers at the highest tax bracket, the primary motivation for most taxpayers is probably other than tax-related, involving philanthropic impulses, a desire to do good, feelings of attachment to particular causes or institutions, and numerous other reasons as well.

In addition, existing relationships among giving, income, and tax rates can change over time in response to changes in social climate, national leadership, or other factors. Analyses such as the present one, which project from previously observed levels for these quantities into the future, must therefore be seen less as predictions of what will happen than as projections of what would happen if these patterns of interaction were to hold under the new circumstances that are projected.

METHODOLOGY AND DATA

To carry out this analysis, four tasks had to be accomplished. First, we had to draw on a suitable model for relating individual giving to changes in income and tax rates. Second, we had to build into this model a way to estimate the effect of rising incomes on individual propensities to itemize deductions, in order to do justice to the full effects of the 1981 law and its projected economic consequences on giving behavior. Third, we had to build in adjustments for the maximum tax on earned income since the elimination of the differentiation between earned and unearned income was one of the principal features of the new law. Finally, we had to locate suitable data and adjust them to make them comparable. This section outlines how these four methodological tasks were handled.

An Economic Model of Giving

The basic estimating equation used in the econometric studies of charitable giving cited above takes the form

$$G = A Y^a P^b X^f e^u \qquad (12\text{-}1)$$

where G is dollars of contributions made, Y is adjusted gross income net of taxes due if no contributions were made, P is the price of giving, X is a vector of other determinants of giving, u is a disturbance or error term, A and e are constants, and a, b, and f are estimated elasticities. Applying this model to the present data yields an equation that predicts one year's contributions as a function of a previous year's contributions, and changes in net income and price:

$$G_{ijt} = G_{io} \left(\frac{Y_{ijt}}{Y_{ijo}} \right)^a \left(\frac{P_{ijt}}{P_{ijo}} \right)^b \qquad (12\text{-}2)$$

where G_{ijt} is predicted average giving for taxpayers in income bracket i, tax status j, in year t. Net income is defined as

$$Y_{ijt} = AGI_{it} - TAX_{ijt} \qquad (12\text{-}3)$$

and is calculated separately for itemizers and nonitemizers, with taxable income for the latter being more at each income level by the average excess deduction claimed by itemizers. Price is defined, following previous empirical work in this area, as the weighted average of the price of giving gifts of cash and assets:

$$P_{ijt} = C_i(1 - M_{ijt}) - (1 - C_i)(1 - M_{ijt} - 0.5MC_{ijt}) \qquad (12\text{-}4)$$

where C_i is the estimated proportion of gifts from the income bracket made in cash, M_{ijt} is the marginal tax rate on ordinary income, and MC_{ijt} is the marginal tax rate on capital gains income. This formulation takes from previous work the assumption that the ratio of appreciation to basis for gifts of assets averages 50 percent. Given the values of net income and price, contributions in Equation (12-1) are calculated in constant dollar terms, translated into current dollars, and summed for itemizers and nonitemizers and by tax status and income class to provide aggregate contributions.

By expressiong Equation (12-1) in logarithmic form, the behavioral parameters can be estimated by standard linear regression methods. In this form, the equation used here is taken from Clotfelter and Steuerle (1981, p. 425):

$$\ln(G + 10) = -1.27 \ln P + 0.78 \ln Y + .26 MRD$$
$$+ .20 DEP + .38 A_{30\text{-}39} + .56 A_{40\text{-}49} - .69 A_{50\text{-}59} + .90 A_{60\text{-}64}$$
$$+ 1.20 A_{65+} - 3.27 \qquad (12\text{-}5)$$

In this equation, G, P, and Y are defined as above; A_{30-39}, A_{40-49}, A_{50-59}, A_{60-64}, and A_{65+} are dummy variables for age groups 30–39, 40–49, 50–59, 60–64, and 65 and older, respectively; and MRD and DEP are dummy variables for taxpayers who are married and who have dependents, respectively. The price elasticity is -1.27, and the income elasticity is 0.78, with standard errors of 0.05 and 0.02, respectively, and R^2 of .47. This equation reflects the most recently estimated parameters for overall individual giving and are in the moderate range of the estimates generated for these elasticities in prior research. This constant elasticity behavioral model underlies the basic simulations presented in this paper.

Because of the importance of these parameters for simulation, however, it is useful to consider an alternative case in which the income and price elasticities vary over the income range. In alternative simulations presented in this paper, we do this by taking elasticities estimated separately by income class.[5] In these estimates, the price elasticity varies from -0.945 for the lowest income groups to -1.779, while the income elasticity varies from 0.393 to 1.089.

Predicting Itemization Status

An important part of the effect rising incomes are expected to have on charitable giving results from the likelihood that the number of taxpayers itemizing their deductions will increase over time if the standard deduction (zero rate bracket) is kept constant. Because it minimizes their tax liabilities, taxpayers virtually always choose to itemize when their deductible expenditures exceed the established standard level. The last 15 years have witnessed periodic increases in the proportion of taxpayers itemizing, punctuated by sharp decreases when the standard deduction is increased. As incomes, expenditures, and prices rise, it is not difficult to predict that the proportion of taxpayers whose deductible expenditures exceed some given dollar amount will tend to increase.

In order to reflect this behavior, itemization behavior was modeled as a function of average income and the zero rate bracket. In specifying the form of the relationship, it was necessary to choose a functional form that would yield predictions of the proportion of itemizers between 0 and 100 percent. The form chosen is a logistical model, which predicts the odds of itemizing as a function of the ratio of average AGI to the zero rate bracket. The following equation was estimated using 1978 data:

$$\ln\left(\frac{I_i}{1-I_i}\right) + c + d \ln\left(\frac{AGI_i}{ZRB}\right) \tag{12-6}$$

where I_i is the proportion of bracket i's taxpayers who itemized, AGI_i is average AGI for the bracket, and ZRB is the zero bracket amount for married taxpayers filing jointly ($3,200 in 1978, more in later years). The estimated value of d was 1.3 (standard error = 0.12) and the R^2 was 0.89. This is the elasticity of the odds in favor of itemizing with respect to the ratio of income to the zero bracket amount. The equation implies, for example, that an increase in this ratio from 5 to 5.5 (10 percent) will tend to result in a 13 percent increase in the odds of itemizing, or an increase in the proportion of itemizers from 39 to 42 percent.[6]

Accounting for the Maximum Tax on Earned Income

Under the pre-1981 tax law, so-called "earned" income is subject to a lower maximum tax rate than other income. One of the principal aims of the administration's tax bill was to eliminate the distinction between "earned" and "unearned" income by reducing the top marginal tax rate on "unearned" income from 70 to 50 percent. Since this change could increase by two-thirds the net price of giving faced by a dividend-receiving high-income taxpayer (from 0.3 to 0.5), this aspect of the tax bill has great potential importance for charitable contributions. Because of the provisions of the present maximum tax, however, the effect of the tax is unlikely to be this simple. In order to calculate marginal tax rates under the previous law, it is important to account for several important features in the calculation of the maximum tax. Under the maximum tax, taxable income is allocated to earned and unearned taxable income, based on the proportion of earned income in AGI (Adjusted Gross Income). The "unearned" portion of taxable income is "stacked" on top of earned income, becoming subject to the highest marginal tax rates.[7] Tax liability is:

$$Tax = T(Y_{50}) + .50\ (ETY - Y_{50}) + [T(Y^*) - T(ETY)] \qquad (12\text{--}7)$$

where $T(\ )$ is income tax as a function of taxable income, ETY is earned taxable income, Y_{50} is the top taxable income subject to the 50 percent marginal tax rate, and Y^* is total taxable income.

$$ETY = \frac{E}{E + U} Y^*$$

where E and U are earned and unearned income, respectively, and

$$Y^* = E + U - D$$

where D is total deductions, including itemized charitable contributions. Differentiation of Equation (12–7) yields the result that the decrease in taxes due to an additional dollar of deductions is:

$$M^* - (M_e - .50)\ \frac{E}{E + U}$$

where M^* is the marginal tax rate on total taxable income and M_e is the marginal rate that would apply to the last dollar of earned taxable income under normal treatment.

In order to calculate tax and marginal tax rate under the maximum tax, it is necessary to estimate the proportion of earned and unearned income by income bracket. This was done by defining earned income as the sum of wages and salaries plus 30 percent of income from businesses, farms, partnerships, and small corporations.[8]

Data

The primary source of data for the analysis reported here is the Internal Revenue Service's annual *Statistics of Income,* which summarizes income, deductions, and related data reported on individual tax returns. Information is also available for selected years regarding the distribution of gifts by recipient group and by form of the gift. Distributions of taxpayers by filing status are also available.

While this source is an invaluable tool, is has a number of limitations. In the first place, the most recently published data available to us were for the 1978 tax year. These data therefore had to be "aged," using standard techniques, to bring them up to date. Average household income in current dollars was assumed to increase at the rate of per-capita national income. Projected price levels were used to express dollar amounts in terms of constant 1980 dollars. In all cases, the Administration's economic assumptions from the 1983 Budget are used for projection. The distribution of taxpayers among filing statuses (e.g., single, married filing jointly) was assumed to remain constant over the period.[9]

In the second place, the *Statistics of Income* reports only aggregate data grouped by income class rather than data for individuals. Fortunately, past research has demonstrated that using aggregate data produces estimates quite close to those obtained using individual data.[10] However, to improve the sensitivity of the analysis, separate simulations were run for taxpayers in each of the five filing statuses and, within each of these, for itemizers and nonitemizers separately.

The third limitation of the *Statistics of Income* is that it provides data on the charitable contributions only of those who itemize their deductions. For nonitemizers, data on charitable contributions were taken from a University of Michigan survey on giving conducted in 1973. These data were aged, to make them applicable to 1978 income classes.[11]

Fourth, because appreciated assets are taxed differently from regular income (they are taxed at special capital gains rates), reported contributions had to be divided between cash and other assets and each had to be analyzed separately. This was done using a distribution based on the 1975 *Statistics of Income* (Table 2.4, p. 52), which provided the most recent data available on the breakdown of gifts.

Finally, the most recent year for which information is available on the distribution of gifts by recipient group is 1962. In that year the *Statistics of Income* (Table E, p. 6) included a breakdown of contributions among five types of recipients: religious organizations, other charitable organizations, educational institutions, hospitals, and other organizations.[12] As above, it was assumed that the proportionate breakdown for each real income level did not change over time, so that the 1962 distributions were interpolated to apply to the 1978 income brackets.

SIMULATION RESULTS

Three sets of results flow from our analysis of the impact of the 1981 tax act on individual charitable giving. The first of these relates to the aggregate impact of the act on the overall level of individual giving. The second relates to the variation in this impact among different income groups. And the third relates to variations in this impact that result for different types of recipient organizations. We examine each of these sets of results in turn.

Because of the attention it has attracted, moreover, we also detail in a separate section how the above-the-line charitable deduction would affect giving if it were fully operational as of 1984. To do this, the 1984 projections were recomputed as if full deductibility for nonitemizers were in effect by that date. In fact, of course, full deductibility is not scheduled to go into effect until 1986. By that date, however, the 1981 law's provision for indexing tax rates, which will affect giving negatively, will also be in effect. Since we have not estimated the effects of indexing, the result under full deductibility presented here should be viewed as suggestive only and not as an indication of the full effects of the 1981 law on giving in the period after 1984.

AGGREGATE IMPACTS

Table 12–1 shows projected total amounts of individual giving for the years 1981–1984 under the two basic assumptions regarding the income and price elasticities of contributions. Under the assumption of the constant income and price elasticities for all households, individual giving for the four years, adjusted for inflation, is projected to be $10.0 billion less under the 1981 tax act than under the previous tax law, with the disparity growing from $0.3 billion in 1981 to $3.9 billion in 1984. Under the assumption that price and income elasticities vary by income level, the projected difference between the two laws is $14.2 billion. In other words, the 1981 tax act will likely depress individual giving compared to what it would have been under the old law. It is important to note, however, that the absolute level of real giving is projected to increase in either case. If one takes the previous level of contributions as the yardstick for comparison—the $40.3 billion level in 1980, for example—giving appears to increase under the 1981 law. It is in comparison to the hypothetical extension of the previous law that the 1981 tax act fares poorly.

Taken together, these aggregate projections imply that individual giving

Table 12–1. Projected Individual Giving, 1981–84, 1981 Tax Act vs. Pre-1981 Law, Two Functional Forms, in 1980 Dollars ($ *billions*)

	Constant Elasticities			Variable Elasticities		
	Pre-1981 Law	1981 Tax Act	Difference	Pre-1981 Law	1981 Tax Act	Difference
1981	$41.0	$40.7	$ −0.3	$41.6	$41.2	$ −0.4
1982	41.9	39.9	−2.0	42.8	39.9	−2.9
1983	45.5	41.7	−3.8	46.4	41.3	−5.1
1984	48.3	44.4	−3.9	49.2	43.4	−5.8
Total	$176.7	$166.7	$ −10.0	$180.0	$165.8	$ −14.2

as a percentage of personal income will continue under the new law the pattern of decline it has exhibited since at least the mid-1970s. As Table 12–2 shows, this pattern is projected to be reversed by 1984, in part because of the expansion of the partial above-the-line charitable deduction in that year. It is far from certain that this turnaround will persist even after full deductibility is in effect, however, because of the potential impact of the indexing provisions that are scheduled to go into effect in 1985.

Variations Among Income Classes

Possibly more important than the overall impact of the 1981 tax act on aggregate levels of charitable giving are the significant variations in impact among income classes. These variations result largely from the fact that the 1981 law reduces tax rates facing upper-income taxpayers more than those for middle- or lower-income taxpayers. As a result, the giving behavior of upper-income taxpayers can be expected to be affected more by the new tax law than that of lower- and middle-income taxpayers, many of whom will be affected by the new deduction for nonitemizers.

Table 12–3 confirms this expectation. What it shows is that a disproportionate share of the reduction in individual giving associated with the

Table 12–2. Individual Giving as a Percent of Personal Income, 1976–80 Actuals and 1981–84 Projections 1981 Tax Act vs. Pre-1981 Law

Year[a]	1981 Tax Act	Pre-1981 Law
1976	1.92	1.92
1977	1.91	1.91
1978	1.91	1.91
1979	1.89	1.89
1980	1.84	1.84
1981 E	1.85	1.86
1982 E	1.78	1.87
1983 E	1.80	1.97
1984 E	1.86	2.03

[a] E = Estimates.

Table 12–3.   Projected Distribution of Individual Giving by
Income Groups, 1981 Tax Act vs. Pre-1981 Law, 1981–84, in
Constant 1980 Dollars ($ *billions*)

Income	Projected Giving, 1981–84		
Group	Pre-1981 Law	1981 Law	Difference
Lower[a]	15.3	15.4	$ + 0.1
Middle[b]	82.6	81.1	− 1.5
Upper[c]	78.8	70.2	− 8.6
Total	176.7	166.7	−10.0

[a] Includes taxpayers with incomes under $6,000, who accounted for about 30 percent of the taxpayers in 1978.
[b] Includes taxpayers with incomes $6,000 to $25,000, who accounted for about 55 percent of all taxpayers in 1978.
[c] Includes taxpayers with incomes $25,000 or more, who accounted for about 15 percent of all taxpayers in 1978.

new law as opposed to the old is concentrated in the upper income brackets. Representing 15 percent of all taxpayers and 44 percent of all individual charitable contributions in 1978, the taxpayers in these brackets account for over 85 percent of the reduction in individual giving associated with the 1981 law as compared with the pre-1981 law over the 1981–1984 period.

Put somewhat differently, the 1981 tax act significantly shifts the burden of giving among income groups over the 1981–84 period compared to what it was in 1980. As reflected in Table 12–4, the share of individual giving for the bottom 30 percent of all taxpayers is projected to increase 3.3 percent between 1980 and 1984 under the 1981 law; and for the middle 55 percent of all taxpayers, it is projected to increase 9.6 percent. By contrast, the share contributed by the 15 percent of all taxpayers in the highest income brackets is projected to *decrease* by 10.4 percent.

Resulting Variations in Impact Among Recipients

What makes these variations in the impact of the 1981 tax act among income classes particularly important is the fact that different income groups

Table 12–4.   Projected Shares of Individual Giving by Income Class
Under the 1981 Tax Act

Income Class[a]	1980	1984	Percent Change 1980–84
Lower	9.0%	9.3%	+3.3%
Middle	45.7	50.1	9.6
Upper	45.3	40.6	−10.4
Total	100.0%	100.0%	—

[a] See notes to Table 12–3.

Table 12–5. Estimated Individual Contributions to Various Types of Charitable Organizations, 1980 vs. 1981 Tax Law Projections, 1981–84, in Constant 1980 Dollars

Types of Organization	1980[c]	Projected Giving, 1981 Tax Law				% Change 1980–84
		1981	1982	1983	1984	
Religious	24.53	24.94	24.85	26.02	27.78	+13.2%
Other charitable[a]	5.82	5.87	5.74	6.00	6.38	+ 9.6
Educational	1.53	1.49	1.33	1.38	1.45	− 5.2
Hospitals	.65	.63	.57	.59	.62	− 4.6
Other[b]	7.75	7.75	7.37	7.70	8.17	+ 5.4
Total	40.29	40.71	39.89	41.71	44.41	+10.2

[a]"Other charitable organizations" here includes such organizations as community chests, American Red Cross, and American Cancer Association.

[b]"Other organizations" includes "literary, educational, and scientific foundations, libraries, museums, and zoos."

[c]The allocations among recipient types reported here are not comparable to those reported in *Giving U.S.A.* because of differences in definitions of types of organizations used.

distribute their contributions differently among various kinds of charitable activities. Generally speaking, lower-income groups give proportionally more of their charitable gifts to religious organizations than do the rich, while the rich give proportionally more to educational and cultural institutions. By altering the distribution of charitable giving among different income groups, therefore, the 1981 tax act may have quite uneven implications for different types of charitable organizations.

Table 12–5 reports the results of such an analysis using the basic simulation model and data originally compiled by the Treasury for 1962. The table compares the amount of giving that five different types of charitable organizations received in 1980 to what they can expect under the 1981 law over the 1981–84 period. As expected, the impact of the new tax law differs significantly among these different types of organizations. In particular, these projections indicate that religious organizations will absorb 79 percent of the real increase in individual giving projected under the 1981 law during 1981–84. As a result, individual giving to religious organizations is expected to increase by 13.2 percent in real dollar terms between 1980 and 1984. By contrast, individual giving to educational institutions and hospitals is projected to *decline* by about five percent *below 1980 levels* in real dollar terms during this period.

The Impact of Above-the-Line Charitable Deduction

Among the many features embodied in the 1981 tax act, and in the simulation results presented above, one deserves special attention because of the interest it attracted within the philanthropic community during the debate over the 1981 bill. This is the provision allowing the 70 percent of all tax-

Table 12–6.   The Effect of the Charitable Deduction for Nonitemizers Illustrated for 1984 in Constant 1980 Dollars ($ *billions*)[a]

| | Projected Giving in 1984 | | | Difference from Pre-1981 Law |
	Nonitemizers	Itemizers	Total	
1981 law with the following portion of nonitemized giving deductible				
25%	14.0	30.4	44.4	−3.9
100%	18.0	30.4	48.3	0
Pre-1981 law	12.7	35.5	48.3	—

[a]Constant price and income elasticities are assumed. Sums of components may not equal totals due to rounding.

payers who do not itemize their deductions to claim a separate "above-the-line" deduction for their charitable contributions anyway. As it was finally incorporated in the 1981 tax act, this above-the-line deduction is scheduled to go into effect gradually over the period 1982–1986. Because our analysis extends only until 1984, it picks up only a partial picture of the potential impact of this feature, and even then only in the 1984 tax year, when 25 percent of the first $300 in contributions by nonitemizers becomes deductible.[13] This approach was taken because of the gross uncertainty of economic projections so far into the future and because the 1981 tax law contains a provision that would index tax rates beginning in 1985, adding a new level of complexity to the analysis and complicating the task of ferreting out the separate impact of the above-the-line charitable deduction when it goes fully into effect in 1986.

Because of the importance of this above-the-line charitable deduction, however, it is useful to assess its fully operational potential impact by itself. To do so, we have recomputed the 1984 results *as if* the charitable deduction were fully in effect in that year. Although these results thus differ in character from the projections of the actual 1981 law presented above, they nevertheless allow us to focus on this one important provision.

As reflected in Table 12–6, a fully operational above-the-line deduction would have a significant effect on giving levels in 1984. In particular, it would increase contributions by nonitemizers from $14 to $18 billion and would virtually offset the $4.8 billion reduction in giving that other features of the 1981 law produce relative to pre-1981 law. By comparison, the partial version of this feature actually incorporated in the 1981 law offsets only about $0.9 billion of this $4.8 billion reduction.

Because nonitemizers are primarily concentrated among middle- and lower-income taxpayers, the above-the-line charitable deduction also has a potential distributional impact. In particular, as shown in Table 12–7, if this provision were fully operational in 1984 it would further alter the distribution of giving away from upper-income taxpayers toward middle- and lower-income taxpayers. Put differently, most of the increase in giving that

Table 12–7. Projected Changes in Shares of
Individual Giving by Income Class Under the 1981
Tax Law, 1984 vs. 1980, With Partial and Full
Deductibility of Gifts by Nonitemizers

	Projected Change in Share, 1984 vs. Actual 1980	
Income Class[a]	With Partial Deductibility[b]	With Full Deductibility
Lower	+ 3.3%	+ 3.3%
Middle	+ 9.6%	+12.9%
Upper	−10.4%	−13.7%

[a]See notes to Table 12–3.
[b]Actual law as enacted.

would result from this feature if it were fully operational in 1984 would
come from middle- and lower-income taxpayers.

Reflecting this, finally, a fully operational above-the-line charitable deduction in 1984 would also alter the results for particular types of organizations. In particular, as shown in Table 12–8, religious giving under this
circumstance would climb 23.9 percent as opposed to 13.9 percent, while
levels of giving to educational institutions and hospitals would remain unchanged. As Table 12–8 also shows, however, using price and income
elasticities that vary with income yields a less favorable result for these latter institutions. Because this formulation assumes that upper-income taxpayers are considerably more price-sensitive than those at lower incomes,
the new deduction has less impact and the tax-rate cuts at the top have
more, resulting in absolute declines for education and hospitals.

Table 12–8. Percentage Change in Individual Contributions to Various Types of
Charitable Organizations, 1980 to 1984, by Tax Law and Elasticity Assumption

	Constant Elasticities			Variable Elasticities
	Pre-1981 Tax Law[b]	1981 Tax Law	1981 Tax Law with Full Deductibility	1981 Tax Law with Full Deductibility
Type of Organization[a]				
Religious	+21.0	+13.2	+23.9	+20.6
Other Charitable	+19.9	+ 9.6	+19.1	+15.6
Educational	+13.1	− 5.2	− 0.1	− 5.2
Hospitals	+12.3	− 4.6	0	− 4.5
Other	+17.4	+ 5.4	+13.5	+ 9.3
Total	+19.9	+10.2	+19.9	+16.3

[a]See notes to Table 12–5.
[b]Incorporates partial deductibility for nonitemizers.

CONCLUSIONS

The Economic Recovery Tax Act of 1981 has already taken its place as one of the most controversial and hotly debated pieces of economic policy in our nation's history. To date, however, the debate over this act has largely ignored one of its more important, if indirect, potential consequences: its impact on the rate of private, charitable giving and, hence, on the strength and viability of the whole private nonprofit sector of national life. This neglect is especially ironic in view of the fact that one of the central tenets of the economic philosophy reflected in the tax act is the belief that fewer social functions should be vested in government and more reliance placed on private institutions to cope with national needs. Yet the evidence developed here indicates that, in certain parts of the nonprofit, charitable segment of the private sector, the tax bill may work in the opposite direction, discouraging private giving and, thus, limiting the capability of private nonprofit institutions to assume an expanded role.

Our projections suggest that aggregate contributions by individuals will decline, relative to the pre-1981 tax law, between 1981 and 1984. When the new deduction for nonitemizers is fully phased in, however, total giving should rise, but probably not to the level it would have reached under the previous act, especially since indexing will by then be in effect. The distribution of that giving will also be affected by the act. The 1981 tax act significantly raises the "price" of giving for upper-income taxpayers. This plus the new incentive for nonitemizers will redistribute the burden of giving from upper incomes to middle and lower incomes. This in turn will lead to disproportionate growth in giving to religious organizations relative to charities favored by the rich, in particular, colleges, universities, and hospitals.

NOTES

1. Data on the expenditures of the nonprofit sector in 1977 are from U.S. Bureau of the Census, 1977 *Census of Service Industries*, SC77-A-53, Part I (January 1981), p. 53-1-3. Data on nonreligious private giving are from *Giving U.S.A.*, 1981 Annual Report (New York: American Association of Fund-Raising Counsel, Inc., 1981), pp. 27 and 29.

2. Under previous law, foundations were required to pay out each year five percent of their assets or all of their earnings, whichever is larger. The 1981 law removes the "whichever is larger" clause, permitting a maximum five percent pay out even when revenues exceed five percent.

3. In 1982 and 1983, 25 percent of the first $100 of gifts will be deductible for nonitemizers. The amount will increase to 25 percent of the first $300 in 1984, 50 percent without limit in 1985, and all contributions in 1986.

4. See, for example, Michael K. Taussig, Economic aspects of the personal income tax treatment of charitable contributions, *National Tax Journal*, Vol. 20 (March 1967), pp. 1–19; Robert A. Schwartz, Personal philanthropic contributions, *Journal of Political Economy*, Vol. 78 (November–December 1970), pp. 1264–91; Martin Feldstein. The income and charitable contributions: Part I—Aggregate and distribution effects, *National Tax Journal*, Vol. 28 (March 1975), pp. 81–100; James N. Morgan, Richard F. Dye, and Judith H. Hybels,

222 The Charitable Deduction

Results from two national surveys of philanthropic activity, in Commission on Private Philanthropy and Public Needs, *Research Papers,* Vol. I (Washington: Department of the Treasury, 1977), pp. 157–323; and Charles T. Clotfelter and C. Eugene Steuerle, Charitable contributions, in Henry Aaron and Joseph Pechman (eds.), *How Taxes Affect Economic Behavior* (Washington: Brookings Institution, 1981), pp. 403–66.

5. In 1975 dollars of net income, Clotfelter and Steuerle (1981, p. 428) present elasticities of $4,000–10,000: −9.45 and 0.393; $10,000–20,000: −1.346 and 0.621; $20,000–50,000: −1.657 and 0.364; $50,000–100,000: −1.360 and 0.668; and $100,000 and over −1.779 and 1.089.

6. Where R is the odds of itemizing, the proportion of itemizers is $R/(1 + R)$.

7. For a more complete treatment of the maximum tax, see Lawrence B. Lindsey, Alternatives to the current maximum tax on earned income, paper presented at the Conference on Simulation Methods in Tax Policy Analysis, National Bureau of Economic Research, January 1981.

8. Earned income may include more or less than 30 percent of business-related income, depending on whether the income is professional and the extent of capital used. The 30 percent figure is used as a baseline in the tax code for dividing business-related income in many cases. The proportion of earned income for the top six income brackets in 1978 was: 0.86; 0.71, 0.63, 0.51, 0.36, and 0.23.

9. See Appendix Table A1 in the original *National Tax Journal* article for economic assumptions and Table A2 for sources of tax return data.

10. For a comparison of estimates from different studies, see Clotfelter and Steuerle (1981).

11. Although more recent data on giving by individuals have been collected, no other survey interviewed such a large number of households (about 1,900 in all), particularly high-income households as did the 1973 University of Michigan survey. The Michigan study found that average contribution levels for nonitemizers generally rose with income. Averages for nonitemizers with incomes over $30,000 are less precise, however, because of the small number of nonitemizers with high incomes. In order to account for the high variability at the upper end, the figures were smoothed by extending the $20,000–$30,000 average up one bracket and simply averaging the figures for the $50,000–$200,000 and above classes together, as shown in column (2).

These income brackets were then inflated by the growth in the GNP price deflator between 1973 and 1978 (141 percent), the average giving estimtes were inflated by the rate of growth per capita itemized charitable contributions between 1973 and 1978 (154 percent), and the resulting averages were interpolated to yield averages for the 1978 income brackets used in the statistics of income.

12. In the IRS tabulations, "other charitable organizations" included such organizations as community chests, American Red Cross, American Cancer Association; while "other organizations" include "literary, educational, and scientific foundations, libraries, museums, and zoos": (IRS, 1962, p. 8).

13. The deduction for nonitemizers in 1982 and 1983 is limited to $100 of gifts, which is below the mean projected giving for nonitemizers at every income level. In 1984, however, the limit is to be raised to $300, and most nonitemizers were projected to give less than $300 without additional incentive. For a discussion of simulating nonlinear rules, see Martin Feldstein and Lawrence Lindsey, Simulating nonlinear tax rules and nonstandard behavior: An application to the tax treatment of charitable contributions, Working Paper No. 682 National Bureau of Economic Research (May 1981).

REFERENCES

American Association of Fund-Raising Counsel. 1981. *Giving USA.* 1981 Annual Report, New York.
Clotfelter, Charles T., and C. Eugene Steuerle. 1981. Charitable contributions. In *How Taxes*

Affect Economic Behavior, eds. Henry Aaron and Joseph Pechman. Washington: Brookings Institution, pp. 403–66.

Feldstein, Martin. 1975. The income tax and charitable contributions: Part I—Aggregate and distributional effects. *National Tax Journal* 28 (March): pp. 81–100.

Feldstein, Martin, and Lawrence Lindsey. 1981. Simulating nonlinear tax rules and nonstandard behavior: An application to the tax treatment of charitable contributions. Working paper no. 682. National Bureau of Economic Research, May.

Lindsey, Lawrence, B. 1981. Alternatives to the current maximum tax on earned income. Paper presented at the Conference on Simulation Methods in Tax Policy Analysis, National Bureau of Economic Research, Palm Beach, Fla., January.

Morgan, James N., Richard F. Dye, and Judith H. Hybels. 1977. Results from two national surveys on philanthropic activity. In Commission on Private Philanthropy and Public Needs, *Research Papers.* Vol. 1. Washington: Treasury Department, pp. 157–323.

Schwartz, Robert A. 1970. Personal philanthropic contributions. *Journal of Political Economy* 78 (November/December): 1967. pp. 1264–91.

Taussig, Michael K. 1967. Economic aspects of the personal income tax treatment of charitable contributions. *National Tax Journal* 20 (March): pp. 1–19.

U.S. Internal Revenue Service. *Statistics of Income—Individual Income Tax Returns.* Washington: Government Printing Office, various years.

13

The Optimal Tax Treatment
of Charitable Contributions

HAROLD M. HOCHMAN and JAMES D. RODGERS

Taking the theory of public goods as its point of departure, this chapter develops the analytical case for fiscal subsidies to charitable giving and, from this perspective, derives their appropriate structure. It deals with whether the existing means of subsidization, through the deduction of charitable contributions from adjusted gross income, satisfies the criteria of Pareto efficiency and distributional neutrality, or whether these objectives are more likely achieved with some alternative mechanism, such as a tax credit.

In 1974, charitable giving amounted to $25.15 billion. Of this, individuals gave some $19.80 billion, and $2.07 billion was transferred through bequests. The remainder was divided between corporate contributions ($1.17 billion) and foundations (2.11 billion).[1] Assuming the marginal rate of tax, on average, to be twenty-five percent, giving by individuals alone reduced federal revenues by some $5 billion.[2] Such subsidies to individual giving are the immediate subject of this chapter. Suitably modified, however, the analysis can be applied to certain other types of deductions, sometimes considered "tax-expenditures," and to corporate giving as well.

Fiscal institutions, in the public choice frame of reference, should reflect citizen-taxpayer preferences. The object of tax policy, as it relates to charitable giving, is to set up a system of subsidies, *provided such subsidies are appropriate,* that is consistent with such preferences.[3] This chapter, in general terms, defines the dimensions of such a system. An important collateral purpose of the exercise is to point out that many other discussions of the tax treatment of charitable giving, in failing to approach the topic from

From *National Tax Journal* 30 (1977): 1–19. The theoretical sections of this paper are based on research supported by the National Science Foundation and The Urban Institute. The policy analysis was prepared at the request of the Department of the Treasury. The comments, suggestions and assistance of Robert Harris, Dick Netzer, Edward Neuschler, Oliver Oldman, John Posnett, Robert Teitel, Richard Wagner, and Burton Weisbrod are acknowledged.
Reprinted by permission of the authors and NTA-TIA.
Editor's note: Portions of this article have been omitted.

the perspective of the theory of public goods, have failed to raise funda-mental issues that are, for policy purposes, logically prior to those on which attention has focused.

This chapter first examines the economic justification of the fiscal sub-sidy to charitable giving. It then presents a theoretical analysis of the ratio-nale for such subsidies, utilizing the theory of public goods, and derives their optimal structure. The incentive effects of subsidization, to which conventional discussion of the tax treatment of charity has devoted most of its attention, are examined, and some of the policy implications of the analysis are spelled out.

THE JUSTIFICATION OF FISCAL SUBSIDIES TO CHARITABLE GIVING

There are two justifications, grounded in the Paretian concept of efficiency, for according preferential tax treatment to charitable giving. The first is the familiar notion that the activities charity finances are not private in the strict sense. Contributions to social, educational, and religious organiza-tions not only benefit the donors, but others, both contributors *and* non-contributors. In other words, contributions produce positive external ef-fects and, in varying degree, possess the characteristics of "publicness." Hence, to rely exclusively on voluntary cooperation among demanders to provide these activities (ingenious though the campaign efforts of some charitable organizations may be) seems likely to result in their undersup-ply. Taking benefits to others into account, the prices faced by individual contributors will be too high, leading them to undercontribute. Moreover, some persons who benefit from these activities at the margin may choose to be "free riders" and make no contributions.

It might be argued that the undersupply of such activities will foster gov-ernment provision, which replaces the voluntarism of charity with the compulsion of taxation. However, even with some "collectivization" of supply, public provision will remain suboptimal if the demanders of the activities that contributions finance are underrepresented in existing polit-ical jurisdictions, and the expenditure decisions of such jurisdictions con-form, approximately, to the median-voter model. Such matters, needless to say, are complex. At issue are (1) just how well the political process re-sponds to constituent demands; (2) the decision rules that political com-munities employ; (3) the tax instruments used to distribute the costs of government-provided goods among the members of the community; (4) the heterogeneity of citizen demands and community composition; and (5) the ease with which political boundaries can be altered and jurisdictions pro-liferated.[4]

To the extent that voluntary cooperation, unassisted, produces subopti-mal levels of provision, the preferential tax treatment of voluntary contri-butions is one way of improving matters. Such "intervention" may be viewed as a means of correcting the voluntary, cooperative outcome, or as a reflection of government failure to assess and implement citizen desires. Through subsidies to charity, political minorities (individuals who feel strongly enough about the social value of certain activities with "public" characteristics) (a) can voluntarily allocate own-income to their provision without fiscal coercion and (b) enlist the aid of the community-at-large in their financing. If individuals who are *not* primary demanders—who do not feel strongly enough about charity-financed activities to support them at the tax-prices implicit in the fiscal structure—benefit from them at the margin, such cost-sharing is a requirement of efficient resource allocation. Indeed, the point of subsidies to charity is to establish sharing arrangements, among primary demanders and the community-at-large, that satisfy the normative criteria of efficiency and distributional neutrality. The community may view such sharing as a compromise between the tyranny of the majority implicit in pure collective action and the polar case of private choice, in which an individual's welfare depends entirely on his own actions.

The second justification of fiscal subsidies to charitable giving is suggested by the economic theory of bureaucracy (see for example, Niskanen, 1971 and Weisbrod, 1976). For at least some government-provided goods, charitable organizations serve as a viable institutional alternative or supplement to public provision. Where they operate at sufficient scale, like major foundations, such organizations compete with government in providing certain services, and, as a consequence, mitigate government monopoly. This has particular import at the national level, where the softening effects of the Tiebout process, which leads individuals to move among jurisdictions when fiscal burdens dominate their expenditure benefits, are weak.

The unique role of private foundations in supporting research and social programs illustrates this argument. In a variety of areas, philanthropic enterprise finances projects that government, by reason of self-interest or law, cannot or will not undertake. Relatively speaking, philanthropy is free from bonds of political accountability, which shackle creative government, and can more readily underwrite risky projects, which hold out the hope of high, though ill-defined, social returns. For the modern scholar and research manager it takes little imagination to see the point.[5]

This line of argument also has a more subtle dimension. For some charitable activities, like those relating to religion, our political constitution precludes government provision, judging its potential costs in terms of conformity to be intolerable. Subsidization, rather than direct provision, thus seems the appropriate means through which to implement the public stake in religious activities.[6]

In the large, these arguments support the way in which charity is now defined for tax purposes. But whether it is appropriate to continue the current system of providing subsidies via deduction from adjusted gross income—so that such subsidies depend on the marginal tax rates of donors—is another matter. Employing assumptions that may approximate reality quite well, we will show that this is unlikely.

To summarize existing practice, the fiscal subsidy to individual charitable contributions in the U.S. now varies with three things. First, it depends on whether taxable income (including contributions) is positive, and whether deductions from adjusted gross income are itemized. If not, the subsidy has no direct worth to the donor, though he may gain from it, indirectly, as a beneficiary of charity, and as a member of the political community if the antimonopoly effects of private philanthropy are important. Second, the subsidy varies with marginal tax rates, which determine the proportions in which the donor and the community share in the costs of a charitable gift. Third, the subsidy is constrained by the limits set on deductibility by the tax code. The general limit of the charitable contributions deduction has been 50 percent of adjusted gross income since 1969; prior to this it was 30 percent.[7]

The discussion that follows focuses on the second aspect.[8] It provides, under specific simplifying assumptions, an analysis of the optimal tax treatment of charitable contributions, and uses this analysis as a basis for assessing how current practice compares with a practical alternative, a tax credit that rebates to all donors a predetermined share of their contributions.[9]

SUBSIDIES TO CHARITY AND THE THEORY OF PUBLIC GOODS

The optimal level of subsidies to private charity depends on how benefits are distributed between donors, the primary sharing group, and secondary demanders, comprising the community-at-large. External benefits must accrue in the demands for the specific services that charity finances or through prior constitutional choice, as with religious activities, to justify the public subsidization of charity. Otherwise, the benefits of giving are private, and no subsidy is warranted.[10]

Assume that charitable contributions finance but one activity, with pervasive "public characteristics," warranting public participation in its financing. The voluntary nature of the contributions has two immediate implications. First, each contributor attains marginal equilibrium, in which *his* incremental benefit and *his* perceived incremental cost are equal. Second, some individuals fail to contribute, not because they place no marginal value on the activity, but because they are better off as "free riders," to wit, they view the cost of its expansion, so long as they must contribute, as excessive and permit others to pay for their benefits.

The first observation implies that *any* equilibrium level of the charity-financed activity, optimal or not, will be one in which all *donors* are in marginal equilibrium. Such a solution can best be described by dividing the community into two groups, those who make voluntary contributions and those who do not. A social optimum requires:

$$\sum_{i=1}^{m} MRS + \sum_{i=m+1}^{n} MRS = MRT \qquad (13\text{--}1)$$

The first term on the left-hand side of Equation (13–1) sums the marginal rates of substitution (MRS's) of contributors and the second sums the MRS's of noncontributors. In the solution described by (13–1) all voluntary contributors are in marginal equilibrium, since $MRS_i = MC_i$, the cost to the individual (as he perceives it) of a unit increment in the activity. The remaining $(n - m)$ noncontributors needs not be in marginal equilibrium. Social optimality (efficient resource allocation) requires that the second *sum*, when added to the first, equal the marginal rate of transformation (MRT) between the public good and some numeraire private good.

The objective of subsidies to charity, defined in terms of an element of the tax base that is a proxy for preferences, is to bring forth the level of contributions that satisfies (13–1) *and* that is also a Lindahl solution, in which, for all persons, contributors and noncontributors alike, $MRS_i = MC_i$. Such an outcome is both efficient and distributionally neutral.

To illustrate how such an outcome may be attained, assume that charity is not subsidized and that the level of contributions is such that the left side of (13–1) exceeds the right. Divide the community, again, into groups. Implicit in the subsidy to charity is a price reduction, which induces those in the first group, who contribute even without subsidy, to increase their nominal contributions, so long as their demands are at all elastic. The price reduction causes a second group, a subset of the initial $(n - m)$ noncontributors, to make some voluntary contributions. Despite the subsidy, individuals in the third group continue to be noncontributors. In addition, as a negative tax, the subsidy reduces federal revenues, leading all groups to contribute indirectly to support of the activity—through some mix of higher taxes and lower expenditures on other programs, assuming full employment.

The tax literature, which dwells on the "incentive effects" of the deductibility of contributions from adjusted gross income, has focused on the net price effects of the subsidy on the first and second groups.[11] Such calculations, however, provide no information about the optimality of this (or any other) subsidy arrangement in terms of the public goods logic. It is to this question that our discussion now turns.

The allocative deficiencies of the no-subsidy situation are examined first. Then the discussion turns to the structure or system of subsidies required to bring about an optimal and distributionally neutral outcome.

Subsidies as a Pareto Optimal Response to Publicness

Assume that a community of three persons (or homogenous groups) is concerned with the financing of a single activity through charitable contributions, without subsidy. Suppose further that both A and B choose to contribute, while the third person, C, does not, even though his valuation of an additional unit is positive at the level that A and B provide.

Consider the choice with which each person is confronted. Assuming that the publicness of the charity-financed good is pervasive, the total quantity, which is available to all, depends on their combined contributions. More-over, with a large number of contributors (the real-world case) strategic behavior is useless, because the individual contributor presumes, ration-ally, that what others give is fixed and independent of his own action. Thus, each person bases his contribution on the amount of the activity it will buy and his own taste for giving, taking the donations of others as beyond his control.

The circumstances just described, for three persons behaving in the mode of the "large-number" case, are illustrated in the three panels of Figure 13–1. The top panel shows A's choice, the middle panel indicates B's, and the bottom panel, C's. Focus first on A's panel. The vertical axis measures A's income, Y^A, and the horizontal axis the quantity of public good, Q. If this good is to be provided at all, it must, by assumption, be financed by voluntary contributions.[12] A's budget constraint is the line EFG. The slope of EFG measures the rate at which A can acquire Q by sacrific-ing own-income (strictly speaking, income available for other consump-tion) and reflects (by its linearity) a simplifying assumption that the mar-ginal cost of Q is constant. The budget line does not extend to the vertical axis, but stops at E, because A has access to the amount of Q that others (i.e., B) finance, whether or not he contributes anything. Initially, there-fore, A's position is at E, given his income Y_0^A and Q_B, the level of the ac-tivity financed by B's contribution. Given his preferences, as described by indifference curve I_A, A contributes $(Y_0^A - Y_1^A)$ and attains equilibrium at F.

B's contribution is similarly analyzed, using the next panel. Given A's contribution of Q_A, B's initial position is H on budget line HJK, which has the same slope as EFG. His contribution secures the provision of an amount Q_B.

Finally, the third individual, C, whose decision is depicted in the bottom panel, contributes nothing, given Q_A and Q_B. C prefers point R because, for him, additional units of the charity-financed good are not worth their cost.

Figure 13–1 describes what Buchanan, in his writings, has called an "in-dependent adjustment equilibrium," in which each person's contribution depends on his private preferences and marginal cost, taking as given the quantities of the public good that others supply. This outcome is analo-gous to the Cournot equilibrium of duopoly theory and results from a sim-ilar adjustment process.[13]

This independent adjustment outcome seems a realistic description of equilibrium in the large-number case, when activities with a significant public or collective-good component are privately financed through unsubsidized voluntary contributions. It is not, however, a Pareto optimal level of pro-vision, much less a Lindahl solution. For a Pareto optimum, it is necessary that summed incremental benefits (over A, B, and C) equal marginal cost, as in Equation (13–1). Here, this condition is not met, because it is A's and B's *individual* (not summed) marginal rates of substitution (*MRS*'s) that equal marginal cost. If, for example, the marginal cost of Q in terms of

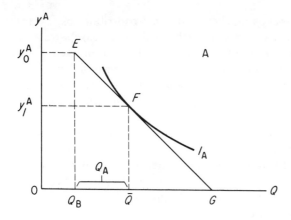

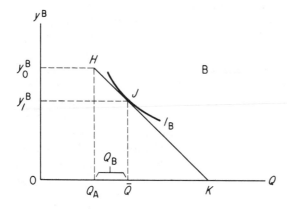

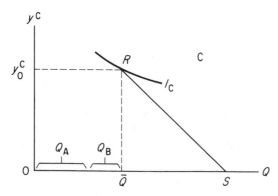

Figure 13–1

other goods is unity, and C's *MRS* at *R* is ½, then at *Q*, the quantity provided,

$$\sum_{A,B} MRS(=1+1) + \sum_{C} MRS(=1/2) > MRT = 1 \qquad (13\text{--}2)$$

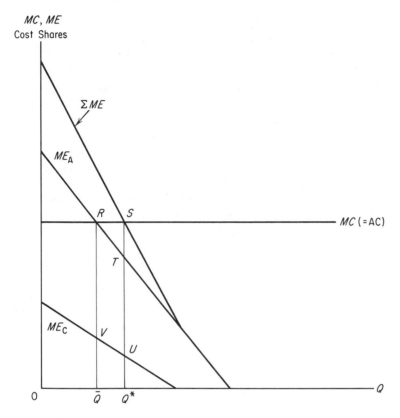

Figure 13-2

Thus, with reference to the Pareto criterion, which defines allocative efficiency, the quantity provided in an unsubsidized, voluntary setting is too small.

Figure 13-2 provides an analysis of the way in which a subsidy can correct such undersupply. To abstract, for now, from the optimal structure of subsidies and focus on cost-sharing between primary demanders and the community-at-large, ignore B, leaving only A, who contributes without subsidy, and C, who does not. The horizontal axis measures the level of the activity. The vertical axis measures: its marginal cost, assumed constant, per unit cost to A and C; and their marginal evaluations, given by the curves labeled ME_A and ME_C. A's private equilibrium is R, at which his marginal evaluation and the marginal cost of providing the good are equal. Because C's marginal evaluation is always less than marginal cost, he contributes nothing. Hence, the quantity provided is $\bar{Q}$, which is less than the optimal quantity Q^*, at which *summed* marginal evaluations, indicated by ΣME, are equal to marginal cost.

To justify public intervention, given the nonoptimality of $\bar{Q}$, our two parties (or groups) must be unable to attain an optimum through voluntary bargaining. While such bargaining might occur in a genuine small-number situation, for most charity-financed activities the large number of small contributors makes it unlikely that optimality will be attained.[14] Hence, efficient allocation requires some external (governmental) modification of the budget constraints with which the participants are faced.[15]

To attain an efficient result, consider a government subsidy, effected, say, through a tax credit that reduces the contributor's income tax liability to a percentage of his gross contributions, S. A fundamental aspect of any such subsidy is that effective tax rates must be raised, public sector activities reduced, or both, to maintain the initial budgetary outcome, be it deficit or surplus. Consequently, through increased tax rates or reductions in service levels, subsidization imposes costs upon both A and C. Assume that the Treasury recaptures this revenue loss through higher effective tax rates, leaving intact the public service budget, and that A is aware that it will do this.[16]

In calculating the effect of the tax credit on the price of his contributions, A will take two factors into account. On the one hand, the tax credit reduces the price of his contributions, because it reduces his taxes, whatever his income, by S per dollar of contributions. On the other, to recoup the implicit revenue loss, A must expect higher general tax rates. The net change in price is a combination of these two effects. The second, indirect component, which operates through higher tax rates, depends on how much the individual contributes; the more he gives, the more revenue the community loses and the higher tax rates must be to maintain a given deficit or surplus.[17]

Figure 13–2 indicates the way in which such a tax credit would function to produce a Lindahl optimum. For optimal allocation, the subsidy must change A's contribution from its no subsidy level $(O\bar{Q} \times R\bar{Q})$ to $OQ^* \times TQ^*$. A's gross contribution must increase to $OQ^* \times SQ^*$. His net contribution, which depends on both the subsidy and the implicit tax change, may be larger or smaller than it was before. This net contribution, plus C's implicit contribution, $OQ^* \times UQ^*$, attributable entirely to the higher effective tax rates required to replace lost revenues, finances the optimal quantity of the activity, OQ^*.

The outcome is necessarily a Lindahl solution. If A is in marginal equilibrium *and* an optimum is attained, C must, in the two-person case, be in marginal equilibrium as well, in the sense that his marginal evaluation $ME_C = UQ^*$ equals the marginal tax cost, to him, of an infinitesimal increase in A's contributions. Ironically, C reaches marginal equilibrium despite making no voluntary contribution at all.[18] For public policy, the issue this raises is that of setting the subsidy rate, S, at the level consistent with the distributionally neutral Lindahl solution.

The Optimal Structure of Subsidies to Charity

Discussion, thus far, has focused on (a) the failure of voluntary behavior to assure sufficient provision of a charity-financed activity and (b) the process through which the subsidies to charity, via a tax credit, can eliminate undersupply and bring about a Lindahl optimum. Attention now turns to the topic of how, if at all, the rates at which charity is subsidized should vary among contributors.

In our previous example, the subsidy took the form of a flat-rate tax credit, invariant with respect to donor income or more generally, donor benefit functions. Under present U.S. law, the subsidy, as a direct function of the marginal tax rate, varies directly with taxable income. Many students of public finance have criticized this on equity grounds.[19] Here, however, the issue of subsidy structure is examined in terms of efficiency, to determine what the public goods rationale for subsidies implies for their optimal structure.[20] We do not consider the equity issue per se, holding, rather, that distributional choice can only be properly discussed in a much broader context than the tax treatment of contributions.

Assume, as in Figure 13–1, a community of three persons: A and B, who contribute to charity, and C, who does not. Suppose, further, that all three have identical tastes, but different incomes, a standard assumption in fiscal design. Let Q^*, as before, be the optimal quantity of the single charity-financed activity, with its price to each contributor being constant over quantity. Ignore, for now, the implicit effects of subsidies on tax rates and, therefore, net contributions, and proceed as if there were some authority, external to the economy in question, that stands ready to assume responsibility for the deficit.

The problem is to decide the appropriate relationship between the rates at which the community subsidizes the contributions of A and B. Given the incomes of the donors, Y_A and Y_B, we can regard their marginal evaluations, at the optimal quantity Q^*, as fixed. To assure provision of the optimal quantity and a distributionally neutral outcome, the price to each person must equal his marginal evaluation; otherwise, (a) the price structure will not induce him to contribute the appropriate amount, so that Q may be under or oversupplied, and (b) the subsidy will not be distributionally neutral (income will be redistributed between A and B).

This equality of marginal evaluation and price is represented, for A and B, by Equations (13–3) and (13–4):

$$\frac{C_A(1-S_A)}{Q^*} = ME_A^* \tag{13-3}$$

$$\frac{C_B(1-S_B)}{Q^*} = ME_B^* \tag{13-4}$$

C_A and C_B are the gross contributions of A and B; S_A and S_B are the subsidy rates: and ME_A^* and ME_B^* are their marginal evaluations at Q^*, the optimal quantity.

To satisfy (13–3) and (13–4), subsidy rates (per dollar of contribution) must equate each individual's marginal (and average) price (his per unit cost share in the absence of monopolistic price discrimination) to his marginal evaluation at the optimal quantity. Such prices, which are obtained by dividing net contributions by Q^*, define the cost shares.

Suppose now that A has the higher income. Then ME_A^* will exceed ME_B^* if Q is a normal good, an assumption the empirical evidence seems to confirm.[21] Inasmuch as quantity is fixed at the optimal level by assumption, and $ME_A^* > ME_B^*$, (13–3) and (13–4) imply that $C_A(1 - S_A) > C_B(1 - S_B)$. To satisfy the Lindahl condition, A's net contribution must exceed B's. However, more precise assumptions, about preferences and income elasticities of contributions (when implicit effects on tax rates are brought back into the discussion) are required to go further and establish, in general terms, the necessary relationship between S_A and S_B.

Suppose, for both A and B, an income elasticity of demand for the charity-financed activity of unity, within the relevant range (levels of output in the vicinity of Q^*). With unit income elasticity, marginal evaluation (or "demand price") rises in proportion to income, so that the elasticity of marginal evaluation with respect to income is also unity.[22] Thus, if B's marginal evaluation is ME_B^* and A's income is $(1 + \lambda)$ times B's ($\lambda > 0$), $ME_A^* = (1 + \lambda) ME_B^*$. Combining (13–3) and (13–4), this produces an exact relationship between contributions and the subsidy schedule required to satisfy the Lindahl condition:

$$C_A(1 - S_A) = (1 + \lambda) C_B(1 - S_B) \tag{13–5}$$

Equation 13–5 indicates that A's net contribution must be $(1 + \lambda)$ times B's if each individual's marginal evaluation is to correspond to his marginal (average) per unit price. Moreover, if $S_A = S_B$, they will face the same prices per dollar of contributions and, with unit income elasticity of demand, A's gross contribution will be $C_A = (1 + \lambda) C_B$. Hence, a subsidy structure with $S_A = S_B$ will satisfy the Lindahl condition, as given by (13–3) and (13–4). Cost *per dollar* of contributions will be the same for the two donors. At the same time their shares in average (= marginal) cost will differ because they contribute different gross (and net) amounts. Other subsidy schedules, which imply different cost-sharing arrangements, violate the Lindahl condition—the public sector analogue of marginal equilibrium in a competitive market—and distort the financing of the collective benefit that A and B support through charitable contributions.

Now consider an income elasticity of one-half. Marginal evaluations rise at but half the rate of income. If A's income is $(1 + \lambda)$ times B's and $\lambda > 0$, $ME_A = (1 + \lambda/2)ME_B$. Combining (13–3) and (13–4), the relationship between A's and B's net contributions to charity must be:

$$C_A(1 - S_A) = (1 + \lambda/2) C_B(1 - S_B) \tag{13–6}$$

Once again the Lindahl condition is satisfied by setting $S_A = S_B$. Since income elasticity is one-half, $C_A = C_B(1 + \lambda/2)$.[23]

This analysis demonstrates that the required increase, with demand, in the fiscal subsidy to a given contributor emerges naturally out of variation in the level of contributions. Attainment of the Lindahl condition does not require the variation of subsidy rates with income, as under present tax law, if the only reason for interpersonal differences in contributions is differences in income. To the contrary, the Lindahl condition requires a flat-rate subsidy, such as a tax credit, under which tax liabilities are reduced by a prespecified proportion of eligible contributions.

Though this demonstration seems simple, it is deceptive. The assumption, contrary to previous argument, that the subsidies are externally financed engenders a conceptual problem. Properly defined, each donor's total contribution must include the compensating increase in his tax payments, inasmuch as contributors as well as noncontributors must share in its fiscal burden. By implication the cost (left-hand) side of (13–3) and (13–4) must be modified to enter the incremental tax. We do this in (13–7) and (13–8). These equations assume that the means of collection is a marginal shift in the individual income tax schedule. The incremental tax function, indicating the implicit increase in the ith individual's marginal tax rate, is denoted by $t'(Y_i)$.[24]

$$\frac{C_A(1-S_A)+t'(Y_A)Y_A}{Q^*}=ME_A^* \tag{13-7}$$

$$\frac{C_B(1-S_B)+t'(Y_B)Y_B}{Q^*}=ME_B^* \tag{13-8}$$

What is of interest here are the implications of different forms of this incremental tax function for the optimal subsidy structure. Specifically, we are concerned with whether this complication reverses our conclusion that a flat-rate subsidy is appropriate (that a tax credit is preferable to deductibility) in terms of the Lindahl condition.

In considering this issue, assume, as before, that the income elasticity of demand is unitary, so that marginal evaluations are proportional to income. An invariant subsidy is optimal, in these circumstances, if and only if the $t'(Y)$ terms in (13–7) and (13–8) are equal. If A's income is twice B's, the increase in A's tax payments must, in dollar terms, be twice the increase in B's. Thus the Lindahl condition requires displacement of the original marginal tax schedule by a constant, a change which makes the effective schedule slightly less progressive.

Matters become more complex when the income elasticity differs from unity, since it is marginal evaluation and not income with which charity must keep in step and, in the present argument, both Y_A and Y_B, the respective incomes of A and B, are fixed. In general, to justify $S_A = S_B$, the ratio of $t'(Y_A)$ to $t'(Y_B)$ must vary with the income elasticity. The higher the elasticity, the more progressive the "increment" in the tax must be. Conversely, with given income elasticity, the more progressive the implied increments in marginal tax rates, the more the subsidy to charity must in-

crease with income—in the direction of its structure under deductibility—
to offset its effect on tax-prices.

In policy, however, it is the magnitude and not the direction of these
effects that is interesting. Cursory analysis provides ample reason to believe that such effects are inconsequential. Charitable giving is less than two
percent of personal income,[25] and the implicit effects of the subsidy on
marginal tax rates are even smaller because part of its cost is diverted to
noncontributors. It thus seems reasonable to think of a small across-the-
board differential in marginal tax rates (a marginal differential, as pointed
out, that is slightly regressive) as the means through which the costs of the
subsidy are offset.[26] Under this, or virtually any other assumption that is
at all realistic, a flat-rate tax credit is likely to provide a good approximation to the Lindahl requirements. It is, in any case, far more likely to
do this than the present structure, under which subsidies to charity are
strongly progressive.

PRICE ELASTICITIES AND COST-SHARING BETWEEN DONORS AND THE COMMUNITY-AT-LARGE

It is important to relate this argument, which considers subsidies to charity
as a means of cost-sharing, to conventional discussion, which centers on
the effect of fiscal subsidies on the incentive to contribute.

Assume, for argument's sake, that a flat-rate tax credit satisfies the Lindahl condition and there is but one charity-financed activity with pervasive
public benefits. Assume, further, that the fiscal authorities have access to a
suitable computational algorithm, which identifies the optimal level of charity
and the terms on which donors and the community-at-large should share
its costs.[27]

A legislature, deciding whether to increase or decrease its subsidy, must
know more than the price elasticity of giving. A unitary price elasticity, for
example, tells it only that a one percent reduction in price will increase
giving by one percent; a price elasticity in excess of unity implies only that
a given reduction in price (increase in the subsidy) will yield a dollar increase in contributions that exceeds its cost in terms of revenue. But it does
not answer the normative question that our analysis considers basic; it does
not tell us whether the price reduction is desirable.

This requires that we must know the relationship between the optimal
sharing ratio, R^*, as defined previously, and the marginal sharing ratio,
R_M, implicit in the incentive effect. R_M is the cost to the community (in
foregoing revenue) of a one percent change in the subsidy, divided by the
increase in gross contributions that accompanies it.[28] If $F_M > R^*$, the subsidy is excessive, with the community (through the fisc) bearing too large
a share in the cost of financing the charity-supported activity. Alternatively
if $R_M < R^*$, the subsidy is too low.

Values of R_M, for price elasticities of *net* giving (cost to the donor) and

Table 13–1.   Community Share of the Incentive Effects on Gross Charitable
Giving *(marginal sharing ratio: R_M)[a]*

Price Elasticity of Charitable Giving	Initial Subsidy Rates = Marginal Tax Rate = 1 − Price to Donor					
	.20	.30	.40	.50	.60	.70
−0.25	.84	.86	.88	.90	.92	.94
−0.50	.73	.77	.80	.83	.87	.90
−0.75	.66	.70	.74	.78	.83	.87
−1.00	.60	.65	.70	.75	.80	.85
−1.25	.56	.61	.68	.72	.78	.83
−1.50	.52	.58	.65	.70	.76	.82

[a]Reported figures average the cost-benefit ratio (marginal sharing ratio) for changes of ±1 percent in the net price of charitable giving.

subsidy rates that span the range of reasonable estimates, are reported in Table 13–1. The price elasticities, which range from −0.25 to −1.50, encompass the Schwartz (1970) and Taussig (1967) estimates at the lower end of their range, and the estimates of Feldstein (1975a) and Feldstein and Taylor (1976), which range between −1.0 and −1.5, at the upper end. The initial subsidy (the complement of the price of charity to the donor) varies from 0.20, as low a marginal tax rate as can be expected to apply on returns which itemize deductions.

The marginal sharing ratios in Table 13–1 are, from the Treasury perspective, cost-benefit ratios. Arithmetically, they are simple averages of the marginal sharing ratios implied by changes of plus and minus one percent in the net price of charity, relative to the price implicit in the subsidy rate at the head of the column (e.g., if the initial subsidy is 0.20, the price is 0.80, and becomes either 0.7920 or 0.8080 as a result of a one percent change). For practical purposes, differences between the marginal sharing ratios implied by positive and negative changes in price (in the one percent range) are insignificant (in other words, less than 0.01).

As might be expected, Table 13–1 tells us that the share of the incentive effect the community must pay through higher taxes declines with price elasticity and increases with the initial subsidy rate. The initial rate of the subsidy makes less difference, the lower the price elasticity; the price elasticity makes less difference, the higher the initial subsidy. In general, R_M is *much higher* than the subsidy rate itself and is quite sensitive to the parameters, because the legislature, in granting subsidies, cannot discriminate between marginal and inframarginal contributions. In other words, changes in the subsidy are not restricted to incremental contributions, but apply to inframarginal contributions as well.

To the fiscal authorities, the point of this numerical exercise is that price elasticity, as a basis for evaluating potential changes in the tax treatment of contributions, can be quite misleading. For the general taxpayer, to whom the Treasury is responsible, liberalization of the tax treatment of contributions is only worthwhile if it has an incentive effect that is worth its marginal tax-price. Public policy involves much more than whether an additional dollar of subsidies can generate more than a dollar of charity.

POLICY IMPLICATIONS

Discussion turns now to specific policy implications. To this point our major conclusion is that the present system, under which contributions are deducted from adjusted gross income, producing subsidies that increase with income and marginal evaluation, may do considerable violence to the requirements of the Lindahl condition. Judged in terms of the public choice logic, this system seems decidedly inappropriate, unless there are large enough increases in the external economies associated with the different activities supported as donor income rises, with no externalities associated with the contributions of persons who do not itemize deductions. This last assumption seems absurd, while there is no empirical support for the idea that the beneficiaries of the rich produce goods with more pervasive external effects. If anything, one would expect charity-financed activities having governmental substitutes (for example, education and social welfare activities) to generate less in the way of positive external benefits than activities that are exclusively financed through charity (for example, religion). Nor does deductibility seem an appropriate way of distributing the costs of privately provided goods which produce collective-consumption benefits between their primary demanders and the community-at-large.

Of the policy alternatives, the simplest, in practice as in theory, is a tax credit, which reduces the income tax liability of the donor by a designated proportion of his contributions, set by the legislature to reflect the extent of their external benefits. While this recommendation is not novel, our reasons for making it are. Students of taxation have often suggested that a tax credit be substituted for the deductibility of contributions under the income tax.[29] As a rule, however, this recommendation has been associated with an aversion to the pro-rich characteristics of deductions from adjusted gross income, and it has rationalized in terms of egalitarian value judgments. To the fiscal economist, concerned with squaring policy with theory, this normative bias in the traditional case for the tax credit is a distinct methodological weakness. In our analysis, with the legitimacy of subsidies to charity (whatever their immediate distributional consequences) as a premise, we avoid this pitfall because we substitute the standard criteria of "efficiency" and "distributional neutrality" for the strong value judgment implicit in traditional use of the "equity" criterion.

It seems appropriate, therefore, to recommend, as a primary reform in the income tax treatment of charitable contributions, the adoption of a tax credit, to replace the deductibility of contributions from adjusted gross income. This seems the most practicable means of approximating the Lindahl condition.[30] To be sure, the case for a tax credit is not cut and dried. It may be vitiated by differences in the substantive composition of giving, though there is no hard evidence on this question, one way or another. Its arithmetic is complicated (as previously described) by the means through which the government raises the tax revenues required to finance the subsidy. But the arguments in opposition to adoption of a flat-rate credit—arguments against moving to a simple and uncomplicated cost-sharing arrangement between donors and the community-at-large—seem nowhere near so compelling, intuitively, as the arguments against the steeply progressive subsidies which deductibility implies. This in no way denies an ultimate need, from a social perspective, for a distributional value judgment. It does imply, however, that the tax treatment of charitable contributions is not the place to implement this value judgment.

The proper level of the tax credit depends, as prior discussion has indicated, on the "external" content of the benefits that charity-financed activities confer; it depends, in other words, on the relationship between the marginal evaluations of the primary sharing group, namely, voluntary donors, and the community-at-large.[31] In academic discussion, though not actual policy, the specification of this proportion can be thought of as a matter for democratic decision-making, which faces the same problems here as in setting tax-prices for conventional public goods.

In practice, however, there is nothing simple about the business of obtaining such an algorithm. As an initial approximation, the legislature might set the tax credit to maintain the budgetary cost of the subsidy at its current level, under deductibility—with an upward adjustment to reflect those contributions that are now subsumed under the standard deduction and thus denied the subsidy. According to Feldstein and Taylor (1976, p. 1219), a 25 percent tax credit would hold both the total volume of contributions and its cost to the Treasury approximately constant. While this approach would ignore the nonoptimality of the outcome under deductibility, our principal reason for advocating reform, it is a starting point that avoids first-order effects on public revenues.[32]

Second, it is not only appropriate, but important, to remove charitable contributions from the umbrella of the standard deduction. So long as charity produces external benefits, there is no logical basis for denying the subsidy to the broad class of donors who do not, for whatever reason, elect to itemize.

Nor do we see a compelling reason to set a quantitative limit, relative to income on any other index of ability-to-pay, on the amount of a taxpayer's contributions (direct *or* through a bonafide foundation, properly monitored) that the community is willing to subsidize, provided it sets the tax credit at its proper level. The present limit is a vestige of an improper interpretation of the rationale for fiscal subsidies to charitable giving, which considers the subsidy to be a tax dodge or loophole, adopted as a matter of political expedience rather than allocative efficiency. No doubt repeal of the limit might enable more of the very rich to pay no tax at all. But to do so, provided the tax credit is less than 100 percent, the rich must assign a larger share of their own income and wealth to social purposes, reducing their expenditures on private goods and, in so doing, producing benefits (through mixed private and public financing) that are valued at cost by the community-at-large.

On these grounds, the twenty percent limit on giving to private foundations seems questionable, assuming, of course, that "the public" has not erred in its definition of eligible foundations. In addition, the efficient use of donations to charity is hampered by the inability of donors to regulate their disposition. As Tullock (1966) has pointed out, individuals have little incentive to acquire such information, since its cost is greater than their private gain. Thus foundations, functioning as intermediaries, acquiring information for donors and monitoring the use of charity by those to whom they dispense funds, play a very significant role in the philanthropic process. The twenty percent limit, by discouraging donor use of the foundation vehicle, not only inhibits efficiency in the disposition of contributions, but, by so doing, reduces the level of giving, even through external benefits might justify additional subsidies.

The final question is whether a "floor" should be placed on eligible contributions, limiting the deduction to persons whose gifts exceed a certain percentage, such as three percent, of adjusted gross income. This limitation has been recommended, among others, by Goode (1964) and Taussig (1967). To rationalize a floor in terms of efficiency, one must argue that activities financed by individuals having deductions lower than the floor generate no positive external effects, or that at least the benefit the floor generates by precluding subsidies to truly private goods offsets the harm it inflicts by stifling contributions to activities with positive external effects. If the former argument is used to rationalize a floor, simply removing these private activities from the list of those that will be subsidized is a better solution. However, either argument requires knowledge about the external effects associated with various charitable activities, and in the absence of such knowledge, no clear position is possible.

In conclusion, it should be pointed out that the logic of this chapter is not limited to the tax treatment of charitable contributions. It can be extended to other deductions allowed by the tax law, referred to (in some cases with inappropriate value connotations) as "tax-expenditures." Such deductions, in contrast to those that reflect costs of earning income, include, among others, medical expenditures, and certain casualty losses, which warrant special tax treatment because they reflect a kind of constitutional decision to share risk. With the medical deduction the case against subsidy rates that vary directly with income seems even clearer than it does for contributions. Though full evaluation of such considerations lies beyond the scope of this chapter, we strongly recommend that the preferential tax treatment of other nonbusiness expenditures of the household be reevaluated in light of analysis of the kind this chapter has developed.

NOTES

1. American Association of Fund-Raising Counsel, *Giving USA: 1975 Annual Report*, p. 6. Foundation giving, of course, derives from prior gifts of corporations and individuals. By 1984 giving had risen to $74.25 billion, with individuals accounting for $61.55 billion, bequests $4.89 billion, foundations $4.36 billion and corporations $3.45 billion. *Giving USA: 1985 Annual Report*, p. 7.

2. The figure of twenty-five percent is taken from Feldstein (1975a). It was calculated by applying the marginal tax rate for joint returns to contributions in each taxable income class.

3. Thus, within the framework of this chapter, it is inappropriate to think of subsidies to charity as a "tax loophole." Such a characterization, pejorative in tone, implies that the community really prefers nominal and effective rates of tax to be one and the same (though there is little evidence that it does) or that the state's claims on the individual's income are logically prior to his own.

4. For a model that discusses these issues in more detail, see Weisbrod (1975). Also see Buchanan and Tullock (1962).

5. We are, of course, ignoring abuses, as occur when the foundation vehicle is used, without social purpose, as a simple tax-dodge, reducing the taxation of private income. But this is a separate issue.

6. If governance and the political process were costless and the federal system ideal, both of these justifications for the subsidization of charitable giving would vanish. There would be no need for "private jurisdictions" of demanders, acting without the coercive powers of government, to provide collective wants. Moreover, individuals would not need charitable organizations as counterpoise to the abuses and inefficiencies inherent in government monopoly.

7. For more detailed discussion of these limits, and the special 30 percent limitation on certain gifts of capital gain property, see Internal Revenue Service Publication 526. Income tax deduction for contributions, 1974 edition.

8. In the policy discussion in the section titled, "Policy Implications," we return briefly to the other two factors.

9. What qualifies as a legitimate contribution (a topic which preoccupies much legal discussion) is ignored, as are abuses of the preferential treatment of contributions, such as gifts of overvalued assets. As a policy issue, questions of legitimacy stand on their own, separate from the concerns of this chapter. Vickrey (1975) examines some aspects of abuse, particularly those involving gifts of noncash assets.

We should note that our analysis does provide a rationale for liberalizing the tax treatment of political contributions and rethinking the present practice of disallowing contributions to organizations engaged in nonpartisan political activity (for example, the League of Women Voters), this despite the ambiguities inherent in the adjective "partisan." Such participation in the political process is itself a public good.

10. If the benefits of a charity-financed activity have a restricted domain in, say, political or spatial terms, those who do not benefit should not be required to help finance it. The members of the "club," as a self-contained community, should be fully responsible for costs. See Buchanan (1965) and Polinsky (1973) for discussion of cost-sharing in a community club context. This implies, strictly speaking, that the subsidization of much charity should be, say, local rather than federal. It has its institutional counterpart in restrictions on deductibility, in some states, to philanthropic organizations that concentrate their activities in-state. Our analysis assumes all this away, implying, in effect, that such differences wash out in the aggregate. To do otherwise would make an already unwieldy analytic framework even more unmanageable.

11. See Feldstein (1975a, 1975b), Feldstein and Taylor (1976), Kahn (1960), Schwartz (1970), Taussig (1967), and Vickrey (1962).

12. The simplest rationalization of this is that public provision requires the acquiescence of a political majority, but that the set of jurisdictional boundaries and opportunity costs of relocation preclude the formation of such a majority.

13. See Breit (1968), Buchanan (1967, 1968), and Fellner (1960).

14. Of course, bargaining may occur if a few large contributors account for a charity's support. For discussion of the possibility of such group bargaining, where the distribution of the relevant characteristic among participants is very skewed, see Stigler (1974).

15. Whether the government has the information to improve matters, rather than make them worse, is not dealt with here. We assume that *some* form of subsidization can improve resource allocation to *some* degree.

16. Introduction of the subsidy will increase the quantity of the charity-financed activity, and alter the optimal amounts of public sector activities that are complementary with it or substitutes for it. Throughout this chapter such interdependence is assumed to be absent.

17. Strictly speaking, this means that A cannot be viewed as a pricetaker, since price varies with quantity. However, in a large-number setting (analogous to a firm in competition) this can be ignored, since an increment in A's contribution will have negligible influence on effective tax rates.

18. Of course, introduction of the subsidy might well induce C to make *some* voluntary contribution, unlike the situation depicted in Figure 13–2, if it reduced his net price, at some levels of contributions, below the corresponding marginal evaluation.

19. See, for example, Schaefer (1968) and Vickrey (1974).

20. We are still assuming that charity finances but a single activity and that the publicness of its benefits is pervasive. Whether subsidy rates should differ among activities because they differ in degree of publicness is essentially an empirical question which is not considered here.

21. This is confirmed in Feldstein (1975a) and Feldstein and Taylor (1976), and by both Taussig (1967), using cross-section data, and Schwartz (1970), in time-series analysis. Although there are wide differences in the estimates of income elasticities of giving reported in these studies, the values are uniformly positive.

22. *Proof:* The elasticity of ME_i, the marginal evaluation of the ith person in the community, with respect to income is defined as:

$$\eta_M = \frac{dME_i}{dY_i} \cdot \frac{Y_i}{ME_i}$$

If person i's net contribution in Lindahl equilibrium is

$$C_i = ME_i Q^*$$

and the change in contribution as income changes (that is, as we move from one person to another) is given by

$$dC_i = d(ME_i) Q^*$$

The elasticity of contributions with respect to income is, therefore,

$$\frac{dC_i}{dY_i} \cdot \frac{Y_i}{C_i} = \frac{d(ME_i) Q^*}{dY_i} \cdot \frac{Y_i}{ME_i Q^*} = \eta_M$$

Thus, with unit income elasticity, $\eta_M = 1$.

23. This exercise can be repeated, with identical effect, for other values of the income-elasticity, such as one and one-half.

24. Note that what we are talking about here are increments in marginal tax rates. It seems reasonable to assume that the individual income tax is the vehicle through which marginal revenue adjustments are made.

25. American Association of Fund-Raising Counsel, *Giving U.S.A.: 1975 Annual Report*, p. 10. Note that personal and not disposable income is the appropriate base. Public choice

theory, which governs this analysis, looks at taxes, which account for the difference between personal and disposable income, as costs to individuals of government-provided services, including charity-financed activities and certain income transfers, Such government-provided services figure in taxpayer utility functions in the same way as private goods.

26. For noncontributors, like C, the Lindahl condition requires that

$$\frac{t'(Y_c)Y_c}{Q^*} = ME_c$$

If a noncontributor places no value on the charity-financed activity at the margin when the optimal quantity is provided (that is, $ME_c = 0$), the incremental tax rate for this person, $t'(Y_c)$, should, strictly speaking, be zero. Hence, unless those with a zero marginal evaluation continue to pay no tax after the across-the-board incremental increase in marginal tax rates, the Lindahl condition will be violated. However, with the assumption that marginal evaluations vary positively with income, the noncontributing individual with the lowest marginal evaluation will pay, correspondingly, the lowest share of the cost.

27. There are, in theory, systematic methods, independent of current giving, through which such information can be obtained. Three suggestive papers are Bohm (1972), Kurz (1974), and Tideman and Tullock (1976).

28. Assume, for example, that there are two individuals, A and C, with A a contributor (subject to 50 percent subsidy) and C a noncontributor. If A has a price elasticity of giving of -2 and initially gives $100 gross, a one percent decrease in price (from 50 to 49.5 percent) would increase net contributions by 2 percent, to $51, and gross contributions to $103 ($= \$51 \div .495$). Initially, the community's share was $50. This share now increases $52 ($= 0.505 \times \$103$). R_M is the ratio of the increase in the community's cost to the increase in gross contributions, that is, $2.00/3.00 \cong 0.67$. Notice that the increase in the community's cost comes about by applying the higher subsidy rate to the new level of gross contributions ($103) rather than the increment of $3.

29. See, among others, Vickrey (1947).

30. Recall the logic of our argument—that charity finances the provision of "goods" and is not an expense of earning income. As to why deductibility was given its present role in the tax treatment of charity, convenience seems the best answer. But one can also point to the failure of decision-makers to understand the public choice logic of the subsidy to charity, inasmuch as the contributions deduction predated full-scale development of the theory of public goods.

31. This also tells us something about the proper relationship between the rates at which the community subsidizes individual and corporate giving. If corporate contributions are passed through to shareowners, imputation problems are confronted, as in any assessment of the distributional implications of corporate income taxation. Such problems are no more (and no less) severe in this context than they are generally. However, to the extent that the corporate tax is shifted forward to the community-at-large through higher product prices, so that the social price of a given sharing ratio is higher for corporate than individual giving, nominal rates of subsidies to corporate giving should be lower.

32. While replacing the current system of deductibility with a 25 percent tax credit would leave the level of giving approximately the same, a substantial change could be expected, again using the Feldstein and Taylor estimates, in its composition. Religious organizations would receive almost 10 percent more and educational institutions 24 percent less in contributions than under the present system. Whether this compositional change represents an improvement or a worsening of resource allocation depends on the optimality (or the size and direction of deviation from optimality) of the present position under deductibility.

REFERENCES

American Association of Fund-Raising Counsel, Inc. 1975. *Giving USA.* New York: American Association of Fund-Raising Counsel.

Atkinson, A. B. 1976. The income tax treatment of charitable contributions. In *Public and Urban Economics, Essays in Honor of William S. Vickrey,* ed. Ronald E. Grieson. Lexington, Mass: D. C. Heath, pp. 13–29.

Baumol, William J., and David F. Bradford. 1970. Optimal departures from marginal cost pricing. *American Economic Review* 60(3): pp. 265–83.

Bohm, P. 1972. Estimating the demand for public goods: An experiment. *European Economic Review* 3(3): pp. 111–30.

Borcherding, Thomas E., and Robert T. Deacon. 1972. The demand for the services of non-federal governments. *American Economic Review* 62(5): pp. 891–901.

Breit, William. 1968. Public-goods interaction in Stackelberg geometry. *Western Economic Journal* 6(2): pp. 161–64.

Buchanan, James M. 1967. Cooperation and conflict in public goods interaction. *Western Economic Journal* 5(1): pp. 109–21.

———. 1965. An economic theory of clubs. *Economica* 32(1): pp. 1–14.

———. 1968. *The Demand and Supply of Public Goods.* Chicago: Rand McNally & Co.

Buchanan, James M., and Gordon Tullock. 1962. *The Calculus of Consent.* Ann Arbor: University of Michigan Press.

Feldstein, Martin. 1975a. The income tax and charitable contributions: Part I—Aggregate and distributional effects. *National Tax Journal* 28(1): pp. 81–100.

———. 1975. The income tax and charitable contributions: Part II—The impact on religious, educational, and other organizations. *National Tax Journal* 28(2): pp. 209–26.

Feldstein, Martin, and Amy Taylor. 1976. The income tax and charitable contributions. *Econometrica* 44(6): pp. 1201–22.

Fellner, William. 1965. *Competition Among the Few.* New York: Augustus M. Kelley.

Goode, Richard. 1964. *The Individual Income Tax.* Washington, D.C.: The Brookings Institution.

Hochman, Harold M., and James D. Rodgers. 1969. Pareto optimal redistribution. *American Economic Review* 59(4): pp. 542–57.

———. 1977. The simple politics of distributional preference. In *The Distribution of Economic Well-Being.* New York: National Bureau of Economic Research.

Internal Revenue Service. 1965. *Statistics of Income 1962: Individual Income Tax Returns.* Washington, D.C.: U.S. Government Printing Office.

———. 1974. *Income Tax Deduction for Contributions.* Internal Revenue Service Publication No. 526. Washington, D.C.: U.S. Government Printing Office.

Kahn, C. Harry. 1960. *Personal Deductions in the Federal Income Tax.* Princeton: Princeton University Press.

Kurz, Mordecai. 1974. Experimental approach to the determination of demand for public goods. *Journal of Public Economics* 3(4): pp. 329–48.

Niskanen, William A., Jr. 1971. *Bureaucracy and Representative Government.* Chicago: Aldine-Atherton.

Polinsky, A. Mitchell. 1973. Collective consumption goods and local public finance: A suggested theoretical framework. Proceedings of the XXVIII Congress of the Institut International de Finances Publiques, Saarbrücken, pp. 166–81.

Schaefer, Jeffrey M. 1968. Philanthropic contributions: their equity and efficiency. *Quarterly Review of Economics and Business* 8(2): pp. 25–34.

Schwartz, Robert A. 1970. Personal philanthropic contributions. *Journal of Political Economy* 78(6): pp. 1264–91.

Stigler, George J. 1974. Free riders and collective action: An appendix to theories of economic regulation. *The Bell Journal of Economics and Management Science* 5(2): pp. 359–65.

Taussig, Michael K. 1967. Economic aspects of the income tax treatment of charitable contributions. *National Tax Journal* 20(1): pp. 1–19.

Tideman, T. Nicholas, and Gordon Tullock. 1976. A new and superior process for making social choices. *Journal of Political Economy* 84(6): pp. 1145–60.

Tullock, Gordon. 1966. Information without profit. *Public Choice* 1 (Fall): pp. 141–59.

Vickrey, William S. 1947. *Agenda For Progressive Taxation*. New York: Ronald Press.

———. 1975. Private philanthropy and public finance. In *Altruism, Morality, and Economic Theory*, ed. Edmund S. Phelps. New York: Russell Sage Foundation, pp. 149–70.

———. 1962. One economist's view of philanthropy. In *Philanthropy and Public Policy*, ed. Frank G. Dickinson. New York: National Bureau of Economic Research, pp. 31–56.

Weisbrod, Burton A. 1975. Toward a theory of the voluntary non-profit sector in a three-sector economy. *Altruism, Morality, and Economic Theory*, ed. Edmund S. Phelps. New York: Russell Sage Foundation, pp. 171–96.

———. 1976. Some collective-good-aspects of nongovernment activities: Not-for-profit organizations. Paper prepared for the 32nd Congress of the Institut International de Finances Publiques, Edinburgh, Scotland.

14

Charity and Dynasty
Under the Federal Tax System

JOHN G. SIMON

TAX TREATMENT OF CHARITY AND THE ALLOCATION OF ECONOMIC POWER

The Problem of "Privilege"

A specter haunts the nonprofit sector of our social order. It is the specter of privilege. It is rarely characterized that way. Indeed, it is a word we seem, as a society, to be quite nervous about using; it is as indelicate, in a socially mobile society, to refer to "privilege" as it was, in a Victorian society, to mention ankles. Although we do not often talk about privilege frontally, traces of the theme show up here and there throughout our public discourse. We have, for example, the suggestion that the charitable deduction in the federal income tax be replaced by a tax credit or by matching grants so that the government will not "subsidize" charitable giving by the rich more than it subsidizes giving by the poor—so that the government will no longer pick up 50 percent of the top-bracket taxpayer's gifts to charity, as compared to 11 percent of gifts made by the bottom-bracket taxpayer or zero percent for the nontaxpayer. Similarly, there are proposals to limit the charitable deduction in the federal estate tax to 50 percent of the gross estate, again reflecting a concern about the extent to which the government "contributes" to charitable giving by wealthy persons. Allusions to the privilege problem found their way into the debate over the regulation of private foundations in 1969 and sometimes they arise when proposals are made to reduce or prevent the exercise of donor control in these foundations.

The specter of privilege is, of course, not confined to those aspects of

From the *Probate Lawyer* 5 (1978):1–92. Reprinted by permission of John G. Simon and the American College of Probate Counsel.

Editor's note: Portions of this article have been omitted. A few passages have been revised to reflect statutory changes or other developments since the article was published.

our federal tax system that relate to the nonprofit world. But problems of privilege applicable to charitable organizations are somewhat different from the issues we normally encounter when discussing other areas of our tax system. For, unlike other aspects of tax reform, our topic does not have very much to do with the ability of affluent taxpayers to shield their wealth and income from taxation. In a sense, the problems I wish to discuss here are issues that remain after other kinds of conventional tax reform have been achieved.

Let us assume, in other words, that we have a tax world unpopulated by preferred stock recapitalizations, installment sales, valuation discounts, charitable front-end annuity trusts, employer-funded life insurance, and other wonders of the estate tax,[1] and that, on the income tax side, the shelters have all been destroyed and, with them, the alchemical conversions of ordinary income into capital gain. What we would be left with, in that utopian world of tax purity, would be a system in which the material rewards of the marketplace, as enjoyed by those who reap them or as enjoyed by those who inherit them, would be recaptured to a greater or lesser degree depending largely on the way Congress fixes the rates. With no change in rate structure, the amount of recapture would substantially increase as a result of these reforms. Would the levelers be satisfied? Or would there be another set of problems they could address under the banner of egalitarian justice? If the trouble with the tax system is that it resembles the process of "dipping deeply into great incomes with a sieve,"[2] then, once we have repaired the sieve, what further systemic work remains to be done? How, one might ask, could there be anything more? I suggest that, even if the sieve were converted into a scoop, causing the estate and income tax systems to do more about leveling the peaks and valleys in the market's allocation of material rewards, an egalitarian dilemma would remain.

[Editor's note: The next section of the original essay spells out this "egalitarian dilemma" in the context of the private foundation, which, with the aid of charitable income or estate tax deductions, permits wealthy persons to maintain a form of dynastic "economic power" over resources. "The dilemma is how to reconcile this retention of power" with the venerable dictum that the tax system is supposed to moderate such economic power. The essay argues that this "power-to-the-rich phenomenon" arises in the case of all deductible giving by wealthy donors—the foundations present only a special case of it—because "the after-tax cost of exercising power and influence in the charitable world is cheaper for the rich than for the poor." Indeed, the author contends that various proposed alternatives to the deduction, such as tax credits and matching grants, would not eliminate the "power-to-the-rich" phenomenon.

The essay then proceeds to study the phenomenon under two headings. First, it is examined "as a matter of consistency or inconsistency with the goals of progressive income and estate taxation." After exploring the "inegalitarian" features of the charitable deduction in the light of several possible rationales for progressive taxation, the author concludes "that the power-to-the-rich aspects of the [deduction] are probably consistent with progressive taxation." The essay next turns to the second branch of the inquiry, in the section reprinted here.]

DO CHARITABLE TAX ALLOWANCES VIOLATE LEGISLATIVE FAIRNESS?

Even if a tax write-off does not violate the goals or rationales of progressive taxation, that cannot be its only test. It may still offend norms of democracy and equity and fairness against which all our legislation must be judged and which transcend the special commands of tax progressivity. Hence, we must consider in these terms a charitable allowance system that permits wealthy citizens to outweigh less-wealthy persons in controlling the disposition of taxable income and wealth and, as a corollary, that makes it easier for wealthy citizens to use taxable income or property to influence the behavior of others. In other words, we must weigh in normative terms the fact that the mechanism that Congress has created for decentralizing into private hands the power to expend taxable resources is a mechanism that is biased in favor of affluent citizens.

The Charge of Inequality

There are some who characterize the vice inherent in such a mechanism in terms of its effects. Thus, William Vickrey has said that the consequence of the present charitable deduction system is that "the choice of the very wealthy" predominates, or as Harvey E. Brazer restates the Vickrey position: "the tastes and preferences of high income people . . . are permitted to exert an excessive influence. . . ."[3] The "tastes and preferences of high-income people" might, of course, lead in the direction of greater benefits for low-income people; pursuing this issue is a major part of any redistributional studies to be conducted in the future. Professor Vickrey's point refers to influence, however, not to benefit—and there does seem to be palpable evidence of an income-biased influence on the distribution of charitable resources. Thus, as a result of the tax system's relatively greater "subsidization" of philanthropy by the affluent, more charitable funds are received by colleges and hospitals than would be the case if power to distribute taxable resources were allocated on a more egalitarian basis; in that event, religion would receive a greater share of charitable contributions. This is one of the messages of the economic studies done for the Filer Commission by Martin Feldstein and his colleagues and by Michael Boskin.[4]

   The only caveat I would enter was suggested to me by a law student who speculated that the giving patterns of lower-income groups may not be fixed; a change in the tax allowance system, intended to favor these less affluent citizens, might, in itself, affect their philanthropic preferences as they were enabled or encouraged to spend more.[5] This point needs further examination. If such a shift in "tastes and influences" takes place, however, some income-biased differences in charitable expenditure patterns would probably remain. For example, it seems clear that if all citizens start to give to higher education, the wealthier donors will favor alma mater institutions more heavily populated by affluent students than the colleges to which less-affluent donors will contribute.

For present purposes, we do not have to resolve this question about the extent to which charitable expenditures in actuality reflect an "excessive influence" of rich "tastes and preferences." The fact that richer prople have a greater capacity to implement their tastes and preferences, as a result of the charitable allowance mechanism, is enough to present an equity issue for democratic theory and legislative policy; the power conferred on more affluent people generates the dilemma, whether or not one can trace the impact of that power on resource allocations.

Upon preliminary inspection, such a nonegalitarian allocation of power does seem to clash with norms of democracy and social equity. Writing from the perspective of political science and economics, Robert A. Dahl and Charles E. Lindblom stated some years ago that

> In the United States the major social evils are probably due less to inequality in consumption, leisure time, or security than to inequality in status, cultural and social opportunities, and control.[6]

And from the perspective of moral philosophy, John Rawls advances as the "Second Principle" of justice:

> Social and economic inequalities are to be arranged so that they are both:
> (a) to the greatest benefit of the least advantaged, consistent with the just savings principle, and
> (b) attached to offices and positions open to all under conditions of fair equality of opportunity.[7]

"Social and economic inequalities" include differences or "hierarchies" in "authority" as well as differences in income and wealth.[8] While Professor Rawls appears to refer to differences in authority that result from organizational arrangements (presumably the hierarchies of governmental or corporate employment), it is probably consistent with his "Second Principle" to include "differences in authority" that arise out of the expenditure power conferred by the charitable allowance mechanism. If so, the charitable allowance system appears to violate the "Second Principle" because, under clause (b), differences in authority are justified only when they are "open to all under conditions of fair equality of opportunity," whereas the ability to take advantage of charitable allowances is "open" only to those of substantial means.[9]

Is Inequality Ever Acceptable?

These and other general statements dealing with equal distribution of power and control do not, however, dispose of the matter. General propositions require refinement before they can be reliably applied. In the case of general propositions relating to social policy, we can seek refinement by reviewing the ways in which the country has treated nonegalitarian legislation in the past.

We can identify examples of legislation that has a built-in class or income bias and yet receives general public approval. For example, Title II of the National Defense Education Act of 1958, as originally enacted, authorized federal contributions to college loan funds for students in need, with "special consideration . . . given to . . . students with a superior academic background" who wished to be teachers or who were strong in science, mathematics, engineering, or a modern foreign language.[10] The inevitable effect of requiring "superior" background or preparation was to favor those students who, although in "need" of college loan funds, came from homes representing a relatively high educational or economic level or who had attended schools whose parent population was relatively well-educated.[11] No egalitarian complaints were heard, so far as I know, in opposition to this provision when it was enacted.

Again, it seems evident that the audiences enjoying performances by symphony orchestras and dance companies subsidized by the National Endowment of the Arts are disproportionately composed of citizens from the upper range of socioeconomic class distributions. Yet, public and legislative support for such grants seems to hold firm and even to increase. On the other hand, one category of state legislation that discriminated on wealth grounds—the poll tax—was too blatant a form of class legislation to withstand Supreme Court scrutiny under the Equal Protection Clause[12] and probably would receive little popular support today. In between these binary examples of acceptance and nonacceptance, there are other examples of legislation with a class bias on which opinion is heavily divided. The student deferment under the military draft is one such case, and large-lot, single-home zoning ordinances—so-called "exclusionary" or "snob" zoning—provide another illustration.

What makes one form on inegalitarian legislation more tolerable than another? We could answer the question simply by counting heads or votes, but a more satisfying answer would look beyond current majorities to principles or criteria that help us to determine the circumstances under which inegalitarian legislation can be justified. For this purpose we are entitled to seek guidance from sources of the kind cited above, i.e., from the social sciences and from moral philosophy. My own research into this aspect of the charity-and-dynasty question is in a highly prefatory stage. Here and there my attention has been invited to suggestive fragments. One example that seems helpful comes from Professor Rawls, in his refinement of the "Second Principle," quoted above. Although he states, in effect, that differences in authority must attach to "offices and positions open to all under conditions of fair equality of opportunity," he appears to allow a departure: "an inequality of opportunity must enhance the opportunity of those with the lesser opportunity." Perhaps the fact that charitable expenditure power is awarded on terms other than those of "equality of opportunity" can be excused if the result is greater opportunity for those who cannot exercise this expenditure power. This result would be consistent with Professor Rawls' "general conception":

> All social primary goods—liberty and opportunity, income and wealth, and the bases of self-respect—are to be distributed equally unless an unequal distribution of any or all of these goods is to the advantage of the least favored.[13]

I am not sure that Professor Rawls meant that his general theory would help us decide specific policy dilemmas of this kind. The Rawls formulations I have quoted do, however, suggest the need for balancing the inegalitarian aspects of any legislation against what the legislation does to redress this same inequality. If we also take into account (as Mr. Rawls seems not to do) the gravity of the inequality, we end up with a balancing test roughly analogous to the "two-tier" test courts use under the Equal Protection Clause of the Constitution: on the first tier, we examine a nonegalitarian measure in light of the governmental purpose to be achieved and bless the measure if rational; on the second tier, where the deprivation of equality is particularly grave—because of the kind of classification used or because of the nature of the interest that is involved—we subject that assertion of governmental purpose to an exceptional standard of "strict scrutiny," insisting that a "compelling" governmental interest be demonstrated.

Home-Grown Test for Acceptable Inequality

My own tentative formula for assessing preferential or discriminatory legislation of the kind we are discussing has something in common with the Rawls approach and even more with two-tier constitutional analysis (although I am not trying to convert this discussion into a constitutional exercise). My formulation runs as follows: legislation that has a preferential "class effect" should be judged in terms of (a) the tendency of the nonegalitarian program or system to serve some important affirmative social purpose, particularly a purpose that benefits the classes of persons who are the "victims" of the inequality; (b) the gravity of the deprivation resulting from the inequality; (c) whether some other equally effective way of reaching the legislative goal would have a less depriving consequence; and (d) the ability of the deprived group to correct the inequality.

Applying the Test to the Charitable Tax Allowance System

Let us now try these criteria on income and estate tax allowances for charitable gifts—referring to any allowance system that provides deductions or credits in generous amounts to generous donors, and also referring to comparable matching grant programs.

Existence of important social goal

Starting with criterion (a), what claim can be made for such an allowance system, having in mind that we are looking for the social benefits that can be ascribed to the nonegalitarian aspects of the allowance system? David A. Good and Aaron Wildavsky have written, of the present charitable deduction, "No one, given a choice today, would deliberately choose (or would publicly defend) subsidizing the rich a lot and the poor a little or not at all."[14] To be sure, no one today would advocate, as an end in itself, preferential treatment for the rich. But I will risk an exploration of the ways in which the inegalitarian structure of a charitable allowance system may be said to advance important social goals.

Programmatic and quantitative goals. There is at the outset a specific, programmatic rationale: an allowance system biased toward upper-income groups produces more money for purposes some of us—perhaps, most of us—may consider objectively "important." Thus, higher education and hospitals receive more as a result of the wealth-correlated giving patterns mentioned earlier. Indeed, the Filer Commission, while advocating an extension of deductibility to lower-income groups, also urged simultaneous retention of the existing deduction provisions partly on the ground that

> eliminating the deduction or replacing it with a tax credit or matching grant system would significantly shift giving away from several current recipient areas at a time when these areas are already undergoing severe economic strain.[15]

But we do not need a general allowance system if our point is to increase private subsidization for particular institutions. A deduction, credit or grant system limited to subvention of such institutions would do the job. Moreover, if we are particularly interested in identifying social benefits that accrue to those deprived by the inegalitarian system—consistent with the Rawls "Second Principle"—then we have to ask how effectively the institutions we wish to favor serve the interests of those deprived of power under the current system; that inquiry, in turn, requires us to seek estimates of the redistributional effects of philanthropy—estimates, unfortunately, that are not yet obtainable. For these reasons, the "help the colleges" or "help the hospitals" rubric does not give us a satisfactory rationale for the inegalitarian nature of the allowance system.

As another rationale, we might consider a second reason urged by the Filer Commission for preserving the present deductions: the "efficiency" of deductions in inducing gifts from the well-to-do as a result of a price elasticity greater than unity (each dollar lost in revenue begets more than one extra donated dollar).[16] The difficulty with affirmatively justifying an allowance system—here we refer particularly to the existing deduction scheme—on these efficiency-elasticity grounds is partly that it involves the redistributional puzzle we have just mentioned: who particularly benefits from the induced extra giving? Perhaps more important, the extra giving—judged, as it must be under this efficiency heading, in aggregate quantitative terms—is not monumental. According to Filer Commission estimates, such induced additional lifetime and testamentary giving exceeds the revenue loss attributable to income and estate tax deductions by about $1–$2 billion.[17] That figure does represent a free ride for the taxpayers, but is it impressive enough, in strictly quantitative terms, to make much of an affirmative case for an inegalitarian piece of legislation? It is hard to provide a nonsubjective answer to such a query. My own response is suggested by the rather rhetorical wording of my question. (The efficiency evidence is powerful, however, in defending the charitable deduction against assaults premised on inefficiency.)

Search for other goals. Turning from these programmatic or quantitative rationales, we search for a more generalized, more powerful and possibly more principled case for charitable allowances and the power they accord to wealthy people. Such a case can be spelled out in three ways, two of which will strike many people as particularly offensive. I list these propositions in order of declining offensiveness:

First, it may be contended that the current system permits these resources to be accumulated in hands of individuals who have more "highly educated tastes"—who are inclined to honor and insist upon the standards of scholarship, artistry, and invention on which civilizations, in the end, find themselves judged. Andrew Carnegie wrote that the millionaire is a

> trustee for the poor, intrusted for a season with a great part of the increased wealth of the community, but administering it for the community far better than it could or would have done for itself.[18]

One can imagine a second, somewhat less elitist, proposition that might go like this: whether or not wealthy givers are better suited to uphold cultural and intellectual standards, affluent individuals are more likely to be idiosyncratic or unorthodox. This differentiation may be a function of economic security or of personal insecurity or of the narcissism attributed to some wealthy people by Robert Coles in his book, *Children of Privilege*. Whatever the reason, such idiosyncracy or heterodoxy is more likely to result in a charitable product that is different from what majoritarian preferences might produce, thus justifying the inegalitarian charitable deduction in the name of pluralism.

"Single-source support" goal. I will not pause to debate either the empirical or ethical validity of these first two propositions, for there is a third rationale that is not only more palatable but less problematic. This proposition is that, quite apart from the "highly educated" or idiosyncratic nature of the donors, the very fact that affluent persons are particularly encouraged and enabled to take advantage of the tax allowance means that charity will receive individual gifts of substantial size; these gifts will com-

bine both the donor's own "private transfer" (net of tax savings) and the government's foregone taxes—the "public share." The advantage of such large gifts lies not in their aggregate amounts; thus, we are not referring to the overall "efficiency" of tax allowances. Instead, the point is that an individual (or that individual's foundation) able to make such gifts serves as a source of substantial financing that does not depend on majoritarian consent or the approval of a large organizational constituency.

If one reason for encouraging private charitable giving is to produce, as an alternative to centralized government planning, what Kingman Brewster called "the calculated anarchy of dispersed initiative, individuality and variety,"[19] that process will not work effectively if initiative, individuality, and variety are expressed only in $5 and $25 contributions. Crucial as these contributions are to the nonprofit organizations that depend on them, these are not often the gifts that launch or give early support to a new enterprise or experiment, a trial balloon in education, the arts, the sciences, social action, or any other field; nor are these often the gifts that will provide support for dissenting or unorthodox ideas. It was not a large donor-pool but a single donor, Louis Schweitzer (individually and later through the Vera Foundation), who launched the bail-reform program now widely adopted; it was a single donor, the Daniel and Florence Guggenheim Foundation, that gave critical support for Robert H. ("Moon-Mad") Goddard's rocket research (rejected by the armed services as chimerical); and it was two medium-sized foundations (Taconic and Field), not a public subscription, that funded Southern voter registration drives in the early 1960s, giving momentum to black political participation.

The amounts needed to finance new enterprises do not necessarily have to be gigantic. Fifteen thousand dollars from the Scaife Foundation was enough to keep Jonas Salk at work developing the polio vaccine when government funds were not available, but $15 would not have been enough. It is conceivable that Dr. Salk could have sold his research program to a thousand $15 contributors, but it seems improbable—even if he could have afforded the solicitation costs.

It is likely, in short, that experimental people and dissenting voices, both those who bravely look ahead and those who bravely look back, will have to be financed, at least in the early stages, out of a single financial pocket, or a very few. The importance of individual control and support was stressed in a 1965 Treasury report:

> Private philanthropic organizations . . . may be many-centered, free of administrative superstructure, subject to the readily exercised control of individuals with widely diversified views and interests. Such characteristics give these organizations great opportunity to initiate thought and action, to experiment with new and untried ventures, to dissent from prevailing attitudes, and to act quickly and flexibly. *Precisely because they can be initiated and controlled by a single person or a small group*, they may evoke great intensity of interest and dedication of energy.[20]

I do not mean to say that a public agency or a broadly based collection of private individuals will never provide this kind of intrepid support. A few community foundations, despite the purposefully "representative" character of their distribution committees, have managed to do so. Recently we have also seen an increasing number of interesting experiments funded by agencies of the federal government and some of the states. For example, some of the grants made by the New York State Council of the Arts meet anybody's test of innovation or bravado; one of the Council's grants paid a troubadour to wander up and down the banks of the Hudson River singing ballads. Senator Proxmire regularly confers his "Golden Fleece" award on one of the more outlandish federal research projects thus at least giving governmental unorthodoxy a form of notoriety. Yet, the pressure that can be applied by such a legislator on a government agency, or by an alumni body or a national membership, suggests that we should not rely on governments or mass-supported nonprofit institutions to provide the kind of cutting edge to which I refer. The very absence of a constituency, the lack of conventional forms of "accountability," is what enables the single-source supplier of philanthropy—the private foundation or the single wealthy individual—to disregard prevailing winds and point out a different way to go.

As we encounter donors occupying extreme positions on the scale of individual or foundation wealth, we may find that caution reasserts itself; the publicity attaching to enormous affluence can be intimidating. The Ford Foundation seemed to display this tendency in a former era, when it was frightened of programs that referred explicitly to civil rights and minority groups. In the past two decades, however, despite the public drubbing it took in the 1969 Tax Reform Act hearings, the Ford Foundation has avoided the blandness that comes from a fear of constituencies, and, on the whole, the "in-the-limelight" syndrome has afflicted very few wealthy foundations or wealthy donors. If they have in fact failed to "make a difference" with their contributions, as often they have, inadequate imagination or care or energy, rather than fright, has been the probable cause.

The distinction between broad-based philanthropic support and single-source philanthropy is one that I believe was not fully respected by The Donee Group of the Filer Commission when it recommended not only that donor control of foundations be phased out, but also

> that organized philanthropies with broad purposes [including foundations] be required by law to expand their governing boards to include significant representation from the general public and non-profit agencies and, in particular, women and minorities. For those philanthropies which have a specialized purpose or geographic or program limitation, we recommend that the law require representation of those communities which are affected by or which have a special interest in those programs or areas.[21]

Mandating such a "representative" governance structure would change the nature of the private foundation, making it resemble more closely the broad-based collectivity that supports most public charities. If foundations begin to conform to the Reece Committee's 1954 request that foundations "be very chary of promoting ideas, concepts, and opinion forming material which runs contrary to what the public currently wishes, approves, and likes,"[22] they will fail to serve the needs of those people, institutions, concepts that the public is not yet ready to embrace. An exclusive reliance on the public charity model of philanthropic support is therefore calculated to reduce the effectiveness of the nonprofit sector in offering "the calculated anarchy of dispersed initiative, individuality and variety." I am not advocating what may be called the "baronial model" of nonprofit governance—the foundation board to which no women, minorities, ethnics, or simply independent thinkers need apply. Every institution needs some degree of ventilation. But it is one thing to ventilate and avoid the "baronial model," and another thing to move to the "majoritarian" or "parliamentary" model that seems to have been advanced by The Donee Group. If we are going to have a private sector, it should not be asked to ape the governance patterns of our public sector.

Encouraging substantial pockets of "single-source" funding not only promotes "individuality and variety" within the world of non-profit organizations; it may also enrich the democratic process in a broader sense. In an era of very big government and very big business (coexisting with big labor), "questions about the balance of forces in society are bound to grow in importance."[23] These questions are not necessarily answered by pointing to the countervailing power mechanism by which government and business are thought to check each other. According to Charles E. Lindblom, the government often fails as a countervailing force because businessmen exercise disproportionate influence over decision-making in the public sector.[24] From a different perspective, others see the government as resistant to taming by the business sector because of the dominance in society of a "new class" that wants to see much of the power that "is supposed to reside in the free market . . . redistributed to government, where *they* will then have a major say in how it is exercised."[25] The business sector, from still another viewpoint, has lost much of its own force because of "the relative passivity, amounting almost to timidity, of business leaders to attacks made upon them."[26]

From any or all of these viewpoints, it seems plausible to argue that the dual—business-vs.-government—"balance of forces" does not operate reliably and can usefully be supplemented by other institutions. Nonprofit organizations provide such supplementation by offering options in addition to those furnished by the government and business sectors—options relating to sources of employment and of housing, opportunities for personal association, provision of goods and services, cultural and educational offerings, even places to be buried. The nonprofit sector therefore serves as a countervailing power. Yet this sector cannot offer this range of alternatives unless it is itself reasonably motley, i.e., pluralistic and differentiated. This motley condition would be difficult to meet without a tax allowance system that encourages major giving by individuals, directly or through their foundations. Legislation providing tax writeoffs for charitable gifts can be defended, therefore, as contributing to the diffusion of power within the larger society, despite—indeed because of—the way this legislation allocates dispositive power to the wealthy.

Responses to the "single-source support" goal. A United States District Judge, Charles Richey, expressed the "countervailing" concept at a Senate hearing; he testified that when a nonprofit public interest law firm appears in his courtroom, he says to himself, "Thank God . . . somebody who does not represent any governmental or private interests."[27] A radical critic of our social order, however, would probably say that the nonprofit organizations and the government and business organizations all represent the very same "interests," and therefore my balance-of-powers point amounts to nothing at all. The critic would argue that the wealthy class, which derives the most power from the charitable tax allowance system, is the same class that also dominates most business and governmental organizations.

This criticism raises issues for another day (and another author!). But I will offer two brief comments. While a majority of the largest donors to higher education do come from the ranks of businessmen,[28] and businessmen, as Professor Lindblom reports, heavily influence government decision-making, many wealthy donors to universities and other nonprofit organizations are not engaged in business. More important, it is not clear that persons of wealth wield dispositive power in the business and government world. About 30 years ago David Riesman wrote:

> Does not wealth, one might ask, exert its pull in the long run? In the past this has been so; for the future I doubt it. The future seems to be in the hands of the small business and professional men who control Congress: the local realtors, lawyers, car salesmen, undertakers, and so on; of the military men who control defense and, in part, foreign policy; of the big business managers and their lawyers, finance-committee men, and other counselors who decide on plant investment and influence the rate of technological change; of the labor leaders who control worker productivity and worker votes; of the black belt whites . . . ; of the Poles, Italians, Jews, and Irishmen . . . ; of the editorializers and storytellers . . . ; of the farmers . . . ; of the Russians . . . ; and so on.[29]

If Professor Riesman's point is correct, wealthy charitable donors do not represent the same "interests" as those who control the rest of the society. But has societal control moved in the directions that Professor Riesman predicted a generation ago? I confess that I do not know where to assemble the information to answer that question. Indeed, this entire discussion of a defense of the charitable allowance—the proposition that substantial-scale giving by individuals and foundations is more likely than public funding or broad-based philanthropy to give us "individuality and variety" and a diffusion of power—rests on assumptions that have some factual support but need a great deal more empirical examination. As it stands, the proposition I have advanced in support of the inegalitarian structure of the charitable allowance must be considered no more than a speculation that strikes this author as reasonable.

Even if it is based on reasonable speculation, however, this rationale may be challenged in terms of the Rawls "Second Principle"; that principle requires us to ask whether the social benefits generated by inegalitarian tax allowance legislation flow to the "victims"—those deprived of expenditure power by such legislation. More knowledge about the wealth redistributional effects of tax blessed charitable giving might provide one set of answers to this inquiry, but, as I have noted, we lack that learning.

As a second response, it might be contended that, although tax allowance legislation withholds expenditure power from lower-income groups, these groups get it back as a result of this same legislation; i.e., some redistribution of power to lower-income groups results from charitable giving, and this phenomenon is particularly true for giving by wealthy individuals. Thus, gifts to voter registration programs (mentioned above), to programs aimed at increasing "accountability" in school systems and other organs of government, to community development corporations, to various civil rights efforts, and to legal service programs for the poor all tend to give lower-income groups a greater degree of power over governmental and economic institutions; and the fact that these programs are largely subvented by private foundation grants, as compared to mass fund-raising, means that they are predominantly supported through the charitable activities of the wealthier members of society.

A study for the Filer Commission, however, reports that, in percentage terms, very few foundation grants support "empowerment" mechanisms or processes such as those listed above.[30] It is arguable that, in the long run, even without resort to specific "empowering" mechanisms, power will be transmitted to lower-income groups through the institutions that wealthy people support, such as higher education and research institutions. It would take more analysis and investigation than anyone has devoted to this subject, however, to allow us to embrace with confidence the proposition that lower-income groups ultimately recapture the power they lose in the short run as a result of charitable tax allowance legislation.

A more general response to the Rawls challenge does seem to make sense, even though I am not sure that Professor Rawls would endorse it and even though I cannot provide rigorous support for it. Very simply, I cannot believe that lower-income groups will fail to share in the advantages of a society in which there is more "dispersed initiative, individuality and variety," more experimentation and more options, and a greater diffusion of power as a result of a robust and heterogeneous "third sector." Once more, I must speculate, but, once more, it seems reasonable to surmise that all of our citizens, including the less-than-rich, will benefit from such a social order—one that is flexible and resilient, able to cope and invent and change to meet the needs of its people. In short, if my speculations are correct, the "victims" will share in the benefits that accrue from a tax system that encourages substantial pockets of private philanthropic capacity.

To the affirmative case that has just been made, I submit this appendage. Facilitating substantial giving on the part of individual donors not only permits them to provide alternative sources of support for experimental or unconventional projects; it also permits them to take a financial leadership role—through "challenge" or "matching" or "pace-setting" grants—in rallying public support for existing nonprofit institutions.[31] I make this point in a supplementary manner because, while such leadership grants are extremely useful to the donee organizations and to the overall level of funding for the "third sector" organizations, the other, option-creating function of large scale philanthropy more directly promotes variety and heterodoxy, heralded as essential attributes of the non-profit world. Moreover, it is conceivable that the "leadership" function could be discharged by large groups of nonaffluent individuals banding together to offer "challenge" or similar grants, whereas we have noted the improbability of using this approach to support experimental or unorthodox enterprises.

Thus, having concluded that an affirmative case can be made for allowing tax forgiveness to the charitable contributions of affluent individuals, I now go on to apply the rest of the four-part formula by which we were seeking to judge the propriety of charitable tax allowances.

Gravity of the deprivation

The second factor I outlined, criterion (b), was the gravity of the inequality. In quantitative terms, the gravity does not appear to be very impressive. True, more money is allocated to education and health, and less to religion, as a result of the presently skewed tax allowance system. Even under the present system, however, the predispositions of the less affluent are given substantial effect. Forty-eight percent of all charitable contributions in 1984 went to religious organizations, and, of the amounts going to educational organizations, some portion was transmitted to religious schools. It should be noted also that only 14 percent went to educational institutions.[32]

In qualitative terms, it is true, the deduction deprives the less rich of a proportionate voice in certain decisions involving public resources. But this is quite different from reducing or diluting the representation of the poor with respect to the fundamental decisions the electorate makes about the form and composition of its government. What is diluted under the charitable allowance system is participation in the distribution of tax-forgiveness dollars, as compared to the kind of participation that is threatened by a poll tax, or by a grossly malapportioned legislature, or by the way the officials of Sunflower County, Mississippi used to behave on registration day. It does not follow, in other words, that inequality of representation presents the same dangers in all contexts. Robert A. Dahl and Charles E. Lindblom point out the importance of making distinctions between governmental and nongovernmental versions of inequality:

> Why, then, is political equality significant in *governments*—that is, in organizations that have a sufficient monopoly of control to enforce an orderly settle-

ment of disputes with other organizations in the area? Precisely because whoever controls government usually has the "last word" on a question; whoever controls government can enforce decisions on other organizations in the area. Thus so long as the condition of political equality is approximated, citizens can always decide in what situations and in what organizations they wish to tolerate hierarchy in order to achieve goals that cannot be satisfied by organization on an equalitarian basis. The condition of political equality assigns to the electorate the position of an ultimate court of appeal to decide where else in society the condition of equality may be enforced or forgone.[33]

Existence of alternative solutions
We move to the third criterion, (c), which asks whether there are alternative, more egalitarian ways of achieving the same legislative goal. Efficiency factors aside, there are other methods by which the legislature could provide governmental support for private, nonprofit institutions—if that were the goal. (For example, the legislature could simply embark on a major grants program comparable to the British and continental systems.) Again, there are probably other methods by which the legislature could stimulate a level of overall charitable giving equal to the present level—if that were the goal. (For example, the government could match, dollar-for-dollar—or three-for-one if necessary—all contributions made by all citizens below certain income categories, either through tax credits or negative-income-tax reimbursements.)

But neither governmental support for nonprofit institutions nor inducement of a given level of charitable giving is the goal we have attributed to a charitable tax allowance scheme. That goal is the decentralized allocation of taxable resources in a manner that enables and encourages individual private decision-makers to commit substantial resources to charitable objectives. In theory, that goal might be achieved in some manner other than through a tax allowance system—i.e., in some manner not related to a person's income or assets. Congress could replace the current income and estate tax deduction program (or that part of it applying to higher-bracket taxpayers) with a statute entitled the "Major Charitable Contributions Enablement Act." The Act could authorize, pursuant to formula, prescribed amounts of federal resources to be turned over to a limited number of individual citizens for them to donate to charitable organizations in their complete discretion, subject only to accounting for full disbursement. In each geographic area a certain number of donors would be appointed in each of several spending categories: for example, some citizens would be $5,000 donors, some $50,000 donors, and, perhaps, some would be given as much as $5 million to enable them to fund, on a five-year basis, a medium-sized, professionally staffed foundation. The donors could be selected (a) by lottery open to all persons over a certain age, or all registered voters, or all holders of high school diplomas or equivalency certificates; (b) by examinations administered by a special commission established by law, with examination criteria established by Congress; or (c) by elections conducted under state law, with federal financing of campaign expenditures.

Such decentralizing procedures would be more costly than income and estate tax allowance systems, not only because of administrative expense, but also because as we have noted, the present deduction system appears to extract from donors more in incremental contributions than the government foregoes in taxes. Moreover, apart from efficiency, I doubt that we would be satisfied with the alternative methods of choosing the donors. For one thing, there may be something of a wealth bias or a socioeconomic status bias in the selection of persons by examination or election and in the self-selection of those willing to participate in any of these methods.

Even if the legislation I have hypothesized freed the decentralizing process from any relationship to affluence, I wonder whether we would be happy with it. The present selection system—albeit based on affluence—may be less divisive than some more purposeful, self-conscious method of selection. The tax allowance method has at least the virtue that it does not call upon the government to play an active role in singling out the chosen few. Elections, lotteries, examinations—each could produce an exorbitant degree of turbulence surrounding issues of fairness in procedure and in criteria. Perhaps the passive, relatively self-executing selection processes are less disturbing, particularly where the power they confer is not, as we have noted, of the most fundamental character. I should like, some day, to explore this point more thoroughly. But even this brief discussion of my hypothetical Act does suggest (at least to me!) the difficulty of finding acceptable alternative methods of achieving the legislative goal we have attributed to a charitable tax allowance system.

Correctability of inequality

Finally, we come to the fourth criterion, (d), the ability of the deprived group to correct the inequality. In contrast to some of the cases we considered when trying out this four-part test, the inequality imposed by a tax allowance system falls on the vast majority of American citizens. Indeed, until 1982, the approximately 75 percent of taxpayers who take the standard income tax deduction could derive no benefit at all from the charitable allowance. Even though legislation due to expire at the end of 1986 permits standard deduction taxpayers to take charitable deductions, they have nowhere near the power to allocate taxable resources that continues to be enjoyed by wealthier taxpayers, who have more discretionary income and who inhabit higher tax brackets; and, of course, such legislation does not benefit those too poor to pay any taxes. Nor can persons with estates smaller than $500,000 benefit from estate tax charitable deductions (as of 1986). Clearly, therefore, the "victims" of the inegalitarian system constitute the bulk of the voting public, who can wipe out the preference if they wish. Their elected representatives did so in the case of the extreme form of that preference—the unlimited income tax charitable deduction, which bit the dust in the 1969 Tax Reform Act, albeit without any rhetoric about power inequality. (The repeal was based simply on the notion that everybody should pay some taxes.)[34]

Why have the dispossessed not risen to wipe out the existing inequality?

Is it because of the "agenda-setting" phenomenon we considered earlier—an exclusion of this form of inequality from the public debates? It is not clear that it has been entirely excluded. To the extent that the territorial strictures imposed on the foundations, restricting their role in business and in government, grew out of a concern with the foundation as the repository of tax-favored power enjoyed by the wealthy, the inequality issue may be entered into the political process. Yet, as we have seen, the power issue was not the explicit rationale for such legislation. Moreover, as far as I am aware, the more general issue of unequal power allocation under the charitable tax deduction system (going beyond the special case of the foundations) was not addressed in any legislative proceedings prior to the mid-1970s. While a few scholars referred to the issue briefly, neither the media nor political candidates touched it.

The matter is now on the public agenda, as far as I can judge. A few bills proposing to substitute a credit for the charitable deduction have been introduced in recent years, and the Filer Commission aired the question. The enactment of the charitable deduction for nonitemizers—and the efforts to keep this law from expiring—are a further symptom that issues of power and privilege have surfaced. The main proponents of this legislation have been charities seeking to increase their revenues, but the Filer Commission and others have proposed the same measure as a way of moderating resentment against the deduction.

Although the matter does appear to be on the agenda, it does not follow that anything will be done beyond adding the deduction for nonitemizers. The allowance system favoring the rich may well continue. Three different national polls in 1984 and 1985 found that 80 to 82 percent of respondents favored retention of the charitable deduction.[35] Perhaps those interviewed were not yet aware of the way the deduction works. Or perhaps the explanation lies in James Tobin's statement that "our society, I believe, accepts and approves a large measure of inequality, even inherited inequality."[36] In any event, the point is that, if hostility to the present system develops, the deprived group has the political capacity to change that system.

Results of test
Measured by my home-built four-part test—and despite the lack of empirical evidence bearing on many of the issues—the charitable tax allowance comes out with passing grades. It seems to present a plausible case for survival in a democratic order, when judged by standards of legislative equity and fairness, despite the fact that its dynastic power aspects fail to live up to an egalitarian ideal.

Of Time and Chance

It may be thought that I do not take the matter of dynastic power and privilege as seriously as one should. I think I do take it as seriously as one should, but not as seriously as some *do*. That, in turn, reflects my general assumption that the inequalities we have been discussing, while far from trivial, will not ultimately shape our ends. Whether we are rich or poor, our individual destinies will be determined by other forces, possibly by other, graver inequalities to be found in the surrounding environment or in our own personal endowments. And, of course, as the Preacher in the Book of Ecclesiastes reminds us, the matter is to a large extent, out of our hands:

> I returned, and saw under the sun, that the race is not to the swift, nor the battle to the strong, neither yet bread to the wise, nor yet riches to men of understanding, nor yet favour to men of skill; but time and chance happeneth to them all.[37]

NOTES

1. The devices are catalogued in Cooper, A Voluntary? Tax New Perspectives on Sophisticated Estate Tax Avoidance, 77 *Colum. L. Rev.* 101 (1977).

2. Simons, *Personal Income Taxation* 219 (1938).

3. Professor Vickrey is quoted by Professor Brazer in *Taxation and Education, Proc. of Spec. Conf. of Amer. Alumni Council* 47 (Finehout ed., Feb. 7–8, 1966).

4. Feldstein and Clotfelter, Tax incentives and charitable contributions in 3 *Research Papers* sponsored by the Commission on Private Philanthropy and Public Needs 1393, 1411 (1977) (hereafter cited as *Filer Commission Research Papers*); Feldstein and Taylor, The Income Tax and Charitable Contributors, in 3 *Filer Commission Research Papers* 1419, 1432–36; Boskin, Estate taxation and charitable bequests, in 3 *Filer Commission Research Papers,* 1453, 1476, 1479. Other studies are reviewed in Clotfelter, *Federal Tax Policy and Charitable Giving* (1985).

5. I am indebted to Donald Susswein for this suggestion.

6. Dahl and Lindblom, *Politics, Economics and Welfare* 145 (1953).

7. Rawls, *A Theory of Justice* 302 (1971).

8. *Id.* 61.

9. *See,* for such an argument, Drewsen, Taxation of foundations and distribution of economic power 15–18 (student paper on file in Yale Law Library, Spring 1974).

10. Pub. L. No. 85–864, §204, 72 Stat. 1584.

11. Coleman et al., *Equality of Educational Opportunity* 295–310, 325 (1966).

12. Harper v. Va. State Board of Educ., 383 U.S. 663 (1966).

13. Rawls, *op. cit. supra* note 7, at 303.

14. Good & Wildavsky, A tax by any other name: The donor directed automatic percentage contribution bonus, a budget alternative for financing government support of charity in 3 *Filer Commission Research Papers,* 2389, 2413.

15. *Giving in America, Report of the Commission on Private Philanthropy and Public Needs* 20 (1977) (hereafter cited as *Filer Commission Report*).

16. *Id.* 129–30, and see note 4, *supra*. On the meaning of "efficiency," see Clotfelter, *op. cit. supra* note 4, at 280–81.

17. The Commission estimates that the figure for lifetime giving would be in the range of $900 million to $1.7 billion. *Filer Commission Report* 129–30. Boskin, *op. cit. supra note* 4, at 1475–76, implies that the figure for bequests would be approximately $100–$200 million.

18. Quoted in Parrish, The foundation: A special American Institution, in *The Future of Foundations* 14 (Heimann ed. 1973). I am grateful to James Douglas for alerting me to this question in connection with the issue under discussion in the text.

19. From an address to the Yale Alumni Fund Dinner quoted in *Yale Alumni Magazine,* Feb. 1965, pp. 10–11.

20. 1965 *Treasury Report* 12 (italics supplied).

21. 1 *Filer Commission Research Papers* 66.

22. *House Select Comm. to Investigate Tax-Exempt Foundations and Charitable Organizations, Report,* H. Rep. No. 2681, 83d Cong., 2d Sess. 20 1954).

23. Douglas and Wildavsky, Introduction—The dilemma of the knowledgeable foundation in the era of big government, in 1976–1977 *Report of the Russell Sage Foundation* 16, 48 (1978).

24. Lindblom, *Politics and Markets* (1977).

25. Quoted in Levy & Nielsen, An agenda for the future, in 2 *Filer Commission Research Papers* 1029, 1063 (emphasis in the original).

26. Bork, Will capitalism survive?, *Yale Alumni Magazine and Journal,* April 1978, 15, 17.

27. Quoted in a leaflet published by the Natural Resources Defense Council, 1977.

28. Brannon and Strnad, Alternative approaches to encouraging philanthropic activities, in 4 *Filer Commission Research Papers* 2361, 2371–72.

29. Reisman, Who has the power?, in *Class, Status and Power* 162 (Bendix and Lipset eds., 1954 ed.).

30. Carey, Philanthropy and the powerless, in 2 *Filer Commission Research Papers* 1109.

31. See *Filer Commission Report* 134.

32. American Ass'n of Fund-Raising Counsel, *Giving USA* 7 (1985).

33. Dahl and Lindblom, *op. cit. supra* note 6, at 42.

34. II.R. Rep. No. 91-413, 91st Cong., 1st Sess. 52 (1969); S. Rep. No. 91-552, 91st Cong., 1st Sess. 79 (1969).

35. Testimony of Brian O'Connell, President, Independent Sector, before the House Ways and Means Committee, July 8, 1985, p. 9.

36. Tobin, On limiting the domain of inequality, 13 *J. Law and Economics* 263 (1970).

37. Ecclesiastes 9:11.

15

The Charitable
Contribution Deduction:
A Politico-Economic Analysis

JEFF STRNAD

Analysis of the tax deductibility of charitable contributions traditionally has focused on two traits of the deduction as a way to fund charitable activities. First, and most prominent, a deduction (rather than devices like a refundable tax credit or a government matching grant) favors high-income individuals by granting them a larger subsidy per dollar contributed.[1] For a high-income taxpayer in the 50 percent bracket, the government in effect pays half the taxpayer's charitable contributions, while for a low-income taxpayer in the 10 percent bracket, the government in effect pays only one-tenth. This disparity is accentuated if the charitable contribution deduction is an itemized deduction.[2] Taxpayers whose itemized deductions are less than the zero-bracket amount will not itemize and, thus, will get no tax benefit from making charitable contributions. A large proportion of low-income taxpayers have been nonitemizers, while most high-income taxpayers itemize.[3]

Second, charitable contributions substantially benefit parties other than the contributors. This trait leads to the claim that the deduction may be defensible even though it apparently favors high-income individuals. Suppose, for example, that the contributions go to an organization that distributes them to the poor. To remove the deduction in that case may be seen as a "tax" on the poor. This type of argument is too limited to justify the deduction. Many of the charitable services that are made possible by donations primarily, or at least partially, benefit high-income taxpayers. For

The numerical simulations in this chapter were made possible through use of equipment provided by the IBM Corporation. I am grateful to Donald Brosnan, Richard Craswell, Harold Hochman, Norman Lane, Roberta Romano, Susan Rose-Ackerman, Alan Schwartz, Matthew Spitzer, and Christopher Stone for their helpful comments on earlier drafts and to John Simon for encouraging me to tackle this subject in the first place. All errors and misjudgments are my own responsibility.

example, higher education, symphonies, and art museums are organizations that are supported at least in part by deductible donations, and the services provided by these organizations substantially benefit high-income individuals.

An additional argument, however, applies to many such services. These services tend to have "public good" aspects that lead them to be undersupplied, absent some form of government intervention. In the pure case of a public good, the good can be consumed by one person without diminishing consumption by another, and it is hard to fund production of the good by charging each person for the benefits that he or she receives from it.

Much of the recent work on the charitable contribution deduction has focused on whether the benefits created by the deduction in the form of helping the poor or producing public goods make the deduction a desirable policy despite the fact that it provides a larger subsidy to high-income individuals than to low-income individuals.[4] Perhaps the most comprehensive effort in this direction is an article by Professor John Simon. Professor Simon points out that charitable organizations produce public goods and notes that the poor consume some of these goods.[5] To determine whether the deduction is good policy he proposes a four-branch fairness test.[6] Three of the branches of his test weigh the added public-goods output and added aid to the poor against the favoritism to high-income individuals that inheres in a deduction.

The last branch of Professor Simon's test asks whether the groups apparently disadvantaged by the charitable contribution deduction (that is, all but a few people in the upper income brackets) could overturn the deduction if they wished. Professor Simon notes that the vast majority of people get little or no tax benefit from the deduction but that in a 1976 Gallup poll 75 percent of those questioned favored the deduction.[7] He speculates that this may be due either to ignorance of the fact that the deduction gives the rich a larger subsidy or to an acceptance of inequality.[8] A more positive view would be that there is awareness of the inequity of the subsidy but that low-income and middle-income voters also are well aware of the additional public-goods output induced by the deduction. Those voters may feel that the benefits to them from the activities generated by the deduction exceed any costs paid by them in the form of additional taxes to make up for the revenue loss caused by the deduction. Alternatively, even if the deduction primarily subsidizes public goods desired by high-income classes, it may be that any revenue loss from the deduction is made up by additional taxes paid by those classes.

This possibility that the charitable contribution deduction is a political bargain that is Pareto improving (that is, benefits some members of society and hurts no one) has important implications for the entire current debate about the deduction. If the deduction plays that sort of role, then the concern about favoritism toward high-income individuals is blunted if not eliminated. Low-income and middle-income individuals would be no worse off as a result of the deduction and might experience substantial benefits.

In the next section I explore the possibility that the deduction is part of a political bargain that meets the norm of not making low-income and middle-income individuals any worse off. The first part of the section gives a qualitative example of how that possibility might come about. Two economists, Harold Hochman and James Rodgers, argue that a political bargain meeting a closely related norm would result in a tax credit rather than a deduction. In the second part of the section (and in the Appendix) I take issue with that viewpoint and conclude that it is plausible (but not certain) that a deduction would be the result under their norm.

In light of that conclusion it is important to ask whether it is likely that the political process produces legislative packages that meet either the norm postulated in this chapter or the one postulated by Hochman and Rodgers. In particular, if groups that ostensibly are harmed by the deduction can protect themselves via the political process, then survival of the deduction suggests that the apparent favoritism toward high-income individuals inherent in a deduction should not be a concern. Conversely, if the political process systematically disfavors those who ostensibly are disfavored by the deduction, then the "inequity" inherent in the deduction cannot be fixed unless the political process is reformed or replaced by some other method of governance.

After developing those arguments further, I go on to examine evidence about how the political process does function. Unfortunately, no clear answer emerges. One cannot tell for sure whether or not the charitable contribution deduction is acceptable under the posited norms. The next section as a whole, however, shows that viewing the charitable contribution deduction as a political bargain may blunt or eliminate the conventional concern about favoritism of high-income individuals. That favoritism is probably the major tax-policy issue concerning the deduction.

Taking a political bargain view of the deduction also affects many other issues surrounding the deduction. The third section of this chapter, entitled "Donor Motivations and the Choice of Policy Instrument," starts from the presumption that the deduction is a political bargain in the interest of many different groups and studies the effects of that presumption on two major issues. I first consider whether there is a serious misallocation of resources arising from donors who give for reasons unconnected with the substantive value of the output of donee organizations. I argue that this "nonsubstantive giving" may not be as serious a problem as commonly imagined.

The second major issue concerns which government mechanisms (such as direct production, tax benefits, or consumer subsidies) should be used to satisfy public goods demand. I address this issue by focusing on a variety of motivations for supporting "170(c) activities." (Contributions to an organization will be deductible as charitable contributions only if the organization is among the organizations specified in section 170(c) of the Internal Revenue Code. It is convenient to refer to these organizations as

"170(c) organizations" or as part of the "170(c) sector" and to refer to the activities of the organizations as "170(c) activities.") Some of the suggested connections between motivations and "policy mix" are speculative. But one can conclude that viewing the deduction as a political bargain has important implications for the optimal policy mix.

THE CRUCIAL ROLE OF THE POLITICAL PROCESS

A Political Equilibrium Approach

A normative structure
This subsection uses a simple norm to express the concern about favoritism toward high-income individuals. If it can be demonstrated that the norm is satisfied by the charitable contribution deduction, then the concern about favoritism in the literature is unwarranted.

Before stating the norm, it is important to make clear the set of legislative policies that must be evaluated under the norm. Viewing the charitable contribution deduction as the result of a political bargain means that other legislation might be passed because of the deduction. This other legislation might include increases in tax rates for those who benefit directly from the deduction or expenditures in favor of those who are not so benefited. The deduction cannot be evaluated in isolation. Evaluation must include the entire package of adjustments made to accompany the deduction. This package is referred to as "legislation accompanying the deduction."

The norm is the following: the charitable contribution deduction, combined with any tax adjustment or other legislation accompanying it, is objectionable if and only if it results in net losses for low-income or middle-income people. This norm would be violated, for example, if those income classes must pay more in taxes to fund the revenue loss from the deduction than they receive in benefits from the additional charitable activity induced by the deduction.

At first glance this norm ignores the fair distribution of the surplus from public-goods production. That surplus is the value to individuals of the goods in excess of the social cost of production. Certain groups may receive disproportionately large amounts of the surplus, and an additional tax adjustment might be used to transfer some of the surplus experienced by those groups to others.

I do not specify how the surplus from public goods production ought to be distributed. Instead, distributional considerations enter at the level of preferences. In other words, preferences for or against provision of any public good include preferences concerning the distributional impacts of such provision. When provision of a public good combined with an allocation of the cost of producing it is unobjectionable under the norm, then low-income and middle-income people experience no net loss where "loss" includes any offense to their distributional sensibilities.[9]

The charitable contribution deduction as a political bargain
It is possible that the charitable contribution deduction and accompanying legislation reflect a political bargain that is in accord with the norm? This subsection shows in a qualitative way that the answer may be yes. In making this argument, I generally assume that all parties to any bargain have reasonably complete information about the effects of the deduction. Those effects include the amount of additional contributions that the deduction induces and the breakdown of those additional contributions between different 170(c) activities. Given this information assumption, the charitable deduction must serve more than a redistributional purpose. Since the value of subsidized goods to a recipient may be less than their market value, cash transfers would be a more efficient redistributional device. This argument does not follow if information is incomplete. Suppose, as is the case, that there is uncertainty about the extra contributions stimulated per dollar of tax revenues lost from the deduction.[10] High-income taxpayers may know that they do not expand their giving much in response to the deduction, while low-income taxpayers believe the opposite. In this case, if taxes paid by low-income individuals partially fund the deduction, then the deduction serves primarily as an income transfer to high-income taxpayers. The information asymmetry may allow high-income taxpayers to fool low-income taxpayers into supporting the income transfer. Although there is a great deal of public information about the incentive effects of the charitable contribution deduction and about the nature of the additional 170(c) activities that tax-induced contributions fund,[11] it is still possible that there is an exploitable information asymmetry.[12] Thus, incomplete information may lead the political process to function in derogation of the norm set out above.

Although the charitable contribution deduction is not a good device for pure redistribution when there is complete information, the deduction may be a good way to encourage provision of public goods by the 170(c) sector. Suppose, for example, that a large number of high-income individuals are interested in increasing the amount of cancer research. Middle-income and low-income individuals would benefit from such an increase and thus might go along with a subsidy to induce high-income people to increase their contributions. Although such groups would block a direct redistribution of income to the high-income group, they might favor a subsidy that on the surface of things seems to benefit high-income people disproportionately. The public-good aspect of cancer research is critical to this political interaction: although one income group funds the research, other groups benefit from it.

Can a Deduction Be an Appropriate Subsidy for Charitable Contributions?

A basic public good analysis: Hochman and Rodgers' model
Beginning with the presumption that the desire to encourage the production of public goods motivates a subsidy for 170(c) organizations,[13] it is

important to ask whether a deduction is an appropriate form of subsidy. The previous subsection raises the possibility that the deduction might be justified as a normatively acceptable political bargain. In pursuing that kind of political analysis, individual motivations for contributing to an organization or for supporting a subsidy for contributions to it are the elementary building blocks.

It is analytically useful to consider a particularly simple motivation first: each donor contributes to the purchase of a good not because of any concern for others or for their consumption pattern and not because of a desire to give for the sake of giving itself but only because the donor values the good for his or her own "private consumption." For example, each person may support cancer research because of the possibility that he or she will be afflicted with cancer in the future. The implications of more complex motivations for the form of the subsidy and for whether the 170(c) sector is the best provider of the services are considered later.

Hochman and Rodgers have developed a model, applicable to the "private consumption" case just defined, to determine the optimal structure of subsidies for 170(c) organizations that satisfy public-good demand.[14] For simplicity the model assumes there is only one public good being produced by the 170(c) sector. Call this one good "the 170(c) good."

The normative structure of Hochman and Rodgers' model is congruent enough with the norm set out above that their result needs to be taken seriously. Consequently, a substantial effort is made in explaining their result (in this subsection) and in showing (in the next subsection and the Appendix) that the result is flawed.

The normative ideal in Hochman and Rodger's model is to achieve a "Lindahl equilibrium." Each individual in the economy pays for the 170(c) good in two ways. First, there is the *net* charitable contribution the individual makes. "Net" means that the part that effectively is paid by the government as a subsidy is subtracted. Second, the individual may have to pay additional taxes to help fund the subsidy. In the model the entire funding for the subsidy is in the form of additional taxes. That is just a conceptual simplification that can stand for the impact on the individual of budget cutbacks, of an increase in national debt, or of other nontax devices for funding the revenue loss from subsidizing contributions.

A Lindahl equilibrium obtains if an optimal quantity of the 170(c) good is produced, and each individual's payment (in the form of net charitable contribution and taxes) equals the individual's marginal valuation of the final unit of the 170(c) good produced multiplied by the amount provided. Thus, when a Lindahl equilibrium obtains, it is as if each individual purchases all he or she wants at a price set at the individual's marginal valuation of the final unit purchased. Unlike a private-goods market, however, this price may differ for different individuals, and all individuals "buy" the same quantity. The optimal quantity of public good will be such that the sum of everyone's marginal valuations of the final unit equals the social cost of producing that unit.

Hochman and Rodgers see two normatively desirable traits in a Lindahl equilibrium. The equilibrium results in an efficient (that is, Pareto optimal) quantity of public good and is "distributionally neutral"[15] in the sense that each person simply buys the quantity she or he wants at a price equal to the individual's marginal valuation of the last unit purchased. However, even when this marginal condition holds it may be true that the surplus generated by public production is distributed very unequally. Thus, it may not be appropriate to call the equilibrium distributionally neutral. Furthermore, including preferences about the distribution of consumer surplus in marginal valuations creates technical problems that in some cases make Lindahl equilibrium an inappropriate equilibrium concept.[16]

It follows from this discussion about consumer surplus that there are at least two instances in which a Lindahl equilibrium satisfies the norm set out above. First, the norm is satisfied when the marginal valuations used to compute an equilibrium incorporate distributional preferences about consumer surplus and there is no technical problem. Second, when such distributional preferences are excluded from marginal valuations, a Lindahl equilibrium will still satisfy the norm if low-income and middle-income individuals do not find the resulting distribution of consumer surplus objectionable.[17] In each case no low-income or middle-income individual is worse off because of provision of a public good through a Lindahl equilibrium. These two instances are significant enough that Hochman and Rodgers' model cannot be dismissed on the basis of the norm set out above.

Hochman and Rodgers argue that a flat-rate credit is a stronger candidate than a deduction for establishing a Lindahl equilibrium. Their technical arguments are detailed in the Appendix, while the core intuition is presented here. Their model has two individuals in it: individual A has a high income while individual B has a low income. For both individuals the "payment" side of the Lindahl equilibrium consists of net charitable contributions plus any tax payments that go toward funding the revenue loss caused by subsidizing the contributions. The net charitable contribution for each individual is the contribution the individual would make without any subsidy multiplied by two factors. The first factor captures the "price effect" of the deduction. Applying this first factor to the amount of contribution in the world without subsidies yields the gross contribution in the world with subsidies. The second factor is one minus the subsidy rate. This factor reduces the gross contribution to a net amount that the individual actually "pays" after subtracting the subsidy portion provided by the government. Finally, individual A's no-subsidy contribution is larger by a particular "income elasticity" factor than B's no-subsidy contribution.

Hochman and Rodgers make a crucial assumption about the tax portion of each individual's payment. They assume that this portion can be ignored because it will be small in any event, and much of it may be shifted to other taxpayers who are not contributors and who may have little or no demand for the public good.[18] This means that for each individual the payment side consists only of that individual's net charitable contribution.

If the rate of subsidy is the same for each individual, then more can be said about the relation between their net charitable contributions. Under the assumption that each person responds to the subsidy with the same intensity, each person will increase his or her gross contributions by the same proportion. ("Responding with the same intensity" means in economic terminology that the two individuals have the same "price elasticity" for charitable giving.) Furthermore, the term converting gross contributions into net contributions will be the same for both individuals. As a result, their net charitable contributions will differ only by the "income elasticity" term: individual A's no-subsidy contribution is higher than individual B's by some proportion due to the fact that A has higher income.

On the "benefits" side, Hochman and Rodgers show that the marginal valuations (the value of the last unit of public good) of A and B are related by the same "income elasticity" term that relates their no-subsidy contribution levels.[19] Thus, individual A's marginal valuation is larger than individual B's by the same proportion that individual A's net contribution exceeds individual B's. As a result, a subsidy with equal rates for each individual (such as a tax credit) enables both individuals to satisfy the Lindahl conditions simultaneously. Hochman and Rodgers conclude that under their assumption neglecting the tax terms "or virtually any other assumption that is at all realistic, a flat-rate tax credit is likely to provide a good approximation to the Lindahl requirements."[20]

An extension of the basic public-goods analysis: an alternative model
The Appendix to this article develops a model similar to that of Hochman and Rodgers: it has two income classes, and the central normative requirement is achieving a Lindahl equilibrium. Rather than adopt Hochman and Rodgers' assumption that the tax part of each individual's payment in Lindahl equilibrium can be ignored, the model considers a range of possible tax structures for funding the revenue loss caused by the charitable contribution deduction. All of these tax structures are "progressive" in the sense that larger increases in percentage rates are imposed on the high-income individuals than on the low-income individuals who contribute.

The striking result that emerges from this model is that when the tax shares used to fund a subsidy for charitable contributions are even *slightly* progressive, very high subsidy rates for A and very low subsidy rates for B may be a Lindahl equilibrium. This type of discrepancy in subsidy rates resembles the discrepancy inherent in a deduction.

Intuitively, these results emerge because high subsidy rates lower the net contribution of the high-income individual. This offsets the progressive tax-rate increase so that the high-income individual makes the correct total payment in a Lindahl equilibrium for the benefits he or she receives from the increase in the 170(c) good.[21]

These results that favor a deduction over a flat-rate subsidy such as a tax credit depend on assumptions about whether the tax part of the payment in Lindahl equilibrium can be ignored and, if not, what the rate structure of that tax part is. Hochman and Rodgers' main justification for their decision to ignore the tax part of each individual's payment is that the tax cost of the subsidy may be diverted to noncontributors outside of their model.[22] In fact, Hochman and Rodgers view it as "reasonable to think of a small across-the-board differential in marginal tax rates . . . as the means through which the costs of the subsidy are offset."[23] If this is what is going on, it is hard to believe in Hochman and Rodgers' conclusion quoted above that a flat subsidy would "provide a good approximation to the Lindahl requirements." Those who had no particular desire for the activities supported by the subsidy would be taxed to fund the subsidy but would not receive benefits that they consider worth the tax costs. That certainly is not a Lindahl equilibrium where each person pays taxes and contributions according to his or her valuation of the activities that are generated thereby.[24]

Moving away from a Lindahl equilibrium in this way does more than block the application of a particular kind of economic analysis. If a substantial proportion of voters were taxed more than the benefits they receive on account of a subsidy for charitable contributions, the political viability of the subsidy would be impaired. A more complex view of the political process, however, suggests that the tax-revenue cost of a subsidy may be shifted onto those who benefit from the additional 170(c) output it induces. Logrolling might serve as a function. Those who do not favor a subsidy for contributions may gain other favorable government expenditures or tax reductions in exchange for supporting the subsidy. The tax-revenue cost of those government expenditures or tax reductions will fall partly on those who want the subsidy for charitable contributions. As a result, individuals or groups that do not favor the subsidy may *effectively* pay a lower tax share to fund the subsidy because they can use their unimpaired political capital to get other government benefits.

This possibility suggests another way to model the question of optimal subsidy structure. The tax cost to individuals who benefit from the 170(c) good will not be neglected, and together they will bear the entire increase in taxes needed to fund the subsidy. This captures the idea that the political process might shift the costs of government programs onto those who benefit from them. There will be no unidentified third parties who will absorb part of the tax revenue cost without a fuss.

Some of the parties who benefit from the 170(c) good may be noncontributors. These individuals should be taxed in a Lindahl equilibrium. My model handles this by splitting the low-income class into two parts. A proportion P of that class contribute, and the rest experience the same benefits as the contributors but make no contributions. The contributors all contribute the same amount. Since noncontributors and contributors experience the same benefits, in a Lindahl equilibrium, the tax increase for noncontributors must be larger than that of the contributors by the amount of the contribution. It is assumed that this tax result within the low-income class is achieved by logrolling or some political device.[25]

The next issue is how to model the distribution of tax revenues between the high-income class and the low-income class. My model leaves this question partially open. The tax-rate increase for each high-income individual is taken to be $1 + \delta$ as large as the tax-rate increase for each contributing low-income individual. If $\delta = 0$, then both taxpayers' rates increase by the same amount. This is an increase that is neither progressive nor regressive; in this model it is the analog of the "across-the-board differential in marginal tax rates" that Hochman and Rodgers consider to be a reasonable assumption.[26] If δ is greater than 0, then the rate increases used to fund the subsidy are progressive with respect to contributors in the sense that the contributor with greater income must pay a greater added percentage of his or her income.

It is plausible to use positive values of δ. Establishing or deciding to continue the charitable contribution deduction is an easier decision *taking as given* that there will be a later overall decision on tax rates. Separating the decision on tax rates means that legislators can focus on the effect of income-tax rates both on incentives to work and on the distribution of income without considering devices such as the charitable contribution deduction for funding public goods. Given the small number of high-income individuals and the egalitarian sentiments in American society, it is not at all unreasonable to anticipate $\delta > 0$ when additional revenues must be raised through the tax system and when raising revenue is the sole focus of legislators.

Using the equations derived in the Appendix, I calculate a subsidy rate for high-income individuals that is consistent with a Lindahl equilibrium if low-income individuals are not subsidized at all. This corresponds to a situation where low-income individuals are not subsidized because the subsidy is an itemized deduction and each low-income individual's total itemized deductions are less than the zero-bracket amount. In the numerical simulations presented in this subsection each high-income individual has six times the income of a low-income individual and there are three times as many low-income individuals as high-income individuals.[27]

The subsidy rates that emerge depend on four more parameters. One is the tax-share parameter δ that has already been discussed. The second is the proportion P of low-income individuals who contribute. The third is α, the "income elasticity" of charitable contributions. This parameter determines how such contributions increase with increases in income. The two values that are used are .75 and 1.0. These values are at the lower and upper ends of the empirical estimates in the literature. The value .75 means that for each one-percent increase in income charitable contributions increase three-quarters of one percent. The value 1.0 means that charitable contributions increase by the same percentage as income does. Finally, a fourth parameter indicating the responsiveness of giving to a subsidy is set for all individuals at the value estimated "for all income classes" in the empirical literature. In other words, the possibility that high-income taxpayers might be more responsive to subsidies for giving is ignored even

Table 15-1. Lindahl Subsidy Rate for High-Income
Individuals When All Low-Income Individuals Contribute
$(P = 1)$

		Income Elasticity	
		0.75	1.0
Tax	$\delta = .1$	.44	.27
Share	$\delta = .25$	.55	.37
Parameter	$\delta = .5$	.75	.53

though, as the next subsection demonstrates, this possibility may increase
the attractiveness of a deduction versus a flat subsidy.

Tables 15-1 and 15-2 report the subsidy rates for high-income individuals required under a Lindahl equilibrium when low-income individuals are
not subsidized. If we assume that the high-income individuals face the current highest marginal rate of .50, then an itemized deduction under current
law consists of a .50 subsidy for high-income individuals and a zero subsidy for low-income individuals who presumably do not itemize. Thus, if
the numbers in Tables 15-1 and 15-2 are large (around .50 or greater),
then the disparities in subsidy rates caused by an itemized deduction do
not appear to be unreasonable on the basis of Lindahl criteria.

The first entry in the Table 15-1, .44, is the subsidy rate that must be
provided to high-income individuals under the Lindahl criteria if low-income
individuals are not subsidized, if $\delta = .1$ and if the income elasticity is .75,
a figure in the lower range of the available econometric estimates. The value
of .1 for δ indicates that the tax increases used to fund the subsidy are not
very progressive: high-income individuals experience a tax-rate increase only
10 percent larger than the increase for individuals with one-sixth the income.

The tables indicate that when the tax increases used to fund a subsidy
for charitable contributions are even *slightly* progressive, the high-income
individual should be heavily subsidized when the low-income individual is
not subsidized at all. The size of the numbers suggest that the disparities
in subsidy rates inherent in a deduction may not be unreasonable on the
basis of Lindahl criteria.[28] Furthermore, comparing the two tables indi-

Table 15-2. Lindahl Subsidy Rate for High-Income
Individuals When Half of Low-Income Individuals
Contribute $(P = .5)$

		Income Elasticity	
		0.75	1.0
Tax	$\delta = .1$	.80	.45
Share	$\delta = .25$	.99	.67
Parameter	$\delta = .5$	>1	.95

cates that a higher subsidy rate for high-income individuals is required when
a larger proportion of low-income individuals contributes. This makes sense.
In place of contributions, the noncontributors pay taxes used to induce more
contributions from high-income individuals via a higher subsidy rate.[29]

Some additional arguments for a deduction as an appropriate subsidy
Hochman and Rodgers' central argument for a flat-rate subsidy such as a
tax credit is the one discussed above: they believe that that type of subsidy
is more likely to approximate a Lindahl equilibrium than a deduction. They
also discuss two other potential justifications for use of a deduction. First,
they consider and reject as unlikely the possibility that giving by high-income
groups involves greater positive externalities than giving by others. A second possible justification for a deduction is that high-income individuals
have a larger price elasticity for contributions so that subsidizing them more
would increase activities that low-income and middle-income individuals
favor at a lower cost to those individuals. Hochman and Rodgers dismiss
this possibility by noting that the evidence for a strong positive correlation
between the absolute value of the price elasticity for contributions and income is weak and that, in any event, providing a greater subsidy to high-
income individuals will shift the composition of giving in the direction that
that group favors.[30]

Hochman and Rodgers may have been too quick to dismiss the second
potential justification. Although the evidence (some of which postdates their
article) is not conclusive, the possibility that the absolute value of the price
elasticity of giving increases significantly with income must be taken quite
seriously.[31] If such an effect exists, and if low-income taxpayers want the
same 170(c) goods that high-income taxpayers support by contributions,
then low-income taxpayers would be better off paying higher taxes to subsidize the contributions of high-income taxpayers than to subsidize the
contributions of their own income class. This possibility is enhanced by the
fact that there is strong (but not conclusive) evidence that for high-income
taxpayers the revenue loss from subsidizing contributions is more than made
up for by the induced increase in contributions. The same cannot be said
about subsidies for the contributions of other taxpayers.[32]

Furthermore, it is not clear how much significance there is in the fact
that providing high-income individuals with a high subsidy shifts giving in
the direction of organizations traditionally favored by that group's contributions. Those organizations (including primarily educational institutions
and hospitals) may provide significant benefits for individuals in other income classes. In addition, the optimal subsidy rate is probably not the same
for all activities, and some activities are supported by government benefits
other than subsidized contributions. It would not be surprising, for example, if contributions to religious organizations are currently adequate despite the fact that contributors to religion generally are subsidized at a lower
rate based on having less income. Exploring that possibility would be a
difficult empirical task.[33]

The Functioning of the Political Process

The previous section discusses several ways in which the charitable contribution deduction might be an unobjectionable political bargain. The discussion is fairly simple and involves some strong assumptions. Nonetheless, an important conclusion follows from the discussion: the deduction's higher subsidy rate for high-income individuals may be just a way of insuring both economic efficiency and an allocative mechanism that accords with the preferences of *all* voters including lower-income and middle-income people who are not the apparent or immediate beneficiaries of the deduction. This possibility raises an important issue: Does the political process function in such a way that the charitable contribution deduction is plausibly an efficient and distributionally neutral device that results in an outcome like Lindahl equilibrium?

This section shows that the two extreme views on this issue are hard to swallow given current knowledge. Under one view the political process produces a result close to Lindahl equilibrium or a related concept. Under the opposite view, the political process systematically ignores the preferences and welfare of low-income and middle-income groups. The deduction is largely a boon for high-income individuals financed by other people's tax payments. The other people, who comprise a rather substantial majority, do not have sufficient political power or political awareness to correct the situation.

Pessimism about the first, "positive," view comes from many sources. First, over the past two decades economists have attempted to design theoretical mechanisms to attain the proper level of public-good production and the proper allocation of costs. There appear to be no mechanisms without theoretical problems.[34] Furthermore, experiments using various mechanisms do not provide reason to be optimistic. Some of the mechanisms seem to result in close to the optimal quantity of public good but with an inappropriate distribution of costs. Other mechanisms fail to come near the optimal overall quantity.[35]

If economists have failed to produce good allocation mechanisms that stand up theoretically or experimentally, it seems unlikely that actual political processes will do any better. In fact, existing knowledge about these processes suggests greater pessimism. Theoretical studies of majority rule and representative democracy reveal that such systems have deep problems. For example, a well-known result for majority rule is that unless voter preferences display certain patterns, the voting process may "cycle" over various alternatives. "Cycling" over three alternatives A, B, and C occurs if A is chosen over B, B is chosen over C, but C is chosen over A. *Any* of the three alternatives may be chosen in a series of pairwise eliminations depending on which alternatives are run against each other first. This result is a simple example of the outcome depending solely on the "agenda." The existing literature reveals many other theoretical problems both with majority rule and with representative democracy.[36] At the same time, empirical studies are at an early stage, and good tests of even the most simple models of the workings of the political process do not exist at present.[37] Finally, there are studies that are more "institutional." These studies focus on the impact of the interests of politicians and bureaucrats on public output, and the studies identify various forces that lead to too much, too little, or the wrong kind of public output.[38]

Given the results of all this work, the assertion that the political process produces a Lindahl equilibrium or an outcome close to it is too bold. Such an outcome cannot even be assured theoretically or in a laboratory where the vagaries of real world processes can be avoided or ignored. In the actual political process a Lindahl equilibrium may be buried by agenda manipulation or may be distorted to serve the interests of politicians or bureaucrats. Thus, it is hard to accept the "positive" extreme view.

But it is also hard to accept the "negative" extreme view that the charitable contribution deduction has served the interest of high-income individuals at the expense of middle-income and low-income individuals since its passage in 1917. High-income groups do not comprise a large proportion of the total population, and it is hard to imagine that the other groups do not have considerable political power.[39] Furthermore, the availability of devices such as logrolling suggest that it is possible to shift the costs of the deduction onto those who benefit from it.[40]

Despite the importance of knowing how well the political process works for judging the charitable contribution deduction, it appears that current knowledge does not offer a definitive answer. There are some elements in the process (e.g., logrolling) that make it possible that the deduction is at least roughly an efficiency-enhancing political bargain. But there is no assurance that a result as normatively pleasing as a Lindahl equilibrium emerges from the process.

DONOR MOTIVATIONS AND THE CHOICE OF POLICY INSTRUMENT

There are two groups that have an interest in a charitable enterprise: the donors who support the enterprise financially and its nondonor-beneficiaries. In the previous section of this chapter, both groups are assumed to be satisfying their own "private consumption" demand for public goods—they are not concerned with the tastes, happiness, or consumption of others. The main goal in that section was to determine whether the charitable contribution deduction and accompanying legislation achieve a Lindahl equilibrium outcome or result from a political bargain that is normatively unobjectionable in the sense that middle-income and low-income individuals are not made worse off. The conclusion is indeterminate on that point: It is possible, but by no means assured, that the deduction and accompanying legislation have those qualities.

Despite this indeterminacy, I assume in this section that the deduction and accompanying legislation provide public goods through a political bargain that is in the interest of many groups. The first subsection describes reasons for using the deduction rather than other methods of government provision to satisfy "private consumption" demand for public goods. The remaining subsections consider the policy mix that would best serve as a political bargain when public-good demand and the desire to make contributions arise from more complex motivations. For analytic ease each of these five subsections considers a single type of motivation that may give rise to charitable giving: nonsubstantive motivations, desires for alternatives to government, utility externalities, consumption externalities, and desires to influence the tastes of others.

The discussion for each motivation is meant to be suggestive and speculative rather than definitive and rigorous. In addition, the set of motivations studied is not meant to be exhaustive. I wish to show that viewing the charitable contribution deduction as the result of a political bargain in the interest of many groups has important implications for the mix of government policies. Many of the implications go beyond or even contradict the conventional wisdom on the subject. Thus, if the political bargain view is correct, then important changes in—and additions to—the traditional approach to issues of policy-mix are in order.

Instrumental Efficiency Justifications in the "Private Consumption" Case

Examining the "private consumption" case allows us to address a basic question. When is the charitable contribution deduction a more efficient instrument for providing public goods than direct government provision?

Suppose, for example, that there is considerable uncertainty about the public's preferences or that tastes fluctuate frequently. In that situation, the charitable contribution deduction serves a "preference revelation" function by allowing contributors to determine the mix of activities while the government retains at least some control over the overall quantity by setting the price of contributions to 170(c) organizations. The uncertainties about what goods to provide may be the very reason why direct government provision of the goods is not feasible. A related rationale for provision through a contribution-funded private sector is "pluralism for efficiency reasons." Efficient provision of the goods may require a diversified, internally competitive private sector unhindered by the bureaucratic and institutional distortions that may affect government provision.

The charitable contribution deduction subsidizes contributions to all eligible activities at the same rate. Generally, however, different activities will have different price elasticities and income elasticities for contributions,[41] different nonsubsidy levels of contributions and different optimal levels of contributions. This suggests that the optimal subsidy-rate structure for contributions may vary substantially across activities. An efficiency problem will exist, therefore, with a deduction, a tax credit, or any other tax incentive that is the same for all activities.

Any efficiency costs of that sort, however, must be balanced against the low administrative costs of a tax deduction. A deduction is a familiar tax device that requires no new government apparatus to administer it. Furthermore, use of a deduction means that the bulk of contributions will come from a relatively small group, high-income taxpayers, and this group will experience the greatest tax incentive to report contributions. It may be easier to monitor such a small group to control practices such as claiming nonexistent contributions or inflating the value of contributions actually made.[42] Finally, activities that are seriously "undersubsidized" by the deduction may be given additional government benefits to correct the situation.

There also may be cases in which a deduction works best as a complement to direct government provision. For example, it may be cheaper to provide the bulk of some good such as primary education by direct government provision but to use subsidized contributions to fund a variety of special kinds of primary education that the government cannot provide efficiently. Alternatively, subsidized contributions may reveal residual demand for more of the kind of education that the government provides.

The next five subsections will consider situations in which the mix of government polities is dictated by particular donor-motivation patterns as well as by instrumental efficiency. For purposes of exposition, instrumental efficiency considerations will be ignored except to the extent that they interact with the particular motivations under examination.

Nonsubstantive Motivations

A donor may be motivated to give for reasons other than an interest in the substantive output of the donee 170(c) organization. This "nonsubstantive giving" may arise in response to pressure from friends, pressure from 170(c) solicitors, and pressure from employers or society generally. Alternatively, the donor may simply enjoy the act of giving itself or may derive prestige from the act of giving. Professor Simon has cautioned that the justification for the charitable contribution deduction would be considerably weakened if giving is "mindless," "sentimentally" motivated, or the result of pressure from family, employer, or 170(c) organizations.[43]

It is not clear, however, that nonsubstantive giving is socially unproductive. "Nonsubstantive donors" may be giving in response to what some other person or institution thinks is desirable. The degree to which nonsubstantive giving will be socially productive depends on how nonsubstantive donors choose one cause rather than another. At least three types of institutional or personal catalysts may influence such donors. First, they may be influenced directly by "substantive donors." This type of influence is probably positive—the substantive donor in effect contributes not only his or her own resources but also those of the nonsubstantive donor. In addition, substantive donors and nondonor-beneficiaries who benefit from the 170(c) activity supported by nonsubstantive donors may favor making those donors eligible for any contribution subsidy, since the goal of such a subsidy is to increase support for the activity regardless of how the increase comes about.

A second catalyst for giving is solicitation by 170(c) organizations. This vehicle raises the specter of self-perpetuating 170(c) organizations surviving on tax-deductible contributions from nonsubstantive donors when substantive demand for the organization's activities is almost zero. Leaving aside the desires of those who run the organization, this condition is not Pareto optimal because nonsubstantive donors could satisfy their desires by giving to 170(c) organizations providing goods and services for which there is substantial substantive demand. Despite these concerns, in the long run the effectiveness of solicitation by 170(c) organizations probably rests to a large extent on social perceptions that ultimately derive from substantive demand for public goods. In addition, solicitation by 170(c) organizations may serve valuable purposes. Solicitation may inform potential contributors and nondonor political supporters about the value of a 170(c) organization's goods and services and, thereby, generate substantive demand for its output.

A third catalyst is general social pressure that is not imposed specifically by donors or by 170(c) organizations. For example, a person may give to his or her alma mater out of a sense that it is proper to do so without specific pressure from the institution or other donors. Individuals themselves ultimately generate these general social pressures by initiating or perpetuating ideas about which institutions should be supported. However, these pressures may operate with a lag. The potential misdirection of resources while nonsubstantive donors adjust to new social perceptions is a potential cost that must be counted in evaluating certain changes in government policy. Suppose, for example, that direct government provision of a 170(c) activity is added to supplement contribution subsidies. The direct government provision lowers the need for provision by 170(c) organizations. But nonsubstantive donors may delay reducing their contributions until new social perceptions have time to lower the social approbation associated with such contributions. As a result, there may be a temporary oversupply of the activity in question.

How does subsidizing nonsubstantive donors fit into the view of the charitable contribution deduction as a political bargain? Substantive donors and nondonor-beneficiaries may have to pay additional taxes to fund the subsidy to nonsubstantive donors. But if the nonsubstantive donors direct their contributions to 170(c) organizations in such a way as to raise the value of the output of such organizations to the substantive donors and nondonor-beneficiaries more than the additional taxes, those groups will benefit from the subsidy. In addition, as long as part of the subsidy is funded by other parties, nonsubstantive donors will be better off. Although nondonor-beneficiaries and substantive donors may benefit from the donations of nonsubstantive donors this way, there is an additional issue. Suppose that nonsubstantive donors' contribution patterns differ substantially from those which would result if nondonor-beneficiaries or substantive donors donated the same money. Might it then be a good idea to disallow subsidies for nonsubstantive donors and at the same time to increase subsidies for substantive donors?

There are several answers to that question. First, it is probably impossible to distinguish between substantive donors and nonsubstantive donors. For many donors substantive concerns blend with pressures from others to dictate choice among potential 170(c) organization donees. Second, even if it were possible to draw such a distinction, it may be desirable to continue subsidizing nonsubstantive donors. Those donors may be more responsive to subsidies than substantive donors. Thus, the "bang" per tax dollar paid by nondonor-beneficiaries and substantive donors to fund contribution subsidies may be greater if nonsubstantive donors are subsidized instead of extending greater subsidies to substantive donors. This effect may outweigh the fact that nonsubstantive donors' patterns of giving are "distorted" in the eyes of substantive donors and nondonor-beneficiaries. Third, if substantive donors know what the pattern of 170(c) organization receipts are, they can redirect their own pattern of contributions to "correct" for the "distortion" caused by the contributions of nonsubstantive donors.[44]

Desire for Alternatives to Government

Where the donor's motivation is a desire to establish alternative institutions that overlap or preempt government functions regardless of the efficiency of those institutions compared with government, pluralism is desired for "preference" as opposed to "efficiency" reasons. Preference pluralism has strong public-good aspects—one person's efforts to set up a private alternative to government will satisfy another's desire for such an alternative even though that other contributes nothing to its creation.

Those who desire alternatives to government will oppose replacing provision by 170(c) organizations with government provision. Viewing provision by 170(c) organizations as a political bargain, the existence of this group would tend to delay the shift of 170(c) activities to the public sector until the efficiency gains or other possible gains from doing so are substantial. Those who are interested in the activities as nondonor-beneficiaries or as substantive donors would face paying extra taxes to make up for losing part or all of the net payments of the preference pluralism group to the activities if such a shift were made.

Utility Externalities

Utility externalities exist when one person's utility depends on another's utility. Utility externalities present a traditional public-good situation. Where persons A and B both desire C to be happier, transfers to C will benefit both A and B regardless of the source of the transfers, and neither A nor B can be excluded from benefiting if either makes a transfer. Where utility externalities are implemented by donations, the donor is best off making a cash transfer since the recipient will use that additional income to maximize his or her own utility. A striking feature of the 170(c) sector, however, is that it almost exclusively provides specific goods as opposed to income transfers.

There are many reasons to believe that 170(c) organizations are extremely inefficient vehicles compared to governments for providing income redistribution even at the margin. Most of these reasons stem from the fact that an income transfer program requires immense administrative resources. It is vital to be able to determine what each individual's income is so that transfers are directed only to those who are truly needy. In addition, if the redistribution program covers a large region or the entire nation, millions of transfers will be involved and the composition of the class of transferees will constantly shift. On the other hand, limiting the program to a small area may be impossible if the benefits are at all significant. Significant benefits may result in migration of poor people to the area with consequences that include financial drain but also extend to straining the area's capacity to place its poor in productive, well-paying jobs as a permanent solution to their plight. That migration would threaten to make the nation poorer by exacerbating inefficiency in labor markets as well as by diminishing the chance of self-sufficiency for some of the poor.

Federal and state governments are uniquely placed to redistribute income. They have a great deal of detailed information about incomes that they must collect to run the tax and welfare systems, and they can ensure at least some degree of national or state uniformity in transfers. It is no surprise that governments have little competition from 170(c) organizations, even for residual demand for income transfers. The sheer size of administrative economies of scale in redistribution programs suggests that a single supplier, government, will most likely provide almost all redistribution.[45]

Consumption Externalities

If person A is concerned not with person B's happiness as evaluated by person B but with what particular mixture of goods B consumes, then there is a "consumption externality" as opposed to a "utility externality" between the two of them. When there is a positive utility externality between groups (that is, members of group A are happier if people in group B feel happier), then there is a basis for legislation setting up transfers between group A and group B since both groups can be made better off by such transfers if the utility externality is strong enough.[46] But the case of a consumption externality offers much less scope for smooth political interactions. Suppose group A prefers that an individual B consumes more of good X and less of all other goods. Group A will be satisfied by legislation that *lowers* B's income and utility so long as consumption of good X is increased. In fact, group A will want to shift B's consumption by means that minimize the transfer of resources from group A to B. For example, group A might desire legislation that taxes B's consumption of goods other than X and reduces B's income taxes by the amount of the revenue from the tax on the goods. This should result in consumption by B of more X.[47] At the same time, ignoring administrative expenses, there is no cost to anyone else since the tax and refund scheme has no net revenue consequences.

There may be several situations in which a contribution subsidy like the charitable contribution deduction might emerge as a political bargain to implement consumption externalities. Consider first the use of a contribution subsidy as an exclusive way to implement consumption externalities. If the As are limited to "donative" instruments (such as subsidies, direct grants of good X, and "rewards" for consuming more X than a fixed quantity) to shift the consumption of the Bs, then the Bs cannot be made worse off by the As' actions. Gifts and positive incentives can always be refused. So limiting As to donative instruments is valuable to Bs who otherwise face the prospect of the use of sticks such as taxation or government sanctions that make them worse off. The Bs, therefore, might favor allowing As to implement their consumption externality tastes through the 170(c) sector and the charitable contribution deduction. The Bs might even pay part of the tax cost of the deduction as applied to these activities in order to steer the As away from using other more direct government devices.

There is one problem with using direct provision of goods to satisfy consumption externalities. If the recipient already buys some of the good, normally the recipient will not increase the total amount of good consumed by the amount provided directly for free. Instead, the recipient will cut back on his or her market purchases of the good and use the extra money to buy other goods. This suggests a possible synergy between government and the 170(c) sector with respect to consumption externalities. The government might provide large quantities of a good X for free to a particular group while taxing the group an amount equal to the total cost of the good so provided. Given this "base" level of provision, additional direct provision might be effective in increasing consumption of X. Contribution-funded 170(c) organizations could then satisfy residual consumption externality demand.

This possibility of valuable coordination of government and 170(c) activity suggests the central role of interactions between the two. Where the government and the 170(c) sector provide the same goods or close substitutes, and donors are aware of the government programs, the size and scope of the 170(c) sector depends on donor expectations about government activity. If the government is expected to maintain a particular policy, such as a given user subsidy or level of provision regardless of 170(c) activity, then added donor contributions will help implement consumption externalities. But it may be the case that additional 170(c) activity will result in a reduction in government activity, and at the extreme it may result in a one-for-one reduction. In such a situation additional giving will be diminished or eliminated. The synergistic use of 170(c) organizations to sop up residual consumption externality demand given a base of government provision will only succeed if the government does not exploit additional giving by changing its provision level.[48]

Desire to Influence the Tastes of Others

In some situations group A wants to change the tastes of another group B. For example, an environmental group might want people to be more conscious of the environment or the old might want the young to adopt certain political beliefs. Taste-changing desired by groups is a public good. If a member of group A spends to change the tastes of group B, all the members of A benefit from whatever changes occur.

At first glance there appears to be no particular reason to distinguish activities aimed at changing tastes from other activities that satisfy public-good demand. There is, however, at least one important practical difference between taste-changing and other public goods.[49] Successful taste-changing measures may result in policy choices with irreversible consequences. Suppose a country goes to war after certain groups in the country engage in a massive campaign to stir up pro-war sentiment. There may be no low-cost method of getting out of the war even if the effects of the taste-changing campaign wear off and the political basis for going to war evaporates.

The case for the existing restrictions on political activity by 170(c) organizations may be partially justified by the political dangers of large short-run fluctuations in tastes. The main restrictions are on overt activity aimed *directly* at the political process: grassroots lobbying is restricted and support of political candidates is banned.[50] These activities have public-good aspects, but such restrictions lessen the danger of a "preemptive" strike by pockets of wealth through a massive campaign to change tastes. Subsidies are aimed at activities that work toward taste-changing more indirectly and slowly by providing information and research. Use of these activities to change tastes allows opponents a fairer opportunity to strike back and allows people time to reflect before agreeing to new leadership or new legislation that may irreversibly affect the course of events. Present restrictions, therefore, allow some forms of taste-changing to be subsidized, yet at the same time discourage taste-changing that short-circuits the gradualism of politics. This position is likely to command wide support and, therefore, it is not surprising that the position has emerged as legislative policy from the current political process.

There is at least one subtle way in which the current system of contribution funding may satisfy demand for taste-changing as a public good. This involves overt and covert donor influence on 170(c) organizations that provide educational services. Educational institutions probably play a significant role in molding the future attitudes and beliefs of students. Donors may attempt to control this belief-shaping process by explicitly tying their contributions to the adoption of particular curricular approaches. Educational institutions may hesitate to teach doctrines that are unpopular with actual or potential donors.[51]

The potential problem with a deduction as a form of contribution subsidy in this instance is similar to the potential problems in other instances. A deduction encourages the contributions of high-income individuals more than the contributions of other individuals, so that it increases high-income group "donor influence" over educational institutions disproportionately. If the high-income group wants to instill beliefs that are not supported by other income groups, the public-good aspect satisfied by the deduction does not extend to those other income groups who may even see encouragement of such beliefs as a "public bad."

There are a range of "political bargain" responses if this situation of conflict between groups occurs. First, those not in the high-income group may demand compensation in the form of lower taxes or higher expenditures on their behalf. This will effectively shift the tax-revenue cost of the deduction to the high-income group. Second, groups other than the high-income group can shift the funding of education more toward direct subsidies for students or other forms of direct government support that are alternatives to donor subsidies. Such a move might reduce the efficiency-motivated pluralism in education because of the greater government role, but it would also dilute the influence of high-income donors over educational institutions.[52] In any event, this is another instance in which the role of the charitable contribution deduction in the overall government policy mix may depend critically on the existing pattern of individual motivations.

CONCLUSIONS

Much of the literature on the tax deductibility of charitable contributions focuses on the claim that the deduction unduly favors high-income taxpayers. In this context, analysts often attempt to assess the fairness of the deduction by calculating the direct costs and benefits to various groups. This chapter suggests that both the concern and the conventional way of addressing it may be misguided. In particular, the chapter shows that the deduction and the legislation accompanying it may be a political bargain that benefits all groups including low-income and middle-income groups. This possibility suggests that in assessing the deduction it is important to focus on the functioning of the political process. If that process allows low-income and middle-income individuals to protect their interests, it seems unlikely that they are harmed by the deduction.

This chapter also shows that if the deduction is part of a political bargain that benefits a wide range of groups, then the appropriate role of the deduction in conjunction with other government policies depends heavily on the particular motivations of donors and of nondonors who benefit from or are harmed by the activities that the donors support. For example, in the case of education, student subsidies may be an attractive alternative to a deduction for contributions to educational organizations if low-income and middle-income individuals are opposed to the added overt or covert influence of high-income contributors on curricula that is a by-product of the deduction.

NOTES

1. This concern has dominated much of the literature concerning the charitable contribution deduction. See, for example, Andrews, Personal deductions in an ideal income tax, *Harv. L. Rev.* 86: 309 (1972) at 310–12, 314–15 (higher subsidy to high-income taxpayers makes charitable contribution deduction indefensible as tax expenditure but tax theory arguments may justify it as a way of measuring income); Simon, Charity and dynasty under the federal tax system, *The Probate Lawyer*, Summer 1978, 20–24, reprinted as Chapter 14 of this volume (dismissing Andrews' tax theory argument and finding high subsidy to high-income taxpayers "a prima facie violation of progressivity").

2. Traditionally, the deduction has been an itemized deduction, but this is changing. For 1982 and 1983 only 25 percent of the first $100 in charitable contributions may be taken "above the line" as a nonitemized deduction. In 1984 this limit is raised to 25 percent of the first $300 in contributions. In 1985 half of all charitable contributions can be taken as "above the line" deductions, and in 1986 all charitable contributions can be so deducted. But after 1986 the law reverts to its pre-1982 state where the charitable deduction is available only as an itemized deduction. See I.R.C. § 170(i).

3. The following table for 1980 is based on data in *Internal Revenue Service, Statistics of Income—1980, Individual Income Tax Returns* (1982):

Adjusted gross income (thousands of $)	Percentage in class versus all returns	Percentage of itemized returns in class
<5	21.38%	2.27%
5–10	19.56	7.30
10–15	15.23	17.99
15–20	11.82	32.36
>20	32.03	69.79
All classes	100.00%	30.83%

4. This recent work includes Hochman and Rodgers, The optimal tax treatment of charitable contributions, 30 *National Tax J.* 1 (1977), reprinted as Chapter 13 of this volume, and Simon, *supra* note 1. Those two articles receive extensive attention in the rest of this article.

5. See Simon, *supra* note 1, 66.

6. See *id.*, 62.

7. See *id.*, 82, 84.

8. See *id.*, 84.

9. This approach gives heavy weight to the concern about favoritism. The preferences and beliefs of the favored group are ignored, and everyone else must be satisfied that the favoritism is acceptable.

There is one significant way in which the norm might not fully capture concerns in the literature. Some high-income individuals may believe that the deduction and accompanying legislation do not provide enough benefits for low-income and middle-income individuals even though these individuals are satisfied with the distributional consequences in light of the benefits they receive. The norm gives no weight to this type of preference on the part of high-income individuals. Nonetheless, this article considers the role that this type of preference may play in a political bargain producing the deduction and accompanying legislation. See text accompanying notes, 44–48 *infra*.

10. For a good summary of the work to date on the price elasticity for charitable contributions, see Clotfelter and Steuerle, Charitable contributions, in H. Aaron and J. Pechman, eds., *How Taxes Affect Economic Behavior* 403 (1981) and the associated comments.

11. For example, volumes III and IV of *Research Papers* sponsored by the Commission on Private Philanthropy and Public Needs (U.S. Department of Treasury, 1977) contain over 30 papers on the effects of the tax system on the amount and composition of 170(c) activities. Many of these papers focus primarily on the charitable contribution deduction. For a discussion of the massive amount of empirical work on the incentive effects of the deduction, see Clotfelter and Steuerle, *supra* note 10.

12. Clotfelter and Steuerle after comprehensively reviewing all the empirical work in the area and presenting their own findings note that the exact econometric specification used has a big impact on the findings so that "caution should be used in making policy prescriptions on the basis of such findings." See Clotfelter and Steuerle, *supra* note 10, 437. Some of the problems with the findings may result in systematic bias. For example, there is the possibility that taxpayers in high brackets tend to overstate their contributions so that empirical studies using tax-return data would find such taxpayers more responsive to the deduction than they actually are. See *id.*, 424, n.38 and *id.*, 446 (comments by John A. Brittain).

13. Some of the nonprofit organizations that are eligible to receive deductible contributions under § 170(c) may "correct" market failures other than public good problems. See Hansmann, The role of nonprofit enterprise, 89 *Yale L.J.* 835, 843–73 (1980), reprinted as Chapter 3 of this volume (discussing various corrective roles). Nonetheless, the public-good rationale for a subsidy applies to many, if not to substantially all, of the organizations.

14. See Hochman and Rodgers, *supra* note 4.

15. See *id.*, 8.

16. This situation can occur because taxes in a Lindahl equilibrium cannot result in a redistribution of consumer surplus. Each person is taxed at a rate per unit that reflects only his or her valuation of the last unit of output. The fact that the person may value earlier units more highly than the last unit has no tax consequences. It is easy to construct examples where Lindahl equilibria exist only at zero public-good production but some positive level of public-good provision is a Pareto improvement over no provision if the consumer surplus from production of the public good is redistributed.

17. At first glance it is not implausible to assume that people ignore the distributional effects of consumer surplus. Concern about the distribution of consumer surplus either for private goods or public goods is rarely voiced at the individual or societal level. This may be the result of a general feeling that each individual's consumer surplus depends on his or her capacity to enjoy and that having a higher capacity to enjoy should not trigger distributional concern. Alternatively, silence about the distribution of consumer surplus may reflect the difficulties inherent in ascertaining that surplus for each individual or even for broad classes of individuals. It makes little sense to talk about redistributing consumer surplus if it cannot be observed.

18. See Hochman and Rodgers, *supra* note 4, 9–10 and note 26.

19. This showing requires an assumption that the income elasticity of marginal valuation is independent of the quantity of public good produced. This point is discussed in the Appendix *infra* at note A2.

20. Hochman and Rodgers, *supra* note 4, 10.

21. This intuitive explanation is worked out more rigorously in the Appendix. See text accompanying note A5 and note A5 *infra*. The Appendix also shows that under current empirical beliefs about charitable giving a flat-rate tax credit would require *regressive* tax-rate changes to be a Lindahl equilibrium. See text accompanying note A6 *infra*.

22. A second justification that Hochman and Rodgers use is that the changes in tax rates would be small since "charitable giving is less than two percent of personal income." Hochman and Rodgers *supra* note 4, 9. Presumably, this is meant to suggest that such changes are

so small that they will be ignored by the individuals concerned. This argument ignores the political visibility of the deduction. Each taxpayer may be unaware of exactly how much he or she pays to fund the deduction each year, but information about the deduction itself is readily available to taxpayers and their political representatives. The 1983 tax-expenditure budget estimates the revenue loss from the deduction at over $10 billion for fiscal 1983. See, *The Budget of the United States Government, Fiscal Year 1983, Special Analysis G*, "Tax Expenditures" (February 1982) (Table G-2). It is hard to imagine that political representatives are unaware that someone must pay for this revenue loss through higher taxes (or through increased deficits, reduced expenditures, or some other device that is modeled as a tax increase in this chapter and in Hochman and Rogers' article).

23. Hochman and Rogers, *supra* note 4, 9–10.

24. Hochman and Rodgers are aware of this problem. They note that under Lindahl equilibrium an individual who makes no contribution and places no value on the final unit of public good produced should pay no extra taxes to fund a subsidy for contributions. See *id.*, 17, n.26. They then point out that in their model the valuation of the final unit of public-good production increases positively with income. If rates are increased by the same percentage for each person, the tax payments required to fund the revenue loss from the deduction will also increase with income. See *id.* Presumably, the idea is that there is not much deviation from a Lindahl equilibrium. Aside from the vagueness of this reasoning, it depends on including the tax part of each individual's payment in the analysis. This article does that in a rigorous way, and the result is that Hochman and Rodgers' conclusions become doubtful.

25. This is a much stronger assumption than the one that will follow for the relation between tax increases for high-income contributors versus low-income contributors. This assumption is necessary, however, if there is to be a Lindahl equilibrium in which a given income class has both contributors and noncontributors who benefit equally from the 170(c) output. The alternatives are to abandon the Lindahl equilibrium norm or to leave the nondonor-beneficiaries out of the formal model as Hochman and Rodgers do.

The reader who is troubled by the strength of the political assumption here can always consider the case $P = 1$ (set out separately below) where all beneficiaries are contributors. That case has some theoretical appeal: if demand for the 170(c) good is considered to be strictly a function of income, it makes sense to model contributions behavior that way too. An additional interesting point is that the results for the case $P = 1$ correspond to at least one Lindahl equilibrium where all members of the low-income class are taxed the same amount. That is true when the contribution of low-income individuals who do contribute is the amount of extra value that those individuals place on the 170(c) good at the margin compared to low-income noncontributors. This is a special case but may be a good approximation: those who contribute may do so because they value the 170(c) good more. In any event, the goal here is not to prove that the charitable deduction is a Lindahl equilibrium but to show that under a political bargain view it is at least as plausible a candidate as a flat-rate tax credit.

26. It is only strictly the analog in the case where all the low-income individuals are contributors or where contributing low-income individuals are modeled to have higher marginal valuations of the 170(c) good than noncontributors by exactly the amount of the contributions. Otherwise, when $\delta = 0$, low-income noncontributors will suffer a higher tax-rate increase than high-income individuals and low-income contributors.

27. The Appendix shows that these exact numbers are not critical to the results. Reducing the income gap tends to make the results less like a deduction. But even if the gap is reduced from six to two times, the results are roughly the same. Changes in size of the low-income class relative to the high-income class also have little effect. See text accompanying notes A4–A5 *infra*.

28. Of course, these results do not *prove* that a deduction provides a good approximation to the optimal subsidy rates under Lindahl criteria. The model is much too simple to have the strength of a proof. But the results indicate that the possibility that a deduction approximates the Lindahl requirements must be taken seriously.

29. In Table 15–2 when $\delta = .5$ and the income elasticity is 0.75, no positive subsidy rate for the high-income taxpayer less than one will suffice for a Lindahl equilibrium to exist. This

is indicated by the entry ">1" rather than an actual number because subsidy rates greater than one are inconsistent with the empirical assumptions about the responsiveness of giving to a subsidy used in the calculations. A subsidy greater than one means that the taxpayer gets more back from the government than he or she contributes. A rational taxpayer would then give all of his or her wealth plus whatever he or she could borrow.

30. See *id.*, 13. It is well known that high-income individuals tend to give more to educational organizations and hospitals while low-income individuals tend to give more to religion. See Clotfelter and Salamon, The impact of the 1981 Tax Act on individual charitable giving, 35 *National Tax J.* 171, 179 (1982) (reprinted as Chapter 12 of this volume); Clotfelter and Steuerle, *supra* note 10, 421.

31. See Clotfelter and Steuerle, *supra* note 10, 426–31.

32. The general conclusion of the econometric work is that the price elasticity is significantly less than zero, but only for the highest income bracket is it fairly certain that the elasticity is less than minus one. See *id.* The additional induced contributions will exceed the tax revenues lost if, and only if, the elasticity is less than minus one.

33. Religious organizations receive the lion's share (around 60 percent) of all individual charitable contributions. See Clotfelter and Salamon, *supra* note 30, 181 (Table 5). But this does not resolve the real issue: whether subsidies expand contributions sufficiently so that religion is provided at an optimal level. Furthermore, determining the optimal subsidy level for contributions is complicated by the fact that religion receives other benefits from government.

34. Many of the mechanisms aim at inducing individuals to reveal their demand for public goods. The mechanisms that succeed at doing this succeed only under limited assumptions, and generally speaking, systematic cheating by coalitions can undermine the revelation properties of such mechanisms. For an elementary discussion, see A. Atkinson and J. Stiglitz, *Lecture on Public Economics*, 513–15 (1980); R. Tresch, *Public Finance: A Normative Theory*, 119–21 (1981).

35. For a discussion of various experimental results see Smith, An experimental comparison of three public good decision mechanisms, 81 *Scand. J. Econ.* 198 (1979).

36. For an elementary and short discussion that includes a more detailed analysis of "cycling," see A. Atkinson and J. Stiglitz, *supra* note 34, 299–310. Good comprehensive surveys are A. Sen, *Collective Choice and Social Welfare* (1970); Mueller, Public Choice: A Survey, 14 *J. Econ. Lit.* 395 (1976); Plott, Axiomatic social choice theory: An overview and interpretation, 20 *Am. J. Political Science* 511 (1976).

37. See A. Atkinson and J. Stiglitz, *supra* note 34, 322–26.

38. See, for example, *id.*, 310–15, 328 (analyzing impact of bureaucratic interests); M. Fiorina, *Congress: Keystone of the Washington Establishment* (1977) (arguing that governments tend to overprovide services due to the interests of politicians).

39. A fact that supports this assertion is that traditionally the charitable contribution deduction has been available only to those who itemize their deductions but the vast majority of taxpayers do not itemize. See note 3 *supra* (30.8 percent itemize in 1980); Clotfelter and Salamon, *supra* note 30, 180 (70 percent do not itemize as of 1981); Simon, *supra* note 1, 82 (75 percent do not itemize as of 1978).

40. See text accompanying note 24 *supra*. Logrolling is no panacea, however. It does not eliminate "cycling," it can lead to overprovision of goods by the government, and it is subject to strategic manipulation. For a good general discussion, see Mueller, *supra* note 36, 406–07.

41. See Clotfelter and Steuerle, *supra* note 10, 419–22.

42. High-income individuals already are audited much more frequently than low-income individuals. See Commissioner of Internal Revenue and the Chief Counsel for the Internal Revenue Service, *Annual Report* (1982) at 44 (in 1981 government audited 7.83 percent of returns of individuals with total positive income over $50,000 versus 1.77 percent of all returns of individuals).

43. See Simon, *supra* note 1, 90–91. Professor Simon is not alone in his concern. For example, considerable scholarly and Congressional attention has been devoted to the fear that

the allocation of contribution dollars among health charities hinges much more on the success of competing public-relations campaigns than on the substantive role of each charity. See Brannon and Strnad, *Alternative Approaches to Encouraging Philanthropic Activities*, IV Research Papers Sponsored by the Commission on Private Philanthropy and Public Needs 2361, 2374–77 (1977).

44. The only problem with this third answer is that nonsubstantive donors may have so favored certain 170(c) organizations that the organizations are funded at or above the optimal level even if contributions from substantive donors have fallen to zero in an attempt to correct this situation.

45. For a related discussion, see Brannon and Strnad, *supra* note 43, 2378–79. See also Roberts, A positive model of private charity and public transfers, 92 *J. Polit. Econ.* 136 (1984) (assuming private organizations are less efficient than government at providing public goods, political equilibrium model predicts zero direct aid to poor by private charity).

46. See Hochman and Rodgers, Pareto optimal redistribution, 59 *Am. Econ, Rev.* 542 (1969); Polinsky, Shortsightedness and nonmarginal Pareto optimal redistribution, 61 *Am. Econ. Rev.* 972 (1971).

47. Using an income-tax reduction to return the revenues from the tax on the goods essentially eliminates any "income effect." Individual B faces a lower price for good X and higher prices for all other goods. The result should be larger purchases of X and lower purchases of other goods.

48. For further discussion of "crowding out" effects and their implications for policy, see Abrams and Schmitz, The "crowding-out" effect of governmental transfers on private charitable contributions, 33 *Public Choice* 29 (1978); Roberts, *supra* note 45; Rose-Ackerman, Do government grants to charity reduce private donations, in M. White, ed., *Nonprofit Firms in a Three Sector Economy* 95 (Urban Institute, COUPE #6, 1981) (reprinted as Chapter 20 in this volume); Steinberg, Voluntary donations and public expenditures, Virginia Polytechnic Institute and State University Working Paper E84-07-01 (July 1984); Weiss, Donations: Can they reduce a donor's welfare? Chapter 2 in this volume.

49. At the theoretical level, there is also at least one important difference. It may be hard to apply a Pareto optimality norm when the public good at issue is taste-changing. See, for example, Marschak, On the study of taste changing policies, 68 *Am. Econ. Rev.* 386 (1978); Weisbrod, Comparing utility functions in efficiency terms, or what kind of utility functions do we want?, 67 *Am. Econ. Rev.* 991 (1977).

50. See I.R.C. §§ 170(c)(2)(D), 501(c)(3), and 501(h) (denying tax-exempt status and ability to receive deductible contributions if organization attempts to influence legislation or participate in or intervene in any political campaign as a substantial part of organization's activities).

51. Overt and covert influences on educational institutions that arise from contribution funding are documented and discussed in Brannon and Strnad, *supra* note 43, 2368–72.

52. For a discussion of the pros and cons of direct subsidies for students as an alternative to contribution-funding of educational institutions, see Brannon and Strnad, *supra* note 43, 2373.

APPENDIX

This Appendix formalizes Hochman and Rodgers' model and presents the alternative model that is the basis for the critique in the text of their conclusions. Suppose there is a single, contribution-funded 170(c) activity that produces a quantity Q of a public good. Consider two people, A and B, who are interested in the public good. Suppose that person A has income Y_A, pays additional income taxes to fund subsidies for contributions to the activity through an increase in rates by $t'(Y_A)$, voluntarily contributes C_A

toward purchase of the good, and is subsidized by the proportion S_A of contributions. When Q of the public good is produced, suppose person A values the last unit provided at $ME_A(Q)$. If an optimal amount Q^* of the public good is provided, then for Lindahl equilibrium to obtain the following relation must hold:

$$\frac{C_A(1-S_A)+t'(Y_A)Y_A}{Q^*}=ME_A(Q^*) \qquad (15-A1)$$

This relation states that for A the price of the good, the sum of total net contributions and extra taxes paid divided by quantity, is equal to his or her marginal valuation of it. For person B there is a similar Lindahl condition:

$$\frac{C_B(1-S_B)+t'(Y_B)Y_B}{Q^*}=ME_B(Q^*) \qquad (15-A2)$$

Hochman and Rodgers assume that A has an income that is higher than B's by the factor $(1+\lambda)$ and that contributions are strictly a function of income when there is no subsidy:

$$Y_A = (1+\lambda)Y_B \qquad (15-A3)$$
$$C_A = (1+\alpha\lambda)C_B \quad \text{when} \quad S_A=S_B=0 \qquad (15-A4)$$

where α is the income elasticity of charitable contributions. This income elasticity is assumed to be independent of income. Although this model with constant income elasticity is fairly simple, it does roughly reflect a reality where there is a positive income elasticity for giving.[A1] Using the assumption that the income elasticity of marginal valuation is equal to the income elasticity of charitable contributions,[A2] the following equality must hold:

$$ME_A = (1 + \alpha\lambda)ME_B \qquad (15-A5)$$

so that

$$C_A(1 - S_A) + t'(Y_A)Y_A = (1+\alpha\lambda)[C_B(1-S_B)+t'(Y_B)Y_B] \quad (15-A6)$$

Hochman and Rodgers assume that the tax terms in Equation (15–A6) can be neglected so that it simplifies to:

$$C_A(1-S_A) = (1+\alpha\lambda)C_B(1-S_B) \qquad (15-A7)$$

Now if $S_A = S_B$ and A and B have the same price elasticity for charitable contributions, then $C_A = (1 + \alpha\lambda)C_B$ and Equation (15–A7) is satisfied since differences between A's and B's gross contributions arise solely from the fact that they have different incomes. This is the mathematical basis for Hochman and Rodgers' conclusion quoted in the text that "a flat-rate tax credit is likely to provide a good approximation to the Lindahl requirements."

The text argues that Hochman and Rodgers' assumption about the tax terms is not a particularly reasonable one. In the rest of this Appendix, I construct a model that specifies the subsidy structure corresponding to a Lindahl equilibrium for any given pattern of tax increases that fund the revenue loss from the deduction. My model begins with the Hochman and Rodgers' framework set up so far, but adds three important features:

1. The tax terms in Equation (15–A6) are not neglected;
2. The model includes a constraint requiring that the tax increases fund the revenue loss from the deduction; and
3. A third class of persons is added who benefit from the 170(c) good but make no contributions.

For convenience, I assume that this third class of persons have incomes equal to Y_B and that their demand for the 170(c) good is the same as others with that income. Suppose that the tax-rate increases for this third group are $t''(Y_B)Y_B$. It follows that in Lindahl equilibrium

$$t''(Y_B)Y_B = C_B(1 - S_B) + t'(Y_B)Y_B. \qquad (15–A8)$$

(That is, since contributors and noncontributors value the 170(c) good the same at the margin, their total payments must be equal).

The model now consists of two income groups with the low-income group divided between contributors and noncontributors. Suppose that the low-income group has N times as many people as the high-income group and that the proportion P of the low-income group are contributors. If we set $S_B = 0$ and choose N appropriately large, we have a rough approximation to the historically typical situation where a large number of nonitemizers receive no tax subsidy while a class of itemizers consisting primarily of high-income taxpayers do receive a subsidy.

Now reconsider Equation (15–A6). Y_A is $(1 + \lambda)$ as large as Y_B. Assume that the tax-rate increase t' (Y_A) for taxpayer A is $(1 + \delta)$ times the tax-rate increase $t'(Y_B)$ for taxpayer B. The parameter δ is a measure of the progressivity of the income-tax increases that will fund the deduction. Now assume that with no deduction B would make C_B in contributions and that η is the absolute value of the price elasticity of charitable contributions for both A and B. Because the income elasticity of giving is α,

$$C_A = C_B(1 + \alpha\lambda) \ (1 + S_A\eta) \qquad (15–A9)$$

Using Equation (15–A9), expressing all tax-rate and income variables in terms of $t'(Y_B)Y_B$ and dividing through by $(1 + \alpha\lambda)$, (15–A6) becomes:

$$C_B(1+S_A\eta)(1-S_A)+\frac{(1+\delta)(1+\lambda)}{(1+\alpha\lambda)}t'(Y_B)Y_B=$$
$$C_B+t'(Y_B)Y_B \qquad\qquad (15-A10)$$

In order for tax increases to exactly cover the revenue loss of a deduction, it must be true that

$$(15-A11)$$
$$C_AS_A = (1 + \delta)t'(Y_B) (1 + \lambda)Y_B + N[(1 - P)C_B + t'(Y_B)Y_B]$$

Here $(1-P)C_B+t'(Y_B)Y_B$ is the average tax share of people with income Y_B. The proportion $(1-P)$ does not contribute and thus pays $C_B+t'(Y_B)Y_B$ in taxes while the rest pay $t'(Y_B)Y_B$.

Using (15-A9), Equation (15-A11) yields an expression for $t'(Y_B)Y_B$:

$$t'(Y_B)Y_B=\frac{C_B[(1+S_A\eta)(1+\alpha\lambda)S_A-N(1-P)]}{[N+(1+\delta)(1+\lambda)]} \qquad (15-A12)$$

Define the parameter γ as

$$\gamma=\frac{(1+\delta)(1+\lambda)-(1+\alpha\lambda)}{(1+\alpha\lambda)[N+(1+\delta)(1+\lambda)]} \qquad (15-A13)$$

Substituting for $t'(Y_B)Y_B$ in (15-A10) using (15-A12) and rearranging we obtain:

$$[\gamma(1+\alpha\lambda) - 1]\eta S_A^2 + [\gamma(1+\alpha\lambda) + \eta - 1]S_A$$
$$- \gamma(1+\alpha\lambda)N(1-P)=0 \qquad (15-A14)$$

The tables in the text are generated using Equation (15-A14) to compute S_A for various values of δ and P. In those computations N is set at 3, η at 1.25, λ at 5, and .75 and 1 are alternative assumptions for α. The values for α are in the lower and upper range of the values found in the econometric literature while the value for η is close to the price elasticities found in studies that pool all income groups together.[A3]

When a real solution exists, Equation (15-A14) generally produces two solutions for S_A. In all the simulations in this paper, $\alpha\leq1$, $\delta\geq0$, and $\lambda\geq0$. When those inequalities hold, one of the solutions for S_A will be negative. This solution is rejected on the ground that the goal is to stimulate charitable donations and a subsidy structure with $S_A<0$ and $S_B=0$ will reduce them.[A4]

The tables in the text take $N=3$ and $\lambda=5$. The result reported in the text is that a high subsidy rate for high-income taxpayers generally is required to meet the Lindahl conditions. Table 15-A1 indicates that this result is not very sensitive to the choice of N and λ. This table is calculated for the case $\delta=.1$, $\alpha=1$, and $\lambda=2$ (except for the "Text" column which

Table 15–A1. Required S_A for $\delta=.1$, $\alpha=1$, and $\lambda=2$ (Text column: $\delta=.1$, $\alpha=1$, $\lambda=5$, and $N=3$)

	$N=1$	$N=3$	$N=4$	$N=10$	Text
$P=0$	.42	.49	.51	.56	.55
$P=0.1$	.41	.48	.49	.53	.54
$P=0.25$	.39	.45	.46	.50	.50
$P=0.5$	.36	.40	.41	.44	.45
$P=1.0$	.28	.25	.24	.22	.27

reports the values for the set of parameters used in the text tables: $\delta=.1$, $\alpha=1$, $\lambda=5$, and $N=3$). The case $\delta=.1$ and $\alpha=1$ results in the *lowest* subsidy rate for high-income taxpayers among the values $\delta=(.1, .25, .5)$ and $\alpha=(.75, 1)$. Furthermore, when λ is reduced, the optimal subsidy rate falls. As a result, Table 15–A1 represents a situation in which we have chosen values of δ, α, and λ that *minimize* the required S_A but are still plausible.

The intuition behind the result that a high S_A is required when $S_B=0$ is apparent from Equation (15–A10). For $\delta>0$ and values of α less than one, as the tax variable $t'(Y_B)Y_B$ increases in order to fund a subsidy for giving, the left-hand side of (15–A10) increases more quickly than the right-hand side. This reflects a "progressive" tax increase falling heavily on A. The result is that A's net payment becomes too large relative to B's net payment. In order to reduce A's net payment, the first term in Equation (15–A10), a term proportional to A's net charitable contributions, must fall. As S_A is increased from 0, this term initially rises. When S_A becomes large enough (greater than .10 for $\eta=1.25$),[A5] the increase in the subsidy effect of the $(1-S_A)$ term outweighs A's tendency to increase gross contributions. As a result A's net contribution falls. As S_A tends toward 1, the net contribution tends toward 0. Thus, in order to offset the "progressive" nature of the tax increase, S_A may have to be set quite high in order to decrease A's net charitable contribution sufficiently.

Another issue is what tax shares would be required if a flat-rate subsidy of the sort Hochman and Rodgers advocate is desired. Consider persons A and B who are both contributors. When $S_A=S_B$, (15–A7) implies $C_A=(1+\alpha\lambda)C_B$ and using that result in (15–A6) implies that

$$t'(Y_A)Y_A=(1+\alpha\lambda)t'(Y_B)Y_B \qquad (15\text{–A}15)$$

But $t'(Y_A)Y_A=(1+\delta)(1+\lambda)t'(Y_B)Y_B$ so that

$$\delta=\frac{1+\alpha\lambda}{1+\lambda}-1 \qquad (15\text{–A}16)$$

This implies that δ must be negative if the income elasticity for charitable contributions is less than one as appears likely from the empirical literature.[A6] If δ is negative, a greater increase in tax rate must be imposed on the contributing low-income taxpayer than on the taxpayer with higher income. Furthermore, Equation (15–A8) indicates that low-income taxpayers who do not contribute must suffer an even greater increase in tax-percentage rate than either class of contributing taxpayers.

APPENDIX NOTES

A1. Empirical studies consistently have found that the income elasticity for contributions is positive. See Clotfelter and Steuerle, *supra* note 10, 410–11, 420–21, 425, and 428. Moreover, those studies suggest that that income elasticity may not be constant with income. See *id.*, 410–11 and 428. This is not a problem for the model here since α can be interpreted as the average income elasticity for incomes between Y_B and $(1 + \lambda)Y_B$.

A2. Hochman and Rodgers "prove" this assumption. See Hochman and Rodgers, *supra* note 4, 16, n.22. Since the goal is to measure the difference between $ME_A(Q^*)$ and $ME_B(Q^*)$, the evaluation is done with Q^* fixed. If N_i is the total net payment (including additional taxes) for person i, then Lindahl equilibrium requires $N_i = ME_i(Q^*)Q^*$. Thus, where Y_i is i's income, $\delta N_i/\delta Y_i = Q^* \delta ME_i/\delta Y_i$ and it follows that the income elasticity of N_i is equal to the income elasticity of ME_i.

This same analysis can be carried out for Q_0 instead of Q^* where Q_0 is the level of output when no subsidy for charitable contributions is provided. In that case $N_i = C_i$ where C_i is i's contribution with no subsidy. But then the income elasticity of N_i is just α. Assuming that the income elasticity of marginal evaluation is independent of Q, α is also the income elasticity of marginal evaluation at Q^*. I make that assumption, so that α is used as the income elasticity of marginal evaluation at Q^*. Use of the assumption considerably simplifies the algebra without substantially changing the results.

A3. See Clotfelter and Steuerle, *supra* note 10, 410–11, 425, and 428.

A4. A more complete model would specify an optimal quantity of contributions and require that the subsidy structure (S_A, S_B) produce that quantity. For simplicity, the optimal quantity aspect of the Lindahl equilibrium calculation is ignored here. But in an earlier version of this chapter I show that in a target quantity model a deduction-like result (a high S_A and a low, but not necessarily 0, S_B) can easily emerge as a Lindahl equilibrium.

A5. More formally, the first derivative of A's net charitable contribution with respect to S_A has the same sign as $(1 - 2S_A)\eta - 1$. The derivative is zero when $S_A = (\eta - 1)/2\eta$. For increases in S_A above that level, A's net charitable contribution falls.

A6. Almost all of the recent estimates of the income elasticity of charitable contributions find values less than one, and in most cases the value is significantly less than one (at the 95 percent confidence level). See Clotfelter and Steuerle, *supra* note 10, 410–11, 425, and 428.

16

Comments

HAROLD M. HOCHMAN

My comment on Jeff Strnad's paper, as he presented it at the conference, consisted of three points. The first two focus on his criticism of my 1977 paper with James Rodgers.[1] Strnad questioned our contention that a tax credit is more likely to be consistent with the public goods rationalization of subsidies to charitable contributions than simple deductibility. Here I contend that Strnad's argument, though provocative, contains a basic flaw. The third point refers to a major aspect of our argument with which Strnad does not deal at all, though it addresses a pervasive defect in the literature on the tax treatment of charitable contributions.

First of all, in our model, the optimal level of subsidies to private charity depends on how benefits are distributed between donors, the primary sharing group, and secondary demanders, who comprise the community-at-large. In order to justify public subsidy external benefits must be produced by the specific services that the charity finances. Otherwise, the benefits of giving are private, and no subsidy is warranted. This argument is adopted from the prior writings of a number of economists, notably Burton Weisbrod.

Strnad, in his political-economic argument, gives little importance to these secondary demanders or treats them as if they were relatively unconcerned with the goods in question, advancing instead a "political bargain" logic. Our model, in contrast, assumes that noncontributors acquiesce *willingly* in fiscal subsidies, because charitable contributions provide noncontributors with private benefits to which they attach positive value, even though this value is but a fraction of the cost. Strnad implies that noncontributors acquiesce *reluctantly*, as the price of obtaining preferred outcomes in a democratic logrolling process.

To be sure, it is difficult to measure publicness, as implicit in nondonor demand, but a number a seminal papers (including Borcherding and Deacon)[2] do suggest ways of approaching the problem. With the political bargain explanation of the subsidy, however, we can think of no evidence that is inconsistent with the hypothesis. By implication, the argument is tautological, and open to the criticism that a theory capable of explaining everything explains nothing.

Secondly, I believe that we were justified in ignoring the increments in individual income-tax burdens needed to sustain the aggregate level of tax revenue, given the subsidy to charity. Rodgers and I ignored these increments because, spread over the community-at-large, they become quite small; the number of taxpayers is considerably greater than the number of tax returns on which contributions are itemized, and contributions are, at most, a few percent of taxable income. It seems to us that nonitemizers would be willing to bear an additional tax burden of this magnitude in the Lindahl-type model we employ, given the public characteristics of the goods and services that subsidized contributions finance.

Third and finally, much of the literature on the tax treatment of charitable contributions focuses on the price elasticity of such contributions and asks, for policy purposes, whether this elasticity is smaller or larger than -1; it asks, in other words, whether a marginal subsidy of $1 (a revenue loss of $1) will raise more or less than $1 in additional contributions. Implicit in this question is the issue of whether the Treasury, in some sense, obtains its money's worth from the fiscal subsidization of contributions. The Treasury, in this connection, represents the community-at-large, as opposed to the particular individuals (the high demanders) who support the goods that contributions finance.

Unfortunately, posing the issue in this way asks the wrong question. The public good justification of subsidies to charity, as outlined in our paper, implies that the fraction of contributions the community-at-large is willing to finance is less than unity. In other words, in a Lindahl cost-sharing scheme the community would only be satisfied if a $1 marginal increment in the subsidy were to bring about much more than a $1 increase in contributions. Table 13.1 of our chapter calculates the community shares of the incentive effects on gross charitable giving implicit in different price elasticities of giving. This table implies that the willingness-to-pay of the community might range from, say, 0.5 to something under unity.

In other words, if the community felt it were worth $1 in revenue to obtain an additional dollar of the benefits produced by charitable contributions, it would simply purchase the good that charity finances through direct government spending. Under unitary government there would be no need for the cost-sharing scheme implicit in fiscal subsidization. If government were not unitary, this might not be the case; but a situation in which a marginal subsidy of $1 gives rise to $1 in additional contributions would imply that the high demanders of the good that charity finances were exporting part of its cost to taxpayers in other jurisdictions. In either case, charitable goods would be oversupplied and the public goods rationalization of fiscal subsidies would not be relevant. The reason all this is so troubling is that so much of both the academic and the policy discussion of the tax treatment of charitable contributions has been couched in terms of the price elasticity issue and has assumed, implicitly or explicity, that an elasticity of -1 has some special normative significance.

NOTES

1. Hochman, Harold M., and James D. Rodgers. 1977. The optimal tax treatment of charitable contributions. *National Tax Journal* 30 (March): pp. 1–18. Reprinted as Chapter 13 of this volume.

2. Borcherding, Thomas E., and Robert T. Deacon. 1972. The demand for the services of non-federal governments. *American Economic Review* 62 (December): pp. 842–53.

V
GOVERNMENT GRANTS

17

The Crowding-Out Effect
of Governmental Transfers
on Private Charitable Contributions

BURTON A. ABRAMS and MARK D. SCHMITZ

Substantial effort has been devoted to developing the conceptual framework and seeking empirical support for the "crowding out" effect of governmental expenditures.[1] While most studies have focused on the economic impact of expansionary fiscal policy actions upon such traditional macroeconomic variables as private investment and the demand for money, some attention has also been directed to assessing the net effect of particular governmental expenditures on private spending behavior.[2] This chapter concentrates on an analysis of a particular category of governmental expenditures—social welfare transfers—and their effect on private charitable contributions.

Table 17–1 reveals the dramatic growth in governmental social-welfare transfers following World War II. Although total private transfers have also grown during this period, they have done so at a slower rate indicating that, over time, governmental transfers have been shouldering a greater relative share of the social-welfare "burden." Table 17–1 also provides the somewhat paradoxical statistic that during this same period real charitable contributions per itemized tax return have remained essentially unchanged despite increases (on average) in disposable incomes, marginal tax rates, and in educational attainment—all factors which presumably encourage charitable contributions. In the following sections we discuss the determinants of private charitable giving and present empirical evidence that suggests that the puzzling constancy of private charitable contributions per taxpayer during recent decades is due, in part, to the growth in governmental social-welfare transfers. The outline for the remainder of this chapter is as follows: (a) alternative models for the analysis of private con-

Reprinted by permission of Martinis, Mijhoff Publishers. A previous version of this Chapter appeared in *Public Choice* (1978), Volume 33, Issue 1, pp. 29–39.

Table 17–1. Federal Welfare Expenditures and Charitable Contributions, 1950–1970 *(1958 dollars)*

Year	Federal Welfare Expenditures ($ millions)	Private Charitable Contributions ($ millions)	Contribution per Itemized Return
1950	$ 6181	$ 4716	$273
1952	4518	5454	327
1954	3968	5967	296
1956	4197	6743	295
1958	4481	7221	285
1960	5046	7639	283
1962	5738	8106	283
1964	7055	8766	298
1966	9484	9317	297
1968	13958	10217	302
1970	17180	10358	284

Source: U.S. Bureau of the Census. 1975. *Historical Statistics of the United States Colonial Times to 1970.* Washington: Government Printing Office, pp. 359, 1123–4. "Federal Welfare Expenditures" includes direct and intergovernmental amounts for welfare, education, and health. "Private Charitable Contributions" are by living donors. Internal Revenue Service. 1950 to 1974. *Statistics of Income: Individual Income Tax Returns* (1948–1972). Washington: Government Printing Office.

tributing behavior; (b) the variables and statistical tests used to measure government's "crowding-out" of private contributions; and (c) the statistical findings.

THE ECONOMICS OF CHARITY

Earlier studies have noted the "public goods" characteristics of charitable donations but have suggested various motives—such as the desire to do "good" and the desire to avoid social pressure—which overcome the free-rider problem and encourage private charitable giving.[3] The "private goods" interpretation of charity permits analysis within the traditional utility-maximization model. The utility-maximizing individual would make private charitable contributions up to the point where the marginal utility of the last dollar donated equals the marginal utility of the last dollar used privately. The extent of an individual's charitable contributions will depend on the individual's utility-preference mapping, his budget constraint, and the relative cost of contributing. The last determinant depends upon the individual's marginal tax rate and whether or not the individual itemizes deductions on his income tax schedules.[4]

Conceptually, the growth in governmental transfers can be expected to exert two distinct influences on private contributions. One is a "substitution effect;" increases in governmental transfers lower (ceteris paribus) the "social need" for additional private contributions thereby encouraging a substitution of private goods for private charitable transfers. The second is an "income effect;" the financing of governmental transfers lowers contributors' disposable incomes and, presumably, the extent of private contributions. Prior theorizing suggests at least three alternative models to formalize these "crowding out" effects.

Ultrarational Case

Applying an ultrarationality assumption developed by David and Scadding (1974), the individual would regard the government sector as an extension of himself. According to this line of reasoning, the individual contributor would perceive the government as an agent or intermediary in the transfer of income from the contributor to the recipient. In the extreme, the ultrarationality assumption would imply the complete crowding out of private contributions by governmental transfers. To illustrate, consider the individual who is allocating $100 of current income to charitable contributions. If the government were to increase this individual's taxes by $100 and then transfer the funds in a fashion consistent with the individual's original private contributions, our taxpayer need merely eliminate an equal amount of private charitable contributions to obtain the same utility as before the tax-cum-transfer. This case is illustrated in Figure 17–1 where both the individual's budget constraint and indifference curves shift horizontally by the amount of the transfer. The individual moves from A to B which maintains the original consumption expenditure but reduces private contributions by the amount of the tax-cum-transfer $(G_0 - G_1)$. His implicit contribution—the sum of his private giving and the amount government gives "in his name"—remains the same. Moreover, the ultrarationality assumption indicates the complete crowding-out case also maximizes the individual's utility at the original level.[5] This model suggests that the appropriate operational measure of governmental transfers for assessing their effect on individual contributing is governmental transfers per donor.

Interdependent Utility Functions

A second model of private contributions that would imply partial crowding out is the assumption of interdependent utility functions between contributors and recipients. If the utility that the contributor received from donations is a function of the utility of the recipient, then increases in governmental transfers, ceteris paribus, would lower the recipient's marginal utility of an additional contribution. If the recipient's marginal utility is lower, the *contributor's* marginal utility from an additional contribution is also reduced and his indifference curves would tend to rotate as shown in Figure 17–2. Thus, higher government transfers alone would lead the utility-maximizing individual to increase expenditures on private goods and reduce charitable transfers until marginal utilities are once again equated, as shown at Point B. Additionally, the tax financing of the transfer would tend to lower the individual's comsumption and contribution spending, moving the donor from Point B to Point C. This model suggests that the appro-

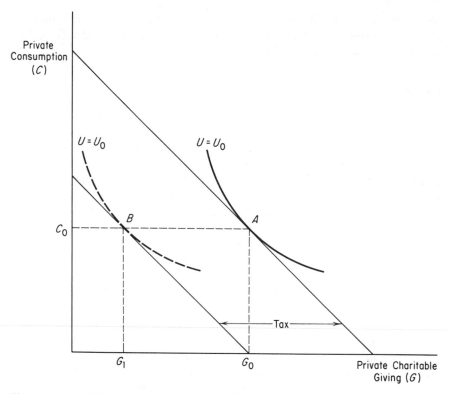

Figure 17–1 The impact of transfers: The ultrarational case. (*Tax* represents the tax-cum-transfer for government contributions. The slope of the budget line is $-p_g/p_c$, where p_g is one minus the marginal income-tax rate for the individual. It follows that $Tax = G_0 - G_1$.)

priate operational measure of governmental transfers for assessing their effect on individual contributing is perhaps governmental transfer per recipient or some other proxy that serves to measure the recipient's well-being.

The Better-to-Give-than-Receive Hypothesis (BGR)

The contributor's utility function may be completely independent of the utility of the recipient. The satisfaction derived from contributing could be intrinsic to the act of giving itself and, consequently, increased governmental giving, ceteris paribus, would have no substitution effect. However, we could still expect an income effect as individuals' disposable incomes are reduced as a result of tax financing of public transfers.

The three models sketched out above suggest respectively that government charitable expenditures substitute completely, partially, or not at all for private charitable contributions. However, these models are merely suggestive and certainly not exhaustive. For example, the implications of

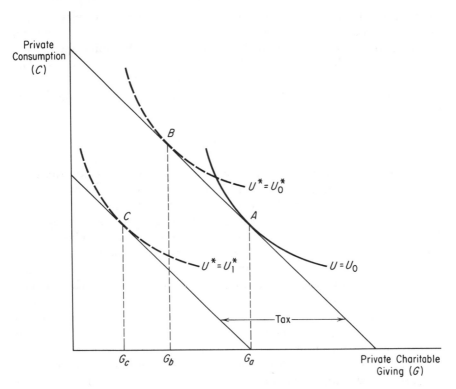

Figure 17–2 The impact of transfers: Interdependent utility case. (The starred indifference curves are post-transfer curves and reflect the negative impact of the transfers on the marginal utility of private giving. The substitution effect from the tax-cum-transfer is $G_a - G_b$, while the income effect is $G_b - G_c$.)

the BGR hypothesis are also consistent with an assumption of complete contributor ignorance of governmental contributions. Prior theorizing, however, tells us nothing about *actual* crowding out and it is to an empirical estimation of this phenomenon to which we now turn.

THE VARIABLES AND REGRESSION MODEL

In order to quantify the crowding-out effect of governmental transfers, we estimated three models using a pooled time series of cross-sectional tax return data for the period 1948 through 1972.[6] The specification for our regression equation takes the following log-linear form:

$$log\ G_{it} = \alpha_0 + \alpha_1 \log Y_{it} + \alpha_2 \log P_{it} + \alpha_3 \log T_t + u_{it} \qquad (17-1)$$

Following Feldstein (1975), the subscript t denotes time and i denotes the adjusted gross income (AGI) class of the contributor.[7] As the dependent variable, private charitable contributing, G_{it}, is the average contribution per itemized federal income-tax return for AGI class i and year t.[8] To control for the actual after-tax cost to the contributor of charitable giving, the "price" of contributing, P_{it}, is calculated by subtracting from unity the marginal tax rate on the first dollar contributed in the class and year. To control for the influence of income, Y_{it} measures the average disposable income (before contributions) per return for each income class.

Governmental Transfers

To capture the influence of government transfers on private contributions to charitable organizations, we introduced several alternative measures of public-sector charitable giving. The measures include only those types of transfers or expenditures that seem on a priori grounds to be substitutes for private donations.[9] The first specification and the one that seems closest to meeting the substitution criteria uses federal expenditures on health, education, and welfare (T_t^1). As an alternative, we added the corresponding expenditures by state and local government units (T_t^2). This offers a broader measure of transfers but some components of state and local transfers might be inappropriate (e.g., state and local subsidies of primary and secondary schools) as perhaps no real private charitable counterparts exist for these expenditures. As a third measure of government giving, we added social security and other federal trust fund expenditures to the health, education, and welfare amounts (T_t^3). While the actual net impact of the social security transfer program is open to question, if individuals *believe* the program helps the needy, the program's growth could affect private charitable giving. Although our prior theorizing suggests a per donor (ultrarational model) or per recipient (interdependent utility model) specification for the government transfer variable, lacking data on the number of donors and recipients, all of our transfer variables were entered into the estimating equations in per capita form.

Other Determinants

Presumably, increases in educational attainment and church membership, ceteris paribus, would serve to encourage increases in charitable contributions.[10] Unfortunately, the strong time trend for these variables poses a multicolinearity problem with our governmental transfer variable. Because of their expected positive influences on private charitable contributions, omission of these variables from our estimating equations would tend to impose a positive bias on the estimate for the coefficient of our governmental transfer variable.

THE FINDINGS

The regression results for the three log-linear models are reported in Table 17–2. Model I uses *federal* expenditures on health, education, and welfare

Table 17–2. Private Charitable Contribution Equations, 1948–1972[a]

	Model		
	I	II	III
Constant	−1.48	−0.35	−2.34
log Y	0.85	0.80	0.81
	(31.37)	(36.75)	(35.91)
log P	−1.00	−1.13	−1.10
	(10.14)	(14.20)	(13.40)
log T^1	−0.18	—	—
	(8.44)		
log T^2	—	−0.27	—
		(13.63)	
log T^3	—	—	−0.25
			(12.80)
R^2	.99	.99	.99
N	136	136	136

[a] Absolute value t-statistics in parentheses. Ellipses denote that variable did not enter that particular model. The dependent variable is private charitable contributions in constant 1967 dollars; Y = disposable income calculated as adjustable gross income less taxes paid plus private charitable contributions times one minus the individual's marginal tax rate; P = 1 minus the taxpayer's marginal tax rate; T^1 = per capita federal expenditures on health, hospitals, education, and welfare in constant 1967 dollars; T^2 = per capita state, local, and federal expenditures on health, hospitals, education, and welfare in constant 1967 dollars; T^3 = T^1 plus per capita social security transfers in constant 1967 dollars.

(T_t^1) for the governmental-transfer variable while Model II enters a broader specification which also incorporates the corresponding state and local expenditures (T_t^2). Model III adds federal trust fund expenditures (comprised mainly of social security transfers) to T_t^1.

The coefficients for the income and price variables have the expected signs and are quantitatively consistent with the findings of Feldstein (1975). The coefficients for the governmental-transfer variables are consistently negative and statistically significant suggesting that increases in governmental transfers have indeed crowded out private charitable giving. The coefficients indicate that a 1 percent increase in governmental transfers (per person) reduces an individual's private charitable giving by approximately .2 percent. Our earlier discussion suggests that a positive bias exists in this coefficient estimate, so this crowding-out effect is perhaps even greater. A second factor that suggests that this crowding-out effect is a lower-bound estimate is that the coefficient for the governmental-transfer variable measures only a substitution effect as real disposable incomes are held constant.[11] Using our Model I estimates, we calculated *total* dollar crowding out for increases in governmental transfers. Substitution and income effects combined indicate a crowding-out effect on the order of 28 percent. This implies that a one dollar increase in governmental transfers lowers private charitable contributing by approximately 28 cents.[12]

The government transfer variable used in the preceding empirical analysis possesses a strong secular trend. Feldstein (1975) had previously established a negative trend for private contributions after controlling for tax rates and disposable income. Consequently, *any* single variable that has risen fairly smoothly over time would be likely to produce a negative coefficient. The transfer coefficients may be merely capturing a time-related factor that we did not or could not control for. To overcome this shortcoming, we tested a similar model using cross-sectional data from 1979 itemized tax returns. Our empirical findings were virtually identical to those reported here.[13]

CONCLUDING REMARKS

The above analysis provides support for the proposition that governmental social-welfare transfers have actually served to attenuate private charitable giving.[14] Our finding of less-than-total crowding out tends to reject both the ultrarational and BGR hypotheses for society as a whole.[15] However, our results do not preclude the possibility that some contributors have been completely crowded out nor that some contributors have been unaffected by increases in governmental transfers.

The highly aggregative data used in this study may conceal substantially different crowding-out effects for particular types of charitable contributions. Further investigation using microeconomic or less aggregative data should help to identify the categories of private charitable contributions most affected by the growth of governmental transfers.

NOTES

1. For a survey of the literature in the macroeconomic area *see* Carlson and Spencer (1975).

2. For examples of microeconomic analyses of "crowding out" *see* for example, Friedman (1962, pp. 80–81), Feldstein (1974), Peltzman (1973), and West (1975).

3. *See*, for example, Ireland and Johnson (1970), Hochman and Peterson (1974), and Long (1976).

4. The effective price of a deductible charitable contribution is one minus the marginal tax rate, Feldstein (1975).

5. An exception occurs when the government's transfer exceeds the initial private contribution. Also, the ultrarational approach does not preclude a redistribution of private contributions to bring the public-private mix in line with the original private allocation of contributions. It is important to note here that the ultrarational approach does not allow us to distinguish between income and substitution effects since individuals know that they must eventually finance the government transfer either through direct taxes, government borrowing, or inflation. Finally, an alternative and equally valid interpretation of Figure 17.1 is that the individual remains at Point A since he views the transfer as part of his own giving, and that the tax remains part of his income. The role of the government is to simply help him spend it.

6. The source of our data is the Internal Revenue Service's, *Statistics of Income: Individual Income Tax Returns*. For even years the volumes provide the value of itemized contributions by adjusted gross income class.

7. The consistent AGI classes reported by the IRS throughout the period 1948–1972 are (in $1000): 0–1, 1–2, 2–3, 3–4, 4–5, 5–6, 6–7, 7–8, 8–9, 9–10, 10–15, 15–20, 20–50, 50–100, over 100. In the actual calculations we excluded observations where real average AGI was below $4,000 or above $100,000. The exclusions make our results consistent with Feldstein and at the lower end generally omit groups with little or no reported contributions.

8. This and all other dollar-denominated variables are translated into real 1967 dollars.

9. In 1962, the Internal Revenue Service (1962, pp. 6–8) reported the following breakdown of itemized contributions: Religious Organizations, 61 percent; Educational Institutions, 4 percent; Hospitals, 1 percent; Other Charitable Organizations (Red Cross, United Fund, etc.), 14 percent; other, 20 percent. It is not clear where contributions to church-related schools and hospitals were classified.

10. Feldstein (1975) acknowledges that the rise in college attendance, the increase in transfers, and the changing role of religion can all be expected to impart some influence. He also suggested that the growth of suburbs is an additional determinant. We make no suggestions over the direction of influence for the last factor, although a study using microdata (Feldstein and Clotfelter, 1976) found a higher giving for person in cities of less than one million persons. No possible link (other than empirical) was suggested between city size and private contributions. The same study also showed education to have a positive but insignificant effect. Our own addition of measures of religion did not affect the crowding-out effects and were generally insignificant and of the wrong sign.

11. We would be amiss, however, if we did not identify several potential specification problems which require us to be somewhat cautious about our findings. First, Feldstein (1975) previously established a negative time trend for individual charitable contributions. Consequently, *any* single variable that has risen fairly smoothly over time would be likely to produce a negative coefficient. Second, a simultaneous equations bias may exist in our estimates. While increases in governmental tranfers may reduce private contributions, it could be argued that falling private contributions might induce increased governmental transfers.

12. The calculations were carried out for mean levels of Model I variables. Nonitemized contributions were not observable but were estimated by adjusting the propensity to contribute on itemized returns for the higher "price" of giving when gifts could not be deducted. We then calculated three separate effects based on the hypothetical assumption that transfers had risen by one percent (i.e., an increase of $72.6 million):

Substitution effects:
Itemized:	Itemized gifts $\times \alpha_3$	$= -\$10.7$ million
Nonitemized:	Nonitemized gifts $\times \alpha_3$	$= - \quad 6.4$
Income effect:	$\dfrac{-\Delta \text{Transfer}}{\text{Income}} \times \alpha_2 \times \text{Total gifts}$	$- - \quad 2.9$
Total crowding out		$-\$20.0$ million

Therefore, we estimated that a $72.6 million increase in government transfers would reduce total charitable contributions by $20 million. We should note that we have said nothing about the inefficiency of the government in actually allocating these funds to needy recipients. *See* for example, Tullock (1971).

13. *See,* Abrams and Schmitz (1984).

14. It is important to note that our crowding-out estimates are only for contributions and neglect any effects on private nondeductible spending. For example, Peltzman (1973) and West (1975) have shown that governmental spending on public education has reduced private expenditures. Our estimates suggest that, in addition to lower private spending, educational institutions may also be receiving less charitable support as a result of increased governmental spending.

15. An alternative test of the ultrarational approach is to define $\hat{G}_{it}$ as the sum of private giving and implied public giving for the group and $\hat{Y}_{it}$ as the income the group would have had if the government had not financed the transfers. Both $\hat{G}_{it}$ and $\hat{Y}_{it}$ are calculated by adding $\hat{T}_{it}$ to the original variables. $\hat{T}_{it}$, in turn, is found by multiplying the share of federal in-

come tax receipts going to transfers times actual taxes paid for the group. The ultrarational hypothesis suggests that the relationship between total giving and total income will not be affected by the government's share of giving or their total expenditure. Our results show that this is not the case—either additional variable has a significant negative effect.

REFERENCES

Abrams, Burton A., and Mark D. Schmitz. 1984. The crowding-out effect of governmental transfers on private charitable contributions: Cross section evidence. *National Tax Journal* December.

Carlson, Keith M., and Roger W. Spencer. 1975. Crowding out and its critics. *Federal Reserve of St. Louis Review* December: pp. 2–17.

David, Paul A., and John L. Scadding. 1974. Private savings; ultrarationality, aggregation, and "Denison's Law." *Journal of Political Economy* April: pp. 225–50.

Feldstein, Martin S. 1975. The income tax and charitable contributions: Part I—Aggregate and distributional effects. *National Tax Journal* March: pp. 81–100.

———. 1974. Social security, induced retirement, and aggregate capital accumulation. *Journal of Political Economy* October: pp. 905–26.

Feldstein, Martin S. , and Charles Clotfelter. 1976. Tax incentives and charitable contributions in the United States. *Journal of Public Economics* January/February: pp. 1–26.

Friedman, Milton. 1962. *Capitalism and Freedom.* Chicago: The University of Chicago Press.

Hochman, Harold, and George E. Peterson. 1974. *Redistribution Through Public Choice.* New York: Columbia University Press.

Internal Revenue Service. (various years). *Statistics of Income: Individual Tax Returns.* Washington, D.C.: U.S. Government Printing Office, even years 1948–72.

Ireland, Thomas R., and David B. Johnson. 1970. *The Economics of Charity.* Blacksburg: Center for the Study of Public Choice.

Long, Stephen H. 1976. Social Pressure and Contributions to Health Charities. *Public Choice* Winter: pp. 55–66.

Peltzman, Sam. 1973. The effect of government subsidies-in-kind on private expenditures: The case of higher education. *Journal of Political Economy* January/February: pp. 1–27.

Schwartz, Robert A. 1970. Personal philantropic contributions. *Journal of Political Economy* November/December: pp. 1264–91.

Taussig, Michael D. 1967. Economic aspects of the personal income tax treatment of charitable contributions. *National Tax Journal* March: pp. 1–19.

Tullock, Gordon. 1971. The charity of the uncharitable. *Western Economic Journal* December: pp. 379–92.

U.S. Bureau of the Census. 1975. *Historical Statistics of the United States: Colonial Times to 1970.* Washington: Government Printing Office.

U.S. Council of Economic Advisers. 1976. *Economic Report of the President.* Washington: Government Printing Office.

West, E.G. 1975. Educational slowdown and public intervention in 19th-century England: A study in the economics of bureaucracy, *Explorations in Economic History* January: pp. 61–87.

18

Do Government Grants to Charity Reduce Private Donations?

SUSAN ROSE-ACKERMAN

Previous research on the relationship between government and charity has examined the stimulative effect of tax exemptions or tax credits.[1] Few studies, however, have looked at either the expenditure side[2] or the regulatory environment. We lack a careful assessment of the impact of government spending and regulatory programs on private donations.[3] As a first step, recent analyses of intergovernmental grants could be extended to cover the case of grants to charity. It is commonplace in the literature on grants to observe that matching programs stimulate lower-level governments to produce more public services than fixed grants with the same dollar cost.[4] Matching grants lower the effective price of public output. Fixed grants do not. Applied to charitable giving, these results imply that fixed grants lead to a fall in private giving so long as donors benefit from the total level of charitable services and not just from the services provided through their own gifts.[5] Direct government production of substitute services will lead to a similar fall in private gifts. Alternatively, matching grants, like deductions and credits, stimulate increased private giving unless taxes increase by enough to swamp the "price effect" of the program.

The results, familiar to students of fiscal federalism and of "tax expenditures," are the direct application of standard neoclassical price theory. They make some strong, simple assumptions about the sector that receives the grants. The following section makes these assumptions explicit and presents a simple model that captures the essential features of the neoclassical analysis. The model has two fundamental weaknesses. First, it fails to

From *Nonprofit Firms in a Three-Sector Economy*, ed. by M. White, Urban Institute, Washington, D.C., 1981 pp. 95–114. Helpful comments were received from Curtis Eaton, Richard Nelson, Sharon Oster, Jeff Strnad, and Dennis Young. The research was partially supported by the Yale Program on Nonprofit Organizations.

capture many of the salient characteristics of the nonprofit charitable sector. Second, it ignores the fact that most grants come with regulatory strings attached. As a condition for receiving public tax money, charities are frequently required to change their behavior. Therefore, I later develop a more realistic model of the charitable social service sector and go on to show that in this model even fixed-sum grants may increase rather than decrease private donations.[6]

NEOCLASSICAL MODEL

The following assumptions are sufficient to produce a model in which either fixed-sum government grants or government production reduce private giving. Nonprofits and the government produce social services of equivalent quality using the same production function. Information is perfect—the public knows exactly what has been produced by public and private agencies, and no one needs to spend resources monitoring the behavior of the nonprofit or the government. I assume that there is only a single social service, called z, which can be supplied for one dollar per unit by both nonprofits and government. The service provides in-kind transfers to needy beneficiaries and is a private good so far as beneficiaries are concerned. Donors and voters do not "consume" z directly, but they benefit from knowing the z is being given to the needy. Thus, the total amount of z satisfies people's taste for redistributive activity and is a "pure public good" to donors and voters. Thus, I have in mind social service charities providing day care, foster care, job training, counseling, etc., and do not discuss cultural or educational institutions where donors are also customers.

The benefits obtained by any donor or voter depend only on the total quantity of z, not on how many other donors and voters also approve the transfer activity (Hochman and Rodgers, 1969). Donors do not benefit from giving per se but only from the overall level of z. Neither donors nor beneficiaries care whether a public or a private organization supplies the services. Finally, this simple model suppresses all intraorganizational complexity and assumes that each nonprofit has a well-defined goal with none of the familiar intransitivities of voting systems or indeterminacies of bargaining regimes. The charity exists solely to further the interests of donors, and all donors have equal incomes and tastes.

Nonprofits are at a disadvantage vis à vis the government. Government can produce the same services as they do and, in addition, has the power to eliminate free riders by levying taxes. Charitable organizations may exist, however, if a group without the power to control government choices has a very high demand for z. Their preferences are so strong that they are willing to contribute voluntarily to an organization that provides increments of z.[7]

Since z can be produced at a constant cost of one dollar per unit, there are no diseconomies of scale within individual charities. Therefore, the efficient number of charities is indeterminate. One million units of z can be produced at the same total cost by 10 charities each producing 100,000 units as by a single large organization producing one million. In addition, no one cares which organization produces z. A donor benefits from the total amount of z, not just from the z produced by the charity he supports. With no loss in generality, then, I can assume that only a single z-producing charity exists that is financed entirely by private gifts and government grants.

Suppose that people have preferences defined over the redistributive activity, z, and spending on private consumption, y. The population is divided into three groups. There are m people with equal incomes and tastes, who have a strong preference for redistributive activity. There are n people with equal incomes and tastes who have low demands for z. Finally, there are the direct beneficiaries of the transfer who pay no taxes and are assumed to have no political role. The n low-demand people are in the marjority, and the government maximizes its chances of staying in power by following their wishes. The only public service of concern to voters is z, and the government's share of costs if financed by a head tax on the $m + n$ people. Clearly, only the m high-demand people will contribute to charity, and even they may be "crowded out" by public subsidy.

Consider first, a government policy of producing z^v or, what amounts to the same thing, providing a grant of z^v to the charity. If donors do not consider the impact of their gift on others' giving, they maximize utility, $U^D(z, y)$, subject to $\bar{y} = y + g + z^v/(m+n)$ and $z = z^v + z^D$, where $y =$ donor's income, $g =$ the donor's gift, and $z^D =$ the level of z financed by private gifts. Then, U^D is maximized at $\partial U^D/\partial z = \partial U^D/\partial y^D$.

If z^v increases, g falls. To see this, suppose, first, that gifts remain constant. Then, z increases and y falls and $\partial U/\partial z < \partial U/\partial y$. Thus, to reestablish the utility maximizing condition, donations must fall. If donors do not anticipate the fall in others' gifts, the actual adjustment mechanism may be a complicated iterative process since each donor initially cuts back too much in response to an increase in z^v.

Second, consider a matching grant where every dollar of private donations generates α dollars of total resources. Thus, for any donor, the cost of an extra unit of z is $1/\alpha$. Then, U^D is maximized at $\alpha(\partial U^D/\partial z) = (\partial U^D/\partial y^D)$. Thus, if α increases, the increase in taxes deters giving, but the fall in the "price" of z stimulates gifts. If the substitution effect dominates the income effect, gifts will increase. This is more likely to happen the smaller m is relative to n and the higher the donors' "price" elasticity of demand for z. Clearly, if we compare two programs with the same tax consequences for donors, a matching-grant program lowers giving less than a fixed-sum grant and may produce increased giving.

GOVERNMENT GRANTS IN A MORE REALISTIC MODEL OF THE CHARITABLE SECTOR

Introduction

A more realistic analysis leads to important changes in the predicted behavior of the charitable sector and its response to grants. I complicate the
model in four ways. First, I assume that there are fixed costs to establishing a charity and that it takes time to set up, operate, and monitor a charity. Second, I allow donors and professional staff to have ideological positions, so that all providers are not thought to be equally effective. Third,
I assume that both quality levels and donor's information about quality
are under the control of charity managers. Fourth, I consider how the
characteristics of clients affect the cost of providing services.[8]

The costs of entry and of starting new projects limit the choices of even
quite well-informed donors. Professional specialists play a critical role in
establishing charities and in deciding what outputs to produce. Given an
existing set of options, busy donors may give little or nothing either because the options available to them look so unpromising, or because it would
take too much time to learn about the alternatives. Charities produce differentiated products whose benefits are uncertain, difficult to measure, and
subject to dispute. Donors may be much better informed about charities to
which they donate and may place a negative value on the output of other
nonprofits because they disagree with the charities' philosophies or have
different understandings of the link between outputs and goals. Thus, poor
information and ideological disagreement reduce the public-good characteristics of charitable activities.

Three groups of people are important to my analysis: donors, managers,
and clients. Clients, however, are as passive in this model as they were in
the simple model shown in the previous section. They consume agency services but do not try to affect policy. I assume that potential donors are like
voters in a Downsian model of politics. Many of them have sufficiently
strong altruistic feelings to lead them to donate to charity, but they do not
take the trouble to monitor their gifts carefully.[9] Their donation patterns
are mainly determined by the symbolic positions of individual nonprofits,
not by a detailed study of their efficacy. Thus, people may have very strong
positions but very little concrete information about the value of a donation
to one charity relative to another. Tastes may differ widely. Services that
some people view as substitutes—for example, caring for the mentally ill
in large institutions or group homes, giving job training in classrooms or
in factories—are viewed as diametrically opposed alternatives by others.

The charity's managers may be professional social workers or others
trained in the "helping" professions, but may also include energetic people
with no particular training, who are strongly committed to the agency's
program. In my framework, most new agencies are founded by potential
managers with a new idea or a perception of a service that needs to be

provided.[10] Charities cannot be established or new services added unless some fixed costs are borne. These are, for example, the costs of setting up an office or facility, and advertising its existence or otherwise seeking clients.

The final characteristic of the production function is the cost of adding new cases as a function of the total number of cases cared for in a given geographic region. The marginal cost of a case to an individual agency may be a function not only of its own size, facilities, and expertise but also of the proportion of the total pool of eligible beneficiaries served by all similar agencies. If agencies try to maximize their caseloads, and if clients can be classified by the cost of treatment, then the marginal cost of an extra client increases as the number of clients served by all agencies in the region increases. Agencies concentrating on "easy cases" can help more people per dollar than those accepting more difficult cases. There is no a priori reason, however, for donors and managers to have utility functions defined over the number of people aided. People may get more satisfaction from aiding a difficult case than from aiding an easy one. Thus, charities might specialize in different types of clients, drawing contributions from those who prefer to use their own contributions to aid the charity's chosen group.

Perfect Information

Ideology and quality

Suppose that ideology is measured by a single, continuous variable, b, and that each donor, k, has a most preferred ideological position b_k. The benefits a donor derives from the services of charity j are a decreasing function of $|b_j - b_k|$. Like the donors in the simple model, people obtain utility from the services of all charities, not just those that receive their donations. However, if $|b_j - b_k|$ is very large, the benefits are small and may even be negative. Donors not only have information about the b_j, but also know each charity's quality level, q_j, client load, s_j, and marginal costs, $c_j(b_j, q_j, s_j)$. Quality is not the same thing as ideology. It is a measure of how well the charity fulfills its goals. Unlike b, more q is unambiguously better than less for all donors. Thus, b might be a measure of the educational "philosophy" espoused by a day-care center, for example, more or less emphasis on discipline, while q measures how well a center succeeds in doing what it set out to do. Therefore, a utility-maximizing donor will not necessarily choose the charity with the smallest $|b - b_k|$. If the charity that minimizes $|b - b_k|$ has high costs and low q_j, then the donor may choose another charity that is less ideologically desirable but that promises more efficient, higher-quality operation.[11]

Charity managers maximize their own utility by choosing b_j and q_j, given their cost curve and an estimate of the level of donations associated with each choice. They also know the levels of b provided by competing charities. Managers care about client loads, quality, and ideology. They may be willing to sacrifice some donations to operate an organization that satisfies their own preferences. They are not simply revenue or client maximizers.

Both Young (1984) and Lubove (1969) confirm this view. Young studied a group of social-service entrepreneurs. Most of them, from an activist nun, to a crusading judge, to a group of innovative social workers, had strong personal commitments to their agency's approach to social service delivery. Similarly, Lubove (1965, 49–52, 159–165, 183–219) discusses the way social workers have sought to control the behavior of charities at the expense of volunteers, board members, and contributors. Managers, however, are constrained by the low level of donations that may result from an idiosyncratic choice[12] and the possibility that donors may become charity entrepreneurs themselves. Entry occurs so long as there are people who expect to be better off as charity managers than in their next, most-preferred occupation.

I assume that there is no shortage of clients so that the level of gift-giving determines s_j given c_j, b_j, and q_j. Individual donors are ideology and quality "takers." No one is a large enough giver to influence the choices of particular charities although the overall distribution of b_j and q_j is, of course, determined in part by donors' preferences. There are fixed costs in establishing charities. This fact combined with the ideological preferences of entrepreneurs implies that many donors can find no charity with $b_j = b_k$.[13] If entrepreneurs' tastes are different from those of most donors, and if charities have positioned themselves to avoid entry by donor-entrepreneurs, then it may be possible to rearrange the charities in ideology space to make most donors better off and increase total gifts.

Donors survey the mixture of existing charities, pick those that provide the highest marginal benefits,[14] and decide how much to give. The behavior of other charities will affect donors' decisions. For example, if a person gives to a charity that has several close "neighbors" along the ideological spectrum, then his gift will be lower the more clients are served by the neighboring charities, and the higher are their q_j. As a second example, suppose that some ideological positions are abhorrent to the donor. He loses utility for every client served by these charities. A devout Baptist might feel worse off the greater the number of children cared for in Roman Catholic day-care centers. He may feel part of a competitive ideological struggle and give more to his favorite Baptist charity, the more clients are served by the Catholic charity.[15] The marginal utility of gifts to the Baptist charity is higher, the higher the level of the Catholic charity's output.

Government grants

Consider now, a government grant with no matching provisions that aids charities if they comply with certain conditions. Some of these conditions can produce an increase in private giving. First, if marginal costs decline as additional clients are added, then a government grant moves a charity down its marginal cost curve. Suppose that at the level of s_j before public subsidy, one dollar bought one extra client. The grant moves the charity along its cost curve so that one dollar now buys more than one extra client. Although the marginal utility to the donor falls as s_j increases, the marginal productivity of a gift increases and giving may increase. If a program of government support permits scale economies to be realized in some charities but not in others with similar levels of b, then gifts will shift toward the more productive producers. The public program may lead to a more concentrated charitable sector as well as a higher level of giving.

Second, the government may state that no charity will receive a grant unless it espouses ideology $\bar{b}$. If $\bar{b}$ is closer to a donor's preferred $\hat{b}_k$ than any b_j that prevailed in the absence of grants, then the donor may shift his gift toward charities that receive grants and may also make a larger gift. The increased client load made possible by the grant lowers the donor's marginal utility of giving, but the movement to a more preferred b raises the marginal utility. Therefore, if the second effect is strong, private gifts may increase even without matching provisions. For example, managers of social-service agencies might prefer to take "professionally interesting" cases regardless of need while donors want to know that clients are, in fact, very poor. If the government insists that the provision of grants depends upon the provision of services to the poor, private gifts may increase when the charity accepts public funds.

Conversely, if donors dislike $\bar{b}$, charity managers may be able to resist government attempts to move them toward an undesirable ideological position. This will be easiest to do if donors and managers are in close agreement so that managers can claim a loss of private giving if they agree to government demands. Suppose that managers choose b_1 but that donors all want $\hat{b}$. The government tries to induce the charity to choose $\bar{b}$ in return for a grant. Suppose that $\bar{b} < b_1 < \hat{b}$. If there are many similar charities all willing to adopt $\bar{b}$, no individual charity has any bargaining power. It must accept $\bar{b}$ or do without the grant. Suppose, however, that $|\bar{b} - b_1| < |\bar{b} - b_j|$ for all $j \neq 1$. Therefore, charity one has some bargaining power vis à vis the government. It can claim that the fall in private gifts will be large if it not only takes a grant but also adopts an ideological position that donors like less than b_1. Similarly, if several government agencies with different ideological positions can provide grants, the manager may be able to play them off against each other if he has some bargaining power. If one agency wants $\bar{b} < b_1$ and another wants $\bar{b} > b_1$, then the manager may be able to accept money from both and stay at b_1.

Finally, suppose that people dislike the ideological stance of some charities so much that increments of service give them negative utility. Suppose that the government "takes sides" and agrees to fund only one kind of charity. For example, suppose there are two competing "philosophies" about how to provide vocational education. Some believe in classroom instruction, while others espouse on-the-job training. A government program supports classroom instruction and funds nonprofits to carry out programs. Some agencies that used to sponsor on-the-job training programs may now shift to classroom instruction, and donors may cut back their contributions. Similarly, agencies that already followed the government's chosen method may also experience a drop in contributions. In contrast, some agencies might refuse public funds and continue to provide on-the-job training. If donors are committed to the agency's program and wish to show that its approach "works" better than the government's approach, then each person may give more when a competitive, publicly supported program begins.[16]

A similar stimulative effect could also occur if charity managers can change their service mix to make it complement, rather than substitute for, publicly subsidized programs. The services provided by the members of the Family Service Association of America, for example, have changed markedly in response to government programs. Over a fifty-year period, they moved from providing relief to an emphasis on advocating the rights of poor families before government social-welfare agencies (O'Connell, 1978). This strategy has apparently permitted them to maintain high levels of private gifts.

Imperfect Information

Information and free riding

There are many different ways in which uncertainty can be introduced into the mode. The most important distinction is between uncertainty caused by a stochastic external environment and uncertainty that arises from an informational asymmetry under the control of charity managers. Since I am interested in the strategic behavior of managers, I concentrate on the latter type of uncertainty.[17]

For simplicity, suppose that uncertainty only affects donors' estimates of q. Thus, suppose that donor k knows b_j, s_j, and c_j with certainty for all j but can only estimate the distribution of q_j, $f_j^k (q_j)$. Managers know q_j with certainty, but they are imperfectly informed about donors' tastes. They know the distribution of preferences across the population, but they have no independent information about the tastes of particular individuals. Those who gave to the charity in the past, however, have revealed that charity j best fits their preferences.

Managers must now decide how much money to spend informing donors about the true level of q_j. Suppose that the strategy of informing a random sample of donors is not worthwhile; that is, donations are expected to be less than fundraising costs for all random samples. Instead, suppose that a charity's manager can benefit from sending messages to the people who donated last period. These people have $\hat{b}_k$ close to b_j and may give more if they have better information about the level of q_j. The only problem with this approach comes from overly optimistic donors who believe that the expected level of $\bar{q}_j$, $\bar{q}_j^k$, is much larger than the true level of q_j. When they find out the truth, they may give less. In general, however, so long as donors are risk averse and do not entirely discount the manager's information as misleading, the added information should lead to increased donations of q_j is not much below $\bar{q}_j$. This fundraising strategy will make it costly for donors to shift to another charity that has not yet provided the donor with any data. Once a person has donated to a charity, he or she will not automatically shift to a new entrant that occupies a preferred point in ideology space. Thus, if the distribution of q_j can be entirely characterized by its mean, q_j, and its variance, v_j, a donor to charity one compares q_1 with the means and variances of competing charities. If the donor is risk averse, he will continue to give to charity one even if q_1 is somewhat less than q_j for some charity j with $b_j = b_1$ and $c_j = c_1$.

A charity manager may have another source of information about donor preferences in addition to his own mailing list. He may be able to purchase or trade mailing lists with charities that have similar b_j's. Other charities, however, will not necessarily agree to a swap or a sale. If b and q are the only factors of interest to donors, a charity will not sell its mailing list to a charity with the same level of b but a higher q. Charities with similar quality levels and close but not equal b's might trade in the hope that gift-giving would increase if donors could be more accurately sorted across charities on the basis of their $\hat{b}_k$. The danger, of course, is that if donors to charity one find out how well charity two is doing, then they will give less and free ride off others' donations.

The charity's provision of information to donors raises the cost of entry. A new organization can only attract enough first-time donors to break even if it can locate a point in ideology space that some donors will support, even given the informational benefits of giving to existing charities. Existing charities will not sell their mailing lists to entrants unless the proceeds from the sale exceed the expected loss of gifts. Obviously, the lower are fixed costs and the more generous are donors, the easier it is to enter ceteris paribus.

Government grants

Suppose that when the government makes grants to charities, it carries out monitoring and information dissemination activities that inform everyone about the actual level of all the q_j. The preceding analysis suggests that this policy will have two contradictory effects on charitable giving. On the one hand, risk-averse people who gave nothing in an uncertain world may now make gifts to charity. Similarly, private gifts will shift toward charities with relatively high levels of q. Even though a fixed grant lowers the marginal benefit of private gifts, total giving may increase because of the reduction of uncertainty. This model could be expanded to include volunteer work designed to improve a donor's estimate of q_i. Then, if the government takes over some monitoring functions, this may raise monetary gifts at the same time as it lowers the level of volunteer activity. Donors do not need to spend so much of their own time monitoring quality. In this case, volunteer labor may be a closer substitute for government grants than private gifts.

On the other hand, imperfect knowledge makes the services of each charity similar to private goods and lowers the incentive to be a free rider. Others' gifts to charity j are not valued highly by a donor to charity one because he does not have an accurate measure of charity j's quality. For fixed $\bar{q}_j$, the larger the variance of q_j; that is, the worse the information about j, the more the risk averse donor gives to charity one. Thus, better information on the q of several similar charities makes charitable services more like Samuelsonian pure public goods. So long as the actual q_j are not much below $\bar{q}_j$, donors will now benefit more from the services of charities to which they do *not* donate.

For example, suppose a presubsidy equilibrium has been established between identical charities. Each organization keeps its existing pool of donors by providing them with differential information about quality. Therefore, no one has an incentive to change charities. Suppose that government grants to both charities are accompanied by monitoring and reporting requirements that produce $q_1 = q_2$ with $q_1 \geq \bar{q}_1$ and $q_2 \geq \bar{q}_2$; that is, uncertainty has been eliminated and actual quality is at least as good as expected quality. This means that the services provided by charity two have the same weight in every donor's utility function as services provided by charity one. Even though information has improved, *all* donors may give less. The public good character of the services has increased, free-rider problems are more severe, and gifts fall (cf. Posnett, 1979).

Government granting agencies do not necessarily publicize the information they obtain from monitoring grantees. Instead, they may keep the information to themselves, a strategy that gives them more control over charitable activities relative to private donors. Suppose, for example, that donors are uncertain, not about q_j, but about b_j. Even after they have given to j, they can only estimate the distribution of b_j. In the absence of a government subsidy, charity managers may purposely keep donors uninformed as a way of increasing their freedom of action even though it reduces gifts. Suppose that the government agencies can learn the true level of b_j and can try to induce the managers to change to $\hat{b}$. Then, the charity's managers may prefer a dollar of private money to a dollar of public money, since it gives them more independence. They may believe that there is a "safe level of tax funds beyond which the voluntary agency is in danger of becoming excessively dependent and risking loss of autonomy and goal deflection" (Kramer, 1966, p. 25). The government's attempt to shift b could lead managers to make an extra effort to secure private funds by giving donors more information and influence on charitable behavior. For example, if the government wants $\hat{b}$, managers want b_1, and donors want $\tilde{b}$ with $\tilde{b} < b_1 < \hat{b}$, then managers could pick b_2 with $|b_2 - b_1| < |\hat{b} - b_1|$ and expend resources to inform donors of the policy shift. In trying to maintain some independence when they accept public money, the professional staff obtains more private gifts and gives greater weight to donors' preferences.[18]

Types of Clients

Hard cases and "cream skimming"

Some donors may care about the type of clients aided by charity. Instead of just counting the number of people served, s_j, they give each client an index, $r_{ij}{}^k$, that measures the marginal benefit to donor k of aiding client i in charity j. For each charity, donors know the distribution of clients over the $r_{ij}{}^k$ or $g_j(r_{ij}{}^k)$. Costs to charity j may depend on $g_j(r_{ij}{}^k)$ or even on $g(r_i)$, the distribution of clients over all agencies. In particular, suppose that clients can be ranked from easy to difficult cases. A difficult case is expensive to treat, but the benefit obtained by the client is large. Charity managers, donors, and government policymakers are assumed to have one of two preference functions. On the one hand, they may only care about the number of clients served.[19] On the other hand, some donors may wish to aid the hard cases first, moving to easier cases only if money is available. Suppose that all charities have identical b_j and q_j. Let y be spending on private goods, and label clients so the marginal cost of helping type i exceeds the marginal cost of helping type $i+1$; that is, $c_1 > c_2 \cdots > c_n$. Then donors' utility functions can be characterized as $U^A(s, y)$ if they care only about client loads, or $U^B(s, g(c_i), y)$ if they favor hard cases. Thus, for those who care about the type of clients served, $U_s{}^B$ is larger, the larger is the c_i of the marginal person. Charity managers have similar preference functions, V, defined over the charities' total revenues, R_j, and either over s_j or over $[s_j, g_j(c_i)]$. Suppose that the cost of serving even the most expensive clients is low enough so that if people have type B preferences, then they want to start with the hardest cases and move to the easier cases only if funds are available. In contrast, those with type A preferences want to "cream skim," that is, they begin with the easiest cases in order to maximize client loads.

Government grants
Suppose now that the government seeks to subsidize the charitable service by giving grants without matching provisions. The public funding agency can be characterized as having either type A or type B preferences. Eight preference combinations are possible and are illustrated in Table 18–1, where $W(s)$ and $W(s, f(c_1))$ represent the government administrators' preferences. To begin the discussion, suppose that only a single charity exists. Then Table 18–1 shows what will happen to private gifts when a government subsidy is introduced. First consider the situations where gifts fall. Cases (2) and (7) are symmetric. In both, donors and charity managers have the same priorities but disagree with government policymakers. So long as the public subsidy is not large enough to absorb the people previously served privately, the charity's marginal cost of treatment is unchanged. However, the number of clients served increases. This fact should reduce private gifts.[20]

Consider next, cases (1), (4), and (5). Cases (1) and (5) are similar. In both, donors and the government agree on maximizing the number of clients. In (1), the marginal cost of serving an extra client falls along with the marginal benefits, while in (5) the marginal cost remains unchanged. Thus, in both cases, gifts fall. In case (4), the government mirrors donor preferences and gifts fall.

Finally, consider (3), (6), and (8) where gifts may go up. In (3) the government and charities agree on maximizing the number treated, but donors want to concentrate on the neediest cases. Thus, government support makes

Table 18–1. Impact of Government Grants on Private Gifts

	Donors			
	(A) $U(s, y)$ Maximize number treated		(B) $U(s, g(c_i), y)$ Treat hard cases first	
	Government		Government	
Charity managers	A $W\,(s)$	B $W(s, g(c_i))$	A $W\,(s)$	B $W(s, g(c_i))$
A: $V\,(s_j, R_j)$	1. Gifts fall	2. Gifts fall	3. Gifts may increase	4. Gifts fall
B: $V(s_j, g_j(c_i), R_j)$	5. Gifts fall	6. Gifts may increase	7. Gifts fall	8. Gifts may increase

it possible for the charity to maximize its client load by treating the easy cases and then moving on to the difficult ones. These clients are more expensive to treat but also provide more benefits to donors. Therefore, gifts may go up. Case (6) is similar in that government and charity managers agree with each other but disagree with donors. As more hard cases are treated, the marginal cost of serving an extra case falls and donations may rise even though s has increased.[21] In case (8), all three groups agree to emphasize hard cases. Nevertheless, once the neediest have been cared for, the marginal cost of helping others falls. This fall in cost could be sufficient to overcome donors' relatively small benefits from helping easy cases.

The analysis can be extended in an interesting way to a geographically distinct charity "market" with several providers. In the provision of social services, the number and admissions policies of other suppliers can affect the costs of any particular charity. The cost of serving one additional client depends upon the pool of people needing service as well as upon the way a charity chooses clients. Therefore, the admissions policies of publicly subsidized facilities may affect the costs of unsubsidized charities. Charities that seek easy, inexpensive cases raise the expected marginal costs of charities that draw from the remaining pool of clients. Those that specialize in difficult cases lower the expected marginal costs of charities open to all types of clients.[22] For example, if the service is the number of children placed in foster-care homes, homes may be more difficult to find or be of a lower quality on the margin as the total number of children placed by all agencies increases. Similarly, the marginal child may be more of a behavior problem. If one organization concentrates on hard cases (for example, in foster care: older children, minority children, or those with handicaps or behavior problems), then others can more easily maximize client loads. If private agencies "cream skim" in order to maximize client loads, the government may be left with the hard cases.

Even if every supplier wants to maximize the number treated per dollar spent, some agencies may find it easier than others to exclude applicants.

A government policy of serving all who apply to public institutions can make it possible for private agencies to turn away hard cases, thus increasing their productivity as measured by donors who seek to maximize the client loads of their chosen charity. If donors obtain few benefits from learning about clients treated in public institutions, then a government policy of accepting "hard" cases can aid private philanthropy. Conversely, if government "cream skims," leaving the residual to the private sector, the opposite result could occur. If donors want to maximize the number treated privately, private giving falls as it becomes costly to add clients.[23]

CONCLUSION

This paper has demonstrated that government grants to charities need not reduce private donations and may even lead to increased private giving. Matching grants stimulate giving by lowering the effective "price" of donations. Fixed-sum grants, however, can also increase giving especially if they are accompanied by regulatory policies that raise the marginal benefits of private contributions. This result can occur if the government is in a stronger bargaining position vis à vis charities than individual donors. Therefore, charity managers may lose relative to both taxpayers and private donors. Public officials may be able to push charities to adopt ideological positions favored by both taxpayers and donors but opposed by managers. This policy could increase private giving. Donations could also rise if public funds give donors better information about charities that receive their donations, or if they permit scale economies to be realized. Alternatively, public subsidy of services that receive little private support could spur increased giving. Thus, if donors strongly dislike the ideology of charities subsidized by government, they may give more to their own favored charities. If government treats "hard" cases in its own facilities, private donors may increase their giving to private providers that can now "cream skim" more effectively.

Nevertheless, in spite of those possibilities for increased private giving, other forces may lower gifts. If government provides everyone with better information about charitable service, free-rider problems increase and private gifts can fall. The more closely fixed-sum government grants substitute private gifts, the more likely is a fall in donations. In the neoclassical model shown earlier, they were perfect substitutes, and gifts were certain to fall. In the discussion in previous section, the final result depends on both the initial preferences and behavior of private charity managers, and on the tastes of taxpayers and government administrators, on the one hand, versus private givers, on the other.

The chapter thus suggests a framework for future empirical work. We know very little about how donors respond either to changing ideological cues or to better information about the quality of charitable activity. We have similarly poor data about the magnitude of scale economies and the costs of improvements in quality, and we need operational measures of the costs of treating people with different "needs." The link between the form of public subsidy and the types of clients served by private nonprofits is also an important but poorly understood issue. Research on all of these questions could be extremely useful to policymakers charged with designing programs that subsidize or compete with the services of nonprofit charities. Even without particular evidence, however, I have shown that, in principle, it ought to be possible to design subsidy programs that encourage rather than discourage private giving.

NOTES

1. For example, Feldstein (1975), Feldstein and Clotfelter (1976). Feldstein and Taylor (1976), Hochman and Rodgers (1969), Schwartz (1970), and Taussig (1967).

2. One exception is Abrams and Schmitz (1978), but they concentrate on government spending on substitute services ("crowding out"), not on government subsidies to nonprofit providers. Their study is essentially a reformulation of previous theoretical treatments of the tax exemption for gifts.

3. This issue is especially important because of the growth of government financing of health, education, and social services, and the public role in providing funds to the nonprofit providers of these services. (See U.S. Department of the Treasury, Commission on Private Philanthropy and Public Needs (1975) and the relevant studies in (1977).) Both the Child Welfare League of America (Haring 1975) and the Family Service Association of America (1977) report an upward trend in government funding of member agencies. The Department of Health, Education and Welfare reported that in the six-month period. April to September 1976, 30 percent of all HEW social-service money was spent by private organizations, mostly nonprofits. The largest category was day care for children which accounted for 40 percent of federal service funds spent by private organizations (U.S. Department of Health, Education and Welfare, 1976). Although in the near future, public funds are likely to fall, they will still constitute a high percentage of nonprofit resources.

4. For example, Oates (1972).

5. See the related discussion in Abrams and Schmitz (1978), and Peltzman's (1973) analysis of the links between public and private spending on higher education.

6. Recent work has also challenged simple models of fiscal federalism. See, for example, Oates (1979) who argues that federal grants will not "crowd out" state and local spending as much as the simple neoclassical models would predict.

7. This is Weisbrod's (1975) explanation of nonprofit activity.

8. This analysis has a rather different focus from recent work on monopolistic competition. It is closest to work on product variety by Eaton and Lipsey (1975) and Lancaster (1979), which assumes that variations in tastes (or physical location) explain product differentiation (or firm location choices). Work by Dixit and Stiglitz (1977) and Spence (1976) is less relevant since it depends upon individuals' desire for variety. My research is also related to a second body of work that stresses buyers' imperfect information and discusses advertising and search behavior (for a review see Stiglitz 1979). However, the fact that donors benefit from others' gifts distinguishes my models from the work on monopolistic competition. Advertising can inform donors both about the quality of services and about the level of others' donations. Unlike models with private goods, the total quantity of each service produced is relevant to donors' choices. All the work on monopolistic competition, also, shares an important difficulty from my point of view. It uses a simple economic notion of optimality that does not seem to me to be appropriate in the charitable context. Instead, my concern is with positive analysis. Given a model of the charity sector, I determine the way private gifts will

respond to a growth in public subsidy. Information about giving can then be used as part of a fuller political-economic analysis of the net benefits of public subsidy.

9. Downs (1957) argues that many citizens will vote but that they will not take much trouble to become informed on political issues. See also Tullock (1966) who observes that individual donors have little incentive to find out about the behavior of charities. Explaining why self-interested people vote when their chance of affecting the outcome is almost zero gives economists as much trouble as explaining why people give to charity when they can free ride off the gifts of others. In both cases, analysts have been reduced to postulating that the acts of voting and gift-giving are valuable in and of themselves (Arrow 1972, Riker and Ordeshook 1968). See Benn (1979) and Singer (1979) for philosophers' attempts to justify voting and gift-giving.

10. This view of charity entrepreneurs is confirmed by most of Young's (1984) case studies of social-service entrepreneurs.

11. If ideology is, in fact, multidimensional, it may be possible to aggregate the diverse characteristics into a single continuous variable with the same properties as b (See Lancaster, 1979, Ch. 2).

12. For example, according to Young (1984), the Florida Sheriff Youth Fund grew rapidly over the past 20 years by tailoring its program carefully to the tastes of its conservative, elderly donors.

13. In Lancaster's (1979) model, fixed costs combined with profit maximization produce a similar compromise between exploiting scale economies and satisfying the diverse tastes of the populace.

14. In most cases, where no two charities have the same levels of b_j, q_j, and c_j, each donor will give to a single charity. His gift is too small to affect the marginal benefit of a gift, so he simply picks the one that maximizes his utility. This result would not apply, of course, if donors do not benefit from a charity's services unless they make some minimum gift. Then donors might want to "buy-in" to several charities. See Rose-Ackerman (1982).

15. This could be modeled by assuming that b is measured around a circle. If a person's $\hat{b}_k$ is at one point on the circle, then draw a diameter that connects that point to a point on the other side of the circle (called $\bar{b}_k$). Then, $\bar{b}_k$ represents the ideology that is the most vehemently opposed by k.

16. This discussion assumes that donors believe strongly in the efficacy of one or another programmatic emphasis. Instead, they may have beliefs that are easily shaken because of their own poor information. If they interpret government support of an activity as evidence of its usefulness, then the above results are reversed. Donors may now give more to agencies that sponsor classroom instruction and most on-the-job training programs will fail for lack of funds.

17. If the first type of uncertainty were important, it could lead to diversification if donors believe that the actual realization of some q_1 in charity one is uncorrelated or negatively correlated with the actual realization of q_2 in charity two. Then, if b_1 is close to b_2 and to $\hat{b}_k$, the risk-averse donor may give a portion of his donation to each charity. For example, suppose a donor does not know which of two mutually exclusive methods of day-care management is correct, and that the chance that the first will work is either independent of, or negatively correlated with, the chance that the second will succeed. He may then give part of his gift to each of two differently managed centers and need never find out whether one of his gifts was, in fact, efficacious.

Alternatively, a charity may not provide the same quality service to all clients. Then donors might know the distribution of service qualities across clients in charity j, e.g., X percent of the clients of j receive a quality of care at least equal to q_j^X. Donors might place a high weight on avoiding either very low quality care or extremely luxurious care.

18. A charity may also have more bargaining power in dealing with one government agency if it also deals with several others. Then, no one agency has responsibility for total agency operations. Managers can tell government agency A that agency B requires them to act in a certain way when the action is really the one preferred by managers. Conflicting quality-control requirements may give managers freedom of action instead of forcing them to specialize. For example, a report on the Jewish Vocational Service in Milwaukee noted that it "has 13 fed-

eral, state and local funding sources, so many, in fact, that auditors appear to be having trouble unscrambling them all" (*Wall Street Journal*, December 28, 1979). This pattern of multiple funding sources is common in the provision of social services.

19. In several of Young's (1984) cases in the child-care field, donors wanted to concentrate on helping people from their own religious or ethnic group. In general, this was synonymous with preferring easy cases to hard cases. See his discussion of Greer Children's Services, Florida Sheriffs' Youth Fund, and Pleasantville Diagnostic Center.

20. If donors want only to help people from their own ethnic group and oppose integration, they may reduce giving if the clientele becomes more diverse.

21. This case is close to Greer Children's Services and Pleasantville Diagnosis Center as both moved to accept increasing public support in the past two decades. Pleasantville's director was, however, worried about donor resistance to integration. He responded to public pressure by setting up a separate diagnostic center for delinquent children and gradually admitted some of these clients to the agency's regular programs (Young, 1984).

22. The effect is very similar to the agglomeration economics and diseconomies discussed in urban economics where the costs of a firm are affected by the presence or absence of other firms in its geographical neighborhood (Segal, 1977, pp. 59–60, 64–68).

23. Interestingly, one reader of an earlier draft suggested that it was unrealistic to suppose that the government would concentrate on hard cases while another suggested that it would never be able to get away with "cream skimming."

REFERENCES

Abrams, Burton A., and Mark Schmitz. 1978. The 'crowding-out' effect of governmental transfers on private charitable contributions. *Public Choice* 33:29–37.

Arrow, Kenneth. 1972. Gifts and exchanges. *Philosophy and Public Affairs* 1:343–362.

Benn, S.I. 1979. The problematic rationality of political participation. *In* Peter Laslett and James Fishkin, eds., *Philosophy Politics and Society: Fifth Series*. New Haven: Yale University Press, pp. 291–312.

Dixit, A., and J.E. Stiglitz. 1977. Monopolistic competition and optimal product differentiation. 1957. *American Economic Review* 67:297–308.

Downs, Anthony. 1957. *An Economic Theory of Democracy*. New York: Harper and Row.

Eaton, E. Curtis, and Richard Lipsey. 1975. The principle of minimum differentiation reconsidered: Some new developments in the theory of spatial competition. *Review of Economic Studies* 42:27–49.

Family Service Association of America. 1977. *Family Service Profiles: Agency Program and Funding: 1976*, New York.

Feldstein, Martin S. 1975. The income tax and charitable contributions: Part I—Aggregate and distributional effects. *National Tax Journal* 28:81–100.

———, and Charles Clotfelter. 1976. Tax incentives and charitable contributions in the United States. *Journal of Public Economics* 5:1–26.

———, and A. Taylor. 1976. The income tax and charitable contributions. *Econometrica* 44:1201–22.

Haring, Barbara. 1975. *Voluntary Member Agency Income: 1974–1975*. New York: Child Welfare League of America.

Hochman, Harold, and James Rodgers. 1977. The optimal tax treatment of charitable contributions. *National Tax Journal* 30:1–19.

Kramer, Ralph. 1966. Voluntary agencies and the use of public funds: Some policy issues." *Social Service Review* 40:15–26.

Lancaster, Kelvin. 1979. *Variety, Equity and Efficiency*. Cambridge, England: Cambridge University Press.

Lubove, Roy. 1969. *The Professional Altruist*. New York: Athenan.

Oates, Wallace E. 1972. *Fiscal Federalism*. New York: Harcourt Brace Jovanovich.

Oates, W. 1979. Lump-sum intergovernmental grants have price effects. *In* P. Mieszkowski and W. Oakland, eds., *Fiscal Federalism and Grants-in-Aid*. COUPE Papers on Public Economics 1, Washington, D.C.: The Urban Institute, pp. 23–30.

O'Connell, Brian. 1978. From service to advocacy to empowerment. *Social Casework* 59:195–202.

Peltzman, Sam. 1973. The effect of government subsidies-in-kind on private expenditures: The case of higher education. *Journal of Political Economy* 81:1–27.

Posnett, John. 1979. The optimal fiscal treatment of charitable activity. Discussion Paper #552 79, Institute for Research on Poverty, University of Wisconsin, Madison, Wisconsin.

Riker, William, and Peter Ordeshook. 1968. A theory of the calculus of voting. *American Political Science Review* 62:25–42.

Rose-Ackerman, Susan. 1982. Charitable giving and 'excessive' fundraising. *Quarterly Journal of Economics* 97:193–212. Reprinted as Chapter 19 in this volume.

Segal, David. 1977. *Urban Economics*. Homeward, Illinois: Richard Irwin.

Schwartz, Robert A. 1970. Personal philanthropic contributions. *Journal of Political Economy* 78:1264–91.

Singer, Peter. 1979. Famine, affluence and morality. *In* P. Laslett and J. Fishkin, eds., *Philosophy, Politics and Society: Fifth Series*. New Haven: Yale University Press, pp. 21–35.

Spence, Michael. 1976. Product selection, fixed costs, and monopolistic competition. *Review of Economic Studies* 43:217–35.

Stiglitz, Joseph E. 1979. Equilibrium in product markets with imperfect information. *American Economic Review: Papers and Proceedings* 69:339–45.

Taussig Michael K. 1967. Economic aspects of the personal income tax treatment of charitable contributions. *National Tax Journal* 20:1–19.

Tullock, Gordon. 1966. Information without profit. *Public Choice* 1:141–59.

U.S. Department of Health, Education and Welfare. 1976. *Social Services: U.S.A.* Washington, D.C.

U.S. Department of the Treasury. 1975. Commission on Private Philanthropy and Public Needs. *Giving in America: Toward a stronger voluntary sector*. Washington, D.C.

U.S. Department of the Treasury. 1977. Commission on Private Philanthropy and Public Needs. Research paper. Washington, D.C.

Weisbrod, Burton A. 1975. Toward a theory of the voluntary non-profit sector in a three-sector economy. *In* Edmund S. Phelps, ed., *Altruism, morality and economic theory*. New York: Russell Sage Foundation, pp. 171–96.

Young, Dennis. 1984. Casebook of Management for Nonprofit Organizations: Entrepreneurship and Organizational Change in the Human Services, New York: Haworth Press.

VI
FUNDRAISING

19

Charitable Giving and "Excessive" Fundraising

SUSAN ROSE-ACKERMAN

Recently, some charities have been attacked for spending an "excessive" portion of their resources on fundraising. This concern has produced a variety of state laws regulating charitable solicitations.[1] Two private organizations that certify charities give heavy weight to fundraising practices,[2] and the United Way justifies its existence by noting the small proportion of its contributions used to conduct the annual campaign.[3] No one, however, has analyzed the problem of excessive fundraising with a model in which nonprofits design fundraising strategies to maximize net expected receipts. This chapter develops a series of such models, and then uses them to assess various regulatory strategies from the dissemination of information to the establishment of a federated fund drive.

In my models, advertising messages are purely informative. They simply tell donors that the charity exists, has a particular ideological position, and spends a certain share of receipts on fundraising. My special concern is donors' attitudes toward solicitation costs. Donors can gain in two ways from fundraising expenses. First, they learn about the charity from the information it provides. Second, the fundraising campaign may cause *other* people to substitute gifts for private consumption or to substitute gifts to a charity the donor likes for gifts to one that he or she dislikes. A donor loses, however, when fundraising diverts funds from one charity the donor likes to another that is equally desirable. This substitution effect is similar to a commonly cited waste of some private advertising that convinces people to choose one of several otherwise identical products without expanding the size of the market (see Schmalensee, 1972).

From *The Quarterly Journal of Economics* 97 (May 1982): 195–212. This research was partially funded by Yale's Program on Non-Profit Organizations. I wish to thank Donald Brown, Franklin Fisher, Evan Kwerel, Richard Levin, Randall Olsen, James Strnad, and a referee for helpful comments on an earlier version.

BASIC ASSUMPTIONS

Why do people give at all, especially when they can take a free ride off the gifts of others? By way of an answer, some analysts (for example, Arrow, 1974) stress the benefits that a person obtains from the act of giving to a worthy cause even if he or she cannot measure the direct consequences of this act in higher service levels. Taken in its extreme form, this explanation converts charitable giving into a private good and avoids all free-rider problems. This perspective seems too narrow. After all, many people give nothing, even though they say they benefit from charitable services, and the vast majority of givers donate small amounts relative to their income and to the charity's budget.[4] Private giving is such a small portion of national income that it seems implausible to eliminate the free-rider problem entirely from a model of charitable giving.[5]

Lacking a more precise social-psychological model of altruism,[6] I shall assume that people have a "social conscience" that is rather unspecific and poorly informed. Their sense of "duty" may lead them to make philanthropic donations based on their income and an estimate of the benefits produced by their gifts. A donation provides two kinds of benefits to a donor. First, if the kth donor's gift to a particular charity is at least equal to some minimum z_k, the donor believes that he or she has "bought in" to the entire range of services provided by the charity. Although donors know about the services provided by all nonprofits that solicit their donations, the psychological benefits they obtain from a charity's total level of services are higher if they have given at least z_k. Second, donors also calculate the marginal benefits of their gifts in providing increases in charitable services. If these benefits are high enough, they may give more than z_k to a few charities. Some charities, however, may produce services that are disliked by some people. These people benefit if *fewer* donations are made to those charities. A donor gives to the charities with the most favorable combination of solicitation practices and philanthropic services. Some charities receive z_k. Others obtain larger gifts.

To characterize a donor's utility function, assume first that fundraising practices are irrelevant and that all donors automatically know about all charities. Suppose that there are n charities and that they can be placed along a single dimension b, which I call "ideology." Each person k has a most preferred ideology b_k, and tastes are single-peaked with respect to b_k.[7] The donor's b_k is independent of his or her income. Each charity j has a fixed level of b, b_j, and announces how many people it served in the last period s_j, as well as c_j, the cost of adding an additional client. Each donor k's utility depends on the levels of the b_j, s_j, and c_j for all j, as well as on k's donations to charity and spending on other goods. Since the charitable characteristics are parameters so far as k is concerned, we can write the utility function as

$$U_k[(y_k, z_1^k, \cdots, z_n^k)/\{b_j\}, \{s_j\}, \{c_j\}] \qquad (19\text{--}1)$$

or k's utility depends on his or her choice of y_k, $z_1^k, \cdots, z_n^k$ conditional on the values of b_j, s_j, and c_j for all j, where

$$y_k = k\text{'s spending of private goods,}$$
$$z_j^k = k\text{'s gift to charity } j, j = 1, \ldots, n$$

Individual k maximizes (19–1) subject to

$$\bar{y} = y_k + \Sigma z_j^k$$

where

$$\bar{y}_k = \text{income of } k$$

The marginal utility of giving to some charity "a" is zero for $z_a^k < z_k$ and then jumps discontinuously to some positive number at $z_a^k = z_k$. The utility gain depends upon the strength of the donor's "buying-in" mentality, the donor's gifts to other charities, and the levels of s_a and b_a relative to b_k and to the set of b_j and s_j provided by other charities. For gifts larger than z_k, the marginal utility of giving also depends on the marginal benefits of the donor's gifts as measured by c_a and by the number of clients already being served s_a. A donor who makes only a minimum donation prefers a charity with a larger client load to one with a smaller number of clients but the same b_j. In contrast, if marginal costs increase with s_j, then a donor concerned with the productivity of his or her own gift might give more to a small organization (see Rose-Ackerman, 1981). In allocating donations, each person trades off the marginal gain from "buying-in" to the total services provided by a charity with a relatively large $|b_k - b_j|$ versus giving a larger donation to a more ideologically attractive charity to permit marginal increments in desirable services.[8]

Now suppose that donors only learn about a charity if it sends them a brochure in the mail. Brochures truthfully announce the charities' b_j, s_j, and c_j and provide information about the share of receipts used for fundraising w_j. The introduction of fundraising changes the specification of (19–1) in two ways. First, it restricts the individual's choice set to include only those charities that have sent brochures. Second, both the minimum gift required to "buy-in" to a charity, and the value to donors of gifts that are greater than the minimum may depend upon the share of gifts used for fundraising.

I consider three attitudes toward w_j. First, donors are indifferent to fundraising expenses. Second, donors believe that high levels of w_j are undesirable. They confuse marginal and average costs and assume that for every dollar they give, only $(1 - w_j)$ of these funds goes to purchase services.[9] Thus, ceteris paribus, donors favor charities with low w_j. Nevertheless, if the w_j of all charities increase, donors may give more if demand for charitable services is price inelastic.

Third, donors are somewhat more sophisticated and recognize that high levels of fundraising may be translated into higher donations from *others*. Donors benefit little if fundraising simply shifts funds between charities that they find ideologically attractive especially if they have given the minimum gift to each one. Therefore, they will want to know what portion of the extra giving comes from private consumption or from charities that are ideologically unattractive.

A final set of assumptions concerns the behavior of charity managers. I assume that each one is very rigid and has a most preferred level of b, b_j, that determines charity j's ideological position. In other words, b_j is not a choice variable for managers.[10] Given their b_j, managers are risk neutral and try to maximize expected revenues net of fundraising costs. Charities can rank donors in terms of the gift expected if they receive a brochure. This expected gift is only a best-guess, however, since the actual gift depends on the behavior of other charities. Given this ranking, charity j can estimate $x_j(\alpha_j, w_j)$. This is the average expected gift from all solicited donors when α_j of the population is solicited and the fundraising share is w_j. It is the probability that charity j is chosen by the average solicited donor multiplied by the size of the average gift. Since donors can be ranked by their expected gift, charities send to the highest expected givers first and then move down the ranking. If the z_k are equal for all k, the highest ranked donors are expected to give more than the minimum gift. Next in line are people who are expected to do no more than "buy-in" to charity j, followed by those who dislike j's ideology or are poor and give nothing. Thus $dx/d\alpha \leq 0$. The total level of gross receipts is $\alpha_j m x_j$, where m is total population. The fundraising technology is very simple: Brochures cost v dollars apiece to all charities. Each charity assumes that the other charities will not change their behavior in response to its choice. The manager must then decide how many brochures to send in order to maximize expected net returns.

I assume that there are no technological or fundraising barriers to entry and that there are potential entrepreneurs willing and able to occupy any b—existing charities cannot monopolize a portion of "ideology space." Neither these conditions nor the assumption that brochures all cost v dollars is meant to be realistic. I have made these extreme assumptions to illustrate the special role of scale economies and entry barriers in a charity "market."

DONORS INDIFFERENT TO FUNDRAISING EXPENSES

In this model (Model I), the charities' fundraising practices determine only the number of brochures a person receives, not the marginal utility of giving. Donors are indifferent to fundraising expenses so that x_j is only a function of α_j.

Suppose that each charity j assumes that the number of other charities is fixed and that none of them changes its behavior to respond to j's choice. Then, the manager of j maximizes

$$R_j = \alpha_j m \ [x_j(\alpha_j) - v] \qquad (19\text{--}2)$$

Net revenue reaches an extreme value, where

$$0 = x_j - v + \alpha_j \frac{dx}{d\alpha} \qquad (19\text{--}3)$$

This is a maximum as long as the α that satisfies (19–3) is less than or equal to one and $2\ dx/d\alpha + \alpha_j d^2 x/d\alpha^2 < 0$. The fundraising share is $w_j = v/x_j$ and is larger, the larger is α_j, i.e., the higher the proportion of the population solicited by charity j. Then, (19–3) can be rewritten as

$$w_j = 1 + \eta_j^! \qquad (19\text{--}4)$$

where $\eta_j^!$ is the elasticity of x_j with respect to α_j, i.e., $\eta_j^! = (dx/d\alpha_j)\ (\alpha_j/x_j) \le 0$. The fundraising share in (19–4) is higher the more inelastic is x_j with respect to α_j.

Suppose that an equilibrium exists given any fixed number of charities n.[11] Then, we can study the relationship between the number of charities and the share of resources spent on fundraising. Although in a range of plausible cases the equilibrium level of w_j increases as the number of charities (n) increases, it is at least possible that, for some n, an increase in the number of charities *reduces* the share of resources that some charities spend on fundraising, thus encouraging even more entry. This could occur if the elasticity of x with respect to α falls by a large amount when entry occurs.

Entry will also affect *total* net charitable resources as well as the *share* of gross resources used for solicitation. Even if α_j falls and w_j increases for all j when n increases, net charitable resources may increase. The added resources generated by new entrants may more than make up for the fall in the net revenues of existing charities. Some donors like the level of b chosen by the new entrant better than that of existing firms and make larger donations. Eventually, however, when the marginal utility of free income is high enough, giving will fall as n increases. As the number of charities increases, the value of an additional brochure to donors falls because donors are already likely to have received brochures from charities with small $|b_k - b_j|$. There is some point where net charitable resources are maximized. Entry, however, will proceed beyond this point. If entry is costless, and if there is an adequate supply of potential charity entrepreneurs, charities will enter until the fundraising share of the marginal charity approaches one, subject to the breakeven condition in each charity.[12] As long as new entrants can pick any point on the ideological spectrum, this also implies that the fundraising share of all charities approaches one. The "charity market" consists of a large number of very small charities. Thus, in a competitive charity market with free entry, the expected level of charitable services provided is very low and a high proportion of revenues will be used for fundraising.

DONORS DISLIKE HIGH FUNDRAISING COSTS

In the second model (Model II), donors dislike high fundraising costs and are less likely to donate to charities that spend a high proportion of their resources on soliciting donations. Charities are required to tell donors the levels of b_j, s_j, and c_j and the fundraising share last period, w_j^{t-1}. Donors assume that the average share of resources spent on fundraising in $t-1$, equals the marginal share in period t. They believe that the larger is w_j^{t-1}, the fewer additional units of service are provided by a given donation. Thus, if the fundraising share differs across charities, donors must trade off this fact against other charitable characteristics. A marginal increase in α_j^t has two effects. First of all, more people receive brochures, and some will choose to give. Second, if the fundraising share of other charities remains constant, the increase in α_j^t will lower the expected gifts of individual donors in the *next* period because w_j^t increases when α_j^t increases.

With the subscript j ignored, expected returns in period t are

$$R^t = \alpha^t m [x(\alpha^t, w^{t-1}) - v] \qquad (19-5)$$

Suppose that charity managers are myopic and ignore the impact of w^t on x^{t+1}. Then, as long as the profit-maximizing α^t is ≤ 1, and the second-order conditions hold, managers maximize R with respect to α^t at

$$0 = x^t - v + \frac{\partial x^t}{\partial \alpha^t}\alpha^t \qquad (19-6)$$

or

$$w^t = 1 + \eta_t^{\mathrm{II}} \qquad (19-7)$$

where

$$\eta_t^{\mathrm{II}} = \frac{\partial x^t}{\partial \alpha^t}\frac{\alpha^t}{x^t} \leq 0$$

The manager's myopia produces an R-maximizing condition similar to that in Model I. In fact, however, this second model is considerably more complicated because the "price" of a unit of charitable services, or $c_j/(1 - w_j^{t-1})$, depends upon the level of gifts received by the charity in the previous period. Thus, an unstable result is possible. For example, suppose that the system is in equilibrium under the conditions of Model I, where donors ignore the level of w_j. Now suppose that donors learn that the price of giving is not c_j, but $c_j/(1-w_j^{t-1})$. If overall demand is price inelastic, then for a given set of $[\alpha_j^t]$, donors give more than in Model I (see Fisher, 1977). The increased giving lowers the fundraising shares, that is $w_j^t < w_j^{t-1}1$, and donors give less. This increases the w_j^{t-1}, and donors give more, etc. Although these oscillations may eventually lead to an equilibrium, it is also possible for the system to be unstable. Conversely, with price-elastic demand, giving is lower in period t, the higher are the w_j^{t-1}. The system may have multiple equilibria, at least one of which is unstable. For some initial conditions, giving may fall over time until the fundraising share equals one and the charity goes out of business. Thus, although stable equilibria are possible with either inelastic or elastic demand, the system can also either entirely unravel or continuously cycle.

Even if overall demand is inelastic, donors favor charities with low levels of w_j^{t-1} (that is, those with high levels of giving relative to fundraising costs). Thus, once a charity begins to lose donations, this may create an unstable situation in which that charity continues to lose relative to others. Similarly, a charity that is successful in one period can build on its low level of w_j^{t-1} to generate more gifts and lower w_j^t still more. Some charities may have fundraising shares that are above those in Model I and may eventually go out of business. Others have lower fundraising shares and use this advantage to expand their "market shares."

Of course, charity managers are unlikely to be so extremely myopic that they fail to recognize that w_j^t affects donations in $t+1$. A manager might instead look T periods into the future and solve a dynamic programming problem that takes account of the links between periods. Thus, first R^T is maximized given w^{T-1}. Then R^{T-1} is maximized given w^{T-2} and so forth. If complete myopia makes managers seem a bit too stupid to be realistic, this second method assumes that they are unrealistically foresighted and technically trained. Thus, suppose instead that managers look only one period in advance and guess that (19–7) holds in $t+1$. They also assume that gifts in $t+1$ relative to gifts in t depend on the level of w^t relative to w^{t-1} and estimate $\alpha^{t+1}x^{t+1}/\alpha^t x^t = \gamma(w^t)$. Ignoring discounting, they maximize

$$TR^t = \alpha^t m(x^t - v) + \alpha^{t+1} m(x^{t+1} - v) \qquad (19\text{–}8)$$

Extreme values occur where

$$0 = x^t - v + \alpha^t \frac{\partial x^t}{\partial \alpha^t} + \frac{d\alpha^{t+1}}{d\alpha^t}\left(x^{t+1} - v + \alpha^{t+1}\frac{\partial x^{t+1}}{\partial \alpha^{t+1}}\right) + \alpha^{t+1}\frac{\partial x^{t+1}}{\partial w^t}\frac{dw^t}{d\alpha^t}$$

But $dw^t/d\alpha^t = (-w^t/x^t)(\partial x^t/\partial \alpha^t)$, and the charity manager guesses that (19–7) holds in period $t+1$, that is,

$$x^{t+1} - v + \alpha^{t+1}\frac{\partial x^{t+1}}{\partial \alpha^{t+1}} = 0$$

Thus we have,

$$w^t = 1 + \eta_t^{II} [1 - \gamma(w^t)\epsilon^{t+1}], \qquad (19-9)$$

where

$$\epsilon^{t+1} = \frac{\partial x^{t+1}}{\partial w^t} \frac{w^t}{x^{t+1}}$$

This is a maximum as long as the α^t and w^t that solve (19–9) are ≤ 1, and the second-order condition holds.

Given w^{t-1}, the level of w^t that solves (19–9) is greater than, equal to, or less than the level that solves (19–7) as $-\eta_t^{II}\gamma(w^t)\epsilon^{t+1} \gtreqless 0$. We know that $\eta_t \leq 0$ and $\gamma(w^t) > 0$. In an atomistic market, the demand curve facing each charity is elastic whatever the elasticity of overall demand; thus, $\epsilon^{t+1} < 0$. Therefore, the above inequality is negative. The fundraising share is lower, and fewer brochures are sent when charity managers are not entirely myopic. Thus, if total market demand is also elastic, the managers' relative farsightedness may reduce the likelihood of a corner solution or at least cause the system to unravel more slowly. If overall demand is inelastic and every charity selects a lower w^t in (19–9) than in (19–7), then overall giving may fall in $t+1$. Thus, w_j^{t+1} may increase for all j. There seems no reason to suppose a priori that these oscillations will necessarily converge to an equilibrium.[13] Instability appears to continue to be possible in spite of the managers' relative farsightedness.

Donors, however, care about ideology as well as w_j. Thus, entry can still occur at levels of b_j favored by donors but not provided by existing charities. Entry leads to more giving from people who received no brochures in the past or who prefer the ideology of the entrant. If potential entrants use the same decision-making calculus as existing charities, then entry occurs as long as net returns are positive over the relevant time horizon. This entry raises the w_j of existing charities at each α_j, and thus erodes their advantage.

To discuss entry more explicitly, we must specify the level of w_j that donors assign to a new charity with no experience in the market. If donors predict that a new charity will have a w_j that is higher than those of existing charities, this is a substantial entry barrier. Entrants can survive only if they pick points in ideology space favored by donors and opposed by existing charities. Entry may cease even though net receipts are large and positive. In contrast, donors may not penalize entrants, and might, instead, assign them the average w_j^{t-1} of the old charities that send brochures. Then, donors' dislike of fundraising pushes donations to a low level as entry proceeds but does not prevent charities as a group from making choices that generate high w_j. Just as in Model I, entry reduces the size of charities and continues beyond the point where net returns are maximized. Because of donors' sensitivity to the "price" of giving, however, entry may cease even though some existing charities have $w_j < 1$.

DONORS JUDGE THE PRODUCTIVITY OF FUNDRAISING

The last model (Model III) assumes the most sophisticated donors. Although they still confuse average and marginal fundraising shares and use w_j^{t-1} as an estimate of future levels of w_j, they realize that a dollar spent on fundraising may raise more than a dollar in new resources. They value these new gifts most highly if they reduce the private consumption of others or come from funds that would otherwise go to charities disliked by the donors. Let $NG_j^{kt}(z_j)$ be the expected net dollar gain in period t for donor k from a gift of z_j^k to j. Then,

$$NG_j^{kt} = z_j^k \, (1 - w_j^{t-1}) + \frac{w_j^{t-1} z_j^k}{v} \, \Theta_j^k \, (1 - w_j^{t-1}) \qquad (19\text{--}10)$$

The first term, $z_j^k(1 - w_j^{t-1})$, is the amount of the donor's gift that the donor believes is spent directly on charitable services by charity j. The term $w_j^{t-1} z_j^k / v$ is the donor's estimate of the number of brochures financed by his gift, and Θ_j^k is an estimate of the value to the donor of gifts generated. In general, this number is less than the total gifts generated because some of the additional giving comes from people who would have given to charities that are almost as good as j as far as the donor is concerned. This value is multiplied by $(1 - w_j^{t-1})$, since the donor estimates that w_j^{t-1} of these new gifts are also spent on fundraising. I assume that the donor does not, however, calculate the whole infinite series. He does not go beyond this second stage to calculate the gifts generated by the additional $(w_j^{t-1} z_j^k / v) \, \Theta_j^k w_j^{t-1} z_j^k$ dollars that he estimates will be spent on fundraising.

For the charity, however, all the gifts generated by fundraising are worthwhile. Thus, $x_j > \Theta_j^k$ for all k, but the x_j depend on the Θ_j^k. Depending upon our assumptions about managers' foresight, the charity maximizes an expression analogous to either (19–5) or (19–8) except that $\partial x^{t+1}/\partial w^t$ is small in absolute value. When w_j^{t-1} increases, the amount of a gift spent *directly* on services falls, but the amount used to generate additional giving increases. The "price" of charitable services is not $c_j/(1 - w_j^{t-1})$, but

$$\frac{c_j}{(1 - w_j^{t-1})} \left[\frac{v}{v + w_j^{t-1} \Theta_j^k} \right]$$

that is, the "price" of giving is lower in Model III than in Model II. The same potential for instability arises here as in Model II, but the problem is less severe the larger are the Θ_j^k, that is, the more the donors benefit from fundraising.

A charity that appeals to a well-defined group of donors who all face the same set of close substitutes is in a very different position from one that tries to reach a broad spectrum of diverse people. Donors are likely to approve a much higher level of fundraising expenses in the latter case because additional gifts are likely to reduce donations to charities a donor does not value highly, that is, Θ_j^k is large.

Entry is more likely to be worthwhile for new charities, the higher are the Θ_j^k of donors. Similarly, if new entrants can draw funds mainly from private consumption, then entry is more likely to occur, since the new charity does not siphon off many funds from other nonprofits that are valued by donors. It remains true, however, that the fundraising share of the marginal charity approaches one as entry occurs. The overall level of charitable services provided depends on donors' attitudes toward entrants and toward fundraising in general. Suppose that donors value fundraising almost as much as charity managers (that is, Θ_j^k is close to x_j). Then even if donors believe that new entrants have high levels of w_j, this will not deter giving very much and net revenues will be pushed toward zero. In contrast, if Θ_j^k is very small, then Model III is almost identical to Model II, and entry is sensitive to donors' beliefs about the w_j of entrants.

CONCLUSIONS: REGULATORY POLICY AND UNITED CHARITIES

This paper demonstrates that the competition for charitable dollars reduces the level of service provision relative to funds raised for all charities. In the absence of entry barriers, the number of charities increases until the fundraising share of the marginal charity approaches one. This result holds even if donors dislike high fundraising expenses.

Of course, in reality, net charitable resources are not close to zero. Entry barriers exist, the supply of charity entrepreneurs is limited, or existing firms monopolize a portion of "ideology space." In particular, donors probably have some "brand loyalty" to existing charities that makes it difficult for new charities to establish a foothold, or perhaps donors assume that new charities inevitably have high fundraising shares. There is no reason to think, however, that existing barriers to entry are in any way optimal. Although entry barriers permit positive levels of charitable services, they also reduce the ideological diversity of the nonprofit sector. The tradeoff between the variety and volume of services is a central policy dilemma.

Not only will advertising be "excessive" in the absence of entry barriers, but, when the fundraising share enters the donors' decision-making calculus, the system may be unstable. In addition, charities that are already large will grow larger, while those that have funding difficulties will contract. These instabilities may be less severe, however, if donors recognize that a portion of advertising expense is productive because it leads other people to give more to charities that they support. The more heterogeneous are donors' tastes, and the higher the marginal utility of giving relative to private consumption in the population as a whole, the more beneficial is advertising to donors and the closer Model III is to Model I where donors are indifferent to fundraising costs.

Since a competitive charity market with no entry barriers does not seem "optimal" in any sense of that word, I consider the efficacy of three different regulatory strategies. The first increases the information available to donors. The second imposes direct restrictions on charities. The third attempts to modify the structure of the charity "market."

A policy of information provision that requires charities to announce the level of w_j will be ineffective if entry barriers are low. The worst results of a system where entry pushes w_j toward one cannot be avoided by simply requiring charities to announce w_j. When donors know w_j, Models II and III prevail, the potential for instability and oligopoly control may be high, and the problem of "excessive" entry remains unless donors believe that new entrants have especially high levels of w_j.

Since this first strategy is inadequate, consider a more aggressive policy where the provision of information about w_j is combined with a limit on w_j. This would be difficult to enforce, however, because charities cannot choose w_j directly. Instead, w_j is determined by the number of brochures charities send and by the productivity of these brochures.[14] Thus, direct restrictions on the number of brochures sent (or α) would seem to be the more effective regulatory mechanism. If not combined with entry restrictions, however, this policy could still produce high levels of w_j. Irrespective of the level of α chosen by individual charities, entry could push the w_j to high levels.

Given the weaknesses of the other options, market structure regulation may be more effective. Although existing entry barriers impose ad hoc controls on market structure, systematic market structure regulation should also be analyzed. To take an extreme example, suppose that a monopoly united charities drive is established where the fund announces in advance the share of receipts that will go to each charity. The fund sends a single brochure to each person so total fundraising costs are mv. Members are not permitted to obtain gifts independently, and no charity can solicit funds unless it joins the united drive. The fund economizes on fundraising costs both by reducing competition between existing charities and by making entry more difficult.

The benefits of reductions in the w_j are not costless, however. A federated drive may make it difficult for ideologically disparate charities to survive and may induce donors to purchase a package of charitable services that does not suit their ideologies. Thus, if the member charities' b_j are very dissimilar and if donors' most preferred b_k are distributed broadly across the ideological range, then fundraising costs aside, the fund increases the price of giving to desirable charities. If donors do not affirmatively dislike some of the b_j, total gifts fall if demand is "price" elastic and increase if demand is inelastic (this is Fisher's result, 1977). If instead donors feel worse off the more money is given to charities with large $|b_k - b_j|$, then even if demand is inelastic, total gifts may fall.

The "price" of giving is pushed *up* by the united fund's "tie-in" sale and pushed *down* by the saving in solicitation costs. For a given set of charities, a monopoly united fund will increase net charitable resources either when demand is inelastic and charities have different (but not directly opposed) ideologies, or when demand is elastic, ideologies are similar, and the w_j are high in an atomistic charity market. Fisher (1977) stresses the first motivation and emphasizes the possibility that donors may be worse off with a united fund because they are being forced to make a tied purchase. This difficulty suggests that public policy should not be directed toward the establishment of monopoly united funds.

Actual united funds do not, however, have such extensive monopoly power. They cannot prevent the entry of independent charities, and people can donate to member charities without going through a fund. The funds' privileged access to the payroll deduction systems at many workplaces gives them some limited monopoly power but not enough to prevent disintegration if donors are very unhappy with the package of services provided by member agencies. Thus, if ideological differences are important, either dissatisfied donors can give to nonmembers whose better b_j's overcome their higher w_j's, or else they can make separate gifts to desirable member agencies. Funds survive by providing a low "cost," ideologically homogeneous package of charities (Rose-Ackerman, 1980). The benefits of combining to reduce w_j appear to be fairly large if one accepts recent estimates showing that giving is "price" elastic (Feldstein, 1975; Feldstein and Clotfelter, 1976; and Feldstein and Taylor, 1976).

Given this chapter's conclusion that high fundraising shares and instability can be expected in an atomistic market with free entry, the united funds' limited monopoly power can perhaps be justified as a realistic compromise between preserving ideological diversity and preventing the competition for gifts from absorbing a large share of charitable resources. This is not to say, however, that the admission procedures and solicitation practices of realistic united funds are entirely benign or that their monopoly power should be increased. United funds impose real costs on nonmember charities and on donors with minority preferences. Thus, the funds' procedures for admitting new charities deserve careful scrutiny to assure that savings in fundraising costs do not overly limit ideological diversity.[15]

NOTES

1. A compilation of state laws is in American Association of Fundraising Counsel (1978).

2. The organizations are the Philanthropic Advisory Division of the National Council of Better Business Bureaus and the National Information Bureau, Inc. Their activities are described in "Rating Charities" (1977) and "Setting Standards for Charity" (1977).

3. A brochure of the United War of Greater New Haven (1978) prominently displays a pie chart showing that only 5.3 percent of campaign dollars was spent on fundraising with another 5.2 percent for "management and services."

4. See Morgan, Dye, and Hybels (1977, 161–64). In their 1973 sample of households, the average gift was $459. Twelve percent of the households gave nothing, and other 67 percent gave less than $500. Giving was from 3 to 4 percent of after-tax income for households with income of $50,000 or less and rose to a high of 14 percent for households with $500,000 of income.

5. Private giving has been 1.5 percent to 2 percent of GNP in recent years (Nelson, 1977, p. 121).

6. Unfortunately, work in social psychology is not very helpful in determining the empirical validity of my hypotheses about giving behavior. Most experimental work on altruism has studied helping behavior, not the donation of money. Even those experiments that did study gift giving concentrated on a single request for aid, not the person's overall donation pattern. The literature is reviewed in Gonzalez-Intal and Tetlock (1977), Krebs (1970), and Macauley and Berkowitz (1970). These studies suggest that variations in advertising strategies may be a powerful determinant of both the level and distribution of total gifts. Unfortunately, this research provides little systematic evidence. For example, we do not know whether people who respond generously to emotional appeals for help give less to other charities or cut-back private consumption. However, Morgan, Dye, and Hybels (1977) in two national surveys of philanthropy found that donors did care about charities' fundraising and administrative costs, but that only higher income people appeared to develop conscious plans for charitable giving. Among the reasons given for giving to charity by frequency of mention were the following: (a) approves of the organization's goals; (b) respondent "belongs" to the organization; (c) respondent gets some benefit from the organization; an (d) pressure or a quota. Money donations are correlated with some sort of personal involvement with the charity or the purpose of the charity. Among the reasons for refusing charitable requests by frequency of mention were the following: (a) other charities were more important; (b) the fund does a poor job; (c) objectionable solicitation including high pressure; (d) dislikes goal of fund; (e) does not know about fund; (f) insufficient income, (g) fund does not need the money; and (h) fundraising and administrative costs are too high.

7. Single-peaked preferences fall off monotonically for $b > b_k$ and $b < b_k$. There are no local maxima. Tastes are separable in the sense that a charity's ideological ranking is independent of its size and marginal costs.

8. The usual marginal conditions for a maximum may not be satisfied because of the discontinuous jump in utility that occurs when a person "buys-in" to a charity. This discontinuity does not, however, present any fundamental problems. Donors simply compare their utility levels with and without a gift of z_k to charity j.

9. This is a realistic assumption. Organizations that rate charities calculate the average fundraising share, not the share of the marginal gift (Rating charities, 1977; and Setting standards for charity, 1977).

10. See Rose-Ackerman (1981) for a discussion of the more general case where managers may trade off the level of b_j against the level of expected receipts. I ignore this complication here in order to concentrate on fundraising choices.

11. An equilibrium exists if no charity wants to change its behavior when it observes the behavior of other charities. Proving the existence and stability of equilibrium in a model of this kind is not a trivial matter, but it is not a problem I am prepared to solve in this paper. Nevertheless, the potential for instability is less here than in Models II and III discussed below. In those models, instability is possible even if only one charity exists.

12. This situation is analogous to the problem of highway congestion where each driver considers only his own driving time not the cost imposed on other drivers. It is also, of course, analogous to entry in a competitive market where profits are pushed to zero. Its normative interpretation is, however, quite different. When profits are zero, the market is efficient. When net charitable revenues are zero, sending brochures is a pure waste.

13. Even in the two-period case, the actual solution of the dynamic programming problem is a complex exercise.

14. Compare a draft bill introduced in the New York State Legislature that attempts to limit fundraising shares to 50 percent of receipts, but does not require charities to tell donors the fundraising share (New York State, 1980).

15. For a fuller discussion, see Rose-Ackerman (1980). See also National Committee for Responsive Philanthropy (1980). This organization is committed to liberalizing United Way admissions practices and opening up the payroll deduction to more charities.

REFERENCES

American Association of Fundraising Counsel. 1978. Special issue: A compilation of state
laws regulating charities. *Giving U. S. A.* Bulletin Number 16, December.

Arrow, Kenneth. 1974. Gifts and exchanges. *Philosophy and Public Affairs* (Summer): 343–
62.

Baumol, William. 1970. *Economic Dynamics: An Introduction*. 3rd ed. New York: Macmil-
lan Company.

Feldstein, Martin S. 1975. The income tax and charitable contributions: Part I—Aggregate
and distributional effects. *National Tax Journal* 28 (March): 81–100.

Feldstein, Martin S., and Charles Clotfelter. 1976. Tax incentives and charitable contributions in the United States. *Journal of Public Economics* 5 (January/February): 1–26.

Feldstein, Martin S., and A. Taylor. 1976. The income tax and charitable contributions.
Econometrica 44 (November): 1201–22.

Fisher, Franklin M. 1977. On donor sovereignty and united charities. *American Economic
Review* 67 (September): 632–38.

Gonzalez-Intal, A. Miren, and Philip Tetlock. 1977. Proposal for organization of literature
review. Program on Nonprofit Organizations, Yale University, New Haven, mimeo.

Krebs, D.L. 1970. Altruism. *Psychology Bulletin* 73:258–302.

Macauley, J., and L. Berkowitz, eds. 1970. *Altruism and Helping Behavior*. New York: Academic Press.

Morgan, James H., Richard F. Dye, and Judith Hybels. 1977. Results from two national surveys of philanthropic activity. In U. S. Department of Treasury, Commission of Private
Philanthropy and Public Needs. *Research Papers: Volume I* (Washington, D. C.), pp.
157–323.

National Committee for Responsive Philanthropy. 1980. *Responsive Philanthropy: Newsletter for NCRP* (Winter).

Nelson, Ralph L. 1977. Private giving in the American economy, 1960–1972. In U. S. Department of the Treasury, Commission on Private Philanthropy and Public Needs, *Research Papers: Volume I* (Washington, D. C.), pp. 115–34.

New York State, Legislative Bill Drafting Commission. 1980. An act to amend the executive
law, in relation to solicitation and collection of funds for charitable purposes and re-
pealing certain provisions thereof. 1-62-35-28, Albany, New York, mimeo.

"Rating Charities," Parts I, II, and III, *Philanthropy Monthly* (May 1977), 19–26; (June 1977),
14–18; (July 1977), 31–33.

Rose-Ackerman, Susan. 1981. Do government grants to charity reduce private donations? In
M. White, ed., *Nonprofit Firms in a Three Sector Economy* (Washington, DC: Urban
Institute), pp. 95–114; COUPE Papers in Public Economics, No. 6. Reprinted as Chapter
18 in this volume.

———. 1980. United charities: An economic analysis. *Public Policy*, XXVIII (Summer), 323–
50.

Schmalensee, Richard. 1972. *The Economics of Advertising* (Amsterdam, North-Holland
Publishing Company, London).

Setting Standards for Charity," *Philanthropy Monthly* (Aug. 1977), 7–11.

United Way of New Haven. 1978. People helping people. New Haven, Connecticut, pam-
phlet.

20

Should Donors Care About Fundraising?

RICHARD STEINBERG

Most donors give because they wish to see services provided, either to themselves (in which case a "purchase" is mixed with a pure donation), or to others. At first thought, it seems, that organizations with higher fundraising levels (or shares) are "bad buys." That is, if a firm spends, on average, 50 percent of its budget on fundraising, it seems that it would cost you $2.00 to purchase $1.00 of "charitable services." In this case, the "price" of $1.00 of charitable services is $2.00, and our intuition is summarized by the statement "the price of charitable services is directly related to the donee's fundraising share." No doubt this intuition underlies state regulation of fundraising.[1]

This intuition is rationalized in Rose-Ackerman's (1982) paper reprinted in this volume. In her model, nonprofit organizations truthfully report average fundraising shares, and donors, lacking information on marginal fundraising shares, assume that the marginal share (the share of an extra dollar of contributions devoted to fundraising) is the same as the average fundraising share (total fundraising divided by total contributions). If nonprofit and donor behavior is accurately described by these assumptions, then the price of charitable services is a monotone increasing function of fundraising share.

I demonstrate below that the intuitive conclusion is generally wrong, for it confuses marginal and average firm behavior, neglects multiplier effects, and ignores cross-donative responses. In particular, I show that if the nonprofit organization acts to maximize any of a broad range of plausible objectives, then the price of charitable service equals $1.00, regardless of the

This research was supported by a grant from the Program on Non-Profit Organizations at Yale University. Additional support was provided by the NSF's grant to the Metropolitan Philanthropy Project at the University of Pennsylvania. Special thanks go to Burton Weisbrod for providing the data and helpful comments, and to Robert Inman, Susan Rose-Ackerman, Henry Hansmann, Dennis Young, Thomas Reiner, Julian Wolpert, Catherine Eckel, Richard Ashley, and William Levis for helpful comments on previous drafts.

level of fundraising. In the more general case, fundraising shares influence the price of charitable services in a very complicated way, and there is no reason to assume that organizations with higher fundraising shares are "worse buys."

To analyze the problem formally, models of donor and firm behavior are developed in the following section of this chapter. The third section of this chapter derives the price of charitable services and demonstrates the general irrelevance of the fundraising share.

The derivation of the expression for the price of services follows directly from the definition of price (here, donative expenditure necessary to obtain a dollar's worth of service). While a normative case can be made that donors *should* use this price in deciding how to allocate their donations across charities, it is not clear whether donors actually do use this price. The fourth section presents evidence on actual donor behavior. It appears that, for whatever reason, the normative theory developed here provides a reasonably accurate description of donor behavior. The final section places the results in some perspective and summarizes. The price of charitable services is related to Hansmann's (1980) concept of contract failure (reprinted in this volume) and to Rose-Ackerman's (1982) notion of excessive fundraising.

THE DONATIVE REVENUE FUNCTION AND NONPROFIT ORGANIZATIONAL OBJECTIVES

This section has two objectives. First, the donative revenue function is characterized. This function relates donations received by a firm to fundraising expenditure by that firm, assuming behavior of other firms remains constant. Second, a one-parameter family of objective functions is proposed. Maximization with respect to this parameter is related to the donative revenue function.

There can be little doubt that fundraising activity affects donations in some way, for how else can we explain large expenditures for this purpose by nonprofit firms? Introspection and anecdotal evidence suggest that fundraising efforts do not have uniform effects—that is, under certain circumstances they encourage donations, while under other circumstances they are counterproductive. The aim here, however, is not to construct a model of donative psychology.[2] Instead, the capability of each charity to estimate the donative response to increases in fundraising expenditures (the donative revenue function) is stipulated.

Consider a donative revenue function illustrated in Figure 20–1, which is a slight modification of Boyle and Jacobs' (1978) formulation. Presumably, some contributions would flow in even if nothing were spent on fundraising—thus, the function is greater than zero above zero. The first few dollars of fundraising expenditure add little to donations received, as they are spent primarily on organizing the campaign and other overhead.

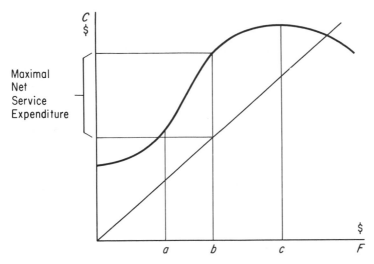

Figure 20–1 The relation between fundraising expenditure and contributions for a single firm.

Additional spending goes primarily to increasing the scope of the campaign, bringing in additional donations with, perhaps, increasing marginal returns. Beyond some point further increases in the scope of the campaign elicit diminishing returns. The campaign can only expand by seeking more doubtful prospects than the prime donors solicited first, or by spending more on each potential donor solicited. There may even come a point where potential donors are so hassled by a campaign that further increases in fundraising would actually reduce total contributions. This possibility covers the range to the right of point *c*. As a practical matter we would expect very few organizations to operate in this range, and these only as a temporary accident.

Net contributions are the difference between contributions received and the funds spent soliciting them, or $C - F$. Diagrammatically, net contributions are the vertical difference between the contributions curve and the 45° line. To find the maximum feasible net contributions, one need merely examine two points—the origin and point *b*. At point *b* the donative-revenue function has a 45° slope, indicating that an additional dollar spent on fundraising adds exactly one dollar to total contributions. To the left of point *b*, additional dollars spent on fundraising more than pay for themselves in additional contributions. To the right of point *b*, even though fundraising is productive, it is not sufficiently productive to cover its costs.

It may be that one can do better by spending nothing on fundraising, since by spending nothing, a charity can avoid the nonproductive setup costs of the fundraising campaign. Thus, one must also look at the origin. Given the assumed curvature of the function, which is reasonable, the origin and point *b* are the only candidates for a maximum, and the charity should select the point with greater net contributions. One must examine curvature as well as slope, for point a is a local minimum despite the 45° slope.

More formally, imagine that fundraising expenditure (F) is the only policy determinant of contributions (C). Volunteer labor is assumed to be exogenous,[3] as are income from sales, dues, and capital account, and expenditures on administration and addition to capital. Net exogenous resources (X) is thus the sum of all categories of exogenous income net of exogenous expenditure. Service maximizers choose F to maximize net service expenditure (S), where:

$$S = X + C - F \qquad\qquad (20\text{--}1\text{a})$$
$$0 \le F \le X + C \qquad\qquad (20\text{--}1\text{b})$$
$$C = C(F) \qquad\qquad (20\text{--}1\text{c})$$

The interior solution to this problem is quite simple. Substituting the donative revenue function (20–1c) into the definition of S, (20–1a), and setting the derivative equal to zero demonstrates that efficient allocations satisfy:

$$dC/dF = 1 \qquad\qquad (20\text{--}2)$$

In words, the marginal donative product of fundraising (MDPF) should be set to 1. In this way, organizations can maximize the net returns from fundraising, a necessary condition for charitable service maximization. Organizations with this objective will be referred to as service maximizers.

Service-maximizing organizations only consider marginal fundraising efforts that are sufficiently productive to pay for themselves. A budget-maximizing firm would do far more fundraising. To maximize a budget, one must maximize contributions. If an additional dollar spent on fundraising brought in an additional penny of contributions, then spending that dollar increases the budget, even though the portion of the budget devoted to services falls by 99¢. Budget maximizers set MDPF to zero.

Why would any organization wish to maximize its budget? At least three reasons have been suggested. Managing a firm with a larger budget might be regarded as more prestigious. Perhaps management salaries are higher, or perhaps self-dealing is more profitable if the budget is larger.

Some organizations are likely to have mixed motives. It may be that the managers would like to maximize their budget at the expense of services, but this makes them feel guilty. Such managers might compromise and adopt an allocation with a MDPF of, say, one half. Intermediate motives may also result if control of the organization is split among managers (or a board of directors) with differing objectives. In such a case, estimated MDPF reveals the predominant objective. Specifically, let maximands belong to the following one parameter family, encompassing convex combinations of the two polar maximands:

$$\psi = k \ (X + C - F) + (1 - k) \ (X + C); \ 0 \le k \le 1 \qquad (20\text{-}3)$$

Efficiency then requires that MDPF be set to k. This means that any organization which maximizes any objective function in this family would select a level of fundraising to achieve a specified constant slope. We shall refer to such firms as "optimizing."[4] The behavior of organizations which do not act to hold MDPF constant is inconsistent with all objective functions in the specified family. Thus, such organizations will be referred to as "nonoptimizing."

HOW SHOULD THE DONOR REGARD INFORMATION ON THE FIRM'S FUNDRAISING?

Maintained Assumptions

In Rose-Ackerman's model, one reason solicitation affects donations is that donors learn the organization's fundraising share. Clearly, this is not the only reason donors respond in the real world, for nonprofit advertising rarely mentions the fundraising share. In addition, donors often obtain such information on their own. Information on fundraising practices thus may have distinct effects from fundraising itself.

To focus on the rationality of individual responses to information on the fundraising share, consider an individual who derives utility only from private-goods consumption and the output of each nonprofit firm. This individual has not been solicited, but is aware of the nonprofit organization and its fundraising share and is considering making a donation. As before, nonprofit output can be measured by total nonprofit expenditures for nonsolicitative purposes.

Nonprofits have three sources of revenue: contributions by the donor under study (C_i); aggregate contributions by others $(\bar{C})$; and other resources (X), which are assumed exogenous. They can spend these resources two ways—on fundraising (F) or on services (S).

First, this section derives the price of services to donor i in the simple case where nonprofit firms are optimizing, donor i contributes a relatively small share of total donations to the firm, and donors other than i respond to total fundraising but not to information on fundraising shares. In this case, I show that donor i should likewise ignore fundraising shares when allocating donations. Then, the price is derived in three more complicated situations—when nonprofit firms are not optimizing, when other donors respond to fundraising share, and when donor i is "large."

When donor i is assumed "small" relative to total contributions, it is rational for i to act competitively. That is, donor i assumes $\partial \bar{C}/\partial C_i$ is identically zero. When i is small, it is also reasonable to assume that $C(F)$ or $C(F/S)$ is locally separable in donor i's donations. That is:

$$\partial^2 \bar{C}/\partial F \partial C_i = 0 \quad \text{or} \quad \partial^2 \bar{C}/\partial (F/S) \partial C_i = 0$$

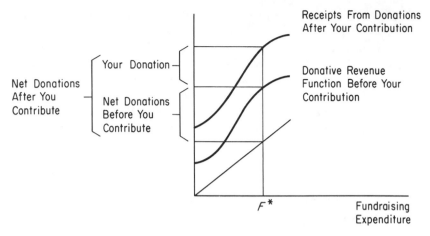

Figure 20–2   Effect of marginal contributions by a 'small' donor.

for the various small donor models in a neighborhood around firm equilibrium.

The Simplest Case

If the recipient nonprofit firm's behavior is consistent with any objective function in the specified family, i is a small donor, and contributions of others depend on F and not F/S, a surprising result follows: exactly 100 percent of i's contribution will be applied to increased services, regardless of how much the organization chooses to spend on fundraising.[5] The reason is that the additional contribution does not change how other donors respond to fundraising. Thus, the contributions curve is shifted upward by the exact amount of i's contribution, while the shape of the curve is unaffected. The optimal expenditure on fundraising is unchanged, so none of the marginal contribution would be swallowed up in increased fundraising expenditures. Figure 20–2 illustrates this case.

Different organizations may find that, because their services and potential donor pools differ, they face different contributions curves. If each were to act as a net-contributions maximizer, they would respond to these different curves by spending different shares of their budgets on fundraising. And yet, a marginal contribution to any of these organizations would have the same marginal efficiency and would be 100 percent applied to increased services. Thus, the "fundraising share" contains no helpful information on how to rationally allocate donations between charities.

Nonoptimizing Firms

Now consider a nonoptimizing nonprofit (that is, one that does not act to hold MDPF constant). In this case an additional contribution has two effects. First, it shifts the contributions curve upward in the manner described before. Second, it will cause the charity to spend more (or, conceivably, less!) on fundraising. If the charity chooses to spend more on fundraising, this may either raise or lower the effective price of my donation, depending on what range of the donations curve the charity is operating in. If the charity would choose to spend an amount like point a in Figure 20–1 in the absence of i's donation, and would choose to spend a greater amount in reaction to i's donation, then donor i's contribution of a dollar leads to a greater than dollar increase in services; the price of service is less than a dollar. Although some portion of their donation is not directly spent on services, that portion was spent on fundraising which brought in more than it cost in donations from others. For example, if the slope were such that an additional dollar of fundraising brought in $10 in additional contributions, and if 50 percent of a marginal contribution were applied to fundraising then donor i would directly purchase 50¢ in services for a dollar spent. But the 50¢ spent on fundraising would lead to $5 in additional contributions which should be attributed to donor i. If 50 percent of these contributions also went to fundraising, donor i would have secured $3.00 additional services for the $1.00 donation after the first round. Thus, the marginal output efficiency is at least 300 percent and the effective price is quite low.

There would, of course, be many more rounds to this process. The new donations cause additional fundraising which causes additional donations, etc. As long as total fundraising remained in the range to the left of point b, each successive round would raise the efficiency of the original contribution still further.

It might seem that this process could continue without limit, leading to an explosive growth in the organization. However, the marginal output is limited for two related reasons. First, each successive round adds a smaller amount of services to the total under certain circumstances (when the share of extra contributions donated to fundraising times the marginal net productivity of fundraising is less than one) so that the total never exceeds a finite limit. Second, because fundraising is subject to diminishing marginal productivity, the process will eventually lead to spending in the range between b and c, where additional fundraising produces more contributions but subtracts from service provision. The two reasons are complementary, as the second insures the necessary circumstances for the applicability of the first.

Without further specification, the exact price cannot be shown except as a local approximation. But, it is clear that organizations initially operating in the range from a to b and responding to increased donations by increasing fundraising expenditures have prices less than $1.00 regardless of the value of the average fundraising share.

If the nonprofit firm were initially operating in the range to the right of point b, and responded to increased donations by increasing fundraising, the price of a dollar's services would exceed a dollar. This would also occur in the range from point b to c if the firm responded to additional donations by reducing fundraising expenditures. This last might occur if the firm had a target service expenditure, in which case additional contributions would reduce the need to spend on fundraising.

There is one additional complication, pointed out in Rose-Ackerman (1982).[6] The value of a marginal donation by donor i depends not just on the marginal output level produced at the target nonprofit, but also on the quantity of resources diverted from other nonprofits and donor i's preferences regarding the relative merits of the services provided by them.[7] A donation, say, to the Democratic Party which induced former Republican contributors to switch allegiance and contribute to Democrats would be valued more highly than one which induced former noncontributors to donate. On the other hand, one benefits little from a donation to Girl Scouts of America which induces others to shift their contributions from Girl Scouts to the Campfire Girls.

The value of marginal output resulting from i's marginal donation can be derived (locally)[8] as follows. Assume the following differentiable functions characterize donor and nonprofit behavior with respect to firm k:

$$F = f(\bar{C} + C_i) \qquad\qquad (20\text{--}4a)$$
$$\bar{C} = g(F) \qquad\qquad (20\text{--}4b)$$
$$S^j = h^j(F) \text{ for all } j \neq k \qquad\qquad (20\text{--}4c)$$

where:

$\bar{C}$ denotes total contributions to nonprofit firm k by all donors except i

C_i denotes donations to firm k by donor i

F represents fundraising expenditure by firm k

S^j represents output of firm j.

Equation (20–4a) characterizes nonprofit behavior. Fundraising is allowed to depend on the exogenous donations of donor i as well as the endogenous aggregate donations of others. The only additional restriction on f necessary for the proof below is that $f' \neq 0$ in the vicinity of equilibrium F conditional on C_i. Thus, the formula derived below does not apply to optimizing firms, where $f' \equiv 0$.

Equation (20–4b) characterizes donor response to fundraising. We assume $g' \neq 0$, at equilibrium, ruling out budget maximizers (they are covered by the previous demonstration). Equations (20–4c) are the "cross-donative response functions," indicating the response of aggregate donations to other firms as a function of fundraising by firm k. The function h is a reduced form simplification. In detail, F^k affects C^j which may affect F^j and, in turn, S^j. We assume that nonprofit behavior is competitive, in the sense that an increase in fundraising by firm k elicits no strategic reaction from other firms. To assume the contrary would further complicate donor i's calculation of rational behavior.

Donor i cares only about nonprofit output (S) at the target firm (firm k) and changes in outputs (S^j) induced at other firms by a donation to k. Using output of firm k as the numeraire good, the value to i of a set of outputs is given by:

$$V_i = S^k + \sum_{j \neq k} \theta^j S^j \qquad (20\text{--}5)$$

where:

V_i indexes the value of the vector of nonprofit outputs to donor i

θ^j is i's marginal rate of substitution between S^j and S^k, assumed locally constant for simplicity.

Finally, budget balance at firm k implies (X is exogenous resources):

$$S = C_i + \bar{C} + X - F \qquad (20\text{--}6)$$

To determine the marginal output attributable to i's marginal donation, Equations (20–4) and (20–6) are substituted into (20–5), and the result is totally differentiated and solved as

$$\frac{dV}{dC_i} = 1 + g'\frac{dF}{dC_i} - f'\left(1 + \frac{d\bar{C}}{dC_i}\right) + \sum_{j \neq k} \theta^j h^{j\prime} \frac{dF}{dC_i} \qquad (20\text{--}7)$$

Some insight can be derived from (20–7). The total impact of a marginal contribution is the initial contribution (the first right hand term) plus induced donations by others (the second term) minus induced fundraising (the third) plus induced output changes at other firms evaluated in terms of output from firm k. Further insight comes from substituting behavioral parameters for the right hand total derivatives. To do this, note that in equilibrium, Equations (20–4a) and (20–4b) must be consistent in that:

$$\begin{aligned} F &= f[C_i + g(F)] \\ \bar{C} &= g[f(C_i + \bar{C})] \end{aligned} \qquad (20\text{--}8)$$

By totally differentiating equations (20–8), substituting the result for the right hand total derivations of (20–7), and simplifying one obtains the desired result in terms of marginal output [price is the inverse of equation (20–9)]:

$$\frac{dV}{dC_i} = \frac{1 - f' + \Sigma \theta^j h^{j\prime} f'}{1 - f' g'} \qquad (20\text{--}9)$$

Note that in this model, donor i could completely determine the effective price of donation without any knowledge whatsoever of the average fundraising share. What matters are three marginal parameters—the marginal donative response of the community to increased fundraising, the marginal fundraising response of the firm to increased donations, and the marginal cross-output response to fundraising.

The average fundraising share would only matter if it was equivalent to marginal fundraising (f'), which would be quite peculiar behavior on the part of nonprofits. It is hard to imagine what objective function would motivate holding the average fundraising share constant, as would be required for equivalence of marginal and average functions. Even with such an objective function, the fundraising share is only one of several determinants of price, and price is not linear or monotonic in the fundraising share.

Unfortunately, the effective price requires donor i to know far more than is reasonable about the behavior of others and of the firm. Might a rational donor conserve informational resources by using $1/(1-F/C)$ as a "rule of thumb" approximation? Perhaps, but such a rule has little to commend it. Those following such a rule would seem to have no advantage over those not following such a rule. Indeed, if legal authorities scrutinized high-share firms more carefully for fraud, such a rule might get things backwards.

When Other Donors Respond to Fundraising Share

Perhaps a problem with the simpler models is that the conclusion—donor i should ignore the fundraising share—emerges from the assumption that other donors respond to total fundraising, rather than a share measure. Consider here the rational response of donor i when total donations of others respond to fundraising share. Then, behavior is characterized by the following equations:

$$F = f(C_i + \bar{C}) \tag{20–10a}$$
$$\bar{C} = g(F/S) \equiv g(Y) \tag{20–10b}$$
$$S^j = h^j(Y) \tag{20–10c}$$

In a fashion similar to that employed above, one can derive the marginal output in terms of total derivatives[9] and behavioral parameters[10]:

$$\frac{dV}{dC_i} = 1 + \left(g' + \sum_{j \neq k} \theta^j h^{j\prime}\right)\left(\frac{1}{S}\frac{dF}{dC_i} - \frac{Y}{S}\frac{dS}{dC_i}\right) - f'\left(1 + \frac{d\bar{C}}{dC_i}\right) \tag{20–11}$$

$$\frac{dV}{dC_i} = \frac{S - Sf' + \Sigma\theta^j h^{j\prime}(f' - Y + f'Y)}{S - f'g' + g'Y - f'g'Y} \tag{20–12}$$

The interpretation of Equation (20–11) is identical to that of (20–7), however in this case, donations of others respond to the change in F/S due to a change in C_i. The interpretation of (20–12) is similar to that of (20–9), but the "multiplier effect" is much more complicated, as the *level* of fundraising is assumed to depend on the level of contributions, while contributions depend on the fundraising *share*. Even though my marginal donation does not directly affect the firm's fundraising, it lowers the firm's fundraising share, ceteris paribus, by an amount that depends on initial F. This induces other donors to increase their contributions at each level of fundraising, which may induce the firm to select a different fundraising level, with subsequent multiplier and cross-donative effects.

Two conclusions emerge from this model. First, as before, the marginal output or effective inverse price of donation is far too complicated and requires far too much information for the average donor. Second, although the fundraising share conveys potentially useful information for allocating donations across nonprofits, this information must be used in a nonlinear and nonmonotonic fashion. Whether a higher fundraising share raises or lowers the efficiency of one's donation depends on the location of equilibrium and the relative magnitudes and signs of the marginal behavioral parameters of both donors and nonprofits. If information on such behavioral parameters is costly, it would seem that donors are better off ignoring information on the fundraising share.

Large Donors

Finally, we will discuss the price of charitable service to large donors. If a donor makes a discrete, large, and advertised donation, both the slope and intercept of the donative revenue function will likely change. For example, if giving by others depends on perceived unmet needs, total donations of others would fall by some fraction of the large donation. If the slope of the revenue function is unaltered, then F^* is unaffected but charitable services still cost the large donor more than a dollar as total giving by others is reduced.

In addition, a large donation may affect the slope of the revenue function, causing F^* to rise or fall, further complicating the price. Generally, we expect that a large donation would flatten the revenue function. If additional fundraising solicited additional donors, and the large donation lowered the level of unmet needs perceived by these additional donors, the MDPF of a given level of fundraising would be lower. However, it is possible that large donations assure other donors that they are contributing to a higher-quality organization, thus increasing MDPF.[11] The conclusion for large donors to optimizing nonprofits is that although the price of charitable services may differ from one dollar, the price depends on the reaction of other donors, and not on the firm's fundraising share.

EMPIRICAL EVIDENCE

The theory suggests that fundraising *levels* may affect donations but the fundraising *share* (or simple measures of price derived from the fundraising share) should not. The theory may provide useful advice to donors who are "rational" in the sense modeled, but the descriptive power of the theory must be demonstrated. Perhaps a high fundraising share discourages donations for psychological or informational reasons not modeled here. Therefore, in Steinberg (1983) I tested the descriptive power of this theory by estimating donative revenue functions. These results are briefly summarized and extended here.

Data were obtained from IRS files, as compiled by Burton Weisbrod of the University of Wisconsin. An extract matching numerical information from publicly available sections of IRS form 990 (filed by tax exempt organizations) and descriptive information from the IRS Exempt Organization Master File was obtained for all filing organizations in four metropolitan areas (Philadelphia, Los Angeles, Houston/Galveston, and Minneapolis/St. Paul) and three years (1974–1976).

A sample of this data was taken, containing all organizations that met all of the following criteria:

1. Gross receipts exceeded $10,000 in each year.
2. Exemption from federal corporate income tax was granted under either section 501-c-3 or 501-c-4 of the tax code (which cover, roughly, charitable, educational, health care, cultural, and research nonprofit organizations).
3. At least some services were provided to nonmembers (ruling out "clubs"), as determined by an algorithm utilizing three self-reported activity codes.
4. Tax forms were filed all three years.
5. The organization had at least one declared nonreligious purpose (as religious sector tax filers are a small and biased sample of all religious nonprofits).
6. The organization was primarily a service provider, rather than a pass-through such as a foundation or a United Way.
7. Contributions to the organization were deductible from personal income taxes. This primarily rules out political lobby groups.

Most of the criteria have obvious justification. Criterion (7) may seem arbitrary, and was employed for convenience, as the data set was originally developed for a separate study.

Remaining organizations were classified into six nonprofit sectors on the basis of their self-declared "activity codes." The classification was, at times, arbitrary, especially for multiactivity organizations. It is hoped that a meaningful partition of reality was obtained. Exact details of the selection and classification algorithms are available from the author.

The sectors are:

1. *Public welfare*—containing, loosely, "charities." Organizations devoted to the care and/or rehabilitation and/or legal protection of children, animals, the poor, minorities, women, criminals, juvenile delinquents, neighborhoods, and others are included here.
2. *Health*—containing hospitals, clinics, mental health groups, and multipurpose organizations whose primary purpose seemed to be provision of medical care. Thus, "old age homes" are classified as Public Welfare, while "medical services for the aged" belong here. Medical research is included in the Science and Research category if it seemed that this was the primary purpose of the organization, while a teaching hospital conducting research was generally classified as Health.

Table 20–1. Marginal Donative Products of Fundraising Level and FPRICE Variables[a,b]

Industry	MDPF	MDP of FPRICE Variant 1: All Variables	MDP of FPRICE Variant 2: Lag F Excluded
Welfare	1.2106	−18.06	300.11
	(0.0770)	(109.96)	(122.66)
Health	0.1269	−1059.84	−1173.76
	(0.0631)	(7662.47)	(7589.58)
Education	1.6286	−20.50	−17.70
	(0.6597)	(594.12)	(593.08)
Arts	2.0795	5.96	−2.17
	(0.5540)	(108.70)	(117.49)
Research	7.5533	−35652.21	30455
	(6.2056)	(141046)	(116881)
Other	0.0989	−37.63	−32.92
	(0.1570)	(48.40)	(56.90)

[a] FPRICE is defined as $1/(1 - F/C)$, where F is lagged fundraising and C is lagged contributions. If reported C were equal to zero, the value was set to 0.01. If reported F/C were equal to 1, FPRICE was set equal to 1000. Both changes were necessary to avoid dividing by zero when computing FPRICE.

[b] Standard errors are in parentheses below parameter estimates.

3. *Education*—containing private schools, ranging from kindergarten to graduate. Tutoring programs, special education, and vocational training programs were included here.
4. *Arts and Culture*—containing performing arts groups, museums, zoos, historical societies, and similar groups.
5. *Science and Research*—containing groups dedicated to medical or other research.
6. *Other*—containing multipurpose organizations for which no tie breaker could be found, international organizations, organizations with no activity codes or errors leading to imaginary codes as well as others which did not logically fit in the above categories.

The marginal donative product of fundraising was estimated for each sector using a variety of specifications, three of which are reported here. In the first (baseline) specification, MDPF was estimated as an individual-effects model with contemporaneous and lagged fundraising effects and variables controlling for administrative and service expenditures. Estimated MDPFs, reported in Table 20–1, are construed as the objective function parameter "k," and most estimates are significantly different from zero. Note that if estimated k *were* insignificantly different from zero, this would not imply that fundraising has no effect on donations, for k measures the impact of marginal, not total, fundraising.

Estimated MDPF is of interest because it "reveals" the predominant objective function of firms in each sector.[12] Welfare, Education, and Art firms seem to behave more like service maximizers than like budget maximizers.

One can confidently reject the hypothesis that MDPF = 0 for each, while we cannot reject the hypothesis that MDPF = 1 for Education or Arts and, although we can reject MDPF = 1 for Welfare, point estimates are numerically close to 1.

On the other hand, Health and Other firms seem to behave like budget maxmizers. One can confidently reject the hypothesis that MDPF = 1 for these sectors and not reject the hypothesis that MDPF = 0. Finally, the standard error for the Research sector is so large that a predominant objective is not revealed.

I tested my theory by appending FPRICE $[1/(1 - F/C)]$ to the list of explanatory variables in the basic specification.[13] FPRICE is a naive measure of the price of output, and would be correct if marginal fundraising equalled the average fundraising share and if multiplier and cross-donative effects were neglected by donors. Prior intuition suggests that FPRICE should have a negative coefficient, while the results of the simplest model presented here suggest that the variable should have a coefficient of zero. Estimated marginal donative product of FPRICE is reported as "Variant 1" in Table 20–1.

Because FPRICE is somewhat colinear with fundraising level, OLS estimates may not detect a significant effect of FPRICE when such an effect exists. "Variant 2" deletes the lagged fundraising level variable but retains FPRICE. This variant attributes all colinear effects to the FPRICE variable, biasing its coefficient towards significance.

In both variants, current FPRICE is excluded. Current FPRICE can only be computed after donations come in, so that this information is unavailable when donors make their decisions. Neither variant had noticeable effects on estimated MDPF or its standard error, thus estimated MDPF is reported for the baseline model only.

If an organization increased its fundraising share from zero to 50 percent, FPRICE rises by only one unit. Thus, the large apparent magnitudes of the FPRICE coefficients reflect primarily the fine scale of measurement. More importantly, in no case was the coefficient of FPRICE significantly negative at the 10 percent level. Indeed, in one case FPRICE was significantly positive at the 5 percent level. Evidence from variant 2 is especially persuasive because this variant provides a conservative test, biased towards detecting significance. While statistical problems remain,[14] the evidence presented here suggests that the marginal fundraising share has no effect on donations. Additional results not reported here find an absence of inframarginal effects as well.[15] Thus, empirical results are consistent with the theoretical results derived above.[16]

SUMMARY AND DISCUSSION

The price of charitable services purchased through donations to a nonprofit organization is generally unrelated to the organization's fundraising share. In those cases where the fundraising share does affect the price, the relation is not linear or monotone increasing. Even when other donors respond negatively to the higher fundraising share, the high fundraising share does not imply that marginal donations are wasted. In any event, a calculation of the price requires far more information than donors can reasonably be expected to possess or process. It would seem that rational donors would not try to take account of the fundraising share when deciding on how to allocate donations across nonprofit organizations.

The intuitive view errs by assuming that marginal donations are allocated to marginal fundraising in proportion to the firm's average fundraising share. However, for those nonprofits which maximize objective functions from a specified family, marginal induced fundraising is zero. Thus, the price of a dollar of charitable output is a dollar.

When nonprofits do not act as if they possessed any objective function in the specified family, behavioral reactions of the firm, multiplier effects on induced donations, and cross donative responses cause the price of output to depart from a dollar. However, the price is essentially unrelated to the firm's fundraising share.

Limited empirical support for this conclusion is provided by estimated donative revenue functions. Estimates summarized here show that marginal fundraising affects aggregate contributions, but a naive measure of price based on fundraising share does not.

The theoretical results are important not only because they provide useful advice to "rational" donors, but because they help extend results explaining the existence of the nonprofit sector. Hansmann (1980) has argued that donors do not purchase charitable services through donations to for-profit firms because a large and uncertain share of their marginal donations may "leak" to stockholder dividends. The "nondistribution constraint" which legally defines the nonprofit form precludes such leaks, so that the price of charitable services purchased through donations would seem to be uniformly lower in nonprofit than in for-profit firms. His theory is incomplete, for if donations to nonprofit firms "leak" to fundraising, there is no guarantee that the nonprofit form will dominate. However, the results derived here indicate that such leaks are generally unimportant.

This chapter argues that small donors should not consider fundraising shares when deciding how to allocate their donations across firms. This does not imply that donors should ignore fundraising when voting for public regulatory policies. Fundraising probably causes a reciprocal marginal external cost to other nonprofit firms—an increase in fundraising expenditure by one firm raises the cost of obtaining donations at other firms by lowering both the intercepts and the slopes of their donative-revenue functions. In general, if an activity produces marginal external costs, the equilibrium level of that activity will be excessive. In addition, entry of new firms may lead to excessive fundraising in the Rose-Ackerman sense, as the net returns of (privately) optimal fundraising programs are driven to zero. Thus, while this chapter suggests an error in the way donors in Rose-

Ackerman's model determine the price of giving, the error does not seem to invalidate her main conclusion.

Thus, donors need not consider fundraising, but government should. However, while derivation of an optimal regulatory policy goes far beyond this chapter, results here suggest that regulatory caps on the fundraising share are too simple, and may be contrary to donor interests.

NOTES

1. See American Association of Fund Raising Counsel, Inc. (1981) for a summary of state laws regulating charitable solicitations (as of Dec. 31, 1980).

2. A number of theories which rationalize individual donative response to solicitation (as distinct from individual donative response to information on solicitative practices) are discussed in Richard Steinberg, Two essays on the nonprofit sector, doctoral dissertation in Economics, University of Pennsylvania, Submitted 1983.

3. Some of these exogeneity assumptions are relaxed in Steinberg, (1983). Absent capital constraints, the conditions derived here are valid in a more general context.

4. While a firm which held MDPF constant at a particular value, k', is acting as if it optimized an objective function with parameter k', we cannot be certain that the firm is succeeding in optimizing with respect to its true (but unobservable) k. Thus, the class of optimizing firms (as defined here) may include firms whose behavior failed to achieve its intended objective. However, there is no ambiguity when MDPF is not held constant—such firms do not act as if they optimized any objective function in the specified class.

5. This result obviously depends on separability. If i's marginal donation flattens the donative schedule ($\partial^2 \bar{C} / \partial F \partial C_i < 0$) then optimal F is lower, increasing marginal output. Optimal F would rise if the schedule became steeper, resulting in a marginal output less than 1.

In addition, this result hinges on the interiority of the optimal solution. Steinberg (1983) shows that if the fundraising level which achieves a marginal donative product of one requires more than available resources, the nonprofit will either spend all or none of its resources on fundraising. If it spends nothing on fundraising, the marginal contribution has 100 percent efficiency, while if it spends everything, efficiency exceeds 100 percent. In this case, although the marginal donation is 100 percent absorbed in marginal fundraising, such fundraising is productive as the marginal donative product exceeds 1, and a multiplier results.

6. Susan Rose-Ackerman, Charitable giving and excessive fundraising, *Quarterly Journal of Economics*, May 1982, p. 197. Reprinted as Chapter 19 of this volume.

7. This complication does not apply to optimizing nonprofits or to budget maximizers, for they hold F constant and, therefore, divert no other contributions when i donates more. Likewise, there is no multiplier effect applying to these nonprofits.

8. Finite approximations are even more complicated (derived as Taylor expansions). Since the principal lesson from the local approximation is that the price is too complicated for i to calculate, this simplification does not damage that conclusion.

9. Denote fundraising share by $F/S \equiv Y(F,S)$, and behavioral relations as in the text. Then, the equivalent value of the vector of nonprofit outputs is given by:

$$V = C_i + g[Y(F,S)] + X - f(C_i + \bar{C}) + \Sigma \Theta^j h^j [Y(F,S)]$$

Totally differentiating, and setting $dX = 0$, one obtains:

$$dV = dC_i + g'(Y_F dF) + Y_S dS) - f'(dC_i + d\bar{C}) + \Sigma \Theta^j h^{j\prime} (Y_F dF + Y_S dS)$$

Noting that $Y_F = 1/S$ and $Y_S = -F/S^2 = -Y/S$ and solving for dV/dC_i, one obtains the result of the text.

10. Three auxiliary relations are necessary. First, note that identically,

$$S = C_i + \bar{C} + X - F$$

Differentiating and setting $dX = 0$, the first relation is obtained:

a. $\dfrac{dS}{dC_i} = 1 + \dfrac{d\bar{C}}{dC_i} - \dfrac{dF}{dC_i}$

Second, note that behavioral consistency requires:

$C = g[Y(f(C_1 + \bar{C}), S)]$

and

$F = f[C_i + g(Y(F,S))]$

Totally differentiating these, one obtains:

b. $\dfrac{d\bar{C}}{dC_i} = \dfrac{f'g'Y_F + g'Y_S(dS/dC_i)}{1 - f'g'Y_F}$

and

c. $\dfrac{dF}{dC_i} = \dfrac{f' + f'g'Y_S(dS/dC_i)}{1 - f'g'Y_F}$

Substituting (b) and (c) into (a), one obtains:

d. $\dfrac{dS}{dC_i} = \dfrac{1 - f'}{1 - f'g'Y_F - g'Y_S + f'g'Y_S}$

When (d) is substituted into (b) and (c), one obtains expressions for all three total derivatives in terms of behavioral parameters only. In turn, these are substituted into expression (20–11) in the text to obtain expression (20–12).

11. Rose-Ackerman (1981) details a variety of reasons why government grants to non-profit organizations might increase aggregate donations. It would seem that all these reasons apply here if "large donor" is substituted for "government grant."

12. Steinberg (1984) argues that the predominant objective is better estimated in a random coefficients framework. Results reported there are consistent with OLS results reported here.

13. In the original formulation (1983), I obtained similar results appending a fundraising share variable (F/C) rather than FPRICE. FPRICE, however, seems more appropriate as a naive determinant of contributions. In addition, FPRICE estimates are directly comparable with those produced by Weisbrod and Dominguez (1984).

14. Steinberg (1983) contains an extensive discussion of relevant statistical problems. Estimates were found to be robust with respect to corrections for endogeneity bias, certain types of measurement error, and certain types of heteroskedasticity. While it is argued there that excluded variable bias is likely to be unimportant, this source of bias cannot be ruled out.

15. To test for inframarginal effects, two linear models without individual effects were estimated across subsamples split at the median FPRICE for each industry. In the first case, the below median intercept was allowed to take a different value than the above median one, but slopes were constrained to be the same for both subsamples. In one industry (Health), the intercept for the low FPRICE firms was significantly lower than that for high FPRICE firms, while in two industries it was significantly higher (Arts at the 5 percent level, Other at the 10 percent level). However, a joint test on the difference in intercepts and the FPRICE coefficient was only significant in the direction predicted by the naive model for the Arts industry.

In the second case, slopes were allowed to vary across the two subsamples, and the lines were not constrained to meet at the median FPRICE. In this case, an appropriate joint significance test found a significant effect (10 percent) in the direction predicted by the naive model only for the Arts industry, while a significant (5 percent) contrary effect was again found for the Health industry. Complete results are available from the author.

16. The contrary results of Weisbrod and Dominguez (1984) should be noted, however. Using a different sample of IRS data, a different and more specific industry breakdown, a log-log functional form, a different error specification, and a different set of explanatory variables, they found that a variable corresponding to FPRICE had a negative sign in six of seven industries which was significant at the 10 percent level in three cases. Robustness analysis conducted in Steinberg (1983) suggests that the difference in functional form is the key reason for differing results, and there is no a priori reason to prefer one form over the other.

REFERENCES

American Association of Fund Raising Counsel, Inc. 1981. A compilation of state laws regulating charitable solicitations. *Giving USA Bulletin* No. 1, January.

Boyle, S.E., and P. Jacobs. 1978. The economics of charitable fundraising. *Philanthropy Monthly* (May).

Hansmann, Henry. 1980. The role of non-profit enterprise, *Yale Law Journal* 9 (April): 835–98. Reprinted as Chapter 3 of this volume.

Rose-Ackerman, Susan. 1981. Do government grants to charity reduce private donations? In *Nonprofit Firms in a Three Sector Economy*, ed. Michelle White. Washington: Urban Institute. Reprinted as Chapter 18 of this volume.

————. 1982. Charitable giving and excessive fundraising. *Quarterly Journal of Economics* 97 (May): 193–212. Reprinted as Chapter 19 of this volume.

Steinberg, Richard. 1983. *Two Essays on the Nonprofit Sector*. Doctoral dissertation in Economics, University of Pennsylvania.

————. 1984. The revealed objective functions of nonprofit organizations. Virginia Polytechnic Institute and State University, Department of Economics working paper # E84-01-03, January.

Weisbrod, Burton, and Nestor Dominguez. 1984. Demand for collective goods in private nonprofit markets: Can advertising overcome free-riding behavior? Social Science Research Institute, U. of Wisconsin, working paper # 8410, April.

VII
CORPORATE TAX BENEFITS

21

The Rationale for Exempting Nonprofit Organizations from Corporate Income Taxation

HENRY HANSMANN

Although most types of nonprofit corporations have been exempted from the federal corporate income tax since that tax was first adopted,[1] we continue to lack a clear rational for the exemption. This was perhaps understandable and acceptable when the nonprofit sector was small and nonprofit organizations were engaged largely in activities of a traditionally charitable nature. Today, however, the nonprofit sector represents a substantial and growing share of the national economy.[2] Nonprofit firms now commonly provide goods and services in direct competition with profit-seeking firms, and in many cases increasingly resemble their for-profit competitors in their manner of organization and operation.[3] The traditional criteria for applying the exemption are, as a result, being stretched beyond recognition, so that the absence of an underlying rationale for those criteria, and indeed for the exemption in general, is becoming increasingly conspicuous. To be sure, various efforts to rationalize the exemption have appeared from time to time. The most comprehensive and thoughtful of these efforts is presented in an article by Bittker and Rahdert.[4] But for a

From *Yale Law Journal* 91 (1981): 54–100. Preparation of the original article was supported by a grant from the Program on Non-Profit Organizations at the Institution for Social and Policy Studies, Yale University.

An earlier and somewhat different version was presented at a meeting of the Committee On Urban Public Economics and appears, under the title "Why Are Nonprofit Organizations Exempted From Corporate Income Taxation?," in the published proceedings of that conference, *The Interaction of the Public, Private, and Non-Profit Sectors* (M. White, ed., 1981).

For helpful comments I am indebted to, among others, Robert C. Clark, Russell Osgood, A. Mitchell Polinsky, Stanley Surrey, Alvin Warren, and Michelle White.

Reprinted by permission of the author, the Yale Law Journal Company and Fred D. Rothman and Company. Portions of text and footnotes omitted. Remaining footnotes have been renumbered.

number of reasons the Bittker and Rahdert analysis, like its predecessors,[5] is ultimately unsatisfying.

This Chapter surveys the various theories that have previously been offered to justify the exemption of nonprofit organizations from income taxation, and discusses the difficulties that those theories present. It then proceeds to offer a novel, and more satisfying, justification for the exemption. In particular, the Chapter argues that the best justification for the exemption is that it helps to compensate for the constraints on capital formation that nonprofits commonly face, and that such compensation can serve a useful purpose, at least for those classes of nonprofits that operate in industries in which, for various reasons, nonprofit firms are likely to serve consumers better than would profit-seeking firms.

Although exemption from federal income taxation extends to nonprofit organizations that assume a variety of legal forms, including charitable trusts and unincorporated associations, the discussion here will be confined, for simplicity of exposition and analysis, almost exclusively to nonprofits that are incorporated. Since nearly all nonprofits of any financial significance are incorporated, this is not a serious limitation.[6] Furthermore, the focus here will be largely on the exemption as it is applied to the primary activities of nonprofit organizations; relatively little will be said about the related issue of taxing, as is now done, an exempt nonprofit's income from wholly owned businesses that it operates at a profit primarily to earn income with which to finance its other activities.[7] Finally, the analysis will be confined to income taxation, which presents relatively distinct issues.

It should be emphasized as well that the concern here is with the exemption from taxation of the income of nonprofit organizations themselves and not with the charitable deduction, which allows an individual who makes a contribution to a qualifying nonprofit to deduct the amount of that contribution from his or her income when computing personal income tax.[8] The charitable deduction and the exemption raise different issues, and it would be quite conceivable for the tax system to embrace one without the other.[9]

Any discussion of the corporate income tax exemption for nonprofits is handicapped by the lack of consensus concerning the purposes and the consequences of the corporate tax even as it applies to ordinary business corporations.[10] Indeed, today the confusion concerning the effects of the corporate income tax is so great, and the critics of that tax so numerous, that one might well ask why we apply a separate tax to corporate income at all, and not just why some kinds of corporations are exempt from the tax. At present, however, the corporate income tax seems well entrenched. Consequently, the discussion that follows will take the existence of the corporate income tax as it applies to business corporations for granted and will simply ask whether it makes sense to exempt some or all nonprofit corporations from that tax. As we shall see,[11] the answer to that question is only partially dependent on the theory one accepts concerning the consequences of the tax as it applies to business corporations.

THE NATURE OF EXEMPT ORGANIZATIONS

It is helpful to begin analysis with a clear image of the essential characteristics of nonprofit corporations and of the exemption from income taxation that applies to them.

A nonprofit organization is, in essence, an organization that is prohibited from distributing net earnings to individuals, such as officers, directors, or members, who exercise control over the organization. In the case of an incorporated nonprofit this "nondistribution constraint" is imposed by the state nonprofit corporation law under which the organization is formed. A nonprofit organization is not, it should be noted, prohibited from *earning* a profit; in fact, many nonprofits show substantial annual net earnings. All net earnings, however, must be plowed back into financing the goods or services that the nonprofit was formed to provide.[12]

Not all nonprofit corporations are exempt from the federal corporate income tax. Rather, only nonprofits that are exclusively dedicated to particular purposes are exempt. The purposes that qualify nonprofits for exemption are explicitly listed in Section 501(c) of the Internal Revenue Code.[13] Any nonprofit corporation whose purposes do not come within this list is, like a business corporation, subject to income taxation.[14] The list of qualifying purposes is extensive, however, and has been broadly interpreted. As a result, there are few significant classes of nonprofit corporations that do not benefit from the exemption.[15] Indeed, the repeated and unreflective reinterpretation of the exemption to accommodate new forms of nonprofit activity,[16] which has kept the scope of the exemption roughly congruent with the outlines of the nonprofit sector as a whole,[17] offers clear evidence of the lack of, and need for, a coherent policy on which to base the exemption.

With these basic characteristics of the nonprofit corporation and its income tax exemption defined, we can now turn to a consideration of the justifications that have been, or could be, offered for the exemption.

DO NONPROFITS HAVE TAXABLE INCOME?

It has been suggested that nonprofits are granted exemption because they have no income in the sense in which that term is used in the Internal Revenue Code.

Can We Construct a Workable Definition of Income for Nonprofits?

Bittker and Rahdert, for example, argue at length that any effort to use ordinary tax accounting to define taxable income for a nonprofit leads to absurdities.[18] Are contributions made to a charity to be included in figuring the organization's gross income? Or should they, perhaps, be treated as ordinary gifts and therefore be excluded for gross income tax purposes?

Should expenditures made by a charity to assist an impoverished individual be deductible as ordinary business expenses? Or are they more correctly treated as nondeductible gifts? There are no satisfactory answers to these and other basic questions, Bittker and Rahdert suggest; the concept of taxable income developed for business organizations simply cannot be carried over to nonprofits in any meaningful way.[19]

But Bittker and Rahdert overstate the difficulties. To begin with, many nonprofits receive little or no income from donations, but rather derive all or nearly all of their income from sales of goods or services that they produce. These organizations—which can conveniently be referred to as "commercial" nonprofits[20]—in fact account for a large portion of the nonprofit sector.[21] For such organizations it would be perfectly easy and natural to carry over the tax accounting that is applied to business firms, taking receipts from sales as the measure of gross income and permitting the usual deductions for expenses incurred in producing the goods or services sold. The resulting net earnings figure could be taxed just as in the case of a business firm. Since nonprofits cannot distribute their net earnings, such a tax would effectively be levied on the sum of (1) earnings saved for expenditure in future years, and (2) net capital investment (i.e., the excess of expenditures on capital equipment over depreciation allowances). Following conventional usage, this sum will occasionally be referred to below simply as "retained earnings."

At best, then, arguments concerning the impossibility of applying ordinary tax accounting to nonprofits apply only to nonprofits that receive substantial income in the form of donations—a class of nonprofits that will be referred to here, for convenience, as "donative" nonprofits[22]—and not to commercial nonprofits.

Yet even for donative nonprofits there is a natural correlate to the concept of taxable income developed for business entities. Consider, for example, a donative organization like the American Red Cross. If an individual makes a contribution to the Red Cross, it is presumably with the intention that the money will be used to provide food, housing, and medical treatment for disaster victims. In other words, the contributor is in effect buying disaster relief. And the Red Cross is, in a sense, in the business of producing and selling that disaster relief.[23] The transaction differs from an ordinary sale of goods or services, in essence, only in that the individual who purchases the goods and services involved is different from the individuals to whom they are delivered.

It follows that we can view the contributions received by the Red Cross and other such donative organizations as sales receipts, and hence—if such organizations were to be subjected to income taxation—as funds that are appropriately includable in gross income. The cost of the services, such as disaster relief, rendered by donative nonprofits would then be deductible, analogously to ordinary business expenses. The result is that donative nonprofits would be taxed annually on the amount, if any, by which their total receipts, from contributions as well as from other sources (such as investment income and amounts received from ordinary sales), exceed their total expenditures on the services to which they are dedicated. As with commercial nonprofits, the tax would therefore effectively be levied on retained earnings.[24]

Will There Be Any Long-Run Tax Liability?

Thus, it seems that without much difficulty we can extend to nonprofits the general principles of tax accounting commonly applied to profit-seeking firms. But will such accounting actually lead to any tax revenue?[25] An argument against taxing the income of nonprofits that one sometimes hears is that, in the long run, nonprofits will necessarily have no net profits, since, by virtue of the nondistribution constraint, they must ultimately spend all of their income on the purposes for which they were formed, and hence their total expenses must ultimately equal their total income.

The strength of this argument depends on several factors, including the detailed accounting conventions employed. In particular, in order for the cumulative net long-run tax liability of a nonprofit to be zero, it must be the case that: (1) all expenditures made by the nonprofit, including distributions upon dissolution, are considered deductible expenses; (2) losses in any year can be carried back to cover gains in any previous year; (3) the nonprofit has relatively free access to borrowed funds, and in particular can, without affecting its ability to borrow for other purposes, borrow funds in any year at least equal to that year's tax liability plus interest due on loans taken out in previous years to cover tax liabilities; and (4) refunds from the Treasury of taxes that were overpaid in previous years are accompanied by payment of interest by the Treasury at a rate equal to the rate that the nonprofit must pay on funds that it borrows. These four conditions, however, do not all hold. At present, losses can be carried back only three years.[26] Further, the Treasury does not pay interest when refunding overpayments from previous years.[27] And, perhaps most importantly, nonprofits do not have unrestricted access to borrowed capital—the consequences of which are explored at length below.[28]

Is the Corporate Tax Just a Tax on Capitalists?

At this point a further objection might be—and sometimes has been[29]—raised. The corporate income tax as applied to business corporations can be viewed as, in effect, a tax on the returns to investors of equity capital, and there is, by definition, no equity capital invested in nonprofit firms. Thus, it might be argued, the net earnings of nonprofits should not be equated, for tax purposes, with the net earnings of business corporations, since only the latter ultimately accrue to the benefit of private investors. In other words, the tax "base" for the corporate income tax simply does not extend to nonprofits.

This argument proves too much, however, for it suggests that *all* nonprofit corporations should be exempt, whereas exemption has in fact always been available only to certain categories of them,[30] and so far even the strongest supporters of the exemption have not suggested that it be extended to all organizations that are legitimately formed as nonprofit corporations.[31] Besides, is it so clear that there is no investor of equity capital in a nonprofit? Can we not view the nonprofit corporation itself as the ultimate owner of its capital, and hence treat *it* as the taxpayer? After all, the income tax even as applied to business corporations has commonly been rationalized on the basis that the corporation itself has taxable capacity apart from its investors—that it is conceptually a separate taxable entity.[32] Or might we not view the patrons of a nonprofit, or perhaps the recipients of its services (if they differ from its patrons), as the benefical owners of its invested capital?

Obviously, simply analogies and metaphors—which are too often the primary analytic tools of lawyers, including tax lawyers—will not yield a satisfying answer as to whether or not we should tax the net earnings of nonprofit organizations. Rather, we must examine and judge the actual consequences of imposing such a tax. That is, we must consider what the world would look like both with and without such a tax, and then decide which world we like better.

COMPENSATION FOR CAPITAL CONSTRAINTS

There is an efficiency rationale for exemption that is more appealing than those discussed above, although it seems never to have been expressly offered before. That rationale is that the exemption serves to compensate for difficulties that nonprofits have in raising capital, and that such a capital subsidy can promote efficiency when employed in those industries in which nonprofit firms serve consumers better than their for-profit counterparts.

Nonprofit organizations lack access to equity capital since, by virtue of the nondistribution constraint, they cannot issue ownership shares that give their holders a simultaneous right to participate in both net earnings and control. Consequently, in raising capital, nonprofits are limited to three sources: debt, donations, and retained earnings. These three sources may, in many cases, prove inadequate to provide a nonprofit with all of the capital that it needs.

Donations are commonly an uncertain source of capital for nonprofits, and an inadequate one as well. Free-rider incentives[33] presumably keep the flow of contributions to donative nonprofits—many of which provide public goods—well below the socially optimal level,[34] and commercial nonprofits, by definition, receive few gifts of any sort. Debt, too, has distinct limits as a source of capital for most nonprofits. Lenders are commonly unwilling to provide anything near 100 percent of the capital needs even of proprietary firms, and are evidently even more conservative in lending to nonprofit firms.[35] One reason for this is that, as debt comes to account for something close to 100 percent of a nonprofit's capital, it becomes increasingly unlikely that the organization's assets will provide adequate security for the debt. Of course, such a lack of security need not rule out debt financing. Debt, like equity, can be used as an instrument for risky investments; one need simply run up the interest rate on loans and bonds as they come to account for a larger fraction of the organization's capital. However, the transaction cost of using debt instruments for capital financing under conditions of substantial risk are high, and presumably prohibitive beyond some point well short of 100 percent debt financing.[36]

As a consequence of these restrictions on external financing, a nonprofit organization's ability to accumulate retained earnings is of substantial importance as a means of capital expansion. The reason for this is twofold. First, accumulated earnings can be used directly to finance capital improvements. Second, the amount of debt financing that a nonprofit can obtain is proportional to some extent to the amount of revenue it can derive from retained earnings, since capital purchased with such earnings provides an extra margin of security for the debt, and since the cash flow from such earnings is evidence to lenders that interest payments on the debt can be covered.[37] To be sure, retained reanings, even when added to the sources of external financing available to nonprofits, are likely to prove an inadequate source of capital where the need for expansion is strong. But at least such earnings have the advantage that they are likely to be proportional to the degree to which demand for the organization's services exceeds its ability to supply them, since excess demand will generally permit the organization to raise its prices (or attract larger donations.)

Therefore, a case can be made against an income tax on nonprofits on the ground that such a tax would (at current corporate rates) cut retained earnings roughly in half, and hence would further cripple a group of organizations that is already capital-constrained. Or, put differently, the exemption can be understood as a subsidy to capital formation.

Of course, the mere fact that nonprofits as a class have difficulty raising adequate amounts of capital does not in itself constitute a justification for providing them with a capital subsidy. Quite the contrary: if the only thing distinguishing nonprofit from for-profit providers of a given service is that the nonprofits have difficulty raising adequate amounts of capital, then a capital subsidy to the nonprofits would simply be wasteful; the industry should be left to the for-profit firms. Indeed, presumably the reason why most sectors of our economy are dominated by for-profit firms is that they constitute, overall, the most efficient means of mobilizing productive resources—including, in particular, capital.

The problem, however, is that often nonprofits are, aside from problems of capital formation, more efficient than their for-profit counterparts in providing those services characterized by contract failure.[38] For such services, the cost of the capital subsidy provided by corporate tax exemption may be more than compensated for by the efficiency gains deriving from the expansion of nonprofit producers that the subsidy encourages.

Thus, the need for capital subsidies provides some justification for exempting nonprofits from corporate income taxation in those industries in which, owing to contract failure, nonprofits have important efficiency advantages over for-profit firms. And this, it appears, is the strongest argument that can be offered for the current policy of exempting many, but not all, nonprofits from taxation.

This argument is not without difficulties. For one thing, as already noted, it is not obvious that the exemption as currently administered is confined to those industries characterized by contract failure. This objection could be met, however, by redefining the contours of the exemption as suggested below.

More importantly, an exemption from income taxation is a crude mechanism for subsidizing capital formation in the nonprofit sector. The extent to which nonprofit firms are capital constrained evidently varies considerably from one industry to another, and, even within industries, from one firm to another. Although direct evidence of the degree of under- or overinvestment among nonprofit firms is largely lacking, there is strong indirect evidence suggesting that nonprofit firms in rapidly growing service industries, such as nursing care, have had their growth noticeably hampered by an inadequate supply of capital.[39] At the same time, there is good reason to believe that in many cases nonprofit firms are substantially overcapitalized; this often seems to be the case today, for example, with nonprofit hospitals.[40] Simply granting or denying income tax exemption will obviously fail to eliminate all such disparity in access to capital among nonprofit firms, or between nonprofit and for-profit firms. The exemption alone can only ameliorate, not eliminate, severe cases of capital constraint, while, in turn, denial of the exemption will in itself be inadequate to insure that a nonprofit does not accumulate capital far in excess of the efficient level of investment.

DYNAMICS OF NONPROFIT GROWTH

In order to get a better grasp of the strengths and weaknesses of the capital formation rationale for the exemption, and to understand the consequences of the exemption in general, it helps to focus on the dynamics of competition in an industry potentially populated with both nonprofit and for-profit firms. The following discussion considers, in general terms, the form that this competition is likely to take, and the way in which tax policy is likely to affect such competition.

For simplicity, let us assume, initially, that the industry in question produces a service that is sold on the market for a price that, following the usual law of demand, is inversely related to the total amount of the service produced and offered for sale by the industry, and that receipts from the sale of this service are the only source of revenue for the producing firms, whether for-profit or nonprofit. Thus, for the moment we shall focus only on commercial nonprofits, and shall defer questions of donative financing. Let us also assume, initially, that the nature and quality of the service do not depend upon whether it is provided by a nonprofit or a for-profit firm.

For-Profit Firms Only

To begin with, suppose that the industry is populated only with for-profit firms. Whether the industry is taxed or not, assuming that there are no substantial economies of scale or other obstacles to effective competition, the forces of competition will tend to lead the industry to expand quickly to the level of production at which all firms (or at least the marginal firms) are just breaking even. This is because additional capital can presumably be obtained readily through the equity market so long as the industry has not yet reached the point at which firms are just breaking even. At this level of production, the price that the service brings on the market will have dropped to the point where each firm is earning just enough from sale of the service to permit it to pay the prevailing market rate of return for all inputs that it employs, including a competitive wage for its workers and a competitive return on invested capital.

If, as is commonly supposed, the corporate income tax, when applied to a for-profit firm, essentially serves as a tax on the return paid to investors of capital, then the effect of imposing such a tax on the industry is to raise the price at which the service must be sold in order for the firm to break even. It follows that the imposition of the corporate tax on this industry will reduce somewhat the amount of the service that is produced and sold.[41]

Nonprofit Firms Only

Now consider, alternatively, what is likely to happen if the service in question is produced only by nonprofit firms.

Capital owned by a nonprofit firm—whether obtained through donations or through retained earnings—is essentially free to the firm, in the sense that the firm need pay no return on that capital, and can turn it to no uses other than production of the services for which the firm was organized.[42] The only capital expenses that a nonprofit must cover, therefore, are (1) interest on borrowed capital and (2) depreciation. To simplify matters, assume for the moment that nonprofit firms do not have the option of borrowing capital. Thus, the only expense facing the nonprofit firms in our hypothetical industry, in connection with a given stock of captial, is the depreciation on that capital.

It follows that a nonprofit firm will be able to break even, while maintaining its current level of production, so long as its income from sale of its services is sufficient to cover the expense of capital depreciation plus wages and other variable costs. If demand for the service is high enough relative to the total amount of the service that the existing firms in the industry can produce, those firms will be able to charge more than enough to cover such expenses, and thus will be able to accumulate net earnings with which to purchase additional capital that can be used to expand production in the future. Indeed, since a nonprofit cannot distribute its net earnings, it has little alternative but to spend its net earnings on additions to its capital stock, and, conversely, firms can add to their capital stock only to the extent that they are able to accumulate such net earnings (again, ignoring for the moment the possibility of using debt).

In the absence of taxes, firms in the industry, therefore, can be expected to expand until total production of the service has reached the point where price has dropped to a level at which each firm has just enough income to cover the costs of depreciation on capital plus noncapital costs such as wages—that is, to the level at which the firms have no net earnings to devote to additions to capital.[43] As long as aggregate demand for the service does not change, this is then the point at which the industry will maintain itself.

The total amount of the service that is produced at this point will, it should be noted, depend somewhat on the preferences of the managers of the nonprofit firms. The reason for this is that the firms will generally be confronted with a tradeoff between present and future production. A nonprofit firm with a given amount of capital can, on the one hand, use the amounts of labor and other variable factors that maximize net earnings, and thus maximize the amount of capital that can be purchased for the purpose of expanding future production. Or, on the other hand, the firm can simply increase the amount of labor and other variable factors that it uses in the current period to the point where the expenses associated with these factors are so large as to consume all potential profits, and thus maximize current production of the service, while providing no opportunity for expansion in the future. Put differently, the "price" that a nonprofit firm pays for the capital it uses for expansion is not the market rate of return, but rather the amount of current production that must be foregone in order to accumulate net earnings.

The point at which the nonprofit firms in the industry stop expanding, therefore, will depend on the extent to which the managers of the firms are prepared to trade off present for future production. A strong relative preference for current production will lead the firms to stop growing at a relatively low level of total industry production (and a high price for the service, which is necessary to cover the high cost of producing with the inefficiently low capital-labor ratio that will characterize such firms), while a strong preference for future production will lead the firms to grow more quickly, and to stop growing only when total industry production is so large, and market price has fallen so low, that a very large amount of present production would have to be foregone in order to obtain the profits necessary to purchase the capital required for even a small amount of future expansion.[44]

Now suppose that a tax is levied on the net income of the nonprofit firms (using the definition of net income offered earlier).[45] What effect will such a tax have on production in our all-nonprofit industry? Note, to begin with, that there will be no tax liability for a nonprofit firm that is not growing, but rather is spending all of its income to cover the costs of capital depreciation and variable costs such as wages. Thus, when the industry has finally reached its equilibrium level of development, in which all firms in the industry are just breaking even, there will be no tax revenues forthcoming from the industry. In contrast, for-profit firms must pay taxes even when they have reached the equilibrium point at which they no longer have an incentive to expand. Thus, income taxes are not a cost to nonprofit firms in equilibrium, and hence have no direct effects on the level of production that the nonprofit firms will ultimately reach, in contrast to the case with for-profit firms. In this respect an income tax levied on a nonprofit differs from a property tax or a sales tax, both of which yield positive tax liabilities for the firm even when the firm is not growing and is just bringing in enough total revenue to cover its costs of production (including taxes).

On the other hand, subjecting nonprofit firms to income taxation *will* have an *indirect* effect on the behavior of the firms. Since such a tax is effectively a tax on retained earnings, it will reduce the rate at which a nonprofit firm can expand. For example, at a rate of fifty percent, an income tax would tax away half of a nonprofit's retained earnings, and consequently reduce by half the amount of capital that a nonprofit could purchase with a given amount of retained earnings. Thus, an all-non-profit industry would expand toward its equilibrium level of production more slowly than it would without the tax. Moreover, the tax has the effect of worsening the tradeoff between present and future production that confronts a nonprofit firm. With a fifty percent tax rate, twice as much present production must be sacrificed for a given increase in future production as would be the case without the tax. The result is that the managers of nonprofit firms will find it less attractive to trade off present for future production at any given level of production, and will put a stop to their firm's expansion at a lower level of total industry production than they would otherwise. Thus, the tax can be expected to reduce not only the rate at which nonprofit firms grow toward their equilibrium level of production, but also the aggregate amount of the service that is produced at equilibrium.[46]

Both Nonprofit and For-Profit Firms

Consider, finally, an industry in which, to begin with, there are only for-profit firms, operating, as a consequence of competition, at the breakeven (equilibrium) point as described above. Suppose, then, that one or more nonprofit firms enter the industry, each with some initial supply of capital. And let us assume, for the time being, that these nonprofit firms can produce the service in question just as efficiently as the for-profit firms in the industry—that is, they can produce a unit of the service with the same amounts of input (capital, labor, etc.) as their for-profit counterparts. Finally, let us assume also, for the moment, that there are no income taxes for either for-profit or nonprofit firms.

At the prevailing market price at which the for-profit firms are just breaking even, the nonprofit firms will be able to produce net earnings, since, unlike the for-profit firms, they need pay no return on the capital that they are employing. What the nonprofit firms proceed to do at this point will depend on the preferences of the firms' managers.

If, on the one hand, the managers of the nonprofit firms have a reasonably strong preference for future expansion over present production, the nonprofit firms will proceed to accumulate net earnings and to grow. The resulting increase in total industry production will tend to drive down the market price for the service, which in turn will cause for-profit firms to start losing money and to begin leaving the industry. By this process the nonprofit firms will continue to supplant for-profit firms until there are only nonprofit firms producing the service. The nonprofit firms will continue to have net earnings, and to expand, however, even beyond the point at which all for-profit firms have been driven from the industry. Such expansion will stop only when the nonprofit firms have increased total industry production to an all-nonprofit equilibrium, as described above, with greater total production and lower market price than that which prevailed before the nonprofit firms took over the industry.

If, on the other hand, the managers of the nonprofit firms have a strong preference for producing as much of the service as possible in the present, without much concern for foregone opportunities for future growth, then they may burn up all of their potential profits by hiring more labor and other variable factors with which to expand current production. The nonprofits will not grow at all, but rather will simply coexist with the for-profit firms at the market price and total level of industry production that would prevail if there were only for-profit firms in the industry. Indeed, if the managers of the for-profit firms were to push their preference for present as opposed to future production to extremes, they might even fail to accumulate sufficient funds to cover depreciation on their existing capital stock, and hence the nonprofit firms would actually decline and would eventually disappear entirely, leaving the industry to the for-profit firms alone.

If the for-profit firms in the industry are subject to income taxation, then it will be more likely that the nonprofit firms will ultimately take over the industry. The reason for this is simply that, as we have seen, imposing a tax on the for-profit firms increases the price at which they must sell their services, and at this higher price the nonprofit firms will face large potential profits and, thus, more favorable opportunities for expansion.

If an income tax is then extended to the nonprofit firms in the industry, it will reduce the likelihood that the nonprofits will ultimately drive out the for-profit firms. As indicated by our earlier analysis, however, the consequences of the tax in this respect will be only indirect. When the firms in the industry, both nonprofit and for-profit, have stopped growing—and, hence, the industry is in a state of equilibrium—the nonprofit firms will be paying no income taxes, whether they have succeeded in taking over the whole industry or are simply coexisting with the for-profit firms. Because the tax does, however, make the tradeoff between present and future production for the nonprofit firms less attractive than in the absence of the tax, it will reduce the incentive for the nonprofit firms to expand production at any given prevailing market price and, hence, will reduce the likelihood that the industry will be taken over by the nonprofits. Moreover, the tax will slow the rate at which the nonprofits grow and, hence, will extend the time it takes for the nonprofit firms to attain their equilibrium level of development, including takeover of the industry, if that is the equilibrium result.

We see, then, that exemption of nonprofit firms from corporate income taxation is not really a subsidy in the usual sense. In equilibrium, nonprofit firms will pay no income taxes whether they are included in the tax base or not. In this respect, as already noted, exemption from the corporate income tax does not give nonprofit firms an advantage over their for-profit counterparts that is of the same character as that which results when nonprofit firms are exempted from a property tax or a sales tax to which for-profit firms are subjected. On the other hand, exemption from income taxation does permit nonprofit firms to grow faster than they could if they were taxed, and it does give them an incentive to grow, and ultimately perhaps to take markets away from for-profit firms, in a broader range of conditions than would be the case without the exemption.[47]

RELAXING THE ASSUMPTIONS

Let us now relax some of the assumptions on which the discussion so far has been premised, in order to understand the consequences of tax exemption in a broader and more realistic range of circumstances.

Growing Demand

We have been assuming so far that demand in the industry is static. If, however, demand for the service is steadily increasing, then the rate at which nonprofits are able to take over an industry initially populated by for-profit firms will be reduced. In fact, if demand for the service increases faster than the rate at which the nonprofits are able to grow, then the nonprofits will not be able to take over the industry at all, and there will continue to be a mix of for-profit and nonprofit firms in the industry so long as demand continues to expand at such a rate. Likewise, if an industry is initially populated only with nonprofit firms, and then the demand for the industry's service begins to grow rapidly, for-profit firms may be able to enter the industry alongside the nonprofit firms, since only the for-profit firms will face no constraint on the amount of capital they can obtain, at market rates of return, for purposes of expansion. The varying percentages over time of nonprofit and for-profit firms in the hospital industry, for example, seem to be explainable at least in part by such variations in the rate of growth in demand.[48]

It follows that tax exemption for nonprofits is likely to have its most pronounced effects in an industry in which demand is expanding. The exemption will have a strong influence on the length of time required for nonprofits to catch up with demand growth, and, hence, on the balance between nonprofit and for-profit producers at any given moment.

Relative Efficiency of Nonprofit Firms

We have also been assuming that both nonprofit and for-profit firms can produce the service in question with the same efficiency. Typically, however, the differences in the form of organization will result in some disparity in efficiency.

In most industries nonprofit firms are probably less efficient than their for-profit counterparts, owing to the decreased incentives for cost minimization that result from the absence of the profit motive,[49] and to the absence of special circumstances—in particular, contract failure—that give nonprofits a countervailing efficiency advantage. If this disparity in efficiency is so large that, at the breakeven price for for-profit firms, nonprofit firms cannot even cover their noncapital costs, then nonprofit firms will not be able to survive in competition with for-profit firms. At more modest levels of inefficiency, however, nonprofits may be able not only to survive in competition with for-profit firms, but also to grow and perhaps even eventually take over the industry, since nonprofits are spared the necessity of paying a competitive rate of return on the capital they employ, and this may compensate for their inefficiency. Whether or not the for-profit firms are subject to income taxation will have an effect here: The higher the rate of tax levied on the for-profit firms, the less efficient the nonprofit firms need be in order to compete with them effectively.

The ability of relatively inefficient nonprofits to survive in competition with for-profit firms will not, however, depend directly on whether or not the nonprofits are subject to income taxation. Rather, as we have seen, nonprofit firms will pay no income taxes in equilibrium and, hence, the exemption will not affect their ability to cover their costs at any given price level for the service that they sell. The exemption will only affect the rate at which nonprofits can grow, and the incentive to grow that faces the firms' managers.

Alternatively, it may be that owing to problems of contract failure, in producing the service in question, nonprofit firms are *more* efficient than their for-profit counterparts.[50] In this case the nonprofit firms in the industry will clearly be able to survive and grow at the price that represents the breakeven point for the for-profit firms.[51] Only if the managers of the nonprofit firms show a strong preference for present production over future expansion, or if demand for the service is growing faster than the nonprofit firms can accumulate earnings, will nonprofit firms fail ultimately to supplant all the for-profit firms in the industry. This will be true, moreover, whether or not the for-profit or the nonprofit firms in the industry are subject to income taxation, though if the for-profit firms are taxed, and if the nonprofit firms are exempt, nonprofit firms will be able to expand at a greater rate, and will have more incentive to expand, than they would otherwise.

Availability of Debt

The preceding discussion has been based on the assumption that nonprofit firms do not have access to debt, but rather must obtain all of their new capital through retained earnings. This is, of course, unrealistic. Nevertheless, the availability of debt capital only partially alters the basic conclusions reached above.

If debt capital were available to nonprofit firms without restriction, then nonprofits would be able to expand rapidly to the point where price for the service has fallen to the level at which it just covers variable costs plus the interest cost of debt capital—which would be roughly the efficient level of operation. Thus, the availability of tax exemption would not affect the speed with which nonprofits could expand to the efficient level of production. Nonprofit firms would, however, still be able to expand beyond this point, using internally generated capital, and such expansion would be governed by the same considerations discussed above.

Of course, it is equally unrealistic to think that nonprofits have unlimited access to debt capital. Rather, nonprofits are, as noted earlier,[52] likely to be able to secure debt financing for a part, but by no means all, of their capital needs. In general, then, we can say that, to the extent that nonprofits have access to debt capital, the importance of tax exemption in facilitating the expansion of nonprofits to their efficient level of production will be reduced.

Donative Nonprofits

For purposes of simplicity and clarity, we have considered here only strictly commercial nonprofits. All that has been said, however, applies with equal force to donative nonprofits. We need simply view the donations that the firms receive as the price that the public is prepared to pay for the services that the firms produce.

IMPLICATIONS FOR TAX POLICY

We are now in a position to formulate the appropriate goals for tax policy, and to consider whether exempting some or all nonprofits from corporate income taxation will bring us closer to those goals.

Policy Objectives

From the perspective of economic efficiency, it is desirable to have non-profit rather than for-profit firms in an industry if and only if the nonprofit firms are more efficient than for-profit firms in producing the service in question. Since the primary efficiency advantage that nonprofit firms have over for-profit firms appears to be in responding to contract failure, this means that, in general, it is desirable to have nonprofit firms develop where contract failure is a serious problem (and one that cannot be dealt with by other means[53]), and not elsewhere.

Assuming that circumstances are such that nonprofit firms are the most efficient producers of the service, the service should generally be produced in that quantity at which the price that it brings just covers the marginal costs of production, such as the costs of the capital, labor, and other factors used in producing the service. Capital, in particular, should be employed in the industry just up to the point at which its marginal productivity equals the costs of diverting the capital from other industries. If there were no tax imposed on the returns to capital in other industries, this would mean simply that capital should be used in an industry populated with nonprofits just to the point where its marginal productivity equals the rate of return that capital is bringing in for-profit industries. With a tax on the return to capital in other industries—in the form of the corporate income tax and the personal income tax—the appropriate standard becomes more ambiguous. A rough approximation is that capital in the nonprofit industry should be used up to the point at which its productivity equals the before-tax rate of return being earned on capital in other industries.[54]

Choosing an Appropriate Policy

It follows that, if tax exemption for nonprofits is to be administered in accordance with the dictates of economic efficiency, two conditions should be satisfied before exemption is granted to the nonprofit firms in a given industry: (1) nonprofit firms must be more efficient producers of the service than are for-profit firms; and (2) the nonprofit firms in the industry must not have expanded to the point at which the productivity of the capital they employ has fallen below the before-tax rate of return being earned on capital in other industries.

As a practical matter, it usually will not be feasible to condition tax exemption for nonprofits on a judgment by the Treasury Department as to whether capital investment among nonprofit firms in particular industries has exceeded the efficient level. Such a criterion would be extremely difficult to administer.[55] Consequently, the best that can be done in this area is probably to focus primarily on the first of the two criteria offered here,[56] and require as a condition of exemption simply that there be convincing evidence that, in the industry in question, nonprofit firms are, owing to contract failure,[57] more efficient than their for-profit counterparts.[58]

Of course, this is not the way that tax policy in this area is, or ever has been, explicitly formulated. Nevertheless, the results achieved with current policy represent at least a crude approximation to those that would be reached following this approach. Thus, the exemption is frequently denied, as it should be, to commercial nonprofits that produce, distribute, or retail standard agricultural and industrial goods, and to those that offer simple services.[59] In such industries it seems extremely unlikely that nonprofit firms are more efficient than for-profit firms and, hence, *any* level of nonprofit development would be inefficient. There would obviously be little point, for example, in granting the exemption to a nonprofit hardware store.

On the other hand, the exemption is quite solidly entrenched for most types of donative nonprofits.[60] This, too, is consistent with the efficiency criterion just suggested. Donative nonprofits, almost by definition, typically provide services that are delivered to third parties or are public goods, and that as a consequence are attended by severe contract failure.[61] Indeed, the wisest course is probably just to assume, absent evidence to the contrary, that all nonprofits that receive a substantial fraction[62] of their income in the form of donations are operating in an environment of contract failure and, therefore, merit the exemption on efficiency grounds. Such a policy—which is essentially what we have now—may well grant the exemption to some organizations for which it is unjustified. But a more refined approach to donative nonprofits would probably not be worth the increase in ambiguity and administrative complexity it would entail.[63]

Between these two extremes—donative nonprofits on the one hand, and commercial nonprofits that provide simple standardized services on the other—we have the troublesome category of commercial nonprofits that provide complex personal services such as education, hospital care, nursing care, and day care. For which, if any, of these services are the fiduciary qualities of the nonprofit form so effective and necessary that tax exemption can be justified on efficiency grounds? It is difficult to offer an authoritative answer to this question, since at present there exist little solid data concerning the relative performance of nonprofit and for-profit firms in providing such services.

For most of these services—including, in particular, nursing care, day care, and education (including vocational education)—continuation of the current policy favoring exemption seems justifiable, though perhaps not compelling. There is, to be sure, debate as to whether in fact the commercial nonprofit firms in these industries, on average, serve consumers better in any important respect than do their for-profit counterparts.[64] Yet in each of these areas nonprofit firms represent a significant fraction of the industry, and this has evidently occurred, in large part, because a substantial subset of consumers feels more comfortable patronizing a nonprofit. Until we have better data suggesting that these consumers are mistaken, there is something to be said for continuing the exemption and, thus, helping to insure that such consumers continue to have the option of patronizing a nonprofit.

On the other hand, it is not at all clear that there is justification for the relatively recent decision to exempt nonprofit hospitals from taxation even if they provide no research, teaching, or subsidized care for indigents; that is, even if they are operated as strictly commercial nonprofits. Problems of contract failure do not seem important in the case of most hospital services. The continued predominance of the nonprofit form in this industry seems, instead, to be attributable to historical and financial factors largely unrelated to the relative efficiency of for-profit and nonprofit institutions.[65] Moreover, there is evidence that, in general, the hospital industry is already overcapitalized.[66] Thus, the hospital industry arguably fails both the criteria suggested above for administering the exemption. The current policy of exempting virtually all nonprofit hospitals may simply further encourage what already appears to be excessive capital investment in this sector.

The Significance of For-Profit Competitors

The preceding analysis throws some light on an issue that has long been a source of confusion in the administration of the exemption for nonprofits: the relevance of the fact that a nonprofit competes with for-profit firms providing similar services. Such competition is frequently cited as a justification for denying exemption. For example, in sustaining the recent refusal of the IRS to grant an exemption to a nonprofit consulting firm, the Tax Court relied on the fact that the firm's business was "of the sort which is ordinarily carried on by commercial ventures organized for profit," and remarked that the firm was "in competition with commercial businesses."[67] "Competition with commercial firms," said the Court, "is strong evidence of the predominance of non-exempt commercial purposes."[68] Yet, as at least one court has noted,[69] the mere fact that a firm competes with for-profit suppliers of the same service cannot be sufficient to justify denial of exemption, since many types of organizations that have long benefited from the exemption, including hospitals, schools, nursing homes, and daycare centers, regularly engage in such competition.[70]

From the discussion above of the dynamics of competition between nonprofit and for-profit firms, it should be clear that the mere presence or absence of for-profit competitors should not be determinative in awarding exemption to a nonprofit. As we have seen, it is quite possible that nonprofit firms, even though less efficient than their for-profit counterparts, could completely take over an industry.[71] Conversely, in industries in which demand is expanding rapidly one might expect to see a large proportion of for-profit firms even if they are less efficient than nonprofits, simply because the nonprofits cannot obtain the capital necessary for rapid expansion. It follows that, in determining whether nonprofit firms in a given industry should have the benefit of the exemption, there is no alternative to inquiring directly into the role that the nonprofit firms play in that industry. If it seems likely that the nonprofit form represents a reasonable response to problems of market failure in that industry, then exemption is warranted under the relative-efficiency test suggested above. If, alternatively, the nonprofit firms seem to serve no function that cannot be served as well or better by proprietary firms, then the case for exemption fails.

In short, the right question to ask in deciding whether to grant an exemption is whether the same service could be provided as well by for-profit firms. The presence of for-profit competitors may well provide evidence in such an inquiry. It is wrong, on the other hand, simply to inquire whether the nonprofit firms in question are in competition with for-profit firms, since in the presence of market failure competition alone cannot be relied upon to sort out the efficient from the inefficient firms.

Redistribution and the Provision of Public Goods

The analysis so far has focused on the existence of contract failure as a prerequisite to granting income tax exemption to nonprofit firms in any given industry. We must now ask whether there are other, independent justifications for granting the exemption. In particular, if a nonprofit organization provides services that redistribute wealth in a socially desirable manner (as by aiding the poor), or that are public goods in some other important respect, does this in itself justify exemption, quite apart from questions of contract failure?

Note, to begin with, that most nonprofits that provide aid to the poor or other public goods are donative nonprofits and, thus, presumably operate under circumstances of substantial contract failure.[72] The exemption can, therefore, be justified for such organizations on that basis alone.[73]

Suppose, however, there were a commercial nonprofit that sold to the poor goods or services, such as food or housing, that were not characterized by contract failure. Would the exemption be justified for such an organization if society felt that such services should be subsidized for the poor? Perhaps, but the case is not a strong one, for in these circumstances there would be no reason to confine the subsidy to nonprofit firms. Indeed, in the absence of contract failure it might be inefficient to provide a selective subsidy to nonprofit providers, since they might well be less efficient than their for-profit competitors.[74]

Similar logic applies to other privately sold services that, for some reason (such as the presence of public-good attributes), are likely to be undersupplied unless subsidized. Vaccinations and, perhaps, vocational education are examples of such services.[75] Absent contract failure, there seems no reason to have a subsidy targeted particularly at nonprofit producers— much less a subsidy that is designed to be proportional to retained earnings.

How Strong a Rationale?

It should be emphasized that, even if the exemption were administered more in accordance with the policy guidelines suggested above, it would remain an extremely crude mechanism for dealing with problems of capital formation in the nonprofit sector.[76] Thus, the strength of the capital subsidy rationale for the exemption should not be overstated. All that is being argued here is that (1) this rationale is the *best* justification that can be given for the exemption, and (2) it is an *adequate* rationale for the exemption in that, so long as the categories of organizations that qualify for the exemption are intelligently delineated, on the whole we are probably better off with the exemption than without it.

CONCLUSION

It has been suggested here that the exemption of nonprofit organizations from federal income taxation should not be viewed simplistically as a subsidy for good works or as a natural consequence of the tax base to which the corporate income tax is applied. Rather, the exemption should be viewed in terms of its consequences for capital formation in the nonprofit sector. Seen in this light, the justification for the exemption is less clear-cut than has commonly been supposed, though it is still possible to rationalize current policy in this area, at least in its broad outlines.

NOTES

1. See Bittker and Rahdert, The exemption of nonprofit organizations from federal income taxation, 85 *Yale L.J.* 299, 301 (1976).
2. The best data available, which are not very good, suggest that the nonprofit sector today accounts for roughly 3 percent of GNP, compared to just over 1 percent fifty years ago. Hansmann, The role of nonprofit enterprise, 89 *Yale L.J.* 835, 835 n.1 (1980). Reprinted in part as Chapter 3 in this volume. Page numbers here and in subsequent footnotes refer to original *Yale L.J.* article.
3. This is true, in particular, of "commercial" nonprofits, such as nursing homes, day-care centers, hospitals, and publications. See Hansmann, *supra* note 2, at 862–68.
4. Bittker and Rahdert, *supra* note 1. See also Bittker, Churches, taxes and the constitution, 78 *Yale L.J.* 1285 (1969), which presents a substantially similar analysis.
5. E.g., Stone, Federal Tax Support of Charities and Other Exempt Organizations: The Need for a National Policy, 1968 *U. So. Cal. Tax Inst.* 27.
6. A few substantial nonprofits, including several of the larger grant-giving private foundations, have been established as charitable trusts rather than as nonprofit corporations. If such organizations were to be denied exemption, there would be a question of the tax rate to be applied. Should they be taxed in the same way as private trusts, or rather as if they were corporations? In any event, the basic issues are the same as for the incorporated nonprofits that are the focus of the following discussion.
7. I.R.C. §511 (tax on "unrelated business income"); I.R.C. §502 (tax on income from "feeder" organizations).
8. I.R.C., §170.
9. Editor's note: The portion of the original article which discusses this issue has been omitted.
10. *See, e.g.*, C. McClure, *Must Corporate Income Be Taxed Twice?* (1979); Stiglitz, Taxation, corporate financial policy, and the cost of capital, 2 *J. Pub. Econ.* 1 (1973).
11. P. 381 *infra*.
12. See Hansmann, *supra* note 2, 838. For an extensive discussion of the application of

the nondistribution constraint under current law, see Hansmann, Reforming nonprofit corporation law, 129 *U. Pa. L. Rev.* 497 (1981).

13. I.R.C. § 501(c) extends exemption to, for example, nonprofit organizations "organized and operated exclusively for religious, charitable, scientific, testing for public safety, literary, or educational purposes . . ." (§ 501(c)(3)); "[c]ivic leagues or organizations . . . operated exclusively for the promotion of social welfare . . ." (§ 501(c)(4)); "[l]abor, agricultural, or horticultural organizations . . ." (§ 501(c)(5)); "[b]usiness leagues, chambers of commerce, real-estate boards, boards of trade, or professional football leagues . . ." (§ 501(c)(6)); "[c]lubs organized for recreation [or] pleasure . . ." (§ 501(c)(7)); "[f]raternal beneficiary societies, orders, or associations . . ." (§ 501(c)(8)); "[c]emetery companies . . ." (§ 501(c)(13)) "[a] post or organization of war veterans . . ." (§ 501(c)(19)).

14. I.R.C. § 11 imposes a tax on the taxable income of "every corporation," without restriction to business corporations.

15. Automobile service clubs, such as the American Automobile Association and its local affiliates, are one of the rare classes of nonprofits that have clearly been ruled not to qualify for exemption on the ground that their activities do not fall within the scope of I.R.C. § 501(c). *See* Chattanooga Auto Club v. Commissioner, 182 F.2d 551 (6th Cir. 1950); G.C.M. 23688, 1943 C.B. 283, *as modified by* Rev. Rul. 69-635, 1969-2 C.B. 126.

16. One example of such expansive reinterpretation of the exemption to accommodate new forms of nonprofit activity is provided by the nursing home industry. The Internal Revenue Service has chosen to interpret the exemption to cover virtually all nonprofit nursing homes in spite of their nonphilanthropic character, on the ground that they are "charitable" organizations and consequently are covered by the language of I.R.C. § 501(c)(3). *See* Rev. Rul. 72-124, 1972-1 C.B. 145. The policy underlying this broad reading of the term "charitable" has never been enunciated.

Nonprofit hospitals provide a similar example. Until recently, a nonprofit hospital qualified for tax exemption—as a "charitable" institution under I.R.C. § 501(c)(3)—only if it provided a meaningful amount of free or below-cost care to the poor. Technological and financial changes in recent decades, however, have changed the character of nonprofit hospitals to the point where the typical nonprofit hospital provides no substantial amount of subsidized care, but rather offers its services only to those who can demonstrate the ability to pay for them. *See* Hansmann, *supra* note 2, 866–68. Rather than continuing to apply its long-standing criterion for the exemption, and thus deny the exemption to most hospitals, the Service chose to reinterpret the term "charitable" so that subsidized care would no longer be required. Rev. Rul. 69-545, 1969-2 C.B. 117. A coherent rationale for this redefinition of the exemption was never expressed by the Service. This imaginative broadening of the statutory category of "charitable" organizations was challenged, but was sustained by the Court of Appeal, in an opinion which sheds no light of its own on the policy issues involved. Eastern Ky. Welfare Rights Organization v. Simon, 506 F.2d 1278, 1288–89 (D.C. Cir. 1974), *rev'd on other grounds,* 426 U.S. 26 (1976). The performing arts are yet another case in point. The performing arts are not covered clearly—or, one might reasonably conclude, even remotely—by any of the various purposes set forth in I.R.C. § 501(c). Nevertheless, rather than deny exemption to such a large and growing class of nonprofits, the Service chose to engage in another act of imaginative reinterpretation, ruling that the performing arts come within the category of "educational" institutions covered by § 501(c)(3). *See* Tres. Reg. § 1.501(c)(3)-1(d)(3)(ii) (example (4) (1959)) (symphony orchestras "and other similar organizations"); Rev. Rul. 64-175, 1964-1 C.B. 185 (repertory theater).

17. As the examples in the preceding footnote suggest, it appears that the exemption has been kept largely coextensive with the scope of the nonprofit sector primarily through the continual redefinition of the exemption to accommodate it to changes in the activities undertaken by nonprofits, and not because nonprofits tend to develop or survive only in industries in which the exemption has already been clearly established. *See* Hansmann, *supra* note 2, 882.

18. Bittker and Rahdert, *supra* note 1, 307–14.

19. Rather surprisingly, the Internal Revenue Service seems never to have addressed, in

general terms, the problem of defining taxable income for a nonexempt nonprofit. One reason for this is apparently that, given the broad view that the Service has taken of the exemption, see p. 369 supra, it has never been forced to give the issue much consideration. Conversely, one suspects that the Service has taken a broad view of the exemption in part, at least, to avoid having to confront the problem of defining taxable income for nonprofits.

20. The terminology derives from the classification introduced in Hansmann, supra note 2, 840–41.

21. In 1976, only 15 percent of the total revenues of nonprofit organizations came from contributions, gifts, and grants; 70 percent came from sales and receipts, and 15 percent came from dues and assessments. Weisbrod, Economics of institutional choice, in The Interaction of the Public, Private, and Non-Profit Sectors (M. White, ed., 1981).

22. See note 20 supra.

23. See Hansmann, supra note 2, 846–48, 872–73.

24. After exploring at length the absurdities of other, less natural definitions of taxable income for donative nonprofits, Bittker and Rahdert, supra note 1, briefly note the possibility of adopting the definition suggested here and summarily dismiss it, saying only that "[s]ince these accumulations and capital outlays are irrevocably dedicated to the institution's nonprofit objectives . . . we do not regard this alternative mode of computing a nonprofit organization's income as very appealing; nor can we see that it has any economic or social advantages over a regime of complete exemption." Id., 312.

Rather surprisingly, Bittker and Rahdert proceed to argue elsewhere in their article that business leagues—which often take the form of donative nonprofits—should be taxed, and suggest that "[t]here would be no great difficulty in applying familiar principles of income computation to their activities. . . ." Id., 357.

25. There appear to be no available estimates of the additional tax revenues that might be collected from nonprofit organizations if the income tax exemption for nonprofits were eliminated. In particular, such a figure has not been included in the "tax expenditure" budgets that have been calculated by the federal government, see Staff of Joint Comm. on Taxation, Estimates of Federal Tax Expenditures for Fiscal Years 1980–1985 (1980), perhaps because of confusion as to (1) whether in fact the exemption amounts to a subsidy, and (2) the related issue of how a nonprofit's tax liability would be computed in the absence of the exemption.

26. I.R.C. § 172(b)(1)(A).

27. Id. § 6611(f)(1).

28. See pp. 372–74 infra.

29. See Bittker and Rahdert, supra note 1, 345.

30. Moreover, we now tax the unrelated business income even of exempt nonprofits, see p. 368 supra—though Bittker and Rahdert, supra note 1, 316–26, are consistent in suggesting a reversal of this policy.

31. Including Bittker and Rahdert. See, e.g., note 24 supra.

32. See C. McClure, supra note 10, 28–38.

33. That is, incentives to refrain from contributing oneself, and simply enjoy without cost the services provided by the donations of others.

34. The charitable deduction induces a substantially more generous flow of contributions to many donative nonprofits than would otherwise be forthcoming. See Feldstein, The income tax and charitable contributions (pts. 1 & 2), 28 Nat'l Tax J. 81, 209 (1975). Even with this incentive, however, the private return to a donation in support of a public good is probably still well below the effective cost of the contribution to the donor.

Of course, some donative nonprofits, far from being underfunded, receive contributions in excess of the amounts they can use constructively. See note 63 infra.

35. See P. Ginsburg, Capital in Non-Profit Hospitals, 26–28, 180–84 (December 1970) (unpublished doctoral dissertation available in Harvard University Library).

36. If a nonprofit's debt is so large that nearly all of its expected income beyond noncapital expenses must be devoted to interest payments, and if the organization's gross income in any given period is uncertain, there is a high probability that in any given period the organization will be unable to meet its interest obligations. When such a default occurs, the lender

must decide whether to foreclose or refinance. Foreclosure is a costly procedure, whether or not the organization's assets are sufficient to cover the debt. Even if refinancing is regularly undertaken in the face of such defaults, the loans must be rewritten and the terms of the refinancing negotiated, which could be extremely awkward and costly. Indeed, the process would be so cumbersome that it would probably be impossible to undertake on a regular basis if the debt instruments involved were bonds rather than bank loans. And even with bank loans there would soon come a point, as the risk of technical default rose, at which the expected transaction costs of continual refinancing would represent an unacceptable portion of the expected return on the loans involved.

Note, too, the awkwardness of the control relationships involved with such high-risk debt financing. The lender will naturally have an ongoing interest in the conduct of the organization's affairs. Yet the only way the lender can exercise some degree of control over the organization, in order to protect that interest, is to negotiate with the organization's management under the threat of withholding further credit or foreclosing in case of technical default. This is likely to be an unsatisfactory method of governing the organization's affairs from the point of view of both the lender and the borrowing organization.

Equity financing via joint stock investments has developed precisely to provide a flexible instrument for capital investment in situations involving risk. To try to use debt instruments to create the same flexibility, and to give the lender the control he needs to ensure that the borrower does not abuse that flexibility, will commonly be so cumbersome that the costs outweigh the benefits. Indeed, if one were to succeed in structuring debt investments in this way, they might well have so many of the properties of ownership shares that the borrowing organization could no longer be deemed to be nonprofit.

37. See Ginsburg, *supra* note 35, 184.

38. The notation of contract failure is developed and discussed extensively in Hansmann, *supra* note 2. There may be circumstances other than contract failure in which nonprofit firms have important efficiency advantages over for-profit firms. Such circumstances have yet to be clearly identified, however.

Some membership organizations, such as country clubs, seem to be formed on a nonprofit rather than a for-profit basis not in response to contract failure, but rather as a means of avoiding simple monopolistic exploitation. See Hansmann, *supra* note 2, 892–94. In these cases, however, the nonprofit form does not seem to be the only, or even the best, way of coping with the problems of monopoly; rather, the cooperative form, which does not suffer from problems of capital formation to quite the same degree as does the nonprofit form, seems adequate, and its broader use in such circumstances could easily be facilitated without any form of special tax treatment. See *id.;* Hansmann, *supra* note 12, 587–99. Moreover, whether organized as nonprofits, cooperatives, or whatever, membership organizations such as country clubs are presumably well situated to raise adequate amounts of capital through their members.

39. Studies of several service industries populated by both nonprofit and for-profit firms suggest that the ratio of nonprofits to for-profit firms varies inversely with the rate of growth in demand. Thus, the percentage of private nursing homes that are nonprofit has been shown to be (as of 1975) significantly lower in those states that have experienced rapid increases in their elderly population. H. Hansmann, The Importance of Property Tax Exemption as an Incentive for Organizing Services on a Nonprofit Basis (unpublished, October 1981) (on file with *Yale Law Journal*). Similarly, the change in the ratio of for-profit to nonprofit hospitals during the rapid expansion of the hospital industry in the 1960s for different states showed a significant positive correlation with the rate of growth in state population. Steinwald and Neuhauser, The role of the proprietary hospital, 35 *Law & Contemp. Prob.* 817, 828 (1970). Differences in access to capital seem to offer the most natural explanation for the difference in growth rates between nonprofit and for-profit firms in these cases. See *id.*, 828. A lack of strong incentives for managers and entrepreneurs in the nonprofit sector to pursue rapid growth may also play a role here, however. See Hansmann, *supra* note 2, 878–79.

40. *See* notes 63 and 66 *infra*.

41. The effects of the corporate income tax, viewing it as an excise on corporate capital,

are explored in Harberger, The incidence of the corporation income tax, 70 *Journal of Political Economy* 215 (1962).

42. We shall ignore here, and throughout, the possibility that a nonprofit might choose to, and be permitted to, invest in unrelated businesses. Allowing for such investment behavior would complicate the analysis considerably without adding importantly to the basic points being made in this Chapter.

43. There is another option open to nonprofit firms facing a high-market price: they can sell their service, not at the market price, but rather at a lower price that is at or below the level that just covers variable costs plus depreciation, and hence accumulate no earnings with which to acquire additional capital for purposes of expansion. (Indeed, if the price thus chosen is below that which is required to cover depreciation on the existing capital, the firms will actually shrink over time.) Since, at such a price, there will be excess demand for the service, firms electing this approach will need to ration their services. This alternative will not be explored here, in part because, in a sense, it does not really add anything new to the problem. We can simply view the service provided by nonprofits that behave this way not as, say, nursing care, but rather as nursing care plus a subsidy of x dollars, the cost of which is x dollars more than the cost of providing nursing care alone; the analysis offered in the text then applies without modification.

44. Owners and managers of for-profit firms, in contrast, are faced with the tradeoff of present for future *profits,* and since, unlike nonprofits, they have relatively free access to the capital markets, they have an incentive to press investment within the firm just to the point at which that tradeoff—which is the internal rate of return on the firm's investments—equals the rate of return (interest rate) on capital in the market. Thus, the capital market constraints the choice of present versus future production in a for-profit firm more strongly than it does in a nonprofit firm.

45. See pp. 369–71 *infra.*

46. These effects will be diminished if depreciation allowances exceed actual decline in value for capital investments. Even if 100 percent of the cost of a capital asset could be deducted in the year of its purchase, however, the consequences of taxing nonprofits described here would continue to some extent if nonprofit firms found it necessary—as presumably they often still would—to accumulate cash reserves over several years in order to finance substantial capital expenditures, for those cash accumulations would still be taxable, and the offsetting deduction for the purchase of the asset could not be taken until the asset was actually purchased.

47. This discussion, it should be noted, ignores questions of risk. The corporate income tax, if extended to nonprofits, might have the effect of making the government a partner in bearing the risks of the enterprise, and consequently could lead nonprofits to undertake more risky ventures than they otherwise would. *See* Stiglitz, The Effects of Income, Wealth, and Capital Gains Taxation on Risk-Taking, 83 *Q.J. Econ.* 263 (1969). If, in the absence of the tax, nonprofits tend to be excessively risk averse, which may in fact be the case owing to the inability of nonprofits to employ equity financing, then imposition of the corporation tax on nonprofits could lead to an improvement in efficiency as far as risk-taking is concerned. Any welfare effects of this sort, however, seem likely to be swamped by the effects that are the focus of the discussion in the text.

48. See Steinwald and Neuhauser, *supra* note 39, 828.

49. Although the separation of ownership and control in large business corporations may create some opportunity for managerial inefficiency, the market for corporate control presumably places some bounds on the extent to which such inefficiency can go. *See* Manne, Mergers and the market for corporate control, 73 *J. Pol. Econ.* 110 (1965). The management of a nonprofit corporation, in contrast, is commonly self-appointing both in law and in fact, and thus is not only beyond the reach of the market for corporate control, but is, in fact, directly responsible to nobody who has a direct interest in the efficiency with which the organization is managed. See *generally* Hansmann, *supra* note 2, 878.

50. *See* note 38 *supra.*

51. Or, what is effectively the same thing, the nonprofit firms will be able to charge a higher

price than will for-profit firms for the same quality of service, since consumers will feel less impelled to undertake costly measures to verify for themselves the quality of the firm's services when the firm is nonprofit than when it is for-profit (or, put differently, will "trust" the nonprofit providers more than the for-profit providers).

52. *See* p. 373 *supra.*

53. *See* Hansmann, *supra* note 2, 868–72.

54. The ambiguity results from problems of second best, deriving from the fact that the corporate tax distorts capital investment in for-profit firms, causing those firms to invest inefficiently small amounts of capital. Of course, if we accept the alternative view of the corporate tax (as applied to for-profit firms) as a tax only on pure profits, then there is no difference between the before-tax and the after-tax marginal rates of return among for-profit firms, and this problem disappears. See Stiglitz, *supra* note 10.

55. It would be very hard to determine with any precision the effective marginal rate of return to investment among nonprofit firms in any given industry; a rough estimate is probably all that could be obtained. Administrative decisions based on rough empirical estimates, however, would always be subject to attack. Moreover, policymaking would be complicated by the fact that the rate of return to capital for nonprofit firms in an industry will often vary from region to region and even from firm to firm.

56. This is not to say, however, that the second criterion need be ignored entirely. See, *e.g.*, note 63 *infra.*

57. If nonprofit firms could be demonstrated to have important efficiency advantages over for-profit firms under identifiable conditions other than contract failure, similar reasoning could justify granting tax exemption to nonprofit firms in those circumstances as well. *See* note 38 *supra.*

58. Of course, focusing just on the first of the two criteria suggested here would yield an unsatisfactory result unless, in fact, the majority of firms that meet the first criterion meet the second criterion as well. There is reason to believe, however, that this is the case. As discussed below, there seem to be two broad classes of nonprofits that arguably meet the first criterion: donative nonprofits, and commercial nonprofits that provide complex personal services. As discussed in note 63 *infra*, donative nonprofits as a class seem more likely than not to suffer from inadequate access to capital. And demand for the services of the second class of nonprofits—which include, for example, nursing homes, day-care centers, and family counseling clinics—has been growing sufficiently rapidly in recent decades, *see, e.g.*, note 16 *supra* (nursing homes), that it seems unlikely that the nonprofit firms in the industries involved are, in general, overcapitalized.

59. *See* Federation Pharmacy Serv., Inc. v. Commissioner, 625 F.2d 804 (8th Cir. 1980) (exemption denied to nonprofit pharmacy); Senior Citizens Stores, Inc. v. United States, 602 F.2d 711 (5th Cir. 1979) (exemption denied to nonprofit store selling used clothing, furniture, and household appliances); People's Educ. Camp Soc'y, Inc. v. Commissioner, 331 F.2d 923 (2nd Cir. 1964), *cert. denied* 379 U.S. 839 (1964) (exemption denied to nonprofit summer resort); B.S.W. Group, Inc. v. Commissioner, 70 T.C. 352 (1978) (exemption denied to nonprofit consulting firm). *But see* Metropolitan Detroit Area Hosp. Serv., Inc. v. United States, 445 F. Supp. 857 (E.D. Mich. 1978) (exemption granted to nonprofit corporation selling laundry services to governmental and nonprofit hospitals).

60. Because, as noted immediately below, donative nonprofits typically provide services that either have desirable redistributive effects or are public goods, it is relatively easy to justify exemption for such organizations on the basis that their services can be classified, for example, as "charitable," I.R.C. § 501(c)(3), "civic," or "social welfare," I.R.C. § 501(c)(4). *See* Hansmann, *supra* note 2, 514.

61. *See* Hansmann, *supra* note 2.

62. Just because an organization receives an occasional small donation, though it relies upon sales receipts for the great bulk of its income, does not mean that it should be considered "donative" for purposes of the analysis offered here. The mere presence of donative income should be considered presumptive evidence of contract failure only when the organization involved is heavily dependent upon such income.

63. Fortunately, the two criteria suggested above for granting the exemption—relative efficiency vis-a-vis for-profits, and existing extent of capital accumulation—often go hand in hand. Not only is it easier to make the case that nonprofit firms are more efficient than their for-profit counterparts would be when the nonprofits in question are donative than when they are commercial, but further, it seems in general less likely that donative nonprofits will exceed the efficient level of capital accumulation than that commercial nonprofits will do so. The reason for this is that the services of donative nonprofits commonly have—at least to some degree, and at least for a limited group of individuals—the characteristics of a public good, and consequently, free-rider incentives are likely to keep the level of donations, and hence the level of capital accumulation and of production, below the efficient level for donative nonprofits. On the other hand, it is not always the case that donative nonprofits are inefficiently constrained by lack of capital. Boys' Town, for example, evidently managed to accumulate, through solicitation of donations, an amount of capital far in excess of any reasonable needs. *See N.Y Times,* April 16, 1974, at 41, col. 1.

64. For example, while some have argued that the widespread abuses that evidently characterize the nursing home industry are primarily attributable to the for-profit firms in that industry, *see* Regan, Quality assurance systems in nursing homes, 53 *J. Urb. L.* 153, 210–14 (1975); Shulman and Galanter, Reorganizing the nursing home industry: A proposal, 54 *Milbank Memorial Fund Q.* 129 (1976), others have argued that, overall, there is not much to choose between nonprofit and for-profit firms in this regard, *see* M. Mendelson, *Tender Loving Greed* 195–212 (1974).

65. Hansmann, *supra* note 2, 866–68.

66. The perception that the hospital industry is overcapitalized was a major stimulus to the passage of the National Health Planning and Development Act of 1974, Pub. L. No. 93-641, 88 Stat. 2225, *codified with amendments* at 42 U.S.C. § 300m and scattered sections (West Supp. 1981).

67. B.S.W. Group, Inc. v. Commissioner, 70 T.C. 352, 358 (1978).

68. *Id. See also* Federation Pharmacy Serv., Inc. v. Commissioner, 625 F.2d 804, 809 (8th Cir. 1980) (exemption denied a nonprofit pharmacy on grounds that, *inter alia,* "it is engaged in competition with for-profit pharmacies"); People's Educ. Camp Soc'y, Inc. v. Commissioner, 331 F.2d 923, 931 (2nd Cir.), *cert. denied,* 379 U.S. 839 (1964) (fact that nonprofit resort was "in active competition with other such businesses" cited among reasons for denying exemption).

69. Metropolitan Detroit Area Hosp. Serv., Inc. v. United States, 445 F. Supp. 857, 861 (E. D. Mich. 1978).

70. For example, roughly 75 percent of all nursing homes in the United States are proprietary. Nevertheless, nonprofit nursing homes, even when (as is commonly the case) they are operated as commercial entrepreneurial nonprofits, have been exempted from income taxation. *See* note 16 *supra.*

71. *See* p. 380 *supra.*

72. *See* p. 383 *supra.*

73. Note, too, that the second criterion for exemption—the current extent of capital investment—is also likely to be satisfied for nonprofit organizations engaging in socially desired production of public goods. The mere fact that greater production of these goods is considered socially desirable indicates that they are presently being supplied at a suboptimal level, which in turn suggests that there is probably too little investment, from an efficiency point of view, in the capital facilities necessary to produce them.

74. *See* p. 383 *supra.*

75. Vocational education may be undersupplied (or, rather, underconsumed) as a result of obstacles facing prospective students in borrowing against their future incomes. *Cf.* Hansmann, *supra* note 2, 859–62 (discussing imperfections in loan markets for higher education).

76. The federal government could presumably use devices other than tax exemption to help alleviate capital shortages confronting nonprofits. Capital grants, loans, or loan guarantees, for example, would provide a much more direct response to the problem. Such devices have, in fact, sometimes been used. Capital grants were provided to hospitals from the 1940s until

the 1970s under the Hill-Burton program. *See The Nation's Health Facilities, Ten Years of the Hill-Burton Hospital and Medical Facilities Program, 1946–56* (Public Health Service Pub. No. 616, 1958). Similarly, capital grants, loans, and loan guarantees have been provided to nonprofit health maintenance organizations under the Health Maintenance Organization Act of 1973, 42 U.S.C. §§300e-2 to 300e-8 (1974 & 1981 Supp.). Devices of this sort might well be superior to tax exemption as a means of allocating capital to the nonprofit sector—though such bureaucratic mechanisms for distributing capital can be quite costly to administer and are subject to constraints and influences that may result in an allocation that is far from efficient.

In any case, the question at hand is not whether it might be possible to design a mechanism for allocating capital to the nonprofit sector that would be superior to tax exemption, but whether, given that no such alternative mechanism is in place, granting tax exemption to certain classes of nonprofits is better policy than not granting such exemption.

22

Unfair Competition and Corporate Income Taxation

SUSAN ROSE-ACKERMAN

"If something is not done . . . , the macaroni monopoly will be in the hands of the universities."[1]

When a group of wealthy graduates donated the Mueller Macaroni Company to the New York University (N.Y.U.) Law School in 1948, the university persuaded a court to give Mueller's profits tax-exempt status because N.Y.U. was a nonprofit entity.[2] Two years later, Congress amended the Internal Revenue Code to narrow this exemption: Henceforth, only the "related" business ventures of nonprofits would be tax exempt.[3]

Very little money has been collected under this provision.[4] Instead, it has channeled the "active" investments of nonprofits into "related" areas. Universities, for example, are no longer in the pasta business, but they continue to sell housing and meals, perform contract research and testing, and operate publishing houses.[5] Of course, the meaning of "related" is not obvious and the Internal Revenue Service (IRS) and the courts have experienced predictable difficulties settling on a definition.[6] The unresolved issue of the law's coverage will be of growing concern to nonprofits since current cuts in marginal tax rates and in government subsidies will undoubtedly induce many nonprofit firms to consider profit-making activities as a way to raise funds.[7] As nonprofits try to enter new fields, such as genetic engineering and cooperative research relationships with private firms,[8] Congress and the IRS will have to decide whether to facilitate or impede these activities, placing new strains on a generation-old policy.[9]

From *Stanford Law Review* 34 (May 1982): 1017–39. Research support for this paper was provided by Yale University's Program on Non-Profit Organizations. I wish to thank Bruce Ackerman, Boris Bittker, George Cooper, Henry Hansmann, and John Simon for helpful comments.

The particular problem of competition from nonprofits raises a more general issue. A variety of tax-favored entities compete with for-profit firms in a broad range of industries.[10] When, if ever, will "unfair" competition by tax-favored firms be a legitimate problem for public policy? Congress's response to complaints of unfair competition has been inconsistent at best. The Internal Revenue Code has all but eliminated the tax advantage of mutual and cooperative banks and insurance companies,[11] but agricultural cooperatives enjoy a relatively favorable tax status.[12] Utilities operated by state and local governments are exempt from the corporate income tax, while private regulated companies are not.[13]

Instead of ad hoc responses to particular claims of unfair competition, we need a framework for analyzing the policy questions that arise whenever a tax-favored firm competes with firms that pay the corporate income tax. Two different claims, both based on the notion of "horizontal equity"[14] are frequently confused in the policy debate.[15] The first approach compares firms within the *same* industry and asserts that it is unfair for the tax system to favor one competitor over another.[16] The second approach compares for-profits across different industries—those with and those without tax-favored firms. Here it is said to be "unfair" for some firms to compete with tax-favored organizations when for-profit corporations in other industries compete only with taxable firms.

The first approach to horizontal equity makes the claim, for example, that N.Y.U. should pay taxes on its Mueller pasta business simply because the Ronzoni Company pays taxes on its macaroni profits. This view assumes that the fairness of tax policy should be assessed by comparing the income statements of the competing companies. But it is obvious that the ultimate impact of N.Y.U.'s pasta activities was not felt by the Ronzoni Company but by the human beings associated with it as investors, workers, and consumers. Sophisticated students of tax policy routinely incorporate this point in their assessments of fairness. Rather than speaking of fairness to corporate entities, they have pierced the organizational veil to consider the interests of human beings.[17] Under this "person-oriented" perspective, the first fairness claim collapses. The different tax treatment of competing organizational forms does not imply that Ronzoni and N.Y.U. would charge different prices for their macaroni or pay different wages to their workers. It implies only that N.Y.U. would keep a larger share of Mueller's profits than would Ronzoni's owners. Once we look beyond the organization, this difference does not seem to violate principles of horizontal equity: Why must a fair tax code treat students and scholars who are the beneficiaries of Mueller's profits as if they were "equal to" Ronzoni's investors?

The second approach to horizontal equity gives a more meaningful interpretation to the complaints of Ronzoni's investors and will be used in the analysis that follows. Under this view, Ronzoni investors would argue that the relevant horizontal comparison is with investors in industries which do not face competition from tax-favored firms. After all, at an earlier point in time, owners of shares in pasta-making companies could have chosen to invest in other businesses instead. In the absence of a tax on unrelated business activities, N.Y.U.'s entry into the pasta business would mean that investors who at one time were similarly situated are now earning different returns. This, at least, raises the possibility of a claim of horizontal inequity: if pasta investors *are* harmed, why should they be called on to bear a greater share than others of the social costs of tax favoritism to nonprofits?

Legally trained commentators have avoided this normative question by doing some inadequate positive economics. They have argued that firms that compete with nonprofits are not generally worse off than those that compete only with for-profits.[18] If this is true, the unfairness issue simply does not arise. I will demonstrate that previous analysts have dismissed the issue of "unfair" competition too quickly. While I agree that nonprofits are no more likely to engage in predatory pricing than for-profits,[19] I will show that for-profit investors may be injured even when predation does not occur. For-profit investors' claims of injury are neither obviously correct nor patently false. Their validity depends both on one's definition of fairness and on a set of factual issues including the market structure of the industry in question, the information available to firms before they enter, the costs of leaving the industry, and the efficiency of capital markets. Both the firms that complain of injury and the legal scholars who minimize the problem of unfair competition have oversimplified the issue and missed critically important features of the problem.

The economic analysis in the first section proceeds in three stages. First, I discuss competition between taxable and tax-exempt firms in a competitive economy where entrants correctly foresee the presence of tax-exempt competitors. Next, I drop the assumption of perfect foresight and show how for-profit firms will be affected by the tax and organizational status of nonprofits in the case of unanticipated competition. To conclude, I assume that the economy is imperfectly competitive, so that nonprofits compete with for-profits in an oligopolistic setting. After specifying in the first section the market conditions under which for-profit investors may be harmed, the second section turns to the normative question. I suggest that the distinctions made in the positive economic analysis will enlighten, if not fully resolve, the problems of identifying "unfair competition." The analysis demonstrates that the present tax on nonprofits' "unrelated" business income is exactly the wrong way to deal with the problem, generating more "unfairness" than it has prevented. While an economically sophisticated definition of unfairness is possible, its application involves subtle empirical issues—so subtle that they may be beyond the administrative capacities of the IRS. As a consequence, outright repeal of the tax on unrelated business activities seems like the best policy response.

THE IMPORTANCE OF MARKET STRUCTURE

The policy debate has tended to view "unfair competition" in black-and-while terms. Either "unfairness" is the inevitable result of nonprofit entry, as for-profit firms and their congressional allies claim, or it almost never happens—as legal scholars assert.[20] If, however, we try to locate the debate within a framework emphasizing market structure and imperfect information, the claims made on both sides seem overly broad.

For-profit firms advance two arguments to justify protection against nonprofit competition. First, they claim that nonprofits will cut prices below the prices that taxable firms could charge. Economically oriented legal commentators have generally dismissed the price-cutting claim by arguing that if price-cutting were profitable, for-profit competitors would do it too.[21] But this argument ignores the possibility that nonprofits can affect market prices without resorting to overtly predatory behavior. Even in a competitive market where firms are too small to affect market prices individually, the entry of nonprofits could lower prices by shifting the overall industry supply curve. Nonprofits may be willing to enter an industry even when marginal for-profit firms are just breaking even. If for-profits cannot easily exit, supply will be larger, returns will be smaller, and price will be lower than in an industry without nonprofit firms. And in an oligopolistic industry, where individual firms *can* affect price levels, equilibrium prices might be lower when one of the major competitors is tax-exempt even though no one ever sets prices below cost.[22]

Second, for-profits argue that nonprofits will grow more quickly than for-profits and be less vulnerable to bankruptcy because they accumulate earnings faster.[23] While these claims have been accepted by most legal scholars,[24] their importance depends critically on the efficiency of capital markets. The more efficiently the capital market operates, the less important are retained earnings. If, however, lenders have difficulty evaluating a firm's investments, the firm may prefer to exploit internal sources of funds, and firms with high levels of retained earnings have an advantage.[25]

To assess the validity of the price-cutting and retained earnings arguments and, thereby, move from critique to contribution, requires a more systematic treatment that models the important market structures separately. To focus on the links among tax status, capital structure, and profitability, I will stylize the differences between firms in an extreme way. There are only two types of firms: for-profit corporations subject to the corporate income tax and nonprofit, tax-exempt corporations that can issue no equity and must raise capital through borrowing or gifts.[26] Nonprofit firms engage in tax-exempt business activity to provide funds to subsidize their primary activities. Therefore, they want to maximize expected profits. I shall also assume that nonprofit firms are, on the average, as efficient as for-profits. Firms need not be identical, but any differences in costs or productivity are not systematically related to organizational form. The production of services by nonprofits is not complicated by ideological commitments or ineffective management.[27] Only tax and capital structure differences are important.

Anticipated Competition from Nonprofits

If an industry were perfectly competitive with easy entry and exit of firms, complaints of "unfair competition" would always be invalid. A for-profit firm that was losing money in competition with a nonprofit would simply leave that industry and earn the competitive rate of return elsewhere.[28]

But in many situations, human and physical capital are not fungible, and exit is therefore costly.[29] Even when exit is difficult, however, there is no reason to assume automatically that for-profit firms are suffering from "unfair" competition from nonprofits. In particular, whenever for-profits could reasonably have expected nonprofit competition at the time of their initial commitment to the industry, they would have included that fact in their calculations of expected returns and made their decision to invest accordingly. They would not have invested unless they expected to do at least as well there as in alternative investments.[30] Therefore, in the case of anticipated competition, no claims of unfairness can be substantiated even if exit is difficult. This argument is independent of any particular model of nonprofit behavior. So long as the entry and subsequent behavior of nonprofits were anticipated, taxable firms could have no grounds for complaint.

The real world, however, frequently does not conform to the stringent conditions imposed here. The next section examines the fairness claims that might arise if exit is costly and if competition from nonprofits is unanticipated.

Unanticipated Competition

Competitive returns represent the opportunity cost of money and time invested in the firm. If entrepreneurs and investors had chosen not to establish a particular firm, they could have invested elsewhere at competitive rates. If a firm earns less than this competitive return and if exit is costly, the owners will suffer losses relative to what they could have earned elsewhere. Thus, one can pose the issue of unanticipated competition in the following way. Suppose that investors, when they decide to enter an industry, anticipate that all competitors will be for-profit firms. When many of the competitors turn out to be nonprofits, under what conditions should we expect the investors to earn "subcompetitive" returns?

In the absence of conscious predatory behavior, the only way nonprofits can affect for-profits is through "excessive" entry. That is, because of the tax treatment of nonprofits and the costs of exit, the industry has more firms, earning lower gross returns, than the for-profit investors expected ex ante. To show how "excessive" entry can occur, suppose that nonprofit entrepreneurial activity is concentrated in a single industry and that the nonprofit sector is small relative to the economy as a whole. Therefore, the sector's investment decisions have no noticeable effect on overall market rates of return. I shall also make the realistic assumption that, despite the tax avoidance potential of 100 percent debt financing, profit-maximizing taxable firms will have capital structures that mix debt and equity.[31]

Given these assumptions, we can derive the formal conditions under which nonprofit entry can depress for-profit returns below competitive levels.[32] Basically, "excessive" entry occurs when non-profits have excess cash to invest and the return they can obtain by lending their money on the bond market is lower than the rate of return on active, entrepreneurial investments.[33] This will often be the case under my assumptions if the corporate tax rate exceeds the tax rate on individual income and if capital-gains taxes are low. Nonprofits will continue to enter until their presence drives down industry returns to the point where marginal nonprofits are indifferent between passive and active investments. When that happens, marginal for-profits will want to leave the industry because they will be earning "sub-competitive" returns that are less than the market return on riskless assets. Because of the costs of exit, those firms will earn less than market returns whether they stay in business, go bankrupt, or sell out.[34]

The importance of this conclusion depends, first, on the concentration of nonprofit investments in particular industries; second, on the number of marginal for-profit firms in any industry earning only competitive returns; and third, on the assumption that nonprofits have excess cash available for investment. If the productive activities of nonprofits are broadly diffused, there will be little impact on profits anywhere in the economy. In fact, if tax-exempt firms have no special efficiency advantages in any industry, one would expect them to seek to maximize returns by establishing firms in a broad range of industries, thus, earning close to a competitive return in each one. Since nonprofits control only a small proportion of the economy's resources,[35] one would not expect them to be able to push returns down much below ordinary competitive rates if their funds were evenly spread across the economy. Further, if most for-profit firms are more than marginally profitable, few firms will want to exit from industries which nonprofits enter, although all will earn somewhat less than they did before the entry of nonprofits.

Finally, if the nonprofits must borrow funds from banks or other lenders, the cost of capital may be too high to make active entrepreneurship worthwhile, even if the corporate tax rate exceeds the individual rate. Nonprofits might, for example, be charged rates that exceed competitive returns because lenders have difficulty monitoring the nonprofits' behavior.[36] Nonprofit managers must then decide whether to use a combination of gifts and loans to start new businesses, taking into account that nonprofits cannot enjoy the tax advantages of debt that accrue to for-profits. The smaller the pool of internal funds available to the nonprofit, the higher the rate of interest charged, and the larger the efficient scale in the industry, the less likely it is that active nonprofit entry will occur. Indeed, if the cost of borrowing is high enough, entry may only occur if the nonprofit is more efficient than existing marginal for-profits.[37] But in that case, if some for-profits were eventually driven out of business, there would be a net efficiency gain.[38]

Of course, there is no reason to believe that a nonprofit's capital structure disadvantages just match its tax advantages. Efficient for-profits may suffer losses if the entry of nonprofits is concentrated in their industry, or efficient nonprofits may fail to enter because they are unable to obtain adequate and affordable capital. If, as I have assumed, efficiency is not systematically associated with organizational form, then the form that is most favored by the tax system and the capital market in a particular situation would be able to exploit whatever opportunities arise. Therefore, it is possible that some efficient for-profit entrepreneurs and investors will earn subnormal returns if nonprofit entry is concentrated in a few industries. The extent of loss cannot categorically be affirmed or denied; it is an empirical issue to be resolved on a case-by-case basis.

Oligopoly

The impact of tax-exempt firms on their taxable competitors can be quite different if an industry is oligopolistic rather than competitive.[39] I shall show that the claims of for-profit firms to suffer "harm" may well be valid in an oligopoly with a fixed number of firms.

Effect of nonprofit status on output

In an oligopolistic market, a firm's tax status may affect its marginal choices, and a tax-exempt firm may have a higher output and a larger effect on market price than a tax-paying firm.[40] To see how this can happen, consider a simple duopoly model in which a for-profit firm, A, faces a single competitor, B, which may be either a tax-exempt nonprofit financed by gifts and debt or a taxable for-profit. Assume, first, that there is no risk of bankruptcy and that lenders require the same minimum rate of return on both bonds and stocks.[41] Lenders require for-profit firms to maintain a ratio of debt to total capital below a specified level, and all firms purchase debt at a fixed rate that is independent of the debt-equity ratio and the level of private giving to nonprofits.[42]

Whatever its tax status, firm B produces the quantity that maximizes profits by equating the marginal revenue gain from an increase in output (after tax for the for-profit firm) with the sum of the marginal increases in operating costs and capital costs from the same increase in output (again, after tax for the for-profit firm). Firm B's profit-maximizing output will depend on its tax status if the tax affects its marginal decisions. This is true under the current system which taxes "accounting" rather than "economic" profits. That is, the tax is levied only on the return to equity, not on capital costs that take the form of interest on debt.[43] So long as some of its marginal capital cost is raised through stock issues, then, it costs the

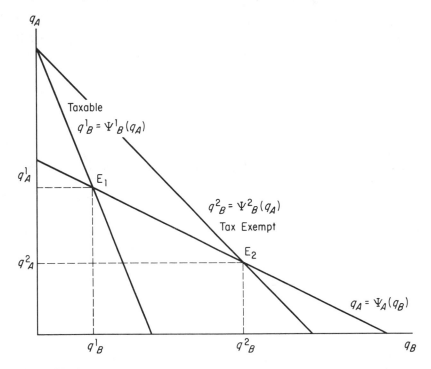

Figure 22-1

for-profit more to expand production than it does a comparable nonprofit. At the level of output that maximizes net profits for the for-profit, marginal revenues would exceed marginal costs for the nonprofit. Therefore, as long as marginal revenue falls with increases in output and marginal operating and capital costs increase or remain constant, the nonprofit will choose a higher level of output than the similarly situated for-profit.[44]

Impact on for-profit competitors

We are now ready to ask how the for-profit firm, A, is affected by the organizational and tax status of its competitor, B. Suppose, for concreteness, that both firms behave as Cournot oligopolists.[45] That is, each one maximizes profits assuming that the output of its rival remains constant. We can then draw reaction functions[46] Ψ_A and Ψ_B that show how firms A and B, respectively, will respond to the output choices of the other firm. Thus Ψ_A shows the profit-maximizing output chosen by A, given its belief about B's output choice.

Figure 22-1 illustrates a possible set of reaction functions where q_A is A's output and q_B is B's output. They have been drawn as straight lines, but all we really know is that they are downward sloping.[47] We established above that, ceteris paribus, B produces more when it is tax-exempt than when it is taxable. Thus, the reaction function of the tax-exempt firm, q_B^1, is everywhere above that of the taxable firm, q_B^2, except when $q_B = 0$.

Since, under the Cournot model, the reaction function for A is unaffected by B's tax and organizational status, the equilibrium of q_B is higher and that of q_A is lower when B is tax-exempt. A is unambiguously worse off when its competitor is a tax-exempt nonprofit.

Importance of bankruptcy risk

But this simple model overstates the injury that a nonprofit can impose on a for-profit. To proceed further, we should take account of the possibility of bankruptcy and default. In general, the interest rate lenders can charge is not fixed for all borrowers. Lenders charge highly leveraged firms higher rates to compensate for their increased risks of bankruptcy.[48] Unless nonprofits are very well endowed or have superior access to donations, they must finance themselves with debt. The risk of bankruptcy may, therefore, be lower for for-profits since they are partially financed by equity investments. This may make for-profit firms more effective competitors because they have superior access to capital funds. The advantages of the for-profit's capital structure and the risk-sharing feature of the corporate income tax[49] may outweigh the for-profit's tax disadvantages. As a consequence, the nonprofit may produce less output than a for-profit because the nonprofit is either rationed in the capital market,[50] or charged high rates by lenders. A may now *prefer* to face a nonprofit competitor.[51]

When bankruptcy is possible, firm managers and shareholders will be concerned not only with expected return but also with risk. In a duopoly or oligopoly, management would, therefore, be concerned both with its own *absolute* level of resources and with its vulnerability to bankruptcy *relative* to other firms in the industry: ceteris paribus, a firm's risk of bankruptcy is negatively related to its competitors' risks. To see this, one need only recognize that if demand is unexpectedly low, everyone faces a heightened risk of bankruptcy, but a firm's risk is lower if there are other firms that are more marginal than it is. Marginal firms, with the smallest cushion of past profits, will exit first, thus pushing up prices and improving market conditions for those that remain.

In this regard, for-profits frequently claim that nonprofits are less likely to go bankrupt than for-profits. Since exit normally implies a loss of wealth and outside sources of capital are not always available to tide a firm over bad years, retained earnings can be an important factor in a firm's survival. Because of their exemption from the corporate income tax, nonprofits are believed to accumulate more earnings in good years to cover losses in subsequent years. If this claim is correct, the relative immunity of nonprofits makes their for-profit competitors relatively *more* vulnerable to bankruptcy. The truth of this claim, however, depends on the availability of loss carryovers in the tax law. If there is full carryover, a firm is never taxed unless it actually earns profits over time. Thus, whether the nonprofit firm has an advantage in the bankruptcy context turns on the existence and completeness of loss carryovers, not on the corporate tax exemption alone. In fact, although loss carryover provisions are not complete, they are quite generous—losses generally can be carried back three years and forward fifteen years.[52] When profits oscillate from positive to negative as time passes, a taxable firm is treated almost like a tax-exempt firm on any gains which are balanced by losses in other years. For-profits will only be disadvantaged when they have a run of losses that lasts more than eighteen years with major losses in the middle of the period—more than three years after the last profit in the past and more than fifteen years before the first profit in future.[53] In short, nonprofits' lower risk of bankruptcy has been overemphasized by their for-profit competitors. Current tax law treats the two organizational forms almost identically.

In conclusion, a for-profit oligopolist would prefer to compete with another for-profit whenever nonprofits have no special difficulties obtaining capital and corporate loss carryover provisions are incomplete. But the for-profit will prefer a nonprofit competitor whenever nonprofits have difficulty raising capital and are, therefore, small and ineffective competitors.[54] Once again, while "harm" is possible, its extent depends upon a set of factual conditions determined by the details of the tax law and the operation of the capital market.

"UNFAIR COMPETITION" AND ECONOMIC ANALYSIS

I have isolated two very different market structures under which for-profit investors may suffer from the presence of nonprofit competition. Each situation requires a different policy analysis. One complaint of unfair competition is easy to dismiss; the other forces us to confront some hard questions of economic justice.

The claims of unfair competition raised by oligopolists should not be taken seriously. American antitrust and regulatory policy makes it clear that there is no public commitment to the maintenance of profits resulting from economic concentration. If successful antitrust litigation forces a cartel to disband, or an oligopolist to divest an acquisition, private investors cannot obtain compensation for their loss of monopoly profits.[55] Similarly, firms should not be entitled to special protection when the production decisions of nonprofits lower their oligopoly returns.

A harder case arises when investors are deprived of competitive returns by the unanticipated entry of nonprofits. It is true that investors in a capitalist economy do not imagine they are guaranteed a competitive return by the government: tastes may change, competitors may develop new technology, and so forth. But when competitive losses can be traced to particular government actions, the state has a special responsibility to justify its conduct.[56] Thus, the fifth amendment requires compensation if the government confiscates private property.[57] Of course, nothing so extreme is in question here. Rather than seizing firm assets, the government is "merely" manipulating the business environment to the advantage of nonprofit firms. Furthermore, it will never be entirely clear how much of the investor's losses are due to the tax-exempt status of some competitors and how much is due to other causes. On the level of constitutional theory, it is not clear what difference the "indirect" character of the government's taking ought to make in assessing the firms' right to compensation.[58] Whatever the theory, however, the case law plainly suggests that contemporary courts would refuse to extend the fifth amendment to cover tax-related claims of "unfair competition."[59]

Courts, however, are not the only institutions concerned with unfair governmental manipulation of the business environment. As the current law indicates, Congress itself has chosen to restrict nonprofits in the name of fairness. But the tax on "unrelated" business income is exactly the wrong way to respond to the problem. The nonprofit sector is, after all, rather small relative to the economy as a whole.[60] If the sector's productive business investments were spread across the economy, they would be unlikely to have much competitive impact.[61] But the tax on "unrelated" business income prevents such dispersion. Tax-exempt firms must now concentrate their profitable endeavors in those few lines of business judged to be "related." For example, the growth of gift shops and vacation tours operated or sponsored by nonprofit organizations may be, in part, a response to the conditions of the tax law.[62] Such concentration in a few areas makes it much more likely that the business activities of nonprofits will impose losses on competitive for-profit firms. Of course, these losses were only unanticipated by firms that were in the industry at the time of the substantial entry of nonprofits. But since the IRS and the courts continue to modify the definition of "unrelated," the statute probably continues to impose new windfall gains and losses on competing for-profit corporations as well as on nonprofits that rely on superseded rulings.[63]

It appears, then, that the tax on unrelated business activity creates more unfairness than it can possibly prevent. It should, therefore, be repealed. It is less clear what, if anything, should be put in its place. If the IRS is to pinpoint instances of "unfair" competition, it would have to carry out an economic analysis that hinges on difficult issues of market structure. Nonprofits might be given the right to enter *any* business subject to a finding by the IRS that further entry is likely to depress for-profit returns below competitive levels. Regulations explicating this standard would emphasize three factors—the prevailing rate of return in the industry, the speed and volume of nonprofit entry, and the costs of exit for for-profit firms. As similar inquiries in antitrust and public utility regulation suggest, this will often require the use of a great deal of discretion.[64] Nevertheless, the principles are clear. First, firms earning supercompetitive profits have no right to protection from "unfair" competition.[65] It is only when this first principle is satisfied that a second issue should be reached. Here, the IRS would determine whether nonprofits are entering at a rate that could have a substantial impact on for-profit returns. Finally, the IRS would have to be convinced that the exit costs of for-profits will be substantial. Once again, the use of discretion is inevitable—but the existence of very specialized human and physical capital would be the focus of concern.

A successful showing of unfair competition would be rare under these guidelines. Indeed, the process seems so cumbersome, and the gains in fairness so elusive, that a simple repeal of the present tax on unrelated income seems the better alternative. By permitting nonprofits to enter any profit-making industry, repeal will reduce the pressure on for-profit firms in areas that are "related" to the primary activities of nonprofits. While this new freedom may increase the overall level of nonprofit entrepreneurial activity,[66] the diffusion of this activity throughout the economy reduces the chance that investors in a particular industry will suffer substantial unanticipated losses from nonprofit entry.[67]

NOTES

1. Revenue Revision of 1950: Hearings Before the House Committee on Ways and Means, 81st Cong., 2d Sess. 579–80 (1950) (remarks of Rep. Dingell), quoted in Note, The macaroni monopoly: The developing concept of unrelated business income of exempt organizations, 81 Harv. L. Rev. 1280, 1281 n.10 (1968) [hereinafter cited as Note, The macaroni monopoly].

2. See C. F. Mueller Co. v. Commissioner, 190 F.2d 120 (3rd Cir. 1951); Note, The macaroni monopoly, supra note 1, 1281. N.Y.U. also owned a leather company, a piston ring factory, and a chinaware manufacturing operation. Other colleges and universities owned enterprises manufacturing automobile parts, cotton gins, and food products, and operated an airport, a street railway, a hydroelectric plant, and a radio station. See Kaplan, Intercollegiate athletics and the unrelated business income tax, 80 Colum. L. Rev. 1430, 1432 (1980).

3. Revenue Act of 1950, Pub. L. No. 81–814, §§ 301, 331, 64 Stat. 906, 947–53, 957–59 (codified at 26 U.S.C. §§ 502–514 (1976)). Several commentators have reviewed this law. See Bittker & Rahdert, The exemption of nonprofit organizations from federal income taxation, 85 Yale L.J. 299 (1976); Cooper, Trends in the taxation of unrelated business activity, 29 Inst. on Fed Tax'n 1999 (1971); Kaplan, supra note 2; Note, Colleges, charities and the Revenue Act of 1950, 60 Yale L.J. 851 (1951) [hereinafter cited as Note, College, charities, and the Revenue Act of 1950]. For a discussion of changes made in the treatment of nonprofit firms by the 1969 and 1976 tax law revisions, see Bittker and Rahdert, supra, 316–30; Kaplan, supra note 2, 1431.

4. See Webster, Effect of business activities on exempt organizations, 43 Taxes 777 (1965). In the last six fiscal years the total tax collected was less than .05 percent of corporate income tax collections. Total fiscal year collections were $24,970,000 in 1977, $27,470,000 in 1978, $24,970,000 in 1979, $27,920,000 in 1980, and $34,310,000 in 1981. Internal Revenue Service, Data on Taxes Collected on Form 990T (unpublished IRS staff calculation).

5. Bromberg, University audits by IRS, Philanthropy Monthly, Feb. 1980, 18 (newsletter).

6. Some of this confusion arises because the law seeks to tax "unrelated" business activity, see I.R.C. § 513(a) (1976), even though the legislative history speaks of "unfair" competition. See Kaplan, supra note 2, 1433–44. See also Treas. Reg. § 1.513-1(b), T.D. 7392, 1976–1 C.B. 162, 168–69. Mansfield, Some aspects of taxation of business income of exempt organizations, in 3 Staff of House Comm. on Ways and Means, 86th Cong., 1st Sess., Tax Revision Compendium 2067 (House Comm. on Ways & Means Comm. Print 1959) [hereinafter cited as Tax Revision Compendium]; Webster, supra note 4. For discussion and commentary on these exercises in definition, see Cooper, supra note 3; Grant, Taxation of exempt charitable organizations engaging in business activities, 4 U.C.L.A. L. Rev. 352 (1957); Green-

baum, *Business dealings by charities*, 14 *Inst. on Fed. Tax'n.* 127 (1956); Webster, *supra* note 4.

7. The cuts will reduce tax incentives for individuals to donate money by decreasing the value of the charitable deduction on the margin. This may well outweigh the "income effect" of the tax cut, that is, taxpayers have more money to spend and may contribute some of this excess to charity. At the same time, government spending cuts will reduce nondonative sources of income for nonprofits and decrease publicly funded alternatives to private largesse. The Economic Recovery Tax Act of 1981 attempts to compensate for its disincentives to donate by means of an "above-the-line" charitable deduction for taxpayers who do not itemize their deductions. Economic Recovery Tax Act of 1981, § 121, I.R.C. § 170 (West Supp. 1982).

8. See, for example, N. Brodsky, H. Kaufman and J. Tooker, *University/Industry Cooperation* (1980); Reinhold, Government scrutinizes link between genetics industry and universities, *N.Y. Times,* June 16, 1981, at 16, col. 1; *Industry's role in academia, N.Y. Times,* July 22, 1981, at D1, col. 3. But see note 66 *infra.*

At present, "all income deprived from research for federal or state governments and, in the case of a college, university or hospital, all income derived from research performed for any person" is tax-exempt under I.R.C. §§ 512(b)(7)–(8). See Myers, *Unrelated business income: A suddenly explosive issue*, in N.Y. *Practicing Law Institute, Seventh Biennial Conference: Tax Planning for Foundations, Tax-Exempt Status and Charitable Contributions* 223 (1978).

9. I address only one of the public policies that differentiate between firms on the basis of organizational form. For example, nonprofits obtain lower postal rates, exemption from property taxes, and favorable treatment on government contracts. *See U.S. Small Business Administration, Government Competition: A Threat to Small Business* 74–79 (1980) (report of the advocacy task group on government competition with small business).

10. Recent data from the Census Bureau's 1977 Census of Service Industries indicate the extent to which taxable and tax-exempt firms coexist in various service industries. *See* U.S. Dep't of Commerce, Bureau of the Census, *1977 Census of Service Industries: Other Service Industries* 53–1–2, 53–1–3 (1981) (Geographic Area Series, No. SC77–A–53, pt. 1 (1981)) (Table 1, Summary Statistics for the United States: 1977) (surveying the major service industries where competition occurs, but omitting competition between subsidiary organizations, such as university book stores or cafeterias, and for-profit firms).

11. In the savings and loan and insurance industries, Congress has responded to complaints of "unfair" competition by equalizing the tax treatment of mutual and for-profit companies. See Klein, Income taxation and legal entities, 20 *U.C.L.A. L. Rev.* 13, 60 (1972).

12. The actual income tax laws facing cooperatives are complicated, but the basic implication of their special treatment is that they face lower tax rates on earnings than corporations. For a summary of the law, see M. Abrahamsen, *Cooperative Business Enterprise* 225–41 (1976). Cooperatives' lower tax liabilities arise mainly because the bulk of patronage dividends paid to members are not taxable to the cooperative. Agricultural cooperatives also have access to low-cost loans from special banks and from members' contributions. They are, however, unable to raise capital through public issues of common stock.

13. *See* Ely, *Federal taxation of income of states and political subdivisions*, in 3 *Tax Revision Compendium, supra* note 6, at 2091; Gilpin, Business income of exempt organizations—Tax equalization—Electric utility service organizations, in 3 *Tax Revision Compendium, supra* note 6, 2077.

14. Horizontal equity is the principle that taxes should be equal for entities in equal positions. *See* A. Atkinson and J. Stiglitz, *Lectures on Public Economics* 353–56 (1980).

15. A third claim should be kept separate because it deals with efficiency, not fairness. Thus when for-profits are harmed as a result of the superior efficiency of tax-favored firms, the claim that the *tax* law gives the successful firms their competitive advantage is obviously unjustified. Rather than restrict this form of "unfair competition," the entry of efficient nonprofits ought to be encouraged. For an analysis of this claim, see Hansmann, *The rationale for exempting nonprofit organizations from corporate income taxation*, 91 *Yale L.J.* 54 (1981). In such markets as daycare, hospitals, and education, for-profits may only be able to survive if they differentiate their product from that provided by nonprofits.

16. Klein, *supra* note 11, 58 ("if the tax system favors one competitor over another without good reason, the unfavored competitor can properly claim injustice").

17. *See,* for example, A. Atkinson and J. Stiglitz, *supra* note 14, 160–226; Warren, *The relation and integration of individual and corporate income taxes,* 94 *Harv. L. Rev.* 717 (1981).

18. *See* Note, *Preventing the operation of untaxed business by tax-exempt organizations,* 32 *U. Chi. L. Rev.* 581, 591–92 (1965) [hereinafter cited as Note, *Preventing untaxed business*]. *See also,* Klein *supra* note 11, 61–68; Note, *The Macaroni Monopoly, supra* note 1, 1281 n.11; Note, *Colleges, charities and the Revenue Act of 1950, supra* note 3, 876.

19. Kaplan, *supra* note 2, 1465–66; Klein, *supra* note 11, 65–66; Note, *Colleges, charities and the Revenue Act of 1950, supra* note 3, 876. In an oligopolistic market prices may be lower if one of the competitors is nonprofit. *See* notes 45–54 *infra* and accompanying text. This price is not predatory in the usual sense of a seller who "cuts price below the level of its rivals' costs and perhaps also its own costs for protracted periods, until the rivals either close down operations altogether or sell out on favorable terms." F. Scherer, *Industrial Market Structure and Economic Performance* 335 (2d ed. 1980).

20. For a summary of the arguments on both sides, see 1 *Tax Revision Compendium, supra* note 6, 3. The most extended discussion by a legal scholar is in Klein, *supra* note 11. *See* also Bittker and Rahdert, *supra* note 3; Kaplan, *supra* note 2; Note, *The Macaroni Monopoly, supra* note 1; Note, *Colleges, charities and the Revenue of Act of 1950, supra* note 3.

Spiro discusses several recent cases where for-profits claimed to suffer from "unfair" competition because of nonprofits' favorable tax status. *See* T. Spiro, "Unfair competition" Between taxable and tax-exempt organizations: Three case studies (Supervised Analytic Writing, Yale University 1979). He looks at an unsuccessful travel industry challenge to the travel activities of the American Jewish Congress and other tax-exempt organizations, Am. Soc'y of Travel Agents v. Blumenthal, 566 F.2d 145 (D.C. Cir. 1977), *cert. denied,* 435 U.S. 947 (1978). After losing in the courts, the travel industry attempted to influence IRS revenue rulings directly. A recent ruling was more favorable to the industry. *See* Rev. Rul. 78–43, 1978–1 C.B. 164 (stating that the University of North Carolina Alumni Association's travel income was "unrelated," and, hence, taxable).

Spiro's second case involves the office products industry, where "sheltered workshops" for the handicapped compete with for-profit firms. The for-profits' trade association, the Office Products Manufacturing Association (OPMA), claimed unfair competition, but a Treasury Revenue Ruling upheld the tax exemption of sheltered workshops. *See* Treas. Reg. § 1.513–1(d)(4)(ii) (1967). Unlike the travel agents, OPMA has brought no court challenges and has concentrated on the important nontax advantages of sheltered workshops. *See* T. Spiro, *supra.*

A third example involves a court challenge brought by a taxable, commercial laboratory against a nonprofit corporation that promotes "manufactures, and the mechanic and useful arts." Structure Probe, Inc. v. Franklin Inst., 450 F. Supp. 1272 (E.D. Pa. 1978), *aff'd,* 595 F.2d 1214 (3d Cir. 1979). Structure Probe alleged that the Franklin Institute violated the Sherman Act, 15 U.S.C. § 2 (1976), in its sale of scanning electron microscope (SEM) services. The suit also claimed that the Institute's sale of SEM services violated its nonprofit charter. The court rejected both claims. 450 F. Supp., 1288, 1290.

21. *See* Kaplan, *supra* note 2, 1466; Klein, *supra* note 11, 65–66; Note, *Colleges, charities and the Revenue Act of 1950, supra* note 3, 876.

22. Price theory demonstrates that marginal firms will be earning a competitive rate of return on their investment. *See* note 28 *infra* and accompanying text. Readers unfamiliar with basic price theory should consult a basic microeconomics text such as J. Hirshleifer, *Price Theory and Applications* (2d ed. 1980).

23. *See* H.R. Rep. No. 2319, 81st Cong., 2d Sess. 579–80 (1950) ("The tax-free status of these . . . organizations enables them to use their profits tax-free to expand operations, while their competitors can expand *only* with profits remaining after taxes."); Klein, *supra* note 11, 255. There is a strong implication that firms do not have access to outside financing. *See generally U.S. Small Business Administration, supra* note 9.

24. *See, e.g.,* Kaplan, *supra* note 2, at 1466. One student commentator argues that a tax-

exempt business can accumulate a larger surplus than a taxable business, which may help it to weather lean years and expand. *See* Note, *Colleges, charities and the Revenue Act of 1950, supra* note 3, 876. Another argues that

> . . . the fast accumulation of capital made possible by tax-free profits is an advantage in any field. Where the market is expanding, the exempt enterprise will have a greater surplus to invest in production and distribution facilities, and, in anticipation of higher net profits, can compete more effectively for supplies, capital assets, and outside financing. Even in an industry with inelastic demand the untaxed business will be able to invest in improvements at a faster rate than its competitors.

Note, *The macaroni monopoly, supra* note 1, 1282. *But see* Klein, *supra* note 11, 66–67 (denying the special importance of retained earnings); Note, Preventing untaxed business, *supra* note 18, 592 (same).

25. I assume here that profit-maximizing organizations will invest in the activities expected to yield the highest return. With perfect information and identical risk preferences, banks and firms would rank investment opportunities in the same way. Firms would be indifferent between borrowing from a bank or using their own funds, and borrowers could obtain funds either from banks or from firms lacking profitable investments within their own company. Asymmetric information changes this result. Banks and other lenders may have trouble monitoring a firm's use of investment funds. Therefore, they will charge an interest rate that takes account of this risk, and they may ration credit to the firm. In that case, retained earnings will be a cheaper source of funds for a firm than bank debt even taking into account "opportunity cost"—the return which the funds could earn if invested outside the firm.

26. Although I do not explicitly discuss the idiosyncracies of cooperatives, mutuals, or government corporations, much of the basic analysis can be applied to these organizations with a suitable modification of the assumptions concerning tax status and capital constraints.

27. I make this assumption not because it is necessarily realistic, but because it permits me to focus on the difference in tax treatment. Bittker and Rahdert suggest that "the business practices of charity-owned enterprises [may be] characterized more by caution than boldness." Bittker and Rahdert, *supra* note 3, 320. Their claim is, however, an empirical assertion that has not been supported by systematic investigation. *See* D. Young, *If Not for Profit, for What?* (1983).

28. In equilibrium in a competitive industry marginal firms earn zero "economic" profits and positive accounting profits. Their accounting profits include both a return to the equity capital invested in the firm, reflecting the opportunity cost of the capital, and the value of the entrepreneurs' time. Economic profits are only positive when a firm's return exceeds what owners could earn by withdrawing their money and time and investing them elsewhere in the competitive economy. On the distinction between economic and accounting profits, see J. Hirshleifer, *supra* note 22, 265. Bankruptcy costs would be small since they include only the administrative costs of going through the procedure. *See* Warner, *Bankruptcy costs, absolute priority and the pricing of risky debt claims,* 4 J. Fin. Econ. 239 (1977) (estimates of the relatively small administrative costs of railroad bankruptcies).

29. Capital is malleable before it is put in place, but once embodied in equipment it cannot be changed easily. A firm has many choices before it has embraced a particular investment strategy. After the plant and machinery are purchased, the firm's choices are limited by the resale market for specialized capital. *See* R. Allen, *Macro-Economic Theory: A Mathematical Treatment* 256 (1967).

30. If all such competition were anticipated by for-profit investors, then the ratio of taxable to tax-exempt capital in the economy as a whole might affect overall rates of return, but taxable firms in *direct* competition with tax-exempt firms would be at no special disadvantage.

Harberger argues that in a competitive economy, a tax on corporate profits will, in the long run, lower overall returns to capital irrespective of where the capital is invested. Harberger, *The incidence of the corporation income tax,* 70 J. Pol. Econ. 215 (1962). See McLure, *General equilibrium incidence analysis: The Harberger model after ten years,* 4 J. Pub. Econ. 125

(1975), for an assessment of Harberger's contribution and a summary and critique of the research spawned by Harberger's original article.

In contrast to Harberger, Stiglitz contends that in the absence of bankruptcy risks the corporate profits tax can be viewed as a lump-sum tax on corporations so long as the personal tax rate on bond interest exceeds the corporate rate. *See* Stiglitz, *Taxation, corporation financial policy and the cost of capital*, 2 *J. Pub. Econ.* 1 (1973). This result depends on features of the tax law Harberger does not consider—that is, "on the interest deductibility provisions and on the fact that capital gains are taxed only upon realization." *Id.*, 33. If interest payments are not deductible, and if depreciation allowances equal true depreciation, then the tax is distortionary and capital flows from the taxed to the untaxed sector. King notes that "[t]his is similar to the conclusions of Harberger's (1962) model except that in our case equilibrium is determined by marginal and not average rates of return." King, *Taxation, corporate financial policy, and the cost of capital: A comment*, 4 *J. Pub. Econ.* 271, 276 (1975). Stiglitz pulls together and extends the discussion by viewing the tax in turn as "a tax on capital in the corporate sector, a tax on entrepreneurship in the corporate sector, a tax on pure profits in the corporate sector, and a tax on risk taking." Stiglitz, *The corporation tax*, 5 *J. Pub. Econ.* 303, 303 (1976).

31. Taxable firms can deduct interest paid on debt, but all returns to equity are taxed. Given this fact, for-profit firms might avoid taxes on profits by relying entirely on bonds to raise capital. If firms were 100 percent debt financed, the corporate income tax would be a tax on the pure or "economic" profits of inframarginal firms. *See* note 28 *supra*. The tax would not affect any firm's marginal choices and, hence, firms would not care about the tax status of their competitors. In a competitive world, the marginal firms earn no excess "economic" profits and, hence, the tax treatment of profits would be irrelevant. For-profit firms would be indifferent to the tax status of their competitors, and no issue of "unfair" competition would arise.

Despite these tax incentives, for-profits do not rely soley on debt for their capital requirements. There appear to be several reasons for this, one of which is the IRS's disfavor of 100 percent debt financing. *See* B. Bittker and L. Stone, *Federal Income Taxation*, 783–785 (5th ed. 1980). In addition, the more highly leveraged a firm is, the more likely are lenders to require higher rates on loans. These higher rates reflect the practical difficulties of monitoring managers and the increased likelihood of bankruptcy as the ratio of loans to equity increases. Therefore, a for-profit firm faces a cost of capital that depends on its capital structure and may well prefer a mixture of debt and equity in spite of the tax advantages of debt.

Modigliani and Miller initiated the current literature on firm capital structure. *See* Modigliani and Miller, *The cost of capital, corporation finance and the theory of investment*, 48 *Am. Econ. Rev.* 261 (1958) (arguing that in a competitive world, with perfect capital markets, no taxes and no risk of bankruptcy, the capital structure of a firm has no effect on its value). Their article was followed by numerous attempts to develop alternative models, including models stressing monitoring and agency costs. *See, e.g.*, Stiglitz, Some aspects of the pure theory of corporate finance: bankruptcies and take-overs, 3 *Bell J. Econ. & Mgmt. Sci.* 458 (1972); Jensen and Meckling, *Theory of the firm, managerial behavior, agency costs and ownership structure*, 3 *J. Fin. Econ.* 305 (1976); Myers, *Determinants of corporate borrowing*, 5 *J. Fin. Econ.* 147 (1977); Ross, *The determination of financial structure: The incentive-signalling approach*, 8 *Bell J. Econ.* 23 (1977).

Miller, however, argues both that bankruptcy costs and agency costs are small and that the tax advantages of debt have been overrated. Miller, *Debt and taxes*, 32 *J. Fin.* 261, 263–64 (1977). He further argues that equity investments are beneficial to high-bracket taxpayers since capital gains are taxed at a lower rate than bond interest payments, and that this fact will be reflected in the market returns to bonds and stocks. *Id.*, 266–68. Thus, the tax laws will determine the debt-equity ratio for the economy as a whole, but there is no optimum ratio for any individual firm. *Id.*, 269. This result, of course, depends upon the assumption of insignificant bankruptcy and agency costs so that lenders are indifferent to the debt-equity ratios of individual firms.

32. Suppose that individual investors all have the same preferences toward risk, and the

capital markets are competitive with market rates set so that individual investors are indifferent between bonds and stocks. To characterize this fact, suppose that there is a riskless asset which earns an after-tax rate of return of v and that all risky assets have nominal or expected returns set so that they are equivalent to a certainty of v. To avoid unnecessary complications, assume that firms issue no dividends, that the personal income tax rate on bond interest is s, that capital gains are untaxed, and that the corporate tax rate is t. This means that the nominal rate on bonds is r where $r = v/(1 - s)$ and that the gross profit rate is w where $w = v/(1 - t)$.

Suppose, further, that a nonprofit has some excess cash to invest. Since its interest earnings are tax-exempt, the nonprofit can earn the equivalent of r if it invests in the bonds of other firms. If it operates a tax-exempt business itself, it will earn w so long as the nonprofit believes that it will be just as efficient as the marginal for-profit.

Thus, in this simple case, it will establish a new business if w is greater than r, that is, if t exceeds s. When this condition holds, the nonprofit obtains tax benefits from either type of investment, but the benefits are greater for productive or "active" investments. If there are many nonprofits in this same situation, they will enter the industry until the marginal nonprofit earns r from its productive investment. At that point, many for-profit firms may want to leave the industry. Any firm that earned a pretax return of w before the entry of nonprofits is now earning r, which is less than w when t is greater than s.

33. If nonprofits were taxed on all productive "business" activities but not on passive investments, then in equilibrium nonprofits would compare the rate of return on active investments with the rate for a hypothetical risk-free investment. If we assume that they can earn no more than the marginal for-profit in an active investment, then nonprofits would only invest in bonds since they would still be tax-exempt. (I assume throughout that nonprofits are such a small force in the bond market that the rate of return is unaffected by their choice.)

Students of public finance may wonder how this rather large change in behavior can be consistent with Stiglitz's claim that, under certain conditions, the corporate income tax does not affect investment choices. See A. Atkinson and J. Stiglitz, supra note 14, 142–46; Stiglitz, supra note 30, 32. Stiglitz considers a case with no bankruptcy risks, where marginal investments are financed by borrowing, interest payments are deductible, and true economic depreciation is deducted to compute tax liability. Then, the firm's marginal investment decisions will remain unchanged whether or not it is subject to the corporate income tax. Furthermore, if the depreciation allowance exceeds economic depreciation, the tax system may actually encourage investment. This result, however, refers only to the *marginal* behavior of existing firms. Stiglitz assumes competitive markets and does not deal explicitly with entry and exit. Thus, while the marginal choices of nonprofits may well be unaffected, they will seek to make a discontinuous change and exit from the industry if their profits become taxable.

34. In the case discussed in text, the nonprofits' impact on for-profits turns on the asymmetric tax treatment of bonds and stocks, not on the nonprofit' tax advantages per se. Suppose, for example, that nonprofits faced the same tax rate on both bonds and stock. Then they would also favor direct investment over bond purchase so long as t is greater than s for other investors. See note 32, supra.

35. See Hansmann, *The role of nonprofit enterprise*, 89 Yale L.J. 835, 835 n.1 (1980) (estimating that the nonprofit sector accounted for about 2.8 percent of national income in 1974).

36. This could happen if lenders believe that nonprofit organizations are particularly untrustworthy users of investment funds. Lenders might prefer to lend to entrepreneurs with some direct ownership interest in the enterprise who will benefit financially if returns are high. See Jensen and Meckling, supra note 31. Compare this supposition about the relative untrustworthiness of nonprofits as borrowers with the argument that nonprofits may be seen as more trustworthy than for-profits by donors and consumers. See Hansmann, supra note 35.

37. Tax disadvantaged firms, see note 34 supra, would be unable to borrow at all unless they were markedly more efficient than ordinary for-profit firms.

38. If as Hansmann, supra note 15, supposes, nonprofit firms are inefficiently capital constrained because of their inability to raise equity capital, then the likelihood that their for-profit competitors will earn subnormal returns is low so long as the two organizational forms are equally efficient.

39. The authors in Note, *Preventing untaxed business, supra* note 18, never go beyond competitive assumptions. Klein, *supra* note 11, 61–66, uses an oligopoly model in which firms do not behave strategically. An oligopoly model is also implicit in Note, *Colleges, charities, and the Revenue Act of 1950, supra* note 3, 876, while competitive assumptions are implicit in Note, *The macaroni monopoly, supra* note 1, 1281.

40. These issues did not arise in Part I–B because the firms were in a competitive industry. No individual firm could affect the performance of the industry by its choice of output level or price. In an oligopolistic industry this is no longer true. The essence of an oligopolistic industry is the close link between the behavior of one firm and the performance of another.

41. I thus abstract from differences in the tax treatment of these individual investments as well as from the relative riskiness of different types of investments.

42. I later consider the risks of bankruptcy and default. *See* text accompanying notes 48–53 *infra*.

43. To an economist, one of the costs of doing business is to provide a "normal" rate of return to invested capital, equal to what could be earned in alternative investments. "Economic" profits are measured as the excess of revenues over these and other costs. *See* note 28 *supra*.

44. If the corporate tax were levied on "economic" profits, firm *B*'s tax status and capital structure would be irrelevant, and firm *A* would be indifferent to the tax status of its competitor. It may look with envy at the higher profits of the tax-exempt firm, but these profits have no effort on its *own* performance.

To see this, suppose that firm *B* acts like a Cournot oligopolist. In other words, *B* maximizes profits holding the quantity *A* produces constant. *See* J. Henderson and R. Quandt, *Microeconomic Theory: A Mathematical Approach* 222–31 (1971).

Let *B*'s profits, Π_B, be

$$\Pi_B = [p(q)q_B - c(q_B)](1-t) \tag{1}$$

where p = price,
    q_A = quantity produced by *A*,
    q_B = quantity produced by *B*,
    q = $q_A + q_B$,
    $c(q_B)$ = total cost of producing q_B,
    t = corporate tax rate.

Then, if the second order conditions hold, *B*'s profits are maximized at:

$$\frac{d\Pi}{dq_B} = (1-t)[p'(q)\ q_B + p \quad c'(q_B)] - 0 \tag{2}$$

In a Cournot model, $p'(q) = \dfrac{dp}{dq_B}$ since firm *B* take *A*'s output as given. Clearly, the level of q_B that solves (2) does not depend upon *B*'s tax rate. Firm *A* does not care about the tax status of its competitor. *See* Klein, *supra* note 11, at 63 (presenting a simple preliminary model); Note, *Preventing Untaxed Business, supra* note 18, at 591–92.

In contrast, when the tax is levied on "accounting" profits, a firm's tax status can affect its behavior. Then in long-run steady state equilibrium, "economic" profits are:

$$\Pi_B = (1-t)[p(q)q_B - \hat{c}(q_B) - r\beta(q_B)] - rE(q_B), \tag{3}$$

where $\hat{c}(q_B)$ = operating costs,
    r = interest rate,
    $B(q_B)$ = dollar value of capital raised by sales of bonds,
    $E(q_B)$ = dollar value of other capital from equity or gifts.

Let $K(q_B)$ = dollar value of capital, let β equal the ratio of debt to total capital required by those who lend to for-profits, and let gifts equal some fixed dollar amount, $\bar{G}$. (I do not analyze the general strategic question of the trade-off between debt financing and the generation of private donations.) We can now ask how a competitor will act if, on the one hand, it is a for-profit with $t > 0$, $\beta < 1$, $B(q_B) = \beta K(q_B)$ and $E(q_B) = (1 - B)K(q_B)$, or, on the other hand, a nonprofit with $B(q_B) = K(q_B) - \bar{G}$, and $E(q_B) = \bar{G}$. Capital raised through gifts has the same opportunity cost as equity capital since it can be invested at rate r. Thus, for the taxable for-profit firm:

$$\Pi_B^1 = (1 - t)[p(q)q_B - \hat{c}(q_B) - r\beta K(q_B)] - r(1 - \beta)K(q_B). \tag{4}$$

For the nonprofit:

$$\Pi_B^2 = p(q)q_B - \hat{c}(q_B) - rK(q_B). \tag{5}$$

Maximizing Π_B^1 and Π_B^2 with respect to q_B, and assuming the second order conditions hold, yields for the for-profit;

$$0 = (1 - t)[p'(q)q_B + p - \hat{c}'(q_B) - \beta rK'(q_B)] - r(1 - \beta)K'(q_B), \tag{6}$$

and for the nonprofit;

$$0 = p'(q)q_B + p - \hat{c}'(q_B) - rK'(q_B). \tag{7}$$

In the short run, if capital is fixed so $K'(q_B) = 0$, both types of competitors make the same profit maximizing output choices. If, instead, capital can be varied, the nonprofit will produce more output. To see this, suppose that each firm produces the same output. But then $-t(p'q_B + p - \hat{c}'(q_B) - \beta rK'(q_B))$ would have to equal zero. Substituting from (7), this implies that $-t(1 - \beta)rK'(q_B) = 0$. But this is impossible so long as the marginal product of capital is positive. Thus, in general, when (7) is solved for q_B so that the nonprofit is maximizing net returns, the for-profit has marginal after-tax costs that exceed marginal revenues. So long as marginal costs increase (or remain constant) with q, and marginal revenues fall, the level of output chosen by the nonprofit is too large for the for-profit. Therefore, firm A is better off if its competitor is a for-profit firm.

The basic idea of this modeling exercise is that nonprofits set marginal revenue (MR) equal to marginal variable cost (MVC) plus marginal capital cost (MKC), while for-profits set $(1 - t)$MR equal to $(1 - t)$MVC$ + (1 - \beta t)$MKC. Since $\beta < 1$, $(1 - t)$ is smaller than $(1 - \beta t)$. Thus MR $-$ MVC is larger than MKC at the taxable firm's profit-maximizing output.

45. *See* J. Henderson and R. Quandt, *supra* note 44, 222–28.

46. *See id.,* 226 (explaining reaction functions).

47. The lines slope downward because firm A maximizes profits at a lower level of output the higher the output of firm B, and vice versa. *See id.* 222–28.

48. The risk is higher because more of the firm's debt takes the form of fixed-rate securities that must be repaid so long as any excess over operating costs is available. With equity investment, a firm's owners and managers have more freedom to decide how much income to pay out in dividends and how much to retain for investment, and as a hedge against losses.

49. *See* Gordon, Taxation of Corporate Capital Income: Tax Revenue v. Tax Distortions (1981) (unpublished manuscript, Bell Laboratories) (stressing the risk-spreading benefits of the corporate income tax); Stiglitz, *The corporation tax, 5 J. Pub. Econ.* 303, 307–08 (1976) (same).

50. *See* D. Jaffee, *Credit Rationing and the Commercial Loan Market* (1971) (attempting to explain why lenders may ration credit rather than raising interest rates); Jaffee and Russell, *Imperfect information, uncertainty, and credit rationing,* 90 Q. J. Econ. 651 (1976) (same).

51. In Figure 22.1, the positions of q_B^1 and q_B^2 would be reversed.

52. I.R.C. § 172(b) (West Supp. 1982).

53. In an inflationary world, loss carryforwards are less valuable than loss carrybacks unless they are somehow indexed to take account of price changes.

In addition to the loss carryover provisions, the Economic Recovery Tax of 1981 provides another benefit to loss-making corporations. The "safe harbor lease" provision of the Act allows them to sell their unused investment tax credits by engaging in sale-leaseback arrangements with business organizations in high marginal tax brackets. *See* Economic Recovery Tax Act of 1981, § 201(a), I.R.C. § 168(f)(8) (West Supp. 1982). Tax-exempt nonprofits are not eligible to participate since the law requires that both sides of the transaction be eligible to receive the investment tax credit. The only exception is for mass transportation vehicles, *id.*, a clause designed to benefit cities with large mass-transit systems.

54. However, in many areas where competition is most brisk, nonprofits cannot be viewed as capital constrained. A fairly common pattern is competition between nonprofits that are "subsidiaries" of large, wealthy tax-exempt organizations such as universities, museums, or churches, and for-profit firms that are small corporations with little or no access to national capital markets. This pattern is common in research and residential care for the retarded or mentally ill.

These cases stand in contrast to nursing homes, hospitals, and publishing houses, where for-profits are frequently organized into chains or are part of larger corporations. Organized child day-care services with a mix of chains, small independent for-profits and nonprofits, and nonprofits affiliated with churches and universities are intermediate cases. *See* C. Coelen, F. Glantz and D. Calore, *Day Care Centers in the U.S.* 3, 83 (1979). Therefore, the for-profit firms that are most likely to complain about "unfair" competition will be those that both face the affiliates of well-endowed institutions and are themselves rationed in the capital market. In fact, this does seem to be the case. The major cases in this area involve travel agents and a testing laboratory. *See* Kaplan, *supra* note 2; T. Spiro, *supra* note 20.

55. The Sherman Act and the Clayton Act both seek to penalize firms which monopolize industries. Instead of compensation, violators may be subject to fines and triple damages awards. *See* F. Scherer, *supra* note 19, 494–95.

The debate in antitrust policy over controlling market structure versus controlling behavior suggests that an active policy to reduce monopoly profits wherever they occur would be controversial. This debate does not imply, however, a public commitment to preserving monopoly returns.

56. *See* B. Ackerman, *Private Property and the Constitution* 140–50 (1977); L. Tribe, *American Constitutional Law* 456–65 (1978); Michelman, *Property, utility and fairness: Comments on the ethical foundations of 'just compensation' law*, 80 *Harv. L. Rev.* 1165 (1967).

Graetz, *Legal transitions: The case of retroactivity in income tax revision*, 126 *U. Pa. L. Rev.* 47 (1977), discusses the issue in the context of changes in the income tax law, but he fails to note the relationship between losses caused by tax law changes and unconstitutional takings of property. Instead he assumes "that any tax law changes considered here do not amount to 'takings.' " *Id.*, 64 n.54. He then goes on to present a range of arguments for and against grandfathering. Although "firm conclusions are difficult," he wishes to make the tax law "flexible" and argues that "[p]eople should make investments with the expectation that political policies may change." *Id.*, 87. On the similarities between taxation and takings, see Ackerman, *Four questions for legal theory*, in *Nomos XXII, Property* 351, 362 (J. Pennock and J. Chapman eds., 1980).

57. U.S. Const. amend. V. *See also* B. Ackerman, *Private Property . . . supra* note 56, 116–118, 133–35; L. Tribe, *supra* note 56, 459–63; Michelman, *supra* note 56.

58. Michelman argues that a utilitarian policymaker would require compensation to be paid only if the public measure "can easily be seen to have practically deprived the claimant of some distinctly perceived, sharply crystallized, investment-backed expectation." Michelman, *supra* note 56, 1233. For a broader view of the takings clause, see B. Ackerman, *Private Property . . . supra* note 56.

59. *See* Alco Parking Corp. v. City of Pittsburgh, 417 U.S. 369 (1974) (tax designed to harm competitive position of for-profit firms does not constitute a taking).

60. *See* note 35 *supra*.

61. *See* Klein, *supra* note 11, 63–64 n.212. If a nonprofit should obtain control of a large firm in some industry, it would be likely to do no more than limit monopoly profits in that industry.

62. T. Spiro, *supra* note 20, details the legal challenges of for-profit providers in these industries.

63. *See* Cooper, *supra* note 3; Greenbaum, *supra* note 6; Kaplan, *supra* note 2; Webster, *supra* note 4. For example, the IRS currently appears to be tightening the definition of "unrelated" at least with respect to universities. *See* Bromberg, *supra* note 5.

64. In Smyth v. Ames, 169 U.S. 466 (1898), the Supreme Court held that a public utility is entitled to a fair return on the value of its investment. It refused, however, to indicate precisely the economic meaning of its standard, saying "[h]ow such compensation may be ascertained, and what are the necessary elements in such an inquiry, will always be an embarassing question." *Id.*, 546. This standard was replaced in the 1940s by a standard that asked whether "the total effect of the rate order [is] unjust and unreasonable." Federal Power Comm'n v. Hope Natural Gas Co., 320 U.S. 591, 602 (1944). Tribe notes that this is a test which "only the most egregiously confiscatory rate structure would have difficulty meeting." L. Tribe, *supra* note 56, 461 n.3 (1978).

65. This is the implication of the antitrust laws and of rate of return regulation for public utilities. *See* F. Scherer, *supra* note 19, 475–94; note 55 *supra*.

66. The increase will be larger if nonprofits are permitted to borrow to finance these investments. Currently, nonprofits can invest in real estate without paying taxes on their earnings, but they are not permitted to borrow to finance these investments. *See* Bittker and Rahdert, *supra* note 3, 322–25. If, in fact, tax-exempt firms took advantage of their favorable tax position to engage in arbitrage so that a major share of the economy's investment funds passed through their organizations, then the hands-off policy recommended in the test would have to be reexamined. However, since lenders do not lend at favorable rates to highly leveraged firms, such arbitrage is unlikely given the limited resources available to tax-exempt firms from private donations.

67. Current changes in the depreciation allowances permitted for tax purposes, *see* Economic Recovery Tax Act of 1981, § 201, I.R.C. § 168 (West Supp. 1982), will reduce the taxes of most corporations. This tax reduction will work against any expansion of nonprofit investments in competitive markets by reducing the tax advantages of debt. It is no longer so likely that nonprofits will find that productive investments will dominate the purchase of bonds for purely tax reasons.

Author Index

Subject Index